Irish America

The Historical Travel Guide
Volume 2

Southern and Border States
Plains and Rocky Mountain States
Western and Southwestern States

Richard Demeter

Cranford Press • Pasadena, California

Irish America
The Historical Travel Guide
Volume 2

Published by
Cranford Press
500 Cliff Drive
Pasadena, California 91107

First Edition

Library of Congress Catalog Card Number: 95-92465

ISBN 0-9648253-1-7

Printed in the United States of America

Dedication

To my father
Géza Demeter
and
to the memory
of
my mother
Catherine Coughlin Demeter
(1918-1996)

¶ **Front Cover Photograph:**

Judge Sarah Garrahan-Moulder, San Antonio's Irishman of the Year 1996, greets those in attendance at the 30th Annual Wreath-Laying Ceremony at the Alamo in honor of the Irish natives who died during its defense in 1836.

¶ **Back Cover Photograph:**

Dick Dowling Statue
Hermann Park, Houston, Texas

This life-size statue of the Confederate officer is part of a granite memorial inscribed with the names of the Davis Guards, the all-Irish unit which repulsed a planned Union attack on the Sabine Pass in eastern Texas.

Contents

Acknowledgments

I wish to acknowledge my use of the research facilities at the Huntington Library in San Marino, California, and the Family History Center in Salt Lake City, Utah. I particularly want to thank the Reader Services staff at the Huntington Library.

I also wish to acknowledge the following individuals and organizations that provided me with some of the information and/or photographs contained in this volume: Carrie Adamson, Augusta Genealogical Society, Augusta, Ga.; Barbara Asmus, University of South Alabama Archives, Mobile, Ala.; Jim Baggett, Birmingham Public Library, Birmingham, Ala.; Patricia Barefoot, Fort Frederica, St. Simons Island, Ga.; Ellen Bilbrey, Arizona State Parks, Phoenix, Ariz.; Mary Bills, Mackay Mansion, Virginia City, Nev.; Jeff Black, Synergy Photo/Graphics, Denver, Colo.; La Vaughan Bresnahan, Trail End Historic Center State Historic Site, Sheridan, Wyo.; Earnest Brin, New Orleans Public Library, New Orleans, La.; Sister Ann Francis Campbell, archivist, Catholic Diocese of Charleston, Charleston, S.C.; Andrew P. Careaga, News Services, University of Missouri-Rolla, Rolla, Missouri; Michelle L. Caron, Mahaffie Farmstead and Stagecoach Stop, Olathe, Kans.; Joseph Carter, Will Rogers Memorial and Birthplace, Claremore, Okla.; Kevin Cherry, Rowan County Public Library, Salisbury, N.C.; Della Clement, Lafourche Parish Library, Thibodaux, La.; Megan Coddington, Kelley House Historical Museum, Mendocino, Calif.; Richard Collier, Wyoming Historic Preservation Office, Cheyenne, Wyo.; Joe Craven, Hampton Plantation State Park, Georgetown, S.C.; J. L. Davis, Yakima Valley Regional Library, Yakima, Wash.; Frank de Loach, Culver & de Loach Company, St. Simons Island, Ga.; Howard Draper, State Capitol, Raleigh, N.C.; Philip Earl, Nevada Historical Society, Reno, Nev.; Gwen Edwards, Magnolia Mound Plantation, Baton Rouge, La.; Rick Edwards, Fort Vancouver National Historic Site, Vancouver, Wash.; Linda Eure, Historic Edenton, James Iredell State Historic Site, Edenton, N.C.; Father William Faherty, S.J., St. Louis, Mo.; Sister Anne Finnerty, Sisters of the Holy Spirit, San Antonio, Tex.; Marty Fleming and Dan Ross, Traveler's Rest State Historic Site, Toccoa, Ga.; Larry Frank, Healy House, Leadville, Colo.; Friends of the Chapel of the Four Chaplains, Valley Forge, Pa.; Henry S. Fullerton, Westfield, N.J.; Mikka Gee, Abiquiu Foundation, Abiquiu, N.M.; Emily Coughlin Giles, Dallas, Tex.; Catherine Gillaspey, Magevney House, Memphis, Tenn.; Ivey Gladdin, Glen Studio, Helena, Ark.; Wayne Godwin, Gamble House, Ellenton, Fla.; Virginia Goodrow, Anderson County Historical Commission, Palestine, Tex.; Robert C. Gray, Virginia & Truckee

Railroad, Virginia City, Nev.; J. Colin Green, Cornelius O'Connor House, Homer, Nebr.; Nina Greenlee, The Carson House, Old Fort, N.C.; Bonnie Greer, Arizona Pioneer Historical Society, Flagstaff, Ariz.; Dennis Grose, University of Montana, Butte, Mont.; Judge Ray Hammond, Garrard County, Ky.; Susan Harris, Bartram Trail Regional Library, Washington, Ga.; Patton Hash, Charleston Historical Society, Charleston, S.C.; Healy-Murphy Center, San Antonio, Tex.; Shelia Heflin, Owensboro-Daviess County Public Library, Owensboro, Ky.; Jim Henley, City and County Archives, Sacramento, Calif.; Jean Hergenrother, College of Agriculture, Topeka, Kans.; Donna Rae Hovatter, Morgantown Public Library, Morgantown, W.Va.; Margaret Huenefeld, Fayette Heritage Museum and Archives, La Grange, Tex.; Jeffrey L. Huntington, Campbell House Museum, St. Louis, Mo.; Roberta Hurley, Hannibal, Mo.; Ann Caraway Ivins, great-great-grandniece of Richard Dowling, Houston, Tex.; Sister Rosemarie Kasper, S.N.J.M, archivist, Sisters of the Holy Names of Jesus and Mary, Marylhurst, Ore.; Amy Kastigar, Brook County Public Library, Wellsburg, W.Va.; Bruce Kaye, Theodore Roosevelt National Park, Medora, N.Dak.; Barbara Keith and Mallory Perry, Stranahan House, Fort Lauderdale, Fla.; Father Cyril Kelleher, O.F.M. Cap., Mission Santa Ines, Solvang, Calif.; Mr. and Mrs. William Kelly, South Pasadena, Calif.; Carol Keninger, Chamber of Commerce, Waterloo, Iowa; Birdie King, Garrard County Public Library, Lancaster, Ky.; Becca Kohl, Montana Historical Society, Helena, Mont.; Mike Krause, Plumas-Eureka State Park, Johnsville, Calif.; Diane Kroner, Idaho State Historical Society, Boise, Id.; Sister Rita Lestelle, Pico Rivera, Calif.; J. J. Lindquist, Smith-Western Inc., Portland, Ore.; Kristina Lindsey, The Molly Brown House Museum, Denver, Colo.; Lisa Littlefield, Atlanta History Center, Atlanta, Ga.; Thomas Lynch, Boys Town, Omaha, Nebr.; Harry Lynn, Big Chimney, W.Va.; Novaline May, Chamber of Commerce, Hope, Ark.; Jess McCall, Fort Douglas Military Museum, Salt Lake City, Utah; Melissa McCann, Victoria Regional Museum Association, Victoria, Tex.; Thomas McEnery, San Jose, Calif.; Hollie McHenry, Wyoming State Archives, Cheyenne, Wyo.; Erick Montgomery, Historic Augusta, Augusta, Ga.; Marilyn Monzo, Nevada County Chamber of Commerce, Grass Valley, Calif.; Hattie Moore, Historical Society, James City, N.C.; Ann Moran, Thomas Gilcrease Museum, Tulsa, Okla.; Carole Mumford, Joel Chandler Harris Association, Inc., Atlanta, Ga.; Betty Newman, Walnut Grove Plantation, Roebuck, S.C.; Valerie O'Brien, Sweetsprings Public Library, Sweetsprings, W.Va.; John O'Reilly, Seattle, Wash.; Jane Pergoli, John Wayne Birthplace, Winterset, Iowa; Robert Perry, Robert Gamble Plantation State Historic Park, Ellenton, Fla.; Anne Post, Charles Town Public Library, Charles Town, W.Va.; Dee Dee Donohue Poteete, San Antonio Convention and Visitors Bureau, San Antonio, Tex.; Judy Price, *The Emporia Gazette*, Emporia, Kans.; Presbyterian Synod Executive Office, Mayaguez, Puerto Rico; Sue Rains, Taylor-Grady House,

Athens, Ga.; Susan Rathke, Emporia/Lyon County Convention and Visitors Bureau, Emporia, Kans.; Maxine Reilly, Refugio County Museum, Refugio, Tex.; Chris Revels, Kings Mountain National Military Park, S.C.; Richard Rice, Sam Houston Memorial Museum, Huntsville, Tex.; Dr. Ronald Ripley, Historical Society, Union, W.Va.; Sue Roeder, St. Mark's Catholic Church, Bottineau, N.Dak.; Michelle Royle, Cline Library, Northern Arizona University, Flagstaff, Ariz.; Burl Salmon, Natchez Historical Foundation, Natchez, Miss.; Suzanne Savery, Department of Tourism, Petersburg, Va.; Father Stephen Schneider, O.F.M., St. Boniface Friary, Louisville, Ky.; Mary Kay Shannon, Magoffin Home State Historic Site, El Paso, Tex.; Rayma Babbitt Sharber, Flagstaff, Ariz.; Debbie Sherwood, Whittier Historical Society, Whittier, Calif.; Monsignor John Simonin, St. Mary's Catholic Church, Charleston, S.C.; Dr. Ron Halloway Snipe, Kansas Postcard Company, Lawrence, Kans.; Sally Stassi, Historic New Orleans Collection, New Orleans, La.; Anne Stewart, Mackay School of Mines, Reno, Nev.; Susan Sutton, Indiana Historical Society, Indianapolis, Ind.; Thomas Patrick Sweeney, General Sweeny's: A Museum of Civil War History, Republic, Mo.; Dr. Ray Swick, Blennerhassett Island Historical State Park, Parkersburg, W.Va.; Sam Thomas, Historical Center of York County, York, S.C.; Tourism Information Center, Isla Verde, Puerto Rico; Thomas Valentine, Rosedale, Ga.; Kathy Vockery, Garrard County Historical Society, Richmond, Ky.; Kate Wacker, Utah State Historical Society, Salt Lake City, Utah; Harry Wallace, Florence, Ala.; Waterford Foundation, Inc., Waterford, Va.; Guto Wenzinger, Mallory-Neely House, Memphis, Tenn.; Susan Whetstone, Utah State Historical Society, Salt Lake City, Utah; Jill Whitten, Brennan House, Louisville, Ky.; and Rick Wilson, Golden Spike National Historic Site, Promontory Point, Utah.

Grateful acknowledgment is also made to:

• Alfred A. Knopf, Inc. for permission to reprint from *Journal of a Residence on a Georgian Plantation in 1838-1839* by Frances Anne Kemble and edited by John A. Scott. Copyright © 1961 by Alfred A. Knopf, Inc.

• The Arthur H. Clarke Company for permission to reprint from "Broken Hand, Chief of the Mountain Men" by Ann Woodbury Hafen found in Volume 7 of *The Mountain Men and the Fur Trade of the Far West* by LeRoy R. Hafen. Copyright © 1969 by The Arthur H. Clark Company.

• McGraw-Hill, Inc. for permission to reprint from "The Ballad of Dick Dowling" by A. M. Sullivan found in *Dick Dowling at Sabine Pass* by Frank X. Tolbert. Copyright © 1962 by Frank X. Tolbert.

• Monsignor Francis J. Weber for permission to reprint from *Mission Dolores: A Documentary History of San Francisco Mission*. Copyright 1979.

• Penguin USA for permission to reprint from *Roughing It* by Mark Twain and edited by Hamlin Hill.

• *The Sacramento Bee* for permission to reprint from *Private Thinks by C. K. and Other Writings of Charles K. McClatchy* edited by Eleanor

Introduction

Like its earlier companion work, this second volume of *Irish America* takes its theme from the boast of Victor Herbert, the Dublin-born musician, that on every page of the history of the United States "you will find the names of some of the most illustrious sons of Erin . . . ." To this litany, of course, can be added the thousands of Irish-American descendants who both individually and collectively left their imprint upon so many aspects of the American story.

Interest in Irish-American history has experienced a renaissance in recent years, prompted in part by the sesquicentennial of the Great Famine. Through an unusual outpouring of dramatic productions and both historical and fictional works, increasing numbers of the 44.3 million Americans of Irish ancestry are learning about the significant influence which their ancestors had in the development of the United States.

When Irish immigration reached its peak during the Famine years in the mid 1800s, the émigrés sought refuge in America – although their Catholicism and appalling poverty and wretchedness caused many native-born Americans to oppose their admission. (It was at this time that the phrase "Scotch Irish" became common, used to distinguish the descendants of the earlier Presbyterian Irish of Scottish ancestry from the more recent Famine-driven arrivals.) In the cities on the East Coast, especially, many of these newcomers endured an ethnic and sectarian hostility which the Irish immigrants of the earlier century had not experienced.

In parts of the South and in the more egalitarian West, however, conditions were more favorable for the Irish immigrants and their descendants. Cardinal James Gibbons, himself born in Baltimore to Irish parents, described the Irish diaspora in those parts of mid-nineteenth-century America: "In the Southern States . . . their number is not so great at present, but with the increasing prosperity of the favored region we may expect soon to see a larger influx of the children of Erin. In many Western states, in communities that have sprung up within this generation, and in which ancient prejudice is weak, or comparatively unknown, the Irish enjoy a high degree of consideration and are among the prominent pioneers of this wonderful complexus of young and vigorous States." The words of the nation's most famous Catholic churchman were echoed in 1869 by the editor of the Irish-Catholic newspaper in San Francisco: "Our Countrymen need not fear . . . that they have to encounter the prejudices against their race or religion, that are such drawbacks to their settlement in many parts of the Eastern States. Irishmen have made themselves a position here fully equal to that of any other nationality in our cosmopolitan population, and the newcomers of the same race need fear to find no prejudice to bar their advancement, unless what any fault of their own may raise against individuals."

Together with a volume published last year, *Irish America (Volume 2)* completes a definitive historical travel guide to landmarks within the United States associated with figures of Irish and Irish-American descent. In addition, the two works are a source of biographical and anecdotal information about those figures and are a chronicle of the memorials erected to those men and women by later generations.

This second volume includes approximately a thousand such sites – houses, churches, monuments, statues, memorials, gravesites, birthplaces, museums, libraries, parks, forts, battlefields, and various other public and private buildings – in three areas of the country: the Southern and Border States, the Plains and Rocky Mountain States, and the Western and Southwestern States. Although this work naturally includes landmarks associated with Irish and Irish Americans well known to a general audience, its emphasis is on the hundreds of others whose Irish ancestry is not known to most readers or whom the Muse of History has overlooked. In all, this work mentions almost six hundred individuals of Irish birth or descent. Because a significant number of these historical figures are mentioned more than once, the reader should consult the index to find multiple listings. In subsequent references to the name, or when an individual's Irish ancestry might be unclear to the reader, I have placed an asterisk in front of the name.

Whether you are of Irish ancestry or not, I hope that *Irish America (Volume 2)* will increase your awareness of the contributions of the Irish and their descendants to American history. I also hope that you will come to appreciate the self-confidence with which an anonymous Irish poet addressed his compatriots in America:

> Fellow exiles! claim your station
> In the councils of the nation;
> Be not aliens in the soil
> Which exacts your sweat and toil.
> For this land your fathers sought,
> With their blood was freedom bought.
> We can boast as brave a stock
> As that which sprung from Plymouth rock . . . .

Richard Demeter
Pasadena, California
May 24, 1996

Landmarks of Irish America

Alabama / 17

Alaska / 30

Arizona / 33

Arkansas / 42

California / 47

Colorado / 141

Florida / 152

Georgia / 169

Idaho / 192

Iowa / 197

Kansas / 210

Kentucky / 225

Louisiana / 245

Mississippi / 266

Missouri / 279

Montana / 308

Nebraska / 326

Nevada / 338

New Mexico / 349

North Carolina / 355

North Dakota / 378

Oklahoma / 382

Oregon / 390

Puerto Rico / 395

South Carolina / 397

South Dakota / 432

Tennessee / 437

Texas / 455

Utah / 509

Virginia / 518

Washington/ 561

West Virginia / 574

Wyoming / 589

ALABAMA

ATHENS

¶ **Houston Memorial Library and Museum,** Market and Houston streets.

Constructed in 1835, this building was the home of George Houston, the first Democratic governor of Alabama after Reconstruction and a descendant of immigrant grandparents who had come to North Carolina from County Tyrone, Ireland, about 1750.

After coming to this part of Alabama with his parents, Houston studied law, was admitted to the bar, and began a political career that took him first to the state legislature and then to Congress (to the latter almost continuously between 1841 and 1861). In 1850 he was reelected to Congress as a Unionist candidate on a platform that declared the unconstitutionality of secession. Although he labored to prevent the dissolution of the Union, when his state seceded he joined the other members of the Alabama delegation in withdrawing from Congress.

During the war Houston refused to serve in the Confederate army, although he was just as adamant in refusing to take the oath of allegiance to the United States. At the end of the war, he was elected to the U.S. Senate but was prevented from serving by the Radical Reconstructionists who dominated Congress. Following his election as governor of Alabama in 1874, he took drastic measures to deal with the state's bankruptcy by slashing public spending and eliminating government positions. Four years later he resigned, however, to take his seat in the U.S. Senate.

§ Open Monday-Friday 10-5, Saturday 9-12. Closed most holidays. Phone: 205-233-8770.

BIRMINGHAM

¶ **Mary Cahalan Statue,** Linn Park, outside the Birmingham Public Library, 2100 Park Place.

This life-size seated statue depicts one of Birmingham's favorite educators in her customary pose – with an open book on her lap. More than 5,000 people attended the dedication of this marble memorial in 1908. The statue was sculpted by Giuseppe Moretti, whose statue of Vulcan is one of Birmingham's landmarks. On March 17, 1993, a plaque unveiling ceremony was held at the Cahalan statue.

Mary Cahalan came to Birmingham in 1872, when, at the age of seventeen, she accompanied her Irish-born parents and her six brothers and sisters from Columbus, Georgia. The Cahalans were among Birmingham's pioneer families, and it was in their home that the first Catholic masses in Jefferson County were celebrated. The family's home was also the city's

*Statue of Mary Cahalan,
one of Birmingham's favorite
nineteenth-century educators.
(Photo courtesy of the Archives
Collection, Birmingham, Alabama,
Public Library.)*

first brick structure.

Two years after her arrival in Birmingham, Cahalan became a teacher at Powell School, the city's first public elementary school. In 1874 she was named principal at Powell and served in that capacity until her death in 1906 from uremic poisoning. During her three-decade career, she was known as an extraordinary teacher, administrator, and humanitarian.

DADEVILLE

❡ Horseshoe Bend National Military Park, 12 miles north on State 49, on the "horseshoe bend" of the Tallapoosa River.

This 2,000-acre park is the site of a decisive victory over the Creek Confederacy in 1814 by Andrew Jackson, the son of immigrants from Carrickfergus, Ireland. Visitors can drive a three-mile interpreted road through the battlefield. The park museum contains a diorama of the battle as well as exhibits on the Creek Indians and the Creek War.

In August 1813 the Creeks massacred approximately 500 settlers at Fort Mims. Seven months later, in March 1814, Jackson's 3,000 Tennessee militia, regular army troops, and Native American allies defeated a force of 800 Creek Indians under Chief Wenawa, killing about 500 of them. Among Jackson's forces were *David Crockett and *Sam Houston.

After his victory Jackson was promoted to major general and was placed in command of the military district on the southwestern frontier. By August 1814 he had pressured the remaining Creek Indians to sign a treaty ceding to the United States 20 million acres in Alabama and Georgia, lands formerly guaranteed to them by treaty.

§ Open daily 8-5:30. Closed January 1 and December 25. Boating, fishing, hiking, picnicking, swimming, visitor center. Phone: 205-234-7111.

FLORENCE

¶ Edward O'Neal House, 468 North Court Street. Private.

This was the residence of Edward Asbury O'Neal and his wife, Olivia Moore, from about 1850 to his death in 1890. Whenever he entered this two-and-a-half-story cottage, his first question was always "Where is the Queen?" – a reference to the nickname he had given his wife ("The Queen of Love and Beauty").

O'Neal, whose father was a native of Ireland, began the practice of law in Florence in 1840 and eventually became a leader in the secessionist movement within the state. At the commencement of the Civil War, he joined the Confederate army at the head of the Calhoun Guards. During the conflict he was promoted through the ranks from captain to brigadier general, an advance matched only by the wounds he received at Seven Pines, South Mountain, and Chancellorsville and for which he was nicknamed "Old Tige."

At Gettysburg, however, O'Neal's five Alabama regiments became scattered because of his inability to control them. As a result of this failure, General Robert E. Lee refused to deliver O'Neal's earlier appointment as brigadier general, and *President Jefferson Davis canceled the promotion. In 1864 O'Neal commanded a brigade in the Atlanta Campaign and then rounded up deserters in northern Alabama.

After the war O'Neal resumed his political career. He served on one of the committees in the state constitutional convention of 1876 and was twice elected governor of Alabama. During his administrations (1882-1886) he successfully promoted prison reform and the creation of additional public schools.

¶ Foster-O'Neal-Rogers House, at the head of Court Street.

This red brick mansion with Greek portico and four white columns was built between 1848 and 1854 by the wealthy planter George Washington Foster. The house, also known as Courtview, was purchased in 1900 by Governor Emmet O'Neal, the son of former governor Edward Asbury O'Neal. (See above entry.) In recent years the building has served as a social center on the campus of the University of North Alabama.

After a career in private law practice and as a U.S. district attorney,

Emmet O'Neal was elected governor of Alabama in 1910 as the candidate of the local option party opposed to prohibition. During his administration the state legislature made large appropriations for education, repealed statewide prohibition, and passed legislation to protect miners and child workers. While attending the national governors' conference in 1911, he delivered a speech in which he attacked the initiative, the referendum, and the recall, a position which prompted a spirited response from *Governor Woodrow Wilson of New Jersey, a strong proponent of those new constitutional mechanisms.

¶ **Jackson Plantation Ruins,** 2 miles north off Cox Creek Parkway (State 133) on Jackson Road (Highway 41) to Dowdy Road.

Although its twenty-four Ionic columns are all that remain today, the Forks of Cypress plantation house was once the centerpiece of a 3,000-acre farm owned by James Jackson. The nineteenth-century mansion was destroyed by fire in 1966.

Jackson, who was born in Ballabay, County Monaghan, Ireland, in 1782, came from comfortable circumstances and was educated as a civil engineer before emigrating at the age of seventeen. From Philadelphia he followed relatives to Nashville, Tennessee, where he was employed in surveying. He quickly acquired property – including a two-story house – and counted *Andrew Jackson among his friends.

In 1810, while still living in Tennessee, Jackson married Sally Moore McCullough, a twenty-year-old widow whose husband had drowned while crossing a stream. Jackson's young wife boasted descent from a founder of Charleston, South Carolina, and from James Moore, the royal governor of South Carolina and himself descended from a leader of the 1641 Irish uprising. The couple had ten children, the eldest of whom they named for their friend "Old Hickory," the future president of the United States.

By 1817 James Jackson and two associates had formed the Cypress Land Company. After purchasing large tracts in what is now Lauderdale County, Alabama, the trio laid out the town of Florence. Andrew Jackson, President James Monroe, and former president James Madison were among those who purchased some of the earliest lots.

With his share of the almost $225,000 which the Cypress Land Company earned from its land sales, James Jackson was in a comfortable position to develop the horse farm which he had always hoped to own. At the junction of Big and Little Cypress creeks – on land which he had bought from the Indian chief Double Head – the Irishman proceeded to build his plantation house. A cousin who spent many boyhood summers at "The Forks of the Cypress" described the flourishing estate: "There were four orchards, two of apples and two of peaches, besides a row of peach trees on each side of the mile-long road that led up little Cypress to the negro quarters. . . . There were only sixty slaves living at The Forks, as the rest were kept on the plantation in Mississippi. . . . Life was simple for those who lived at The Forks. They read many good books, as four times a year a publisher in Philadelphia sent to The Forks a box of the best of the new publications. The negroes of that day suffered much from a fearful epidemic now apparently unknown – 'misery in de back.' It attacked them when there was much work to do, and numbers would be affected at the same time. Fortunately, it never killed, and there was but one cure, plenty of good food and a complete rest. The negroes always took this prescription cheerfully."

In developing his horse-breeding enterprise, Jackson acquired some of the best thoroughbreds available in England. In 1830, for instance, he purchased from Lord Chesterfield the famous horse Leviathan, for which the king of England had once paid 2,000 guineas. Five years later the Irishman bought Glencoe, formerly the property of George IV.

❡ **Old Florence Cemetery,** at the east end of Tennessee Street.

This burial ground contains the graves of Alabama governors *Edward Asbury O'Neal and *Emmet O'Neal.

MOBILE

❡ **Father Ryan Burial Site,** Catholic Cemetery, 1700 Dr. Martin Luther King Jr. Avenue.

The tomb of Father Abram Ryan, an Irish-American Catholic priest known as the "Poet of the Confederacy," is engraved with the words "Poet, Patriot, and Priest." The grave is also adorned with these lines from "The Conquered Banner," probably his most famous poem:

> Furl that Banner, for 'tis weary;
> Round its staff 'tis drooping dreary:
> Furl it, fold it, – it is best;
> For there's not a man to wave it,
> And there's not a sword to save it,
> And there's not one left to lave it
> In the blood which heroes gave it,
> And its foes now scorn and brave it:
> Furl it, hide it, – let it rest!"

❡ **Father Ryan Statue,** Father Ryan Park, at the junction of Spring Hill Avenue, Scott Street, and St. Francis Street.

The life-size bronze statue of Father Abram Ryan, the "Poet of the Confederacy," was donated by the children of Mobile in 1913.

Father Ryan was born in Hagerstown, Maryland, in 1838, the son of Matthew Ryan and Mary Coughlin of County Tipperary, Ireland. He was

Statue of Father Abram Ryan, the "Poet of the Confederacy." (Photo courtesy of the University of South Alabama Archives.)

educated at the Christian Brothers' School in St. Louis, Missouri, where he fell in love with a young girl named Ethel, who, like him, however, had decided to enter religious life. About their brief romance the budding poet wrote: "They met to part from themselves and the world. . . . / And in the heart of that last parting hour, Eternity was beating." He later described her as "A fair, sweet girl, with great brown eyes / That seemed to listen just as if they held / The gift of hearing with the power of sight." In preparation for the priesthood, he attended St. Mary's Seminary in Perryville, Missouri, and Our Lady of the Angels Seminary in Niagara Falls, New York.

Following his ordination in 1860, the young priest began a career that encompassed educational, pastoral, and editorial duties. At first he was a professor at various seminaries until his appointment as pastor of St. Mary's parish in Peoria, Illinois. Subsequent pastoral assignments took him to the Nashville diocese, to St. Patrick's Church in Augusta, Georgia, and to both the cathedral and St. Mary's Church in Mobile, Alabama. After the Civil War he variously served as editor of the *Banner of the South* in Augusta and of the *New Orleans Morning Star*. Because of poor health he retired to Biloxi, Mississippi, in 1881.

Ryan was an ardent supporter of the South during the Civil War. Although he failed to secure an official military chaplaincy, he seems to have served in an unofficial capacity. According to one authority, Ryan was at the Battle of Marye's Heights at Fredericksburg, Virginia, in mid December 1862. (It may have been here that he reputedly seized a musket and fought side by side with the Confederate troops.) Four months later he was mourning the death of his brother on the battlefield, a personal tragedy that prompted him to write the poems "In Memory of My Brother" and "In Memoriam – David J. Ryan C.S.A." Toward the end of the war, when no other clergyman would do so, he ministered to smallpox victims at the Gratiot Prison in New Orleans. While still in the Crescent City, he was accused of refusing to bury a dead soldier because he was a Yankee. When the priest was ordered to appear before Benjamin Butler, the Union general in charge of the occupied city, Ryan defended himself. "Why, I was never asked to bury him and never refused," he said, adding gratuitously, "The fact is, General, it would give me great pleasure to bury the whole lot of you." (The same incident is related about *Father James Mullon, the pastor of St. Patrick's Church in New Orleans [q.v.].)

Ryan achieved more lasting fame because of his verse. In addition to poems of a religious nature, he penned some lines with an Irish theme:

Unroll Erin's flag! Fling its folds to the breeze!
Let it float o'er the land, let it flask o'er the seas!
Not a stain on its green, not a blot on its gold,
Tho' the woes and the wrongs of three hundred years
Have drenched Erin's Sunburst with blood and with tears!

He is better known, however, for his Civil War poetry, the most familiar works being "The Conquered Banner," "The Sword of Robert Lee," "The Lost Cause," and "March of the Deadless Dead." Despite the popularity of his verse, he viewed his work as of little importance. He described his efforts as "written at random – off and on, here, there, anywhere – just when the mood came, with little of study and less of art, and always in a hurry."

In a letter to Francis F. Browne quoted in an 1886 edition of *Bugle-Echoes*, Ryan provided insight into his most famous work. "I wrote 'The Conquered Banner' at Knoxville, Tenn., one evening soon after Lee's surrender," he explained, "when my mind was engrossed with thoughts of our dead soldiers and dead cause. I never had any idea that the poem, written in less than an hour, would attain celebrity. No doubt the circumstances of its appearance lent it much of its fame. In expressing my own emotions at the time, I echoed the unuttered feelings of the Southern people; and so 'The Conquered Banner' became the requiem of the Lost Cause." In fact, Ryan believed that the duty of a Southern poet was to keep alive the memory of the Confederacy.

After what he regarded as the War of Southern Independence, the priest-poet toured the country on the lecture circuit, sometimes to raise funds for the relief of plague victims and Southern orphans and widows.

It was not until the late 1870s that he seems to have reconciled himself with the victorious North. He did so after the South's former enemies sent money, nurses, and doctors to help fight the yellow fever epidemic that devastated parts of the South in 1878. His final rapprochement was expressed in "Reunited" and "Requiem for the Federal Dead." Ryan died in Louisville, Kentucky, in 1886, while engaged in writing a life of Christ.

¶ Government Street Presbyterian Church, 300 Government Street.
The oldest church in Mobile, this Greek Revival structure was built in 1836 according to designs of James Gallier and Charles Dakin.
Gallier, who was born in County Louth, Ireland, attended the School of Fine Arts in Dublin before coming to America in 1832. After working as a draftsman and an architect in New York City, he formed a partnership with Dakin while they both lived in New Orleans. Gallier was involved in the reconstruction of St. Patrick's Church and the U.S. Mint in the "Crescent City" and designed the Merchants Exchange, City Hall, Christ Church, and many large residences there. After traveling in Europe and North Africa between 1850 and 1868, he was drowned in a shipwreck off North Carolina in May 1868. (See New Orleans, Louisiana.)

¶ Immaculate Conception Cathedral, Clairborne Street, between Conti and Dauphin streets.
*Father Abram Ryan was an assistant here from 1870 to 1877. He lived for part of that period in the residence of Bishop Michael Portier, a Creole cottage built in the 1830s and still standing at 307 Conti Street. In 1877 Ryan became pastor of St. Mary's Church, which stood on the southwest corner of Lafayette Street and Old Shell Road. A modern church now occupies the site.

MONTGOMERY

¶ First White House of the Confederacy, 644 Washington Avenue, across from the Capitol.
The house contains period furnishings, war relics, and heirlooms connected with the family of Jefferson Davis and Varina Howell Davis, both descendants of emigrants from northern Ireland. The residence was originally located on Lee and Bibb streets and was built by William Knox, a native of Ireland and one of Montgomery's leading citizens. He and his family lived in this house for a number of years. (See Knox House below.)
Following his election as president of the Confederate States of America, Jefferson Davis and his wife lived in this house during the four months that Montgomery was the capital of the Confederate government. At that time the house was located at another site in the city.
Mrs. Davis left an account of her husband's reaction when he learned

of his election. "Upon reading the telegram he looked so grieved that I feared some evil had fallen our family," she recalled. "After a few moments of painful silence he told me, speaking as a man might speak of a death sentence. As he neither desired nor expected the position, he was more deeply [de]pressed."

At the first reception which Mrs. Davis hosted in the Confederate White House, she wore a "rich brocaded silk, with wide flowing sleeves from which drooped delicate lace." After attending a later reception, William Howard Russell of the *London Times* wrote: "There was no affectation of state or ceremony in the reception. Mrs. Davis, whom some of her friends call 'Queen Varina,' is a comely, sprightly woman, verging on matronhood, of good figure and manners, well dressed, ladylike, and clever, and she seemed a great favorite with those around her."

§ Open Monday-Friday 8-4:30, Saturday and Sunday 9-4:30. Closed January 1, Easter, Thanksgiving, and December 25. Phone: 205-242-1861.

¶ **Knox House,** 419 South Perry Street. (Enter on South Lawrence Street.)

Although now occupied by the Reid and O'Donahue public relations firm, this antebellum structure was once the home of William Knox, a native of Strabane, County Tyrone, Ireland. He constructed the house about 1848 at a cost of $50,000.

After immigrating to America in the 1820s, Knox first settled in Winchester, Tennessee. There he married Anne Octavia Lewis, whose father had been wounded at the battle of King's Mountain during the Revolutionary War. It was probably at the time of his marriage that Knox, a Methodist, converted to Catholicism. He and his wife had fourteen children.

After the Knoxes' arrival in Montgomery sometime in the 1830s, William established the Central Bank of Alabama on the northeast corner of Dexter Avenue and Court Square, where its building still stands. A Democrat and an ardent secessionist, Knox accommodated the Confederacy with its first loan – borrowed from his bank on February 26, 1861, to pay for food and blankets for the new government's first volunteers. During the war, Mrs. Knox organized a woman's auxiliary association and opened up her house for the group's various activities.

¶ **Scott and Zelda Fitzgerald Museum,** 919 Felder Avenue.

The museum features a videotape presentation about the Fitzgeralds and contains exhibits and memorabilia connected with the flamboyant pair.

Located in Zelda Sayre's home town, the museum occupies the house in which the colorful couple lived in 1931 while she wrote *Save Me the Waltz* and while he penned *Tender Is the Night*. The material in Zelda's book was frequently autobiographical and revealed her spats with her famous Irish-American husband. Fitzgerald felt insulted by her book and wrote angrily to his publisher: "Turning up in a novel by my wife as a somewhat anaemic portrait painter . . . puts me in an absurd . . . position. . . . Using the name of a character I invented to put intimate facts in the hands of the friends and enemies we have accumulated en route – my God, my books made her a legend and her single intention in this somewhat thin portrait is to make me a non-entity."

Fitzgerald had first met the eighteen-year-old Zelda at the Montgomery Country Club in July 1918, where she performed the "Dance of the Hours" while allegedly drunk. At the time, he was a lieutenant with the 67th Infantry Regiment stationed at Camp Sheridan near Montgomery . Perhaps because of his naivete, he was often the object of practical jokes played on him by his fellow officers. One such prank occurred when the officers suggested that Fitzgerald sleep late in order to be rested for his late-night socializing. During a barracks inspection the next morning, the commanding general was chagrined to find Fitzgerald still in bed.

Fitzgerald's most autobiographical work is *This Side of Paradise*, published two years later and generally regarded as the first realistic American college novel. Besides containing references to the sixty-four books and ninety-eight writers that influence Amory Blaine – the Fitzgerald-like protagonist – the work chronicles the influence of Monsignor Darcy, a character based on Monsignor Cyril Fay, who had become for Fitzgerald something of a surrogate father in St. Paul, Minnesota.

In the summer of 1917, Fay – who often recited mass in Gaelic and had been enlisted in a plan to provide American Catholic support for the Allies in exchange for Irish independence – wrote an unusual letter to Fitzgerald. In it he advised the eighteen-year-old young man to obtain a passport and be ready to accompany him on a secret mission to Russia to bring the Church there into union with Rome. As things turned out, however, although Fitzgerald secured his passport for "secretarial work" in Russia, Fay was unable to take his young protégé. Three months later, when it appeared that Fitzgerald might be sent overseas with his infantry unit, Fay wrote the second lieutenant a poem entitled "A Lament for a Foster Son, and He going to the War Against the King of Foreign." Part of the poem, which Fitzgerald later incorporated into *This Side of Paradise*, includes these lines: "May Patrick of the Gael and Columb of the Churches and the / five thousand Saints of Erin be better than a shield to him / And he go into the fight. / Och Ochone."

§ Open Wednesday-Friday 10-2, Saturday and Sunday 1-5. Phone: 205-264-4222.

❡ State Capitol, Dexter Avenue.

A statue of *Jefferson Davis stands on the front lawn of the capitol near where he took the oath of office as president of the Confederacy in February 1861. The approximate location is marked by a brass star embedded in the pavement in front of the west portico.

On the north lawn is the Confederate Monument, whose cornerstone was laid by Davis in April 1886. The monument was executed by *Alexander Doyle.

Born in Steubenville, Ohio, in 1857, Doyle became familiar with monument making through his father, who was employed in the quarrying business. The younger man later studied sculpture in Italy, initially while living there with his parents and then when he returned on his own to study at the national academies in Rome, Florence, and Carrara. After establishing himself in New York City, he quickly earned a reputation as a sculptor of monuments. An Indiana newspaper once opined that at the age of thirty-five Doyle had created more public monuments than any other American sculptor and that 20 percent of such monuments in the United States were the product of his hand and chisel.

Other examples of Doyle's work are the Francis Scott Key monument (Frederick, Md.) and statues of *Henry Grady (Atlanta, Ga.), *Sergeant William Jaspar (Savannah, Ga.), *Horace Greeley (New York City), General Philip Schuyler (Saratoga, N.Y.) and General James Garfield (Cleveland, Ohio). Four of his most significant works are in New Orleans: the marble statue Calling the Roll and statues of *Margaret Haughery, General Albert Sidney Johnson, and General Robert E. Lee.

TUSCUMBIA

¶ **Ivy Green,** 300 West North Commons.

Ivy Green was the birthplace and home of Helen Keller, who, at the age of nineteen months, was left blind, deaf, and mute following an attack of scarlet fever. She overcame her physical disabilities, however, to become a world-famous author, lecturer, and advocate for the handicapped. She was descended from Alexander Moore, a soldier of possibly Irish ancestry and an aide to the Marquis de Lafayette.

The frame house on the property was built about 1820 by Helen's grandfather, David Keller. Helen was born in 1880 in the adjacent plantation office, which also served as living quarters for her and her teacher, Annie Sullivan, from 1887 to 1896. The story of the women's early relationship is told in The Miracle Worker, which is performed at Ivy Green on Friday and Saturday nights from late June through July.

Desperate for assistance in raising his daughter, Arthur Keller in 1887 had welcomed Annie Sullivan into his home as Helen's governess and teacher and later constant companion. Annie was the daughter of impoverished and illiterate immigrants from Limerick, Ireland. Following the death of her mother and the desertion of her father, the ten-year-old Annie – almost blind from a childhood fever – was committed to a public almshouse. Four years later, however, she enrolled in the Perkins Institution for the Blind in Boston and soon underwent an operation that restored a limited degree of eyesight.

Within weeks of her arrival at Ivy Green, Annie tamed the unruly Helen and began to teach her by spelling the names of objects into the young girl's hand with the manual alphabet. In the famous incident at the pump still located at Ivy Green, Annie spelled out the word "water" while pumping the liquid over the girl's hand. This technique – immortalized in a scene in *The Miracle Worker* – was the beginning of Annie's effort to develop her pupil's vocabulary through continuous manual communication.

Through the financial generosity of friends and with Annie as her constant support, Helen was able to pursue a formal education. In 1894 the pair moved to New York so Helen could attend a school where deaf children were taught oral speech. After her acceptance to Radcliffe College, Helen fulfilled the requirements for a bachelor's degree in four years and was graduated *cum laude*. Annie all the while had accompanied her to classes, spelled the words of the lectures into her hands, and spent five to six hours a day reading to her. This regimen, however, had its toll on Annie's eyesight, which continued to deteriorate.

While still a college student, Helen began a prolific writing career and adopted the role of an activist on a variety of issues. First appeared her autobiography – *Story of My Life* – published in 1902 with the assistance of John Albert Macy, who subsequently married Annie. The following year Helen published *Optimism*, which over the next thirty years was followed by *The World I Live In*, *A Song of the Stone Wall* (a 600-line patriotic poem), *Out of the Dark* (a collection of her socialist essays) *My Religion* (an apologia of her Swedenborgian views), and the autobiographical *Midstream*. In bringing the public's attention to ophthalmia neonatorum, a blindness in newborn infants caused by venereal disease, she broke a taboo against discussing such topics. She went on to become a militant suffragist, a pacifist, and a member of the Socialist Party. She likewise used her fame to call for the abolition of child labor and the death penalty and to support the birth control movement, the National Association for the Advancement of Colored People, and federal assistance for the blind.

In the meantime Annie had experienced marital strains and the beginning of additional medical problems. Although Macy walked out on the marriage in 1913, Annie refused to grant him a divorce, perhaps because of religious scruples, although she had abandoned Catholicism long before. Despite the discovery that she had tuberculosis, she continued to make the lecture circuit with Helen. Her eyesight became even worse, until she was totally blind by 1935. After her death the next year, her cremated remains were buried in the National Cathedral in Washington, D.C.

After Annie's death Helen continued her travels throughout the world on behalf of the blind. She visited Japan twice – once before World War II, when she gave ninety-seven lectures in thirty-nine cities, and again after the war, when she spoke at Hiroshima and Nagasaki against the nuclear holocaust. The inveterate sojourner also traveled to Australia, New Zealand, South Africa, the Middle East, and Latin America. She subsequently received an Academy Award for The Unconquered, a documentary about her life. In an interview on her eightieth birthday, she expressed her plans for the future: "I will always – as long as I have breath – work for the handicapped." After her death in 1968, her remains were laid to rest next to those of her "Teacher" and "Miracle Worker."

§ Open Monday-Saturday 8:30-4:30, Sunday 1-4:30. Fee. Phone: 205-383-4066.

WETUMPKA

¶ **Fort Toulouse/Fort Jackson Park,** 12 miles northeast of Montgomery and 3 miles west of U.S. 231.

The park is the site of two forts, one built by the French in 1717 and the other constructed by *Andrew Jackson during the Creek War. By the Treaty of Fort Jackson in August 1814, the Creek Indians ceded to the United States 20 million acres in Alabama and Georgia.

§ Open April-October, daily 6 a.m.-9 p.m.; rest of the year, daily 8-5. Campground, boat ramp, nature trail, picnicking, visitor center. Fee. Phone: 205-567-3002.

ALASKA

BARROW

¶ **Post-Rogers Memorial,** across the street from the Mark Air terminal at the airport.

This memorial commemorates the death of the famous humorist Will Rogers and his pilot, Wiley Post, in a 1935 plane crash twelve miles south along the coast.

The actual site of the crash is marked by another memorial on a high cliff above the Walatka lagoon, facing the Arctic Ocean. The marker – made of stone from Rogers' home state of Oklahoma – is inscribed with these words: "Will Rogers and Wiley Post ended life's flight here, August 15, 1935." Rogers boasted of his mixed Irish and Native American ancestry. (See Claremore, Oklahoma.)

DENALI NATIONAL PARK AND PRESERVE

¶ **Mount McKinley.**

Named for William McKinley, one of the fourteen Irish-American presidents of the United States, this mountain was known to the early Athabaskan Indians as Denali, "the high one." The famous mountain actually has two peaks: the 19,470-foot North Peak and – two miles away – the 20,320-foot South Peak (the true summit and the highest in North America).

President McKinley was a fifth-generation descendant of David McKinley, a weaver from County Antrim, Ireland, who immigrated to Pennsylvania, about 1743. The president's grandfather, James McKinley, was born at Conacher's Farm in Dervock, County Antrim, in 1783.

SKAGWAY

¶ **Klondike Gold Rush National Historical Park.**

In 1897-98 the Klondike was the scene of a mad scramble by hundreds of fortune hunters who hoped to strike it rich in the newly found gold fields. One of the most fascinating figures among these hardy argonauts was Nellie Cashman, an Irish native already legendary among the miners of Nevada, British Columbia, and Arizona. (See Tombstone, Arizona.)

After sailing to Skagway from Victoria, British Columbia, in February 1897, Nellie and her nephew set off for the headwaters of the Yukon River, 150 miles away. As they trekked through the thirty-three-mile Chilkoot Pass, the defile was so steep for their pack animals that the pair had to carry their provisions on their back. Nellie remained at the headwaters until spring broke up the ice, when she and her companion built boats and navigated the 560-mile journey down river to Dawson City.

At first Nellie operated a restaurant and a grocery store, the latter becoming known as "The Prospector's Haven of Rest" because of the free cigars and the reading and writing facilities that she offered the miners. Her reputation for helping the needy was so well appreciated that "her entrance into a saloon or dance hall was the signal for every man in the place to stand." Her opinion of the miners was reciprocal: "I have mushed with men, slept out in the open, washed with them and been with them constantly, and I have never been offered an insult. . . . A woman is as safe among the miners as at her own fireside. If a woman complains of her treatment from any of the boys, she has only herself to blame. . . . I can truthfully say that there was never a bigger-hearted class of men than the genuine sourdoughs of Alaska."

Except for brief visits south, Nellie spent the rest of her life in the Far North. It was at Dawson that she apparently enjoyed her greatest success as a prospector, extracting an incredible $100,000 from one of her claims. When asked what she had done with that amount of money, she said: "I spent every red cent of it buying other claims and prospecting the country. I went out with my dog team or on snowshoes all over that district looking for rich claims." In 1904, in her mid fifties, she left Dawson for Fairbanks – in the even harsher interior of Alaska – and opened another grocery. Three years later her wanderlust took her sixty miles north of the Arctic Circle, where she bought and operated a dozen mines, although without much to show for her backbreaking labor.

In 1924, at the age of 75, Nellie became the champion woman musher of Alaska, covering 750 miles in seventeen days. On her last trip to the Arctic Circle, she became ill with pneumonia and was taken to Fairbanks. After her recovery, however, she set out again for the Arctic, but weakness forced her to abandon her plans, but not before she had come within eighty miles of her camp. This time she asked to be taken to the hospital in Victoria which she had helped the Sisters of St. Anne to establish many years before with a $500 donation from the miners in British Columbia. Not long before her death, she waxed philosophical: "You never quite know what's going to happen next, or when your time will come to cash in your checks. It all adds interest and variety to life." She is buried in Ross Bay Cemetery in Victoria.

§ The visitor center at Broadway and 2nd Avenue offers exhibits, films, interpretive programs, and walking tours daily, mid May-mid September. Phone: 907-983-2921.

¶ **Mollie Walsh Statue,** Mollie Walsh Park, near 6th Street and Broadway.

The inscription on the marble base of this portrait bust tells the tragic – if incomplete – story of this Skagway pioneer: "Alone, without help, this courageous girl an a grub tent near Long Cabin during the Gold Rush of 1897, 1898. She fed and lodged the wildest, gold-crazed men generations shall surely knew. This inspiring spirit – murdered, Oct. 27, 1902."

Mary "Mollie" Walsh was born in either Wisconsin or Iowa in 1872, one of three children born to Patrick and Susan Walsh, emigrants from Ireland. At the age of nine she moved with her parents and her two brothers to St. Paul, Minnesota. Nine years later, however, she and a girlfriend headed off on their own, doubtlessly to seek their fame and fortune.

According to some sources, Mollie was a dance-hall queen in the Irish community of Butte, Montana, before moving on to Alaska. In October 1897 Mollie – now twenty-four – arrived in Skagway aboard the S.S. *Quadra*. Among the passengers was the Reverend R. M. Dickey, through whose efforts Walsh was introduced to Skagway's proper society. Although that winter she worked with other Christian women to establish the town's first church, the following spring she departed for Long Cabin on the White Pass Trail. There she set up a grub tent for the miners in the area.

As perhaps was inevitable in an environment in which women were at a premium, Mollie had numerous suitors, the most ardent of whom were Jack Newman and Michael Bartlett, two regular customers at her restaurant. Newman, head packer for one of the large pack trains on the White Pass Trail, was so passionately in love with her that he killed a Skagway faro dealer over her affections. Newman also quarreled with Mollie over one of her other admirers – Michael Bartlett, also a trail packer. Although Newman ordered her not to see his rival, Mollie ignored his command and married Bartlett. The new couple later moved to Dawson City, where he made a fortune as a packer. In 1902, while the two were living in Seattle, Bartlett killed his twenty-nine-year-old wife, apparently in a jealous rage because of the attentions offered her by another man. In the subsequent legal trial, Bartlett was acquitted on the grounds of temporary insanity. His wife was buried in Calvary Cemetery in St. Paul, Minnesota.

In 1930 the jilted Newman – still full of remorse because of his ill-fated argument with Mollie – erected this monument in her honor.

ARIZONA

FLAGSTAFF

¶ Riordan State Historic Park, 1300 Riordan Ranch Road.

This historic park is dominated by a forty-room log mansion, constructed in 1904 by Michael and Timothy Riordan, brothers who owed their fortune to the success of the Arizona Lumber and Timber Company.

The structure, which actually consists of two similar wings with differing roof lines, was christened *Kinlichi* (from the Navajo for "red house"). Each brother and his family lived in one of the two-story wings, which were joined by a one-story recreation facility known as the billiard room. Each wing contains about 5,000 square feet of living space.

The exterior of this Craftsman-style structure incorporates wooden shingles, volcanic stone, and log-slab siding, while the interior is furnished with hand-crafted furniture, a grand piano, stained-glass windows, and a swinging settee suspended from the ceiling.

Natives of Chicago, the two brothers had come to Arizona in 1884 to join their brother, Daniel, who at the time was the Indian agent at Fort Defiance. After arriving in Flagstaff, Timothy became associated with the Ayer Lumber Company, eventually rising to manager soon after his brother acquired ownership of the milling enterprise. In 1887, however, the company's mill was destroyed by fire. Once a new and improved struc-

Riordan Mansion.
(Photo by Princely Nesadurai and courtesy of Riordan Mansion State Historic Park.)

ture was completed, Daniel changed the name of the company to Arizona Lumber & Timber.

By 1897 Timothy had become president of the company but was immediately faced with the challenge of rebuilding after a second disastrous fire. The reconstructed mill facility incorporated state-of-the-art precautions against future fires and was considered the finest sawmill in the western part of the country. (It boasted the first bandsaw in Arizona and the second in the United States). The forty to fifty houses which the company constructed for its employees ranged from one-room cabins to larger structures with as many as ten rooms.

The Arizona Lumber Company also owned a second mill eighteen miles from town, one that had a capacity to produce 60,000 board feet per day. In addition, the company acquired the Central Arizona Railroad, a line that extended twenty-four miles into the region's timber belt. Timothy Riordan later served as president not only of that rail line but also of the Flagstaff Electric Light Company. He was also a shareholder in the Howard Sheep Company and the Crespi and Flagstaff oil companies.

In a letter to his daughter in 1921, Timothy described the only significant fire which damaged *Kinlichi*. "[W]e found that Mr. Mike's house had been destroyed by fire," he wrote. "It appears that the fire broke out under the roof on the corner adjoining the cabin. . . . [O]ur hose and the town hose were coupled together and the new fire engine was turned loose and bursted [*sic*] the hose in many places. . . . The astounding thing is how did it miss burning the cabin and our house, as the wind was blowing that direction and the water supply was bum. Anyway . . . practically everything in the house was saved and is now piled up in the billiard room and in the garage, and all the family are in our house. . . . Very little . . . burned[,] only what was up in the attic. There were ten trunks destroyed there and Uncle Mike's fur lined overcoat and an Irish overcoat and things of that kind that had been stored up there for the summer . . . ."

§ Open mid May-mid September, daily 9-4; rest of the year, daily 1-4. Fee. Phone: 602-779-4395.

GRAND CANYON NATIONAL PARK

❡ **Buckey O'Neill Cabin,** now part of Bright Angel Lodge.

The oldest remaining building on the rim of the Grand Canyon, this simple log cabin was built by *William "Buckey" O'Neill, one of the organizers of the famous Rough Rider cavalry unit during the Spanish-American War. (See Prescott, Arizona.)

O'Neill had come to this area in 1897, when he staked several claims along the canyon rim near Cyclorama Point. He also staked some additional claims about fourteen miles south of the rim at a place which he named Anita. The copper ore in the latter claims was so rich that a year later a Chicago engineering firm bought out his interests.

PRESCOTT

¶ **The Rough Rider Memorial Monument,** in front of the Yavapai County Courthouse, Montezuma Street.

The work of the sculptor Solon Borglum, this bronze memorial was dedicated in 1907 and is inscribed with the following words: "Erected by Arizona in honor of the first U. S. Volunteer Cavalry, known to history as Roosevelt's Rough Riders, and to the memory of Captain William O. O'Neill and his comrades who died while serving their country in the war with Spain."

Born in Ireland in 1860, William O'Neill had come to Phoenix in 1879 and eventually became that uniquely western type of Renaissance man: editor, gambler, newspaper owner, lawyer, sheriff, miner, explorer, politician, soldier, and hero.

Despite his Irish origins, O'Neill usually gave his birthplace as either Washington, D.C., or St. Louis. During the Civil War his father, John Owen O'Neill, had been a captain in the 116th Pennsylvania Volunteers, a unit in the famous Irish Brigade. He was wounded a total of fourteen times in the conflict, five times at Fredericksburg alone.

After heading out west in 1879, the younger O'Neill worked as a typesetter for the *Phoenix Herald*, during which time his skill at the card game faro or "bucking the tiger" earned him the nickname "Buckey." He later became the editor of the *Arizona Gazette* and a reporter for the *Tombstone Epitaph*. After moving to Prescott in 1881, he served as the editor of the *Prescott Miner* and became the owner-editor of *Hoof and Horn*, a cattleman's journal. While sheriff of Yavapai County, O'Neill led a posse that nabbed four cowboys who had stolen $1,300 from an Atlantic & Pacific train at Diablo Canyon, east of Flagstaff, in March 1889. The 600-mile, three-week pursuit ended with a shootout before the outlaws were taken to Kanab, Utah, for trial.

In the meantime O'Neill was becoming moderately wealthy from an investment in an onyx mine near Prescott. He later uncovered copper deposits near the south rim of the Grand Canyon. Following two unsuccessful attempts to be elected Arizona's territorial representative in Congress, O'Neill was elected mayor of Prescott in 1898. With the outbreak of hostilities between the United States and Spain, he helped organize the Arizona Volunteers, a group which later became part of the First U.S. Volunteer Cavalry Regiment, also known as the "Rough Riders." When enlisting in the army, O'Neill for the first time revealed his Irish birthplace.

O'Neill's enthusiasm for supporting the war effort against Spain may have been the result of his belief that Arizona would secure statehood and "stardom" if her young men rallied to the flag. In a letter written to a friend some time in May 1898, O'Neill asked the rhetorical question, "Who would not gamble for a new star in the flag?"

Whatever O'Neill's aspirations for Arizona, the Fates had decreed otherwise for Captain O'Neill of A Troop. Not long after he and his men landed in Cuba, the popular officer was cut down by enemy fire on San Juan Hill. Theodore Roosevelt, the colonel of the First U.S. Volunteer Cavalry, recorded the tragic episode of July 1, 1898: "The most serious loss that I and the regiment could have suffered befell just before we charged. Buckey O'Neill was strolling up and down in front of his men, smoking his cigarette, for he was inveterately addicted to the habit. He had a theory that an officer ought never to take cover – a theory which was, of course, wrong, though in a volunteer organization the officers should certainly expose themselves very fully, simply for the effect on the men; our regiment toast on the transport running, 'The officers; may the war last until each is killed, wounded, or promoted.' As O'Neill moved to and from, his men begged him to lie down, and one of the sergeants said, 'Captain, a bullet is sure to hit you.' O'Neill took his cigarette out of his mouth, and blowing out a cloud of smoke laughed and said, 'Sergeant, the Spanish bullet isn't made that will kill me.' A little later he discussed for a moment with one of the

The Rough Rider Monument.
(Photo courtesy of Sharlott Hall Museum Library/Archives, Prescott, Arizona.)

regular officers the direction from which the Spanish fire was coming. As he turned on his heel a bullet struck him in the mouth and came out at the back of his head; so that even before he fell his wild and gallant soul had gone out into the darkness."

O'Neill's death was all the more ironic because of another tragic episode which had occurred when American troops first landed at Daiquiri, Cuba. During the landing, two black cavalrymen were pulled under the water by the surf. Although O'Neill tried to rescue the two men, he was ultimately unsuccessful. After his death, his widow received condolences from Prescott's African-American citizens, who described their mayor as a true and tried friend. O'Neill was first buried in Cuba, but his body was reinterred in Arlington National Cemetery in Virginia on May 1, 1899.

Arizona's most famous Irishman is the subject of "Rough Rider O'Neill," a poem by Joseph I. C. Clarke, for many years the president of the American Irish Historical Society. Three of that work's four verses are printed below:

> When the cresset of war blazed over the land
> And a call rang fierce thro' the West,
> Saying, "Rough Riders, come to the roll of the drum,"
> They came with their bravest and best,
> With a clatter of hoofs and a stormy hail –
> Sinewy, lean, tall and brown;
> Hunters and fighters and men of the trail,
> From hills and plains, from college and town;
> With the cowboys' yell and the redman's whoop,
> Sons of thunder and swingers of steel;
> And, leading his own Arizona troop,
> Rode glad and fearless "Bucky" O'Neill.
>
> In the ranks there was Irish blood galore,
> As it ever is sure to be
> When the Union flag is flung to the fore,
> And the fight is to make men free.
> There were Kellys and Murphys and Burkes and Boyles –
> The colonel owned an O'Brien strain –
> And the lift of the race made a glow on each face
> When they met on the Texan plain;
> But the man of them all, with the iron will –
> Man and soldier from crown to heel;
> A leader and master in games that kill –
> Was soft-spoken Captain "Bucky" O'Neill.
>
> On the watch in the valley or charging the height,
> In a plunge 'cross the steep ravine,
> San Juan or Las Guasimas, battle or fight,

Or a such thro' the jungle screen,
Where the wave of the war took the battling host
The Rough Riders fronted the storm,
And their dead on the rocks of red glory tossed
Amid spray with their life-blood warm.
What wonder, then, holding his chivalrous vow
To stoop not, nor crouch not, nor kneel,
That Death in hot anger struck full on the brow
Of the dauntless "Bucky" O'Neill.

¶ **Sharlot Hall Museum and Historical Society,** 415 West Gurley Street.

Among the restored buildings in this outdoor museum is the Governor's Mansion, a two-story log structure that served as the first capitol building and executive mansion of Arizona Territory. During the mid 1860s, territorial governor John Goodwin lived in one wing of the pine log building while Richard McCormick, the territorial secretary, lived in the other.

Born in New York in 1832, McCormick was descended from an emigrant who had left Londonderry, northern Ireland, for Pennsylvania sometime before 1735. Although McCormick's early education prepared him for Columbia College, his poor health caused him to seek relief in travel, principally in Europe and Asia. While in the Crimea in the mid 1850s, he covered the conflict there for several New York journals, and he later published two accounts of his experiences in that part of the world. Upon his return to the United States, he continued his journalistic career – initially as the editor of the *Young Men's Magazine* and later as a correspondent for the *New York Evening Post* covering the Army of the Potomac in the beginning months of the Civil War.

In the meantime McCormick's antislavery views had led him into the Republican Party. His subsequent friendships with President Lincoln and Secretary of State Seward resulted in his appointment in 1863 as secretary of the newly organized Arizona Territory. Soon after their arrival there, McCormick and Governor Goodwin took part in a ceremony marking the official creation of the Territory. In an address during a snowstorm that day, McCormick struck the appropriate tone: "After a long and trying journey, we have arrived within the limits of Arizona. These broad plains and hills form a part of the district over which, as representatives of the United States, we are to establish a civil government. Happily, although claimed by those now in hostility to the Federal arms, we take possession of the Territory without resort to military force. The flag which I hoist in token of our authority is no new and untried banner. For nearly a century it has been the recognized, the honored, the loved emblem of law and liberty. From Canada to Mexico, from the Atlantic to the Pacific, millions of strong arms are raised in its defense, and above the forts of all foreign and domestic foes, it is destined to live untarnished and transcendent."

Once settled in Arizona, McCormick became the territory's leading political force, known for his red hair, natty attire, and extraordinary energy. He founded the *Arizona Weekly Miner* (with the press he had brought from the East), suggested that the new capital be named for the Western historian Walter Prescott, and promoted the territory through his articles in Eastern publications and through his investments in mining and real estate. For his efforts McCormick was appointed territorial governor in 1866. During his three-year tenure he was an outspoken advocate for the creation of an educational system, the development of agriculture and mining, and the construction of roads and railroads to California and New Mexico.

To gain political support in his quest to be named the territorial delegate to Congress, McCormick urged that the capital be transferred to Tucson. Although after his election in 1868 he was accused of organizing a "ring" that profited from government contracts, while in Congress he worked for the territory's good by promoting irrigation, forest conservation, and restrictions on buffalo hunting. With regard to the Indians in Arizona, he urged sure and swift punishment for the brutal tribes and monetary compensation for those which worked on the reservations. By 1874 he had returned to the East, where he was elected to Congress.

§ Open April-October, Tuesday-Saturday 10-5, Sunday 1-5; rest of the year, Tuesday-Saturday 10-4, Sunday 1-5.

TOMBSTONE

¶ **The Nellie Cashman Restaurant,** 115 South 5th Street.

Although the interior of this adobe structure was renovated after a fire destroyed the ceiling, the exterior looks much as it did in the 1880s, when the building was known as Russ House. At that time it was operated by Nellie Cashman, renowned from Alaska to Mexico for her prospecting feats and her many acts of charity toward her fellow miners. The restaurant features a copy of the famous portrait of Cashman, made in China by Sam Lee, her Chinese Cook, on a visit to his native land.

Nellie, whose slight frame and barely five-foot stature belied her enormous energy, was born in Queenstown (now Cobh), Ireland, in about 1850. By the age of seventeen, however, she and her sister Frances had immigrated to Boston, where Nellie found work as a bellhop in a local hotel. After the pair had moved on to San Francisco, Frances married a man by the name of Cunningham and subsequently had five children.

Nellie first succumbed to the lure of gold in 1874, when she joined a stampede of fortune hunters to the mining fields around Dease Lake in upper British Columbia. After operating a boardinghouse for miners there that season, she visited Victoria, British Columbia, but immediately returned at the head of a relief expedition after learning that many of the men at Dease Lake were ill from scurvy. Although it was the dead of winter, Nellie and her party of six set out with 1,500 pounds of food and supplies. Using a harness device around her neck, Nellie dragged her share of the provisions in a sled, although she weighed less than a hundred pounds herself. She recalled that one night during the seventy-six-day trek "the men put my tent up on the side of a steep hill where the snow was 10 feet deep. The next morning one of my men came to where my tent was to bring me coffee. It had snowed heavily in the night, and, to his surprise, he couldn't find the tent. Finally they discovered me a quarter of a mile down the hill, where my tent, my bed and myself and all the rest of my belongings had been carried by a snowslide." After arriving at Dease Lake, she nursed back to health the 75 of the 200 miners who suffered from scurvy.

By 1879 Nellie had moved to Tombstone, Arizona, although she was less attracted by the silver mines than by the commercial opportunities that the boomtown offered. At first she sold groceries and supplies at the Tombstone Cash Store and at Nellie's Nevada Boot and Shoe Store. Later, however, she and a partner opened the Russ Hotel, whose menu offered a surprisingly *haute cuisine*: trout, lamb with caper sauce, fricassee à la creme, corned beef, dressed veal, lobster salads, beef à l'Español, New York plum pudding, calf heads, and beets with horseradish. (When a stranger in town complained about the beans, a miner sitting nearby forced him to eat them – at gunpoint.) Nellie later sold her interest in the hotel to help her widowed sister operate a boardinghouse known as the American Hotel. When her sister died, Nellie took it upon herself to raise and educate her five nieces and nephews. For a while Nellie ran the Cashman Hotel in Kingston, New Mexico, where one of her dishwashers was the future oil millionaire, Edward Doheny, the son of an Irish immigrant father. (See Doheny Mansion, Los Angeles, California.)

During the years she lived in Tombstone, Nellie became a well known civic leader and fund-raiser for a variety of causes. She once raised $500 for a prospector who had broken both legs during a fall into a mine shaft. She later came up with $700 as part of a bargain she had struck with the bishop in Tucson: If she raised the money to build a church, he would supply a priest. To raise the money, the strong-willed Irishwoman had organized Tombstone's first amateur theatrical production – a musical comedy called *The Irish Diamond* followed by a ball. (Some of the funds came from habitués of the town's red light district.) She was also instrumental in organizing the Miner's Hospital Association and a branch of the Irish National Land League.

In 1883 Nellie decided to sell the Russ Hotel when she heard the Siren call of the gold fields once again. According to one tradition, she and twenty other prospectors headed for the Baja California peninsula after a Mexican stumbled into her hotel and, before dying, mumbled the words ". . . go to Mulege." The gold nuggets in the expired man's pockets must have clouded the argonauts' minds, for they set off across the desert rather impetuously and soon realized that they were almost out of water. After volunteering to seek help, Nellie made it to a Catholic mission and returned with a water-bearing rescue party just in time to save her companions from dying of thirst. It was no accident that she was known as the Angel of Tombstone, the Frontier Angel, the Miner's Angel, and the Saint of the Sourdough.

Another incident illustrates the preeminent standing which Nellie enjoyed in Tombstone. In 1884, when five men awaited execution for the murder of four bystanders during a robbery of the Goldwater store in Bisbee, she assisted the priest in ministering to their spiritual needs. And when a local carpenter expressed his intention to charge admission to the grandstand which he had built near the site of the hanging, Nellie reacted with indignation. After rounding up some of her miner friends, she led them on a midnight raid to dismantle the stands. (She herself reportedly swung the first sledge, an episode that gave rise to the saying that she was an angel with a temper.)

Both during her lifetime and after her death, Nellie was the object of unusual eulogy. In October 1895 the *Arizona Star* reported: "Yesterday Tucson was visited by one of the most extraordinary women in America, Nellie Cashman, whose name and face have been familiar in every important mining camp or district on the coast for more than twenty years. She road into town from Casa Grande on horseback, a jaunt that would have nearly prostrated the average man with fatigue. She showed no sign of weariness, and went about town in that calm businesslike manner that belongs particularly to her." John Clum, who founded the *Daily Arizona Citizen* and who knew Nellie personally, wrote that "Her principal business was to feed the hungry and shelter the homeless, and her chief divertissement was to relieve those in distress and to care for the sick and afflicted." Many years later a resident of Tombstone added: "In every place where I knew her she was the queen of the Irish miners, and held the high respect of the 'Cousin Jacks' (Cornishmen) as well. . . . I have always regarded Nellie as a most remarkable and admirable woman."

§ Phone: 520-457-2212.

ARKANSAS

BERRYVILLE

¶ **Saunders Memorial Museum,** 115 East Madison Street.

Besides Oriental rugs, Tiffany lamps, and American silverware, the museum contains the largest private gun collection in the country, including weapons that belonged to Annie Oakley, Pancho Villa, and the Irish-Americans Jesse James and Henry McCarty ("Billy the Kid").

§ Open March-October, Monday-Saturday 10:30-5. Fee. Phone: 501-423-2563

EUREKA SPRINGS

¶ **Hatchet Hall,** 35 Steele Street.

Between 1908 and 1911 this was the home of *Carry Nation, the famous temperance leader who was known for her hatchet-wielding attacks against saloons. The house had originally been built by some of her followers as an academy devoted to the training of future prohibitionists. Nation died in Eureka Springs soon after giving a speech in Basin Park. Today Hatchet Hall contains memorabilia associated with the fiery activist and her crusade. (See Bryantsville, Kentucky.)

§ Phone: 501-253-7324.

HELENA

¶ **Patrick Cleburne Burial Site,** Confederate Cemetery in Maple Hill Cemetery, 1801 North Holly Street.

The grave of Patrick Cleburne, an Irish-born Confederate general known as the "Stonewall Jackson of the West," is adorned by a monument surmounted by a sixteen-foot urn. The front of the monument is inscribed with his name and the Latin verse "Dulce et decorum est pro patria mori." The other three sides are inscribed with the names of the battlefields on which Cleburne fought: Shiloh, Shelton House, Richmond (Ky.), Chicamauga, Missionary Ridge, Ringgold Gap, and Franklin. On the base is a stanza from a poem by Naomi Hays: "Rest thee, Cleburne; tears of sadness / Flow from hearts thou'st nobly won; / Mem'ry ne'er will cease to cherish / Deeds of glory thou hast done."

The present monument to Cleburne was dedicated on May 10, 1891. During the ceremonies Virginia Frazer Boyle read her poem "The Death of Cleburne."

> 'Tis midnight's hour, and through the lifting clouds
> The struggling moonbeams gaze on Franklin's field,
> Upon the war-stained corpse of friend and foe,

And weirdly kiss the lips forever sealed.

The ghastly calm seems steeped in human gore,
The ditch bears in its depth the bloody tide;
The cold December winds mourn round the spot
Where Cleburne, with his charger, nobly died.

No more for him rings out the battle-cry,
No more the stern lips echo back its tone;
And as in life he led the Irish bands,
In death his life-blood mingled with his own.

Patrick Ronayne Cleburne was born in County Cork, Ireland, on St. Patrick's Day 1828. Although he apprenticed himself to a druggist at the age of eighteen, he failed the apothecaries' exam administered at Trinity College, Dublin, primarily because of his deficiencies in the classical languages. To escape this humiliation, he sought anonymity in a British infantry regiment, although after three years he left the service for America in 1849. He eventually obtained a job as a druggist's clerk in Helena.

While living here, Cleburne had an opportunity to demonstrate the skill with a pistol which he had learned in the British service. One day, it seems, a disgruntled local resident – angry that the Irishman had supported a friend in a recent controversy – shot him in the back from a doorway. Cleburne was dangerously wounded when the ball passed through his body, but as he fell he drew his pistol and killed his assailant.

Life in Helena also exposed Cleburne to practical jokes which a newcomer to America should have expected. After seeing and buying his first watermelon from a youngster named Joseph Maxey, the Irishman inquired of the lad how he should eat it. Seizing the chance to pull the paddy's leg, the young dissembler replied, "You must stew it." Cleburne readily followed the recipe and with kettle and flame dutifully boiled the odd-shaped fruit. To his question about the next step, Maxey replied with moxie, "Put it into dishes and eat it with a spoon." After obtaining the needed implements from his neighbors, the ingenue prepared to serve the concoction to a pair of local doctors who happened to visit him. Hardly had he proffered his "nice treat" to his guests than one of them made the understated observation, ". . . you have spoiled a nice melon, Cleburne." By then Maxey was nowhere to be found.

As national events rushed headlong toward civil war, Cleburne threw in his lot with the Confederacy. He first enlisted in the Yell Rifles and then in the 1st Arkansas Regiment, whose men elected him captain. In a letter of May 7, 1861, he proclaimed his devotion to the Confederacy: "I am with the South in life or in death, in victory or defeat. . . . I believe the North is about to wage a brutal and unholy war on a people who have done them no wrong, in violation of the Constitution and the fundamental principles of the government. They no longer acknowledge that all government derives its authority from the consent of the governed."

About his personal qualities it was agreed that Cleburne was essentially shy but also able to assert his authority when necessary. A member of his staff admitted that the Irishman was not a good conversationalist "except when in the company of congenial friends whose intimacy freed him from all shackles of embarrassment." Although Cleburne was a strict disciplinarian, he insisted that his men be treated with respect and he never condoned punishment that disgraced the individual. As punishment for minor offenses, he ordered extra guard duty, loss of privileges, or assignment to a cleaning detail. On one occasion when he learned that one of his drunken soldiers had been whipped with the buckle end of a belt, he took steps to ensure that the officer who had ordered the punishment lost his commission. Although Cleburne rarely used foul language and his speech normally betrayed little of an Irish accent, when he became angry he sometimes cursed and lapsed into a thick brogue.

In 1863, during a battle at Richmond, Kentucky, the Irishman was wounded in the mouth. The bullet which entered his left jaw destroyed two lower teeth and lodged in his mouth, rendering him incapable of speech and thus useless as a commanding officer during that engagement. Although Cleburne later fought in Alabama and Tennessee, he showed

Patrick Cleburne Monument
in Helena, Arkansas.
(Photo by Ivey S. Gladin.)

the most daring at Chickamauga, where he and his men repulsed Sherman and covered the retreat of General Braxton Bragg from Lookout Mountain at Ringgold Gap in Georgia. For his actions during these crucial engagements, he became known as the "Stonewall Jackson of the West."

As the fortunes of the Confederacy waned during the last year of the war, Cleburne risked military advancement with what some regarded as a dangerous suggestion. Seeing that the Southern ranks were becoming thinner, he proposed that the slaves in the South should be enlisted in the Confederate army and that they be granted their freedom for serving. Although his commanding officer refused to forward the proposal to Richmond, a fellow officer of Cleburne's thought that the suggestion was so controversial that he sent a copy to the Confederate president. *Jefferson Davis thought the proposal inexpedient and took no action on it. The Irishman was vindicated, however, when his suggestion was embodied in a bill which the Confederate Congress passed on March 3, 1865.

A year after the battle at Richmond, Cleburne was shot and killed during an engagement at Franklin, Tennessee. Before the battle he said to a companion, "Well, Govan, if we must die, let us die like men." The Irishman's last words were spoken to a fellow officer: "We will resume this conversation at the first convenient moment." Ironically, his death on the battlefield occurred only fifteen minutes after an unusual act of charity toward one of his men. As he rode into battle he had noticed that one of his Irish boys was leaving tracts of blood on the ground while walking barefoot over the frozen cornfield. Cleburne took off his boots and gave them to the soldier, dying soon later in his own bare feet. After hearing of Cleburne's death, Robert E. Lee compared him to "a meteor shooting from a clouded sky."

During the battle at Franklin, the Confederates suffered staggering losses. In addition to the deaths of more than 6,000 soldiers, the South lost the services of a dozen of its generals. One of the men who discovered Cleburne's body the next day wrote: "He lay flat upon his back, as if asleep, his military cap partly over his eyes. He had on a new gray uniform . . . . It was unbuttoned . . . a white linen shirt . . . was stained with blood on the front part of the left side, or just left of the abdomen. This was the only sign of a wound. . . ."

Cleburne was first buried in Rose Hill Cemetery in Columbia, Tennessee. He was reburied in the graveyard at St. John's Episcopal Church at Ashwood, Tennessee, about which he had only recently before said, "It is almost worth dying for, to be buried in such a beautiful spot." In 1869 his remains were moved to Helena, Arkansas.

§ To reach the cemetery, go north off U.S. 49 (Business Route) to Columbia Street, 2 blocks east on McDonough Street to Holly Street, and then 4 blocks north to Maple Hill Cemetery (1801 North Holly Street). Open daily 9-5.

HOPE

℘ Clinton Birthplace House, 117 South Hervey Street.

Now in the process of being restored, this house was where President Bill Clinton lived with his mother (Virginia Dell Cassidy) and his grandparents until he was four years of age.

The youngster's father had died in an automobile accident three months before the birth of his son, whom his mother named William Jefferson Blythe IV. When Virginia moved to New Orleans to study nursing, she left her two-year-old son with his grandparents. The family moved to Hot Springs, Arkansas, after she married Roger Clinton, who became young Bill's stepfather and whose last name the future president took.

According to authorities in Northern Ireland, President Clinton is descended from Lucas Cassidy, who had emigrated with his wife, Rachel, from Roslea, County Fermanagh, in 1750. Their son, Levi, was born in Chesterfield, South Carolina, forty years later. These same sources assert that Lucas Cassidy's descendants have been traced to Alabama, Arkansas, and Nevada and that he may have been the 4th-great-grandfather of Clinton's mother, who was born in 1923.

The man who claims to be President Clinton's closest living relative in Ireland is Mike Cassidy, a sixty-five-year-old bachelor living in County Fermanagh. He is the owner of the cottage in Crockada from which Lucas Cassidy purportedly emigrated in the middle of the eighteenth century. Anticipating the president's visit to Ireland in November and December 1995, Mike Cassidy said, "It would be nice to meet the President, show him around a bit like when President Kennedy came. He'll need the wellies, up here in the winter – the wind would blow your head off."

The American Embassy in Dublin and the Department of the Taoiseach dismiss the Roslea-Cassidy claim as "a leap of faith" without genealogical basis. A spokesman for the department concedes instead that Clinton's Irish connection may be through such names in his family tree as Hayes and Ayres. As a result of still inconclusive evidence, the American president will have to settle for recognition from the Irish Heraldry Office in Dublin that he is "of uncontested Irish descent" and that he "incontrovertibly has Irish blood."

Before entering politics, Bill Clinton earned a bachelor's degree in international affairs from Georgetown University, attended Oxford University on a Rhodes scholarship, and was graduated from Yale Law School. During the 1970s he worked for the presidential campaigns of George McGovern and Jimmy Carter. At thirty Clinton was elected attorney general of Arkansas and two years later became governor of the state, the nation's youngest chief executive.

§ Hope Chamber of Commerce: 501-777-3640.

CALIFORNIA

ANGELS CAMP

¶ **Angels Hotel,** 1287 South Main Street.

According to tradition, it was at this hotel that *Mark Twain first heard of a legendary jumping-frog contest, a tale that he reworked into "The Celebrated Jumping Frog of Calaveras County." Twain allegedly heard the original story from the hotel's bartender, Ben Coon. Twain initially marketed his own version of the story as "Jim Smiley and His Jumping Frog." Angels Camp annually celebrates a frog-jump contest in his honor. (The local high school's athletic teams are known as the "Jumping Frogs.")

¶ A statue of Mark Twain is located in Utica Park (Utica Lane and Sams Way). (See Florida, Missouri.)

BEL AIR

¶ **Reagan Home,** 668 St. Cloud Road. Private.

This one-acre, $2.5 million estate is the home of former president *Ronald Reagan and his wife, Nancy. The 6,500-square-foot house contains three bedrooms, a dining room, a library, servants' quarters, a swimming pool, and a three-car garage.

BELMONT

¶ **Ralston Hall,** Notre Dame College, 1500 Ralston Avenue.

This structure was formerly the country residence of William Ralston, one of the most powerful financiers on the Pacific Coast and the "man who built San Francisco." Ralston had purchased the estate in 1864 from Count Leonetto Cipriani, an Italian political refugee. A dozen years earlier the Italian had dismantled the villa in his native land and shipped the crated pieces to San Francisco.

Ralston proceeded to enlarge the Cipriani house into an eighty-room mansion, the largest private residence on the West Coast. He adorned it with chandeliers, parquetry floors, solid silver doorknobs, and mirror-paneled walls, transforming it into a magnificent showplace for weekend balls and banquets. In addition, he constructed greenhouses, a gymnasium, a Turkish bath, mahogany-paneled horse stables, and a fifty-room house for his servants. The property also had its own gasworks and water reservoir.

In 1923 the estate was acquired by the Sisters of Notre Dame, who moved their convent and college here from San Jose. The mansion then became known as Berchman's Hall, so named for one of the founding nuns, and Ralston's famous ballroom became the school chapel. In recent years the building was restored to its appearance during the Ralston era.

A native of Ohio, William Ralston was a descendant of Robert and Margaret McBride Ralston, emigrants from County Down, Ireland. When he first learned of the California gold rush, he headed west via Panama, like thousands of others inspired by dreams of quickly acquired wealth. But unlike the vast majority of those argonauts, the twenty-three-year-old hoped to strike it rich not by breaking his back in the mines but by providing food, provisions, and transportation to the miners. To this end he accepted a position as agent in Panama for Garrison & Morgan, a firm which operated a steamship line between New York and San Francisco.

By 1856 Ralston had settled permanently in San Francisco and was a partner in an increasingly successful banking firm. When Joseph Donohue and Eugene Kelly joined the partnership at the beginning of the Civil War, the name of the enterprise was changed to Donahue, Ralston & Company. Since almost all bullion shipments from the mines in Nevada and California passed through the firm, Ralston and his partners profited handsomely.

In 1864, however, Ralston withdrew from the firm and established the Bank of California with Darius Mills, the city's foremost financier. The new financial house quickly became the premiere banking institution in the West. After opening an office in the mining capital of Virginia City, Nevada, Ralston prepared to take advantage of the slump caused by flooding in the mines. Facing bankruptcy because production had come to a standstill, some of the owners borrowed money from the Bank of California, offering shares in their mines as collateral. Through these loans and the inevitable foreclosures, the bank obtained a controlling interest in many of the mines. In addition, the increasingly rapacious "Ralston Ring" gained control over the mines' lumber supply by buying up the nearest forests and building sawmills and water systems. And when the bank built the only railroad to Virginia City, the monopoly was complete. Within two years the bank earned $1 million in net profits, paid dividends of 12 percent, and doubled its initial capitalization of $2.5 million. To cap it all off, when the mines returned to full production, Ralston and his partners shared in the incredible wealth which the mine shafts began to yield in the early 1870s.

The bank's other investments were equally diversified. Besides loaning $3 million to the Central Pacific for the construction of the first transcontinental railroad, the bank invested heavily in real estate, irrigation and reclamation projects, hydraulic mining, Alaskan fisheries, and San Francisco factories and refineries. It also financed construction of the California Theater and the Grand and the Palace hotels. (Today the site of the latter hotel is occupied by the Sheraton Palace Hotel, built in 1909 and renovated several times since.)

In the end, Ralston overextended himself and the bank. When the public sensed that he could not meet his obligations, a "run" on the bank forced it to close in August 1875. The ripple effect was so wide that the bank's failure caused a suspension of the San Francisco and the Pacific stock exchanges. Ralston himself resigned as president of the Bank of California and transferred his $15 million of personal holdings to an agent, with instructions to use that sum to help satisfy the claims of his creditors. The following day, however, while taking his accustomed swim in the bay, he died of an apparent stroke.

§ To inquire about tours, call Monday-Friday 9-4. Fee. Phone: 415-593-1601, extension 201.

BENICIA

¶ **Walsh House,** 235 East L Street.

One of the earliest Carpenter Gothic houses built in California, this 1850 structure was the home of John Walsh, a sea captain from Prince Edward Island. The house was a favorite gathering place for local society, including military and naval officers stationed in the area. Today the house is a bed and breakfast establishment.

Referred to as an Irishman, Walsh may have been in the San Francisco Bay area as early as 1818, when he was the first officer of the *Houqua* bound for China. He seems to have had shipping interests in South America, and it was from Valparaiso, Chile, that he and his family arrived to settle in Benicia in 1849. When Benicia was raised to the status of a port of entry, Walsh was made deputy customs collector. Although he was at first a trustee of the local Presbyterian church, he later became affiliated with St. Paul's Episcopal Church, serving the latter as vestryman and senior warden. He was also the commissioner of county schools before his death in 1884 at the age of eighty-seven. His wife, Eleanor Frisbee Walsh, managed his shipping interests and was one of the first women to be registered in Solano County as a married woman doing business in her own name.

BERKELEY

The inspiration for the name Berkeley came from Frederick Billings, the chairman of the board of trustees of the University of California in the mid 1860s. When the trustees were considering names for the proposed site of California's new university, Billings suggested "Berkeley." He said that the city's location on the western perimeter of the country reminded him of the prophetic lines written by the Irishman George Berkeley about a golden age in the New World :

> There shall be sung another golden Age,
> The rise of Empire and of Arts,
> The Good and Great inspiring epic Rage,
> The Wisest Heads and Noblest Hearts . . . .

Westward the Course of Empire takes its Way;
The four first Acts already past,
A fifth shall close the Drama with the Day;
Time's noblest Offering is the last.

Berkeley was a native of County Kilkenny, Ireland, where he was born in 1684. Following his appointment as dean of the cathedral in Londonderry in 1724, he became an advocate for the conversion of the Native American. After resigning his deanery, he left Britain in September 1728 to establish a college in Bermuda to provide pastors for colonial parishes and to train missionaries to the Indians. His ship lost its direction and landed instead in Newport, Rhode Island, the following January. There he erected a large clapboard house on a ninety-acre farm. After realizing that his educational plan would never receive the financial support he had expected from England, Berkeley returned to Ireland and bequeathed his farm to Yale College. (See *Irish America, Volume 1.*)

¶ **Hearst Memorial Mining Building,** north of Mining Circle on the University of California campus.

The funds for the construction of this building were provided by Phoebe Apperson Hearst in honor of her husband, George Hearst. Born in 1820 near Sullivan, Missouri, George Hearst was of Scottish ancestry on his paternal side but was Irish through his mother, Elizabeth Collins Hearst. Mrs. Hearst's family had settled in Georgia after emigrating from Galway, Ireland.

After attending a mining school in Missouri, George Hearst crossed the continent by foot, taking up quartz mining and later placer mining in California. Although he met with little success there, he eventually made a fortune from his mining holdings elsewhere: the Ophir in Nevada, the Homestake in North Dakota, the Ontario in Utah, and the Anaconda in Montana. He lived lavishly on his newfound wealth but was correspondingly generous in his charity.

In 1882 Hearst acquired the *San Francisco Daily Examiner*, which he used in his unsuccessful attempt to secure the Democratic nomination for governor. Although he subsequently allied himself with the Democratic boss of San Francisco, he lost a bid for the U.S. Senate to Leland Stanford. Hearst was later appointed to the Senate to fill a vacancy and was elected for the full term two years later. Although while in the Senate he took an active interest in legislation pertaining to mining, agriculture, land grants, and railroads, he seldom spoke on the floor and even dubbed himself "the silent man of the Senate." Despite his mixed legislative record, he was known and admired for his honesty, humor, and expertise as perhaps the nation's best geologist. Four years before his death in 1891, his twenty-eight-year-old son, William Randolph Hearst, had assumed management of the renamed *San Francisco Examiner*.

Fifteen years earlier George Hearst's wife, Phoebe, had traveled to Europe with their young son, known to the family as "Willie." While touring Ireland, the pair saw unbelievable poverty, which Phoebe tried to describe to her husband in a letter from Belfast. "Many of them are highly educated, warm hearted and hospitable," she wrote about the Irish people, "but the poor classes are terribly poor. Willie wanted to give away all his money and clothes, too, and really, I felt the same way. If we could have relieved half of them. . . . Willie says he does not like this country very much because the men are so bad to the women and horses. He saw the women working out[side] barefooted and thinly clad. The horses in the south of Ireland are so poor and overworked. The whole country is beautifully cultivated."

A century later Willie's own son, William Randolph Hearst Jr., wrote in his autobiography that he had interviewed the famous Irish nationalist Eamon De Valera on numerous occasions. After mentioning that De Valera had led Ireland for thirty-five years – twenty-one as prime minister and another fourteen as president – the journalist mentioned the statesman's claim that Hearst's father had "helped us to be a nation."

❡ The Greek Theater, in the eucalyptus grove above Gayley Road, was a gift of William Randolph Hearst and was first used in 1903.

BEVERLY HILLS

❡ **Greystone Mansion,** 501 Doheny Road. Not open to the public.

Described as the largest and most impressive home ever built in Beverly Hills, this fifty-five room mansion was completed in 1927 by the oil millionaire Edward Doheny at an estimated cost of $4 million. The house is built on a twenty-five-acre piece of property that was originally part of Doheny Ranch, now Trousdale Estate.

The 46,000-square-foot mansion, whose reinforced-concrete walls are three feet thick, derives its name from its outer coating of Indiana limestone. During its heyday the inside of the house was noteworthy because of its grand dining room (with an orchestral balcony), chapel, gymnasium, movie theater, billiard room, bowling alley, and servants' quarters for a staff of thirty-six. The estate also boasted a fire station, a swimming pool, riding stables, dog kennels, tennis and badminton courts, a sixteen-acre garden, and a seven-room English-style cottage (used by the Doheny children as a "doll house").

Doheny's son, Edward Jr. ("Ned"), moved into the house with his wife and family in 1928. The very next year, however, the thirty-six-year-old heir was murdered in the house by his male secretary, Robert Plunkett. Because the murderer immediately killed himself, no confirmation could be given to the subsequent rumors that Doheny was killed because he had resisted a homosexual advance from Plunkett. Doheny's widow remarried and remained at Greystone until the mid 1950s.

A decade later the house was purchased by the city of Beverly Hills, which built a nineteen-million-gallon reservoir under the estate's upper parking lot. At one time the city got 45 percent of its water from this facility. In 1971 the estate was dedicated as Greystone Park, and five years later the house was placed on the National Register of Historic Places. Today Greystone is used for a variety of events, among them private social gatherings.

BODIE

¶ **Bodie State Historic Park,** 20 miles southeast of Bridgeport via State 270 and U.S. 395.

In the 1880s this former community of 5,300 was one of the West's most lawless gold-mining towns, although in its heyday its mines produced almost $100 million in ore. The town's 170 buildings are preserved in a state of arrested decay.

According to the 1880 U.S. Census, the Irish-born made up sixteen percent of Bodie's population, and a sizeable number of the other inhabitants had Irish surnames. To be sure, the Irish were found in every aspect of the town's rambunctious life, most notably as lawmen, outlaws, and publicans. Three members of the infamous Daly Gang, for instance, were William Buckley, John "Three-Fingered" McDowell, and James Masterson. For killing a settler, though, they found justice at the end of a rope. Before meeting his Maker, Buckley dictated a letter to a brother in San Francisco: "Give my first and last love to my mother in Ireland. Don't let her know that my death was by the ignominy of the gallows. . . . God bless you all. I have hope yet in a merciful God and savior." The outlaw's last words were, "Adieu, boys . . . all of you must go to my wake in John Daly's cabin tonight."

For a time Brodie was home to Patrick Reddy, who in 1879 established his law practice in what the *Bodie Standard* called the "most imposing law office outside of San Francisco." The forty-year-old lawyer had been conceived in County Carlow, Ireland, but was born in Woonsocket, Rhode Island. After journeying to California in 1861, he worked in the mines in Placer County and then in Virginia City. In 1864, while living in a camp in that Nevada silver-mining capital, he was so severely injured by an assailant that his arm had to be amputated. He later made the most of his remaining limb by challenging all comers to arm-wrestling.

To complement his practice in Bodie, Reddy in 1881 opened another office in San Francisco. Although he was a state senator during the mid 1880s, he continued to defend the underdog and often without fee, just as he had done in Bodie. In the 1890s he even traveled to Idaho to speak out for the rights of the hundreds of miners who had been imprisoned during an attempt by the mine owners to destroy the workers' union. According to the *San Francisco Bulletin*, Reddy "distinguished himself against the best legal talent in the Northwest in the numerous cases which grew out of those labor troubles."

By the time of his death in 1900, Reddy had made more than $3 million and was known as the most famous trial lawyer west of the Mississippi. Except for the $250,000 that remained in his final estate, however, he had given most of his wealth away, often to provide medical treatment for his old mining friends who were incapacitated because of old age, sickness, or accident.

Despite their distance from the mother country, the Irish in Bodie never forgot their Irish roots. Shortly after the Irish nationalist leader Charles Stewart Parnell visited the United States seeking funds for the Land League back home, the Bodie Irish established a chapter of the organization. At the league's first meeting in December 1880, Judge John Ryan played on all the ancient resentments: "For seven centuries, Ireland has been fighting for liberty. . . . Those who have gathered here tonight should not respond as Irishmen, merely, but as citizens of the leading republic of the earth and aid in liberating the oppressed people from English rule."

§ Open Memorial Day weekend-Labor Day, daily 9-7; rest of the year, daily 9-4. Fee. Phone: 619-647-6445. The park is often inaccessible during winter.

CALISTOGA

¶ **Sharpstein Museum,** 1311 Washington Street.

On the grounds of the museum is one of the twenty-five cottages which were part of a summer resort built here in the 1860s by Samuel Brannan. Two other cottages are located nearby: one a bed and breakfast establishment on Cedar Street and the other a private residence on Wapoo Street. Brannan's general store is located on the corner of Wapoo and Brannan streets.

Brannan was a native of Saco, Maine, the grandson of Patrick Brannan of County Waterford, Ireland. The San Francisco entrepreneur had come to California at the head of a Mormon expedition in 1846. In coming to the Calistoga area, he hoped to promote the tract of land which he had bought near the local hot springs as a rival to the famous springs in Saratoga, New York. According to one story, Brennan was drunk and garbled his words when he proclaimed, "I'll make this place the Calistoga of Sarafornia."

Brannan promoted the region in other ways as well. The Napa Valley Railroad Depot in Calistoga is a reminder of his ability to persuade the people of the Napa Valley to finance a branch railroad to his resort. For the grand opening of the Calistoga Hot Springs in 1868, the new rail line brought about 3,000 people from San Francisco and the surrounding regions. Brennan was also one of the early vintners in the Napa Valley, whose slopes he planted with cuttings of superior wine and table grapes.

As a youngster, Brannan had served an apprenticeship in the printing business and had visited most of the country as a journeyman. After converting to Mormonism in 1842, he moved to New York City, where he published two organs for the new sect. When a group of Mormons decided to set up a colony in Mexican California, they chose Brannan as their leader. Leaving New York aboard the Brooklyn, the 238 emigrants sailed around South America and arrived in Yerba Buena (later called San Francisco) at the end of July 1846.

By that time, however, hostilities between Mexico and the United States had been going on for several months. When the emigrants saw the Stars and Stripes flying over Yerba Buena, they realized that California had been captured by American troops. Having hoped to escape the persecution which they had experienced in the United States, the Mormons were disappointed at the new political reality on the West Coast and probably agreed with Brannan when he uttered an oblique curse: "There's that damn flag again!"

Much of Brannan's subsequent career was a litany of firsts. He not only performed the first non-Catholic wedding in California but also preached the first sermon in English and operated the first flour mills in the new territory. In addition, he published San Francisco's first newspaper (the *Yerba Buena California Star*), was a member of the first city council, and was the first president of the San Francisco Committee of Vigilance. When the vigilantes ordered the execution of John Jenkins for stealing a safe in broad daylight, Brannan found himself a codefendant in the state's first jury trial.

Between 1847 and 1849 Brannan operated a store at Sutter's Fort in Sacramento. Soon after gold was discovered nearby, he was apparently the first to inform San Franciscans about the earth-shaking event, making the long journey from the goldfields himself and proclaiming the news throughout the old plaza: "Gold! Gold from the American River!" A special edition of his newspaper also carried one of the first reports about the discovery: "It was discovered in December last, on the south branch of the American Fork, in a low range of hills forming the basin of the Sierra Nevada, distant thirty miles from New Helvetica [Sutter's Fort]. It is found at a depth of three feet below the surface, and in a strata of soft sand rock. Exploration made southward the distance twelve miles, and to the north five miles, report the continuance of this strata and the mineral equally abundant. The vein is from twelve to eighteen feet in thickness." During the ensuing Gold Rush, Brannan store's did an incredible $150,000 a month in business.

Brannan at first invested much of his newfound wealth in real estate, but he eventually branched out into other enterprises. Although at first he opposed renaming Yerba Buena, he later supported the city's new name, calling San Francisco "the Liverpool or New York of the Pacific Ocean." He eventually owned one-fifth of the exploding city, including almost all the property adjoining Market Street. In addition, he owned a quarter of Sacramento when it was laid out, and he staked a claim on an island in the nearby American River. At one point Brannan's holdings extended to Hawaii and Southern California. In 1868 he purchased a 17,000-acre piece of property in Los Angeles County. From Europe he introduced sheep and blooded horses, and he invested in banks, railroads, and express and telegraph companies. By the time of his death, he was California's first millionaire.

(As an elder in the Mormon Church, Brannan collected tithes from his coreligionists who worked his gold diggings. But when he was ordered by Brigham Young to turn over the tithes to the Church, the feisty Irish-American said, "I'll give up the Lord's money when [Brigham] sends me a receipt signed by the Lord.")

When the French installed a puppet ruler as emperor of Mexico in 1866, Brannan armed and equipped a military force known as Brannan's Contingent to fight in Mexico on the republican side. Fifteen years later, when the American's fortunes had begun to fade, the Mexican government granted Brannan two million acres in Sonora. Although he planned to establish an American colony there, he lost most of the property when the surveyors he had hired took most of his land in payment for their work. He later paid off some of his debts with a $9,000 gift from Mexico.

For more than a year after Brannan's death in 1889, his corpse lay in the receiving vault at Mount Hope Cemetery in San Diego because there was no money to bury him. Finally a stranger named Alexander Bledon bought a plot for Brannan's burial. In 1926 a granite marker was erected over his grave with the inscription: "Sam Brannan / 1819-1889 / California Pioneer of '46 / Dreamer / Leader / and Empire Builder."

COLUMBIA

¶ Columbia State Historic Park.

The park covers a dozen square blocks in the historic section of Columbia, one of the most important mining towns in the Mother Lode and home to many Irish fortune hunters. Between 1850 and 1870 the placer mines near the town produced $87 million in gold.

A number of buildings from the Gold Rush days have been restored: a bank, a newspaper building, a schoolhouse, a theater, saloons, the City Hotel, a Masonic Temple, a church, and the Wells Fargo Express Company. A slide show on Columbia's history is presented in the museum.

Two structures, in particular, have Irish associations:

• The Fallon House Theater, at the corner of Broadway and Washington streets, was built in the early 1860s by James Fallon. Today the theater presents stage productions Thursday-Saturday at 8 p.m. and Sunday at 2 p.m. during scheduled performances. Fee. Phone: 209-532-4644.

• St. Anne's Church, on Church Lane (off South Broadway Street), was constructed between 1853 and 1856 on property donated to the church by Norton Kane and his two mining partners (Maguire and Finn). Located atop Kennebec Hill, the church was paid for by the local miners, many of whom were Irish. The mural at the back of the altar was painted by James Fallon. The nearby cemetery contains many marble gravestones.

The church, which can hold 600 worshippers, was completed under the direction of Father Daniel Slattery, its first pastor. Elizabeth Sanborn, a parishioner who attended the dedication of St. Anne's on November 2, 1856, recorded her impressions of Father Slattery's eloquence that day: "But such a sermon as he could preach! Everybody was eager to hear every word of his never-to-be forgotten discourses. Everybody went to the Catholic church; standing room inside as well as outside, people standing on tiptoe to get every sound from his wonderful voice."

Slattery was one of thirty-six children born to an Irish family in County Kerry, Ireland. After studying at St. Patrick's College in Maynooth, County Kildare, he came to California in September 1854 and was ordained two months later in San Francisco. In July 1855 he was named pastor of Columbia, Angel's Camp, and Murphys. Two years later he was assigned to St. Joseph's Church in Marysville, where he died in 1860. Two of his brothers were also pioneer missionaries in northern California.

An edition of the *Sonoma Democrat* in 1856 reported that the two major holidays in Columbia every year were the Fourth of July and St. Patrick's Day. The paper went on to quote a presumably Irish orator as he ended his Fourth of July speech with the customary prediction: "And through the veil of the not distant future I see the vision of a great Republic of the Emerald Isle, and I behold a tyrannical England sunk in the slough of insignificance and degradation."

§ Park open daily 8-6. Stagecoach and horseback rides available Memorial Day-Labor Day, daily 8-6; rest of the year, Saturday-Sunday and holidays 8-6. Stagecoach fee. Phone: 209-532-0150 (park office) or 209-532-0663 (livery).

CULVER CITY

¶ **Holy Cross Cemetery and Mausoleum,** on Slauson Boulevard near Jefferson.

This consecrated ground is the final resting place of such well known Irish-American entertainment celebrities as Ray Bolger, Jackie Coogan, Bing Crosby, Dennis Day, Helen O'Connell DeVol, John Ford, Joe Flynn, Jack

Haley, Pat O'Brien, Edmund O'Brien, Walter O'Malley, and Rosalind Russell.

DANVILLE

¶ **Tao House,** 1.5 miles west at the end of Kuss Road.

From the end of December 1937 to February 1944, this California-Spanish ranch house was the home of *Eugene O'Neill and his actress wife, Carlotta Monterey. It was here that O'Neill, the first American playwright to win the Nobel Prize in literature, wrote his last five dramas.

O'Neill and his wife had come to the West Coast in December 1936, soon after he was awarded the Nobel Prize. The famous Anglo-Irish playwright Bernard Shaw had said that he was "very pleased" about the choice of O'Neill, while two other Irish authors weighed in with praise: Lennox Robinson ("O'Neill's contribution to the drama is very valuable indeed") and William Butler Yeats ("I have the greatest admiration for his work"). But in O'Neill's eyes the greatest recognition came from the Irish ambassador in Washington, who praised him on behalf of the Irish Free State for adding, along with Shaw and Yeats, to the credit of old Ireland. Yeats had earlier flattered O'Neill by requesting his permission to stage his *Days Without End* at the Abbey Theater in Dublin.

With the $40,000 award from the Nobel Committee, $75,000 from the sale of a house off the coast of Georgia, and $3,000 from the sale of other properties, O'Neill decided to build a house in northern California. For the most part, construction on the fifteen-acre site proceeded according to Carlotta's desire for "something primitive on the outside but with a Chinese interior" and with space for 8,000 books and 300 pairs of shoes. Although the exterior's adobe-like concrete masonry gave the structure its Spanish Revival look, the black tile on the roof was definitely á la oriental, as were the interior doors painted Chinese orange or red. The price tag for the O'Neill's new home – which they named Tao after the Chinese word for "the right way of life" – was $100,000. During their six years here O'Neill completed *The Iceman Cometh, Hughie, Long Day's Journey into Night, A Moon for the Misbegotten,* and *A Touch of the Poet.*

On the property of Tao House is the grave of the O'Neills' beloved Dalmatian, Blemie. The marble headstone is inscribed with the legend, "Sleep in Peace, Faithful Friend." About the dog, Carlotta once acknowledged to a confidant that "Gene and I spoil him no end, but always say he is the only one of our children who has not disillusioned us. . . . " (When O'Neill's seventeen-year-old daughter, Oona, married Charlie Chaplin, then fifty-four, the playwright severed all connections with her.)

On the day of the dog's burial, O'Neill helped himself through the grieving process by writing a panegyric to Blemie entitled "The Last Will and Testament of Silverdene Emblem O'Neill." Echoing sentiments which

Whitman had expressed about "man's best friend" in "Song of Myself," O'Neill adopted the persona of his faithful Fido. Although the 250-word testament describes the dog's weariness with a life plagued by blindness and deafness, it may actually express the playwright's battle with Parkinson's disease. The first few lines suggest the vanity of vanities: "Dogs are wiser than men. They do not set great store upon things. They do not waste their days hoarding property . . . [and] worrying about how to keep the objects they have, and to obtain the objects they have not. There is nothing of value I have to bequeath except my love and my faith . . . ."

§ Tours are conducted twice a day seven days a week at 10 a.m. and 12:30 p.m. Visitors can reach the house only by a van provided by the National Park Service. Reservations are required. Phone: 510-838-0249.

DOWNEY

This city of 89,000 people in Los Angeles County bears the name of John Gately Downey, at thirty-two the governor of California (1860-62) and the first Irish-born chief executive of any state in the Union.

When Downey, a native of Castlesampson, County Roscommon, came to America, he first settled in Maryland, where his two half-sisters operated a female academy. For a while he attended a Latin school under the tutelage of a Mr. Cochran, perhaps intending to fulfill his relatives' desire that he become a priest. He later turned his attention to learning about pharmacy from John Callan in Washington, D.C., thus becoming a journeyman pharmacist and beginning a twenty-year odyssey that finally ended in California. En route to his destiny on the West Coast, he was employed in a drug and stationery store in Vicksburg, Mississippi, and then conducted a business in Cincinnati. When he began to consider going to California, an acquaintance asked him, "What do you want to go there for with your drugs? It is the healthiest country in the world." Downey replied, "Well, tell me how many people are now there, and I will teach them how to take medicine."

After finally arriving in San Francisco after an eighty-nine-day journey from New Orleans by way of Panama, the Irishman was forced to sell his gold watch in order to pay his way to the mines. Since his efforts there bore little, if any, fruit, he returned to San Francisco, virtually penniless. By chance, though, he saw a newspaper article advertising a consignment of drugs in San Pedro just waiting for a buyer. After finding an investor to stake him, he bought the drugs at 24 percent less than their original cost and opened the first pharmacy in Los Angeles (and the only such shop between San Francisco and San Diego).

Although he had tried to avoid involvement in politics, like many Irishman he succumbed to the temptation. In 1859 he was accordingly nominated for lieutenant governor of the state, primarily to lend ethnic balance to the Democratic ticket. Although Downey and his running mate were successful, the latter resigned the governorship – after only a week in office – to accept election to the U.S. Senate seat recently made available by the death of *David Broderick. (See Broderick-Terry Duel Site in San Francisco, California.) Downey thus succeeded to the governorship.

As the state's chief executive, Downey was faced with several major challenges as well as opportunities to guarantee the state's prosperous future. He first of all eliminated the staggering $4 million debt which he had inherited from the previous administration. Although a Democrat, he supported President Lincoln's war effort and guaranteed California's loyalty to the Union despite opposition from secessionists and Confederate sympathizers. He also threw his support behind the granting of agricultural subsidies intended to increase the production of corn, cotton, and flax. In addition, the governor helped finance a trip to Europe by the Hungarian winemaker Agoston Haraszthy to obtain the cuttings that would respond to the climate and soil conditions in northern California. It was also during Downey's tenure that a permanent site for the capital building in Sacramento was finally selected.

Following his two-year term in office, Downey devoted himself to various commercial and real estate ventures. He was particularly keen to develop the Santa Gertrudes Rancho in the San Gabriel Valley. When Downey donated land worth $1 million toward the creation of a Methodist college known as the University of Southern California, the Catholic bishop asked him whether he had left the Catholic Church. Downey replied magnanimously that "the work these men are doing was just as acceptable in the sight of God as the work of our Church, and I have already done a great deal for the Catholics all around here and at San Bernardino – giving them land and money."

DUBLIN

¶ **Irish Heritage Park,** behind St. Raymond's Church at 6600 Donlon Way.

The park contains many historical markers and gravestones that tell the story of Dublin's early settlers. Among those buried here are Michael Murray and Jeremiah Fallon, natives of Ireland who had come west in 1846. A marker next to the grave of Fallon's son Rodger, reads: ". . . renowned for his honesty and integrity and proficiency with the *riata* [rawhide rope] which sometimes was up to 70 feet in length." The grave of Thomas Donlon, killed at the age of twenty-five while helping build St. Raymond's church, is marked by a historical plaque.

The large eighteen-foot monument in the park marks the grave of James Witt Dougherty (1813-1879) and his dog, Carlo. Dougherty, an American-born Protestant, was one of Alameda County's second largest landowners, with 17,000 acres. In the census taken the year after his death, he was described as the head of a household of five children, two Chinese cooks, two servants, and nineteen farmhands.

• In the park is Murray School, now a museum maintained by the Dublin Historical Preservation Association. Phone: 510-828-3377.

• A short distant from Heritage Park, on land once owned by James Dougherty, is the Dublin Howard Johnson Hotel (6680 Regional Street), which features a small museum about the town's Irish settlers. Phone: 510-828-7750.

• On the west side of U.S. 50 is the two-story Amador Hotel, which was erected in 1870 by James Dougherty with redwood lumber brought from Redwood City.

• A mile south from Dublin, along the eastern base of the Pleasanton Ridge and the western edge of Amador Valley, is the Jeremiah Fallon House, built in 1850 of redwood timbers.

⚓ St. Raymond's Church, 6600 Donlon Way.

This Catholic church was constructed in 1859 on property donated by the Irishmen Michael Murray and Jeremiah Fallon. The original list of subscribers to the building fund contains forty-eight names, thirty-six of them Irish. The largest subscription – $50 – was made by Thomas Donlon, who unfortunately fell from the roof of the church while he was working on its construction.

ESCONDIDO

⚓ San Pasqual Battlefield State Historic Site, 8 miles east on State 78.

This fifty-acre site commemorates an important episode in the American conquest of California during the Mexican War. It was here on December 6, 1846, that *General Stephen Watts Kearny, at the head of sixty-two dragoons, clashed with 150 Californians under General Andres Pico. The visitor center presents a film about the battle.

Besides listing the names of the American casualties, the bronze marker at the site of the engagement reads: "The State of California honors with this monument the American soldiers who under the leadership of Brig.-Gen. Stephen Watts Kearny, Capt. Abraham Johnston, Capt. Benjamin Moore, Edward Beal, and Kit Carson the Scout gave their lives in the Battle of San Pasqual between the Americans and Mexicans. Dec. 6-10, 1844."

At the beginning of the engagement on December 6, the Californians seemed to retreat, but they suddenly turned and charged with muskets and sharpened willow lances. The Americans, whose ammunition was wet from the morning rain, attempted to counter the charge with hand-to-hand combat. Although Kearny's rear guard brought up howitzers to repel the attack, at the end of the skirmish twenty-two Americans lay dead and sixteen were wounded. Kearny suffered two serious lance wounds.

The next day, after dispatching Kit Carson and Lieutenant Edward Beale to seek reinforcements in San Diego, Kearny positioned his men on a nearby hill. There they remained until help arrived on December 11, but not before being forced to eat their mules in order to survive. The eminence, now known as Mule Hill, is located east of U.S. 395, four miles south of Escondido, and is noted by a historical marker on a side road.

Stephen Kearny was born in New Jersey, the fifteenth and last child of Philip and Susanna Kearny. On his paternal side he was descended from an Irish immigrant who had settled in Perth Amboy, New Jersey, in 1720. Although Stephen's father was a wealthy landholder, his estates were confiscated during the Revolutionary War because of his Loyalist activities.

The young Kearny served in the War of 1812, suffering injury and capture, but his military career was otherwise spent on the western frontier. During more than two decades he accompanied various expeditions, many of them to open new areas of the West to effective American control. In this service he was frequently placed in command of frontier posts or was charged with their construction (e.g., Fort Towson, Oklahoma; Fort Des Moines, Iowa; and Fort Kearny, Nebraska).

In June 1846 Kearny was promoted to the rank of brigadier general in command of the Army of the West. As part of the American strategy during the Mexican War, he led almost 1,700 men from Fort Leavenworth, Kansas, to assist in the capture of the Southwest from Mexican control. After entering Santa Fe without opposition, he served as military governor until he could organize a civil government. He then continued his march to the Pacific Coast, although he ordered 200 of his 300 dragoons to return once it was learned that California had been conquered.

After Kearny's setback at the battle of San Pasqual, a relief force sent by Commodore Robert Stockton allowed him to reach San Diego. Now in command of 600 troops, Kearny marched them to Los Angeles, which fell after two minor engagements and only one American casualty. In the meantime the Californios had surrendered to Lieutenant Colonel John Charles Frémont, who almost immediately came into conflict with Kearny. Having been appointed civil governor of California by Stockton, Frémont refused to obey Kearny's orders, an act of insubordination for which he paid dearly.

Before leaving California, Kearny issued a proclamation promising protection of property and representative government. "California," the proclamation read, "has for many years suffered greatly from domestic troubles; civil wars have been the poisoned fountains which have sent forth trouble and pestilence over her beautiful land. Now ... the star-spangled banner floats over California ... and under it agriculture must improve and the arts and sciences flourish, as seed in a rich and fertile soil. The Americans and Californians are now but one people. .... Let us, as a band of brothers, unite and emulate each other in our exertions to benefit and improve this our beautiful, and which must soon be our happy and prosperous home."

§ Open Thursday-Monday 10-5. Closed January 1, Thanksgiving, and December 25. Phone: 619-238-3380 or 489-0076.

EUREKA

❡ **Carson House,** southwest corner of M and 2nd Streets. Private.

Erected in 1885 by William Carson, a local lumber magnate, this towering landmark is regarded as the most perfect example of Victorian architecture in the United States today. While the exterior of this eighteen-room mansion is constructed of fir and redwood, the interior is finished in oak and two kinds of mahogany. The three-story house is a riot of gables, turrets, cupolas, pillars, finials, and balconies and is crowned by a tower from which Carson espied incoming ships. The most notable interior features of the house are its onyx fireplace, baronial dining room, ballroom, and stained-glass windows. Today the mansion belongs to the Ingomar Club, an organization of business people formed to preserve the historic structure.

Carson, the son of an immigrant from northern Ireland, was born in New Brunswick, Canada, in 1825. Although in his youth he helped his father in the timber export business, in 1849 he and several other woodsmen sailed for California. During the summer of 1850, they worked the Trinity gold fields north of San Francisco. While spending the winter along the coast in Humboldt County, however, Carson and his companions contracted to supply logs for a recently built sawmill. Although the would-be miners returned to the Trinity fields the following spring, they were again in Humboldt a year and a half later.

By 1854 Carson had gone into the lumber business permanently. That year he was operating the Muley Mill in Eureka, filling the triple roles of sawyer, foreman, and salesman. That fall he exported the county's first cargo of redwood lumber, and in due course his company owned 20,000 acres of the finest redwood in the world. Although the major terminus for his lumber was the growing metropolis of San Francisco, his ships carried the product to Los Angeles, San Pedro, and San Diego as well as across the Pacific to Hawaii, Australia, and Asia.

Carson followed an unusually enlightened policy toward his employees. Besides paying his loggers adequate wages, he kept them at work even when business was slow and he offered them board at the company cookhouse. Just before Labor Day in 1890, in fact, he reduced the men's work day from twelve to ten hours. (In gratitude the loggers marched to his house, serenaded him with a band, and offered three rousing cheers for their boss.) When 2,000 loggers and mill hands from other local companies went on strike for better wages, a closed shop, and improved working conditions, Carson's employees ignored efforts to enlist their support, an indication of their satisfaction with their situation.

Using the profits he enjoyed from his logging business, Carson invested in a variety of entrepreneurial undertakings. Besides helping capitalize three Humboldt County banks, he was a founder of the North Mountain Power Company and an incorporator of the Eel River & Eureka Railroad Company. He also promoted two other local rail lines and owned partial interest in two lumber companies in Southern California. In 1890 the lumber giant built Eureka's first modern brick structure – a three-story building known as the Carson Block – at a cost of $100,000.

¶ **Fort Humboldt State Historic Park,** Highland Avenue, off U.S. 101.

The fort established here in 1853 served as the headquarters for the Northern California District of the Humboldt. *Ulysses S. Grant served here briefly in 1854 as captain of the 4th U.S. Infantry. In a letter home he complained of the loneliness of the place: "You do not know how forsaken I feel here!" Ironically, the future Civil War general resigned from the army that May rather than face dismissal for excessive drinking while stationed at the fort. Today the only original building is the redwood hospital, now used to house the visitor center. The officers' quarters are indicated by markers on the site.

GLENDALE

¶ **Forest Lawn Memorial Park,** 1712 South Glendale Avenue.
  • *Signing of the Declaration of Independence,* Court of Freedom.

This mosaic reproduction of John Trumbull's heroic painting includes the figures of the six Irish-Americans who were present as delegates to the Continental Congress when the Declaration of Independence was adopted: Thomas Lynch (4th from left), Charles Carroll (16th), Robert Treat Paine (21st), George Read (44th), Edward Rutledge (46th), and Thomas McKean (47th). (The three Irish-born signers – James Smith, George Taylor, and Matthew Thornton – were not present when the Declaration was adopted but signed the document later that year.) The mosaic measures twenty by thirty feet – three times the size of the original painting – and includes about 1,500 pieces of glass mosaics.
  • Temple of Santa Sabina, Lot 4116 Sunrise Slope.

Originally an altar and baldachino in the Basilica of Santa Sabina in Rome, this "temple" was erected to house the remains of Edward Doheny Jr., the only son of the famous Irish-American oil tycoon. The architectural grouping consists of an altar surrounded by four polished granite columns that rise thirty-four feet to a marble cornice which in turn supports an octagonal dome and a turret surmounted by a cross. (See Doheny Mansion, Los Angeles, California.)

The altar and baldachino had come into the possession of Dr. Herbert Eaton, the founder of Forest Lawn, about a decade before the younger Doheny's untimely death. It was Eaton who suggested that the "temple" be used as a memorial to the young man.

Santa Sabina, one of Rome's oldest churches, dates from the fifth century and is located near St. Paul's Outside the Walls. The basilica is named for Sabina, the wife of the Christian convert Valentinus, who was martyred for his faith sometime before A.D. 126.

§ Memorial park open daily 9-5 (9-6 in summer). Phone: 213-254-3131.

GRANADA HILLS

¶ **O'Melveny Park,** off Interstate 5 at Balboa Boulevard to Sesnon Boulevard.

Although the law firm of O'Melveny & Myers is well known in Southern California, few people are aware of this expansive park located at the base of the Santa Susana Mountains and named for one of the Southland's most prominent attorneys, entrepreneurs, and civic leaders.

Henry O'Melveny was born in Illinois in 1859, the grandson of an Irish emigrant who had come to America before 1795. O'Melveny was graduated from the University of California at Berkeley in 1879 and two years later was admitted to the state bar. After a brief tenure as deputy district attorney for Los Angeles County, the young lawyer entered into a series of law partnerships, the last under the name O'Melveny & Myers from 1939 until his death two years later. Among the firms' clients were the Goodyear Tire & Rubber Company of California, Shell Oil Company, Proctor & Gamble, Union Pacific Railroad, Paramount Pictures, and Johns-Manville Company. He was among the founders of several municipal electric companies that were later merged as the Pacific Light & Power Company, the forerunner of today's Southern California Edison. Besides helping create the Los Angeles Abstract Company, he served as either director or president of at least ten enterprises, among them banks and land, oil, and water companies.

O'Melveny's civic involvement was equally diverse. He was the founder of the Los Angeles Civil Service Commission and served as its first president. He also was a trustee for such institutions as the Los Angeles Public Library, California Institute of Technology, the Salvation Army, and the Southwest Society. In 1912 he presented $50,000 to the Southwest Museum and for a time was director of that institution. His interest in preserving the state's redwoods and beaches led him to serve on the Los Angeles and the California State park commissions.

GRASS VALLEY

¶ Lola Montez House, 248 Mill Street.

Now occupied by the Nevada County Chamber of Commerce, this structure is a replica of the house in which the Irish-born dancer Lola Montez lived between 1851 and 1853. Although the exterior has been restored to its earlier appearance, the only original portions of the house are the front door and an interior sliding door.

Born Marie Dolores Eliza Rosanna Gilbert in Limerick, Ireland, this internationally known beauty was the daughter of a British army officer and his wife, a woman of reputedly Spanish descent. Following the death of her father from cholera, her mother remarried, and the young Eliza was sent to her stepfather's relatives in Scotland for her early education. At the age of eighteen, Eliza demonstrated her independence by eloping with a young army lieutenant named Thomas James. When the new bridegroom soon eloped with the wife of a fellow officer, Eliza returned to Scotland, but en route she had an illicit affair with the aide-de-camp to the governor of Madras.

After a brief period of training in Spain, Eliza transformed herself into Lola Montez – Spanish dancer. As she performed her way through the major capitals of Europe, she became notorious for her sexual liaisons. She counted among her paramours the musician Franz Liszt, the novelist Alexandre Dumas, and Bavaria's King Ludwig, the last of whom granted her 20,000 florins a year and conferred upon her the title of Countess of Lansfeld. In return she infected him with syphilis and generally so dominated him that his government was mocked as the Lolaministerium.

Montez was also known for her exotic Spider Dance, a feature of her famous dance tours. Dressed in flesh-colored tights over which she wore a series of full, short skirts, she began her dance by recognizing that her ankles were becoming entangled in the filaments of a spider's web. When she discovered a spider on her petticoat, she tried to dislodge it by jumping gracefully into the air. Through her pantomime she continued to be plagued by more arachnids, examining and shaking her skirts and at the same time revealing a variety of colored petticoats. By dancing herself into a frenzy, she shook the imaginary spiders out of her skirts and onto the floor, where she crushed them under her feet.

In the meantime Lola had married an Irishman named Patrick Purdy Hull, part owner of the *San Francisco Whig* and a reputed relative of Patrick Purdy Brontë, the father of the famous female authors. When she first met Hull aboard a ship en route to San Francisco, she was captivated by his wit and his resemblance to a former lover. Marriage to such a celebrity sometimes brought Hull to the point of desperation, though, since his wife continued her usual eccentric behavior (e.g., carrying a pistol, smoking cigars, and humiliating and assaulting men).

After touring the United States in a stage show, Montez settled for two years in Grass Valley. Here she converted a brothel formerly operated by an Irish madam named Jennie Moore into a more suitable home for herself and her husband. One can imagine Hull's surprise when miners unaware that Jennie's was no longer in business arrived at the Hulls' door seeking to stay overnight with one of Jennie's "girls." To fend off these interlopers, Lola bought a brown bear named Major and chained it to a nearby tree. Hull, however, disliked Ursus Major intensely, especially when his wife insisted that the animal accompany them on their customary walks. (Her menagerie also included dogs, cats, parrots, and monkeys.)

During the last years of her life, Montez underwent an amazing transformation. As a well known lecturer throughout the United States and Great Britain, she spoke on such topics as "Beautiful Women" and "Heroines of History." Hers was a quietly militant approach to feminism: "One woman going forth in independence and power of self-reliant strength to assert her own individuality . . . ," she proclaimed, "will do more than a million convention women to make herself known and felt throughout the world." She later lived a spartan existence in New York City, ministering to fallen women at the Magdalen Asylum and warning them of the dangers of syphilis, which at the time ravaged her own body. A paralytic stroke left her incontinent, subject to seizures, and unable to talk. At the end she received spiritual consolation from an Episcopal priest, who later attested to the sincerity of her repentance and religious conversion. About her own life, Montez once said, "I have always been notorious, never famous."

§ Open daily 9-5. Phone: 916-273-4667.

HOLLYWOOD

¶ **Walk of Fame,** on both sides of Hollywood Boulevard (from Sycamore Street to La Brea Avenue) and both sides of Vine Street (from Yucca to Sunset).

Since its creation in 1960, Hollywood's Walk of Fame has grown to include 2,062 names of celebrities embedded in pink terrazzo stars in the sidewalk along the city's two most famous streets. Besides the name of each personality, the star contains an emblem identifying the category in which the entertainer was honored: radio, motion pictures, television, recording, and live theater. Since 1960 an average of one star per month has been added to Hollywood's star-studded walk, which now covers more than five acres.

The Walk of Fame includes stars in honor of each the following Irish or Irish-American entertainers: Brian Aherne, Gene Barry, Ethel Barrymore, John Barrymore, John Drew Barrymore, Lionel Barrymore, Brian Beirne, Ray Bolger, Alice Brady, Walter Brennan, Billie Burke, James Cagney, James

Cain, Art Carney, Rosemary Clooney, George Cohan, Kevin "Chuck" Connors, Dolores Costello, Lou Costello, Bing Crosby, Norm Crosby, Dennis Day, Walt Disney, Brian Donlevy, James Dunn, Irene Dunne, Jerry Dunphy, Dustin Farnum, William Farnum, Mia Farrow, Alice Faye, Barry Fitzgerald, Geraldine Fitzgerald, Errol Flynn, John Ford, William Frawley, Janet Gaynor, Judy Garland, Jackie Gleason, James Gleason, Leo Gorcey, Jack Haley, Helen Hayes, Susan Hayward, John Huston, Buster Keaton, Gene Kelly, Grace Kelly, Patsy Kelly, Arthur Kennedy, George Kennedy, Burt Lancaster, Angela Lansbury, Aline MacMahon, Amy Madigan, Dorothy Malone, Mary Margaret McBride, Mercedes McCambridge, Leo McCarey, Ed McConnell, Fibber and Molly McGee, Victor McLaglen, Thomas Meighan, Thomas Mitchell, Mary Tyler Moore, Audie Murphy, Hugh O'Brian, Edmond O'Brien, George O'Brien, Margaret O'Brien, Pat O'Brien, Donald O'Connor, George O'Hanlon, Maureen O'Hara, Walter O'Keefe, Michael O'Shea, Gregory Peck, Mary Pickford, Anthony Quinn, Ronald Reagan, Mickey Rooney, Mickey Rourke, Rosalind Russell, Mack Sennett, Preston Sturgis, Margaret Sullavan, Barry Sullivan, Ed Sullivan, Gene Tierney, Regis Toomey, and John Wayne.

In addition, the Hollywood entertainment industry brought stardom to these other Hollywood personalities of Irish descent: Sara Allgood, Ed Begley, Peter Boyle, Pierce Brosnan, Nancy Carroll, Walter Connelly, Jackie Coogan, Maurice Costello, Helen O'Connell DeVol, Richard Egan, Joe Flynn, William Gargan, Richard Harris, Lloyd Hughes, Alice Joyce, Gregory Kelly, Paul Kelly, Edgar Kennedy, May McEvoy, Frank McHugh, Colleen Moore, Erin O'Brien Moore, Tom Moore, Victor Moore, Jack Mulhall, Lloyd Nolan, Carroll O'Connor, Dan O'Herlihy, Dennis O'Keefe, Ryan O'Neal, Peter O'Toole, Mary Philbin, Tyrone Power, Tom Powers, Robert Ryan, Arthur Shields, Hal Skelby, and Spencer Tracy.

JOHNSVILLE

¶ **Moriarity House,** Plumas-Eureka State Park and Museum, 4 miles west on County A14 at 310 Johnsville Road.

Built sometime between 1870 and 1880, this wooden frame structure was the home of John Moriarity and his family from 1896 to 1917. The house is furnished to reflect life before the introduction of electricity and the railroad in 1909 changed the isolated nature of the area. Despite the fact that the house has only four rooms, it was home to Moriarity and his wife and their eight children. (While some of the children slept in the attic, the rest of the family crowded into one bedroom.)

Moriarity's parents – Maurice and Catherine (O'Neil) Moriarity – had emigrated from Ireland sometime prior to 1860. Soon after their marriage in West Virginia, they journeyed to California, settling in Howland Flat, one of many mining camps that had sprung up in the Sierras. John, the eldest of the couple's three children, was born in Howland Flat in 1867. At the age of twenty-one, he married Margaret Ann Hayes, the daughter of an Irish immigrant father and an American-born mother. By 1893 the young couple had three children of their own.

When Maurice Moriarity died two years later, John led his family and his widowed mother across the mountains to a new home near Johnsville, anther mining community. The area in which John and the members of his family settled was known as Echo Flat and was most likely located on property owned by the Plumas Eureka Mine. It was there and at the Jamison Mines – as well as possibly at the Morning Star and the Bluenose mines – that Moriarity worked to support his growing family.

In 1898 the thirty-year-old miner was described in a voter's register as being a California native, with a dark complexion, gray eyes, and black hair. While he and his wife lived in their house near Johnsville, the couple had five more children. Moriarity died in 1913 in San Francisco, where he had gone for treatment of a cancerous growth on his face and neck.

§ Museum open mid June to mid September, daily 8-4:30. Park open year round. Closed January 1, Thanksgiving, and December 25. Fee Memorial Day-Labor Day. Phone: 916-836-2380.

LIVERMORE

¶ **Concannon Winery,** Interstate 580E to the North Livermore Avenue exit and then south three miles to 4590 Tesla Avenue.

The winery's headquarters is the former residence of James Concannon, a native of the Aran Islands off the west coast of Ireland and the founder of California's oldest winery in continuous operation.

Concannon's ancestors were originally from County Roscommon, Ireland, but fled to Galway during Cromwell's conquest of Ireland in the middle of the seventeenth century. James Concannon's great-great-grandfather subsequently fled to one of the Aran Islands rather than pay tithes to the Protestant established church. His son moved the family to Inishman, the most westerly of the islands, where "the English flag had never flown."

By 1865 James Concannon had immigrated to Boston and was working for the Singer Sewing Machine Company. After marrying Ellen Rowe, a native of Castlecomer, County Kilkenny, the couple traveled to Oregon, where James lived the life of a sheepherder for a brief time. Disliking the loneliness of such a rural life, Concannon and his wife and son soon moved to San Francisco. It was there that the Irishman found work as a traveling salesman, covering the entire West Coast for a rubber stamp company.

In 1883, between business trips, Concannon purchased almost fifty acres of land in the Livermore Valley for $1,200. Although he retained his sales job, he actively pursued the study of viticulture and winemaking and imported the first of the grape cuttings from the Sherry and Burgundy regions of France. The archdiocese of San Francisco quickly became the winery's first customer for altar wines.

Through frequent visits to Mexico, Concannon became fluent in Spanish. On one occasion he received from the Mexican dictator Porfirio Diaz a concession to supply Mexican growers with cuttings from his California winery. The Irishman frequently visited the haciendas himself, distributing the cuttings as well as a tract on viticulture which he had written in Spanish. (When the Irishman visited Archbishop Joseph Alemany in San Francisco, the two conversed in Spanish.)

Despite the long distance between California and his homeland, Concannon kept in contact with his family in Ireland. His brother Martin had early come to California to supervise the winery's operations while James was traveling. Concannon himself returned to the Aran Islands several times, the last in 1909 after recovering from a stroke. Although his doctor at first counseled against such a trip, he soon realized that not going would be extremely harmful to his patient. On that final trip Concannon also visited Dublin, where he met such republican leaders as Arthur Griffith, Douglas Hyde, and Patrick Pearse and had the honor of giving a speech in Irish.

Following Concannon's death in 1911, operation of the business fell to Joseph, one of the Concannons' ten children. Although the business almost failed during Prohibition, Joseph's diversification into farming and stock raising saved the family's fortunes. The winery remained in the family until 1980, when it was purchased by outside interests. Concannon wines received an extraordinary public relations boost during *President Ronald Reagan's visit to Ireland during his first term. When he was greeted by Prime Minister Garrett FitzGerald, the president presented him with a six-litre bottle of Concannon Petite Sirah (1979 vintage).

§ Open Monday-Friday 9-5, Saturday-Sunday 10-5. Phone: 510-447-3760.

LOS ANGELES

¶ Audie Murphy Memorial Plaques.

America's most highly decorated veteran was honored in 1971 with the erection of bronze tablets in the lobby of Patriotic Hall (the veterans memorial building) on South Figueroa Street and on the Veterans Memorial Coliseum on Exposition Boulevard.

¶ Boyle Heights, bounded by Interstate 10, Interstate 5, and State 60.

Although this area is now a heavily Hispanic section of East Los Angeles, it is named for the Irish immigrant Andrew Boyle, who first settled in his part of the city in 1858.

A native of County Galway, Boyle (or O'Boyle) had come to New York

City in 1832, at the age of fourteen. With him were his seven brothers and sisters, come in search of their father, Hugh, who had emigrated from Ireland following his wife's death. For two years Andrew worked in New York, but he seems to have accompanied his siblings to Texas, where they became part of the famous San Patricio Colony on the Nueces River.

Having failed to find his father, Boyle at eighteen joined the Texas revolution against Mexico, enlisting in an artillery unit in the Texan army. While serving under Colonel Fannin, he was wounded and captured at the battle of Coleto and expected to be executed with 400 of his comrades. Happily for Boyle, however, the Mexicans were under the command of Captain Carlos de la Garza, who had recently been entertained by the Irishman's brother and sister at San Patricio. At that time the officer had promised Boyle's siblings that he would treat their brother well if the Galway native should ever fall into his hands. (See Goliad, Texas.)

After his rescue Boyle sailed to New Orleans, where he obtained employment at $2.50 a day and soon found his father. The younger man was still attracted to military life, however, and before long took passage on a schooner bound for the mouth of the Brazos River in Texas. After walking 150 miles to the Texan camp, Boyle was in such ill health that he was discharged from the army. He subsequently returned to New Orleans.

During the 1840s Boyle was engaged in the mercantile business, on the Red River initially and in Mexico some time later. In 1848, while attempting to make his way back home, he fell from a skiff at the mouth of the Rio Grande, barely escaping with his life but losing the $20,000 in cash which he was carrying. Upon his safe arrival home, however, he found that his wife had died of a fever contracted after receiving the false news of his drowning.

By 1851 Boyle had traveled to San Francisco, there opening a boot and shoe business that unfortunately suffered extensive damage in the two fires that befell the city that year. Although he was able to rebuild the business, after seven years he moved to Los Angeles, where he paid $3,000 an acre for a vineyard on the east side of the Los Angeles River. By doing so he became the first American to settle in that vicinity and to build the first brick house there. In the following years he achieved considerable success in the manufacture and sale of wine.

¶ **Calvary Cemetery,** 4201 Whittier Boulevard.

Among the well known figures in Los Angeles history who are buried here are the following: Irish native Cardinal Timothy Manning, the Anglo-Irish actors Lionel and Ethel Barrymore, and Irish-Americans Edward Doheny, John Reagan (the father of the president), Lou Costello, Irene Dunne, and Cardinal James McIntyre.

¶ **Doheny Mansion,** 8 Chester Place.

This French rococo mansion is now occupied by the Sisters of St. Joseph of Carondolet, but in the 1920s it was the home of oil producer Edward Doheny and his wife, Carrie Estelle Betzold.

Doheny was the son of an Irish immigrant father who by 1856 had settled in Fond du Lac, Wisconsin, with his Canadian-born wife, Eleanor Quigley. At sixteen the son ran away from home to fill a succession of jobs as booking agent, mule driver, fruit packer, and waiter. At eighteen, though, he began what would turn out to be his life's work – extracting wealth from beneath the soil. As a gold prospector he met with erratic success while wandering through Texas, New Mexico, Arizona, and Mexico for the next twenty years. He easily adapted to the gun-slinging ways of the West, and in New Mexico he became a legend for disarming a local bandit who had fired sixteen bullets at him.

In 1892 Doheny made his way to Los Angeles, where, virtually penniless, he one day noticed a wagonload of dark brown earth being carted through the street. After inquiring about the strange substance, he learned that it was *brea* (Spanish for "pitch") and that it bubbled from the ground near Hancock Park. Aware that the pitch was crude oil, the old prospector leased a vacant lot nearby and within months tapped a well 225 feet below ground. Hailed as one of the city's first oil wells, it produced forty-five barrels of oil a day. From this fortuitous start Doheny went on to control almost all the state's oil production within five years.

Doheny next turned his attention to Mexico, where he ultimately leased a million acres. Through his Mexican Petroleum Company, he cleared the jungles and built the infrastructure for an extremely lucrative enterprise, made possible because of bribes to Mexican officials. By 1922 his Mexican operations had netted him $31 million, while his total worth was three times that amount.

That same year Doheny obtained two choice government concessions. One was a contract to construct a large naval fuel station at Pearl Harbor, while the other granted him the drilling rights to 32,000 acres in the naval oil reserve in Elk Hills, California. (The California site was estimated to hold as much as 250 million barrels of oil.) Doheny had acquired this latter windfall for a mere $100,000 cash "loan" to Albert Fall, the secretary of the interior and an old friend of Doheny's. After obtaining the rights, Doheny said about the future: "We will be in bad luck if we do not get $100 million in profit."

During the lengthy congressional hearings and court cases which ensued, Doheny at first claimed that he had never given Fall any money. (Technically speaking, the oilman's son, Ned, had given the interior secretary the "loan.") The elder Doheny later explained that he had loaned Fall $100,000 partially out of gratitude for an act of kindness that had happened thirty-five years before. In 1886, Doheny claimed, Fall had lent him some law book to study while he was recuperating from a fall down a

The Doheny Mansion.

mine that had broken both his legs.

Doheny's attorney reached such oratorical heights in defense of his client that he alluded to the valiant service which Ned had given his country in World War I. According to his lawyer's peroration, Doheny Sr. had not only provided America with unbelievable underground riches but had also "offered that young man's life upon the altar of patriotism. He went on the turbulent and submarine-invested oceans in his country's service – the only son, the only child. And you are asked to believe that when Edward L. Doheny, near the end of his life, corruptly intended to bribe Albert B. Fall . . . he deliberately used as an instrument therefor his son, the pride of his youth, the hope of his maturity, the solace of his old age!"

In March 1930 the jury rendered a verdict whose irony only the law could countenance. Although the jurors convicted Fall of receiving the bribe, they acquitted Doheny of offering it. In addition, another court ordered Doheny to pay the government $47 million for the oil which his company had extracted from the Elk Hills site.

Although before his fall Doheny was considered the richest man in America, he was not particularly philanthropic. He did contribute to the Democratic party and the Irish independence movement, but whatever large-scale philanthropy is associated with the Doheny name was really the work of his wife. In addition to providing funds for the construction of St. Vincent's Catholic Church in Los Angeles, she established a million-dollar library at the University of Southern California in Los Angeles in memory of her son.

§ Mansion open to visitors during an open house each Christmas. Reservations required. Phone: 213-746-0450.

¶ Gene Autry Western Heritage Museum, 4700 Western Heritage Way.

The history of the American West is traced through paintings, artifacts, statuary, cowboy films, and audiovisual materials. The museum contains a number of exhibits with an Irish-American connection:

• Thomas Moran's heroic-size painting of *The Mountain of the Holy Cross*, a scene near Leadville, Colorado;

• artifacts once owned by "Billy the Kid" (Henry McCarty) and "Buffalo Bill" Cody; and

• the dress helmet, spurs, shoulder knots, and forage cap of General Miles Keogh, an Irish-born officer at the battle of the Little Bighorn. (Most of Keogh's effects were obtained from members of the cavalryman's family, who still live in Clifton Castle, Ireland.)

In addition, a large mural by Guy Deel depicts the following well known Irish-Americans: John Ford, Grace Kelly, William Hart, Will Rogers, Theodore Roosevelt, and John Wayne.

§ Open Tuesday-Sunday 10-5. Closed Thanksgiving and December 25. Fee. Phone: 213-667-2000.

¶ Joseph Scott Statue, in front of the Los Angeles County Courthouse, 110 North Grand.

This standing bronze statue commemorates Joseph Scott, a lawyer of Irish descent who for sixty-five years was a major influence in the growth of Los Angeles and of the Catholic Church in Southern California.

Scott was born in Penrith, England, in 1867, the son of a Scotch Presbyterian father and his Irish-born wife, Mary Donnelly. After attending St. Cuthbert's College (Durham) and London University, the younger Scott immigrated to America in 1889. There he found his first job, although working in a paper mill for twelve and a half cents an hour hardly seemed appropriate for a man with a college education. His second job – as a hod carrier in New York City – paid twice as much and provided Scott with a favorite story. Years later he told how, on that first day carrying bricks, his knees wobbled as he walked to a ladder to make the ascent for the fifth time. The weather that autumn and winter in New York made another lasting impression: "And was it cold? If you have ever caught the wind from the frozen North River up five stories, with a hod of bricks you will love the balmy breezes of California as I have ever since I got here." Within a year, however, Scott's employment situation changed dramatically with his appointment as a professor of rhetoric and English literature at St. Bonaventure's College in Allegany, New York.

After moving to Los Angeles in 1893, Scott studied law and began a long public career as one of the city's most prominent citizens. In legal circles he was best known as a trial attorney, and in one of his most sensational cases he represented Joan Berry in her paternity suit against Charlie Chaplin. Scott was the first Catholic member of the Los Angeles Board of Education, to which he was elected five times and on which he served as president for five years. In addition, he founded the Los Angeles Chamber of Commerce and was the honorary vice president of the Panama-Pacific International Exposition in San Francisco in 1912. Besides receiving a Ph.D. from Santa Clara University, he was the recipient of several papal honors, including the knighthoods of Malta and the Holy Sepulchre.

In recognition of his legal prominence, Scott was named dean of Loyola University Law School in Los Angeles in 1930. Two years later, at the Democratic national convention, he nominated Herbert Hoover for the presidency. At a testimonial dinner marking the fiftieth anniversary of Scott's arrival in the United States, the honored guest reminded his listeners of his Irish roots: "When I was three months old, so that you may know why my heart is with the Irish, three boys were swung off from a gallows at Manchester. They were no more felons, no more criminals than any of you good, wholesome men here. They had an idea they wanted Ireland to be

Statue of Joseph Scott, renowned Los Angeles attorney and civic leader.

free. They believed with Lincoln that God Almighty never made a man good enough to keep his fellow man in subjugation, and they tried to rescue one of their fellows in a prison van; one of them blew the lock of the van open with a pistol killing a policeman who had his ear to the keyhole. These three boys Allen, Larkin and O'Brien were swung off from the scaffold at Manchester. When they were called to account by the judge, and when the jury's verdict was rendered, they shouted from the dock, 'God save Ireland.' The day those boys were hung my little mother . . . pulled the curtain down from my little bedroom, and the tears from her Irish eyes fell upon my face, and she prayed her rosary for her three fellow countrymen."

¶ Mulholland Drive, a 22-mile stretch of road from Hollywood to the Pacific Ocean.

Opened to public use in 1924, this Southern California landmark honors William Mulholland, the Irishman credited with "inventing" Los Angeles because he assured its survival by providing it with an adequate water supply for the future.

¶ Mulholland Memorial Fountain, Riverside Drive and Los Feliz Boulevard, at the entrance to Griffith Park.

Among all the memorials in Los Angeles, few could be as appropriate as this fountain, dedicated in 1940 to the memory of William Mulholland, whose Owens River Aqueduct channeled water from the Sierra Nevada Mountains to a thirsty Los Angeles.

Born in Belfast, Ireland, in 1855, Mulholland had run off to sea at the age of fourteen. During four or five years before the mast, he crossed the Atlantic nineteen times, sailing the triangle between Glasgow, the West Indies, and the United States. Although he came to America permanently in the early 1870s, he was not yet prepared to abandon his sea legs, preferring instead to work on lumber ships that plied the Great Lakes.

Attracted to California by tales of its healthful climate, Mulholland arrived in the state in 1876 to begin what turned out to be a long career in the engineering of water-supply projects. While seeking work in Los Angeles, he learned that the city's water system consisted of twenty-four miles of water mains and an undetermined length of wooden pipes, known in Spanish as *zanjas*. His first job with the Los Angeles Water Company was as a ditch tender, keeping the system's main ditch – the *Zanja Madre* – free of debris and weeds along its course from the Los Angeles River to a reservoir in Elysian Park. He lived at this time in a wooden shack near the site of the memorial fountain in his honor.

In his free time, meanwhile, the Irishman studied mathematics, hydraulics, and civil engineering, thus acquiring the preparation that helped him become the water company's chief superintendent in a very short time. Once in a position of responsibility, he rebuilt most of the city's water distribution system and installed water meters that led not only to a dramatic decrease in per capita water consumption – from 300 gallons per day to 200 – but also to a 10-percent reduction in rates. In this latter regard he was a prudent watchdog of the public's money: "The dollar that I spend I consider to be the greasy, dirty dollar of the workingman."

By 1904 Mulholland had become convinced that a city with such potential for expansion could not depend for its water supply on either the clouds or the "tricklish" Los Angeles River. He accordingly proposed creation of a massive aqueduct system stretching 240 miles from Owens Lake at the base of the Sierra Nevadas to Los Angeles. In searching for a suitable starting site, he made a 500-mile journey to Owens Lake in a mule-drawn buckboard.

After persuading Los Angeles voters to approve a bond issue to finance the huge undertaking, Mulholland began actual construction in 1909. Considered second only to the building of the Panama Canal in scope, the project encompassed the laying of 3,800 miles of pipe and the building of sixty-five reservoirs and twenty-seven earth dams. The aqueduct's terminus is four miles north of San Fernando, near Interstate 5, and is known as "The Cascades."

When the hydraulic miracle was completed in 1913 – at less than the estimated $24 million cost, by the way – a two-day celebration was held at the San Fernando Valley spillway where the aqueduct came to rest. A crowd of 40,000 had gathered to watch the arrival of the precious liquid down the spillway and to hear the project's creator declare from the rostrum: "This rude platform is an altar, and on it we are here consecrating this water supply and dedicating this aqueduct to you and your children and your children's children – for all time!" Even the *New York Times* reported the faraway event, noting that the aqueduct would provide the San Fernando reservoir with 260 million gallons of water a day.

The last decade of Mulholland's life was marred by a devastating tragedy for which he accepted full responsibility. In the dead of night on March 12, 1928, almost 500 people were killed when the St. Francis Dam, part of the Owens Valley water system, collapsed and sent a tidal wave through the valley of the Santa Clara River. In what was the state's worst natural disaster since the San Francisco earthquake, the flood destroyed everything in its path as it made its way to the ocean, sixty-five miles away. Hundreds of homes were washed away, and almost 8,000 acres of farmland were inundated, resulting in $20 million in damage.

During the recriminations which followed the catastrophe, the *Los Angeles Record* attacked Mulholland for his engineering incompetence. The *Los Angeles Times*, however, was more compassionate: "His Irish heart is kind, tender, sympathetic and the tragedy for the people in the canyon and the Santa Clara Valley is the tragedy of William Mulholland." For his own part, the Irishman said that, although he had taken the usual precautions in constructing the dam, he had "overlooked something here. If there is an error of human judgement, I was the human." To his credit Mulholland accepted blame for having built the dam on a weak and friable bedrock and clay substratum. Although a coroner's jury ruled that he was responsible, it did not prosecute him, having heard evidence that the dam might have been deliberately dynamited. When Mulholland suffered a stroke in December 1934, his doctors expected him to die anytime. Instead, he fought on for six months, saying, "The Irish never give up."

¶ **St. Vincent de Paul Church,** at the corner of Adams Boulevard and Figueroa Street.

When a fund-raising campaign began in the early 1920s to build a new church on this site, the oil magnate *Edward Doheny and his wife agreed to finance the new structure but only if it was modeled after the church of Santa Prisca in Taxco, Mexico.

The resulting Spanish Renaissance church was designed by the Boston architect Ralph Adams Cram, known at the time as America's greatest designer of churches. The reredos on the main altar contains images of the Apostles and a statue of St. Edward, which, interestingly, bears a very close resemblance to Doheny himself. An early architectural guidebook for Los Angeles advises its readers that "no one has seen Los Angeles until he or she has visited and prayed in Saint Vincent's Church."

¶ The Dohenys had earlier contributed substantially to the construction of St. John's Episcopal Church diagonally across from St. Vincent's.

¶ **Washington Memorial,** Forest Lawn Memorial-Park – Hollywood Hills, 6300 Forest Lawn Drive, west of Griffith Park.

This sixty-foot-high bronze and marble tribute to the first president is surrounded by portrait busts of George Washington's most capable generals: *Henry Knox, the Marquis de Lafayette, Benjamin Lincoln, and Nathanael Greene. Four colossal seated figures represent oppression, revolution, victory, and peace (symbolized by Cincinnatus). The work of Thomas Ball, the memorial was exhibited at the Chicago World's Fair in 1893 and formerly stood in Methuen, Massachusetts.

Knox, who was Washington's secretary of war, was descended from Scotch-Irish settlers who emigrated from Londonderry, Ireland, to Boston in 1729. It was Knox who proposed to Washington the creation of a fraternal organization of military officers that became known as the Order of the Cincinnati.

§ Memorial park open daily 9-5 (9-6 in summer). Phone: 818-241-4151.

MENDOCINO

¶ Kelly House Historical Museum, 45007 Albion Street.

This restored 1861 house is the former home of William Kelly, a native of Prince Edward Island, Canada, and one of the most influential early settlers in the Mendocino region. The museum contains photographs, paintings, and a research library.

The oldest of eight children, Kelly was born in 1821 to Peter Kelly, a shipbuilder on Prince Edward Island. For a time the younger man worked in the province's lumber industry but eventually left the island to work in Westport, Maine, and then the Bermudas. Lured to California by the discovery of gold, Kelly and his brother James set sail in 1850 for the Golden West via the Isthmus of Panama. While awaiting passage there, however, the pair realized the commercial opportunities presented by the thousands of argonauts who made the Isthmian crossing. The brothers therefore abandoned their intention of going to California and instead opened a store. For almost a year their enterprise enjoyed phenomenal success until they both fell victim to cholera.

Following his brother's death from the disease, William shipped for California. Repelled by the congestion and general chaos of San Francisco, though, he moved up the Sacramento River to Benecia, where he worked as a shipbuilder. He later sailed aboard the *Ontario* with forty other men who had been hired to construct the first sawmill in Mendocino, where they arrived in 1852.

Kelly at first worked with the other men as a logger, contracted to supply logs to the California Lumber Manufacturing Company. Within a year, however, he and a partner began Mendocino's first general store, which they operated under the name of Kelly & Woodward. In a succession of other partnerships, Kelly later operated a sawmill at Caspar, a livery stable, and several saloons and pool halls. In the meantime he had acquired almost the entire Mendocino peninsula for just under $2,700. His vast real estate holdings later included timberland and a ranch.

In 1855, at the age of thirty-four, Kelly returned to Prince Edward Island with the intention of bringing his fiancée back with him to Mendocino. She, however, was unwilling to leave her family and friends for an uncertain life in the West. Kelly therefore turned his romantic attention to Eliza Lee Owen, who agreed to accompany him to California. After the grueling journey – by schooner to Panama, by railroad across the isthmus, and by schooner again up the West Coast – the two were married in Mendocino, still a primitive lumber town with only three other married couples.

Either on this trip or on a subsequent one, Kelly brought his father and his brothers and sisters to Mendocino. The father was an accomplished preacher and for many years served as an elder for the town's first Presbyterian church. Although William was also a Presbyterian, as a tribute to his wife, a Baptist, he donated the property on which was constructed a Baptist house of worship. (The church was completed in 1894 and is still in existence on Ukiah Street.)

William and his wife lived for six years in what is now known as the Heeser House on Albion Street until their home – Kelly House – was completed. Although Kelly died in 1895, his widow continued to reside in the family home until her death in 1914 at the age of eighty-nine.

§ Museum open June-September, daily 1-4; rest of the year, Friday-Monday 1-4. Library open Tuesday-Friday 9-4. Fee. Phone: 707-937-5791.

MILL VALLEY

¶ Reed Sawmill, Old Mill Park on Throckmorton Avenue.

Surrounded by towering redwood trees, this early nineteenth-century sawmill was erected by John Read (or Reed), a native of Dublin whose early arrival in this part of California earned him the nickname "Father of Pioneers."

Read had left Ireland in 1820, presumably as a boy of fifteen in the company of a sailor-uncle who took him to Mexico. By 1826 the young man had made his way to California, first to Los Angeles and then to Sausalito in the northern part of the Mexican province. Although he applied for a land grant in that area, his request was denied by the government authorities. His second attempt to acquire land – this time in Sonoma County – was equally unsuccessful, the Indians having driven him off the land and destroyed his crops.

At the suggestion of a Catholic priest, Read proceeded to San Rafael,

The Reed Sawmill in Mill Valley.

where he accepted the post of major-domo at the mission there. By 1832, however, he had again moved north to Sausalito. It was from there that he developed the first ferry service to Yerba Buena (the future San Francisco) on the opposite shore. Finally, in 1834, a month after becoming a naturalized Mexican citizen, he received his coveted land grant from Governor José Figueroa.

The 7,800-acre grant was known as Rancho Corte de Madera del Presidio, named for the redwoods cut down for use at the garrison in Yerba Buena. Besides planting orchards and introducing imported cattle to his land, Read constructed a sawmill powered by water from a nearby creek. With this new technology, he whipsawed lumber for the construction boom which the Gold Rush brought to San Francisco.

Soon after acquiring his rancho, Read married Señorita Hilarita, the youngest daughter of Don José Antonio Sanchez, commandant of the presidio in San Francisco. When Read died from excessive leeching, his widow married Bernardino "Three-fingered Jack" Garcia, a bandit friend of Joaquin Murrieta.

MURPHYS

This small community of 1,200 people in Calaveras County was named for John and Daniel Murphy, the sons of Martin Murphy Jr., a native of Wexford, Ireland, and a member of the first immigrant group to bring wagons over the mountains to California.

When the two sons arrived in this area near the Stanislaus River, they were members of Charles Weber's Stockton Mining Company, which had already established several trading posts in the nearby gold fields. The Murphys first resided at Dry Creek near Valecito (Murphys Old Diggins) but later moved north to Angels Creek at Murphys New Diggins (now known simply as Murphys). At both sites John engaged in trade with the Native Americans, to whom he traded blankets and trinkets for gold dust or nuggets. In less than two years he made more than $2 million before leaving Murphys in December 1849. He later married Virginia Reed, a survivor of the ill-fated Donner party, and had nine children.

A visitor's description of Murphys in the 1850s presents a picture of a typical Gold Rush community on the ascent from mere respectability to civilization: "Although consisting of tents, [Murphys New Diggins] had, during the summer of 1849, been raised to the rank of a real town, where an alcalde, a sheriff, and a constable were duly elected. The whole town comprised about fifty tents, two or three blockhouses, and a house built of planks; yet, it already boasted nearly as many 'bars' as tents, besides three American and four French dining rooms, two doctor's shops, at least twenty gambling tables, and a skittle ground where you might have three throws for the reasonable price of twenty-five cents." Only two years later

Murphys had made the transition, as another visitor recorded its attractions: 500 frame houses, a "permanent and floating population" of 3,000, nine carpenter shops, eight taverns, seven blacksmith shops, five butcher shops, four bakeries, two restaurants, two steam sawmills, one livery stable, one express and banking house, one cider and syrup factory, one bowling alley, and "dance and drinking houses innumerable."

Modern-day visitors to Murphys can see the Wells Fargo Express Office, the Sperry Hotel, the Traver Building, the Jones Apothecary, and St. Patrick's Church.

PACIFIC PALISADES

¶ Will Rogers State Historic Park, 1501 Will Rogers State Park Road.

This 186-acre site includes the ranch home where the famous cowboy humorist lived from 1928 to 1932. The thirty-one-room house contains his trophies and various memorabilia. The property still has the original stables, corrals, riding ring, roping arena, and trails laid out by Rogers.

§ Park open daily 8-7 in summer, 8-6 in winter. Home open daily 10-5, depending on staff availability. Closed January 1, Thanksgiving, and December 25. Fee per vehicle. Phone: 310-454-8212.

SACRAMENTO

¶ McClatchy Park, 33rd and 5th streets.

Named for James McClatchy, this urban park honors the memory of the Irish-born founder of a famous newspaper chain that included *The Sacramento Bee*.

A native of County Antrim, McClatchy immigrated to America in 1842 and gained his early newspaper experience while working for the *New York Tribune*. After reaching San Francisco at the time of the Gold Rush, the Irishman served briefly as the paper's California correspondent. McClatchy was later associated with various newspapers in Sacramento, including the *Bee*, which he helped establish in 1857. In the meantime he had married Charlotte McCormick, whose Irish parents were from Prince Edward Island, Canada.

In the weeks preceding the Civil War, James McClatchy played a singular role in helping secure California for the Union cause. In 1861 he made the acquaintance of Edmund Randolph, at the time visiting Sacramento in hopes of being elected one of the state's U.S. senators. Despite his Virginia birth, Randolph was a strong unionist. For that reason he informed McClatchy that General Albert Sidney Johnston, then in command of the U.S. military in California, planned to betray his post in the event of civil war by turning over to the South the 30,000 weapons in the federal arsenal at Benicia. Alarmed by this news, McClatchy dispatched a Pony

Express rider with a letter to Colonel E. D. Baker with the request that he forward the information to President Lincoln. The chief executive, in turn, dispatched Brigadier General Edwin Sumner to California, where he assumed command from Johnston, later one of the Confederacy's foremost commanders.

Beginning in 1875, McClatchy's sons – Charles Kenny and Valentine Stuart – became associated with their father in the operation of the *Bee*. Nine years later, soon after the founder's death, the sons assumed complete control. As editor, Charles continued his father's outspokenness in a column variously known as "Notes by C.K." or "Private Thinks by C.K."

Never a partisan follower of any political party, Charles McClatchy generally supported the populist-progressive candidate no matter what his affiliation. In 1908, for instance, he supported *William Jennings Bryan for president. He later supported the Progressive Republican candidates Hiram Johnson and *Theodore Roosevelt in their respective gubernatorial and presidential bids. Following the Stock Market Crash in 1929, he blamed President Herbert Hoover and Wall Street for the nation's economic woes and threw his support behind Franklin Roosevelt.

McClatchy generally advocated passage of the Progressive agenda. In his newspaper columns he enthusiastically supported female suffrage, curbs on monopolies, direct election of the president and U.S. senators, municipal ownership of utilities, and adoption of the referendum on the federal level. Unlike most Progressives, though, he favored American participation in World War I and opposed entrance into the League of Nations. He likewise attacked prohibition and called for the repeal of the Eighteenth Amendment.

In addition to political issues, his columns were filled with topics about which he was equally straightforward. He consistently attacked anti-Semitism and religious bigotry and occasionally opined that universities promoted atheism and radicalism. He condemned modernism in literature and art, preferring instead Shakespeare, Dickens, and Poe.

McClatchy was thoroughly modern, however, in his ability to both see and seize commercial opportunities. Between 1925 and 1931 he was operating four radio stations in California (Sacramento, Fresno, Bakersfield, and Stockton) and one in Reno, Nevada. During that same period he founded the *Fresno Bee* and purchased the *Modesto Herald*, which he renamed the *Bee*.

In 1936 McClatchy's daughter Eleanor helped compile a sampling of his editorials and opinion pieces into a book called *Private Thinks by C. K.* In a dispatch written from Dublin in May 1911, McClatchy described the poor economic prospects for his father's native land: "There is no work in Ireland for the Irish people. Practically Ireland has no industries. Ireland was once a land of many industries. When . . . she came under English domination, her industries were throttled; . . . A change of government will not start the mills in Ireland unless mill owners can . . . feel confident that their goods will not be driven out of Irish and English markets by American and German goods which will be allowed to come in free of any duty – and which will continue to be sold in Dublin and Glasgow, and Liverpool, and London cheaper than the local manufacturers can sell similar goods."

In an article written from Sligo a decade later in the midst of the Irish civil war, McClatchy denounced the atrocities committed on both sides. "And while the government has been . . . acting in Ireland in a manner that is a sin against civilization and a crime against humanity," the editor wrote, "the Sinn Feiners also have committed deeds that should cry out to high Heaven for vengeance against their perpetrators. In this matter the pot calls the kettle black, and the kettle responds by proving the pot is just as soot-coated. . . . Each side accuses the other of having inaugurated these devilish deeds. Each asserts it has been forced to act as it does, in self-defense or in 'reprisal.'" Then, alluding to a character in one of Shakespeare's works, a practice which he frequently repeated in his writing, McClatchy added: "Each satisfies its own conscience with the words of Shylock: 'The villainy you teach me I will execute; and it shall go hard but I will better the instruction.'"

◖ Sacramento History Museum, 101 I Street.

The museum's permanent exhibits include a Mother Lode gold collection worth $1 million, a historic print shop, and photographs of various ethnic groups which contributed to the state's development. The museum also displays the façade of a building constructed in 1900 as the headquarters of *The Sacramento Bee*, founded and managed by successive generations of the McClatchy family. The façade, which is about thirty feet wide and twenty-five feet high, contains the first level and entry dome of the originally three-story structure. The building was erected in honor of James McClatchy. The present headquarters of *The Sacramento Bee* is located at 21st and Q streets.

§ Open Wednesday-Sunday 10-5. Closed holidays. Phone: 916-264-7057.

SAN CLEMENTE

◖ La Casa Pacifica, Del Presidente Avenue. Private.

Formerly known as the Cotton Estate, this five-acre property on a bluff overlooking the ocean was purchased by *Richard Nixon for $349,000 and renamed La Casa Pacifica. This Spanish-style western White House was constructed in the 1920s, has fifteen rooms, and is built around a central patio. The estate was sold soon after Nixon resigned the presidency.

SAN DIEGO

⚶ **House of Pacific Relations International Cottage Inc.,** Balboa
Park.

This complex of fifteen cottages represents thirty-one nationality
groups, with each cottage containing exhibits on specific ethnic groups.
The Irish cottage displays a nineteenth-century kitchen as well as artifacts
and memorabilia from the old country.

§ The cottages are open Sunday 12:30-4:30 and the fourth Tuesday of
the month noon-3. Music and dance programs are presented mid March-
October 31, Sunday 2-3. Phone: 619-234-0739.

⚶ **Whaley House,** 2482 San Diego Avenue.

Constructed in 1856, this two-story landmark was the first brick house
built south of San Francisco. Besides being the home of Thomas Whaley, it
variously served as a store, a courthouse, and a theater.

Whaley, who was born in New York City in 1823, was descended from
an originally English family which had settled in Londonderry, northern
Ireland, in the seventeenth-century. After attending the Washington Institution in New York, Whaley spent two years on the Grand Tour of Europe
with his tutor. When gold was discovered in California, however, he took
passage aboard the *Sutton* – the first ship to leave New York for the gold
fields – and arrived in San Francisco after a 204-day voyage around the
Horn. En route he wrote numerous letters to his mother and kept a journal that exceeded a hundred pages in length. In one of the letters he described San Francisco's famous weather: "The mornings are damp and
cool. Sometimes misty. About nine o'clock it is pleasant enough, and continues so til noon, then it grows warm, and before two o'clock sometimes
it is exceedingly hot, and continues so til four, when the land breeze sets
in blowing great guns. . . . The evenings are cold, so that overcoats are
indispensable."

By 1851 Whaley had moved to San Diego, where he joined two business partners in opening a general store on the old plaza, the first of several such ventures which he undertook in that border town. During a subsequent visit to New York, he married Anna Lannay and returned with
her to California. It was at that time that he broadened his commercial
interests by engaging in brick making, a move that naturally led to the
construction of a brick home for his recent bride. The couple had six children of their own and apparently acted as foster parents to several others.

Following a fire which destroyed his store in 1858, Whaley was ab-
sent from San Diego for a decade, living first in San Francisco as a government commissary and then in Alaska after the United States acquired that
frozen territory. When his later commercial ventures in San Diego were
unsuccessful, he returned to New York. Upon his return to San Diego five

The Thomas Whaley House.

years later, he served as city clerk in 1881-82 and city trustee in 1885. His foray into real estate during this decade was so successful that he was able to retire in 1888.

According to local San Diegans, the Whaley House is haunted by at least five ghosts. The most colorful is that of "Yankee Jim" Robinson, who was hanged in 1852 on a scaffold erected in the house. The execution went so poorly that the thief strangled for fifteen minutes before expiring. Three of the other ghosts are said to be members of the Whaley family: Whaley's wife, Anna, whose spectre likes to sit in the kitchen; their son Thomas Jr., who died at the age of seventeen months; and their youngest daughter, Corrine Lillian, who lived in the house until 1953 (when she was eighty-nine). While alive, Corrine had her bed moved to the first floor of the house when one ghost continually obstructed the stairs with its bodily presence. The fifth spectral inhabitant of the house is Sheriff James McCoy.

§ Open Wednesday-Sunday 10-4:30. Closed holidays. Fee. Phone: 619-298-2482.

SAN FRANCISCO

¶ Archbishop's Residence, 1000 Fulton Street.

Although now a bed and breakfast establishment, this fifteen-room mansion was built in 1904 as the residence of Patrick Riordan, the second archbishop of San Francisco.

Riordan was born in 1841 in Chatham, New Brunswick, Canada, where his parents had first settled after arriving from Kinsale, Ireland. After moving with his parents to the Chicago area, Riordan was graduated from the University of Notre Dame in South Bend, Indiana. Although he was one of the first dozen students selected to attend the North American College in Rome, poor health forced him to leave the Eternal City and continue his education in Paris and Belgium. Following his ordination, he taught theology and canon law at St. Mary of the Lake University in Chicago before doing pastoral work in several Illinois parishes.

Riordan's appointment as archbishop of San Francisco in 1884 led to the tremendous growth of the archdiocese. Besides building St. Mary's Cathedral and more than forty churches in the city, he established St. Patrick's Seminary, which for more than twenty-five years was the only major seminary on the West Coast. He also created a parochial school system and established Newman Clubs at Stanford University and the University of California at Berkeley. His fluency in six languages symbolized the polyglot nature of the city's inhabitants, many of them immigrants, for whom he supported the creation of national churches ministering to them in their native tongue.

Much of the archdiocese's physical growth was brought to ruin, however, in the earthquake of 1906. Although Riordan was in Chicago when the disaster struck, he rushed back to the city to oversee relief efforts. With a dozen parish churches and schools destroyed, the archbishop visited his displaced parishioners by automobile and celebrated mass in the open air. Incredibly, within two years all but one of his parishes were rebuilt. By the end of his stewardship, the number of parishes had more than doubled and the number of priests had tripled.

Prior to the 1906 earthquake, Riordan played a major role in two thorny legal issues. He successfully led a campaign to exempt churches from the taxation to which they had been subject since 1868. In addition, he brought suit against the Mexican government for failing to completely indemnify the Catholic Church for property seized when Mexico secularized the Missions in California. The suit, which was the first case of international arbitration brought before The Hague Tribunal, resulted in a unanimous decision in favor of the Church. Although the Mexican government complied with the decision for a decade, it defaulted in 1913.

§ Phone: 415-563-7872.

¶ **Brannan Street,** running west from the Embarcadero to 10th Street.

This thoroughfare was named for Samuel Brannan, a Mormon elder of Irish descent who arrived at Yerba Buena (the earlier name for San Francisco) in 1846. (See Calistoga, California.)

¶ **Breen Place,** perpendicular to McAllister Street between Larkin and

Hyde streets.

This short street cross from the San Francisco Public Library was named for *Patrick Breen, one of the survivors of the horrors which befell the Donner party during the winter of 1846-47. (See Truckee, California.)

¶ **Broderick Street,** running north from Buena Vista Park to Marina Boulevard.

This mile-and-a-half stretch honors the memory of David C. Broderick, one of three U.S. senators of Irish descent who were elected from California prior to 1890.

Broderick was born in Washington, D.C., in 1820, the son of an immigrant from County Kilkenny who had come to America to work as a stonecutter on the Capitol. Other than an apprenticeship as a stonecutter, the boy had little formal education, apparently because he was forced to provide for his mother and younger brother after the death of his father. His ruling ambition, however, was politics. By the time he was twenty, his involvement with New York City's Tammany machine and his control of Ward Nine had brought him a coterie of followers. As the owner of a saloon, he earned a good living as well as additional political prominence. His first campaign for Congress, however, failed.

Hoping to create a political career for himself in California, Broderick in 1849 sold his saloon and took passage to San Francisco. Before leaving New York, however, he took the unusually drastic steps of emptying his casks in the street and promising never again to "sell or drink liquor, smoke a cigar or play a card." Once at the Golden Gate, he entered into partnership with an assayer for the purpose of supplying coin-scarce San Francisco with a reliable medium of exchange. According to their ingenious device, the scarcity was to be solved through the coining of "slugs" worth either $4 or $8 (based on the value of the metallic content). The partners hoped that the public would purchase and use the "coins" as either $5 or $10 coins in their commercial transactions. The gamble paid off, and from the differential Broderick made a substantial profit.

Broderick's first entry into California politics came with his election to the state constitutional convention at the end of 1849. Within months he was appointed by the governor to a vacancy in the state senate, beginning a hegemony during the 1850s that caused him to be called "the Democratic party of California." Although his ultimate goal of being elected to the U.S. Senate divided and deadlocked the California legislature for two years, that body finally voted to send him to Washington. Once in the nation's capital, however, the California senator came into open conflict with *President Buchanan over the issues of patronage and slavery. When the president denied him the right to dispense federal patronage in California, Broderick attacked the administration for its pro-slavery stance and its alleged corruption. The debate split the state Democratic party and tainted the gubernatorial election of 1859, when Justice David Terry, a pro-slavery member of the state supreme court, deliberately provoked an incident by publicly insulting the senator. Broderick's reciprocal insult resulted in a challenge to a duel. (See next entry.)

¶ **Broderick-Terry Duel Site,** 1100 Lake Merced Boulevard, near the San Mateo County line.

Two granite shafts mark the positions of the two contestants in California's most famous politically inspired duel. A granite memorial ten yards north gives the facts of the unfortunate incident: "United States Senator David C. Broderick and Judge David S. Terry fought a duel on this ground in the early morning of Tuesday, September 13, 1859. Senator Broderick received a wound from which he died three days later. The affair marked the end of dueling in California. . . ."

Although Broderick had previously been friendly to Terry, the chief justice of the California Supreme Court, trouble began when the judge accused the senator of helping defeat his attempt to be reelected to the bench. When Broderick learned of Terry's accusation before the convention of the state Democratic party, he responded by saying that "I have said that I considered him the only honest man on the supreme bench, but now I take it all back." When the senator refused to comply with Terry's demand for a retraction, the judge demanded satisfaction.

On the dueling field that foggy morning, each of the antagonists was provided with a Lefoucheux pistol, chosen, as custom dictated, by the challenger. As Broderick fingered the hair-triggered weapon nervously, he accidentally discharged it at the count of "one." Obviously at a tremendous advantage, Terry deliberately fired into the senator's right breast. Broderick lingered for three days before dying, the first U.S. senator to be killed in a duel. His last words were, "They killed me because I was opposed to the extension of slavery, and a corrupt administration." His funeral oration by Colonel E. D. Baker drew 30,000 citizens to Portsmouth Square. Because of the Catholic Church's ban on dueling, however, Broderick was not allowed to be buried in consecrated ground. As a result, he was interred in Lone Mountain Cemetery.

§ From Lake Merced Boulevard, turn in at the sign "Lake Merced Hill, Private Club." Park across from the tennis courts and walk to the historical marker at the end of the lot. Go past the small granite plinth to the two stone markers.

¶ The pistols used in the Broderick-Terry duel are on display at the Museum of Money of the American West, located in the Bank of California, 400 California Street. Open Monday-Thursday 9-4, Friday 9-6. Phone: 415-765-0400.

¶ *California Star* **Site,** 743 Washington Street, off Portsmouth Square.

A plaque embedded in the sidewalk near the door of the Bank of Canton marks the site of the office in which *Sam Brannan published the *California Star*, San Francisco's first newspaper. (See Sharpstein Museum, Calistoga, California.)

¶ **California Theater Site,** 444 Bush Street.

A tablet at this site marks the location of the old California Theater, constructed in the late 1860s by a syndicate that included *William Ralston, the "man who built San Francisco." Despite the efforts of the architect to design a building that could withstand fire and earthquake, the 1,600-seat auditorium was a casualty of the 1906 catastrophe that hit the city.

¶ **Donahue Monument,** Battery, Bush, and Market streets.

Although at first sight this memorial seems indecent, its five bronze figures of half-naked men struggling to force a mechanical punch through a metal plate actually are quite appropriate. Executed in 1894 from a model by the sculptor Douglas Tilden, the bronze pile was erected in memory of Peter Donahue, "the Father of the Industrial Revolution in the Far West." A gift of Donahue's son James, the monument weathered the 1906 earthquake.

Although born in Glasgow, Scotland, in 1822, Donahue was of Irish descent, his parents having emigrated from Ulster about twenty-five years earlier. When he was eleven his parents immigrated to America and eventually settled in Paterson, New Jersey. There he became an apprentice millwright and engineer in the factory of Thomas Rogers, Ketchum & Grosvenor, the largest manufacturer of railroad engines in the country. His two brothers, meanwhile, learned the allied skills of molding and boilermaking.

In 1845 Peter moved to New York City and was hired by the Novelty Iron Works to help build the first steam gunboat for the Peruvian navy. After accompanying the completed ship to its destination, he remained in the country until the eve of the California Gold Rush. Succumbing to "argonautical fever," he embarked for California aboard the *Oregon*. When the ship had mechanical problems en route, Donahue earned $6,000 for repairing them but turned down a $1,000 bonus to remain in the employ of the ship's owners.

After spending about five months in the placer mines north of Sacramento, Donahue abandoned his quest for gold and returned to San Francisco. The *Chronicle* later described his decision to leave: "His thrifty nature would not allow him to be content with taking his chances in the lottery of the mines." Instead he joined his brothers in opening the first machine shop and foundry in the western half of the country. Their first major contract was to make 200-pound castings for the drive shaft of an iron steamship dating from the Mexican War.

Operating as the Union Iron Works, the fledgling company eventually expanded its business to include the repairing of engines and the construction of quartz mills, mining machinery, and gas-works. In fact, the brothers' new technology – amalgamating pans, compressed air drills, and powerful pumps – facilitated the transition from placer mining to deeper quartz mining throughout the West. (The company made one of the largest mining pumps in the world for $500,000.)

By the middle of the 1850s, Donahue had acquired his brothers' interest in the business. During the Civil War he produced the first printing press ever manufactured in California as well as the first two vessels produced under government contract on the West Coast. In 1865, meanwhile, he completed for the San Francisco & San Jose Railroad the first locomotive built in the state. The "California," as it was called, was forty-two feet long and weighed twenty-nine tons unloaded with wood and water and forty-six tons when loaded. On a run from Palo Alto to San Francisco, the locomotive hit a top speed of sixty-seven miles per hour.

In the meantime Donahue had begun to diversify his commercial interests. As early as 1852 he and his brothers obtained a fifteen-year franchise to erect a gas works, lay pipes under the streets, install street lamps, and light the city of San Francisco at the rate of 32.5 cents per lamp per night. On February 11, 1854, part of the city was lighted by gas for the first

The Donahue Monument.

time. The *Alta California* duly reported the historic event: "In traveling over the muddy sidewalks and in wading through the street crossing, there was a light ahead which showed the pedestrian how to pick his way and seemed as a sort of guiding star through the mud. . . . Besides the greater accommodation, the safety of the streets and property will be very much increased, and when the streets are more generally lighted, the frequent midnight robberies and burglaries will materially decrease in number."

Although during the next quarter century Donohue's Gas Light Company dropped its rates from $15 per 1,000 cubic feet to $3, important voices began to call for more competition. Frank Pixley, the publisher of the *Argonaut*, for example, urged the city to encourage competition against Donahue's company by granting additional franchises. In 1874 Pixley tweaked the nose of the San Francisco Gas Light Company by explaining why the churches in the city did not substitute gas lights for candles: "At the present rates for gas, few churches . . . can really afford that precious fluid. . . . It has been suggested that, by an arrangement with the directors of the Company, the surprising bills might be paid in salvation; but as corporations have no souls, and the equivalent of even the most remarkable gas bill would not go very far toward saving the individual mortal parts of the directors, the proposition was not met with favor."

Donahue also became more involved in the burgeoning transportation industry in California. In 1861 he organized the first streetcar line in San Francisco and eventually acquired two-thirds ownership of the San Francisco & San Jose Railroad. In addition, he was either an owner or a director of the Union Pacific, the San Francisco & North Pacific, and the San Francisco & Colorado River lines.

Donahue became so enamored of trains, in fact, that the Union Iron Works built him a six-wheeled private car. Known as the "Silver Palace," it was ten feet wide and fifty-one feet long and could accommodate fifteen passengers. Besides a drawing room, it boasted a sleeping compartment and an observatory. The *Alta California* rhapsodized about its elegance: "It was, in truth, a marvel of architecture, though with its walls and panelling unadorned except by the rich hues of native California wood, the beautiful California coloring of the white pine and the mammoth redwood. The furniture, hangings, and upholstery were in excellent taste; the ladies' apartment fitted for the accommodation of a princess, and all the apartments supplied with every convenience that human ingenuity could devise."

On the car's inaugural run to the East Coast, Donahue enjoyed the company of two Irish Americans: James Flood, one of the famous Bonanza Kings, and Patrick Murphy, the owner of Rancho Santa Margarita in San Luis Obispo County. When the Silver Palace reached Chicago, however, Donahue learned that the car's gauge was different from that of the tracks going east. As a result, workmen had to jack up the private car and replace its wheels with others of the proper gauge.

¶ **Downey Street,** running north between 17th and Waller streets.

This hilly street was named for John Gately Downey, governor of California from 1860 to 1862 and the first Irish-born chief executive of any state in the Union. (See Downey, California.)

¶ **Fairmount Hotel,** Mason and California streets, at the top of Nob Hill.

One of San Francisco's most famous landmarks, the Fairmount was named for James Fair, one of the legendary Bonanza Kings. Although this American-born son of Irish immigrants had intended to build his personal residence on this site, a divorce from his wife and his own untimely death ended any such possibility. Theresa Fair, one of his two daughters, later built a hotel on the property, naming it in honor of her father. When the 1906 earthquake struck, the interior of the almost-completed structure was gutted by fire, but the walls and the foundations were unharmed.

¶ **Father Peter Yorke Way,** between Post and Geary streets and Franklin and Gough streets.

This short lane with the long name honors San Francisco's famous "labor priest," a controversial champion of the organized labor movement.

Yorke was born in Galway, Ireland, in 1864, the son of Captain Gregory and Brigid (Kelly) Yorke, who provided their son with a secondary education steeped in the classics. After studying theology at St. Patrick's College in Maynooth, he completed his training for the priesthood at St. Mary's Seminary in Baltimore, Maryland, where he was ordained in 1887. Before taking up full-time pastoral duties in San Francisco, however, he completed advanced degrees in theology from the Catholic University of America in the nation's capital. Many years later he received a doctorate in theology from the Holy See for his numerous polemical works.

Once in San Francisco, Yorke quickly advanced along the clerical *cursus honorum*. In rapid succession he became personal secretary to *Archbishop Patrick Riordan, chancellor of the archdiocese, and editor of the *Monitor*, the official archdiocesan newspaper. From its pages he waged war against the xenophobia and religious bigotry promoted by the American Protective Association. He also organized the Catholic Truth Society to counter the A.P.A.'s anti-Catholic bias. He even criticized what he called the sectarianism of both the state university system and Stanford University. Three years later the governor appointed him a regent of the University of California. The energetic cleric also founded a home for working girls and was a leader in the temperance movement.

Yorke fell from grace with the archbishop, however, when the priest became involved in an embarrassing public feud with mayoral candidate

*James Duval Phelan. (In Yorke's eyes the politician's accommodating views about the British prime minister bordered on a betrayal of the cause of Irish independence.) When Riordan dismissed his former protégé as editor of the *Monitor*, Yorke in 1902 founded a publication of own – the *Leader*. He used this weekly journal to promote Irish nationalism and to argue the rights of labor. He had already publicly defended the teamsters' strike of 1901, but now he wholeheartedly preached the principles of economic justice enunciated in Pope Leo XIII's encyclical *Rerum Novarum*.

Although many employers regarded him as a demagogue, the priest-editor continued to support the working class, most notably during the street car strike of 1906-07. In an editorial during the labor unrest, he proclaimed the necessity of strikes because, "Except in isolated cases, employers have never freely and voluntarily given to their employees the things that justice and humanity require that men should have. . . . When labor organization has become perfected or nearly so there will be no unsuccessful strikes, because capital will grant the just and honest demands of labor freely and without compulsion."

As with most Irishmen, Yorke's heart was never far from his native land and its desire for political independence. He was a popular lecturer on Irish history and literature and organized an Irish fair in San Francisco as early as 1902. He was also an influential champion of the Gaelic revival, establishing the California branch of the Gaelic League and collecting $20,000 to promote the language in Ireland itself. As vice president of Sinn Fein in the United States, he did his utmost to bring about the dream of an Irish republic. When the Easter Rising in Dublin was brutally crushed by the British in 1916, he organized a $50,000 relief fund for its victims, one of whom was his cousin – John McBride – executed as a ringleader of the uprising. A few weeks before Yorke died, he sponsored a public reception for Mary MacSwinney, whose brother, the mayor of Cork, died as a result of a hunger strike in 1921 when he was imprisoned by the British.

¶ Father Yorke is buried in Holy Cross Cemetery in Colma, south of San Francisco. For many years the anniversary of his death in 1925 was celebrated by a memorial service at his grave.

¶ **Flood Building,** at the corner of Market and Powell streets.

Named for the bonanza king *James Flood, this twelve-story building was erected on the site of an earlier structure destroyed by fire in 1898. The Flood Building sits on a wedge-shaped property and is noted for its rounded corner decorated with columns in bas-relief.

¶ **Flood Mansion,** on the northwest corner of California and Mason streets. Private.

Now the headquarters of the Pacific Union Club, San Francisco's first "gentlemen's club," this large brownstone mansion was built by *James

The Flood Mansion.

Flood at a cost of $1.5 million. The forty-two room mansion was noted for its Moorish smoking room and its Louis XV drawing room. The house is surrounded by the original $30,000 brass fence, whose polishing was a full-time job for one of Flood's servants.

Although the interior of the house was gutted in the 1906 fire, its sandstone exterior walls were spared. As a result, the residence was the only great mansion on Nob Hill to survive that catastrophe. After the fire and earthquake, semicircular wings were constructed on each side of the house, a third floor was added, and the tower at the front was lowered ten feet.

Flood's extraordinary wealth was derived from his phenomenally successful mining ventures in Virginia City, Nevada. Like the other three "Bonanza Kings," he had come to California during the Gold Rush. While in San Francisco, he met William O'Brien, like himself a native of Ireland and the man with whom he operated a popular saloon named the Auction Lunch. After forming a partnership with *John Mackay and *James Fair, the four paid $100,000 for a controlling interest in a Virginia City mine which the seller thought was worthless. (More than a $1 million had already been expended in unprofitable exploration.) When a new ore vein was discovered in the mine, the Irishmen used their newfound wealth from this strike to buy up smaller mines at the northern end of the Comstock Lode. The luck of the Irish blessed this new venture when miners digging a thousand feet below ground discovered the "Big Bonanza," a stratum of silver ore 400 feet deep. Between 1873 and 1882 the mine yielded $65 million in silver.

¶ Flood and his son, James Leary Flood, built two other mansions in the city. The one at 2120 Broadway is now the Hamlin School, and the other, at 2222 Broadway, is Sacred Heart High School.

¶ Hayes Street, running west from Market Street to Stanyar Street.

Located in the Hayes Valley district of the city, this street was named in memory of Thomas Hayes, whose study of Spanish land grants led him to the discovery that hundreds of acres in the center of the city were still unclaimed and available at no cost.

After emigrating from his birthplace in Rosscarbery, County Cork, Ireland, in 1820, Hayes worked in New York City as a clerk in the U.S. Customs Office. While still a young man, he entered local politics and soon was elected alderman for the Fourth Ward. Ardent in his support for the cause of Irish independence, he accompanied the editor of the *Irish Volunteer* to Canada in order to enlist recruits in an ill-conceived plan to end British rule in Ireland.

When the venture failed to attract much support north of the border, he cast his eyes on California, where he hoped to make money by providing the '49ers with food and supplies. After sending a shipment of provisions to California, Hayes and his brother took passage around the Horn, joining the more than 100,000 argonauts who headed for California in 1849. The brothers quickly sold their consignment of merchandise at a considerable profit.

Not long after arriving in San Francisco, Hayes discovered a well in the sand dunes surrounding the city. Eager to purchase the extremely desirable site – near the present City Hall – the Irishman studied old Spanish land grants, presumably to determine the property's owner. To his surprise he learned that no claim to the site had ever been registered and that hundreds of acres of land in the center of the city still lay unclaimed. He quickly surveyed 160 acres around the well and filed a claim with the city.

Before long he built a large house near the well, at first calling it "Travelers' Rest" but renaming it "The Hermitage" after people jokingly compared it to a nearby cemetery. It was most likely after this name change that he became known as "Old Hickory," a reference to *Andrew Jackson and his own Hermitage in Nashville, Tennessee. Hayes later set aside part of his property for use as the city's first outdoor recreation park. Two years later, in 1863, it was the site of an Irish festival honoring St. Patrick's Day and featuring a hurling match between "The Emmets" and "The Wolfe Tones."

¶ Hibernia Savings and Loan Society, corner of McAllister and Jones streets.

Although now a police station, when completed in 1892 this Greek

Revival structure was the headquarters of the Hibernia Savings and Loan Society, founded thirty-three years earlier by John Sullivan. This one-story granite structure is noted for its gilded dome, mosaic floor, and Corinthian colonnade pilasters inside.

A decade after its founding, Hibernia Savings had assets of more than $10 million from almost 15,000 depositors. Although the bank survived the 1906 fire, it could not escape the merger mania of more recent history. The Hibernia is now part of Bank of America.

John Sullivan had left his native Ireland at the age of six when he and his parents immigrated to Canada. He later found work as a logger in Maine before moving to Missouri in 1842. Two years later he joined the Murphy-Miller party on its overland trek to California. After settling in San Francisco, he worked as a teamster, a trader, a woodcutter, and a dealer in firewood. He was assisted in the woodcutting trade by two of his brothers and several Mexican workers.

By 1846 Sullivan was associated with William Leidesdorff in supplying wood for galleys aboard the whaling ships that visited San Francisco. He later took advantage of the gold rush to open a general store in Tuolumne County to cater to the needs of the increasing numbers of miners who poured into the area. Although there is no evidence that Sullivan himself engaged in mining, his presence in the region is recalled by a creek and two arroyos named for him.

Even before he went into the merchandising business, Sullivan had begun to invest his money in San Francisco real estate. In 1847, for instance, he bought two lots on the southeast corner of Pacific and Dupont streets for $31. In 1850 he married Catherine Farrely, who before her death only four years later, gave birth to their two sons. Sometime before her untimely death, she and her husband donated land on the northeast corner of California Street and Grant Avenue for the construction of Old St. Mary's Church.

¶ **James D. Phelan Memorial Beach State Park,** in the Seacliff District, between Lincoln Park and the Presidio.

This popular recreational park is named for the famous San Francisco merchant capitalist who bequeathed $50,000 toward its purchase.

¶ *Jeremiah O'Brien,* Fort Mason Center, Building A.

During World War II the *Jeremiah O'Brien* was one of almost 3,000 emergency cargo steamers built in response to the massive German sinking of Allied shipping. The vessel is the last surviving "Liberty Ship" and today serves as the National Liberty Ship Memorial. The *O'Brien* is also the sole survivor of the armada of 5,000 ships which participated in the D-Day invasion of Normandy Beach.

At its launching in South Portland, Maine, in June 1943, the *Jeremiah*

The Liberty Ship Jeremiah O'Brien.

O'Brien was christened in honor of the Irish-born hero of the first naval encounter of the Revolutionary War. One hundred and thirty-two years before, in June 1775, O'Brien and his brothers had led a band of Patriots from Machiasport, Maine, in the capture of a British frigate which had arrived off the coast. (See *Irish America, Volume 1*.)

The World War II career of the *Jeremiah O'Brien* included seven extended voyages as a transport ship. Like her sisters, she is approximately 440 feet long and could carry almost 10,000 tons of cargo (e.g., 2,800 jeeps, 440 light tanks, and 230 million rounds of rifle ammunition). Her first four sailings were between the United States and Britain as part of a convoy. During the fourth cruise, however, she was pressed into service for the invasion of Normandy and made eleven shuttle runs carrying troops and supplies between Britain and the Omaha and Utah beachheads. At one point she carried part of General Patton's Fifth Division from Belfast to the Normandy coast. The ship's fifth voyage took her from New York via the Panama Canal to Chile, Peru, and New Orleans, while her next trip was a short one to the Philippines and back to San Francisco. The famous Liberty Ship's last wartime cruise took her on a round trip from San Francisco to Australia, Calcutta, Shanghai, and Manila.

After the war the *Jeremiah O'Brien* was one of 300 Liberty Ships docked in San Francisco. In 1962, when Captain Thomas Patterson was ordered to scrap the ships, he reported that the "*O'Brien* is in excellent shape as if she had just returned from World War II." As a result of that observation, efforts were launched to save at least one Liberty Ship for posterity. The National Liberty Ship Memorial, a non-profit corporation created to restore and preserve the *Jeremiah O'Brien*, was thus established in 1978. Since that time the vessel has been placed on the National Register of Historic Places, and the foundation has received grants from the National Trust for Historic Preservation, the Department of the Interior, and various maritime industries.

In 1994, during the fiftieth anniversary of the Allied landings in Normandy, the *Jeremiah O'Brien* embarked on a commemorative voyage to draw public attention to her role in that crucial naval maneuver. During the voyage she visited the following ports: Portsmouth, Southampton, Chatham, and London (England); Cherbourg, Rouen, and Le Havre (France); Portland, Maine; Baltimore, Maryland; Jacksonville, Florida; and San Diego and Los Angeles, California.

§ Open Monday-Friday 9-3, Saturday-Sunday 9-4. Fee. Phone: 415-441-3101. In May the annual five-hour Bay Cruise includes a buffet luncheon and the Seamen's Memorial Ceremony in honor of sailors lost in World War II.

¶ **Kate Kennedy Children's Center,** 1670 Noe Street, in the Noe Valley District.

This local landmark honors the memory of the pioneer San Francisco educator who successfully championed tenure for teachers and equal pay for women.

Born in 1827 in Gaskinstown, County Meath, Ireland, Kennedy obtained her early education at a cottage school two miles from her home. She later attended a convent school in Navan, where she learned to speak German, French, Italian, and Spanish. When the death of her father meant that the family could no longer afford to send her five younger sisters to school, Kate instructed them herself at home.

When the Great Famine helped Kate, her sister Alice, and their brother Patrick decide to emigrate in 1849, the trio sailed for New York. There the girls found work in an embroidery factory and gladly used their French-speaking skills to serve as interpreters for the many francophone women on the job. Kate herself continued her informal studies, intent upon becoming a public school teacher.

By 1856 the two Kennedy sisters had made their way to San Francisco, where Kate received her first teaching assignment, in a small town on the outskirts of San Francisco Bay. The next year, however, she was assigned to San Francisco itself and quickly became principal of a school that provided multilingual instruction to its varied student body. Despite the heavy responsibilities of this new job, Kennedy discovered that women were paid less than men in similar positions. For the next fifteen years, she devoted herself to the cause of equal pay for women, a crusade that finally bore fruit when the state legislature passed a law requiring such compensation for female teachers in the public schools. She later succeeded in obtaining legislation which made it illegal to remove a fully accredited teacher without a formal hearing.

In 1878 Kennedy took a leave of absence from her job to travel through Europe. In one of the many letters which she sent the San Francisco Bulletin for publication, she described a visit to Killarney while she was in Ireland. "The view [from Ross Castle]," she wrote, "extends over the lakes and a great part of the surrounding country, embracing the mansion of Lord Kenmare and many other stately edifices, and is one of indescribable loveliness. The castle is said to be the last stronghold which held out against Cromwell, and the cannon used in its defense are still seen, half embedded in the soil and overgrown with ivy. . . . [We] shall long remember the Fourth of July at Killarney as one of the happiest days of our lives."

In addition to performing her educational responsibilities, Kennedy became a spokesperson for a variety of political and social issues. Foremost among them were women's suffrage, unionism, proportional representation, land reform, and taxation. With regard to the latter two, she became a strong supporter of the Knights of Labor, Henry George's Single Tax, and the Land Reform League. She also wrote Short Sermons to Workingmen, a series of articles championing labor unions as the only vehicle to guarantee the rights of workers.

As a result of her activism, however, Kennedy made quite a few enemies. When she sought a brief leave of absence to rest and recover her health, her opponents used this opportunity to marginalize her. In 1887 the board of education transferred her from the school at which she had been principal for two decades to a school much like the one at which she had first taught. And along with the demotion came a reduction in salary – from $100 a month to $75. Although the students at her San Francisco school held a protest gathering – staged a riot, according to one source – she was later dismissed outright, clearly in violation of the law which protected a tenured teacher from dismissal except for misconduct or incompetence. After a three-year legal battle, the state supreme court sided with Kennedy and ordered that the board reinstate her and pay her back salary ($5,700). Two decades after her death, the Kate Kennedy Schoolwomen's Club was founded to further the cause of teachers' rights.

At her interment in Laurel Hill Cemetery in San Francisco, Kennedy was eulogized by *Judge James Maguire. On her behalf he told the world that "she sympathized with the poor and oppressed of her brethren; that she labored and hoped for the restoration of them to their natural heritage, of their natural opportunities, believing firmly that the greatest portion of human miseries, in the present age, springs from the exclusion of the poor from the resources which the Creator has so generously and bountifully provided."

¶ **Kearny Street,** running north from Market Street to Columbus Avenue.

This major thoroughfare was named for *Stephen Watts Kearny, the military commander whose Army of the West helped conquer California during the Mexican War. (See Escondido, California.)

¶ **Knights of the Red Branch Hall,** 1133 Mission Street.

Although today the Knights number but a handful compared to the thousands of members it boasted in the second half of the nineteenth century, the Irish fraternal organization still holds its meetings in this historic hall. The current structure dates from 1909, when it was built to replace the earlier meeting place, destroyed in the 1906 earthquake.

Founded in 1869, the Knights of the Red Branch were an offshoot of the Fenian movement, an attempt to secure Irish independence and the creation of an Irish republic by force of arms if necessary. The name of the organization comes from a fraternity of warriors presided over by Conor MacNessa, king of Ulster at the time of Christ. Although the deeds of the knights merited continual retelling in the Irish chronicles, it was Conor whom the herald MacRoth described to Queen Maeve: "This most beautiful of the kings of the world stood among his troops with all the signs of obedience, superiority, and command. He wore a mass of yellow, curling, drooping hair. He had a pleasing, ruddy countenance. He had a deep, blue, sparkling, piercing eye in his head and a two-branching beard, yellow, and curling upon his chin. He wore a crimson, deep-bordered, five-folding tunic; a gold pin in the tunic over his bosom; and a brilliant white shirt, interwoven with thread of red gold, next his white skin."

After a lifetime of glorious deeds, Conor was felled by a "brain-ball" to the skull, fired by the Connaught warrior Cet MacMagach, during a cattle raid. Conor lingered for seven years until suddenly one day his kingdom was plunged into utter darkness and the heavens were rent by lightning and the earth was rocked by thunder. Asked to account for the startling phenomena, Conor's chief druid explained that they marked the execution of a divine man who had performed miracles during his life in one of the easternmost dominions of Rome. Infuriated at such an injustice, Conor unsheathed his sword and cried out, "Show me the accursed wretches who did this base deed!" Rushing out of the palace and into a grove of trees, the king began to cut their branches, all the while shouting, "Thus would I treat the slayers of that noble Man, could I but reach them."

Another version of the story says that it was Conal Cearnach, a Knight of the Red Branch, who informed Conor of Christ's death. According to this version, the knight had been a Roman prisoner in Jerusalem on the day of the crucifixion and had witnessed the event. "A representative of every race of mankind," says the legend, "was on the Hill of Calvary at the dreadful hour." Conal Cearnach represented the Gael.

¶ **Lefty O'Doul's,** 333 Geary Street.

This famous restaurant and watering hole has been a popular gathering place for sports fans and tourists since it was established in 1958 by Francis Joseph ("Lefty") O'Doul, baseball player and manager.

O'Doul had grown up in an Irish neighborhood of San Francisco called Butchertown, near the later site of Candlestick Park. Years later he attributed his success in baseball to Rosie Stoltz, an elementary school teacher of his, who taught him the fundamentals of the game. Before his father insisted that he leave school to work in a slaughterhouse, the youngster had pitched two semiprofessional clubs to city championships.

O'Doul's professional career began in 1917 when he joined the San Francisco Seals. Even then he was known as a colorful figure who delighted the children in the stands by tossing them baseballs that he had stuffed into his pockets before taking the field. Later while with a team in Iowa, he lost the tip of one finger when he was hit by a line drive.

After serving in World War I, O'Doul joined the New York Yankees, thus beginning a major league career in which he was optioned or traded by thirteen different professional clubs. He enjoyed his greatest season in 1929, when he set the National League's batting record (.398) and hitting record (.254). (His career batting average was .349.) After playing for the Brooklyn Dodgers and the New York Giants, he entered the record books as one of the few who had played for all three New York City teams.

When his major league career ended, O'Doul successively managed four teams in the Pacific Coast League. He was later a batting coach for the Giants when they made the move to San Francisco. Among his protégés were Willie McCovey and Joe DiMaggio. When O'Doul's fans tried to credit him with developing DiMaggio, the manager replied, "Nobody taught Joe DiMaggio how to hit. . . . I was just smart enough to leave him alone." In the meantime the Irish-American had become known as "the man in the Green Suit" because of his customary attire. (His wardrobe included 200 suits and 200 ties.)

Beginning in 1931, O'Doul became the unofficial ambassador of baseball to Japan. During more than twenty trips to that country, he promoted the sport by leading all-star teams in competition against Japanese squads. Besides coaching teams from the Japanese University League, he organized the Tokyo Giants, the first Japanese professional team.

§ Phone: 415-982-8900.

¶ **McCoppin Park,** in the Parkside District, between Taraval and Santiago streets and 22nd and 24th streets.

This urban park honors the memory of Frank McCoppin, elected in 1867 as San Francisco's first Irish-born mayor.

The election illustrated the strong political influence of the city's Irish at that early date: New York City did not have an Irish mayor until 1880, and Boston's first mayoral sweep by an Irish candidate did not occur until four years after that.

Except that Frank McCoppin was born in Longford, Ireland, in 1834, little is known about his early life until he arrived in New York City at the age of eighteen with his parents. Despite his poor origins, he somehow managed to marry into the family of the aristocratic former mayor of New York, James Van Ness. Before moving to California, the young Irishman studied engineering, the aspect of his curriculum vitae that most likely secured him an appointment to oversee construction of the Market Street Railroad, the city's first transit system. While serving four terms on the board of supervisors, he consistently opposed municipal ownership of the street railroad but instead favored its regulation.

When the Democrats swept to power in the statewide elections of 1867, McCoppin rode on their coattails into the mayor's office. The major positive development for the city during his tenure was the construction of the largest dry-dock on the Pacific Coast, an undertaking that was financed by *William Ralston's Bank of California. Although the completion of the transcontinental railroad in Utah in 1869 was greeted by San Franciscans with rejoicing, the influx of Chinese who had formerly worked on the line only added to the numbers of unemployed in the city. The Chinese were later blamed for the depression which hit the manufacturing sector of the city's economy.

In the mayoral campaign of 1869, McCoppin came under vicious personal attack. The press, for instance, charged that his election to the board of supervisors nine years before had been illegal because he was not a naturalized citizen at the time of the balloting. He was also accused of rigging the Democratic convention that had nominated him for mayor. In addition, to counter slurs about his mother, he was forced to send to Ireland for evidence that he was not a bastard. Despite the attacks, he lost the election by only 116 votes out of approximately 20,400 cast.

Even in the defeat of one of his own, the editor of the Irish-Catholic *Monitor* could take consolation in the relative enlightenment of the San Francisco electorate. "Our Countrymen need not fear," he wrote, "... that they have to encounter the prejudices against their race or religion, that are such drawbacks to their settlement in many parts of the Eastern States. Irishmen have made themselves a position here fully equal to that of any other nationality in our cosmopolitan population, and the newcomers of the same race need fear to find no prejudice to bar their advancement, unless what any fault of their own may raise against individuals."

McCoppin remained involved in political life until the end of his life. In 1871 he sought the Democratic nomination for governor and was an official at several of the party's conventions. His election to the state senate in the mid 1870s led to his inclusion in a political directory of the time. There he was described as "a singularly handsome and *distingué* gentleman; tall and straight as a poplar, and although but 43 years of age his hair is white as snow. . . . He is one of those high-toned Irish gentlemen who remind one of the Burkes and the Sheridans. . . . [T]he more of Senator McCoppin's class, and the less of the opposite, that immigrate to this country from the Green Isle, so much the better for the reputation of the Irishmen in America, and the more fully will the people of this country realize the fact that an Irish gentleman is the peer of any man."

¶ **McKinley Monument,** St. James Park, North 1st, North 3rd, St. John, and East St. James streets.

This bronze monument to *William McKinley, the twenty-fifth president of the United States, was erected in 1902, the year after his assassination in Buffalo, New York.

¶ **McKinley Monument,** Baker Street between Fell and Oak streets, near the entrance to Golden Gate Park.

Erected to honor *President William McKinley, this bronze female figure symbolizing the Republic towers thirty-five feet above a granite base.

¶ **Mission Dolores,** on Dolores between 16th and 17th streets.

Founded at the end of June 1776, this Roman Catholic mission is the oldest religious structure in the city. Its adjoining cemetery contains reminders of San Francisco's Hispanic heritage as well as evidence of the city's influential Irish population during the nineteenth century. Among those buried here is Captain Luis Antonio Arguello, the first governor of Alta California under Mexican rule, while statues of the Native American saint Katherine Tekawitha and Father Junipero Serra, the founder of California's mission system, stand in the small enclosure.

Although the cemetery contains the graves of numerous Irish immigrants, the most famous are James Casey and John ("Yankee") Sullivan, victims of the infamous and extralegal Vigilance Committee. The monument over Casey's grave was erected by his fire company and is adorned with stone bas-reliefs of firemen's helmets and bugles.

The international nature of the cemetery is reflected in a poem by Bishop Merlin J. Guilfoyle, a former pastor of the Dolores Mission:

> There are names like Casey, Cora,
> DeHaro and Arguello,
> French, Italian, Spanish, Slavs
> On stones which ages mellow.
> And when each county of Old Ireland
> Sought a judgment day's position,
> It chose slightly south of Market
> And a little west of Mission.

Casey had come to San Francisco in 1851, soon after his release from

Sing Sing Prison in New York after serving time for grand larceny. Like other contemporary politicians, he found the road to political power via one of San Francisco's fire companies, but he increased his power base through his own weekly newspaper. By 1855 he was inspector of elections in the Sixth Ward, a position that proved embarrassing when, after a number of electoral irregularities, he was elected to the Board of Supervisors – even though he had not been a candidate for the office.

The result of the election caused a bitter exchange of editorials between Casey and James King of William, the editor of the *San Francisco Bulletin.* In an attack that appeared in the paper on May 14, 1856, King argued that his antagonist should have "his neck stretched" for ballot-box stuffing and alluded to his earlier incarceration in New York. That same afternoon, when King was leaving his office, Casey confronted him and fired a gun into his chest.

The next day 2,000 citizens answered the call to form the Second Vigilance Committee and within a short time assumed physical control of the city. Bowing to the obvious intimidation, the militiamen who were guarding Casey resigned and threw in their lot with the vigilantes, as did the local National Guard unit. Fearing that Casey's friends planned to free him, a mob of 2,600 armed men stormed the jail and easily seized the prisoner from the thirty deputies who remained his last defense. In short order the committee tried him and publicly hanged him from the second floor of the organization's headquarters. His reputed last words – "May God Forgive My Persecutors" – are engraved on his tombstone.

The Vigilance Committee next came after John ("Yankee") Sullivan, renowned in happier times as a boxing champion but now accused of ballot-box irregularities in connection with Casey's "election." (Sullivan had created a ballot box with a false side and a false bottom into which ballots were stuffed before the voters came to the polls.) While awaiting trial in the committee's jail, he was deprived of his reputed eight shots of liquor a day and apparently went into hallucinations. Fearing that a mob was about to hang him, he took his own life.

§ Open daily 9-4. Closed Thanksgiving and December 25. Fee. Phone: 415-621-8203.

¶ **Native Sons Monument,** at the intersection of Market, Montgomery, and Post streets.

The work of Douglas Tiden and a gift of *James D. Phelan, this memorial commemorates California's admission to the Union. Dedicated in 1897, the memorial shaft is surmounted by a bronze angel holding aloft a book inscribed with the date of admission (September 9, 1850). At the base is a bronze statue of a miner, holding in his right hand a pick and in his left an American flag, its field spangled with a new star for California.

¶ **O'Farrell Street,** running west from Market Street to Masonic Avenue.

This major east-west artery was named for Jasper O'Farrell, an Irish engineer and surveyor who revised the street survey completed for the city in 1839 by the Frenchman Jean Jacques Vioget.

O'Farrell, who had come to Yerba Buena in 1843, was selected four years later to correct the angles laid out in the earlier survey. Besides extending the streets in all directions, O'Farrell laid out Market Street, a 120-foot-wide boulevard. The new street ran diagonally to the Frenchman's earlier grid and stretched from the waterfront to Mission Dolores and Twin Peaks, both prominent landmarks to the west. South of Market Street, the Irishman laid out new streets, making them parallel and perpendicular to his new boulevard rather than to the blocks on the north side. It is for this reason that few of the streets on either side of Market Street connect with each other. In addition, his decision to make the blocks on the south side of Market Street twice the size of those on the north consigned that area of the city to industrial development.

O'Farrell's odyssey toward San Francisco began in Dublin, when at the age of twenty-four he joined a surveying expedition to the west coast of South America. After spending six months charting the serrated coast line of Peru, he headed north to survey the coast of Mexico. It was while there that he learned Spanish, a skill which placed him in good stead when "Don Gaspar" arrived in Yerba Buena aboard an American survey ship.

Since Alta California was still under the control of Mexico, O'Farrell offered his services to Mexican officials there. The newcomer must have been pleasantly surprised when he was not only offered a surveying job but was also named the government's chief engineer and surveyor. He was entrusted with the task of measuring the land grants in the Yerba Buena area, particularly in Marin and Sonoma counties.

In 1847, however, he came under attack when his plan to revise San Francisco's street survey became public. Not everyone favored wider streets, while some objected to his grand diagonal boulevard because it would cut off the present city from its expected expansion on the south. Warned that an angry mob intended to lynch him, O'Farrell wisely left the city for his ranch near Sebastopol in Sonoma County.

In the meantime O'Farrell had married Elena McChristian, the daughter of a prominent figure in the Bear Flag Revolt that declared northern California's independence from Mexico. Attracted by the news of gold near Sacramento, O'Farrell, his father-in-law, and a few other men headed for the gold fields near the Yuba River. Within only three months the miners had extracted $75,000 worth of gold. With this newfound wealth the Irishman eventually expanded his rancho to almost 60,000 acres. In 1858 he was elected a state senator from Sonoma.

¶ Phelan Building, Market and O'Farrell streets.

This landmark five-story building was constructed in 1881-82 by James Phelan, the San Francisco merchant and capitalist whose will disposed of an estate worth almost $7.5 million. The structure, which originally contained five million bricks and two million board feet of timber, was severely burned during the fire that ravaged the city after the 1906 earthquake, but it was completely restored. A bust of Phelan is located inside the lobby. He is buried in Holy Cross Cemetery in San Mateo County.

A native of Queen's (now Laois) County, Ireland, Phelan had immigrated with his father and two brothers in 1824, at the age of three. Forced to quit school when his father's business in New York failed, James found work as a grocery store clerk. Despite its poor pay this experience gave him the business sense and the initial capital which he ultimately parlayed into a fortune. With savings from his clerking job, the young Phelan was able to start his own merchandising business. So successful was it that by 1848 he had saved about $50,000.

Although the Irishman was attracted to the California gold fields, he was not destined to become a miner. Instead he hoped to make his fortune by selling the California argonauts the supplies which, in their haste, they had often left behind. After selling most of his usual inventory, he resupplied himself with articles and utensils that would be in demand in the California mining communities. Showing the caution that characterized him, he sent off his cargo on three ships. Although one of the vessels sank during its voyage around Cape Horn, the other two sailed into San Francisco Harbor about the time he arrived after a life-threatening journey across the Isthmus of Panama. (He almost died of malaria there.)

Phelan's arrival in San Francisco coincided, of course, with the spectacular boom which that city experienced as a result of the Gold Rush. He invested the $100,000 profits which he subsequently made from his mercantile trade into real estate and the wholesale liquor business. During the Civil War he diversified his operations to include the exportation of wool and wheat to the East Coast and foreign markets.

After a year spent in traveling with his family in Europe, Phelan returned in 1870 to begin a new phase in his career. With a capitalization of $1 million, he established the first national bank in California – now the Crocker First National – and presided as its president when it paid out $2 million in dividends over the next dozen years. He later helped organize the Mutual Savings Bank of San Francisco and two insurance companies.

§ Open during business hours Monday-Friday.

¶ Phelan Mansion, 2150 Washington Street.

The San Francisco residence of James Duval Phelan was built after the 1906 earthquake and is a duplicate of his Villa Montalvo in Saratoga, California [*q.v.*]. Phelan, the son of the Irish-born entrepreneur James Phelan, served three terms as mayor of San Francisco and one as U.S. senator.

¶ **Phillip Burton Memorial,** Fort Mason.

This larger-than-life bronze statue of Phillip Burton depicts the U.S. congressman with outstretched arms as if in animated debate, a not unusual stance for a self-described "fighting liberal."

Born to an Irish mother and a father of Irish-German descent, Burton was a graduate of the University of Southern California in Los Angeles and of Golden Gate Law School in San Francisco. He began his political career in 1956, when at the age of thirty he was elected to the California legislature, there earning a reputation as a deal maker. Republicans did their best, though, to unseat the San Francisco congressman because of his controversial redistricting plan for California's delegation in Congress. Described by Burton himself as his "contribution to modern art," the gerrymandering plan allowed Democrats to increase their margin in the delegation from 22-21 to 28-17 in the subsequent election. Under the plan Burton's own Fifth District in San Francisco was 62 percent Democratic.

After this veteran of World War II and the Korean War was first elected to Congress in 1964, Burton used his position to oppose the Vietnam War and to attack the House Un-American Activities Committee. He also supported efforts to weaken the power of committee chairmen because their views were generally more conservative than his. After his election in 1974 as chairman of the Democratic caucus, he was described as "a young curmudgeon" by an admiring critic. The next year he missed being chosen his party's majority leader by one vote. Nevertheless, he continued to be acknowledged as a leader of the Democrats' leftist wing, and he succeeded in obtaining legislation that created the Occupational Safety and Health Administration and greatly expanded federal welfare programs. One of his favorite targets was corporate lobbyists: "I've got to put the squeeze on the *cojones* of the exploitative industries in my state. You have to learn how to terrorize the bastards. . . . They have no limits on their greed or their view of their own self-worth and power. . . ."

¶ **Ralston Monument,** Marina Park, near Fillmore Street.

This marble memorial was erected in 1941 to commemorate *William Ralston, financier and builder of the California Theater and the old Palace Hotel. The monument is ten feet high, seven feet long, and five feet wide. (See Belmont, California.)

¶ **Robert Emmet Statue,** Academy of Science Drive, Golden Gate Park.

Designed by *Jerome Connor soon after the 1917 Easter Uprising in Dublin, this statue is one of four such works by the Irish-born sculptor. The seven-foot-high bronze statue honors the famous Irish Protestant patriot who led an unsuccessful insurrection of United Irishmen in his na-

Statue of the Irish patriot Robert Emmet by Jerome Connor.

tive land in 1803. Emmet had entered Trinity College in Dublin a decade earlier but resigned in protest against its inquisitorial examination of its students' political views.

The pedestal displays the coat of arms of the United Irishmen and is inscribed with extracts from Emmet's final speech before his execution: "I wished to procure for my country the guarantee which Washington procured for America. . . . I have parted from everything that was dear to me in this life for my country's cause. . . . When my country takes her place among the nations of the earth, then, and not until then, let my epitaph be written . . . ."

The statue was presented to the city by *James D. Phelan in 1919, probably to atone for remarks considered overly sympathetic to Britain. Eamon De Valera, the president of the Irish Free State, gave the dedicatory address. The United Irish Societies annually gather here to commemorate Emmet's birthday, an event that includes a recitation of the Irishman's "Speech Before the Dock." Duplicates of this statue are in Washington, D.C.; St. Stephen's Green, Dublin, Ireland; and Emmetsburg, Iowa [*q.v.*].

Jerome Connor was born in County Kerry, Ireland, in 1876 and as a young child came to America with his family. Because his parents were so poor, he was forced at age thirteen to earn his own living. After working successively as a sign painter, a machinist, and a stonecutter, he lived and worked in a craftsman colony near Buffalo, New York, where he did metal work, plaster casting, and sculpture. After opening his own studio in Syracuse, he received his first major commission – a marble memorial to Walt Whitman. He later set up a studio in the nation's capital, which today boasts three of his works: the Nuns of the Battlefield Memorial and statues of *Bishop John Carroll and *Robert Emmet.

Connor was a strong advocate of the Irish independence movement. In 1921 he exhibited a portrait bust of Eamon De Valera, the president of the Irish Free State, at the Philadelphia Exhibition of Fine Arts. Four years later he returned to Ireland to work on a memorial in County Cork to the victims of the Lusitania sinking, which had occurred off Cobh in 1915. While occupied on this project for fourteen years, he completed a series of relief portraits of the cabinet members of the Irish Free State government. He died in Dublin in 1943 and was buried in Mount Jerome Cemetery in the Irish capital.

¶ St. Patrick's Church, 756 Mission Street.

Although overshadowed in size by the modern skyscrapers to the west, St. Patrick's stands tall because of its heritage as the focus of the city's first Catholic parish. Founded in 1851, the parish in those early years was served by Father John Maginnis, a native of Duleek, County Meath, Ireland.

The present brick church on this site was constructed to replace an earlier edifice built in 1870 and destroyed in the 1906 fire. Although it is strengthened by buttresses and steel girders and lacks the earlier structure's graceful spire, the present building is dimensionally like the 1870 church. Its interior, however, reflects the wish of Monsignor John Rogers, its Wexford-born pastor during the 1920s and 1930s, that it be the Irish national church on the West Coast. For that reason the predominant colors are green, white, and gold, while the statuary and stained glass are eloquent expressions of Ireland's religious history.

The clerestory windows of the church portray mainly pre-Christian traditions. The windows on the west side of the nave depict (left to right) the following scenes: the Death of King Connor Macnessa, the Death of Milcho, Connla of the Golden Hair, Cormac MacArt, Ith at the Palace of Aileach, the Building Emania, Osisin in Tir-na-Nog, and the Prophecy of Conn Cead Cathach. The windows on the left portray the Pursuit of the Gilla Dacker, Dermot O'Dyna in Tir-fa-tonn, the Children of Lir, Moran the Just, the Voyage of St. Brendan (the only Christian scene among these lights), Amergin's Triumph-Song, the Voyage of Maeldun, and the Voyage of the Sons of O'Corra.

The lower windows in the nave depict episodes in the life of St. Patrick and images of various Irish saints. Clockwise from the northwest, the four corner windows in the nave depict scenes from the life of St. Patrick: responding to the invitation of the Irish to come among them, expelling the spirit of evil from Ireland, establishing his church at Armagh, and lighting the pascal fire on the Hill of Slane.

The intervening windows along the two sides of the nave show Ireland's patron saints, seen in alphabetical order by counties: MacNissi (Antrim), Celsus (Armagh), Lasserian (Carlow), Felim (Cavan), Senan (Clare), Finbar (Cork), Colmcille (Derry), Adamnan (Donegal), Malachy (Down), Lawrence O'Toole (Dublin), Molaise (Fermanagh), Jarlath (Galway), Brendan (Kerry), Brigid (Kildare), Canice (Kilkenny), Fintan (Laois), Benignus (Leitrim), Munchin (Limerick), Mel (Longford), Mochta (Louth), Colman (Mayo), Finian (Meath), Macartan (Monaghan), Kieran (Offaly), Coman (Roscommon), Attracta (Sligo), Ailbe (Tipperary), Eoghain (Tyrone), Carthage (Waterford), Fechin (Westmeath), Aedan (Wexford), and Kevin (Wicklow).

The litany of Irish saints continues in the cluster of figures on the church's three altars: Patrick, Brigid, Colmcille, and Columba on the High Altar; Adamnan, Declan, Fursey, Jarlath, Brendan, Enda, Grellan, and Kevin on Our Lady's Altar; and Lawrence O'Toole, Nesson, Ruadhan, Tussach, Malachy, Oengus, Senan, and Ultan on St. Joseph's Altar. The High Altar is also adorned with the coats of arms of Ireland's four provinces: the Eagle of Connacht, the Red Hand of Ulster, the Three Crowns of Munster, and the Harp of Leinster.

ℐ Stanwood Hall, The Hamlin School, 2120 Broadway.

Stanwood Hall, one of several buildings on the campus of The Hamlin School, was constructed in 1901 for James Leary Flood, the son of the Nevada silver king *James Flood. The exterior of the twenty-four room house is noted for its pilasters, Ionic columns, and pedimented windows.

The younger Flood and his wife moved into the three-story Italian Baroque mansion in 1906, after the San Francisco earthquake and fire gutted the Flood mansion on Nob Hill. (That residence is now the Pacific-Union Club.) When James Leary Flood and his wife later moved to 2222 Broadway, Flood's sister Cora Jane remained at the 2120 Broadway address until 1924, when she moved to the Fairmount Hotel. Three years later the Baroque mansion was purchased by Mrs. Edward Stanwood, who converted the principal rooms into classrooms.

ℐ Sullivan Firehouse, 870 Bush Street.

The front of this still active fire station is adorned with a memorial plaque to *Dennis Sullivan, San Francisco's fire chief at the time of the 1906 fire and, ironically, a victim of the earthquake which precipitated it.

At the time of the disaster, Sullivan had been a member of the San Francisco Fire Department for twenty-nine years. During most of his fourteen years as chief, he had warned city officials about the possibility of such a catastrophe but had been unsuccessful in persuading them to provide his department with more modern fire-fighting equipment, including machinery that could pump sea water.

During the earthquake Sullivan and his wife were asleep in adjoining upstairs rooms in this firehouse (Engine Company #3). As the quake began, the turret from the California Hotel next door fell through the ceiling of Mrs. Sullivan's room, making a gaping hole in the floor and taking her with it. She escaped serious injury, however, because the mattress to which she clung cushioned her fall.

As Chief Sullivan ran into his wife's room, he, too, fell through the floor and suffered two broken ribs, an injured head, and a punctured lung. He also was severely burned when he landed against hot radiator pipes. The chief was rescued only after several hours of effort and died three days later. Although he remained conscious during that time, his attendants told him nothing about the fire. As he had predicted, the city's fire hydrants ran dry as soon as the water mains were broken by the quake.

℧ William O'Brien Burial Site, Calvary Cemetery, Lone Mountain.

During the 1930s this serene-looking mausoleum was home not only to its long-dead builder and rightful inhabitant but also to a group of impoverished itinerants. In their desperate quest for shelter, these homeless men had pried open the mausoleum's bronze door and set up housekeeping, replacing the tomb's stained-glass window with a stovepipe. The wealthy San Franciscan whose peace these interlopers disturbed doubtless would have enjoyed the company had he been alive, for William O'Brien was renowned for his congeniality and was universally called "The Jolly Millionaire."

Born in Queen's (now Laois) County, Ireland, about 1826, O'Brien had come to American sometime before his twenty-first birthday. For a while he worked in New York City as a store clerk but, bitten by the gold bug, was one of the first argonauts to head for the West Coast. To pay his passage around the Horn, he did duty as a deck hand aboard the *Tarolinta* and arrived in San Francisco in the summer of 1849. From then on, O'Brien annually celebrated his arrival by hosting his former fellow passengers to a glorious banquet. In 1878, the last year of his life, he chartered a boat for fifty of his friends and comrades for an outing to Angel Island in San Francisco Bay.

At the time of his actual landing, however, O'Brien was penniless and the object of charity from a bystander on the wharf who gave him a pair of shoes. The young adventurer was so desperate that he offered to help unload the ship's cargo in order to earn a few dollars. Once on his feet, though, he headed for the mines at Poor Man's Gulch on the Feather River, where he met a man with whom he started a commercial enterprise in San Francisco.

This partnership ended four years later, however, when O'Brien met a fellow Irishman named James Flood, with whom he opened a saloon on Washington Avenue. Dubbed the "Auction Lunch" because, like other such establishments at the time, it provided its drinking customers with a free lunch, the business became an overnight success. With Flood pouring the stout and O'Brien using his charm to draw patrons into the place, the two proved a winning combination and made quite a fortune.

While they were dispensing good cheer, though, the two Irishmen were learning about sluice boxes and options from their clients, mostly miners and stock brokers. Confident that they could succeed on their own in the world of hard hats and green visors, the partners sold their saloon in 1866 to devote their attention to mining. In a subsequent partnership with *John Mackay and *James Fair, who had already made a fortune in the mines, the four "Silver Kings" purchased the Consolidated Virginia Mine in Nevada. Their luck in the mines was so phenomenal that within four years after selling their pub O'Brien and Flood were enjoying an income of more that $500,000 a month. With their growing wealth the Silver Kings opened the Bank of Nevada, whose initial capitalization of $5 million quickly doubled.

For a man like O'Brien, however, wealth meant less than the companionship of friends and relatives. When he died a bachelor at the age of fifty-two, he left his vast fortune – except for $100,000 for charities – to his sister and their children.

SAN JOSE

¶ Murphy Building, 36 South Market Street.

Located at the center of old San Jose, the Murphy Building was constructed in 1862 by Martin Murphy Jr. as a multipurpose commercial structure. With its large cornice, ornamented window surrounds, and pedimented windows, the building is a fine example of sixteenth-century Italian style. The 63-by-40-foot room on the upper floor was constructed as part of Murphy's agreement with the county that the chamber be fitted out as a courtroom.

Murphy was born near Wexford, Ireland, in 1807, the oldest of the eight children of Martin Murphy Sr. and his wife, Mary Foley Murphy. When the family patriarch decided to immigrate to Canada, he set sail in 1820, bringing with him his wife and four of their children. Martin Jr. and his sister Margaret remained behind to work the family farm until a buyer could be found.

Not until six years later was the property sold, at which time the brother and sister were finally able to join the rest of the family in an Irish settlement outside Quebec. There Martin Jr. met and married Mary Bolger, the daughter of a family that the Murphys had known in Wexford. While living in Quebec, the couple had six children, but after their two youngest died in a cholera epidemic the family fled the city for the open farm lands. Murphy bought several hundred acres near his father's property.

The harsh weather and the developing political conditions in Canada during the 1830s, however, caused the Murphys to consider a move to the United States. Once again led by their patriarch, the family made the trek, this time settling on farm land near St. Joseph, Missouri. Again two members of the family fell victim to disease – this time malaria. Therefore, when a frontier missionary told the Murphys about the attractions of California, they prepared for the arduous journey across the continent.

During that 1844 migration, the fifty-one members of the Miller-Murphy-Stevens party, as they were called, made history with a number of firsts. Not only were they the first immigrant group to bring wagons over the mountains to California, but they were also the first to cross the Sierra Nevada Mountains through what would later be called the Donner Pass. Like the ill-fated Donner party who tried to cross the Sierras five years later, the Murphy group reached the summit late in the season and decided to spend the winter there until the snow melted. Fortunately, though, two of the elder Murphy's sons – John and Daniel – were able to obtain food and other supplies from across the mountains.

Soon after the party arrived safely at Fort Sutter (now Sacramento) in March 1845, Martin Murphy Jr. purchased about twenty square miles along the Consumnes River, about fifteen miles away. There he established the first successful wheat farm in the Sacramento Valley, marketing the amber grain at John Sutter's famous trading post.

About fifteen months after Murphy's arrival in California, his ranch witnessed the first skirmish between Americans and Mexicans for control of California. According to the historian Herbert Bancroft, a Mexican military force used Murphy's corral to stable the 125 horses which they were driving to the San Joaquin Valley. During the night a party of Americans under General John Frémont made off with the horses and headed for Sonoma, where they declared independence from Mexico and created the Bear Flag Republic. Luckily for the Mexicans staying at Murphy's ranch, the Irishman was able to provide each of them with a new mount. A historical marker on the site of Murphy's ranch commemorates the event.

Martin Murphy Jr. farmed his ranch near Sacramento until 1849, when he moved south to Santa Clara County. There he purchased the 4,000-acre Pastoria de la Borregas (Sheep Pasture) Rancho for $12,000. After changing the property's name to Bay View Ranch, he constructed the wood-frame building that served as his family's residence in Sunnyvale until 1953, when the city acquired the ranch for public use. The house itself was destroyed in 1961, but the site is marked in the Murphy Historic Park in Sunnyvale [q.v.].

Before his death in 1884, Murphy had acquired land holdings larger in extent than all of County Wexford, his birthplace in Ireland. In all, he owned a total of almost 79,000 acres spread over six ranchos in San Luis Obispo, Santa Barbara, and Santa Clara counties. In 1874 alone he harvested 1.5 million bushels of wheat. Besides developing a superior type of grain, he introduced a new breed of cattle that was better adapted to California's heat and dry terrain.

In addition to achieving renown for his innovations in agriculture and animal husbandry, Murphy was known for his philanthropy. He was particularly generous in the field of education, being one of the original founders and benefactors of the Jesuit-run Santa Clara College and of Notre Dame Academy in nearby San Jose. Even in his money-lending transactions he was generous, charging interest at rates well below the average (e.g., 1.5 percent on loans above $25,000).

¶ Thomas Fallon House, 175 St. John Street.

Since its construction by Thomas Fallon in 1859, this structure has served a variety of functions: private residence, kindergarten, boarding house, and popular restaurant known as The Italian Cellar. In 1978 the building was restored to its mid-nineteenth-century appearance.

Many of the details of Fallon's life have been preserved in his correspondence, much of it skillfully woven into a quasi-fictional "journal" created in 1978 by Thomas McEnery, a former mayor of San Jose. In the introduction to the journal, McEnery relates Fallon's childhood recollection of dead bodies piled high along a road near Kinsale, Ireland, the land of his birth in 1824. To these images of famine and desolation, Fallon added his father's fear of an uprising in Ireland, a concern that caused the older man to take his family to Canada. Recalling his feelings at the age of three – as the family was about to emigrate – Fallon painted a poignant picture of Cork, their port of embarkation. "To me it was the biggest gathering of people and buildings I had ever seen," he wrote, "and the ship we were to sail on was a true Leviathan to my eyes. At the foot of the lower quay it tugges [sic] at its moorings and we carefully were packed aboard and deposited beneath the deck. All I could recall after that was the sight of the roofs as we sailed and shortly the old head of Kinsale was briefly in view. . . . [I]t was the last thing my eyes saw in Holy Ireland."

Once in Canada, the family settled in London, Ontario, a town of 1,200 people, where the young Fallon eventually served an apprenticeship with a Dublin-born saddler. About his master, Fallon recalled: "What he lacked in business sense, he made up in a vast knowledge of Ireland, her history and stories." Following his father's death the eighteen-year-old decided to take the money which the older man had set aside for him and travel to the United States. After leaving his mother in his brother's care, Fallon crossed the border and for a time practiced his trade in Detroit and Cincinnati. Eager to experience the excitement of the West, however, he soon headed down the Ohio River to the Mississippi and into Texas. Upon his arrival there, he found the region racked by the war for Texan independence. He remained in Texas long enough to serve with the rebels under Sam Houston at the battle of San Jacinto.

By the summer of 1843, Fallon was at Fort Lancaster, Colorado, where he had just killed a Frenchman under mysterious circumstances. Fallon subsequently joined the topographical survey party led by John C. Frémont and headed for California. He later claimed that he was the first white man to see Lake Tahoe.

After his arrival in Santa Cruz the next year, Fallon resumed his saddlery trade and soon became famous for his craftsmanship, especially in making the Mexican saddle tree. At the news of the Bear Flag Revolt in Sonoma County – where a group of Americans had declared independence from Mexico in June 1846 – he enlisted twenty-two men to join the insurrection. "Captain" Fallon proceeded to lead these men across the mountains to Santa Clara, all the time carefully avoiding a clash with Colonel Jose Castro and a 200-man force of Californios sent to crush the revolt.

In the meantime war had broken out between Mexico and the United States. Perhaps emboldened by this news, Fallon led his band of men into San Jose, taking control of the Mexican government there and on July 14 raising the American flag in front of the *juzgado* (courthouse). Although an American by the name of James Stokes had apparently raised the Stars and Stripes before Fallon's arrival, the flag had been cut down and carried away by angry Californios. In a subsequent letter to an American naval officer, Fallon wrote: "I am happy to inform you that we have . . . hoisted the star spangled baner [*sic*] on the 14th ins, and we hope it may wave & dispense its blessings throughout this country." After taking control of San Jose for the United States, Fallon led his men to Mission San Juan Bautista, where they met Frémont, now in command of the California Battalion. Before long, the Irishman disbanded his troops and joined Frémont's expedition to San Diego.

At the conclusion of the Mexican War, Fallon returned to Santa Cruz and married Maria del Carmen Lodge, the sixteen-year-old daughter of Martina Castro and Michael Lodge, a sailor from Dublin. In a notation of February 22, 1848, Fallon described his future wife as having "the beautiful full face of an Irish lady and the dark shades of her mother." Together the young couple headed for the gold mines, where they operated a store and made a fortune in a matter of months. With the proceeds, Fallon bought the Eagle Hotel in San Jose and used it as a residence, hotel, and store.

When Maria inherited about 3,800 acres from her mother, Fallon sold the Eagle Hotel for $3,500 and moved with his wife to Texas. After the death of three of their nine children, however, the couple returned to San Jose in 1854. It was at this time that Maria divorced her husband, apparently because of his roving eye. Four or five years later, after his election as mayor of San Jose, Fallon built the house on St. John Street. At the time, it was one of the town's finest residences and boasted a formal garden on its front lot.

When Fallon remarried in 1875, Annie, the youngest of his three surviving daughters, came to live with him and his new wife. This marriage lasted only seven years, however, and ended in a divorce which Fallon initiated. He later moved to San Francisco, where, it seems, he promised to marry Elmira Dunbar. When Fallon – now in his late fifties – reneged on his word, the aggrieved brought suit for breach of promise of marriage. A San Jose jury subsequently awarded a $10,000 judgment against him, a decision he was in the process of appealing when he died in 1885. In the litigation which followed his death, the bulk of his estate was awarded to two of his children. Events were further complicated by reports after his death that he had been seen in London, Dublin, New Orleans, and Denver.

❡ A marker at the corner of Market and Post streets commemorates Fallon's capture of San Jose during the Mexican War: "On this spot stood the *juzgado* of 1798. Over its roof Captain Thomas Fallon raised the stars and stripes July 14, 1846."

SAN JUAN BAUTISTA

❡ **Castro-Breen House,** on the south side of the Mission Plaza.

This two-story residence was built in 1840-41 by former governor Jose Castro and is considered the best example of California adobe construction remaining from the Mexican era. The central hallway is flanked by a living room and a large dining room, and each of the bedrooms upstairs opens onto a balcony.

Sometime prior to 1854, Castro turned use of the house over to the Irishman Patrick Breen and his family, one of only two families in the Donner party to survive intact after spending the winter of 1846-47 trapped in the snows of the Sierra Nevadas. (See Truckee, California.)

After their rescue the Breens had first convalesced at Sutter's Fort in the Sacramento Valley before moving to Murphy's Ranch on the Consumnes River near the fort. The family spent the following winter at Mission San Jose, but in February 1848 they settled in the fertile San Juan Bautista Valley, becoming the first American family to settle there. Initially the family stayed in the mission buildings but later moved into Castro's adobe.

Good fortune smiled on the Breens when their sixteen-year-old son discovered gold worth $12,000 in the Mother Lode. With a portion of that money, Patrick Breen bought the Castro house, which he proceeded to operate as "The Inn." The hotel quickly became a favorite stop-off for travelers making the journey from Monterey to the gold fields to the north. (Breen advertised his rate as "Five dollars a night per horse and man.")

The Castro-Breen House.

He also purchased 1,000 acres of land, approximately half of it almost adjacent to the Mission.

During the twenty years that Breen and his wife lived in San Juan Bautista, the Irishman was a prominent figure. Besides serving as the postmaster and a school trustee, he was one of the three county supervisors. At his death in 1868, he owned real and personal property worth more than $110,000. The Breens' only daughter, Isabella, was the last survivor of the Donner party to die.

❡ On a hill southwest of the Old Mission is a cemetery in which Breen, his wife, and other members of their family lie buried. Several monuments mark the graves.

SAN PEDRO

❡ John T's Tavern, 331 West 6th Street.

Constructed in 1925, this San Pedro watering-hole was formerly the office of John Tracy Gaffey, a pioneer California newspaper editor, real estate developer, and civic leader.

Gaffey was born in Galway, Ireland, in 1860, the son of Thomas and Ann (Tracy) Gaffey. While his father was of Scotch-Irish stock, his mother was from an old Norman-Irish family. At the age of seven Gaffey accompanied his mother and his six brothers and sisters to San Francisco. From there the family moved to Santa Cruz, where they bought a cattle and sheep ranch. After completing his elementary and high school education in San Francisco, Gaffey attended the University of California at Berkeley for a year.

Gaffey began his public career at the age of twenty-one, when he founded the *Santa Cruz Herald*. Over the following decade he served in a succession of governmental positions: undersheriff of Santa Cruz County, clerk of the California Supreme Court, and member of the Board of Equalization. Once after returning from Mexico, where he had been attending to his mining interests, he learned that he had been elected to the Los Angeles School Board. When the remaining months of his term expired, he resumed his position as managing editor of the *Los Angeles Herald*, later resigning to serve six months on the Los Angeles City Council.

Perhaps Gaffey's most enduring contribution to the future of Southern California, however, was his support for *Stephen Mallory White. As the latter's campaign manager, he succeeded in canvassing enough votes in the state legislature to win White's election to the U.S. Senate in 1892, despite the opposition of Collis P. Huntington, the powerful head of the Southern Pacific Railroad. Even after the election White and Gaffey continued to battle the railroad giant as they fought his efforts to divert a $3 million congressional harbor appropriation from San Pedro to Santa Monica. In the end, the Irish-American senator and his Irish-born ally succeeded in assuring San Pedro's future as the site of man-made Los Angeles Harbor. Appropriately enough, Gaffey was later appointed customs collector for the new harbor by *President Grover Cleveland, although he declined the position.

In the meantime Gaffey had married Arcadia Bandini, reputedly the most beautiful woman in Southern California and a descendant of two of the state's most prestigious Mexican families. This daughter of Don Juan Bandini was related through her mother, Esperanza, to the famous Sepulveda family, whose claim to what is now the San Pedro area and Rancho Palos Verdes derived from a land grant from the king of Spain.

For his beautiful wife Gaffey constructed a Spanish-style twenty-two-room mansion on a seven-acre site known as "Hacienda La Rambla." Formerly at Bandini and Third streets in San Pedro, the house boasted a wine cellar, a circular driveway, a chapel, an interior courtyard, and a library. Together with his office on 6th Street, the library housed some of the 20,000 books which Gaffey brought back from a trip to Europe. (The Irishman could read in several languages and was said to be interested in everything from Roman history to Spanish architecture.)

At his death in 1935, Gaffey left $236,000 to his wife and their two children, an inheritance that derived primarily from his real estate investments. "La Rambla" was subsequently turned into a restaurant by Gaffey's son but was demolished in the 1960s to make way for a new Y.M.C.A. building. Nearby Gaffey Street, the major traffic corridor to the Harbor

Freeway, honors the San Pedro pioneer.

¶ Stephen Mallory White Statue, Stephen White Drive, near the Cabrillo Marine Aquarium.

This large bronze statue depicts one of California's most influential U.S. senators in an oratorical pose, standing in front of a chair of state and extending his right arm as if to emphasize a debating point. The work of the sculptor Douglas Tilden, the statue was unveiled in 1908 at its original location in the Los Angeles civic center. The sculpture was moved to San Pedro in 1989 to mark the ninetieth anniversary of the city's selection as the port of Los Angeles, a choice which White had championed in Congress for a decade.

White was born in San Francisco in 1853, the son of Irish immigrants who had come to America as children. Although his grandfather had been a successful farmer along the Shannon River, he left his native country in disgust after British authorities there inflicted a savage injustice upon two of his farm laborers. After arriving in San Francisco, the future senator's father, William, became a newspaper writer and the author of *A Picture of Pioneer Times in California*, written under the pseudonym William Grey. After two decades as an official of the state Democratic party, he changed his allegiance to the Workingmen's party and was its gubernatorial candi-

Statue of Stephen Mallory White, champion of San Pedro as the port of Los Angeles.

date in 1879. William's wife, Fannie Russell, was related to *Stephen Russell Mallory, the Confederate secretary of the navy.

A graduate of Santa Clara College, Stephen White was admitted to the bar in 1874 and began practice in Los Angeles. One of his most personally memorable experiences was his role in helping the U.S. attorney general win a case in the Supreme Court upholding the constitutionality of the Chinese Exclusion Act. In rapid succession he was district attorney of Los Angeles County, state senator, and U.S. senator. White identified with the populist wing of the Democratic party and rivaled *William Jennings Bryan in his denunciation of corporate monopoly and in his support of free silver. He consistently opposed U.S. imperialism and on the floor of the Senate opposed a declaration of war against Spain in 1898.

White also attacked American efforts to annex Hawaii and Cuba. In his view annexation would benefit only big business, permitting the trusts to exploit the annexed territories and bringing an influx of cheap labor into the Unites States. Most likely with an intentional pun, he charged that those Americans who wished to annex Hawaii "saw a good deal of sugar in the proposition." In a speech after his retirement from the Senate, he expressed his belief that America had a destiny higher than imperialism: "I think that her destiny is something more than to subjugate snakes, boa constrictors, Filipinos or Cubans. I look upon her as the typification of the republic of the ages. I regard her as containing within her mighty bosom the truths of centuries, received from those who have striven to elevate virtue, to take women and men and build them up to be higher and better things in the struggling story of mortality."

White is most prominently remembered in California history for his success in obtaining a $3 million appropriation from Congress which effectively gave Los Angeles a man-made harbor. In the culmination of a titanic battle during the mid 1890s, White defeated the plans of Collins P. Huntington to divert the appropriation to Santa Monica, a site favored by the Southern Pacific Railroad but farther to the west of Los Angeles. White's three-day debate with Senator William Frye of Maine – a supporter of the Santa Monica site – was one of the most spirited in the history of the U.S. Senate. Upon his return to California after the successful vote in Congress, White was hailed as a hero and was feted with parades, speeches, and fireworks in both Los Angeles and San Pedro.

Actual construction of the harbor began on April 26, 1899, when the first barge-load of rocks was dumped into the sea off San Pedro Point to begin the 9,250-foot breakwater. The event was attended by between 10,000 and 15,000 people, among them White himself. In his remarks to the crowd, the former senator described the role which the future harbor would play in the latest unfolding of America's "manifest destiny." "When this great work is done," he predicted, "it will again be proved that the control of the American people does not . . . 'stop with the shore,' but that we move onward in those paths of conquest where the sword does not gleam and the bullet does not kill, but where the inventive and progressive American subdues by the force of his energy and the magnetism of his personality. . . . Whatever I have done or can do will not be only for the advantage of my section and State, but for my country. . . ."

Although White lived for five years after his victory on the harbor issue, his health was permanently impaired. According to the former senator's secretary, it was White's indefatigable work habits that killed him. "Every night until 11 or 12 o'clock, many nights until 2 or 3 o'clock and sometimes all night in winter and summer," the secretary said, "we toiled side by side, and sometimes I have awakened him from asleep at his desk only to be told that he could not go home yet but must finish some particular piece of work." In a remark which White reportedly once made to the president of the United States, the former senator wrote his own epitaph, saying that he "would rather be a lawyer whose word was as good as the rich man's bond, and whose opinion upon intricate questions of judicial science were valued . . . than to hold in his hands all the honors that were ever won by appeals to the passions and prejudices of men."

SAN RAFAEL

¶ **St. Vincent's School for Boys,** U.S. 101 to the St. Vincent's Drive exit.

This Catholic orphanage for boys was erected in 1855 on almost 1,000 acres deeded to the archdiocese of San Francisco by Timothy Murphy, one of the earliest foreigners to come to this part of California. One of the school buildings is named for the 300-pound Irishman, and a historical marker in his honor is located in front of the main entrance to the institution.

Murphy was born in 1800 in Coolaneck, County Wexford, and apparently received a commercial education good enough to allow him to obtain a position with a business firm in Dublin. In a short time, however, he sailed to Lima, Peru, to work for Hartnell & Co., a British meatpacking firm. In 1829 the company sent him to Monterey, California, to manage its packing and exporting operations there.

When this California venture proved unsuccessful after a year or two, Murphy turned to the commercial hunting of otter, selling the animal's pelts for between $40 and $50 apiece. While engaged in this trade, he operated out of either the Presidio in San Francisco or the Mission in San Rafael. Dr. Quigley, in his work *The Irish Race in California*, described the burly Irishman as "a man of commanding appearance, [who] stood six feet two and one-half inches high; muscular and straight with a fair, florid complexion and an aquiline nose. He was a famous 'shot.' Even up to the day of his death, he could kill a deer or antelope at a distance of one-fourth of a mile with his rifle. He also kept a large kennel of beagles and greyhounds, thirty-five of which he had at one time sent to him, by sea, by his cousins, the Conroys of Callao."

Following the secularization of the California missions by the Mexican government, Murphy served as administrator at San Rafael Mission between 1837 and 1842. Ironically, though, one of the government officials who visited the mission during that time commented that Murphy was illiterate. The historian Bancroft, however, says that the Irishman was "a good penman, but his Spanish was peculiar, and his letters too often contained vulgar expressions and insults to all with whom he did not agree; yet he was on the whole a good-natured and popular man." In addition, as agent and commissioner of the Nicasio Indian tribe, he was a faithful guardian of their interests.

During this period Murphy had become a friend of Mariano Vallejo, and had even been considered a candidate for marrying his daughter. Perhaps as a result of this relationship, the Irishman in 1844 received from Governor Manuel Micheltorena a grant of almost 22,000 acres encompassing San Pedro, Las Gallinas, and Santa Margarita ranchos. Following the Mexican War, the adobe house which "Don Timotheo" built in San Rafael was visited by General William T. Sherman on his way from Monterey to Sutter's Fort in Sacramento.

A lifelong bachelor, Murphy at his death bequeathed his extensive real estate holdings to his brother Martin and to his nephew John Lucas. He also left between $200 and $400 to each of his Indian servants: Candeliria, Josavius, Alevasia, and Dick.

§ Open Monday-Friday 8-3. Tours of the campus available by prior arrangement. Phone: 415-507-2000.

SAN SIMEON

¶ **Hearst-San Simeon State Historical Monument,** 1 mile east off State 1.

This property was originally part of a 48,000-acre tract acquired by *George Hearst in 1865 and on which he built a ranch house and raised cattle. By 1919 Hearst's son – William Randolph – had created a newspaper empire known for its "yellow journalism. That year the younger Hearst began to construct "The Enchanted Hill," an extensive estate intended to house the tons of furnishings, statuary, and other *objets d'art* which he had acquired in Europe.

Following completion of three palatial "guest houses," work was begun on the twin-towered Spanish-Moorish castle, constructed of concrete faced with limestone. Eight years in the building, "La Casa Grande" contained 115 rooms, thirty-one bathrooms, two libraries, and an assembly hall eighty-three feet in length. By the time most of the project was completed in 1947, Hearst had spent an estimated $30 million. In the meantime the newspaper magnate had expanded his property to 240,000 acres and had added terracing, broad gardens, arboretums, and a zoo.

During the 1920s and 1930s, Hearst entertained hundreds of political leaders, business figures, and celebrities, including his mistress, actress Marion Davies. In 1943 Hearst closed up "the Ranch" to reduce expenses and to guard against a feared Japanese submarine attack.

§ Open by tour only, daily 8-5 in summer and daily 8:20-3:20 in winter. Closed January 1, Thanksgiving, and December 25. Four different tours available. Reservations recommended. Fee. Phone: 800-444-4445.

SANTA BARBARA

¶ **Rancho del Cielo,** Rufugio Canyon. Private.

Located in the Santa Ynez Mountains, this 688-acre ranch was purchased by Ronald Reagan in 1974 for $574,000. During his presidency the "Ranch in the Sky" served as the California White House and afforded the president an opportunity to relax by chopping wood and riding his horses.

SANTA CLARITA

¶ **William S. Hart County Park and Museum,** 1.75 miles northwest of State 14 via San Fernando Road.

This recreational site contains the home and 265-acre ranch of the famous Western movie star. In addition to original furnishings, the house features historical objects, Native American artifacts, and examples of Western art. (See Billings, Montana.)

§ Park open daily 8-dusk. Closed January 1, Thanksgiving, and December 25. House open mid June-mid September, Wednesday-Sunday 11-4; rest of the year, Wednesday-Friday 10-1, Saturday-Sunday 11-4. Phone: 805-254-4584 or 259-0855.

SARATOGA

¶ **Villa Montalvo,** 0.5 mile southeast on State 9 and then 1 mile southwest on Montalvo Road.

Approached by a winding driveway, this Italianate villa is set in an expanse of broad lawns and formal gardens landscaped with fountains and marble statuary and 400 species of plants (including Italian cypress and Irish yew). The mansion was formerly the summer home of James Duval Phelan, a U.S. senator and the son of the famous Irish-born entrepreneur James Phelan. The villa was named for Ordañez de Montalvo, the fifteenth-century Spanish writer in whose work *The Exploits of Esplandian* the name "California" first appeared.

The younger Phelan was born in San Francisco in 1861 and studied law at the University of California at Berkeley. Bowing to the wishes of his father, however, he abandoned his legal and literary plans and assumed a dominant role in the older man's real estate and banking enterprises, chiefly as chairman of the United Bank and Trust Company.

Despite his lack of previous political experience, Phelan in 1897 was selected as the mayoral candidate of San Francisco's reform movement. During his three terms in the mayor's office, he rooted out graft on the board of supervisors and saved the city more than $300,000 by nixing a variety of patronage "jobs." Besides taking steps which later allowed San Francisco to bring its water supply from Hetch-Hetchy Valley, he also was responsible for much of the city's beautification in the form of parks, fountains, and plazas. In addition, he laid the groundwork for the city's impressive civic center of Renaissance-style buildings. When he was criticized for his handling of the teamsters' strike in 1901, however, he decided not to seek a fourth term. Even though he sustained tremendous personal losses during the 1906 earthquake, he was at the forefront of the effort to aid its victims and rebuild the city.

Five years after the earthquake, Phelan began construction of Villa Montalvo on 160 acres in the Saratoga foothills. In 1914, when the first visitors came to the lavish estate, they marveled at the exotic wood used in the entry doors, the hallway, and the library. Here, like a modern Lorenzo de Medici, he patronized aspiring painters, musicians, sculptors, and literati and feted them at his annual "Day in the Hills."

The same year in which Phelan saw the completion of his beloved villa, he became the first U.S. senator from California to be elected by popular vote. During his single term in the Senate, he advocated the exclusion of Chinese and Japanese from the country and supported *President Wilson's war effort.

Following his retirement from the Senate, Phelan returned to Montalvo to enjoy its sybaritic pleasures. Although he never married, in later life he enjoyed the almost constant companionship of the novelist Gertrude Atherton, who, however, was jealous of his attention to the tennis star Helen Willis. Among the other celebrities who enjoyed Phelan's estate were *Alfred E. Smith and Franklin Roosevelt.

Phelan's death became the occasion for what the newspapers described as the largest and most imposing funeral ever seen in San Francisco. One of the two largest bequests in his will was $1 million to a charitable foundation. The other was Villa Montalvo itself, given to the San Francisco Art Association for the development of the arts by promising students.

§ Arboretum open Monday-Friday 8-5, Saturday-Sunday 9-5. Gallery open Thursday-Friday 1-4, Saturday-Sunday 11-4. Tours of the home April-September, Thursday and Saturday at 10. Fee for tour. Phone: 408-741-3421.

SAUSALITO

¶ **O'Connell Memorial,** Bulkley and Harrison avenues.

This crescent-shaped cement bench was erected in honor of Daniel O'Connell, the Irish-born political refugee and poet and one of the founders of the Bohemian Club. The circular wall behind the bench is inscribed with O'Connell's last poem, "The Chamber of Sleep." The first stanza establishes the controlling metaphor used throughout the work:

I have a castle of silence, flanked by a lofty keep,
And across the drawbridge lieth the lovely chamber of sleep;
Its walls are draped with legends woven in threads of gold,
Legends beloved by dreamland in the tranquil days of old.

Born in 1849 in Ennis, County Clare, O'Connell was the grandnephew of the illustrious Irish patriot of the same name. The older man was appreciatively known as the "Great Emancipator" for his successful efforts to eliminate some of the civil disabilities under which Irish Catholics labored. Although the younger man was eventually to break ranks with his great-uncle's nonviolent and constitutionalist approach to reform, he was a frequent visitor at the Emancipator's home in Derrynane, County Kerry.

After his mother and sister drowned in the Dublin Grand Canal, the young O'Connell enrolled in Clongowes Wood College in the Irish capital. There, under the tutelage of the Jesuits, the young student studied the Greek and Latin classics and developed the love for literature that remained with him the rest of his life. His influential father, however, hoped to direct his son into a naval career by obtaining for him a commission in the English navy.

Although O'Connell was eager to see the world, he soon abandoned the navy and headed to California on his own, sailing from New York around the Horn. Not long after his arrival on the West Coast in 1868, he was offered a teaching position at Santa Clara College. To the questions of inquisitive students, he replied – perhaps facetiously – that he had left the navy because of his involvement in a duel with a Frenchman. The Irish newcomer later taught at old St. Ignatius College in San Francisco. Eager to express his writing talent more fully, he left teaching for a career in journalism, first with the *San Francisco Chronicle* and then with *The Evening Post*. (He had helped establish the *Post* with the social reformer Henry George.)

In the meantime O'Connell had become associated with a group of artists, journalists, and writers known as the Bohemian Club. Created in 1872 to promote camaraderie and friendship, this social organization allowed its members to express their wit and creativity through poetry, song, and drama. For a man of O'Connell's talent, the club was the perfect incubator, and it was at his suggestion that the members adopted the name "Bohemian," probably because of their somewhat unconventional ways.

In recognition of his Irish birth and punditry, O'Connell was dubbed the "King of Munster," the lord of the club's monthly "High Jinks."

Soon after the King's death in 1899, D. M. Delmas, a member of the Bohemian brotherhood, penned an unofficial epitaph:

"His Epitaph shall outlast the chiseled tracery of crumbling granite or corroding marble, for as long as a votary of Bohemia kneels at her shrine, his bosom will heave with grief, and his eyes be drowned with tears as he mourns the loss of dear old Dan.

> The king of Munster is dead
> Long live the king!
> O'Connell was a true Celtic spirit
> who left his mark wherever he roamed.
> That billowing band of the woodlands,
> The *maitre d'* of high jinks,
> The high priest of hilarity,
> One of a kind, Daniel O'Connell, Prince of Bohemia."

❡ O'Connell's house in Wildwood Glen still stands, modernized and enlarged, at 41 Cazneau Avenue. Private.

SIMI VALLEY

❡ Ronald Reagan Presidential Library, 40 Presidential Drive.

Constructed in Spanish Mission style, the library stands on a hilltop that commands a panoramic view of the surrounding countryside. The museum displays photographs and memorabilia of the president's life, a replica of the Oval Office, gifts of state, and a large piece of the Berlin Wall, a reminder of Reagan's influence in ending the Cold War.

President Reagan's paternal ancestors came from Ballyporeen, County Tipperary, Ireland. In 1847 his great-grandfather, Michael O'Regan, immigrated to London, where he married Catherine Mulcahy and adopted the present spelling of the family name. The couple moved to Canada with their sons in 1858 and later took up farming near Fairhaven, Illinois.

The future president was born in his family's apartment above a bakery in Tampico, Illinois, in 1911. According to family tradition, when the infant's father – John ("Jack") Reagan – saw his son for the first time, he made the comment: "He looks like a fat little Dutchman. But who knows, he might grow up to be president some day." In his autobiography Reagan explains that his parents had originally intended to name him "Donald" but ended up christening him "Ronald" after one of his aunts beat them to it by giving her son the name "Donald." Because Reagan never thought that "Ronald" was "rugged enough" for a boy's name, he asked people to call him "Dutch."

In 1920 Reagan's father moved his family to Dixon, Illinois, the first of many moves that Jack made in search of a better life. The former president paid special tribute to his father's ability as a storyteller, describing him as "endowed with the gift of blarney and the charm of a leprechaun." He also acknowledged his father's influence on the formation of his ideals: "Among the things he passed on to me were the belief that all men and women, regardless of their color or religion, are created equal and that . . . it's largely their own ambition and hard work that determine their fate in life."

As Reagan related in his autobiography, as a youngster he occasionally defended his father's honor with his fists. It seems that some of the boy's classmates ridiculed "Dutch" because of his father's Catholicism and claimed that the local Catholic church was storing weapons to be used to complete a planned papal invasion of the country. When "Dutch" asked his father about this charge, Jack told his son that the story was "baloney." After some of the boy's classmates called his father a liar, "Dutch" was led "to engage some of them in hand-to-hand combat on the playground."

In 1984, when President Reagan visited Ballyporeen, he was shown his great-grandfather's 1829 baptismal record. He also hoisted a pint in a pub named after him and learned that he was distantly related to *John F. Kennedy and Queen Elizabeth II. About this visit to his ancestral home, Reagan later wrote in his autobiography: "I had a flood of thoughts, not only about Michael Reagan, but about his son, my grandfather whom I had never met. I thought of Jack and his Irish stories and the drive he'd always had to get ahead; . . . What an incredible country we lived in, where

The Ronald Reagan Presidential Library.

the great-grandson of a poor immigrant from Ballyporeen could become president. I couldn't help but think that maybe Jack would have been proud that day."

The former president enjoyed telling another story connected with his 1984 Irish visit. While passing a tombstone near where St. Patrick had erected his first cross in Ireland, Reagan noticed that the grave marker bore two inscriptions. The original carving read: "Remember me as you pass by, for as you are so once was I, but as I am you too will be, so be content to follow me." A hand-scratched rejoinder appeared below: "To follow you I am content, I wish I knew which way you went."

In contrast to his warm reception in Ireland, President Reagan encountered bitter opposition from his fellow Irish-American, Thomas "Tip" O'Neill, the Speaker of the House of Representatives. About their first meeting after the president's inauguration, Reagan wrote that "Tip didn't try to hide the fact that he thought I had come to Washington to dismantle everything he believed in – things he and other liberals had spent decades fighting for, starting with the New Deal." When the president once expressed his surprise and disappointment at a personal attack which O'Neill had made against him and his policies, the Speaker replied, "Ol' buddy, that's politics. After six o'clock we can be friends; but before six, it's politics." Reagan later confided in his autobiography: "Until six o'clock, I was the enemy and he never let me forget it. So, after a while, whenever I'd run into him, whatever time it was, I'd say, 'Look, Tip, I'm setting my watch; it's six o'clock.'"

§ Open Monday-Saturday 10-5, Sunday noon-5. Closed January 1, Thanksgiving, and December 25. Fee. Phone: 805-522-8444.

SOLVANG

J Old Mission Santa Ines, 1760 Mission Drive.

During the 1932 Olympics in Los Angeles, this mission was the scene of an unusual act of homage by one of the teams entered in the competition. That summer the members of the Irish Olympic team traveled 150 miles north from Los Angeles by automobile to place a wreath at the grave of Father Albert Bibby, the famous Irish patriot and exile. During the athletes' visit, a reporter from the *Santa Maria Valley Vidette* asked one of the Irishmen whether he had known the priest personally. "All Ireland knew him" was the young man's proud reply.

Born Thomas Francis Bibby in Bagenalstown, County Carlow, in 1878, the youngster grew up near the Capuchin abbey in Kilkenny. Upon joining the Capuchin Order at Rochestown, County Cork, in 1894, he took the religious name of Albert and was ordained eight years later. After taking graduate courses at Royal University, he was appointed professor of philosophy and theology at St. Kieran's College in Kilkenny. From 1913 to

1919 he served as secretary at the provincial headquarters in Church Street, Dublin, where he was known for both his piety and his wisdom as a confessor. He was also an early promoter of the Gaelic League.

During the Easter Rising in Dublin in 1916, Father Albert ministered to the Volunteers who had seized the North Dublin Union area and for a time was with them in the Four Courts. In a diary which he kept during the ill-fated insurrection, he described the shelling of the building "as so heavy and so deafening that it was almost impossible for the priest [i.e., Father Albert] who was hearing confessions to carry out his duties. The firing was carried on furiously for seven and a half hours. We have been heartened by the girls of Cumann na mBan and nurses and doctors who are here unselfishly giving their services to the wounded."

Father Albert was later one of the Capuchin priests who attended four prisoners just before their execution at Kilmainham Jail in Dublin the following May 4. One of the condemned was the poet Joseph Mary Plunkett, who, according to his mother, addressed the following words to Father Albert: "Father, I want you to know that I am dying for the glory of God and the honour of Ireland."

Father Albert later recounted his final meeting with Sean Heuston, one of four other prisoners who were executed three days later. After entering the young man's cell in Kilmainham Jail, the priest found Heuston kneeling beside a small table with his rosary beads in his hand, having just finished writing some letters to his relatives and friends. "We said together short acts of faith, hope, and contrition and love," wrote the Capuchin. "[W]e prayed together to St. Patrick, St. Brigid, St. Columcille and all the Saints of Ireland. . . . But though he prayed with such fervor for courage and strength in the ordeal that was at hand, Ireland and his friends were close to his soul."

Finally at about 4 a.m. a British soldier arrived at the cell. Father Albert recounted Heuston's last minutes: "We now proceeded towards the yard where the execution was to take place, my left arm was linked in his right, while the British soldier who had handcuffed and blindfolded him walked on his left . . . . A soldier directed Sean and myself to a corner of the yard. . . . He was perfectly calm and said with me for the last time, My Jesus, mercy! I scarcely had moved away a few yards when a volley went off, and this noble soldier of Irish freedom fell dead. I rushed over to anoint him. His whole face seemed transformed, and lit up with a grandeur and brightness that I had never before noticed." From then on, Father Albert was thoroughly identified with the Irish independence movement and became a chaplain of the Irish Republican Army. His outspoken views aroused the displeasure of British authorities in Ireland, however, and he was exiled from the country in 1924.

That same year, by an unusual coincidence, the Irish Capuchins were entrusted with Mission Santa Ines in distant California. Few places in the world could have been farther away from Father Albert's beloved Ireland, but it was there that the priestly exile was assigned. (Strangely enough, he had always practiced a special devotion to St. Agnes, known in Spanish as Santa Ines.) The new pastor was at the mission for less than a year, however, before he died in Santa Barbara, California, in February 1925. In a letter of January 25 he bid adieu to his friends and fellow Capuchins in Dublin, and on his deathbed he renewed his allegiance to the ideal of an Irish republic. At his death one of the Catholic publications in Ireland proclaimed that "the Catholic Church has lost a gifted scholar and a saintly priest; Ireland a loyal and devoted patriot." Although he was first buried in the cemetery at Mission Santa Ines, thirty-three years later – in accordance with his lifelong wish – his remains were returned to his native land and interred in the friars' cemetery at Rochestown.

One of the Capuchins whom Father Albert mentioned by name in his final letter home was Brother Brendan Green. During the 1916 Easter Uprising, the two had been stationed at the Capuchin friary in Dublin. Like Father Albert, Brother Brendan espoused the cause of Irish nationalism and spent the last years of his life at Mission Santa Ines, dying there in 1966. In accordance with his request, Brendan was buried in the grave formerly occupied by Father Albert. The site in the mission cemetery is still marked by the cross erected over the priest's original resting place.

§ Museum open May-October, Monday-Friday 9-5, Saturday 9-4:30, Sunday noon-5; rest of the year, Monday-Saturday 9:30-4:30, Sunday noon-4:30. Closed January 1, Easter, Thanksgiving, and December 25. Fee. Phone: 805-688-4815.

STOCKTON

❡ **The Haggin Museum,** Victory Park, Rose Street and Pershing Avenue.

In addition to vintage farm and firefighting equipment, a Native American basket collection, and the Storefronts Gallery, this regional museum features works by the American painters Albert Bierstadt, William Bradford, Thomas Hill, George Inness, and *Thomas Moran. (See Tulsa, Oklahoma.)

§ Open Tuesday-Sunday 1:30-5. Donations, Phone: 209-462-4116.

SUNNYVALE

❡ **Murphy Historic Park,** 252 North Sunnyvale Avenue.

A historic marker indicates the site of the wood-frame building that Martin Murphy Jr. erected here in 1851. The structure had been built to his specifications in Maine and was shipped around Cape Horn to California. The building served as his family's residence in Sunnyvale until 1953, when the city acquired part of his ranch for public use. The house itself was destroyed in 1961. (See Murphy Building, San Jose, California.)

TAHOE NATIONAL FOREST

ℑ Mount Lola.
This mountain peak bears the name of Lola Montez, the internationally known Irish-born beauty who transformed herself into a Spanish courtesan and exotic dancer. (See Grass Valley, California.)

TRUCKEE

ℑ Donner Memorial State Park, 1 mile west on Donner Pass Road.
This 353-acre park is located near the site where the eighty-one members of the ill-fated Donner party were stranded during the winter of 1846-47. Almost 35 percent of the emigrants had Irish names – among them Breen, Dolan, Halloran, McCutchen, Murphy, and Reed. In all, two-thirds of the men, one-third of the children, and one-quarter of the women perished.

• The Pioneer Monument. Erected by the Native Sons and Daughters of the Golden West, this impressive memorial commemorates the members of the Donner party. The pedestal, which is surmounted by four bronze statues representing a pioneer family, stands about twenty-two feet, the height of the snow in this area during that frightful winter. The monument is located near the site of the cabin used by the Irish immigrant Patrick Breen and his family, one of only two families to survive the horrifying episode without loss of life.

Breen, who was born in County Carlow, Ireland, had immigrated to Canada in 1829, settling in Southwold (near Toronto) and there marrying Margaret Bulger, whom he had known in the old country. Soon after his arrival Breen was a member of a committee which formally requested the bishop of Kingston to provide the Catholics in the Southwold region with a priest. When the bishop was unable to satisfy that request, Breen took his family into the United States. The Irish couple and their children resided successively in Illinois and Iowa Territory, where Patrick was deeded 320 acres of land near Keokuk. He became a naturalized citizen in 1844, his Irish-born neighbor Patrick Dolan having testified that Breen had lived in the United States for at least five years.

In April 1846 the nine members of the Breen family and their friend Dolan set out from Keokuk, bound for California. With children ranging in age from fourteen years to infancy, the Breens traveled in three wagons, while Dolan drove a wagon of his own. At the beginning of July, they arrived at Fort Laramie. There they were joined by several other families, including those of George Donner and James Reed, both of whom had arrived from Springfield, Illinois. Reed, an Irish-born Protestant, soon found himself banished from the party for killing another emigrant. Reed, it seems, had gotten into an argument provoked by John Snyder, who struck Reed and his wife with a heavy whip stock. Reed pulled out a knife and stabbed his assailant.

On July 20 Donner made the tragic mistake of leading the wagons onto the unfamiliar Hastings Cutoff around the south side of Great Salt Lake. Because of delays along the way, they arrived at Truckee Lake in the eastern Sierras at the end of October, dangerously late in the season to attempt a crossing. As they feared, snow prevented their passage, and they resigned themselves to spending the winter at the base of the mountains. The Breens built cabins at the lake, while other families encamped at Alder Creek, five miles away.

Faced with starvation, fifteen emigrants tried in December to cross the Sierras on snowshoes in what they called the "Forlorn Hope" party. One of their number was the bachelor Patrick Dolan, who had a sizeable quantity of meat from his slaughtered oxen. Before leaving with the party, he asked Breen to use the meat for Mrs. Reed and her family. This request prompted Breen to take the Reed family into his cabin.

In her diary the Reeds' daughter Virginia recorded her experience in the Breens' cabin. "The Breens were the only Catholic family in the Donner party and prayers were said aloud regularly in that cabin night and morning. . . .," she wrote. "I was very fond of kneeling by the side of Mr. Breen and holding . . . [little torches] so that he might be able to read. . . . One night we had all gone to bed . . . but I could not sleep. . . . All at once I found myself on my knees with my hands clasped, looking up through the darkness, making a vow that if God would send us relief and let me see my father again I would be a Catholic. That prayer was answered." And the girl kept her promise.

Virginia's banished father eventually discovered the stranded group. Reed came upon his wife and Virginia and one of her brothers as they were making their way out of the camp. As Virginia explained in her account, when Reed "learned that two of his children were still at the cabins, he hurried on, so fearful he was that they might perish before he reached them. He seemed to fly over the snow, and made in two days the distance we had been five in traveling, and was overjoyed to find Patty and Tommy alive. . . . He filled Patty's apron with biscuits, which she carried around, giving one to each person. He had made soup for the infirm, and rendered every assistance to the sufferers." He later set out with seventeen of the survivors but immediately ran into a "perfect hurricane" of a snowstorm for three days and nights.

In the meantime the "Forlorn Hope" party, on the sixth day out, decided that they might have a chance to survive if one of their number was sacrificed. They agreed that whoever drew the longest slip would be their victim. Dolan, who drew the death card, said: "I am ready; take my life and save your own." When no one in the group would kill him, though, it was agreed that they would struggle on until death brought one of them down.

On Christmas Day Dolan became delirious, escaped from his blankets, and ran out into the storm. After being brought back to the shelter, he became even more deranged, pulling off his boots and most of his clothes and running out into the storm again. When he wandered back to the shelter, he was pulled inside, only to die that evening. The next day some of the group cut the flesh from Dolan's arms and legs, roasted it over the fire and ate it, "averting their faces from each other, and weeping." Of the fifteen members of the "Forlorn Hope" party, only seven survived.

An abbreviated account of the Donner party's ordeal in the Sierra Nevadas first appeared in the *California Star* in 1847. A fuller account was contained in a twenty-nine-page diary which Breen kept between November 20, 1846 and March 1, 1847. The extreme hardships faced by the emigrants at the lake camps are evident from these selected excerpts from the diary:

• Nov. 20, 1846: ". . . we again took our teams & waggons & made another unsuccessful attempt to cross in company with Stanton   we returned to the shanty it continueing to snow all the time we were here   we now have killed most part of our cattle having to stay here untill next spring & live on poor beef without bread or salt   it snowed during the space of eight days with little intermission . . . ."

• Dec. 25: "Began to snow yesterday about 12 o clock   snowd. all night & snows yet rapidly   wind about E by N   Great difficulty in getting wood   John & Edwd. has to get   I am not able   offerd. our prayers to God this Cherimass morning   the prospect is appalling   but hope in God Amen"

• Jan. 17, 1847: "provisions scarce   hides are the only article we depend on, we have a little meat yet, may God send up help."

• Feb. 9: ". . . Pikes child all but dead   Milt [Elliot] at Murphys not able to get out of bed   Keyburg never gets up says he is not able. John went down to bury Mrs. Eddy & child"

• Feb. 26: ". . . Mrs. Murphy said here yesterday that [she] thought she would commence on Milt. & eat him. I dont [know] that she has done so yet, it is distressing   The Donn[ers] told the California folks that they commence to eat the dead people 4 days ago, if they did not succeed that day or next in finding their cattle then under ten or twelve feet of snow & did not know the spot or near it. . . ."

• Feb. 28: ". . . 1 solitary Indian passed by yesterday come from the lake had a heavy pack on his back gave me 5 or 6 roots resembleing onions in shape   taste some like a sweet potatoe, all full of little tough fibres."

After their rescue the Breens stayed for a short time at Sutter's Fort before moving to the ranch of *Martin Murphy Jr., a member of an emigrant group which had crossed into California three years earlier. In September 1847 the Breens moved to Mission San Jose and later to San Juan Bautista, becoming the first American family to settle there. (See San Juan Bautista, California.)

• Murphy Cabin Site, 200 yards from the Emigrant Trail Museum. A huge boulder marks the location of the cabin which sheltered the members of the Murphy family. The bronze tablet on the rock reads: "Donner Party, 1846-7. The face of this rock formed the north end of the fireplace of the Murphy Cabin. General Stephen W. Kearny, on June 22, 1847, buried under the middle of the cabin the bodies found in the vicinity." The tablet also lists the names of the members of the Donner party, both those who perished and those who survived.

§ Park open June-September 30, daily 8-dusk. Museum open Memorial Day-Labor Day, daily 10-5; rest of the year, daily 10-12 and 1-5. Closed January 1, Thanksgiving, and December 25. Fee. Phone: 916-582-7892.

TUTTLETOWN

℥ Mark Twain Cabin Replica, 1 mile west on Jackass Hill.

Built in 1922, this cabin is a replica of the one in which *Mark Twain lived for several months during the winter of 1864-65. The original structure was built by Dick Stoker, the model for the character Dick Baker in Twain's classic *Roughing It.*

The famous author had prudently come to this area to escape the ire of the enemies he had made in San Francisco by writing about that city's police corruption for the *Territorial Enterprise* of Virginia City, Nevada. During his brief sojourn here, Twain gathered material that later became the basis for such stories as "The Californian's Tale," "What Stumped the Blue Jays," and "The Celebrated Jumping Frog of Calaveras County." (See Florida, Missouri.)

WHITTIER

℥ Pat Nixon Memorial Fountain, Colima Road and Mar Vista Street.

A plaque on the fountain commemorates the former first lady, born Thelma Catherine Ryan, the daughter of an Irish-American mining engineer. (See Yorba Linda, California.)

℥ Richard Nixon Law Office Site, Old Bank of America Building, 13002 East Philadelphia.

A plaque on the ground outside the building marks the location of Wingert and Bewley, the law firm which *Richard Nixon joined in July 1937.

Following his graduation from Whittier College in 1934, Nixon attended Duke University School of Law. He was hired by Wingert and Bewley for $50 a month, a stipend which was to increase to $100 at the beginning of his fifth month there. Only then would he begin to receive an annual salary.

Nixon's law office desk diaries for 1938 and 1939 show appointments related to such matters as estate taxes, wills, divorce petitions, defaults, and oil company registrations. Only eighteen months after entering the firm, Nixon was made a partner. "I was on my way to becoming a young pillar of the community in which I had grown up," he wrote. "I had become a grown-up and to people I met for the first time I was no longer Frank and Hannah Nixon's son – I was Mr Nixon, the new partner in Wingert and Bewley."

WOODSIDE

¶ **Filoli,** off Interstate 280 via Edgewood Road to Cañada Road.

The mansion on this 654-acre estate was completed in 1919 by William Bourn as a wedding gift for his daughter, who was about to marry an Irishman. Bourn chose this site because it reminded him of the area around the Lakes of Killarney in Ireland, where he had recently bought the famous Muckross House. Bourn created the name "Filoli" as a acronym from the words in his family's motto ("Fight, Love, Live"). The Georgian house is built of white stone and glazed terra-cotta and is surrounded by extensive French and Italian gardens.

Bourn really had ulterior motives for building the mansion. By offering it to his daughter Maud and her husband, Arthur Vincent, he hoped to dissuade his son-in-law from accepting an appointment as a magistrate in Zanzibar with the British civil service. The ploy worked, and Vincent agreed to accept the house.

In 1921 Bourn suffered a debilitating stroke that left him confined to either his bed or a wheelchair for the rest of his life. Sadly aware that her husband would never be able to visit his beloved Muckross again, his wife, Agnes, decided to bring Muckross to Filoli, in a manner of speaking. She accordingly commissioned the San Francisco artist Ernest Peixotto to visit Killarney to sketch the Muckross House with the intention of reproducing his work throughout the Filoli mansion.

The artist's work can be seen today in the mansion's French-style ballroom. Among the huge murals are scenes depicting the Lakes of Killarney, Brickeen Bridge, Torc Mountain, and, of course, Muckross House itself. The mural that shows Arthur Vincent standing in a boat fishing contains – according to his son, A. W. B. Vincent – an inaccuracy: The elder man never stood up while fishing because one leg was shorter than the other. During a visit to Filoli, the Irish poet W. B. Yeats expressed his feelings about the estate in an entry in the guest book: "A place so beautiful it seems. / Neither from waking life, nor dream. / A mystery of those mysteries."

As things turned out, Bourn's original plan to prevent his daughter from going off to Africa with her husband was largely frustrated but for another reason. The Vincents spent little time at Filoli, living much of the time instead at the Muckross House in Killarney. In 1931, two years after Maud's death, Vincent presented the Muckross property to the newly independent nation of Ireland.

§ Two-hour mansion and garden tours are offered Tuesday-Saturday at 9:30, 11:30, and 1:30 (April-June) and at 10 and 1 (February-March and July-November). Fee. Reservations required for tour. Self-guided tours are available Friday and the first Saturday and second Sunday of each month (mid February-early November). Phone: 415-364-2880.

YORBA LINDA

¶ **Richard Nixon Presidential Library and Birthplace,** 18001 Yorba Linda Boulevard.

This $21 million, nine-acre complex includes a museum, gardens, and the small clapboard house in which *Richard Nixon was born in 1913. The former president and his wife, Pat, are buried in the garden.

The museum offers a variety of films, interactive video displays, and memorabilia connected with the president's life and political career. A room devoted to world leaders features life-size statues of ten of the twentieth century's most famous: Charles de Gaulle, Konrad Adenaeur, Winston Churchill, Yoshida Shigeru, Anwar Sadat, Golda Meir, Chou En-Lai, Mao Tse-tung, and Nikita Krushchev.

Richard Nixon's ancestry was Irish on both sides. His Nixon forebears were Ulster Protestants, originally from Fermanagh and South Tyrone. The first Nixon to come to America was James Nixon, the president's great-great-grandfather, arriving in the early years of the eighteenth century. He died in Delaware in 1773.

The president's Milhous ancestors, meanwhile, were originally of German descent, although by the end of the seventeenth century some family members were living in Ireland. The president's fifth-great-grandfather, a Quaker by the name of John Milhous, was born in Carrickfergus, County Antrim, in 1699. It was there that his son Thomas was born before the family moved to Timahoe, a village twenty miles northwest of Dublin. And it was from Timahoe that Thomas and his wife and young family left for Pennsylvania in 1729.

A direct descendant of these Irish Quaker emigrants was Hannah Milhous, the president's mother. Hannah was born on a farm in Butlerville, Indiana, and at the age of twelve accompanied her family to Whittier,

The Richard Nixon Birthplace House.

California, the Quaker colony where her son Richard was born.

With a $3,000 loan from his father-in-law, Nixon's father bought twelve acres of land and an $800 build-it-yourself house from Sears. When completed, the 700-square-foot home had one upstairs bedroom (for the future sons), one downstairs bedroom (for the parents), a living room, and a kitchen. The house was devoid of any modern conveniences like electricity, running water, indoor plumbing, and refrigeration. It was here that the Nixons' second son was born, named for Richard the Lionheart. (Four of the five Nixon sons bore the names of English kings – Harold, Richard, Arthur, and Edward.)

Nixon's wife – born Thelma Catherine Ryan on March 16, 1912 – was the daughter of Will Ryan, a wandering Irish-American who first began to see the world when he signed aboard a whaling ship. After working as a surveyor in the Philippines, he headed for Alaska, hoping to find his fortune in the recent Yukon gold strike. Success in the mines eluded him, however, and he moved on to the Black Hills of South Dakota, where his brother was a miner. Unable to shake his bad luck, he headed for Ely, Nevada, where he was hired as a silver-mining engineer. It was here that his wife of three years gave birth to their first daughter, Thelma Catherine.

Ryan had been working in the mines when the infant was born, but when he returned home after midnight to find that his daughter had been born so close to St. Patrick's Day, he added the name "Patricia" to the other two and called her his "St. Patrick's babe in the morn." Although he called her by no other name than Pat, she herself never adopted it until she attended Whittier College. On the few occasions when Pat became angry, her father would laugh and exclaim, "You stubborn Irishman!"

When President Nixon and his wife visited Ireland in October 1970, they had mixed results when it came to meeting family relations. Although officials found and introduced the first lady to purported cousins, they failed to find a single Milhous. As a result, when the president was taken to Timahoe, where his fifth-great-grandfather had once lived, he had to content himself with a visit to the Quaker cemetery where that ancestor was buried. Even that visit was anticlimactic, however, because the burial ground contained no individual grave markers but only a large slab with a list of those who were buried there. Nixon's dog at the time – an Irish setter called Timahoe – was named for the president's ancestral home.

§ Open Monday-Saturday 10-5, Sunday 11-5. Closed January 1, Thanksgiving, and December 25. Fee. Phone: 714-993-3393.

YOSEMITE

¶ Mahan Peak, Tower Peak.

This 9,146-foot-high peak was named for Dennis Mahan, a professor of engineering at the U.S. Military Academy from 1832 to 1871.

Born in New York City soon after the arrival of his parents from Ireland, Mahan sought and obtained an appointment to the U.S. Military Academy primarily because of his interest in studying drawing there. Following his graduation from West Point in 1824, he pursued further study at the School of Application for Engineers and Artillery in Metz, France. Upon his return to the academy four years later, he was appointed professor of civil and military engineering. Because he was hampered by the unavailability of textbooks for his courses, he developed his own, some of which his students used as manuals when they commanded troops during the Mexican War and the Civil War.

¶ Moran Point, Yosemite Valley, on the old Four-Mile Trail, just east of Union Point.

As early as the 1880s this point bore the name of Thomas Moran, an artist of Irish ancestry who was famous for paintings that captured the grandeur of the American West. (See Tulsa, Oklahoma.)

¶ Mount Broderick, Yosemite Valley.

This 6,706-foot-high peak was named for *David Broderick, an outspoken opponent of slavery and the first U.S. senator to be killed in a duel. (See Broderick-Terry Duel Site in San Francisco, California.)

¶ Mount Conness (and Conness Creek, Lake, and Glacier), Tuolumne

Meadows.

Mount Conness, 12,590 feet in height, honors the memory of John Conness, the man responsible for introducing legislation in Congress which led to the establishment of Yosemite and Yellowstone as national treasures.

The youngest of fourteen children, Conness was born in County Galway, Ireland, in 1821 but ran away from home in his early teens. After immigrating to America, he worked as a piano maker until 1849, when he succumbed to the lure of the Gold Rush. Within a brief time he had struck it rich, and with his new wealth he went on to become a leading merchant and civic leader in the mining community of Georgetown in El Dorado County. In 1853 he was elected to the California legislature.

Following his election to the U.S. Senate in 1863, Conness assumed the mantle of support for the Union and opposition to slavery formerly worn by his fellow Irishman Senator David Broderick. In a gesture of support for Lincoln's Emancipation Proclamation, Conness presented the president with a polished cane of California live oak, a memento which Conness had received from Broderick himself. Conness, in fact, enjoyed an unusually close relationship with Lincoln, as the Washington correspondent for *The Sacramento Bee* explained: "Mr. Conness became his fast friend and a confidential adviser of President Lincoln, conferred with him freely upon the policies of the Pacific Coast, the strength of the union sentiment there, and especially in regard to the support of the administration in the extreme war measures which might be inaugurated or become necessary." During his second presidential campaign, Lincoln chose Conness to address a mass meeting of Union supporters in San Francisco. Besides describing what the president had done to preserve the Union, the senator expressed his own opposition to slavery in terms favorable to the working class, many of them Irish. Countering the belief that the emancipation of black slaves would adversely affect white workers, Conness told his listeners that "capital has its foot and its heel upon labor, as long as such a mill stone weight as slavery hangs around the neck of labor."

During his legislative career, Conness advocated several visionary pieces of legislation for which he rarely receives credit. More than anyone else he persuaded the California legislature to organize a state geological survey. He also introduced a bill in the U.S. Senate to turn Yosemite Valley and Mariposa Forest over to California for use as a state park. In the same vein it was he who first proposed setting aside Yellowstone Park as a national preserve. In addition, he was the first to propose a transcontinental railroad, an idea that earned him an honored place in the ceremonies marking its completion at Promontory, Utah, in 1869.

Mount Conness was officially named in 1931 by Clarence King, the director of the U.S. Geological Survey. In honoring Conness, the director said that because of its "firm peak with titan strength and brow so square and solid it seemed altogether natural we should have named if for California statesman, John Conness."

¶ **O'Shaughnessy Dam,** at the Hetch-Hetchy Reservoir, 9 miles north of Mather (on the northwest side of Yosemite National Park).

Named for a native of County Limerick, Ireland, O'Shaughnessy Dam is the centerpiece of a vast aqueduct system that supplies San Francisco with water from the Sierra Nevada mountains 200 miles away.

The system's creator, Michael Maurice O'Shaughnessy, received a degree in engineering from the Royal University of Ireland before coming to the United States in 1885. Almost immediately he obtained a position in California as assistant engineer with the Southern Pacific Railroad Company. Contracts for a variety of other projects occupied his time until 1898, when he began a seven-year engagement in Hawaii as a construction hydraulic engineer on twenty sugar plantations, building some of the largest irrigation systems ever undertaken. After returning to the mainland, the Irishman accepted engineering positions with numerous water companies in New Mexico, Southern California, and Mexico.

In 1912 O'Shaughnessy was appointed city engineer for San Francisco. In that position he either built or completed the city's municipal railways, three tunnels in the city (Stockton Street, Twin Peaks, and Sunset Railway), five dams, and the Hetch-Hetchy water and power supply plant. He also engineered several of San Francisco's major arteries, including Marina, Twin Peaks, and Junipero Serra boulevards. During this time he also engineered the construction of several dams throughout the state, as well as the Lake Tahoe Dam in Nevada.

O'Shaughnessy's greatest achievement, however, was his completion of the Hetch-Hetchy water contract. Twenty years in the making and costing $100 million, the project is known principally for the O'Shaughnessy Dam, standing 312 feet above the Tuolomne River and creating a reservoir eight miles long. The system also boasts a diversion tunnel through solid granite, seventeen more miles of tunnel, a forty-five-mile pipe siphon, a power plant, and a twenty-nine-mile subterranean waterway. Water first flowed through the system in October 1934, sixteen days after O'Shaughnessy's death. Between 1935 and 1938 the height of the dam was raised eighteen feet.

§ The dam can be reached from Yosemite Valley by a 38-mile drive on Big Oak Road. A nine-mile road from Mather leads to the dam, where a plaque stands near the summit. Although Yosemite National Park is open daily all year round, not all entrances are accessible during the winter.

COLORADO

AVONDALE

¶ **Fort Reynolds Site,** 1 mile east on U.S. 50.

A marker on the highway indicates the site of old Fort Reynolds, named for General John Reynolds, who was killed at Gettysburg in 1863.

The grandson of an Irish immigrant who came to America in 1762, Reynolds was a graduate of the U.S. Military Academy and had been breveted for gallantry at Monterey and Buena Vista during the Mexican War. Between that conflict and the Civil War, his tours of garrison duty were interrupted by an overland expedition to Salt Lake City and participation in the campaigns against the Rogue River Indians in Oregon and the Mormons in Utah. On the eve of the Civil War, he was named commandant of cadets at West Point, where he was also a tactics instructor.

During the war Reynolds was placed in command of the I Army Corps of the Army of the Potomac. If his plan to attack the enemy's left flank at Chancellorsville had been adopted, the victory might have gone to the Union. In the face of General Lee's expected incursion into the North, Reynolds was ordered to occupy Gettysburg. There, on the first of the three-day struggle that followed, he was killed by a sharpshooter as he led the 2nd Wisconsin Regiment near the Chambersburg road.

COLORADO SPRINGS

¶ **Hall of the Presidents Living Wax Studio,** 2 blocks south of U.S. 24 at 1050 South 21st Street.

Among the more than 130 wax figures by Madame Tussaud are those of all the U.S. presidents, including the fourteen of Irish or Scotch-Irish ancestry: Andrew Jackson, James K. Polk, James Buchanan, Andrew Johnson, Ulysses S. Grant, Grover Cleveland, Benjamin Harrison, William McKinley, Theodore Roosevelt, Woodrow Wilson, John Kennedy, Richard Nixon, Ronald Reagan, and Bill Clinton. The figures are part of tableaux depicting some historical event associated with each chief executive. The nation's First Ladies are also represented.

§ Open Memorial Day-Labor Day, daily 9-9; rest of the year, daily 10-5. Fee. Phone: 719-635-3553.

¶ **Will Rogers Shrine of the Sun Memorial,** on the Cheyenne Mountain Highway.

This medieval-looking stone tower was erected as a memorial to *Will Rogers by Spencer Penrose following the humorist's death in a plane crash in Alaska in 1935. (See Barrow, Alaska.) Penrose, a friend of Rogers', located the tower in such a way that the rays of the sun light it from sunrise to sunset. Penrose and his wife are buried in the rose granite structure. (See Claremore, Oklahoma.)

CRIPPLE CREEK

¶ Isabella Mine, off Gold Camp Road.

This gold mine, still recognizable by its head frame, was one of the first successful investments of Mollie O'Bryan, an astute mining entrepreneur and the only female broker on the Cripple Creek Mining Stock Exchange.

Mary "Mollie" O'Bryan was born in Missouri in 1873 and moved to Colorado with her parents in the 1880s. She first worked in Lake City as a stenographer with various mining and brokerage firms, a position which allowed her to learn not only about the mining business but also about investing, corporations, and even mine management. Attracted by tales of gold, the young woman headed for Cripple Creek, where she opened a small stenographic office of her own. Perhaps using "insider information" gleaned from the various businessmen for whom she worked, O'Bryan bought up multiple blocks of 1,000 shares in the Damon Gold Mining Company for $5. When she sold the stock for twice the price three weeks later, the local mine owners and stock jobbers marveled at her business acumen. They were again amazed when she quadrupled her money after investing in stock in the Acacia and Isabella mines. According to the newspapers, she had such "rare good judgment that brokers began to defer to her intelligence in making investments."

With her profits O'Bryan proceeded to buy a share of the Big Four Gold Mining Company, an operation which owned four mines in the area. Through her contacts with the members of the town's leading brokerage company, she was elected to the Cripple Creek Mining Stock Exchange, although she was able to post the $5,000 security bond and pay the $400 membership fee herself. In syndication with other investors, O'Bryan formed the Teutonic Consolidated Gold Mines Company. After several promising veins and rich ore pockets were discovered in one of its mines, she bought the claim for $3,500. Within a month she was offered $35,000 for the property but refused the offer.

Hoping to gain better control over their assets, O'Bryan and her partners consolidated the Big Four, the Juanita, the New Century, and the Transvaal into a new organization called the Amalgamated Gold Mining Company. When O'Bryan was named the company's new president, the press ranked her "among the leaders of the mining world." The consolidation occurred at an inopportune time, however, as the mining industry was paralyzed by a number of serious labor strikes at the end of 1903. As a result, O'Bryan sold off Amalgamated but retained control over the Gold Bond, the Trilby, and the Teutonic. By 1910, though, she had been forced to sell everything but the Teutonic. After her fall from gold-plated grace, O'Bryan continued to live in Cripple Creek, working as a broker and a stenographer and living with her sister.

DENVER

¶ **Molly Brown House,** 1340 Pennsylvania Street.

From 1894 until her death in 1932, this three-story, stone Victorian mansion was the home of philanthropist and socialite Maggie Brown, more popularly known as the "Unsinkable Molly" Brown. She and her husband, mining magnate James Joseph ("J.J.") Brown, bought the residence for the incredible sum of $30,000.

Almost immediately the irrepressible Molly began a campaign to attain her rightful place in polite society. After her "Shanty Irish" background prevented her easy ascent into the *haute-monde*, however, she began to promote herself through stories of her own making. She once claimed, for example, that Samuel Clemens had saved her from a cyclone while she traveled on the Mississippi. In another "tall tale" she alleged that she had accidentally set fire to $300,000 which her husband had squirreled away in their potbellied stove. (Modern authorities estimate that a mere $75 in coin was scorched.)

Maggie never wavered in her attempt to scale the wall of social respectability. Against her husband's wishes, she enrolled their two children in expensive boarding schools. She spent lavishly on draperies, furniture, and carpets for the house, and seamstresses, designers, and gold-embroidered gowns for herself. Besides immersing herself in the study of art, music, and languages, she frequently traipsed to Europe, often taking the children out of school to accompany her. ("J.J." complained that she was raising two "no-account" children.) On her excursions she acquired an ever-growing circle of acquaintances all too eager to accept her invitations to enjoy the good life provided by her husband's wealth. (The Browns' daughter Helen said that her mother's love of fame and high society – which she hoped to achieve with that wealth – led ironically to her parents' divorce.)

When Maggie and her husband traveled together, she usually leased the house to well-placed members of society. A perhaps apocryphal account spread by her detractors involved the use of her home by a former state governor while she was traveling in Europe. When she returned – so the story went – she was dismayed to find that the expectorating ex-governor had freely used the floors of the mansion as the object of his disgusting habit. When Molly expostulated with the ungentlemanly man's wife, the latter replied, "You didn't provide any cuspidors, so what did you expect?"

Even after her husband tired of her pretensions and the pair separated, Molly continued her efforts to become a member of the "Sacred 36," the inner circle of Denver socialites. Despite their snubs, she entertained lavishly, a hobby equaled only by her frequent redecoration of the house. Eventually Molly's "betters" were forced to recognize her philanthropy to the city's charities and to admire her for visiting the scene of the "Ludlow Massacre," where several striking miners in the southern part of the state had been killed by state militia. In the latter instance she rushed from the pleasure palaces of Cannes to provide food, clothing, and money for the orphans and widows of the victims, dismissing concern for herself with the words, "To hell with the danger or the cost!"

Maggie earned her famous sobriquet after showing her mettle during the sinking of the *Titanic* in April 1912. While sightseeing with the John Jacob Astors in Egypt, Maggie had decided to accompany them home to America on the famous luxury passenger liner, advertised at the time as perfectly safe and "practically unsinkable." On the fifth day out, however, the ship hit an iceberg. Although at first the 2,224 passengers seemed assured of the ship's lifesaving equipment, when it became known that the vessel had only twenty lifeboats – each capable of holding fifty passengers – panic ensued. Because of the confusion, only 717 people were placed in the lifeboats. In the meantime, Maggie had been lowered into lifeboat #6 with other women and one man. After doing more than her share in

The Molly Brown House.
(Photo by Jeff Black,
Synergy Photo/Graphics)

rowing the dinghy away from the vortex swirling around the *Titanic*, she proved equally invaluable when the *Carpathia* arrived and rescued the survivors in the lifeboats. Because of her skill with foreign languages, she was able to help the officers aboard the *Carpathia* talk with the survivors, many of whom were immigrant women whose husbands had remained on the ship and were drowned. In addition, she was able to raise $10,000 from the wealthier survivors for distribution among the needy. Even when the *Carpathia* reached New York five days later, she remained with the survivors until she had completed sending messages to their relatives and found some type of assistance for many of them. It was therefore not without too much exaggeration that she could boast that she was "unsinkable." (After "J.J." heard about her exploits – when she wired him for money – he remarked that she was "too mean to sink.")

The acclaim which Maggie received for her heroism during the sinking of the *Titanic* finally brought her the social distinction which she had so long sought. Three weeks after the tragedy, she was honored at the Denver Country Club by a delegation from the "Sacred 36." In addition, the *Rocky Mountain News* wrote that perhaps "to one who has looked death calmly in the face and forgotten her own peril in order to comfort the weak and stricken . . . it does not seem so great a thing . . . to be 'taken up' by prominent society folk as it does to those who are doing the gracious act."

§ Open June-August, Monday-Saturday 10-4, Sunday noon-4; rest of the year, Tuesday-Saturday 10-4, Sunday noon-4. Fee. Phone: 303-832-4092.

¶ Museum of Western Art, 1727 Tremont Place.

Although originally built in 1880 as the first coeducational college west of the Mississippi River, this red-brick Victorian structure was later a notorious gambling hall and house of prostitution. Today the building houses more than 100 works of art depicting landscapes, buffalo hunts, and Indian scenes by such famous western artists as *Thomas Moran, *Georgia O'Keeffe, Frederic Remington, and Charles Russell.

§ Open Tuesday-Saturday 10-4:30. Fee. Phone: 303-296-1880.

ESTES PARK

¶ William Allen White House, 6 miles west in Rocky Mountain National Park. Private.

This complex of a studio, cabins, and other buildings was the summer home of *William Allen White, the crusading editor of the *Emporia (Kansas) Gazette*. Although the compound is not open to the public, a guided walk during the summer takes visitors to one of the cabins. (See Emporia, Kansas.)

GOLDEN

¶ **Buffalo Bill Memorial Museum,** atop Lookout Mountain Park, 5 miles west of town on State 5.

Located near the grave of *William "Buffalo Bill" Cody, the museum exhibits numerous items associated with the famous showman's life and career, including rifles, posters, photographs, clothing, Western art, and Wild West Show posters. Many of the items on exhibit were collected by Johnny Baker, a close friend of Cody's and a member of his Wild West Show. (See Cody, Wyoming.)

§ Open May-October, daily 9-5; rest of the year, Tuesday-Sunday 9-5.

• Every summer in mid July, Golden celebrates Buffalo Bill Days with a parade, crafts, and a mountain men camp.

¶ **Territorial Capitol,** 12th Street and Washington Avenue.

While Golden served as the state capital from 1862 to 1867, this structure was the scene of various legislative sessions. Today the building is a restaurant that features the bar where *James Butler "Wild Bill" Hickok allegedly hoisted his last drink. (See Abilene, Kansas.)

GREELEY

¶ **Greeley Municipal Museum,** 919 7th Street.

Besides housing a variety of historical documents, this museum is a local archive of *Horace Greeley's correspondence.

The town was named for the famous editor of the *New York Tribune,* who in 1870 helped found the experimental Union Colony on this site. Greeley and his agricultural editor had selected this area because its location near the South Platte River offered the possibility of a successful irrigation system. Within months the colonists had dug a ditch nine miles long and six feet wide. The colony's prohibitionist roots were reflected in one of its rules: "Thou shalt not sell liquid damnation within the lines of the Union Colony."

§ Phone: 303-350-9220.

LEADVILLE

In 1879 the Irish and their American-born children were the largest group among Leadville's 5,000 inhabitants. The Irish presence was evident even in the names of the mines in which they labored and of course in their social organizations, particularly the Ancient Order of Hibernians. While some of the underground diggings were christened for the Irish revolutionaries O'Donovan Rosa, Robert Emmet, and Wolfe Tone, the memory of the last two heroes was further enshrined in the names of such fraternal organizations as the Knights of Robert Emmet and the Wolfe Tone Guards.

Among the town's 328 Irish immigrants at the time was John McComb, a native of County Offaly who had come to the United States in 1853. After working in Buffalo, Detroit, and the Great Lakes area, he arrived in Leadville with ten cents in his pocket. In two years time, though, he discovered ten mines, two of which he named the Maid of Erin and the Parnell. Once rich, he spent thousands of dollars to buy gifts for his friends and relatives in Ireland. He finally sold the Erin for $43,000.

Within a year of their arrival in the area in 1876, the three Gallagher brothers had made a small fortune from their five silver, gold, and lead mines. Mrs. Patrick Gallagher, newly arrived among the *nouveaux riches*, playfully depreciated her husband's humble background and announced her next step up the social ladder. "Pat isn't Irish at all, " she said. "He is an Inglishman, but comin' over to Ameriky in a shteamer he got in wid a lot o' Irish, and got their damned brogue; and faith, he can't git over it. . . . Shure, the Irish up the gulch here are not fit for we'uns to assoscheat wid. We are goin' to move down to Leadville and put up a brick house in the latest style. . . ."

Another Irishman who struck it rich in Leadville was the Connaughtman John Morrisey, who had come to the mines as a special agent of Diamond Joe Reynolds. After discovering a pair of mines for Reynolds, the illiterate Morrisey was made his manager. When the Irishman became a successful mine boss himself, his crew gave him a gold watch. Morrisey disguised his inability to tell time by saying to inquirers after the time: "Here, look fer yourself. Ye wouldn't belave me if I told ye." On another occasion, when asked to register at a hotel, he wrapped his hand with a handkerchief and shamelessly lied: "I just slammed a cab door on me hand and hurt it." Morrisey eventually toured Europe, squandered a fortune, and died in the poorhouse in Denver.

At the end of the 1880s, fate chose Leadville for the intersection of two personalities whose lives would soon intertwine. The first to arrive was James Joseph Brown, a native of Pennsylvania who had learned mining there and had prospected in Dakota before coming to Leadville in 1885. He quickly became a mine foreman and seemed content with his life until Margaret Tobin arrived from Missouri and swept him off his feet. (See Hannibal, Missouri.) After a brief courtship, they were married in the Catholic church in Leadville. (She was nineteen years old, and "J.J." was thirty-one.) The couple first lived in a log cabin near the mine in which Brown worked, but after Maggie gave birth to their first child, the coupled moved to a comfortable house at 300 East Seventh Street in Leadville.

In 1893 "J.J." was made superintendent of the Little Johnny Mine, one of several properties owned by Ibex Mining Company. He was well on his way to wealth when he was given 12,500 shares in the company after discovering high grade copper and sheet-gold among the lead-silver ores of the mine. The following year the company paid $1 million in dividends, and Brown's fortune was made. It was then that Maggie – intoxicated by the reality of wealth and the prospects of social preferment – decided that she and "J.J." and the children should move to Denver. (See Molly Brown House, Denver, Colorado.)

¶ **Healy House Museum,** 912 Harrison Avenue.
     Originally a two-story structure, this house was built in 1878 for August and Emma Meyer. A decade later, however, it was purchased for $4,000 by Daniel Healy, a prominent businessman, for use as a boardinghouse. To accommodate more residents, Healy added the third story in 1898. Among the twenty-one boarders who lived here were Healy himself, his cousin Nellie Healy, and several men employed by the railroad. Today the house is a museum highlighting the Victorian lifestyle of the late 1800s mining period.
     Healy was born in County Kerry, Ireland, in 1860 and came to America with his parents at the age of five. The family settled in Hancock, Michigan, where the youngster worked in the stamp mills. With money he saved from his job in the mills, Healy attended Valparaiso University in Indiana and seems to have been particularly interested in philosophy. He was fond of saying, "A man can never go afield if he follows the teachings of Epictetus." After his graduation he taught school for three years in Marquette, Michigan.
     By 1885 Healy was living in Leadville, where he worked as a law clerk and a mail carrier. After several years as assistant postmaster, he bought a failing real estate and insurance business, which he soon turned into a profitable venture. He was also an agent for several other insurance companies and for some of the best known commercial blocks in Leadville. His enterprises were so successful that at his death he left investments and property worth between $20,000 and $25,000. The general opinion of Healy's integrity was expressed by John Curley, the state mine inspector and a close personal friend: "The quality of honesty was more emphasized in him than in any man whom I think I have ever met. He was absolutely reliable and I never heard of anyone's doubting his integrity. Anything that savored of underhandedness was foreign to his nature. He could not conceive of stooping to a dishonest act."
     For many years Healy was active in several social and political organizations. In addition to belonging to the Knights of Robert Emmet and the Knights of Pythias, he was at various times a member of both the state and the county central committees of the Democratic party. Although he first failed to win election as senator of Lake County, he was victorious in a second attempt against Jesse McDonald.
     In 1908 Healy made an extensive tour through Europe as the guest of

his brother Patrick and his wife. The invitation may have been an expression of gratitude for the financial assistance which Daniel had given his brother when the latter suffered severe losses to his sheep- and cattle-raising business in Wyoming. Healy died four years later after suffering an attack and drowning in Turquoise Lake while fishing with two companions. He left his estate to be divided among his sister, Belle Healy Young, his two nieces, Belle and Claire Kelly, and his cousin, Nellie Healy.

¶ Matchless Mine Cabin, one mile east on East 7th Street.

This museum chronicles the history of the Matchless Mine, which netted its owner, Senator H. A. W. Tabor, $10 million in 1878. (A single shipment of ore from his mine assayed 10,000 ounces of silver a ton.)

When the Irish author Oscar Wilde descended the mine shaft in 1882, a dozen bottles made the rounds among a dozen miners and their guest – "the first course being whiskey, the second whiskey, and the third whiskey." After all the toasts were drunk, the nearly inebriated miners were surprised at Wilde's ability to hold his liquor and declared him "a perfect gentleman."

§ Open June 1-Labor Day, daily 9-5. Fee. Phone: 719-486-3900.

¶ Tabor Opera House, 308 Harrison Street (U.S. 24 at 4th Street).

In 1882 the Irish-born playwright Oscar Wilde addressed an audience here on "The Practical Application of the Aesthetic Theory to Exterior and Interior House Decoration, with Observations on Dress and Personal Ornament." Wilde himself was dressed in a suit of "elegant black velvet, with knee breeches and black stockings, a Byron collar and white neckhandkerchief. . . . On his shirt front glittered a single cluster of diamonds."

After reading to the miners from the autobiography of Benvenuto Cellini, the Irishman later wrote: "They seemed much delighted. I was reproved by my hearers for not having brought him with me. I explained that he had been dead for some little time, which elicited the inquiry, 'Who shot him.'"

§ Open Memorial Day-October 1, Sunday-Friday 9-5:30. Fee. Phone: 719-486-1147.

MANASSA

¶ Jack Dempsey Museum, 3 miles east of U.S. 285 on State 142 at 410 Main Street.

This is the restored home of Jack Dempsey, the heavyweight boxing champion of the world from 1919 to 1926. The story of the famous fighter's boxing career is told through photographs and other memorabilia on display.

Christened William Harrison Dempsey in 1895, the Manassa native was one of eleven children born to sharecropper parents and was of mixed Indian, Irish, and Scottish ancestry. Showing little aptitude for book learning, he preferred to box with classmates after school and ended his formal education after the eighth grade. Having made up his mind to become a fighter, he followed a regimen that included gum chewing (to strengthen his jaw) and dousing his face and neck with brine (to toughen his skin).

Dempsey began his boxing career at the age of twenty, having exchanged his personal names for "Jack," apparently in honor of an earlier boxer by the name of Jack Dempsey. The press began to take notice when the 185-pound Dempsey easily bested opponents up to seventy pounds heavier and six inches taller. Such was the case when the "Manassa Mauler" won the world championship by trouncing Jess Willard – shattering the giant's cheek bone in thirteen pieces and bringing him to the canvas seven times. Over the next seven years Dempsey beat his challengers six times, until he was finally defeated by Gene Tunney in a bout that attracted a record 100,000 spectators.

Although the former "Giant Killer" tried to make a comeback in the early 1930s, he realized that it was time to hang up the gloves. During his career he had earned an estimated $5 million. Of his sixty-nine professional bouts, he won forty-seven by knockouts, seven by decisions, and one on a foul; he drew four times, lost four by decisions, and was knocked out once; there was no decision in five bouts. His advice to future champions was: "Keep your guard up, your chin down, and your seat off the canvas."

After 1932 Dempsey tended to his numerous business interests and took an active role in World War II. Besides owning hotels in New York City and Miami, he was the proprietor of a liquor house, a clothing store, and two restaurants in the Big Apple. Within months after Pearl Harbor, though, he tried to enlist but was rejected because of his age and lack of military experience. He subsequently joined the Coast Guard to oversee its physical fitness program. According to Dempsey, his greatest wartime experience occurred just before he landed with the assault troops on Okinawa. The understandably nervous men seemed to relax when they saw the considerably older ex-fighter among them. "This can't be so tough if they send old men like Dempsey along with us," one of the boys said.

§ Open Memorial Day-October 1, Monday-Saturday 9-5. Donations. Phone: 719-843-5207.

MANITOU SPRINGS

ℐ Buffalo Bill Wax Museum, 404 West Manitou Avenue.
The museum displays wax figures of thirty-two Western pioneers – including *William Butler Cody – in lifelike tableaux.

§ Open June-August, daily 9-9; April, May, and September, daily 10-5. Fee. Phone: 719-685-5900.

OURAY

¶ **Camp Bird Mine,** south on State 550 to the first road on the right.

The mines in the Ouray area were originally silver claims until the Irishman Thomas Walsh discovered gold in much of the discarded ore. After buying up several claims west of Ouray in 1896 for $20 million, he named them Camp Bird and proceeded to extract between $3 million and $4 million in gold annually for the next six or seven years. In 1902 he sold the mine to a British concern for $5.2 million.

After coming to the United States at the age of nineteen, Walsh helped construct bridges for the Colorado Central Railroad near Golden. He later mined at Del Norte and Central City, Colorado, and Deadwood, South Dakota. Upon his return to Colorado, he settled in Leadville, married Carrie Bell Read in 1879, and lived with his wife in an abandoned boxcar in Sowbelly Gulch. (The new bride so disliked the name of the gulch that she tried to get it changed to "St. Kevin's.") In 1880, meanwhile, Walsh discovered a silver mine that produced $75,000 worth of the precious ore in just two months. During the silver crash of the early 1890s, however, Walsh suffered severe financial losses and headed for Ouray in 1895 to rebuild his fortune.

Following his successful development of the Camp Bird Mine, Walsh moved to Washington, D. C. and took his place among both the *nouveau* and *vieux riches*, building a $1 million mansion on Massachusetts Avenue. He later joined King Leopold of Belgium in various mining operations in the Congo and died in the nation's capital in 1909. (See *Irish America, Volume 1*.)

Before the mining magnate's death, he had acquired a reputation for foolish generosity to his daughter, Evalyn. When the young girl complained that having to walk to school in Washington was "trying for my dignity," she asked her father to hire a horse and carriage. Within days the doting father presented her with a blue victoria, a pair of matched sorrels, and a coachman decked out in a silk hat. In later years he gave his dear Evalyn a $100,000 wedding gift and succumbed to her desire that he purchase the Hope Diamond for her. As it turned out, though, the $154,000 investment (and its reputed curse) had tragic consequences: her son was killed in a car accident (after being the object of repeated kidnap threats), her daughter died because of a drug overdose, she herself became addicted to morphine, and her adulterous, alcoholic husband went insane.

FLORIDA

APOPKA

¶ **Rock Springs and Kelly Park,** 6 miles north on State 435 to Kelly Park Road.

This park was donated to the city by Dr. Howard Kelly, an eminent obstetrician and pioneer at Johns Hopkins Medical School in Baltimore, Maryland.

Descended from an Irish immigrant who had settled in Philadelphia in the mid 1700s, Kelly was a graduate of the University of Pennsylvania's medical school. In 1884 he established what became the Kensington Hospital for Women, where he specialized in the surgical treatment of pelvic and abdominal diseases. Here he performed the first successful caesarian section conducted in Philadelphia under antiseptic conditions.

After serving as associate professor of obstetrics at the University of Pennsylvania, he accepted an invitation to become the chief gynecologist at Johns Hopkins Hospital as well as professor of gynecology at Johns Hopkins Medical School. So significant were his contributions to the early development of these two institutions that he was included in John Singer Sargent's famous painting *Four Doctors* (now in the Welch Medical Library at Johns Hopkins).

During his career Kelly was an innovator, experimenter, and social reformer. Not only did he invent many new procedures and instruments but his was the first X-ray machine used in Baltimore. He was also one of the first American physicians to use radium in the treatment of cancer. He was well known for his *pro bono* medical treatment of the poor, and he was a generous benefactor of many missionary efforts and public charities.

§ Open April-October, daily 9-7; rest of the year, daily 8-6. Swimming, picnicking, hiking, and camping. Fee. Phone: 407-889-4179.

DRY TORTUGAS NATIONAL PARK

¶ **Fort Jefferson,** on Dry Tortugas Key, 68 miles west of Key West. Accessible by seaplane from Key West.

Located in the Dry Tortugas Islands off Key West, Fort Jefferson was intended to protect the shipping lanes in the Gulf of Mexico, but advances in military technology made it obsolete even before it was abandoned in 1874. In 1865 four of the so-called "Lincoln Conspirators" were imprisoned here for their alleged complicity in the assassination of President Abraham Lincoln.

One of the four prisoners was Michael O'Laughlin, a childhood friend of Lincoln's assassin, John Wilkes Booth. In fact, O'Laughlin and his Irish Protestant family had lived in a house owned by Booth's mother. He was described by a contemporary diarist as someone who "might have been mistaken for a native of Cuba, short and slender, with luxuriant black locks, a delicate moustache and whiskers, and vivacious black eyes." The Irishman had served briefly in the Confederate army but later took the oath of allegiance to the U.S. government. In September 1864 he agreed to join Booth's plan to kidnap Lincoln while the president was on his way to the Soldiers' Home in Washington. Once captured, Lincoln would be taken to Richmond and held hostage for the release of Confederate prisoners.

In early January 1865 Booth entrusted O'Laughlin with pistols, knives, and handcuffs for the planned kidnapping. A planned seizure on March 17 failed to materialize because Lincoln did not attend the play at the Soldiers' Home that evening as expected. On March 27 Booth telegraphed O'Laughlin to come to Washington for the kidnap attempt scheduled for two days later. As it happened, however, Lincoln was out of town that day, on a trip to Petersburg and Richmond. It was probably at that time that Booth decided to change the venue of the planned kidnapping from the Soldiers' Home to Ford's Theater, a change that the other conspirators strongly opposed. Booth ultimately changed plans again, this time for an assassination attempt.

Within a week of Lincoln's death, O'Laughlin was arrested. He and nine others were charged with conspiracy to assassinate the president, *Vice President Andrew Johnson, Secretary of State William Seward, and *Lieutenant General Ulysses S. Grant. O'Laughlin was charged specifically with lying in wait to kill Grant on the night of April 13-14. Although O'Laughlin admitted that he had been connected with the plot to kidnap Lincoln, he denied any knowledge of or involvement in the assassination plot. According to the prosecution, O'Laughlin had been in Washington on April 13 making inquiries about Grant. Testimony also claimed that the Irishman called on Booth at his hotel on April 14 and that he was in the city on the night of the murder. The commission conducting the case found O'Laughlin guilty of intent to kill Grant and sentenced him to life imprisonment at Albany, New York. President Johnson later changed the venue to Fort Jefferson. There O'Laughlin died of yellow fever on September 23, 1867, two years before Johnson released the other three convicted conspirators on Dry Tortugas.

§ Open daily 8-dusk. Phone: 305-242-7700.

ELLENTON

¶ Gamble Plantation State Historic Site, 1 mile north and 3 miles east on U.S. 301, at 3708 Patten Avenue.

The plantation house on this site was built between 1844 and 1856 as the home of Major Robert Gamble, whose great-great-grandfather had emigrated from Londonderry, northern Ireland, about 1735. The two-story house is built of red brick and tabby brick (shells, sand, and oyster-shell lime) and is fronted on three sides by eighteen huge columns. The house had ten rooms.

Gamble, who had been cited for bravery during the Seminole War and later attended West Point, arrived in this area in 1844. Although the terrain of this region reminded him of the frontier of Middle Florida where he had served during the war, he was pleasantly surprised to find it occupied by "intelligent men, nearly all mechanics of great skill." "There were blacksmiths, boiler makers, workers in iron in the higher branches of the art, cabinet makers, carpenters, bricklayers &c., &c.," he wrote, "and by availing myself of the services of these men, I was enabled to overcome, when I commenced the erection of my buildings, what otherwise, in a country so entirely cut off and remote from the resources of civilization, would have proved almost insuperable obstacles."

After Gamble's brother John Grattan Gamble Jr. arrived in the region, the pair began to acquire acreage from some of their neighbors. By 1849 the Gambles had obtained title to 1,500 acres, 320 of which they had brought under cultivation by clearing the land and erecting an extensive network of drainage ditches. The crops which they eventually planted were a varied lot: sugar cane, corn, sweet potatoes, grapes, citrus, guava, and rice.

To process their first sugar cane harvest, the brothers erected three frame structures to boil, drain, and mill the produce of the fields. The mill itself was – in Robert's words – "a gigantic affair": an arrangement of three horizontal rollers five feet long, the largest weighing five tons. But disaster struck almost immediately. With the cane cut, milled, and boiled, and the granulated sugar packed into barrels, a fire consumed the whole operation, destroying forty tons of sugar and 4,000 gallons of molasses.

Within three years, however, Robert Gamble had erected a new mill and refinery, the largest of several in the area and equipped with modern machinery from New Orleans. Constructed of fire-resistant "tabby" and clay brick, the new buildings stretched 340 feet and boasted a fifty-horsepower engine-driven mill. Gamble proudly described its operation: "While the mill was in motion a solid mass of cane five feet wide and 14 inches high passed continuously between the rollers, and was so effectually crushed that the bagasse as it passed from the rollers was nearly as dry as timber, cut in two at every point, and if applied to the mouth, while inhaling would produce partial suffocation by its fine, dry impalpable powder." Gamble's operation also included an eight-horsepower engine that powered not only the vacuum pans in his mill but also his grist mill and the circular saw used in making barrels which held about 1,000 pounds of sugar.

Gamble's operation enjoyed considerable success, at least until 1856. In his first year of operation with his new facilities, for instance, Gamble produced 231,000 pounds of sugar and 11,500 gallons of molasses. Although severe cold destroyed a third of the next year's production, the figures for 1853-54 show a 30 percent increase over those of 1850-51: 363,000 pounds of sugar and 15,000 gallons of molasses.

At the height of his success, Gamble's plantation encompassed 3,450 acres, almost a third of it cleared and in production and worked by 190 slaves. The slaves – the oldest of whom in 1860 was a 105-year-old woman – lived in fifty-seven structures that lined the main road from the river. By 1856, however, falling sugar prices and crop losses had forced Gamble to sell the estate for $190,000 to two buyers from Louisiana.

Even before sugar prices began to fall, Gamble – like other planters in the region – had began to diversify. In 1851 he employed a gang of axemen – under the direction of "a happy-go-lucky sort of a character who found his way into our wilderness" – to cut down 3,000 cubic feet of timber for ships. That same year Gamble hired a New England shipwright and a dozen laborers to help his axemen cut down 6,000 cubic feet. Although the risk of losing a cargo on its sea voyage to ports like New Orleans and Key West was always present, the trade was extremely lucrative, one timber cargo being valued at $3,500. Most likely prompted by such returns, Gamble in 1853 purchased a $7,000 brig to transport timber to New York.

• Today the Gamble Plantation State Historic Park is Florida's major Confederate memorial, so designated because of its association with Judah Benjamin, the Confederate secretary of state. In May 1865, at the conclusion of the Civil War, Benjamin eluded capture by federal troops by posing as a French journalist on his way from Richmond, Virginia, to Florida. Having arrived at the former Gamble Plantation – then the home of the Confederate deputy commissary for the area – Benjamin somehow escaped detection, even though a reward of $40,000 brought pursuers to the plantation. With the commissary's help he eventually escaped to London at the end of August. Once in England, he enjoyed a second career as a distinguished member of the bar, at one time being asked to handle half the appeals to the House of Lords.

§ Site and visitor center open daily. Tours of the mansion Thursday-Monday at 9:30, 10:30, 1, 2, 3 and 4. Fee for mansion. Picnicking. Phone: 813-723-4536.

FORT LAUDERDALE

¶ **Stranahan House,** 1 Stranahan Place, south of Las Olas Boulevard.

Built in 1901, this was the home and trading post of Frank Stranahan, reputedly the first white settler in this region and the grandson of an immigrant from County Antrim, Ireland. The 2,000-square-foot wood-frame building has been restored to its 1913-15 appearance. It is noted for its fine wood paneling throughout the interior.

Stranahan, a native of Ohio, had come to Florida in 1887, primarily to restore his lungs, impaired during his employment in a steel mill. By February 1893 he had accepted a job managing New River Camp, a tourist facility in what is now Fort Lauderdale. His first night sleeping under the stars near the New River proved something of a surprise for the newcomer, though, when he awoke to find himself surrounded by thirty sleeping Seminoles. His later remark to his brother – "I think I will get along with them all right" – proved prophetic, since the house he soon built along the banks of the river also served as a post for trading with the natives.

After acquiring almost eleven acres along the river, Stranahan built his first trading post on this site – a complex that included a one-story frame structure, a wooden bulkhead, and a dock. It was here that as many as 150 Seminoles arrived by canoe to sell pelts, alligator hides, and egret plumes, gathered during weeks of hunting in the Everglades. And it was here that they spent the money on food, traps, fabric, and ammunition. Stranahan, who resolutely refused to sell liquor to the Indians, was also the local postmaster and operated a ferry across the New River.

The Seminoles usually stayed at Stranahan's trading post for between four and seven days. To accommodate the extremely large number that came, he allowed them to sleep on his veranda or under a canvas roof he erected. "I've often laughed to myself at the comment of the verandas of this house having been built to conform with the old Southern style," Stranahan said. "The truth is I put them there for the Indians to sleep on

The Robert Stranahan House. (Photo by Woodbury and Associates.)

when they would come in from their hunts, tired out and needing a place to rest off the ground. And there were many nights when these floors were so crowded with sleeping Indians that you could hardly step between them."

Frank Stranahan's other ventures in banking and real estate were quite successful until the collapse of the Florida "Land Boom" in 1928 literally broke the bank. Crushed by his own financial losses and feeling responsible for those of his friends, he drowned himself in the New River. Two of his cousins – Robert and Frank Stranahan – established the Champion Spark Plug Company in 1908.

§ Open September-June, Wednesday, Friday, and Saturday 10-3:30. Closed January 1, Thanksgiving, and December 25. Fee. Phone: 305-524-4736.

FORT MEYERS

¶ **Edison-Ford Winter Estates,** Interstate 75 exit 22 to 2350 McGregor Boulevard.

This complex includes the adjacent winter homes of Thomas Edison and Henry Ford, the latter the son and grandson of immigrants from County Cork, Ireland. Ford's 3.5-acre estate was known as "Mangoes."

Ford became familiar with the Fort Meyers area in 1914 when he and his wife spent a winter vacation with Thomas Edison at the famous inventor's estate, "Seminole Lodge." During that visit Ford toured the Everglades and the cypress forests and so enjoyed studying the native birds and exotic flowers that he soon purchased a house and property worth $34,000 next to Edison's estate.

Ford's paternal grandfather, John Ford, had been a Protestant tenant farmer near Clonakilty in County Cork. In 1847 he left his homeland for America, bringing with him his wife and their seven children. One of the sons, William, subsequently met and married the daughter of Patrick O'Hern, also a native of Cork. Their son Henry was born in 1863.

In the early 1920s this son – by then a famous car manufacturer – visited Ireland to open his company's first factory outside the United States. During the visit he pledged £5,000 for the Hospital Building Fund in Cork. The next day, however, the local press reported that he had promised to donate £10,000. When officials from the hospital fund offered to correct the error with a new headline ("Henry Ford Did Not Give £10,000 to Hospital"), the American manufacturer realized that he had been "taken in" and promised to make the larger donation. His only condition was that he be allowed to choose the biblical quotation that would adorn the hospital: "I came among mine own – and they took me in."

§ Open Monday-Saturday 9-3:30, Sunday noon-3:30. Closed Thanksgiving and December 25. Fee. Phone: 813-334-3614/7419.

KENNEDY SPACE CENTER

Along with Cape Canaveral Air Force Base, the Kennedy Space Center is the headquarters of the nation's space program. The 140,000-acre combined site is forty-seven miles east of Orlando on either State 50 or the Bee Line Expressway and is accessible via U.S. 1 to State 405 (east) to State 3 (north).

The Kennedy Space Center, on Merritt Island, was built in honor of *President John F. Kennedy, who in May 1961 committed the United States to landing a man on the moon "before this decade is out." It was from here that the country's *Gemini* and early *Apollo* space missions were launched.

One of the early *Gemini* astronauts was *James McDivitt, while *Michael Collins piloted the Apollo 11 spacecraft which put a man on the moon in 1969. Collins later became director of the National Aeronautics and Space Museum in Washington, D.C. The first American woman to walk in space was *Kathryn Sullivan, during the 1984 flight of the *Challenger* space shuttle.

¶ **Spaceport USA,** 11 miles east of Interstate 95 on State 405.

In addition to space films shown on a five-and-a-half-story screen, the center features multimedia displays, a moon rock, and various spacecraft. Tickets for the two-hour bus tours of the Kennedy and Cape Canaveral sites can be purchased here. Tours depart daily from Spaceport USA every fifteen minutes from 9:45 until two hours before sunset (except December 25 and certain parts of launch days).

The Astronauts Memorial is accessible through the entrance to Spaceport USA. Known as the Space Mirror, this memorial honors the American astronauts who died while involved in the space program. The monument rotates with the sun in such a way that the sun's rays shine though the names of the astronauts.

§ Open daily 9-sunset. Closed December 25 and during certain parts of launch days. Fee for theater. Phone: 407-452-2121.

¶ **U.S. Astronaut Hall of Fame,** 6224 Vectorspace Boulevard, 1/4 mile east of U.S. 1 on State 405.

This building features photography and memorabilia associated with the Mercury and Gemini astronauts.

§ Open daily 9-5. Closed December 25. Fee. Phone: 407-269-6100.

KEY BISCAYNE

¶ **Florida White House,** 500 and 516 Bay Lane. Private.

Following his election to the presidency in 1968, *Richard Nixon sold his apartment in New York City and purchased these adjoining residences for $250,000. The compound served as the Florida White House when the president and his wife stayed here.

KISSIMMEE

¶ **Wild Bill's Wild West Dinner Show,** east of Interstate 4 at 5260 West Irlo Bronson Memorial Highway (U.S. 192).

This two-hour dinner show is modeled after the famous traveling Wild West Show of "Buffalo Bill" Cody, whose mother boasted that her ancestors were descended from Irish nobility. (See Cody, Wyoming.)

After a career as a scout for various expeditions to the West (including one under *General Philip Sheridan), Cody opened the Wild West "Exhibition" in Omaha, Nebraska. For the next thirty years, it visited thousands of towns and cities in the United States and Europe, its 500 buffalo complemented by a troupe of 600 Indians, Pony Express riders, cowboys, stagecoach drivers, broncobusters, and sharpshooters.

§ Performances daily at 7 p.m. Museum open daily 10:30-8:30. Fee. Phone: 407-351-5151.

MIAMI BEACH

¶ **Ancient Spanish Monastery,** 16711 West Dixie Highway at 167th Street, N.E., in North Miami Beach.

Now known as St. Bernard of Clairvaux Episcopal Church, this twelfth-century Spanish monastery was shipped from Europe in the 1920s by *William Randolph Hearst. The famous publisher had intended to reassemble its 36,000 stones – shipped in almost 11,000 crates – at his mansion in San Simeon, California. However, when customs officials ordered that the crates be opened – on the suspicion that the straw packing material was contaminated with hoof-and-mouth disease – the blocks became hopelessly misidentified and Hearst abandoned the project.

Hearst was born in San Francisco in 1863 into a politically influential family that traced its descent primarily to Scottish ancestors who had immigrated to America in 1680. Hearst's mother (Elizabeth Collins), however, was of Irish ancestry, her family having emigrated from Galway. According to a family story, Hearst's Irish Catholic governess, Eliza Pike, was concerned that his mother had not had the infant baptized. One day when the mother was out of the city, Eliza spirited young Willie to a Catholic church, where he was baptized by a priest. When the boy's mother returned and learned what the governess had done, Mrs. Hearst reminded her employee that the family was Episcopalian. Eliza replied: "It doesn't matter so long as the baby is Christian."

After assuming ownership of the *San Francisco Examiner* from his father, a U.S. senator and mining entrepreneur, the younger Hearst made it a financial success. In 1895 he bought the *New York Journal* and proceeded to wage a circulation battle with the *New York World*, using such devices as sensationalism, editorial crusades, banner headlines, and color comics. By 1937 he owned twenty-five large dailies throughout the country.

§ Open Monday-Saturday 10-4, Sunday noon-4. Closed Easter, Thanksgiving, and December 25. Fee. Phone: 305-945-1461.

¶ Jackie Gleason Theater of the Performing Arts, 1700 Washington Avenue and 17th Street.

Beginning in 1964, Miami Beach became synonymous with Jackie Gleason after he moved the production crew of his Saturday-night television program to what he enthusiastically promoted as the "fun and sun capital of the world." At the time, the hour-long program was beginning the eighth of an eighteen-year run.

Gleason – known on his birth certificate as Herbert John Gleason – was born in Brooklyn in 1916. His father, an insurance clerk who abandoned his family when "Jackie" was almost ten, was apparently a native of Cork, while his mother (May Kelly Gleason) came from County Kilkenny. Forced to support herself and Jackie, the future comedian's mother worked in the change booth of a New York subway until her death six years later.

Gleason's early career boasted a varied resumé. As a youngster he showed off his wit in school drama productions, and at sixteen he worked as master of ceremonies at Brooklyn's Folly Theater. Stints as a carnival barker, disc jockey, and cabaret performer led to his Broadway musical comedy debut in 1940 in *Keep Off the Grass*.

During the next decade the ambitious entertainer became increasingly well known to theatergoers for small comedic and melodramatic parts. In two years he appeared in five motion pictures, among them *Larceny, Inc.* and *Springtime in the Rockies*, and in 1943 he began the first of 882 performances in *Follow the Girls*. By now known for his girth, the 250-pound actor rounded out the 1940s by appearing in the musical *Along Fifth Avenue*.

Gleason made the transition to the new medium of television in 1949, when he appeared for twenty-six weeks in the *Life of Riley* series. Despite competition from TV prize fights, Gleason's popularity began to soar during his appearance on the *Cavalcade of Stars*. It was during this two-year run that he was able to display the range of his comedic skills through his portrayal of such psychological studies as Joe the Bartender, the Poor Soul, and the playboy Reggie Van Gleason III. "I give each character a saving grace, a touch of sympathy," he said about his many personae.

After a year as the star of NBC's Sunday-night *Colgate Comedy Hour*, Gleason hit pay dirt when he was offered a $400,000 production contract to do his own program. Earning the actor a cool $10,000 a week, the *Jackie Gleason Show* ran for eighteen years and etched his intensely physical comedy in the minds of the American public. His trademark "And awaaaay we go!" as he sidled off the stage – arms swinging – was matched only by the deliciousness he exclaimed ("How sweeeet it is") after sipping presumably alcoholic spirits from an incongruous-looking tea cup.

Gleason reached the height of his popularity, however, as the bus driver Ralph Kramden in *The Honeymooners*. In contrast to the pathetic poormouth figure he played in the show, though, "The Great One" enjoyed a three-year contract that promised to make him the highest paid star on TV. In response to suggestions that he was not worth the high-flying salary he was offered, the comedian replied with a mixture of pride and uncharacteristic humility. "People seem to think I should be ashamed of making $11 million," he said. "I'm not. . . . I came a long way in a very short time and I still remember the lean years and the hopeless years. There is no point in kidding anybody by hanging my head coyly and murmuring, 'I was lucky.'. . . I've sweated for perfection and for any success I've won. But I don't take all the credit. I still stop in at St. Patrick's Cathedral and get on my knees and say, '*You're* the greatest.'" As it turned out, the show's sponsor backed out after the first year, although reruns continued until 1971.

Gleason's star was tarnished in 1983, however, when he amazed CBS and his former costars by producing the so-called "lost" episodes of *The Honeymooners*. Totaling more than seventy hours, the shows had never been lost but had been the object of Gleason's extravagant solicitude. (He had spent $5,000 a year to provide air-conditioned storage.) Hoping to deflect the cynicism which his contrived "discovery" had produced in the public, he resorted to humor. "Until Ralph found them under the backseat of the bus," he joked, "we didn't know they were there." "I think this is the right time. I'm sick of watching those other ones," he added.

Following his television career, Gleason returned to motion pictures. Although most of the fifteen films he made at this time were far from unforgettable, he received Oscar nominations for his portrayals of the pool shark Minnesota Fats in *The Hustler* (1961) and of a mute janitor in *Gigot* (1963). He was frustrated, however, in his desire to play the Irish mayor Frank Skeffington in the film version of Edwin O'Connor's novel *The Last Hurrah*. Two years before his death in 1987, Gleason was elected to the Television Hall of Fame.

Although "The Great One" was described by two critics as "a bucket of Irish charm" and "a king-sized leprechaun," he had no romantic love for Ireland itself. He did, however, appreciate its language and literature, treasures to which his mother had introduced him. When the Irish author Brendan Behan came to the United States, Gleason was so taken by the man that he accompanied him for much of the rest of his visit. Yet on one occasion, while Gleason was drunk and belligerent, he urged Behan to drink, fully aware that the author was an alcoholic and risked death if he "took a drop of the drink." Gleason later tried to make amends by challenging Behan to a buttermilk-drinking contest for charity. The Irishman observed that he liked Gleason because his jokes always contained "a certain amount of sadness, of truth." He especially liked Gleason's remark that "Loneliness is particularly wretched to the actor because there is no audience to witness his misery."

§ Box office open Monday-Friday 10-5. Phone: 305-673-7300.

¶ Villa Serena, 3115 Brickell Avenue. Private.

Built by *William Jennings Bryan in 1916, this red-tiled house was his permanent home from 1921 until 1925. From here he left to serve as prosecutor in the Scopes Trial in Dayton, Tennessee, where he died a few days after the famous "Monkey Trial." (See Dayton, Tennessee, and Lincoln , Nebraska.)

¶ Wolfsonian Museum, 1001 Washington Avenue.

One of the museum's newest acquisitions is the Geneva Window, a work of eight panels by Harry Clarke, Ireland's greatest stained-glass artist. The window was commissioned by the government of the Irish Free State in the 1920s to celebrate the country's modern literary heritage. The window was originally intended to grace the International Labor Office at the League of Nations headquarters in Geneva, Switzerland.

The completed window depicted figures from the works of such contemporary authors as Joyce, O'Casey, O'Flaherty, Shaw, Synge, and Yeats. Although there was a stir about some of the characters that Clarke included – among them St. Joan, Joxer Daley, Pegeen Mike, Countess Cathleen, and the Playboy of the Western World – it was the artist's inclusion of a drunk and a partially undressed dancer that caused the government to ultimately reject the work. Clarke died, however, in the midst of the controversy.

Born in 1889, Clarke was introduced to the stained-glass craft by his father, who owned a company in Dublin which created the popular glass work, primarily for churches. As a youngster, Clarke displayed a special talent for drawing, and by his early twenties he had become a respected illustrator and artist in the vitreous medium. During the subsequent two decades, he became renowned for the glass work in numerous churches throughout his native land. A major influence in the Celtic Revival, he celebrated Ireland's rediscovery of her heritage, primarily through his depiction of the country's saints and heroes (e.g., St. Brendan the Navigator and St. Gobnait, the patron of beekeepers).

The Geneva Window went on exhibit at the Wolfsonian in November 1995. After exhibitions in Los Angeles, Seattle, Pittsburgh, and Indianapolis, the window is scheduled to return to Miami Beach in the spring of 1998. Although the work is part of the Wolfsonian's collection, it will not be permanently on display at the museum. Clarke's works can be found in only one other place in the United States – in St. Vincent de Paul Basilica in Bayonne, New Jersey.

§ Open Tuesday-Thursday and Saturday 10-6, Friday 10-9, and Sunday 12-5. Fee. Phone: 305-531-1001.

OLUSTEE

¶ Olustee Battlefield State Historic Site, 2.5 miles east on U.S. 90.

On February 20, 1864, this site was the scene of the largest Civil War engagement fought in Florida. The decisive Union defeat was due, in large part, to Brigadier General Joseph Finegan, the commander of the Confederate forces in East Florida.

Finegan, born in Clones, Ireland, in 1814, had immigrated to America during the famine. After settling in Florida, he established himself as a lawyer and a planter and later operated a lumber mill in Jacksonville. He also was associated with U.S. Senator David Yulee in railroad construction. During the constitutional crisis that culminated in civil war, the Irishman openly advocated secession and attended the state convention which voted to withdraw from the Union. Loyalist support was nevertheless still strong in Florida and led to the dispatch of Union troops to the state in the hope of establishing a provisional government loyal to the Union.

As the ranking Confederate military official in the state, Finegan prepared to counter the arrival of a 5,000-man Union force in Jacksonville in February 1864. While these federal troops burned and pillaged their way across the Florida panhandle, the Irishman gathered and dispatched a force of 6,000 Confederate troops to the vicinity of Olustee. Although, as Finegan suspected, the nearby rail junction was the intended target of the Union advance, the Northern troops were slow to engage the enemy. Finegan, however, showed no such hesitancy and instead ordered one of his two brigades to take the offensive. During almost five hours of combat, Finegan's men broke the Union line and forced the Yankees to retreat.

The following May, Finegan was assigned to the Army of Northern Virginia. In an engagement at Cold Harbor, the Irishman's regiments filled the breach that Union troops had made in the Confederate line and succeeded in driving back the attackers. After the war he resumed his law practice, served a term in the state senate, and worked as a cotton broker in Savannah. He is buried in Old City Cemetery in Jacksonville.

§ Site open daily 8-5. Museum open Thursday-Monday 9-5. Phone: 904-752-3866.

PALM BEACH

❡ Kennedy Winter Home, 1113 North Ocean Boulevard. Private.

This white stucco villa was purchased in 1933 by *Joseph P. Kennedy, whose son John Kennedy recuperated here in 1955 after a back operation. Here the young Kennedy wrote much of *Profiles in Courage*, which won a Pulitzer Prize but prompted questions about its authorship. In 1995 the mansion was purchased by a New York banker and his wife. The "Kennedy Winter White House" will be designated a historic landmark.

Among the schoolgirl mementos which Joseph Kennedy's daughter Kathleen kept in her scrapbook were numerous newspaper clippings about the children's parties at the family's winter estate. One article read: "Kennedy's Palm Beach villa was the setting for one of the most enjoyable parties given for members of the visiting school set when John, Kathleen, Rosemary and Joe Junior were hosts at a buffet supper for a large group of their school and college friends. Tables were set for six and later motion pictures were shown. Guests included Charles Amory, Lem Billings, Randolph Hearst and Jeffrey Roche."

Many years later, while visiting Cork, Ireland, President Kennedy joked about his family's privileged enclave. In introducing one of the members of his American entourage, he said: "And now I would like to introduce to you the pastor at the church I go to. He comes from right here in Cork – Monsignor O'Mahoney. He is the pastor of a poor, humble flock in Palm Beach, Florida."

PENSACOLA

❡ Andrew Jackson House Site, on the southeast corner of Palafox and East Intendencia streets.

While *Andrew Jackson was serving as the first territorial governor of Florida after its purchase from Spain, he and his wife lived in a house formerly on this site (now marked by a bronze tablet).

Mrs. Jackson strongly disapproved of what she regarded as the profane observance of the Sabbath among the city's Spanish population. As a result of her influence, when this part of Florida came under American rule the authorities outlawed gambling and other abuses on Sunday.

❡ Andrew Jackson Statue, Plaza Ferdinand VII, South Palafox Street, between East Government and Zaragoza streets.

This statue commemorates the role that *Andrew Jackson played in reaching the agreement by which Spain sold Florida to the United States in 1821.

❡ Stephen Mallory Burial Site, St. Michael's Cemetery, Alcaniz and

Garden streets.

Stephen Russell Mallory, the Confederate secretary of the navy, was born in Trinidad about 1813, the son of a civil engineer who had married Ellen Russell of County Waterford, Ireland. After the family moved to Key West about 1820, the younger Mallory spent three years at the Moravian school in Nazareth, Pennsylvania, before taking up the study of law. Toward the end of the 1830s, he saw military service in the Seminole War and married Angela Moreno. During his subsequent legal career, he was appointed customs collector at Key West by *President James K. Polk. His political aspirations came to fruition when he was elected to the U.S. Senate and served as chairman of the naval affairs committee. Perhaps because of his fluency in Spanish, he was offered the post of U.S. minister to Spain, although he declined *President James Buchanan's offer.

After throwing in his lot with the Confederacy, Mallory oversaw the creation of a naval force – literally from scratch – although he failed to develop the fleet of ironclad vessels that he had hoped to build. As the last days of the Confederacy approached, he accompanied *President Jefferson Davis as they and their wives sought refuge from pursuing federal troops. At La Grange, Georgia, Mallory was hauled out of bed by armed men and spirited off to prison in New York. When released on parole almost a year later, he returned to Pensacola, where he practiced law until his death in 1873.

ST. AUGUSTINE

¶ Cathedral of St. Augustine, Cathedral Street, facing Plaza de Constitución.

This church is the center of the oldest Catholic parish in the United States, dating from the beginning of the Spanish regime in 1565. Despite its Spanish origins, however, this church and an earlier one on this site both had connections with Irishmen named Moore.

The earlier church was destroyed when James Moore, the governor of South Carolina, raided St. Augustine during Queen Anne's War (1702-13). The present church, which was built in the 1790s and partially destroyed by fire in 1887, was rebuilt in the Spanish style by Bishop John Moore. The church contains a gold tabernacle from Ireland and a side altar dedicated to St. Patrick.

Governor Moore was reputedly descended from Roger Moore, a leader of the 1641 Irish uprising who had immigrated to Charleston, South Carolina, about 1675. The younger Moore became a well known Indian trader who, as governor, tried to get the colonial assembly to grant him a monopoly of the Indian trade. Failing in this brazen maneuver, he dissolved the legislature, a tactic which he repeated every time that body attempted to investigate alleged voting irregularities. When, as a private citizen,

*St. Patrick's altar
in the Cathedral
of St. Augustine.*

Moore was denied his request that the legislature counteract French influence by waging an offensive war against the Apalachee Indians, he gathered a military force of his own and carried off a successful raid upon the
natives, carrying off many of them as slaves.

Bishop John Moore, meanwhile, was a native of Rosmead, County
Meath, Ireland. Before coming to St. Augustine, he had served as a curate
in Charleston, South Carolina, during the Civil War. Because of his strong
loyalties to the South and the Confederacy, he refused to swear allegiance
to the United States and thus became the object of mail censorship by
Union authorities.

§ Tours daily at 1 and 3. Phone: 904-824-2806.

¶ **O'Reilly House,** 131 Aviles Street. Private.

Constructed about 1763, this two-story building is one of the city's
oldest and was willed by Don Miguel O'Reilly to the Catholic Church,
which at one time used it as the rectory of St. Augustine Cathedral.

Don Miguel was actually Father Michael O'Reilly, a Catholic priest
born in Longford, Ireland, in 1752. After studying theology at the Irish
College in Salamanca, Spain, he was one of twenty Irish priests recruited
to serve the Spanish missions in Louisiana and Florida. For a brief time he
was the chaplain to Spanish troops in Cuba and the Bahamas. In 1783 he
was appointed assistant to Father Thomas Hassett, the Irish-born pastor
of St. Augustine parish in East Florida. Thirteen years later O'Reilly was
named vicar, and during his pastorate he established a school and saw the
completion of a church erected by the royal governor.

On one occasion O'Reilly found himself the object of a matrimonial hoax of sorts. It seems that Lieutenant John O'Donovan, a member of the Hibernian regiment of the British garrison in the city, had his eyes on a young Spanish woman named Dominga Zéspides. After her father rejected O'Donovan's suit because of the Irishman's lack of noble birth and his unpromising financial prospects, the enamored pair concocted a ruse in order to get married. After Dominga stole away to meet O'Donovan at the home of a friend near the barracks, she sent a messenger to O'Reilly, imploring him to attend to her dangerously ill mistress. When the priest arrived at the house, he was surprised to find the mistress in good health and to unwittingly witness the young lovers recite their nuptial vows in his presence, a trick that supposedly assured the validity of the marriage. The Irish priest died in 1812 – after twenty-eight years in St. Augustine – and was succeeded by Father Michael Crosby, a native of Wexford, Ireland, who had studied at the Dominican College in Seville, Spain.

ST. MARKS

¶ San Marcos de Apalachee State Museum, off State 363 and 1 mile south on Canal Street.

The museum is on the site of a fort built by the Spanish in 1679 and captured by *Andrew Jackson in 1818 during a campaign against the Seminoles. The remains of the fort and its earthworks are still visible. The museum displays Native American, Spanish, and Civil War artifacts.

TALLAHASSEE

¶ San Luis Archaeological and Historic Site, Mission Road, 0.25 mile northwest off U.S. 90.

This is the site of one of five seventeenth-century Spanish missions and Apalachee Indian villages near Tallahassee which were destroyed in 1703-04 by English troops under *James Moore, the former governor of South Carolina. (See the Cathedral of St. Augustine, St. Augustine, Florida.)

Excavations already done on the site are visible and interpreted. Continuing excavation work is done Sunday through Thursday from late February to early June.

§ Open Monday-Friday 9-4:30, Saturday 10-4:30, Sunday noon-4:30. Closed Thanksgiving and December 25. Phone: 904-487-3711.

WHITE SPRINGS

¶ Stephen Foster State Folk Culture Center, 3 miles east of Interstate 75 on U.S. 41.

This 250-acre wooded preserve on the Suwannee River celebrates Stephen Collins Foster, the famous Irish-American composer, and the river he immortalized in his song "Old Folks at Home." The visitor center features animated dioramas depicting scenes from Foster's musical compositions. Among the special events held at the center is the National Stephen Foster Day Celebration, held on a date near January 14, the anniversary of his death.

Foster was born in Pittsburgh in 1826 of Scotch-Irish parentage on both sides. His paternal great-grandfather had emigrated from Londonderry to Lancaster, Pennsylvania, about 1728, and his grandfather had fought in the Revolutionary War.

As a young man, Stephen Foster attracted public attention through the popularity of his early Negro ballads – "O Susanna," "Louisiana Belle," "Uncle Ned," and "Away Down South." This unexpected success led him to consider musical composition as a full-time career and to determine to become "the best Ethiopian song writer." Beginning in 1852, some of his ballads became part of the repertory of the minstrel companies of the day, including the famous Christy's. His fame increased with the appearance of "The Old Folks at Home," "Massa's in the Cold Ground," "My Old Kentucky Home," and "Old Black Joe." Following an unhappy marriage and excessive drinking, however, he died in poverty in New York City in 1864.

According to Foster's brother Morrison, the famous composer chose the Suwannee River as the locale of "Old Folks at Home" as if by instinct. The composer began his search for a name by asking his brother, "What is a good name of two syllables for a Southern river?" Morrison recorded the rest of the exchange: "I asked him how Yazoo would do. 'Oh,' said he, 'that has been used before.' I then suggested Pedee. 'Oh, pshaw,' he replied. 'I won't have that.' I then took an atlas from the top of my desk and opened the map of the United States. We both looked over it and my finger stopped at the 'Swanee,' a little river in Florida emptying into the Gulf of Mexico. 'That's it, that's it exactly,' exclaimed he delighted, as he wrote the name down; and then was finished, commencing, 'Way Down Upon de Swanee Ribber.'"

Despite this generally accepted version, old residents in this part of Florida claimed that Foster was familiar with the name of the river from a visit he had made to Columbus, an old town in the Suwannee area, in the 1850s.

§ Park open daily 8-dusk; buildings open daily 9-5. Fee. Phone: 904-397-2733.

GEORGIA

ATHENS

¶ **Taylor-Grady House,** 634 Prince Avenue.

This exquisite antebellum house was constructed sometime between late 1838 and June 1839 by Robert Taylor, a native of Cookstown, County Tyrone, Ireland. The house was built to replace an earlier residence which Taylor had built but which had been destroyed by fire only a few weeks before its expected completion.

Taylor, who was born in Ireland in 1787, had come to the United States as a child when his parents moved here to join relatives already living in Savannah. Although his uncle, Robert Holmes, wished to provide him with a European education, the fourteen-year-old youngster decided to join his father in business in Savannah. Eleven years later he became a partner in that firm, renamed Taylor, Davis, and Taylor to reflect his promotion.

In 1816 Robert Taylor married Harriot Caroline Jones, the daughter of an aristocratic family from Beaufort, South Carolina. The couple's permanent residence was Savannah, where Taylor was inducted into the Hibernian Society and where two of their three sons were born. (Only one, however, survived childhood.) After only five years of marriage, Mrs. Taylor herself died at "Innisfail," the family's plantation in Morgan County. Like her sons, she was buried in the family vault in Madison, Georgia, where her husband erected a monument to her memory.

In 1827, six years after his wife's death, Taylor married Elizabeth Bolling Deloney Berrien, a widow whose daughter by her first marriage joined the Taylor household. Three sons were born to the couple in rapid succession, although one died in infancy.

Taylor in the meantime was beginning to take a prominent place in Georgian society. Already a member of a charitable organization known as the Union Society, he was appointed in 1833 to a committee to prepare the celebrations surrounding the inauguration of *Andrew Jackson. The following year he was among the two dozen men who drew up resolutions for the Union Republican Party. In addition, in 1841 he was commissioned a brigadier general in the state militia. To more than 700 acres in Morgan County, he added extensive real estate holdings in Athens itself. By 1850 his wealth was placed at $200,000, much of it in the form of property in four additional counties, including plantations named Bolling Brook, Erin, Mayo, and Peru.

Taylor's wife Elizabeth died in 1840 after a lengthy illness. Her husband survived for another eleven years before becoming involved in a freak train accident that led to his death a few days later. An article in the *Southern Banner* described the unfortunate incident: "The train reached the Madison depot at eight o'clock, and Gen. Taylor, who was an infirm man and afflicted with paralysis, in attempting to leave it, fell between the cars with his feet resting upon the track. The train was moving off slowly from the depot at the time, and the trucks of the last car passed over both his feet, cutting one of them and crushing the other." He died four days later, after his attending physicians amputated one of his legs.

In his will Taylor left detailed wishes about his burial and expressed his undying love for his spouses. "I design and enjoin as a sacred duty upon my children and upon my executors named," he began, "to cause my body to be interred in my family vault . . . that my inanimate may rest and moulder with those of my two once lovely, excellent and ever beloved wives; the worthy objects of all my kindness and finest love and adoration . . . . No matter where or in what region I may die, let this be done . . . that I may rest in death as I lived in life, with objects so gentle, so endearing, and so much beloved and now mourned by me, until we may all be called together to our last account."

Taylor's house in Athens remained in the family until 1863, when it and a 338-acre farm were purchased by William Simmons Grady. The new owner was of Irish ancestry also and had organized a company of soldiers to fight for the Confederacy. He was killed at Petersburg in 1864, having suffered wounds to the head, the chest, and each arm. His son, Henry Grady, lived in the house for three years while he attended the University of Georgia. The younger Grady later became the managing editor of the *Atlanta Constitution* and promoted reconciliation with the North following the Civil War. The Henry Grady School of Journalism at the University of Georgia is named for him. (See Henry Grady Statue in Atlanta, Georgia.)

§ Open Tuesday-Friday 10-3:30. Closed holidays. Fee. Phone: 706-549-8688.

ATLANTA

J Atlanta-Fulton County Public Library, 1 Margaret Mitchell Square, at Peachtree and Forsythe streets.

The library exhibits memorabilia connected with the production of the film *Gone With the Wind*, based on the famous novel by Margaret Mitchell and featuring the fiery coquette Scarlett O'Hara.

As a youngster listening to tales from members of her parents' families, Mitchell had developed an intense interest in their history. Her father's Catholic ancestors had been in the Atlanta region since the Revolution, while her mother's Irish relatives had settled in the state in the early 1800s. In fact, Mitchell's mother was descended from Phillip Fitzgerald, a native of County Tipperary who had fled with his family to France following the abortive uprising in Ireland in 1798. By his early twenties, however, he had immigrated to America, eventually settling in Taliafero County, Georgia, and marrying Eleanor McGhann. That the marriage produced seven daughters but not a single surviving son was attributed to a curse hurled upon Fitzgerald when he bought the foreclosed property of a local farmer. At the time of the sale – so ran the family story – the farmer's wife directed a prophecy toward the new owner: "You'll never raise a man child on this land." Despite the "curse," the Irishman eventually acquired an estate of 3,000 acres and thirty-five slaves.

One of Fitzgerald's seven daughters was Annie Elizabeth, a headstrong girl who refused the convent education which her sisters received. In describing her, her grandson used such words as "authoritative step," "determination," "arrogance," and "temper" – characteristics that make it likely that she was the model for Margaret Mitchell's famous virago, Scarlett O'Hara. Whatever the case, she seemed no match for her husband, John Stephens, a native of King's County, Ireland, and, like his father-in-law, a man of learning and puritanical leanings. From this mismatch, however, came twelve children, one of whom was Mitchell's mother, Mae Belle Stephens.

Educated in the Quebec convent school which her mother had refused to attend, Mae Belle was known for her intelligence, even as a child. She was particularly attracted to the songs of the Irish balladeer Thomas Moore and shared with her classmates "the story of Robert Emmet, of Tara and the Bards." Thoroughly Irish in her identification, she delighted in the literature and history of "my Father's and my Grandfather's country – the country of a Burke, a Curran, and of an Emmet."

Beginning in 1926, when Margaret Mitchell started work on her novel about the antebellum and postbellum South, she did extensive research in the newspaper files of this library. For the next ten years she continued to add to the growing novel, working in her apartment on 10th and Peachtree streets and once using the manuscript to bolster a swaybacked coach. To her surprise the Macmillan Company purchased the publishing rights and began a massive effort to publicize the book.

Within the first year of its publication in 1936, the book sold a record 1.383 million copies and won the Pulitzer Prize for literature. Most reviewers lavished unqualified praise on Mitchell's work, and during the next quarter of a century the book sold more than 10 million copies, supplanting *Uncle Tom's Cabin* as the nation's best-selling novel. Yet some critics continued to complain that the book portrayed a romanticized view of plantation life, despite Mitchell's claim that she had attempted just the opposite.

§ Open Monday 9-6, Tuesday-Thursday 9-8, Friday and Saturday 10-5, Sunday 2-6. Phone: 404-730-1700.

¶ **Atlanta History Center,** 130 West Paces Ferry Road N.W.

Among its collections the center has works by the Irish-American authors Joel Chandler Harris, Sidney Lanier, Margaret Mitchell, Flannery O'Connor, and Mark Twain. Some of Mitchell's personal effects are also on display.

§ Open Monday-Saturday 10-5:30, Sunday and holidays noon-5:30. Closed January 1, Thanksgiving, and December 24-25. Fee. Phone: 404-814-4000.

¶ **Benjamin Hill Statue,** State Capitol, Washington Street, between Hunter and Mitchell streets.

Located in the north wing of the capitol, this large marble statue of Benjamin Hill honors a leading member of the Confederate Congress and an outspoken critic of the Reconstruction policies imposed on the South after the Civil War. The statue is the work of *Alexander Doyle.

According to a family tradition, Hill's paternal ancestors had come from Ireland. After graduating from the University of Georgia in 1843, Hill began a legal career which, in the eyes of his contemporaries, had no rival. When he was elected to the Georgia Assembly in 1851, he was a Whig dedicated to preserving the Union through the sectional compromises embodied in the omnibus bill passed by Congress the year before. As the sectional conflict over slavery reemerged in the Kansas-Nebraska debates, however, he abandoned the Whigs for the American or "Know Nothing" party. In the fateful presidential campaign of 1860, he opposed Lincoln and actually tried to unite the other three candidates against the "Black Republican." Although he fought against secession at the subsequent state convention, he accepted that body's decision and signed the secession ordinance.

As a member of the provisional congress that gathered in Montgomery, Alabama, Hill helped organize the fledgling Confederate government. Elected to the Confederate senate during the Civil War, he was a consistent champion of the policies of *President Jefferson Davis, defending conscription, in particular, as a necessary wartime measure. Toward the end of the war, he was arrested and detained for three months in Fort Lafayette, New York.

Once returned to his home in Georgia, Hill became a vigorous opponent of the Reconstruction Acts passed by the Republican Congress. In a series of speeches, he denounced the Radicals' attempt to punish the South and effectively extirpate its social, political, and economic systems. He gained national attention for his views with the publication of *Notes on the Situation* in 1867. In one of his addresses he accused the Radicals of using the postwar situation "to destroy the Constitution because they hated the Constitution." The result, Hill continued, was the "preservation of a *territorial* Union, but the utter destruction of a *Constitutional Union*. Consent was the beauty of the old Union; force is the power of the new."

By 1870, however, Hill was urging his fellow Georgians to accept the Reconstruction policies of abolition and black suffrage now that those changes had become part of the Constitution. For his "treachery" he was virtually ostracized by conservatives in the state until 1875, when he was elected to the House of Representatives despite strong opposition. There he resumed his former role as a champion of the South and a defender of the Confederacy against charges of inhumanity. He was also influential in persuading President Hayes to withdraw federal troops from the South in 1876. He was elected to the Senate the following year but died of tongue cancer in 1881. (See Lagrange, Georgia.)

§ Open Monday-Friday 8-5:30. Closed holidays. Phone: 404-656-2844

¶ Church of the Immaculate Conception, on the corner of Central Avenue and Hunter Street.

The first members of this congregation were Irish railroad builders. The present church was built in 1869 to replace a structure that was almost destroyed by General William Sherman's invading Union troops. In 1864, when a detachment of Sherman's Yankees was about to set fire to the original church, the parish priest, Father Thomas O'Reilly, confronted the troops and warned that no Catholic could remain in the regiment if the building was torched. Because most of the men in the detail were Catholics, the church was spared. O'Reilly laid the cornerstone of the present church and is buried under the main altar.

For many years on April 28, the church was the scene of funeral services for the members of the Irish Horse Traders and their families who had died since the previous spring. The first of these families had arrived in the United States in the 1850s and in time numbered eight: the Carrolls, Costellos, Dartys, Garmons, McNamaras, O'Haras, Rileys, and Sherlocks. Like some of the families, the O'Haras became itinerant traders, making Atlanta their home for a time and buying up property in the growing community. They seem to have settled here because the city was a good place to buy and sell horses and mules. But it was with the burial of John McNamara in Oakland Cemetery in 1881 that the traders established the tradition of bringing their dead to Atlanta each year.

Because of their itinerant nature, most of the Irish Horse Traders had no permanent address. The story is told of how the local draft board registered sixty-eight young men in a row, each indicating his address as 869 Peachtree Street in Atlanta. When draft officials inquired about the address, they discovered it was that of a local mortuary – where the bodies of clan members were shipped when they died and where they were stored until the mass funerals at Immaculate Conception Church. Traders tell the story of one of their own who, after losing his wife, sent the body to the Atlanta mortuary with a $2,000 check to cover the funeral arrangements. After he remarried several months later, his new wife died in a relatively short time. He dutifully dispatched her body to Atlanta with another $2,000 check for the funeral expenses. On April 28 that year the trader grieved for both wives at a single service.

• A marker outside the church summarizes its unique position in the history of Atlanta: "First Catholic Church in the Atlanta area and the oldest complete building standing in downtown Atlanta. The church was established in 1848. The first building, a frame structure, was erected here in 1851. Father Thomas O'Reilly, its pastor, successfully appealed to Union General H. W. Slocum in 1864 to spare his church and the neighborhood. Thus, the church, four other churches, and the City Hall-Court House were saved from destruction when Atlanta was burned. Cornerstone of this structure laid in 1869. Completed and dedicated in 1873. Designated a Shrine in 1954."

§ Open Saturday 8-3 and before and after mass. Guided tours by arrangement. Phone: 404-521-1866.

¶ Confederate Memorial Carving, Georgia's Stone Mountain Park, just east off Interstate 285 via U.S. 78.

Stone Mountain Park is a 3,200-acre recreational and historic area. Among its attractions is the Confederate Memorial Carving – three gigantic equestrian statues of *President Jefferson Davis, *General Thomas "Stonewall" Jackson, and General Robert E. Lee carved into the northern face of Stone Mountain. Although the entire sculpture occupies an area the size of a city block and each figure is equal in height to a nine-story building, the figures are dwarfed by the 583-acre mountain side. The world's largest sculpture was begun by Gutzon Borglum and took fifty-seven years to complete.

Among the park's many other attractions are the Civil War Museum, the Antique Auto and Music Museum, an antebellum plantation, the riverboat *Scarlet O'Hara*, a scenic railroad, a laser show, hiking trails, swimming, fishing, tennis courts, boat rentals, golf courses, ice-skating, picnicking, restaurants, and a campground. The film *Miracle of the Mountain* is presented during the summer.

§ Park open daily 6 a.m.-midnight. Fee. Phone: 404-498-5600.

¶ Henry Grady Monument, Marietta Street, near Forsyth Street.

This ten-foot-high statue honors *Henry Grady, who revitalized the *Atlanta Constitution* as its managing editor and used the paper to promote his concept of the "New South" after the Civil War. The statue depicts Grady in an oratorical pose, while female figures representing History and Memory are seated on either side of the pedestal, which is inscribed with selections from his speeches. The monument was designed by *Alexander Doyle and was dedicated in 1891.

Grady's first forays into journalism produced mixed results. While attending the University of Virginia soon after the war, he penned gossipy news items for the *Atlanta Constitution* under the *nom de plume* of King Hans (derived from the German for his own name and from his fiancée's last name). Later, when, as editor of the *Rome (Ga.) Courier*, he was forbidden by his publisher to attack local political corruption, he purchased the two other newspapers in town and combined them into a bully pulpit. Although this venture was a financial failure, he and two associates tried again with a publication of their own, the equally short-lived *Atlanta Herald*. After a stint with the *New York Herald* and with the help of a $20,000 personal loan, Grady bought a 25 percent interest in the *Constitution*.

As managing editor, Grady helped make the *Constitution* the most popular newspaper in the region and the vehicle for promoting his vision of the postbellum South. He urged Southerners to develop local resources, diversify their crops, and promote manufacturing. He realized, however, that the economic resurgence of the former Confederacy would be impossible without the help of Northern investors. In turn, financial backing would not be forthcoming until the South had achieved social stability by resolving the race issue. In this regard Grady believed that white Southerners would acquiesce to the political rights granted African Americans after the war in return for an acknowledgment of white supremacy and

*Statue of Henry Grady
by Alexander Doyle.*

the maintenance of segregation.

Grady preached his gospel not only on the editorial page but also in a series of speeches throughout the country. Before addressing the New England Society of New York in 1886, he betrayed his trepidation at speaking where no Southerner had ever appeared before: "I have thought of a thousand things to say, five hundred of which if I say they will murder me when I get back home, and the other five hundred of which will get me murdered at the banquet." In his actual address he lauded Lincoln as "the typical American" and jokingly pointed out that his fellow speaker, William T. Sherman, was "considered an able man in our parts, though some people think he is a kind of careless man about fire." The central message of the address, however, was that Southerners had accepted the results of the Civil War, bore no animosity toward the North, and were interested in economic development and racial and national harmony.

❡ Henry Grady's association with Atlanta is also commemorated in the Grady Memorial Hospital (80 Butler Street) and Grady Stadium (8th Street and Monroe Drive).

❡ **John C. Calhoun Plaque,** Trust Company of Georgia, 25 Park Place.

A bronze plaque outside the bank contains the words of a speech given in 1845 by *John C. Calhoun in which he prophesied the creation of an extensive railroad network in the South. (See Clemson, South Carolina.)

❡ **Margaret Mitchell Apartment,** 10th Street and Crescent Avenue.

This shell of a structure is currently undergoing reconstruction. The front portion of the building will be restored to its appearance in 1899 when it was a single family dwelling, while the back will be reconstructed to look like the apartment building in which *Margaret Mitchell lived during the 1920s when she started work on *Gone With the Wind*.

§ Phone: 404-249-1358.

❡ **Margaret Mitchell Square,** Peachtree and Forsyth streets.

The nearby Georgia-Pacific building occupies the site of Loew's Grand Theater, where *Gone With the Wind* made its film debut on December 15, 1939, after a three-day festival. In less than a year, 25 million people had seen the movie.

Despite its popularity, the motion picture only alluded to some details in the book. The heroine's full name, for instance, was Katherine Scarlett O'Hara, and her father – Gerald O'Hara – was a native of County Meath, Ireland. The book tells the story of his adventures in the New World, his marriage to a French Creole woman from New Orleans, and his eventual acquisition of a plantation, which he named Tara for the ancient seat of Ireland's high-kings. The film version does include an interesting scene in which Scarlett teases her father for talking like an Irishman when he speaks about his attachment to the land. He, in turn, reminds her of her Irish heritage and, like Steinbeck in *The Grapes of Wrath*, stresses man's bond to the soil.

Much has been made of the alleged similarities between the fictional Gerald O'Hara and the real-life Phillip Fitzgerald, Mitchell's maternal great-grandfather. While resemblances exist in the two men's Irish surnames as well as in their religion, economic status, and place of birth, their personal qualities are quite different. On the one hand, O'Hara is uncultured, barely literate, and unmindful of religion while Fitzgerald was a bibliophile, a member of the Irish gentry, and a Jansenist in his religious sensibilities.

¶ Oakland Cemetery, 248 Oakland Avenue.

• This is the final resting place of *Margaret Mitchell, who, despite the popularity of *Gone With the Wind*, did not continue her writing career and even destroyed an unpublished earlier work. Until her death in 1949, she spent much of her time answering her mail and doing charity work. She died five days after being struck by an automobile while helping her husband cross Peachtree Street.

• The cemetery is also noted for the unusually large and highly decorated monuments marking the graves of many Irish Horse Traders and the members of their families. (See Church of the Immaculate Conception above.)

¶ P. J. Kenny Statue, Kenny's Alley, Underground Atlanta.

This bronze statue of a mustachioed barkeep represents P. J. Kenny, the Irish owner of a saloon on what was formerly Alabama Street, the location of several public houses and livery stables in the late 1800s.

¶ Road to Tara Museum, The Georgian Terrace, 659 Peachtree Street, Suite 600.

As its name suggests, this museum contains one of the largest collections of *Gone With the Wind* memorabilia in the country. Among its attractions are a twenty-two-minute film on the life of *Margaret Mitchell, autographed and foreign editions of her famous novel, a hundred *Gone With the Wind* dolls, reproductions of costumes used in the famous film, and a gift shop.

§ Open Monday-Saturday 10-6, Sunday 1-6. Closed January 1, Thanksgiving, and December 25. Fee. Phone: 404-897-1939.

¶ Westview Cemetery, 1680 Westview Drive, S.W.

This beautifully landscaped cemetery contains the graves of *Henry Grady (Section 50) and *Joel Chandler Harris (Section 1).

¶ **The Wren's Nest,** off Interstate 20 west via exit 19 to 1050 Abernathy Boulevard, S.W.

For many years this was the home of Joel Chandler Harris, the author of the famous Uncle Remus stories, masterpieces of African-American humor and dialect. The Victorian house received its name from the wren which had built its nest in the author's mailbox and which he allowed to reside there to hatch its annual brood. The memorabilia in the house includes Harris's writing table, his favorite rocking chair, and his old-fashioned typewriter.

Harris was the son of Mary Harris, who gave birth to the child in 1848 after his Irish father had abandoned her. While listening to his mother read from *The Vicar of Wakefield*, the youngster developed a desire to follow a career in writing. At age fourteen he learned how to typeset for a newspaper published at "Turnwold," a nearby plantation. After he began to sneak short items of his own into the paper, the publisher offered to teach him how to write more formal prose. The boy's education was cut short, however, when General Sherman's invading army devastated the county.

After the war the aspiring journalist worked for several other newspapers, including the *Savannah Morning News*. One of the other employees there described Harris as "of small stature, red-haired, freckle-faced, and looked like a typical backwoodsman. . . . But that night when his copy came out, we knew he was a writer." When yellow fever threatened the

"The Wren's Nest," the home of Joel Chandler Harris.

city, however, Harris fled with his wife and two children. He was later hired by the *Atlanta Constitution* to write feature articles, political editorials, fiction, and book reviews. He was eventually asked by his editor to compose daily humorous sketches involving African-American characters. In meeting this challenge, Harris drew upon his experiences from "Turnwold" – observing the animals and listening to the black slaves tell stories in African dialects. The resulting sketches formed the basis for his first book, *Uncle Remus: His Songs and Sayings*, published in 1880 and turned many years later into the Disney motion picture *Song of the South*. Probably the most famous of the sequels in the Uncle Remus cycle were *The Tar Baby* (1904) and *Uncle Remus and Br'er Rabbit* (1906). During the last year of his life, he was the editor of the unsuccessful *Uncle Remus's Magazine*.

Despite almost three decades of literary celebrity, Harris was painfully shy. His voice frequently failed him when he was expected to speak to strangers, and on one occasion his retiring nature prevented him from reading aloud to a gathering of children. He was baptized into the Catholic Church only weeks before his death and was buried in Westview Cemetery in Atlanta.

§ Open Tuesday-Saturday 10-4, Sunday 1-4. Closed holidays. Fee. Phone: 404-753-7735.

AUGUSTA

¶ **Confederate Monument,** Broad Street, between 7th and 8th streets.

This seventy-eight-foot-high Italian marble shaft is surrounded by life-size figures of Confederate generals T. R. R. Cobb, *Thomas "Stonewall" Jackson, Robert E. Lee, and Leroy Walker.

¶ **Kennedy O'Brien Marker,** St. Paul's Church, 605 Reynolds Street.

This marker mentions that the site of Augusta was selected by the Irish fur trader Kennedy O'Brien as a trading post. O'Brien erected the first storehouse at his own expense and eventually became the most prominent of the pioneer settlers.

To protect Kennedy and the other colonists, General James Oglethorpe in 1735 built Fort Augusta on this site. (A Celtic cross to the exterior rear of the church marks the location.) Four years later Oglethorpe recognized O'Brien's contribution to the development of this area by recommending to the trustees of the Georgia colony that he be granted 500 acres of land. O'Brien's trading associates at Fort Augusta were most likely Irish also: William Callahan, Daniel Clarke, Patrick Clarke, Charles Dempsey, Michael Garvey, Peter McHugh, and Daniel McNeil.

¶ **Magnolia Cemetery,** 3rd Street.

Established about 1800, this cemetery counts many Irish settlers among the 35,000 people buried here. Both the Scotch-Irish (who came to Augusta at the turn of the nineteenth century) and the later "Famine Irish" are represented among the graveyard's "permanent residents."

¶ **Poets' Monument,** Greene Street, between 7th and 8th streets.
This granite shaft honors four Georgia poets: *Father Abram Ryan, *Sidney Lanier, Paul Hamilton Hayne, and James R. Randall.

¶ **Woodrow Wilson Boyhood Home,** 419 7th Street. Private.
This was the home of young *Woodrow Wilson from 1857 to 1870 while his father was the pastor of the First Presbyterian Church in Augusta.

BRUNSWICK

¶ **Lanier's Oak,** a mile north on U.S. 17.
According to tradition, it was under this tree overlooking the marshes that the poet *Sidney Lanier was inspired to write his most famous work, "The Marshes of Glynn." (See Macon, Georgia.)
¶ Lake Sidney Lanier in the northern part of the state honors the Georgia poet.

EATONTON

¶ **Br'er Rabbit Statue,** Courthouse Square, U.S. 441.
This unusual work of art recalls one of the most famous characters in the Uncle Remus stories of *Joel Chandler Harris.
• Just west of the square is the house in which Harris was probably born. The private structure at the corner of West Marion and West Lafayette streets is marked by a sign.

¶ **Uncle Remus Museum,** south on U.S. 441 in Turner Park.
This museum was made from two slave cabins that were part of the home of Joseph Sidney Turner, the "little boy" in the Uncle Remus stories by *Joel Chandler Harris. The museum is decorated to illustrate the way of life depicted in the famous author's animal stories. On display are first editions of Harris's works and paintings as well as woodcarvings of some of the characters in his stories (e.g., Br'er Bear, Br'er Fox, Br'er Rabbit, and Uncle Remus). (See the Wren's Nest, Atlanta, Georgia.)
The author's Uncle Remus character was based largely on Uncle George Terrel, an old African-American slave who told stories to the local children as he baked ginger cookies to sell in Eatonton on Saturdays. Other characters were based on borrowings from African Ashanti and Housa folklore. The wily rabbit of the Ashanti people, for instance, became the American Br'er (Brother) Rabbit, while the African leopard and zebra were

transformed into the American buzzard and woodpecker. And the powerful African sky god Nyame was personified in the plantation owner in Harris's stories.

§ Open May-September, Monday-Saturday 10-12 and 1-5, Sunday 2-5; rest of the year, same hours (except closed Tuesday). Fee. Phone: 706-485-6731.

FAYETTEVILLE

¶ **Margaret Mitchell Library,** 165 Johnson Avenue.

The library is named for *Margaret Mitchell, the author of *Gone With the Wind*. While doing research for her book, Mitchell met several women in this area who were involved with the construction of a library. When the building was dedicated in 1940, it was named for Mitchell, who by then had become even more famous with the debut of the film based on her novel. (See Atlanta-Fulton County Public Library, Atlanta, Georgia.)

§ Phone: 404-461-8841.

FITZGERALD

¶ **Blue and Gray Museum,** in the Municipal Building downtown.

Besides exhibits about the experiences of the Civil War soldier, this museum chronicles the town's founding in 1896 by a group of Union army veterans under the leadership of Philander Fitzgerald, an Indianapolis attorney and editor.

Fitzgerald, whose paternal ancestors had come from Ireland, was born in Greensburg, Indiana, in 1847. During the Civil War the youngster served in the Union army as a drummer. In 1864, however, he began the study of law, a pursuit that was followed by a clerkship in the U.S. Claim Agency. He eventually opened his own private practice, specializing in pension law and the prosecution of all manner of claims arising from the war. In this practice he gained national renown and sometimes required the services of thirty-five clerks to handle his correspondence. In 1887 he purchased the *Veteran's Review*, a publication dedicated to serving Northern veterans. After changing its name to the *American Tribune*, Fitzgerald was able to increase its circulation from 300 to 28,000 in only five years.

In the meantime Fitzgerald had conceived the idea of establishing a veterans' settlement somewhere in the South. In 1894, when a drought ravaged the Middle West, the governor of Georgia organized a relief effort to supply the area with flour, meat, and corn. This gesture of reconciliation to a former enemy so impressed the Union veterans that they decided to settle in the Peach State.

After forming a joint stock company known as the *American Tribune* Soldier Colony Company, the veterans bought 50,000 acres in Georgia and headed with their families for a site which Fitzgerald had in the meantime selected. Within sixty days of its founding, the population of the colony exploded from 100 to 4,000 and included both Northerners and Southerners. The conciliatory origins of the new town can be seen in its Lee-Grant Hotel and its Blue and Gray Park. In addition, the streets are named for Union and Confederate generals and battleships.

§ Open April-October, Monday-Friday 2-5. Closed holidays. Fee. Phone: 912-423-5375.

IRWINVILLE

¶ Jefferson Davis Memorial Park, 1 mile south on State 32.

This state park includes the site where *Jefferson Davis, the president of the Confederacy, was captured by Union troops on May 10, 1865. His capture by Michigan cavalrymen frustrated his plan to continue the war after Lee's surrender at Appomattox. On the grounds is the Davis Monument, a granite shaft topped by a bronze bust of the Confederate president and faced with a bas-relief panel depicting his capture.

Just before his capture the president had attended his last cabinet meeting in Washington, Georgia, and was on his way with his family to a Southern port. When the Union troops approached him, Davis covered himself with his wife's raincoat, in the dark thinking that it was his own. Mrs. Davis then covered his head and shoulders with her shawl. From here Davis was taken to Fortress Monroe, Virginia.

JEFFERSON

¶ Crawford Long Medical Museum, 28 College Street in the public square.

This museum honors Crawford Long, a doctor of Scotch-Irish background who in 1842 performed painless surgery using sulfuric ether as an anesthetic. The museum, located on the site of Long's office, features exhibits about the history of anesthetics and includes an apothecary shop, a doctor's office, and a general store. The museum also displays a diorama illustrating Long's first anesthetic operation. Crawford Long Day is held the first Saturday in November.

Long, whose Presbyterian grandfather had emigrated from Ulster about 1761, received a medical degree from the University of Pennsylvania. After achieving a reputation as a skilled surgeon in New York, he returned to his rural roots in Georgia. Once, when some of his young friends wanted him to host a "nitrous oxide frolic" – at which they hoped to become lightheaded from the laughing gas – he substituted sulfuric ether. Since this gas was equally effective when inhaled, his guests experienced the desired state of hilarity, but many of them were bruised during their rambunctious "frolic." When Long noticed that these bruises were unaccompanied by pain, he concluded that sulfuric ether was an anesthetic. In eight subsequent operations – including the removal of three tumors and the amputation of two digits – he showed that patients to whom the ether had been administered felt no pain during the procedures.

§ Open Tuesday-Saturday 10-1 and 2-5, Sunday 2-5. Closed major holidays. Phone: 706-367-5307.

LAGRANGE

¶ **Bellevue,** 204 Ben Hill Street.

Built in the early 1850s, this Greek Revival mansion was the home of *Senator Benjamin Hill, a member of the Confederate Congress and a spokesman for the rights of the defeated South during the Reconstruction period. The house is notable because of its Ionic columns, porticoes, and ceiling medallions. (See Benjamin Hill Statue, Atlanta, Georgia.)

§ Open Tuesday-Saturday 10-noon and 2-5. Closed January 1, July 4, Thanksgiving, and December 25-26. Fee. Phone: 706-884-1832.

MACON

¶ **Sidney Lanier Cottage,** 935 High Street.

This Gothic Revival house was the birthplace in 1842 of the poet Sidney Lanier, best known in Georgia for his series of verses about the marshes in the state, most notably "The Marshes of Glynn."

Lanier, whose mother was of Scotch-Irish descent, dreamed of pursuing music and studying at a German university, but such plans were derailed by the onset of the Civil War. In his exuberance for the Southern cause, he believed that the Confederacy was on the brink of a prosperity unknown to any other nation. While serving in the war as a scout, he considered pursuing a literary career, but the catastrophe wrought by the war, his own worsening health, and the need to provide for a wife and children prevented him from becoming a first-rate literary figure.

Lanier summarized the eight years of his life after the war as "merely not dying." He once described his artistic frustration to a friend: "My head and my heart are so full of poems which the dreadful struggle for bread does not give me time to put on paper, that I am often driven to headache and heartache purely for want of an hour or two to hold a pen." In 1879, however, he was named professor of English literature at Johns Hopkins University. Over the next twenty years, in addition to poetry he wrote a series of boys' adventure books as well as works on English verse, the English novel, and music and poetry.

§ Open Monday-Saturday. Closed holidays. Phone: 912-743-3851.

❡ Lanier's memory is also recalled in Macon by a park and a high school named in his honor. The Washington Memorial Library, on Washington Avenue at College Street, has a first edition of Lanier's poems, one of his flutes, and a marble bust of the poet by Gutzon Borglum.

MILLEDGEVILLE

❡ **Flannery O'Connor Room,** Dillard Russell Library, Georgia College.
The library contains manuscripts, letters, first editions, and other memorabilia of author Flannery O'Connor, perhaps the greatest twentieth-century American Catholic writer of fiction and the first woman to be included in the prestigious Library of America series.

Unlike her contemporary Margaret Mitchell, O'Connor inherited Irish ancestry from both sides of her family. Her mother, Regina Cline, was descended from Patrick Harty, a native of County Tipperary who had settled in Taliafero County, Georgia, in 1824. The Tipperary connection was strengthened when one of Harty's granddaughters married Peter James Cline, the son of an Irish school teacher from Roscommon. Although the younger Cline attended St. Vincent's College in Pennsylvania, during the Civil War he returned to his home in the South, where he managed to eke out an existence as a crockery salesman and a railway brakeman. For antagonizing federal authorities in Nashville, however, he spent five weeks in jail. He later formed a partnership to sell broadcloth and silks from a wagon (his "traveling store") before eventually settling in Milledgeville.

On her paternal side Flannery O'Connor was descended from Patrick O'Connor, an Irishman who had operated a carriage and wagon manufacturing business in Savannah, where the future author was born. It was one of his grandsons – Edward O'Connor Jr. – who married Flannery's mother. During World War I, Edward served in France as a lieutenant with the American Expeditionary Force. He later became extremely active in the American Legion and at one time was elected statewide commander of the organization.

Few people are aware that Flannery O'Connor's first name was actually "Mary." She dropped this name, however, in favor of "Flannery," an allusion to one of her other Irish ancestors. At the age of sixteen John Flannery had emigrated from Ireland and landed in Charleston, South Carolina, in 1851. After working as a bookkeeper in Savannah, when the Civil War broke out he enlisted in the Irish Jasper Greens and advanced to the rank of captain. Following the war, he returned to Savannah and founded the Southern Bank of Georgia and began to engage in the cotton trade. Besides serving as president of the John Flannery Company, he was a director of the Savannah Cotton Exchange and a generous contributor to the construction of St. John the Baptist Cathedral in Savannah. Flannery was also a member of the Jasper Memorial Association, the Hibernian Society, and the Irish-American Historical Society. In 1867 he married a granddaughter of Patrick Harty, Flannery's O'Connor's first Irish ancestor in America.

Even as a youngster Flannery O'Connor was intent upon a writing career, although she early knew the sting of disappointment. In her high school yearbook, for instance, she described her hobby as "collecting rejection slips." It was not until she attended Georgia State College for Women (now Georgia College) in Milledgeville that several of her stories attracted serious attention. As a result, she received a fellowship from the University of Iowa and completed a master's degree in literature there in 1947. Her literary fame grew with the publication of two novels and additional short stories. The latter were collected in *A Good Man Is Hard To Find*, *Everything That Rises Must Converge*, and *The Complete Stories*.

Despite O'Connor's Catholicism, few of her characters are Catholic but, instead, reflect the Protestant fundamentalism of the South. According to Caroline Gordon, O'Connor's characters are "lost in that abyss which opens for man when he sets up as God," a description which echoes the author's claim that she was indebted to Nathaniel Hawthorne, though "with less reliance on allegory." About her identity as a Catholic author, O'Connor wrote: "When people have told me that because I am a Catholic, I cannot be an artist, I have had to reply, ruefully, that because I am a Catholic I cannot afford to be less than an artist." She was equally paradoxical in describing her role as a Southern regionalist: "To know oneself is to know one's region. It is also to know the world, and it is also, paradoxically, a form of exile from that world."

In 1950 O'Connor began to show the effects of disseminated lupus. This condition caused her to move with her mother to "Andalusia," the family farm outside Milledgeville, where she resided almost continuously until her death in 1964.

§ Open by request Monday-Friday 8-5. Phone: 912-453-5573.

¶ Andalusia Farm, 5 miles north on U.S. 441.

In 1951 the author Flannery O'Connor and her mother moved to this 500-acre former plantation which the older woman had inherited. Here the pair adhered to the advice which Flannery proposed to her mother: "You run the farm, and I'll do the writing." It was while living here that Flannery completed all of her published fiction. She also occupied herself with painting and raising swans, peacocks, and geese.

¶ O'Connor House, 305 West Green Street. Private.

Once the state executive mansion, this 1820 white frame house was the home of Regina O'Connor, the mother of the author Flannery O'Connor. Following the death of the author's father (Edward Francis O'Connor Jr.)

in 1950, mother and daughter lived in this house for a year before moving to Andalusia Farm.

ROSWELL

¶ **Bulloch Hall,** State 400 exit 4, 1 mile west to Alpharetta Street and then 2 miles south to 180 Bulloch Avenue.

This 1840 Greek Revival mansion was the childhood home of Martha Bulloch and the site of her marriage in 1853 to Theodore Roosevelt Sr. Their son – the future president of the United States – was born in New York City. In 1905 President Roosevelt addressed a crowd of townspeople in Roswell when he visited his mother's childhood home.

The president's mother was descended from John Dunwoody, who had emigrated from Londonderry, northern Ireland, in 1730. After first settling in Chester County, Pennsylvania, Dunwoody moved with his family to Georgia.

§ Open Monday-Friday 10-3. Closed holidays. Fee. Phone: 404-992-1731.

ST. SIMONS ISLAND

¶ **Hampton Plantation,** on the northern tip of the island, north on Couper Road (which turns into Hampton Point Drive).

Although little now remains of the estate formerly owned in the nineteenth century by Major Pierce Butler, one of the larger structures on the plantation is visible along Hampton Point Drive. Other structures – including the ruins of a tabby cotton barn and some cabins – are scattered throughout the property of a nearby gated residential community known, appropriately, as Butler's Plantation.

The estate was originally one of two plantations in Georgia owned by Major Pierce Butler, an Irish-born member of the Continental Congress and of the Constitutional Convention and one of South Carolina's first U.S. senators. Born in County Carlow, Ireland, in 1744, Butler was the third son of Sir Richard Butler, an Irish baronet.

Denied the family title and fortune by the law of primogeniture, the younger man followed a military career and was a major in His Majesty's 29th Regiment when he first visited South Carolina. During his stay in that southern colony, he married Mary Middleton, the daughter of a wealthy planter whose luxurious plantation house still stands outside Charleston. Just before the Revolution the Irishman sold his commission and used the proceeds to purchase what became known as Hampton Plantation, a potentially valuable piece of land on St. Simons Island at the mouth of the Altamaha River.

While a delegate to the Constitutional Convention, Butler was a champion of a strong central government, although he defended the rights of the South with regard to slavery and was the author of the fugitive slave clause in the Constitution. He also insisted that black slaves should be included equally with whites in determining a state's population for purposes of representation "in a Government which was instituted principally for the protection of property."

From 1795 to 1815, Butler spent each winter on Hampton Plantation. Because of its 700 slaves, the property was self-sustaining, producing not only rice, cotton, and sugar but also clothing and leather. In 1804 it was host to Aaron Burr, who had fled south after his duel with Alexander Hamilton in New Jersey. After amassing a fortune, Butler moved to Philadelphia, where he erected a large Georgian townhouse. He is buried in Christ Church cemetery in that city.

Hampton Plantation eventually passed into the hands of Butler's grandson, Pierce Butler Mease, who also inherited a fortune of $700,000. The younger Butler, whom one biographer called a "wastrel," dropped his last name, presumably out of a desire to be identified with his famous ancestor. Whatever the case, when he and his wife, the English actress Frances (Fanny) Kemble, visited the plantation for the first time in 1839, they found the mansion house in shambles and the infirmary "a wretched abode of wretchedness." It was during the subsequent year that Fanny kept a diary about life on Hampton Plantation and Butler Island – *Journal of a Residence on a Georgian Plantation*.

To the great annoyance of her husband, Mrs. Butler propounded "radical" ideas about marriage and slavery. "She held that marriage should be companionship on equal terms," he once complained. In addition, she excoriated slavery both to him and to the pages of her journal. She detested the use of the lash on her husband's slaves and protested the plight of the female Negroes, especially their return to work immediately after childbirth and the high mortality rate among their children. This issue became such a contentious one between Fanny and her husband that he finally forbade her to intercede on the slaves' behalf. "Why do you listen to such stuff?" he asked her. "Why do you believe such trash? Don't you know that niggers are all damned liars?" (Seven years earlier Butler had been instrumental in persuading the Pennsylvania legislature to disenfranchise free blacks in that state.) The stormy marriage finally ended in divorce.

In her journal Mrs. Butler also expressed some insightful comments about the Irish, especially in comparison to African-American slaves. "It strikes me with amazement," she wrote, "to hear the hopeless doom of incapacity for progress pronounced upon these wretched [black] slaves, when in my own country [England] the very same order of language is perpetually applied to these very Irish, here spoken of as a sort of race of demigods by Negro comparison. And it is most true that in Ireland nothing can be more savage, brutish, filthy, idle, and incorrigibly and hopelessly helpless and incapable than the Irish appear; and yet, transplanted to your Northern states, freed from the evil influences which surround them at home, they and their children become industrious, thrifty, willing to learn, able to improve, and forming, in the course of two generations, a most valuable accession to your laboring population. How is it that it never occurs to these emphatical denouncers of the whole Negro race that the Irish at home are esteemed much as they esteem their slaves . . . ."

Many years later, when Pierce Butler had followed his grandfather into the U.S. Senate, he figured in one of the most notorious events in the history of that body. In 1855, as sectional differences over slavery were reaching an explosive level, Senator Charles Sumner, the leader of the New England abolitionists, attacked Butler in a speech on the floor. After referring to the "harlot Slavery" as Butler's mistress, Sumner went on to declare it the duty of decent men "to dislodge from the high places that tyrannical sectionalism of which the senator from South Carolina is one of the maddest zealots." Preston Brooks, a congressman from South Carolina and an admirer of Butler, decided to punish Sumner for his remarks. A few days later he entered the Senate, approached Sumner at his desk, and denounced the speech as a "libel on South Carolina and Mr. Butler." Preston then proceeded to strike the older man over the head with his cane until it broke and Sumner fell to the floor, bleeding and unconscious.

Five years later, soon after the election of Lincoln, Butler returned to Philadelphia, "eager for secession." According to the diarist Sidney George Fisher, the South Carolinian had arrived "only to buy arms and intends to return immediately and join the army. He will take his daughter Fanny with him and has bought a rifle for her, too, for he says even the women in the South are going to fight."

❡ A historical marker on U.S. 17/State 25 south of nearby Darien indicates the site of Pierce Butler's other Georgia plantation, this one on Butler's Island.

SAVANNAH

❡ **Celtic Cross,** Emmet Park, East Bay Street.

This cross honors Savannah's inhabitants of Irish descent. For more than 165 years, the city has been hosting a St. Patrick's Day Parade. Of the 125 such parades in the United States, Savannah's parade is the largest after New York City's.

❡ **Flannery O'Connor Home,** 207 East Charlton Street on Lafayette Square.

This three-story house where the famous author lived as a youngster is now a literary and educational center, offering films, readings, and seminars devoted to O'Connor and other Southern authors.

¶ William Jasper Statue, Madison Square, Bull and Harris streets.

In the square is a bronze statue of William Jasper, clutching in his hands the regimental colors which he risked his life to save during an engagement with British troops in Charleston.

Jasper, whose exploits with the 2nd South Carolina Regiment ranked among the most heroic of the Revolution, was born in South Carolina about 1750 to Irish parents. During the British attack on Fort Sullivan in Charleston in June 1776, he showed his bravery in a dramatic way by endangering his life to save the patriot flag. For this exemplary act he was awarded the sword of *Governor Edward Rutledge. On another occasion he and a comrade overpowered five British guards in order to release a number of prisoners, and he later spent eight days in the enemy camp as a spy.

During the assault on the British lines around Savannah in October 1779, Jasper was mortally wounded while trying to fasten the regimental colors to a parapet on the Spring Hill redoubt. Due to his efforts the banner was prevented from falling into the enemy's hands. As he lay dying, he pointed to his honorary sword and said: "Give it to my father and tell him I have worn it with honor. If he should weep say to him that his son died in the hope of a better life. Tell Mrs. Elliott that I lost my life supporting the colors which she presented to our regiment."

Statue of William Jasper in Madison Square.

The monument in Madison Square honors Jasper for this last act of daring and is inscribed as follows: "To the Heroic Memory of Sergeant William Jasper Who Though Mortally Wounded Rescued the Colors of his Regiment in the Assault on the British Lines about this City October 9th 1779. A Century Has not Denied the Glory of the Irish American Soldier Whose Last Tribute to Civil Liberty Was His Noble Life 1779-1879."

When the cornerstone of this monument was laid in 1879, Governor John Gordon eulogized Jasper and his Irish compatriots: ". . . I invite the Irish-Americans and the patriots of Ireland everywhere to regard the column which shall be erected to Jasper as a monument also to the spirit of resistance to tyrants, which though baffled in Ireland and victorious in America, is still older and as abiding in Ireland as in American hearts. Ireland and Irishmen in every quarter of the globe . . . will rise up with one accord to do honor to the principles of freedom for which . . . Jasper fell and for which this monument is to be dedicated. . . . What does America not owe Ireland for the monuments of Irish industry and for Irish contributions to bar and bench and battlefield; for Jasper and Montgomery, martyrs to American independence; for Shields and the Irish-born soldiers who in every war followed the flag of this Republic? What does the South not owe to Ireland for enriching her soil with the blood of Cleburne, and her literature with the genius of Ryan, that gifted Irishman who is at once the thunderbolt of oratory and rainbow of poesy. . . .?"

SEA ISLAND

¶ Eugene O'Neill House. Private.

Known as Casa Genotta, this beach cottage on this resort island off the coast was built by the playwright Eugene O'Neill with money he had earned from his successful drama *Mourning Becomes Electra*. While living here with his wife, Carlotta, from 1931 to 1936, O'Neill rarely went into town, preferring instead to spend most of his time writing, occasionally for twenty-four hours at a time. Here he wrote much of *Days Without End* and his only comedy, *Ah, Wilderness!* He also outlined a cycle of eleven projected plays, finishing the first draft of *A Touch of the Poet* and creating dialogue for *More Stately Mansions*, although these two works were not completed until 1958 and 1964, respectively.

TOCCOA

¶ Traveler's Rest State Historic Site, 6 miles east off U.S. 123 on Riverdale Road.

Originally built in 1815, this plantation house was purchased in 1833 by Devereaux Jarrett IV as a home for his family. He later enlarged it to its present 6,000 square feet and operated it as a post office and a stagecoach inn. In addition to the main building, the property today includes two original structures (the dairy house and the slave cabin) and two reproductions (the wellhouse and the meathouse).

Jarrett, whose great-great-grandmother was "a lady from Ireland" and whose mother (Dorothy Mallory) was most likely Irish, had grown up in South Carolina. After coming to this part of Georgia in the early 1800s, he accumulated thousands of acres of farm land and became known as the richest man in the Tugaloo Valley. His many enterprises included a country store, a blacksmith shop, a cotton gin, a ferry, a grist mill, a saw mill, and a tanyard.

In 1836 an Englishman who stopped at Jarrett's Inn recorded his impressions: "I got an excellent breakfast of coffee, ham, chicken, good bread and butter, honey and plenty of good new milk for a quarter of a dollar. The landlord cultivated an extensive farm . . . and was a quiet, intelligent, well-behaved man, a great admirer of Mr. C. [John C. Calhoun], and seemed anxious to do what was obliging and proper, more from good feeling than for the poor return he chose to take for his good fare. What charming country this would be to travel in, if one was sure of meeting with such nice clean quarters once a day."

When Jarrett died in 1852, his four children inherited his 14,000 acres of land and ninety-seven slaves. Traveler's Rest passed to his youngest son, Charles Kennedy Jarrett, who maintained it as an inn and a residence until he died in 1877. It remained in the family until 1955.

§ Open Tuesday-Saturday 9-5, Sunday 2-5. Closed January 1, Thanksgiving, and December 25. Fee. Phone: 706-886-2256.

IDAHO

BOISE

¶ **O'Farrell Cabin,** 4th and Fort streets.

This one-room cabin was built by John O'Farrell in 1863 for his seventeen-year-old bride, like him a native of Ireland. The wooden house was the site of Boise's first Catholic mass and its first school.

O'Farrell was born in County Tyrone in 1823, the son of a military engineer who had served in the British army and had fought at the battle of Waterloo. At the age of fifteen, the youngster went to sea for the first time, beginning a naval and merchant marine career that spanned twenty years before he settled permanently in the American West. During early steamship voyages to Calcutta, St. Helena, and Australia before he was twenty, O'Farrell became a master ship-smith and later plied that trade in the Philadelphia navy yards.

At the outbreak of the Mexican War, O'Farrell took passage on the *Lexington* bound for Monterey, Alta California, a journey that took 198 days around the Horn. While in California, the Irishman spent some time in the Mexican settlement of Yerba Buena – the future San Francisco – where he met James Marshall and John Sutter, the principal celebrities in the Gold Rush which was the sweeping the territory. (Marshall, still fresh from his golden discovery at Sutter's Mill, presented the twenty-four-year-

The O'Farrell Cabin. (Photo courtesy of the Idaho State Historical Society.)

old Irishman with three grains of gold dust.) Himself struck with the "Gold Fever," O'Farrell found work in the mines, earning $40 to $50 a day.

Beginning in the winter of 1850, however, while snow made mining impossible, O'Farrell again followed the lure of the sea. At first he shipped on coal steamers that sailed between New Zealand, Australia, and San Francisco, but by 1853 he was in England, aboard a man-of-war bound for service in the Crimea. During the Anglo-French attack upon Sebastopol, he was wounded and was cited for his valiant conduct.

With a speed that seems incredible for the age of steam, the Irish adventurer had returned to the American West by 1857. After a brief stay in the California gold fields, he organized a prospecting expedition to Pike's Peak in what is now Colorado. (His discovery of the precious metal was among the first in that future state.) After further peregrinations that took him to mining camps in Oregon, Washington, Idaho, Montana, Wyoming, Utah, Nevada, New Mexico, and Arizona, he arrived at the site of modern-day Boise. This time, however, he was at the head of a train of fourteen wagons that carried his new wife – Mary Chapman – and her mother and brothers.

Many years later Theresa O'Farrell, one of the couple's seven children, left an account of an incident prompted by a premonition which her mother experienced. "One beautiful summer afternoon," she wrote, "my mother was standing outside of our log cabin, which had just been completed, when two travel-stained horsemen rode past. . . . [M]y mother called to my father, who was nearby, to go after and bring them back, for she was confident they were priests. My father thought she was mistaken, as there was nothing in their garb to bespeak their clerical calling, as they were dust covered and dressed in the rough style of the pioneer. . . . By that time, the two horsemen were far on their way, and my father went after them on horseback, and as he approached, he called 'Father,' and they both stopped and he found to his great delight and surprise that they were two young French missionaries . . . on their way to Oregon . . . [T]his small incident, however, changed their plans, and they returned with my father, and the new log cabin was quickly converted into a chapel, and for many years served as such." As the number of Catholics in Boise increased, the O'Farrells donated a piece of property for the construction of a more suitable church.

MOSCOW

¶ **Latah County Historical Society,** 110 South Adams Street.

Now the headquarters of the local historical society, this Gothic Revival mansion was built in 1886 as the home of William McConnell, Idaho's first U.S. senator and third governor.

McConnell was born in Michigan in 1839, the son of emigrants from northern Ireland. At about the age of twenty, he moved to California, where he tried his hand at mining and teaching school. After the discovery of gold in Boise in 1862, however, he walked to Idaho and took up farming, perhaps to supply the large number of adventurers attracted to the mines. Sometime after the Civil War, he was again on the West Coast, for a time in the cattle-raising business in California and then as a member of the Oregon state senate. By 1874, however, he had returned to Idaho, this time to follow a career as a merchant in Moscow. Fourteen years later he was the area's largest grain dealer.

McConnell subsequently became one of Idaho's most prominent political figures. He was involved in efforts to gain statehood for Idaho and was an effective member of its constitutional convention. Although elected one of the new state's first U.S. senators, he served only three months (having been elected in an off year and having drawn the short term). He later completed two terms as governor (1893-1897). A Republican, he generally disagreed with the Democratic-Progressive legislature, although he did support and sign its bill to recognize the right of workers to unionize. He and the legislature also cooperated to create two teachers' colleges, to accept a million acres from the federal government, and to allow female suffrage. After retiring from the chief executive's office, he served as Indian Inspector from 1897 to 1901.

One of the colorful figures whom McConnell mentioned in his history of Idaho was John Kelly, a renowned fiddler at a gambling house saloon in Idaho City. Because he was in such high demand, the Irish musician successfully negotiated a contract that allowed him to perform from a swinging platform suspended from the ceiling. Since tempers often flared among the disgruntled gamblers, Kelly wanted to be literally above the fray – and the flying bullets. Yet, when such a disturbance broke out, Kelly invariably rose to his feet as he placed the fiddle behind his back, thereby exposing himself to the danger below. In McConnell's view, it was as if Kelly preferred that a "stray bullet should find lodgment in his body rather than in his violin."

Despite the fiddler's unusual priority, McConnell spared no praise for the musician. "As an artist with the bow he had no equal in that way," the former governor wrote. "[H]e could make his pet instrument tell a plaintive tale of home and mother, or of tearful ones who awaited, oft in vain, the return of father, brother or lover; . . . He was a big hearted son of the Emerald Isle and although untoward circumstances had made him the leading attraction of a den of iniquity, he loved best to play those tender chords that awakened the memories of other days. . . ."

It was this same John Kelly who adopted a six-year-old Piute Indian who had survived a reprisal attack by white settlers in early 1863. Besides dressing the child in a down-sized version of a Confederate uniform, the musician taught the boy how to be a contortionist. Always his adoptive father's constant companion, the boy even appeared at Kelly's barroom recitals and occasionally exhibited his contortionist skills. As the years passed, the boy also became an accomplished violinist, at eighteen already the equal of his father. While the pair were on a visit to Ireland, however, the boy contracted a congestive chill and died. McConnell described the older man's response to the tragedy: "Kelly had no children of his own, and while he related to the writer the story of the boy's life and death, his furrowed face was deluged with tears."

§ Open Tuesday-Saturday 1-4. Closed holidays. Donations. Phone: 208-882-1004.

PRESTON

¶ **Bear River Battleground Monument,** 3 miles northwest on the east side of U.S. 91.

This monument marks the site of the most devastating defeat ever experienced by Native Americans in North America – the battle of Bear River on January 29, 1863.

The prelude to the battle was the effort of local Indians to stop further encroachment by white settlers. Even the local Indian agent attributed the Indians' grievances to the scarcity of game and the loss of fertile land, both caused by the tribes' imminent dispossession. "It is not to be expected that wild and warlike people will tamely submit to the occupation of their country by another race," the agent reported, "and to starve as a consequence thereof." Nevertheless, after the Indians had ambushed several wagon trains, Irish-born Colonel Patrick Edward Connor and the California Volunteer 3rd Infantry moved into Shoshoni territory, indiscriminately killing unarmed Indians en route. The Shoshoni responded with an ultimatum of death to any whites who crossed Bear River.

When the Indians kept their word by killing a number of white miners as they tried to ford the river, Connor prepared for a final showdown. Despite the freezing weather and deep snow, the American officer left Salt Lake City at the head of approximately 200 men, marching them a distance of 120 miles in just six days. (Seventy soldiers were disabled by frozen feet.) After arriving at the Indian encampment in a gorge at the mouth of the river, the soldiers were met by volleyfire and immediately lost fourteen of their own. As the battle developed, however, the Americans outflanked their opponents and virtually annihilated them with their gunfire.

In his report about the episode, Connor summarized his role in the massacre: "I ordered the flanking party to advance down the ravine upon either side, which gave us the advantage of an enfilading fire and caused some of the Indians to give way and run toward the north end of the ravine. At this point I had a company stationed who shot then as they ran out. . . . Few tried to escape, however, but continued fighting with un-yielding obstinacy. . . . The most of those who did escape from the ravine were afterwards shot in attempting to swim the river." After four hours Connor's unit suffered fourteen killed and forty-nine wounded. A local white settler was critical of Connor's tactics: "Instead of offering the Indi-ans a chance to surrender, and be taken peaceably, General Connor issued a very cruel order to his men – 'Take no prisoners, fight to the death; nits breed lice.'"

The next day civilian visitors to the battlefield counted 364 Shosoni dead on the ground and in the river. Two-thirds of the dead on the battle-field were women and children stacked eight deep, so that "You could walk on dead Indians or quite a distance without touching ground." Many of the Mormons in the area saw the Indians' defeat as "intervention of the Almighty," and Connor himself was promoted to brigadier general within a few months. (See Colonel Connor Statue, Salt Lake City, Utah.)

IOWA

CEDAR RAPIDS

¶ **St. Paul's United Methodist Church,** 1340 3rd Avenue Southeast.

The Chicago architect *Louis Sullivan was commissioned to design this landmark church in 1910, although his plans to include a semicircular front and a tower to the rear made construction too expensive. The church was later completed by one of Sullivan's former designers as closely to the original plans as possible.

Sullivan was born in Boston, the son of an Irishman who had promoted himself from a wandering minstrel to the owner of a dancing academy in London and who had prospered in the same line of work after arriving in Boston in 1847. Determined upon a career as an architect, the younger Sullivan entered the Massachusetts Institute of Technology, but his study of architecture produced in him a distaste for the classical and a preference for the Romanesque revival in vogue in Boston at the time. After leaving M.I.T., he worked briefly in architectural firms in Philadelphia and Chicago before sailing for Paris with hopes of matriculating at the Ecole des Beaux Arts. For six weeks he studied eighteen hours a day in preparation for the entrance test. After less than a year at the Beaux Arts, however, he returned to Chicago, still without having discovered the underlying architectural law which he sought.

In 1881 he became the second half of Adler and Sullivan, a new architectural firm which soon became the second most sought after practice in Chicago. As his clientele grew, Sullivan became increasingly absorbed with answering the major question facing designers of large buildings: how to provide increased light for such structures and how to raise them to greater heights. Sullivan found his answer in what was called the Chicago School of Architecture, a movement which pioneered the use of iron and steel skeleton frames. Particularly through the Wainwright Building in St. Louis and the Gage Building in Chicago, he illustrated his discovery of the architectural principle which he had so long sought: "Form follows function." Convinced that such a modern form as the skyscraper required a new method of expression, he incessantly pointed out the incongruity of clothing such a structure in the classical accoutrements of the past. More than any other man he helped make the skyscraper America's most significant architectural contribution.

CLINTON

¶ **Van Allen and Company Department Store,** 200 5th Avenue South, at 2nd Street (U.S. 67).

This four-story brick building is the last multistory steel-frame structure designed by *Louis Sullivan, whose work set the standard for American skyscrapers. The building was completed in 1914 and bears Sullivan's famous terra-cotta decoration. The structure, which is now a museum, exhibits 100 photographs of works which Sullivan designed.

§ Open Wednesday-Sunday noon-4. Closed holidays. Phone: 319-242-2000.

DENISON

¶ **McHenry House,** 1428 1st Avenue North.

Built in 1885, this Queen Anne mansion was the home of the jurist William Harrison McHenry Jr. The house is noted for its interior woodwork.

McHenry was a direct descendant of James McHenry, a native of Ballymena, Ireland, and secretary of war under George Washington and John Adams. The nineteenth-century McHenry attended Iowa College of Law, helping defray expenses by conducting a local orchestra. During his subsequent private practice, he served on the faculty of his alma mater and later was elected to a state district court. After retiring from the bench, he represented various corporate interests, most notably the Des Moines City Railway Company.

§ Phone: 712-263-2693.

DES MOINES

¶ **Allison Memorial,** east of the Soldiers' and Sailors' Monument on East Walnut Street.

Erected in 1913, this eight-foot symbolic marble figure of the Republic honors William Allison, who served in the U.S. Senate from 1873 until his death in 1908. Six bronze figures surround the pedestal.

Born in 1829 to descendants of Scotch-Irish immigrants to Pennsylvania, Allison was admitted to the bar at the age of twenty and promptly took *Horace Greeley's advice to go west. He eventually gravitated to Dubuque, Iowa, where he joined a law firm and succumbed to the seduction of politics. As a Republican in a Democratic stronghold, he was like a fish swimming against the tide, but the circumstances of a newly created district contributed to his election to Congress in 1862. There he supported the Republicans' agenda, whether it was Lincoln's amendment to abolish slavery or the impeachment of the new president and the Radicals' reconstruction plan. During his subsequent thirty-five years in the Senate, Allison became – as Senator Aldrich observed – "a master of the arts of conciliation" on such issues as the tariff and the currency. For most of his Senate career he served on both the appropriations and finance committees, on the former as chairman.

¶ **Flynn Farm Mansion and Barn,** 2600 11th Street. Private.

This High Victorian and Italianate residence was built in 1867 by Martin Flynn, an agricultural and business leader in the state from 1870 to 1906.

At the age of eleven, Flynn had accompanied his two older brothers to New York City, where they arrived in 1851 from their native County Waterford, Ireland. After moving on to Westmoreland County, Pennsylvania, the three found employment with the Pennsylvania Railroad: Tom as a construction foreman, John as a laborer under him, and Martin as a water boy. Five years later the boys' parents arrived in America and settled in Dubuque.

Having learned the rudiments of railroad construction while working for the Pennsylvania line, Flynn decided to become a railroad contractor. After completing the Dubuque & Southwestern Railroad, he was awarded a contract to do preliminary construction work for the Union Pacific Railroad. (For four months he had the sole responsibility for the project until Indians drove his crew from the right of way.) During the 1860s and 1870s, he constructed the Northwestern Railway, the Cincinnati & South Railroad, the Eastern Tennessee Railroad, forty miles of the Wisconsin Central, and two lines for the Rock Island Railroad. Building the Ratou tunnel in New Mexico for the Atchison, Topeka & Santa Fe was his most difficult undertaking.

In the meantime Flynn had become involved in several other business and commercial enterprises. After purchasing 640 acres outside of Des Moines, he introduced the first Shorthorn cattle in the state. His later real estate investments brought his holdings to 1,700 acres. Besides building the Flynn Block at the corner of 7th and Locust streets in Des Moines, he helped organize the People's Savings Bank (Des Moines), the Des Moines Brick Manufacturing Company, and the Flynn Sheep Company (Douglas, Wyoming).

DUBUQUE

¶ **Kelly's Bluff,** at the south end of Cardiff Street.

This section along the river was named in honor of Thomas Kelly, a reclusive eccentric who settled in Dubuque in 1832 and lived in a cave at this location. The next year, working alone, he opened a shaft and within three days extracted 1,400 pounds of lead ore. The wealth which he acquired after later discovering the main lode allowed him to bring his relatives from Canada and to build a smelting furnace on the bluff. At the time of his death in 1867, the value of his property was estimated at between $50,000 and $200,000. Rumors that he had buried large sums of gold on the bluff led to occasional forays by search parties, until they were stopped by the authorities. Nevertheless, sums ranging in amount from

$500 to $10,000 were discovered in the ground.

¶ **New Melleray Abbey,** 12 miles southwest on Rural Route 1 to 6500 Melleray Circle in Peosta, Iowa.

The story of this Trappist monastery goes back to early 1849, when Bishop Mathias Loras of Dubuque visited Mount Melleray Abbey in County Waterford, Ireland. While there, he expressed his desire to establish such a Trappist community on 500 acres of prairie and timber land in his American diocese.

By the middle of the following July, six members of the Irish Trappist community had arrived in Dubuque. When its superior, Abbot Bruno, laid the foundation for the new abbey, he was joined in witnessing the historic event by the other Irish monks: Father James O'Gorman, Father Clement Smythe, and the lay brothers Timothy, Barnaby, and Macarius. When the abbot soon returned to Ireland, Father O'Gorman became the first superior of the newly established monastery.

In September a larger contingent of sixteen Irish monks from Mount Melleray arrived in Dubuque. Although the group's one priest (Patrick Mahon), two choir brothers, and thirteen lay brothers survived the crossing from Liverpool to New Orleans, six died of cholera during the steamboat ride to St. Louis. In April of the next year, one French and twenty-two more Irish Trappists made their way to America under Father Francis Walsh, who became the new monastery's second abbot.

From the beginning, New Melleray experienced an uneasy cycle of expansion and contraction. In 1863 the monastery was raised to the status of an abbey, and by 1870 it had added two new wings in thirteenth-century Gothic Revival style. While its original property had expanded to 3,000 acres in 1918, the number of its monks had fallen to seventeen that year (from sixty-one in 1860). Nevertheless, under the subsequent abbacy of Dom Bruno Ryan, the establishment paid off its capital debt and grew in number to fifty monks. A boom in vocations among former servicemen after World War II helped increase the abbey's membership to 135, of whom 40 were priests. This rapid expansion allowed the abbey to modernize its farming program and double the size of its physical plant. In 1995 the abbey had thirty-nine monks.

§ Church and guest house open to visitors. Gift shop open Monday-Saturday 9-11 and 1-3. Phone: 319-588-2319.

EMMETSBURG

¶ **Robert Emmet Statue,** in front of the county courthouse.

Like the other three statues of Emmet by the Irish-born sculptor Jerome Connor, this bronze likeness depicts the famous Irish patriot with outstretched hand pleading his case before the court which condemned him to death for his part in the 1798 uprising against British rule. (See Robert Emmet Statue, San Francisco, California.)

One of several Irish settlements in Iowa, Emmetsburg was established in 1856 and was long known as a center of Irish culture in this part of the country. Although its famous statue of Emmet was presented to the city as early as 1919, the memorial was officially erected in its present location only in 1958. During that intervening time the statue had lain in obscurity in the basement of a local grocery store because of disagreements among the townspeople about where it should be erected. In the 1930s the statue was sold to the Ancient Order of Hibernians in Minnesota.

When residents began to prepare to celebrate the centennial of Emmetsburg's founding, they made overtures to the statue's owners to effect the return of the monument. When negotiations proved fruitless, however, a group of Emmetsburg residents simply stole the statue.

GREENFIELD

¶ **Catalpa,** southeast of Greenfield. Private.

This nineteenth-century frame house belonged to Henry C. Wallace, U.S. secretary of agriculture and the owner and editor of *Wallace's Farmer*, a local agricultural newspaper. His son, Henry A. Wallace, who also served as secretary of agriculture as well as vice president of the United States, was born here in 1866.

Henry C. Wallace was the grandson of Irish emigrants who had come to America in 1832. After learning the printer's trade in Winterset, Iowa, he attended Iowa State Agricultural College, where he later held a professorship. In 1894 he joined his father and his brother in purchasing *Farm and Dairy*, an agricultural journal to which they soon added their surname. Featuring a rare mixture of religion and agricultural topics, the newspaper became one of the nation's foremost agricultural publications.

As one of the most visible spokesmen for farm interests, Wallace championed the equalization of railroad rates for agricultural products and advocated the inclusion of agricultural courses in high school curricula. As secretary of agriculture under President Calvin Coolidge, he worked for farm relief and used his department to help farmers become more efficient and develop improved marketing systems.

GRINNELL

¶ **Brenton National Bank,** 4th Avenue and Broad Street.

Despite its status as a small town, Grinnell boasts one of Iowa's most famous structures. Constructed in 1914 from a design by *Louis Sullivan, Brenton National is known for its austere geometric form and the terracotta cartouche with its recessed circular window above the entrance.

HAMPTON

¶ **Franklin County Historical Society,** on the county fairgrounds on State 3 West.

The society's museum displays memorabilia and photographs dealing with William Daniel Leahy, one of only five men to be named a Five-Star Fleet Admiral, the U.S. Navy's highest rank.

Leahy was born in Hampton, Iowa, in 1875, the grandson of Irish immigrants Daniel and Mary (Egan) Leahy. After graduating from the Naval Academy in 1897, Leahy sailed aboard the U.S.S. *Oregon* when it made its historic voyage around Cape Horn from Bremerton, Washington, to join the American fleet in Cuba during the Spanish-American War.

Over the next decade Leahy served in a variety of theaters. After participating in naval operations connected with native uprisings in the Philippines and in China, he did a brief stint as a physics and chemistry instructor at the Naval Academy. In 1912 he served as chief of staff of naval forces in the occupation of Nicaragua and three years later was assigned command of the *Dolphin*, one of the ships which helped execute the American punitive action against Mexico and the occupation of Santo Domingo and Haiti. Soon after the U.S. entry into World War I, he commanded the *Princess Matoika* in the dangerous business of transporting American troops and supplies to France, a mission for which he received the Navy Cross.

For the next twenty years Leahy followed a career that alternated service at sea with duties in the naval bureaucracy. In rapid succession he was appointed Rear Admiral, chief of the Bureau of Ordnance, chief of the Bureau of Navigation, Vice Admiral, and Admiral. As ordnance chief he improved anti-aircraft guns and argued the superiority of battleships over the claims of naval aviators. Finally in 1937 he was named Chief of Naval Operations, the Navy's highest command. In this last capacity he lent his support to the naval expansion program that was adopted in 1938 and allowed a strategic reappraisal to deal with a possible two-ocean war.

Following his retirement from the Navy in 1939, Leahy was recalled to serve his country on the diplomatic front. A brief tenure as governor of Puerto Rico preceded his appointment as ambassador to unoccupied France. This latter posting required delicate diplomatic skills, especially in dealing with the Vichy government under Marshal Pétain. Although he succeeded in blocking the transfer of the French fleet to Germany, he failed in his efforts to minimize German pressure on the Vichy regime.

When the United States entered the war at the end of 1941, Leahy returned home to become Chief of Staff to the Commander-in-Chief. In this newly created post, Leahy advised President Roosevelt on military issues and represented him on the Allied Command Combined Chiefs of Staff. Although he advocated an invasion of France from Britain, he opposed support for Charles de Gaulle and the French underground. In addition, he was a presidential advisor at all the international conferences, including Yalta and Potsdam, although he was wary of Roosevelt's concessions to the Soviets. For his wartime services Leahy was named a Five-Star Fleet Admiral, one of only five men in American naval history to be so honored. After the war he was instrumental in reorganizing the nation's armed services under a single cabinet position, the secretary of defense. He also opposed the accommodationist policy of *Secretary of State James Byrnes toward the Soviet Union and vigorously supported the Nationalist Chinese in their war against the Communists.

During his career Leahy received numerous honorary degrees and foreign decorations. The international esteem which he enjoyed is evident in the variety of the latter awards from Portugal, China, Ecuador, Poland, Great Britain, France, Belgium, Italy, the Netherlands, Panama, Chile, and Brazil.

§ Open during the summer, Saturday and Sunday 1-4; rest of the year by appointment. Fee. Phone: 515-456-5668 (Hampton Chamber of Commerce).

LE CLAIRE

¶ Buffalo Bill Cody Museum, 201 North River Road.

This museum contains memorabilia associated with *William "Buffalo Bill" Cody, who was born in the family home near Le Claire in 1846. The house in which he lived until 1851 is now located in Cody, Wyoming, which he helped establish in 1895. (See Cody, Wyoming.)

§ Open mid May to mid October, daily 9-5; rest of the year, Saturday-Sunday 9-5. Fee. Phone: 319-289-5580.

McCAUSLAND

¶ Buffalo Bill Homestead, 3 miles southwest on F-33.

Built in 1851 by Isaac Cody, Buffalo Bill's father, this limestone house was the famous scout's boyhood home until the family moved to Kansas two years later. Buffalo and Texas longhorn cattle can be viewed on the property.

§ Open April-October, daily 9-5. Donations. Phone: 319-225-2981.

OSAGE

¶ Hamlin Garland Marker, on Route 218.

A marker directs visitors to the boyhood home of the author *Hamlin Garland. Located four miles northeast of Osage, the property still has the house that Garland's father built a century ago as well as the trees that the father and his son planted there. The younger Garland attended a country school just north of Osage and was graduated from Valley Seminary in Osage in 1881. His early life in this area is the subject of his 1899 book *Boy Life on the Prairie*. (See Aberdeen, South Dakota.)

WATERLOO

¶ **Sullivan Brothers Convention Center,** 4th and Commercial streets.

Waterloo's convention center is named for five native sons – the Sullivan brothers – who were killed during the battle of Guadalcanal in November 1942. The five ranged in age from twenty to twenty-nine. Memorabilia connected with the Sullivans are on display in the convention center.

The brothers – Albert, Madison, Joseph, Francis, and George – had enlisted in the U.S. Navy together the previous January on condition that they not be separated during the war. After the local recruiter had refused to guarantee their request – reminding them that the Navy placed members of the same family in different assignments – the brothers wrote a letter of protest to the Navy Department in Washington. In its official reply the Navy agreed to waive its rule and allow the four unmarried brothers to serve together. But when the same Navy reply mentioned that Albert was exempt from military service because he and his wife had a child, the youngest of the Sullivan brothers was furious. After additional correspondence with the Navy bureaucracy, Albert was finally permitted to join his brothers.

In the meantime, the brothers' determination had become even more fixed when they learned that Bill Ball, their closest friend, had been killed aboard the U.S.S. *Arizona* during the Japanese attack on Pearl Harbor. The boys' mother knew that she would be unable to dissuade them, especially now that they were also intent on joining to avenge the death of their friend. She therefore consoled herself with the belief that George and Francis – who had already served in the Navy – would be able to assure not only their own safety but that of their brothers. In her heart, though, she realized that the boys were fatalists. "They felt that when your number was up, there was nothing you could do about it but die fighting," she later said. "They would take their chances together." Even George had presciently observed: "If the worse comes to worst, why we'll all have gone down together."

The brothers perished after their ship, the U.S.S. *Juneau*, was sunk by Japanese fire in the Solomon Islands. Four of the brothers died immediately from the explosion, while George was among the 140 of the ship's 700 men who initially survived. For days George lay adrift on a raft, crying out for his missing brothers and becoming increasingly deranged from drinking salt water and from exposure to the burning sun. In his madness he told one of his companions on the raft that he was going to swim to an island some fifty miles way – "to get some buttermilk and something to eat." Although his comrades tried to dissuade him, the last Sullivan brother jumped overboard – only to be ripped apart by three sharks as he screamed "Help me! Help me!" At the time of the sinking, a spokesman for the Navy said that the loss of the Sullivan brothers was the heaviest blow suffered by any American naval family.

Subsequent events catapulted the martyred brothers into the national spotlight. In February 1944 they were honored by a mass at St. Patrick's Cathedral in New York City and by the announcement that a newly built destroyer would be named for them. That same month the Sullivans' forty-three-year-old uncle, Patrick Henry Sullivan, joined the crew of the new destroyer, while their sister, Genevieve, took her brothers' place in the war effort by joining the WAVES. Today *The Sullivans* is one of several naval vessels on display in the Naval and Servicemen's Park in Buffalo, New York.

The brothers gained further recognition with the 1944 Hollywood film *The Sullivans* (later retitled *The Fighting Sullivans*). Although their parents at first hesitated about granting permission for the movie, they consented when they realized that the film would highlight the importance of the war effort. Mr. and Mrs. Sullivan were honored guests at the film's premiere in New York City, and during the intermission they sold war bonds in the lobby.

• During ceremonies marking the fiftieth anniversary of the Sullivans' deaths, five flowering crab apple trees were planted in their honor at the Grout Museum in Waterloo (on West Park Avenue at South Street along U.S. 218). The trees were actually grafts from five trees planted in 1951 on the Capitol Plaza in Washington, D.C., in memory of the Sullivan brothers.

• In August 1995, Albert Sullivan's granddaughter, Kelly Sullivan Loughren, participated in ceremonies marking the launching of a new destroyer, *The Sullivans*. As she smashed a bottle of champagne against the ship's prow, she said: "In honor of my grandfather and his brothers, I christen thee *The Sullivans*. May the luck of the Irish always be with you and your crew." *The Sullivans* and its crew of twenty-six officers and 315 sailors were invited to visit Ireland in the summer of 1996 to coincide with the gathering of the O'Sullivan clan and to mark the fiftieth anniversary of the Irish navy.

❡ Sullivan Brothers Memorial Park, East 4th Street.

• A bronze plaque marks the site of the home in which the five Sullivan boys grew up. Across the street is the Illinois Central roundhouse where the boys' father, Thomas, worked as a freight conductor. Thomas, whose parents had settled in Iowa after emigrating from County Cork, Ireland, had struck out on his own at the age of sixteen. When he was unable to find work as a cowboy, he took a job in a Colorado mine but eventually came to Waterloo to work as a railroad brakeman.

In January 1943, when Thomas was informed that his sons were missing in action, he was, of course, devastated by the news. He nevertheless decided to continue on his way to work, never having missed a day for thirty-three years, except for serious illness. His wife, who had urged him to go, later recalled her thoughts: "I knew that his train was carrying war freight. If that freight didn't reach the battlefronts in time, it might mean more casualties. Dad holding up the train might mean that other boys would die, that other mothers might have to face such grief needlessly."

• At the center of the park is a landscaped memorial area consisting of a pentagonal concrete dais surrounded by a water-filled moat. On top of the dais stands a circular granite pedestal which, in turn, supports the bronze shamrock insignia from the destroyer U.S.S. *The Sullivans*. Each of the five facets of the monument displays a bronze plaque with the name of one of the brothers.

℥ Sullivan Brothers Memorial Plaque, St. Mary's Catholic Church, East Parker and East 4th streets.

A plaque on the statue of the Virgin Mary in front of the church honors the five Sullivans brothers who worshipped here before joining the Navy in 1942. Following the receipt of official news about the brothers' deaths, a pontifical mass was celebrated here in their honor. Albert, the only one of the brothers who was married, left behind his wife and their one-year-old son, James. When the youngster turned seventeen, he entered the Navy. He still lives in Waterloo today.

WEXFORD

℥ Father Thomas Hore Window, Church of the Immaculate Conception, on State X52, 8 miles south of Lansing.

This stained-glass window honors the founder of a successful Irish colony in Wexford and was a gift of the original settlers at this site. The present stone church was erected in 1870 to replace the earlier log church dedicated to St. George. (That this earlier Irish church was named for England's patron saint seems incongruous, but its name was due to the custom of christening a church for the saint on whose feast day it was established.)

A native of the barony of Forth in County Wexford, Ireland, Hore attended St. John's Seminary in Kilkenny before sailing to Virginia in 1820. There he was ordained by Patrick Kelly, the first bishop of Richmond and a former instructor of his at the seminary. When poor health forced the young priest to return to Ireland six years later, he served as pastor of Kilaveny and Annacurra during the height of the great famine.

When approximately 1,200 local parishioners expressed their desire to emigrate, Hore agreed to accompany them and suggested that they settle in Arkansas. The priest may have suggested that state because of his acquaintance with Andrew Byrne, the first bishop of Little Rock, who had twice returned to his native Dublin in quest of priests and nuns for his new diocese. Whatever the case, the *Boston Pilot* described Hore's colonists as a "most respectable and respect commanding body" headed for the fertile plains of Arkansas. After landing in New Orleans at the end of 1850, Hore and seventy-five families (of 450 colonists) sailed up the Mississippi to their intended destination, Fort Smith. Disappointed either because no land was available or because it proved unsuitable, most of the colonists decided to abandon the state and sail for St. Louis.

Undaunted and unwilling to give up his scheme, Father Hore traveled to Dubuque, Iowa, hoping to find a suitable site. At the suggestion of that city's bishop, the Irish priest obtained title to several thousand acres in Allamakee County, near Prairie du Chien. Despite these arrangements, most of the original colonists preferred to remain in St. Louis or had already moved farther west. Nevertheless, Hore persisted, finally establishing a colony in the spring of 1851 with only eighteen families, a quarter of those who had left Ireland with him. They named the site Wexford in honor of their common homeland. When Hore returned to Ireland six years later, he deeded his property interests in the colony to the New Melleray Trappist monastery near Dubuque, Iowa.

WINTERSET

¶ John Wayne Birthplace, 224 South 2nd Street.

This four-room house has been restored to its appearance when Marion Robert Morrison (John Wayne) was born here in 1907. The birthplace displays memorabilia and photographs associated with the famous actor.

Wayne's original name honored both his grandfathers – Marion Mitchell Morrison and Robert Emmet Brown. When Wayne's mother named her other son Robert Emmet, Wayne's middle name was changed to Mitchell. As a child, Marion was nicknamed "Duke" (for his pet Airedale). To confuse matters even more, when Wayne became famous as "The Duke," he deliberately misled biographers by claiming that his middle name was Michael.

Wayne's paternal great-grandfather, Robert Morrison, was born in County Antrim, Ireland, in 1782 and immigrated to New York at the age of nineteen. Like many of his compatriots who came to America, the young man fled when his part in the unsuccessful 1798 uprising was discovered. After working briefly with two uncles in the weaving business in South Carolina, he moved to Kentucky. During the War of 1812, he was an officer in a cavalry unit that saw action against the Indians. He was later named a brigadier general in the Ohio militia and served for four years in that state's legislature. Before his death he had fathered fifteen children by two wives.

In 1905 Wayne's father, Clyde Leonard Morrison, married Mary (Molly) Alberta Brown, whose mother was a native of County Cork and whose father bore the name of the famous Irish patriot Robert Emmet. While Wayne's mother had the fiery temper, it was from his more even-tempered father that the future actor received some advice about the art of fisticuffs. The older man acknowledged the chivalric virtues ("Always keep your word. A gentleman never insults anyone intentionally") but leavened them with the caveat: "Don't look for trouble, but if you get into a fight, make sure you win it." Wayne later confessed to following a modified version of the second rule: "A gentleman never insults anyone *unintentionally*."

While working in the prop department at Fox Film Corporation in Hollywood, Wayne first appeared on screen in bit parts in three silent films produced by *John Ford. (See Monument Valley, Utah.) After a succession of westerns during the 1930s, Wayne achieved stardom when Ford, who considered him "a splendid actor who has had very little chance to act," cast him as Ringo Kid in *Stagecoach*. During the 1940s Wayne starred in a number of sea roles and action pictures, although he continued in the western genre. He was particularly proud of General Douglas MacArthur's remark about his performance in *She Wore a Yellow Ribbon*: "Young man, you represent the cavalry officer more than any man who was in uniform." His most memorable role for Irish-Americans, however, was as Sean Thornton in Ford's *The Quiet Man*. Filmed in Ireland, this classic tells the tale of a retired American prizefighter who returns to his native Erin and finds himself in a contest for the affections of a feisty colleen (*Maureen O'Hara).

In the face of criticism against his later Vietnam War film *The Green Berets*, Wayne replied in kind. "The little clique back there in the East has taken great personal satisfaction in reviewing my politics instead of my products," he said. "And they've drawn up a caricature of me, which doesn't bother me. Their opinions don't matter to the people who go to movies." Finally in 1969, after a career of more than 200 films, he received an Academy Award for his role in *True Grit*. Not content to let anyone else write his epitaph, he composed his own: *Feo, fuerte, y formal* (which he translated as "He was ugly, was strong, had dignity").

At the time of Wayne's death in 1979, it was reported that the actor had converted to Catholicism. His daughter Aissa, however, doubted such a possibility, insisting that – despite her own upbringing as a Catholic – her father had never attended church with her or her mother. In fact, she claimed that he had never shown an inclination toward organized religion, as proof quoting her father: "I don't belong to any church. I believe in God and Jesus Christ, and I pray. If anything, I guess I'm a Presby-goddamn-terian." With regard to the visit of the archbishop of Panama to Wayne's deathbed, Aissa acknowledged seeing her father "slightly" nodding his head as the cleric prayed in Latin. But she pointed out that, since her father was heavily drugged at the time, she did not think that he was aware that a conversion was being attempted. "It may comfort certain people to believe John Wayne died a Catholic," she conceded, "but I was a witness and I don't think so."

§ Open daily 10-5. Closed January 1, Thanksgiving, and December 25. Fee. Phone: 515-462-1044.

The birthplace of Irish-American actor John Wayne.
(Photo courtesy of John Wayne Birthplace, Winterset, Iowa.)

KANSAS

ABILENE

¶ **Old Abilene Town and Western Museum,** 6th Street and Buckeye.
This historical reconstruction of Texas Street, Abilene's main thoroughfare, contains original log buildings and a schoolhouse as well as replicas
of several commercial buildings from the days of the cattle drive. Two of
these replicas are the Merchant's Hotel and the Alamo Saloon, the latter
frequented by James "Wild Bill" Hickok, the legendary town's marshal in
1870. Abilene's annual Wild Bill Hickok Rodeo takes place in August.

James Butler Hickok was born in Troy, Illinois, in 1837, the grandson
of an Irish immigrant who had fought at Plattsburgh in the War of 1812.
Even as a youth Hickok was considered the best shot in that part of the
state. At eighteen he headed for Kansas, where he joined the paramilitary
forces intent upon bringing the territory into the Union as a free state and
where he briefly served as a lawman. His first job as a stagecoach driver
on the Santa Fe Trail was short lived, however, after he was attacked by a
bear. Although he killed his attacker with a bowie knife, Hickok was injured so severely that he was not expected to recover. The young adventurer defied the odds, though, and recovered enough to work for the Overland Stage on the Oregon Trail. While in Nebraska in 1861, he was almost
killed again, this time in a gunfight with the McCanles Gang.

With the outbreak of the Civil War, Hickok began his varied career as
scout and lawman. During the war itself he served as a Union scout and
was several times captured and sentenced to death as a spy but invariably
escaped. After the hostilities he served as a scout and Indian fighter on the
frontier for generals *Philip Sheridan, Winfield Scott Hancock, and George
Custer. As deputy U.S. marshal at Fort Riley, Kansas, he was responsible
for enforcing the law over a 200,000-square-mile territory. He later was
marshal for Hays City and Abilene, Kansas. Although he killed many outlaws and recovered hundreds of stolen horses and mules, he never killed
anyone except in self-defense or in the execution of his duties. On one
occasion, when he was attacked by three men, he killed all of them. His
most famous act of self-defense was when he killed Phil Coe, the owner of
a saloon and gambling house in Abilene.

Although for a while Hickok toured with *"Buffalo Bill" Cody and his
troupe, he eventually returned to the Wild West, this time to Deadwood
City, North Dakota, where he was killed by Jack McCall. Hickok is buried
in Mount Moriah Cemetery in Deadwood. Each year in late August,
Abilene celebrates the Wild Bill Hickok Rodeo.

§ Phone: 913-263-4194.

COFFEYVILLE

❡ Condon National Bank, 811 Walnut Street.

This brick building was the site of one of two bank robberies committed in Coffeyville on October 5, 1892, by the Dalton Gang, composed of the three Irish-American Dalton brothers and two of their confederates. The façade of the bank is scarred by bullets which the townspeople fired at the robbers.

When Grattan Dalton, Jack Moore, and William Powers entered the Condon Bank soon after 9:30 a.m. and demanded cash, they were told that the safe – which was operated by a time lock – would not open until 9:45. (The safe had actually been opened at 8 that morning, but the teller tried to stall the bandits with his lie.) Over at the First National Bank across the street, meanwhile, Robert and Emmett Dalton had netted $21,000 in gold and currency after forcing the staff to open the vaults.

As the bandits tried to make their escape, however, they were met by a barrage of gunfire from citizens who had armed themselves with weapons provided by two hardware store owners. After escaping with his brother through the back door of the National Bank, Emmet Dalton shot and killed three citizens and wounded another. When the Daltons joined their confederates in "Death Alley," where their horses were waiting, additional gunfire resulted in the death of the city marshal and each member of the gang except Emmett, who somehow survived twenty-three hits. The Coffeyville *Journal* later editorialized: "The city sat down in sack cloth and ashes to mourn for the heroic men who had given their lives for the protection of property . . . and the maintenance of law in our midst."

• The old city jail, where sixteen-year-old Emmet Dalton was held while he received medical assistance, is still located in Death Alley. Dalton later served fourteen years of a life sentence before moving to California, where he died in 1937.

❡ Dalton Defenders Museum, 113 East 8th Street.

The museum features items connected with the Daltons and their bank robberies in Coffeyville in 1892. Among the items are photographs, some of the stolen moneybags, and the guns used in the holdups.

§ Open Memorial Day-Labor Day, daily 9-7; rest of the year, daily 9-5. Fee. Phone: 316-251-5944.

❡ Elmwood Cemetery, two blocks west of U.S. 169.

Two members of the Dalton Gang – Robert and Grattan Dalton – are buried here. The Daltons' father evidenced his Irish roots in his choice of names for his sons, Grattan and Emmet having been named for famous Irish patriots. The Daltons were descended from early French-Norman immigrants to Ireland. (The name was originally spelled "D'Alton.")

EMPORIA

❡ *Prairie Passage,* Lyon County Fairgrounds, 6th Avenue (U.S. 50) and Industrial Road.

These four sets of paired limestone sculptures – known collectively as *Prairie Passages* – were designed by Richard Stauffer of Emporia and were produced by the 1992 Kansas Sculptors Association Team Carve. The eight pylons present a variety of images about nature, people, the soil, education, and technology. The unusual shafts range from ten to fifteen feet in height and weigh between five and nine tons. The paired pylons are sculpted with significant names and images from the history of the region:

• "WAW," for *William Allen White, the editor of the *Emporia Gazette;* carved images of railroads, gears, hammers, finance, and a mortar board;

• "Alahe," from the Indian for "people of the east wind"; carved hands gesturing the sign language for "I come in peace";

• "Lyon," for the Civil War general Nathaniel Lyon, whose name is recalled in Lyon County; carved symbols of clouds, rain, lightning, creeks, hills, turkey, and fish;

• "Plumb," for Preston Plumb, a founder of Emporia and an early state legislator; carved images of wheat, cattle, sheep, wagon wheel, cowboy hat, iron, shovel, and church.

§ Open year round, all hours. Phone: 316-342-1600.

❡ **William Allen White Home,** 927 Exchange Street. Private.

Known as "Red Rocks" because of its red sandstone ashlar exterior, this two-and-a-half-story house was purchased in 1899 by William Allen White, the crusading editor of the *Emporia Gazette.* The Pulitzer Prize winner lived in this house for forty-five years.

White, whose mother was born in Quebec to Irish parents, early became acquainted with issues of social reform through his parents' advocacy of prohibition and woman suffrage. After gaining experience on two Midwestern newspapers, the young White borrowed $3,000 to purchase the *Emporia Gazette* in 1895 and for the next half century produced most of that paper's editorials. His original uncompromising Republicanism appeared in an especially vitriolic editorial attack on the Populist movement and by implication on its champion, *William Jennings Bryan. (The editorial – "What's the Matter With Kansas" – brought him national recognition.) Through his acquaintance with *Theodore Roosevelt, however, the editor moved leftward in his political views, calling for government regulation of the trusts, for instance, and eventually following the former president into the Progressive Party, at least temporarily.

Although White nominally returned to the Republican tent, he enthusiastically supported the Progressive elements in the agenda of the Democratic president *Woodrow Wilson, particularly the League of Nations. During the 1920s White attempted to move the Republicans toward the left, although without any real success. While he was attracted to Calvin Coolidge as the epitome of small-town American values, he disliked the president's servility to the business interests. (White's editorial in support of the unions and free speech during the 1922 railroad strike earned him a Pulitzer Prize.) It is true that White later criticized much in Franklin Roosevelt's New Deal program, but on the whole he supported its direction: "Much of it is necessary. All of it is human. And most of it is past due."

In addition to his renown as an editor, White enjoyed a reputation as a successful author. His first work of fiction – a collection of stories about life in Kansas – appeared as early as 1896, and he yearly contributed about two dozen articles and reviews to the nation's magazines. His biography of Coolidge – *A Puritan in Babylon* – appeared in 1938, and his autobiography earned him a second – although posthumous – Pulitzer.

⁋ Emporia has several other attractions related to its most famous celebrity. They are located along the four-mile-long William Allen White Memorial Drive and are marked by signs bearing White's silhouette.

• The *Emporia Gazette* Museum (517 Merchant Street) displays equipment used to print the paper during William Allen White's tenure as editor. Among the items are drawers full of type, a hand-fed printing press, and a Linotype machine. Today the *Gazette* is published by a third genera-

William Allen White Bust.
(Photo by Michael K. Dakota and
courtesy of the Emporia Gazette.*)*

tion of the White family – Paul and Barbara White Walker and their son Christopher.

• White Memorial Park (6th and Merchants streets) was dedicated in 1988 and contains a bust of White's son, William Lindsay White. The son was a noted journalist in his own right and the author of several books. *What People Said* was based on a 1933 Kansas bond scandal, while *They Were Expendable* was the story of a U.S. boat squadron in the Pacific during World War II. His award-winning radio broadcast from the Mannerheim Line in Finland in 1940 inspired Robert Sherwood to write the play *There Shall Be No Night*. White succeeded to the editorship of the *Gazette* in 1944 and continued to publish the family newspaper until his death in 1973.

• William Allen White Elementary School (902 Exchange Street) was built in 1950 to replace Union School, where White's daughter, Mary Katherine, was once a student.

• William Allen White Library (Emporia State University) features books, manuscripts, correspondence, photographs, and other materials by or about the famous journalist. The library also contains the Mary White Collection, which honors White's daughter, the victim of an accident that took her life at the age of sixteen.

• William Allen White Bust and Memorial (Peter Pan Park, South Rural Street and Kansas Avenue) was dedicated in 1950 by former president Herbert Hoover. The bust is flanked by large bronze plaques engraved with his moving editorial "Mary White," written after his daughter was killed in a horseback-riding accident in 1921. (She was struck by an overhanging limb.) In the editorial he expressed his admiration for his daughter for refusing to exchange her pigtails for a more sophisticated look: "The tom-boy in her, which was big, seemed to loathe to be put away forever in skirts. She was a Peter Pan, who refused to grow up." White and his wife donated the park to the city in honor of their daughter.

❡ William Allen White and his family are buried in Maplewood-Memorial Lawn Cemetery on Prairie Street. His grave – like the graves of his son and his daughter – is marked by a marble composing stone once used by the *Gazette*.

HAYS

❡ **James "Wild Bill" Hickok Statue,** Union Pacific Park, 10th and Main Streets.

After becoming sheriff of Ellis County in the summer of 1869, *James Butler Hickok made his headquarters in Hays. During his five months as a local lawman, he killed two lawbreakers. He suddenly left town the following summer after engaging in a brawl with several members of the 7th Cavalry, one of whom was killed.

¶ William "Buffalo Bill" Cody Monument, 12th and Main Streets.

A stone statue depicting the upper torso of *William "Buffalo Bill" Cody with arms crossed on his chest sits atop an engraved pedestal. The monument commemorates his role as cofounder of Rome, the predecessor of Hays, in 1867. Cody also supplied nearby Fort Hays with buffalo meat, a task that earned him his famous nickname.

LAWRENCE

¶ Museum of Natural History, Dyche Hall, University of Kansas, 14th Street and Jayhawk Boulevard.

This Romanesque Revival building on the campus features exhibits on vertebrate animals. Its most famous mounted exhibit is "Comanche," the horse ridden by *Captain Myles Keogh during the battle of the Little Bighorn in June 1876, when the Seventh Cavalry was defeated by Chief Crazy Horse. Keogh's mount was the only surviving member of the cavalry unit after its humiliating defeat. (See Hardin, Montana.)

§ Open Monday-Saturday 8-5, Sunday 1-5. Closed January 1, Thanksgiving, and December 25. Phone: 913-864-4540 or 864-4450 (Saturday and Sunday).

LEAVENWORTH

¶ Fort Leavenworth, 7th Street and U.S. 73.

This 5,600-acre active military post was established in 1827 to protect caravans moving along the Santa Fe Trail. The fort played a major role in the Indian Wars, the Mexican War, and the Civil War, serving as a base for numerous expeditions west. During the conflict with Mexico, *Colonel Stephen Kearny set out from here on his way to capture Santa Fe and help wrest control of California from Mexican control.

Seventy years later, in November 1917, the little-known writer *F. Scott Fitzgerald arrived here to undergo officer training in the U.S. Army. Since his desire to enter combat in the last year of World War I was never realized, he spent much of his enlisted time writing a work that was published in 1920 as *This Side of Paradise*, This popular portrayal of the generation that grew up during the Jazz Age was Fitzgerald's first novel.

Today Fort Leavenworth contains 110 buildings dating from the late nineteenth and early twentieth centuries. The post features a national cemetery, a chapel, the old Oregon and Santa Fe Trail markers, the Frontier Army Museum, and the U.S. Army Command and General Staff College.

§ Fort open all year. Phone: 913-684-5604. Museum open Monday-Friday 9-4, Saturday 10-4, Sunday and holidays noon-4. Closed January 1, Easter, Thanksgiving, and December 25. Phone: 913-684-3767.

¶ **General Grant Monument,** Scott and Grant avenues.

Designed by Lorado Taft, this bronze statue of *Ulysses S. Grant was erected in 1889.

MANHATTAN

¶ **Fort Riley,** 10 miles southwest on State 18 or at Interstate 70 exit 301.

The original garrison on this site was built in 1853 to protect the pioneers and settlers heading west along the Oregon and Santa Fe trails. The fort was appropriately named for Major General Bennett Riley, who twenty-six years earlier had led the first military escort down the Santa Fe Trail. By 1855 the fort had become a cavalry post; General George Custer's famous Seventh Cavalry was organized here right after the Civil War. Fort Riley is now a 100,000-acre military installation.

Riley, born in 1787 to Irish Catholic parents in St. Mary's County, Maryland, began a career in the U.S. military during the War of 1812. After the rifle regiment which he commanded was disbanded in 1821, he was transferred to the infantry and spent the next two decades fighting Indians: in the Dakotas, along the Santa Fe Trail, in the Black Hawk War, and in the swamps of Florida against the Seminole.

During the Mexican War, Colonel Riley distinguished himself at Cerro Gordo and with *General James Shields stormed the fortified convent-church of San Mateo at Contreras-Churubusco in August 1847. There they captured Major John Riley, described as the leader of the so-called "Irish deserters" and one of the most hated figures during the war.

After the conflict with Mexico, Major General Riley and his regiment were transferred to California. As the provisional governor of that vast new territory, Riley in 1849 called the convention at Monterey which drew up a constitution for California and applied for admission to the Union.

• The infamous John Riley of the "Irish deserters" was born in County Galway probably in 1817. His first military experience was in the British army in Canada, but following his desertion in 1843 he settled in Michigan. There he worked as a laborer and earned a less than sterling reputation, at least in the eyes of his employer, Charles O'Malley. Near the end of the Mexican War, O'Malley wrote to General Winfield Scott: "The said Riley worked in my employ off and on for the space of two years, with whom I had more trouble than all the other men who worked for me . . . for he was always in variance with every one he had any thing to do with."

Perhaps because of his bad relationship with his employer, Riley in 1845 traveled to Fort Mackinac and enlisted in the U.S. Army as a private. His regiment immediately headed for Texas, encamping with General Taylor's troops along the Rio Grande opposite Matamoros. From across the river came seductive promises to Americans who deserted, blandishments that must have reawakened Riley's desire to "attain my former rank [in the British Army?] or Die."

Whatever his motivation, in April 1846 Riley obtained permission to attend a Catholic mass which he claimed was being said on the Texas side of the river north of the camp. When he was captured two and a half years later, he said that he had not deserted but had been captured by the Mexicans on his way to the religious service. Almost immediately, though, he was commissioned as a first lieutenant in the Mexican Army, receiving $57 per month instead of the $7 month he had been paid as an American private. During his tenure in the service of Mexico, he eventually rose to the permanent rank of major: "I have had the honor," he wrote to O'Malley, "of fighting in all the battles that Mexico has had with the United States and by my good conduct and hard fighting I have attained the rank of major." Riley's enthusiastic tone contrasts with his later contention that he had been forced into service for Mexico.

Because the American deserters in the Mexican Army preferred their own unit, Mexican military officials allowed Major "Juan Reyle" to organize just such a contingent. Although the Mexican government regarded Riley's two companies as a foreign legion, its American members called it the San Patricio Company. Patrick Dalton, an Irishman who had deserted the U.S. Army in October 1846 while stationed along the Rio Grande, was named captain of one of the companies.

Despite its name and the strikingly Celtic features of its major (almost 6' 2" with dark hair, blue eyes, and ruddy complexion), the battalion was not exclusively Irish. Of the approximately 200 men in its ranks at the end of the first year, only 40 percent of them were from Ireland. The remainder of the men were British, European, American, and Canadian. Nevertheless, the Irish character of the unit remained in the public's perception, as indicated by the fact that it was known informally as the Irish Volunteers and the Colorados or Red Guards (because of so many red heads or red-faced members). In 1848 it officially became the San Patricio Battalion.

The San Patricios distinguished themselves at the Battle of Churubusco in the last days of the war. Holed up in the steeple of the convent of San Pablo, they defied capture until their Mexican comrades had fled and their ammunition was depleted. Despite the odds, they reportedly pulled down the white flag of surrender three times, and General Santa Anna himself commented that he would have won the day if he had had a few hundred more men like Riley's. Of the eighty-five San Patricios taken prisoner, seventy-five were charged with desertion from the American army.

A newspaper reporter at the time described the San Patricio flag captured during the battle: "The banner is of green silk, and on one side is a harp, surmounted by the Mexican coat of arms, with a scroll on which is printed *Libertad por la Republica Mexicana*. Underneath the harp is the motto 'Erin go Bragh.' On the other side is a painting . . . made to represent St. Patrick, in his left hand a key and in his right a crook, or staff resting upon a serpent. Underneath is painted 'San Patricio.'"

At their court-martial none of the accused justified their desertion on religious or political grounds or on the desire for military promotions, cash bonuses, or land grants. Forty percent of the defendants claimed that they had been drunk when they were captured by the Mexicans, and more than half swore that they had not fired at the Americans at Churubusco. Riley himself submitted a six-page defense claiming that he had been captured, imprisoned, and questioned by the Mexican generals Ampudia and Arista for information about Taylor's army. "[Arista] told me that he would give me four days for to consider whether I should take arms in defense of the Republic of Mexico or not. If not, that I should suffer. . . . I thought fit to accept the commission for fear of being immediately shot."

The American judges, among them Colonel Bennet Riley, sentenced all but two of the defendants to death. A petition signed by twenty American citizens and foreign nationals in Mexico City asked General Scott to grant Riley a reprieve. "We speak to your Excellency particularly of O'Reilly," the document stated, "as we understand his life to be in most danger. His misconduct might be pardoned by your Excellency in consideration of the protection he extended to this city to the persecuted and banished American citizen whilst in concealment, by notifying [us of] an order he held to apprehend them and not acting on it. We believe him to have a generous heart admitting all his errors."

Scott confirmed the sentence of death for fifty San Patricios but pardoned five and reduced the sentences of fifteen others. Riley himself was among those spared the death sentence because he had deserted before the U.S. Congress had actually declared war against Mexico. Riley and the other fourteen with reduced sentences were to be given fifty lashes and to be branded with a two-inch letter "D."

On September 10, 1847, the first group of deserters was flogged in the village of San Angel. A Yankee private described the bloody business: "[Those] that were to be stripped and branded were tied up to the tree in front of the Catholic church on the plaza, their backs were naked to the waist band of the pantaloons, and an experienced Mexican muleteer inflicted the fifty lashes with all the severity he could upon each culprit. Why those thus punished did not die under such punishment was a marvel to me. Their backs had the appearance of a pounded piece of raw beef, the blood oozing from every stripe as given. Each in his turn was branded . . . ." Riley, as it happened, was branded twice. Because the first brand was done upside down, he was branded on the other cheek also.

The first sixteen to be executed were hanged from a forty-foot-long scaffold fourteen feet off the ground. The remaining thirty were hanged under the supervision of Colonel Selby Harney, an American officer with a reputation for extreme brutality and tyranny. Although one of the condemned – Francis O'Connor of Cork – had lost both legs as a result of

Churubusco and was expected to die shortly, Harney ordered that he be taken to the gallows and hanged with the rest. With an eye for the dramatic, Harney demanded that the hangings not take place until the American flag was seen replacing the Mexican banner over Chapultepec Castle in Mexico City.

Following the signing of the peace treaty between Mexico and the United States, John Riley and the other imprisoned San Patricios were released, but not before they were stripped of their buttons, had their heads shaved, and were paraded to the tune of "Rogue's March." Riley and his companions rejoined the Mexican Army in June 1848 as part of the newly created San Patricio Battalion, perhaps attracted by the terms of service: thirty pesos per month, 170 acres of land after five years of satisfactory service, and a pension if wounded while in service.

Riley and his men had hardly signed up for the new battalion when they were accused of plotting to overthrow the Mexican government. Riley spent six weeks in prison but later did two years of military service in Vera Cruz and Puebla. He was honorably discharged in the summer of 1850 and may have returned to Ireland.

MEADE

J Dalton Gang Hideout and Museum, 4 blocks south of U.S. 54 on Pearlette Street.

The museum contains an opening to a ninety-five-foot tunnel that leads to the barn where the members of the Dalton Gang kept their horses. (See Coffeyville, Kansas.)

§ Open Memorial Day-Labor Day, Monday-Saturday 9-6, Sunday 1-6; rest of the year, Monday-Saturday 9-5, Sunday 1-5. Fee. Phone: 316-873-2731 or 800-354-2743.

MEDICINE LODGE

J Carry Nation Home, 211 West Fowler Avenue at Oak Street.

Beginning in the late 1880s, this one-story gray stone building was the home of the militant temperance leader *Carry Nation and her husband. When she sold the house in 1902 for $800 (at a $1,700 loss), the proceeds were used to support a home in Kansas City for wives and mothers of drunkards. Today the house is a museum operated by the Woman's Christian Temperance Union.

Mrs. Nation's first public demonstration in favor of prohibition occurred in Medicine Lodge in 1899. On that Sunday afternoon she and a few of her followers conducted a prayer meeting in front of one of the seven saloons in town. After inveighing against the evils of liquor and leading her supporters in the singing of hymns, she stormed the door of the saloon. Finding that it was locked, she pounded on the door and railed against the proprietor: "You are a child of Satan. You will go to Hell!" Apparently defeated but certainly undaunted, she returned home, leading her followers with her uplifted umbrella and singing "John Brown's Body Lies A-mouldering in the Grave." As she later admitted, it was then that she experienced "the birth pangs of a new obsession and realized that she was to become the 'John Brown of Prohibition.'"

Early the next year she attacked a saloon in nearby Kiowa with bricks and stones. During an attack on a saloon in Wichita later that year, she used her trademark hatchet for the first time. (See Bryantsville, Kentucky.)

§ Open Wednesday-Saturday noon-5, Sunday 1-5. Fee. Phone: 316-886-3553.

OLATHE

¶ **Mahaffie Farmstead and Stagecoach Stop,** 1100 Old Kansas City Road.

This two-story stone residence was built in 1865 by James Beatty Mahaffie, a descendant on both his maternal and paternal sides of immigrants from northern Ireland. The house – the last remaining stagecoach stop on the Santa Fe Trail – is built of two-foot-thick limestone. A cornerstone on the second story bears the date "1865" and the initials "J.B.M." The fifteen-acre property also includes a limestone ice house and a wood peg barn.

Mahaffie had come to Kansas in 1857, arriving from Indiana with his wife and five children. Within six months he bought a 160-acre farmstead near Olathe for $1.25 an acre. By the end of the Civil War, he owned 570

The Mahaffie House.
(Photo by Ronald Holloway Snipe © and courtesy of Mahaffie Farmstead.)

acres and was the largest landowner in eastern Kansas. Since Mahaffie's farm was located just north of the Santa Fe Trail, his house became a natural stopping-off place for travelers heading west by stagecoach. (The basement in Mahaffie's house served as a travelers' dining room.)

With the extension of the railroad to Olathe at the end of the 1860s, the Mahaffie Farmstead was no longer used as a stagecoach station. Mahaffie helped assure the future of this area of the state, however, through his influence as an incorporator and director of the Kansas Neosho Valley Railroad.

§ Open September-May, Monday-Friday 1-5; rest of the year, Wednesday-Saturday 10:30-3:30, Sunday 12:30-3:30. Closed major holidays. Fee. Phone: 913-782-6972.

ST. PAUL

¶ Osage Mission Site, State 57.

St. Francis Catholic Church stands on the site of a nineteenth-century school founded by Mother Bridget Hayden for girls of the local Osage Indian tribe. The church cemetery contains her remains as well as those of the other sixteen nuns who served at various times at the mission.

The bodies of the seventeen nuns were buried here in 1930 following their exhumation from the original Sisters of Loretto cemetery at the mission. At the time of the transfer, sixteen of the graves were found to contain bones, scapulars, and penitential cords. In the seventeenth grave, however, was the preserved body of Mother Bridget, still clad in her habit.

Born Margaret Hayden in Kilkenny, Ireland, in 1814, the future Mother Bridget came to the United States with her parents when she was six. The family first lived in Perryville, Missouri, where the young girl attended the Sisters of Loretto school. She completed her education at the nuns' school in Cape Girardeau, Missouri. It was there that Margaret returned – at the age of twenty-seven – as a postulant, exchanging her earlier life for a religious habit and a new name.

Sister Bridget was stationed in Loretto, Kentucky, when a Jesuit missionary arrived to plead for nuns willing to work with the Osage Indians in Kansas. Eager to accept the challenge, she and three other sisters traveled to the frontier in ox-drawn lumber wagons, arriving there in the fall of 1847. A dozen years later Sister Bridget became the superior of the Loretto community, a position which she retained until her death in 1890.

Besides teaching the traditional academic subjects, the nuns taught the Osage girls domestic skills. The religious women also tended to the Indians' medical needs as best they could. Sister Bridget, in fact, possessed such effective healing powers that the Indians called her the "Medicine Woman." The story is told of the old squaw who one day asked the nun to cure her illness, promising to be baptized in return. Noticing that the squaw's body was covered with sores, Bridget dutifully washed and bandaged the woman's body and presented her with some new clothes and a blanket. When the Indian returned nine days later – her sores gone and her body healed – she proceeded to keep her promise. After taking religious instruction, she was baptized, accepting the new name "Mary."

By 1870 many of the Osage had left the mission, forced to move to Oklahoma by the terms of another treacherous treaty. In time, the school came to be attended mostly by white children and was renamed St. Ann's Academy. The school attracted students from as far away as St. Louis and San Antonio, many drawn by its musical program and fine arts curriculum. Despite the demographic change, Mother Bridget continued to employ a half dozen Indian girls, whom she allowed to attend classes. Known for her blue eyeglasses with octagonal frames, Bridget continued to teach until she was no longer able to do so. She remained in the classroom, though, visiting other teachers at their work or sitting quietly in the back of the room doing her needlework.

In 1890, at the age of seventy-six, Mother Bridget fell ill from bronchitis. After a week of confinement, a Jesuit priest who visited her reminded her that the end was near. "Oh, no, Father," she replied, "I have not yet had my agony." After her death she was eulogized by Noble Prentis, a visitor to the Osage mission two decades before. After recalling the nun's striking white hair, Prentis continued: "She had passed through, in her early years in the wilderness, quite enough to change its color. She was a woman of commanding look, and spoke in a firm, resolute but quiet way, as one should, accustomed to impress herself on human creatures brought to her as wild as any bird or beast in all their native prairies; this she had done and more – she had gained their affections. [She spoke to the visitor] like a mother indeed, not of churches and creeds but of the necessity of personal righteousness."

SEDAN

¶ Emmett Kelly Museum, Main Street.

Once owned by the Missouri-Pacific Railroad, this house was the birthplace in 1898 of the world famous circus clown Emmett Kelly. His father, an Irish immigrant who worked as a section foreman for the railroad, named him for the Irish patriot Robert Emmet.

Aware of her son's artistic abilities, Kelly's mother enrolled him in a correspondence art course at the Landon School of Cartooning. His first job involved presenting "chalk-talks" in which he converted words into cartoons or illustrations, usually for the entertainment of informal social groups. In 1921, however, he obtained a position as a cartoonist with a Kansas City company which specialized in creating animated advertisements for use in movie theaters. It was while working at this job that he developed his clown figure "Weary Willie." In his autobiography, *Clown*, Kelly described his creation as "a forlorn and melancholy little hobo who always got the short end of the stick and never had any good luck at all, but who never lost hope and just kept on trying."

In addition to his love of cartooning, Kelly was enamored of "trouping," or living and working with the circus. Early in his life he had learned to work on a single trapeze, but it was not until 1921 that he received his first real circus contract – to perform as a trapeze aerialist and to double as a clown with a London-based circus. He subsequently married an aerialist named Eva Moore. When the couple's two children were old enough, the family appeared together on the double trapeze as the "Aerial Kellys."

With the downturn in circus business during the Great Depression, Kelly abandoned the trapeze to concentrate on perfecting his clown persona. Unwilling to be "just another clown," he developed something special by literally becoming his earlier cartoon figure Weary Willy. Unlike the traditional clown in motley apparel, Willie wore a tattered and baggy suit, a "costume" that seemed ready made for the down-in-the-heels 1930s. Kelly's most famous Weary Willie routines saw him trying to crack a peanut with a sledge hammer or trying to sweep a spotlighted circle of light off the stage. Despite his enthusiasm for the role, Kelly knew that it was tinged with irony. "I don't feel funny when I'm this hobo character. . . . ," he confessed. "Maybe it's Willie's attempt at a little dignity in spite of everything that tickles folks. Incongruity, they say, is one of the main ingredients of humor."

Kelly was also an innovator in taking his clown persona beyond the flaps of the Big Top. He routinely performed in night clubs and small theaters, for instance, and in 1950 he played the murderous clown in the film *The Fat Man*. He also appeared as Weary Willie in the Cecil B. DeMille's 1952 epic *The Greatest Show on Earth*. Besides performing in a Broadway production of *Keep Off the Grass*, Kelly served as the Brooklyn Dodgers' mascot for a season and appeared in European movies and on American television. In 1989 he was posthumously inducted into the Clown Hall of Fame in Delavan, Wisconsin.

§ Open April-October 31, Monday-Saturday 10-5, Sunday 1-4. Donations. Phone: 316-725-3470.

TOPEKA

¶ **State Capitol,** Capitol Square, 10th Street between Harrison and Jackson streets.

The interior of the capitol building is decorated throughout with murals painted by *John Steuart Curry at the end of the 1930s. His mural *The Settlement of Kansas* is dominated by a fanatical figure of the abolitionist John Brown astride a scene of violent confrontation between pro- and antislavery contenders. The Bible and the rifle in Brown's outstretched hands seem to signify the abolitionist's role in promoting the violence that racked Kansas during the late 1850s.

Curry, who traced his lineage to an eighteenth-century ancestor from County Tyrone, Ireland, had studied at the Art Institute of Chicago. His first commissions came from Wild West journals that expected him to capture the spirit of that most characteristic of American regions. After further study in Paris, Russia, and New York, he was accepted as a serious artist with the exhibition of his *Baptism in Kansas* in Washington, D.C., in 1928. With *State Fair, Hogs Killing a Rattlesnake,* and *Tornado,* he became a leading exemplar of Regionalism and the darling of eastern critics eager for purely American representational art. His other major pieces are *Kansas Stockman, The Line Storm, Spring Shower, The Gospel Train,* and *Return of Private Davis.*

§ Open daily 8-5. Phone: 913-296-3966.

WICHITA

ℐ Carry Nation Fountain, Cowtown.

To commemorate the famous temperance crusader's attack on the bar in the Hotel Carey in 1900, members of the Woman's Christian Temperance Union erected this fountain. Originally located in Union Station Plaza, the memorial is adorned with a hatchet on one side and a Bible on the other. In 1945 the fountain was suspiciously knocked down by a beer truck, although the driver claimed it was an accident. Not until 1970 was enough money raised to move the memorial to its present site.

ℐ Eaton Hotel, 525 East Douglas Avenue.

Formerly known as the Hotel Carey, this late nineteenth-century establishment attracted national attention when *Carry Nation attacked its elegant bar on December 27, 1900. As she smashed bottles and shattered mirrors, she cried out, "Glory to God and peace on earth, good will to men."

Although not the first time she trashed a drinking establishment, this attack was Nation's first use of a hatchet as a weapon of choice and led to the coining of a new word – "hatchetation." (See Medicine Lodge, Kansas.)

KENTUCKY

BARDSTOWN

¶ **My Old Kentucky Home State Park,** 1 mile southeast on U.S. 150.

Known as "Federal Hill," this Georgian colonial house was the centerpiece of a plantation owned by John Rowan. His cousin, *Stephen Collins Foster, visited the mansion in 1852 when he and his wife were on their way to New Orleans. A probably apocryphal story says that Foster wrote his famous song "My Old Kentucky Home" during that visit. At the very least he may have been inspired to compose the work while staying at the estate.

Rowan, who was of Scotch-Irish ancestry, was renowned as an orator and pleader at the bar in criminal cases. He always defended the accused, except in one unusual case in which he was assigned the task of prosecuting a man accused of larceny. After successfully winning a conviction, Rowan resigned as prosecuting attorney, secured a new trial, and obtained the acquittal of the recently convicted thief. One of Rowan's early biographers described his hold upon a jury: "Many jurymen who sat under his eloquence, have said that there was in the manner and oratory of Rowan a force that overcame them ere they could steel themselves against it, – nay, that they believed to resist him in a capital case was almost impossible."

Although Rowan himself ran afoul of the law when he killed a man in a duel, this unfortunate episode did not prevent the Kentucky lawyer from subsequently enjoying a prestigious political career. In 1801 Rowan and Dr. James Chambers – both equally vain about their classical learning – challenged each other to a duel, the result of an earlier fist fight over who was the "best master of the dead languages." In the ensuing duel Chambers was wounded and died the next day. Although Rowan was arrested, the state attorney general resigned rather than prosecute a case against him. Despite this blot upon his character, Rowan went on to serve as Kentucky's secretary of state and to be elected successively to the U.S. House of Representatives, the Kentucky Assembly, and the state court of appeals. While in the U.S. Senate, he participated in the Webster-Hayne debate, arguing an extreme states' rights position against Senator Daniel Webster by claiming that "the States remain plenary sovereigns as much so as they were before the formation of the [U.S.] constitution." He is buried in the family cemetery near "Federal Hill."

• Near the cemetery is a small seated bronze statue of the Irish-American songwriter Stephen Collins Foster. (See White Springs, Florida.)

§ Open June 1-Labor Day, daily 8:30-6:30; March-May and day after Labor Day-December 31, daily 9-5; other months, Tuesday-Sunday 9-5. Closed January 1, Thanksgiving, and December 23-27. Fee. Phone: 502-348-3502.

Statue of the songwriter
Stephen Collins Foster.

• The musical drama *The Stephen Foster Story* is presented nightly (except Monday) in the park amphitheater from early June through Labor Day. The presentation features fifty of Foster's melodies. Information: 502-348-5971 or 800-626-1563.

BOWLING GREEN

§ **St. Joseph's Church,** 430 Church Street.

Although this Catholic church was built between 1870 and 1884, its original congregation dates from 1859 when it was composed mostly of Irish workers on the Louisville and Nashville Railroad.

BRYANTSVILLE

§ **Carry Nation Birthplace,** Carry Nation Road. Private.

The fiery temperance advocate Carry Moore Nation was born in this stone house in 1846. Her father, George Moore, was descended from a pioneer Irish settler in the area, while her mother was a manic-depressive who fancied that she was Queen Victoria. Carry Moore later used her own mystic experiences to justify her temperance mission as divinely inspired.

Shortly after moving with her parents to Belton, Missouri, in 1867,

Moore married Charles Gloyd, a man whose alcoholism destroyed the marriage. Once she had left him, she supported herself by teaching school – until she was fired, reputedly after a dispute over the correct pronunciation of the letter "a." Before long, however, she married David Nation, a minister, lawyer, and newspaper editor. Although this second marriage lasted twenty-four years, it was generally unhappy for both spouses. When Mrs. Nation moved to Kansas to become the pastor of a church, her husband divorced her on the grounds of desertion. About her place in history, Mrs. Nation later reasoned, "Had I married a man I could have loved, God could never have used me."

In the late 1890s Carry Nation began having the visions which prompted her to start a crusade against the evils of drink. As a member of the Woman's Christian Temperance Union, she was known throughout the world for her hatchet, which she used without mercy in her saloon-smashing sprees. These were all the more threatening because of her 175-pound, almost six-foot physical presence. In Wichita, for example, she trashed the Hotel Carey and other distinguished saloons, destroying quantities of liquor worth thousands of dollars. She justified her hellion habits on the theory that, wherever saloons were illegal, any citizen had the right to destroy not only their demon rum but also their furniture. She, in turn, was the victim of violence, often being shot at, clubbed, or cut. Although she was arrested about thirty times, she was able to pay her fines from the proceeds of her lectures and the sale of souvenir hatchets.

After making a public speech in 1911, Nation suffered a mental breakdown, caused, no doubt, by the illness which prompted her visions. As a result, she spent the last five months of her life in a hospital in Leavenworth, Kansas. In reviewing her life, she once mused: "I can see where I have made mistakes – many of them – but they were mistakes of the head and not of the heart." She lies buried in Belton, Missouri [q.v.], under a monument inscribed, "She hath done what she could."

§ To reach the house, go south on State 27, right on State 34 for 2.5 miles, right on Fisher Ford Road for 4 miles, and then right on Carry Nation Road.

CARROLLTON

¶ **General Butler State Resort Park,** 2 miles southeast on State 227.

This state park was named for William Orlando Butler, a grandson of Thomas Butler of Kilkenny, Ireland. The elder Butler's five sons were so illustrious for their military prowess that General Lafayette said of the family, "When I wanted a thing well done, I ordered a Butler to do it."

William Butler served as a captain during the War of 1812 and was promoted to the rank of major for his service at the battle of New Orleans. He later served in the Kentucky legislature and the U.S. Congress before being appointed major general of a group of volunteers for General Zachary Taylor's invasion of Mexico. Toward the end of the Mexican War, Butler succeeded General Winfield Scott to the chief command of American forces in Mexico. In 1848 Butler was the vice presidential candidate on the Democratic ticket.

The land which makes up this park was first acquired in 1797 by William Butler's father, Percival, a Revolutionary War soldier. Although the property was later divided among the elder man's children, William Butler subsequently consolidated the estate before selling a portion of it to Philip Turpin, his brother's son-in-law. Turpin subsequently built the two-story brick house in the park for his wife, Eleanor Butler Turpin. Members of the Butler family are buried in the adjoining cemetery, including Percival Butler.

§ Park open daily 24 hours. Closed December 25-27. Swimming, fishing, boating, nature trails, golf, tennis, picnic sites, and campgrounds. Butler House open Memorial Day weekend-Labor Day, daily 9-5. Fee. Phone: 502-732-4384.

COVINGTON

❡ **Big Bone Lick State Park,** 26 miles southwest on Interstate 75 or U.S. 42 and west on State 338.

Paved trails in the park lead to dioramas of prehistoric beasts which perished in the mud when they came here to lick the salt produced by the springs. Visitors can also observe a herd of buffalo.

Irishman James McAfee and his two brothers spent July 4, 1773, here while floating down the Ohio River. During their encampment they made seats and tent poles of the mastodon ribs and backbones which they found. On July 9, after one of the other men in their party fired at a buffalo herd off in the distance, the "lords of the prairie" headed straight for him and James McAfee. While his companion had time to find safety in the branches of a tree, McAfee was barely able to shield his body behind another tree close at hand. Because this second tree was so narrow that it barely covered his body, McAfee was almost impaled by the horns of the stampeding beasts as their lumbering bodies scraped against the bark.

§ Park open daily dawn-dusk. Museum open April-October, Monday-Thursday 10-6, Friday-Sunday 8-8; rest of the year, Thursday-Monday 9-5. Fee for museum. Phone: 606-384-3522.

CRAB ORCHARD

❡ **Whitley House State Historical Site,** 2 miles west on U.S. 150.

The first brick house built by Anglo-Americans west of the Alleghenies, this residence takes its name from *William Whitley, the pioneer scout and state legislator who completed it in 1792. The house, which he constructed on land granted him for his service in fighting the Indians, has several security features: two-foot-thick walls, an unusually high placement of the first-floor windows, a secret hiding place, an easily secured central kitchen, and a hidden interior staircase. Also known as the "Guardian of the Wilderness Road," the residence was a favorite meeting place for pioneers heading west and for such famous frontiersmen as Daniel Boone and George Rogers Clark.

In 1788 Whitley, who called his estate "Sportman's Hill," built on it the first circular racetrack in the state, although he used clay instead of turf and reversed the English custom of racing in a clockwise direction. The breakfast which Whitley served his guests after early morning races included salmon, possum, turkey, duck, beef, squirrel, bear, sweet potatoes, pies with rum sauce, and Old Bourbon Whiskey.

Whitley, whose mother was from Ireland, had been born in Virginia in 1749 but had moved with his wife and children to Kentucky about 1775. While living on the frontier, he took part in more than twenty raids or engagements against the Indians, frequently to avenge their earlier attacks. (Despite many close calls, he was wounded only once, when the tip of his nose was shot off by a bullet.) On at least three occasions, he guided expeditions under the command of George Rogers Clark, once as part of a complement of 1,000 men who defeated the Indians. In 1783 he was captured by a group of Native Americans while he attempted to obtain the

The William Whitley House.

release of prisoners taken during the Revolution. Although Whitley was at first received kindly enough, one warrior stirred up the others against him, but when the American showed that he would fight in self defense if he had to, Chief Otter Lifter complimented him for his bravery and let him go with several prisoners. Some years later Whitley was appointed a major in the Kentucky militia and led a force of 200 men against a Chickamauga village near Nashville, Tennessee.

When the War of 1812 came to the frontier, Whitley volunteered for service even though he was sixty-four years old at the time. On the eve of the battle of the Thames in October 1813, he expressed the fear that he would die the next day. As if to climax his life as an Indian fighter, he swam across a river to retrieve the scalps of three Indians he had killed earlier. His premonition about his fate turned out to be accurate – he was killed in battle but not before reputedly killing the famous Chief Tecumseh.

• A memorial near the base of the hill on which Whitley's race track originally stood summarizes his career and emphasizes his role in developing Kentucky's horse racing tradition.

§ Open June-August, daily 9-5; March-May and September-December, Tuesday-Sunday 9-5. Fee. Phone: 606-355-2881.

CUMBERLAND GAP NATIONAL HISTORICAL PARK

Located at the juncture of Kentucky, Tennessee, and Virginia, this historic gap was the entrance to the long-sought *Ken-ta-ke* or "great meadow" of the Indians. Although Daniel Boone was the most famous explorer to head west through the Cumberland Gap, he had been enticed to the region by the tales of an Irishman named John Finley. In fact, Finley served as Boone's guide when he and some other hunters passed through the gap in 1769. Despite Finley's crucial role in opening up Kentucky to colonial settlers, he was eclipsed by the more famous Boone. As a former governor of the state said, "Of all the pioneers, the least justice has been done to Finley."

A native of northern Ireland, Finley had by 1740 settled with his parents near Lancaster, Pennsylvania, where he was granted a license to trade with the Indians. By 1748 he was trading as far as the Alleghenies and had set up a trading post at what is now Pittsburgh. He first visited Kentucky on a trading expedition down the Ohio River, during which he proceeded as far as the present Louisville. In 1752 the Shawnee in the area took him to the "great meadow," where he built either a cabin or a trading post at Eskippakithiki. Three years later, after joining General Edward Braddock's campaign against the French and their Indian allies, the Irishman met Boone and aroused his curiosity about *Ken-ta-ke*. After this brief military experience with Boone, however, Finley participated in a trading expedition that took him as far as Illinois. It was therefore not until 1769 that he was able to visit Boone's cabin in Yadkin County, North Carolina, and propose to lead a small group of frontiersman into Kentucky. He intended to find his old camp at Eskippakithiki by following the Warriors' Path through a gap in the Cumberland range.

DANVILLE

❡ **McDowell House, Apothecary, and Gardens,** 125 South 2nd Street.

This restored eighteenth-century structure was the home and shop of Dr. Ephraim McDowell, the grandson of an Irish immigrant to Pennsylvania. After studying anatomy and surgery in Virginia, McDowell attended the University of Edinburgh and returned to Danville to practice. In 1806 he performed a gallstone operation on fourteen-year-old *James Polk, the future president of the United States.

§ Open March-October, Monday-Saturday 10-12 and 1-4, Sunday 2-4; rest of the year, Tuesday-Saturday 10-12, and 1-4, Sunday 2-4. Closed January 1, Easter, Thanksgiving, and December 25. Fee. Phone: 606-236-2804.

❡ **McDowell Park,** 5th Street, between Main and Market streets.

In the park are monuments to *Dr. Ephraim Dowell and Jane Todd Crawford, the woman on whom he successfully performed an ovariotomy, the first such operation in the United States.

In 1809 McDowell was called to the Lexington area to help Mrs.

The McDowell House and Apothecary.

Crawford give birth to what were expected to be twins. His examination, however, led him to believe that she was not pregnant but suffered from a large abdominal tumor. Although he confessed that he had never performed an ovariotomy before, he was willing to undertake the procedure if she would come to Danville. Even though Mrs. Crawford was forty-seven years old and in intense pain, she made the sixty-mile journey on horseback in a few days.

During the ovariotomy, Mrs. Crawford had to be held down on the operating table because she had to endure the procedure without anesthesia. Twenty years later McDowell described the procedure: "I opened her side and extracted one of the ovaria which from its diseased and enlarged state weighed upwards of twenty pounds; the Intestines, as soon as an opening was made ran out upon the table [and] remained out about thirty minutes and, being upon Christmas day[,] they became so cold that I thought proper to bathe them in tepid water previous to my replacing them; I then returned them [and] stitched up the wound and she was perfectly well in twenty-five days." Mrs. Crawford lived another thirty-two years.

ELKTON

⁋ McReynolds House, South Main Street. Private.

This was the boyhood home of James Clark McReynolds, U.S. attorney general and associate justice of the U.S. Supreme Court. He was born here in 1862 of parents descended from Scotch-Irish Presbyterians who had first come to Pennsylvania in the mid 1800s.

As attorney general for *President Woodrow Wilson, McReynolds brought antitrust action against AT&T and the Union Pacific Railroad. He had earlier shown his "Trust-Busting" zeal against the American Tobacco Company while he was assistant attorney general under *Theodore Roosevelt.

FAIRVIEW

⁋ Jefferson Davis Monument State Historic Site, east on U.S. 68.

A 351-foot-high obelisk marks the site where Jefferson Davis, the president of the Confederacy, was born in 1808. (His mother, Jane Cook, was of Scotch-Irish descent.) The room at the base contains a bas-relief panel with a life-size figure of Davis. Visitors can take an elevator to the top.

The twenty-two-acre park also includes a replica of the two-room log cabin birthplace, distinguished by the fact that it was the first in the area to have glass windows. The original cabin was torn down in 1886 to make room for the Bethel Baptist Church next to the park. When Davis was two years old, his father, who raised tobacco and horses on his 600-acre farm here, moved his family to Rosemont, Mississippi.

§ Open May-October, daily 9-5. Fee for elevator. Phone: 502-886-1765.

FORT KNOX

This 100,000-acre U.S. military reservation south of Louisville was created in 1918 and was named for *Henry Knox, a Revolutionary War general and the first U.S. secretary of war. Fort Knox is the site of the U.S. Gold Depository, constructed of steel, granite, and concrete. (It is not open to the public.)

FRANKFORT

¶ **State Capitol,** on the south end of Capitol Avenue.

Three illustrious Kentuckians are honored with statues in the capitol rotunda: *Jefferson Davis, Abraham Lincoln, and *Dr. Ephraim McDowell.

§ Open Monday-Friday 8-4:30, Saturday 8:30-4:30, Sunday 1-4:30. Phone: 502-564-3449.

¶ **Frankfort Cemetery,** 0.5 mile east on U.S. 60/460 at 215 East Main Street.

• In addition to the Kentucky Veterans War Memorial, this cemetery contains the graves of Daniel Boone, Theodore O'Hara, and seventeen of the state's governors. O'Hara, a well known editor and military officer, lies buried under a monument inscribed with verses from his ode "The Bivouac of the Dead."

O'Hara was born in Kentucky, the son of Kean O'Hara, one of three brothers who had fled Ireland when they were implicated in a conspiracy against the British government in 1798. The son attended St. Joseph's College in Bardstown, Kentucky, and then studied law before beginning a journalistic career that included positions in Frankfort, Louisville, and Mobile. During the Mexican War he took part in the battle of Chapultepec and was breveted major for gallant conduct at Churubusco. His famous dirge "The Bivouac of the Dead" was written in 1848 for the dedication of the Kentucky Veterans War Memorial in honor of the Kentuckians killed in various Mexican campaigns. Four lines from that poem were later chosen by the War Department to grace the entrance to each of the country's national cemeteries: "On Fame's eternal camping-ground / Their silent tents are spread, / And Glory guards, with solemn round, / The Bivouac of the dead."

O'Hara's subsequent military career included a filibustering expedition to Cuba and service with the Confederacy during the Civil War. In 1849-50 he commanded a regiment of volunteers who had joined an expedition to liberate Cuba. After O'Hara and his men landed on the island, he

*Theodore O'Hara Grave
and Memorial.*

ordered them to charge the Spanish barracks. As he led his men in the
attack, however, he was shot in the leg, thus becoming the first foreigner
to shed his blood for Cuban independence. During the Civil War he raised
a company of light dragoons, helped seize Fort Barrancas in Pensacola
harbor, and was colonel of an Alabama infantry regiment and staff officer
to two Confederate generals. Despite these achievements, he was not rewarded with advancement, a neglect which he brought to the attention of
the Inspector General in 1862: "I think I may safely refer to my record in
this war to prove that I have not deserved this fate. I am sure that I have
not been behind anyone in zeal for the cause in which we are struggling. I
was among the very first to take up arms in it, and as far as I have been
allowed the opportunity, I have served it faithfully and diligently." After
the war he became a cotton merchant in Columbus, Georgia.

   • The cemetery also contains the remains of Presley O'Bannon, a native of Virginia whose forebears had come from County Tipperary, Ireland. After advancing to the rank of second lieutenant in the U.S. Marines, he commanded the marine detachment aboard the *Argus* during its
service against the Barbary pirates in Tripoli in 1804. In April of the following year, he and a detachment of Marines led the attack against the
town of Derne, Tripoli, in a successful effort to rescue 180 American seamen held for ransom by pirates. During the battle he was the first Ameri-

can to raise the U.S. flag on foreign soil. (His detachment's daring achievement is alluded to in the reference to the "shores of Tripoli" in the Marine's Hymn.)

After retiring from military service in 1807, O'Bannon moved to Kentucky. His bravery at Derne was recognized four years later when he received from the State of Virginia a jeweled sword. (Although the hilt depicted him holding a flag in one hand and a sword in the other, it unfortunately misspelled his first name as "Prietly.") He later served in the Kentucky legislature before his death in 1850. During World War I a destroyer was christened in O'Bannon's honor, while the World War II destroyer named for him sank a Japanese battleship at Guadalcanal and earned sixteen battle stars.

§ Open daily 8-dusk. Phone: 502-227-2403.

HARRODSBURG

¶ **Old Fort Harrod State Park,** U.S. 127 and Lexington Street.

The park features a reproduction of Fort Harrod, built in 1775 by frontiersmen led by Captain James Harrod and destined to become the first permanent English settlement west of the Alleghenies. Among the structures inside the fort are replicas of pioneer cabins and the state's first schoolhouse, while three corners of the stockade contain blockhouses. The blockhouse at the southeast corner is known as the McGinty house, named for Ann Kennedy Wilson Poague Lindsay McGinty, reputedly the first white woman in Kentucky and most likely of Scotch-Irish descent.

Ann McGinty, whose maiden name was Kennedy, survived each of her four husbands, three of whom were killed by Indians on the frontier. Her second husband was William Poage, whom she married in Virginia in 1760. After living in various places in the southwest corner of that colony, the couple settled in 1774 near Abingdon, Virginia, where Poage was in command of a fort. When Ann and her husband moved to Fort Harrod the following year, she brought with her the first spinning wheel to be introduced into the wilderness. With this device she wove the region's first linen from nettle lint, which she later combined with buffalo wool to produce "linsey-woolsey."

In 1781, three years after Poage's death at the hands of local Indians, his widow married Colonel Joseph Lindsay, who as the commissary general to George Rogers Clark, unfortunately died at the battle of Blue Licks the very next year. Sometime later his widow married James McGinty, one of the founders of Lexington, Kentucky. Following her death in 1815, Mrs. McGinty was buried in the cemetery to the north of the fort. An unknown author paid tribute to Kentucky's first female pioneer with these words:

She who had braved the red man's hate –

With Harrod, Clarke and Boone,
First of her sex within the State,
Before a way was hewn,
Who heard the savage whoop and yell
With dead around her strewn –
And helped the savage horde repel
To save the place from ruin.

• The museum in the George Rogers Clark blockhouse contains a large oil painting of an incident in the life of *Simon Kenton, the frontier scout who served with Clark and Daniel Boone in several campaigns against the Indians. (See Washington, Kentucky.)

• Along the south side of the cemetery wall is a plaque marking the McAfee Memorial Stile, honoring the five sons of James McAfee Sr., a native of Armagh, Ireland. The marker reads as follows: "Sons of James McAfee Sr. and Jane McMichael McAfee, the McAfee brothers came to Kentucky in 1773 and were the original founders of the Salt River settlement. Several of the brothers were with George Rogers Clark on memorable expeditions. They were in the vanguard of those civilizing agencies which were to redeem the wilderness and make it a fertile field and the home of a Christian people. They brought with them not only the axe, the hunting knife, and the rifle, but the implements of peace and beneficent industry and above all the Bible, respect for law and order, and reverence for the Sabbath day. They established a community in 1779 where the town of McAfee stands."

§ Fort open mid March-October, daily 8:30-5 (Friday and Saturday until 8 p.m., mid June-Labor Day); February 1 to mid March and November-December, daily 8-4:30; rest of the year, Tuesday-Sunday 8-4:30. Closed Thanksgiving and Christmas week. Check times for amphitheater, museum, and store. Fee. Phone: 606-734-3314.

• From mid June-late August, the James Harrod Amphitheater behind the fort is the site of the outdoor drama *The Legend of Daniel Boone*, presented Monday through Saturday at 8:30 p.m. Fee. Phone: 800-852-6663 or 606-734-3346.

KUTTAWA

¶ **Kelly's Iron Furnace,** 2 miles north on State 810.

A plaque marks the ruins of a brick office and store that are the remains of a furnace complex built here in 1851 by William Kelly, who discovered the pneumatic process of refining iron for making steel.

Born in Pittsburgh in 1811, Kelly was the son of John and Elizabeth (Fitzsimons) Kelly. After setting up a commercial forge in nearby Eddyville, Kelly accidentally discovered the process of converting pig and cast iron into steel but was unable to perfect the procedure because of insufficient blast pressure. While experimenting later at an iron furnace, he found that, when the carbon in molten cast iron is subjected to air blast, the carbon itself raises the temperature of the molten mass. This discovery was pirated, however, by one of the Englishmen whom he had hired as an assistant. As a result, a patent for the perfected process was granted to Henry Bessemer, by whose name the process is generally known. After convincing patent officials that he had actually developed the process, Kelly received a U.S. patent and was recognized as the original inventor. Nevertheless, Kelly received only $450,000 from the commercial use of his invention, while Bessemer received about $10 million in royalties.

LANCASTER

¶ **Kennedy House Site,** 9 miles east on State 52.

The house formerly on this site was the centerpiece of a 15,000-acre plantation owned by General Thomas Kennedy. The famous author Harriet Beecher Stowe is said to have visited the estate when she was gathering material for *Uncle Tom's Cabin*. The book's character Eva is reputedly based on Kennedy's daughter Edna, who raised ten children here. George Harper, another character in the book, was based on Lewis Clark, one of the general's 200 slaves, while Kennedy's son Tom and his wife were the basis of the Mr. and Mrs. Shelby in the book.

¶ General Kennedy is buried in the graveyard of the Paint Creek Presbyterian Church, about three miles from the site of the plantation house. Although Kennedy's forebears were of Scottish origins, his branch of the family had resided in Ireland for several generations before his grandfather John was kidnapped from that island and sold into bondage as a ship master in America. After completing his term of indenture, he studied medicine and became one of the most distinguished men in Maryland.

His grandson Thomas, meanwhile, was born in North Carolina in 1757. During the Revolution he was appointed captain of dragoons and fought in several engagements, including the battle of Kings Mountain. Wounded and captured by the British at Ramour's Hill, he was held prisoner for about seven months. After the war he settled in what is now Kentucky. He twice was elected to the Virginia legislature and attended the convention which drew up a constitution for the new state of Kentucky. After his appointment as brigadier general of a militia brigade, he served on a committee which selected Frankfort as the state capital. He was subsequently a member of the state legislature for twenty-five years, as either a senator from Madison County or a representative from Garrard County.

Tradition has it that after Kennedy's death supernatural events conspired to deprive him of eternal rest. When family members gathered to discuss erecting a memorial shaft over his grave, a robed angel appeared and warned them that the monument would be destroyed, allegedly because of his cruelty to his slaves. Although prudence persuaded the family to place a simple flat stone over the grave, even that minimal *memento mori* was struck and shattered by lightning. An identical fate befell the second and third gravestones which the family placed over the site.

LAWRENCEBURG

❡ **Kavanaugh Academy,** 241 Woodford Avenue.

This structure was originally built as the residence and office of Dr. Charles Kavanaugh, a physician whose first American ancestor was Philemon Kavanaugh, an immigrant born in Ireland in 1705. From 1903 to 1945 the house was also the site of a school conducted by Dr. Kavanaugh's wife. The academy gained national recognition as a preparatory school for the U.S. military and naval academies.

LEXINGTON

❡ **John C. Breckinridge Statue,** Fayette County Courthouse, on East Main Street between Mill and Upper streets.

Breckinridge, a major force in American politics and a presidential candidate against Lincoln in 1860, traced his ancestry to two Irish sources. His paternal great-great-grandfather, Alexander, emigrated from northern Ireland in 1728, while his maternal great-grandmother was Lettice Preston, a native of Ireland and a member of an influential South Carolina family.

In 1849, at the age of twenty-eight, Breckinridge made his debut in politics by winning election to the state legislature from Fayette County. Two years later he was sent to Congress, where, despite his usual equanimity, he almost became involved in a duel after a heated debate with a representative from New York. Despite this incident, his eloquence and record in Congress resulted in his selection as the vice presidential running mate for *James Buchanan in the election of 1856.

The nation's youngest vice president, Breckinridge presided over the Senate and gave the valedictory when that body moved into its new chambers in the Capitol in 1859. In that address he sketched the history of the Union and made an eloquent plea for its preservation. Ironically, though, he was accused of disunionist sympathies after his selection in 1860 as the presidential candidate for the Southern wing of the Democratic Party. In his defense he proclaimed, "I am an American citizen, a Kentuckian who never did an act nor cherished a thought that was not full of devotion to the Constitution and the Union."

Following the election of Lincoln, Breckinridge used his influence to obtain the adoption of the Crittenden Compromise, a last-ditch effort to keep the Southern states in the Union. Although he believed in the right of secession, he opposed such a course at that time. He was equally insistent that the federal government had no authority to coerce a state. After the firing on Fort Sumter, however, he realized that the Union was effectively dissolved. He consequently claimed that Kentucky was free to go her own way, although he was disappointed when the legislature adopted a policy of neutrality.

Having earlier been elected to represent Kentucky in the U.S. Senate, Breckinridge duly served in that body but opposed Lincoln's war policy by voting against his requests for troops and appropriations. When Kentucky abandoned its neutrality after an invasion by Union troops, the senator returned to his state, but he soon had to flee from the agents of the military regime who sought his arrest. At the request of the state legislature, he resigned from the Senate but not before castigating those who had betrayed the state to the Union army and declaring, "I exchange with proud satisfaction a term of six years in the Senate of the United States for the musket of a soldier." For his later efforts to organize a provisional Confederate government in the state, he was indicted for treason in the federal district court in Frankfort. The U.S. Senate likewise declared him a traitor and went through the formality of expelling him, even though by then he was a brigadier general in the Confederate army.

During the war Breckinridge saw action in a wide variety of theaters. After participating at Shiloh, Vicksburg, and Port Hudson, he covered Bragg's retreat at Murfreesboro and later commanded a division at Chicamauga and Missionary Ridge. Between assignments in southwest Virginia, he was with General Jubal Early in a raid on the outskirts of Washington in July 1864. Six months later, however, he was appointed the Confederate secretary of war.

After Lee's surrender at Appomattox, Breckinridge fled with the Confederate cabinet and later made his way to Florida in a successful escape to Europe via Cuba. In 1868, however, he arrived in Toronto, where he later received permission from American authorities to return to Lexington. Never freed from the constitutional disabilities imposed upon former Confederate officials, he forswore involvement even in state politics and preferred instead to return to his law practice. He later became an influential advocate for railroad development within the state.

¶ **John McGarvey House,** 362 South Mill Street. Private

This is the former residence of Dr. John McGarvey, the president of the College of the Bible and the son of an Irish immigrant who operated a dry-goods business.

McGarvey, an ordained minister of the Disciples of Christ, gained renown for his missionary work in Missouri. At the start of the Civil War, he was one of the ministers of his sect who declared that Christians should not participate in the conflict. In 1865, probably because of the scholarship he had shown in a number of his published biblical commentaries, he was made professor of sacred history at the College of the Bible, at that time still affiliated with Kentucky University. During his tenure there he published works of apologetics and vigorously attacked the methods and assumptions of biblical exegesis known as higher criticism. Following a tour of Egypt and Palestine in 1879, he published *Lands of the Bible*. He served as president of the College of the Bible from 1895 to 1911.

LOUISVILLE

¶ **Brennan House,** 631 South 5th Street.

This mid-nineteenth-century Victorian townhouse was the home of Thomas Brennan and his descendants from 1884 to 1969. The house still contains furnishings of the Brennan family, including family portraits, a glass chandelier, a hand-carved mantel, and an ornately carved bedroom suite.

Brennan, who was born in Queen's County, Ireland, in 1839, had come to America at age three with his grandmother, who first settled in New Orleans. Before he was seventeen, he had worked in various factories in St. Louis and Cincinnati, but in 1857 he moved to Louisville to help construct the first locomotive engine for the Louisville & Nashville Railway Company. Before long he had established Brennan & Company, one of the city's earliest iron foundries. In 1882 he merged his enterprise with the Southwestern Agricultural Company, serving as president of the new venture for the next ten years. In addition to machine tools, the new company manufactured a variety of agricultural implements.

Known for his inventive genius, Brennan was the holder of numerous patents and was the winner of twenty-seven first prizes for his inventions, two of them at the Chicago World's Fair in 1893. Probably his most famous invention was his perfection of a seed drilling machine. Following his retirement in 1897, he and his wife and some of their nine children traveled extensively through Europe and the Near East. During his declining years he was known as "the oldest foundryman in Louisville."

§ Open Tuesday-Saturday 10-4. Fee. Phone: 502-540-5145.

¶ **Father Ryan Plaque,** St. Boniface Church, 527 East Liberty Street.

A bronze plaque on the front wall of the church notes that *Father Abram Ryan, the "Poet-Priest of the Confederacy," died here on April 22, 1886. Also known as the "Tom Moore of Dixie" and the "Poet of the Lost Cause," Ryan had retired to the nearby Franciscan friary a few weeks before his death and was engaged in writing a life of Christ when he was called to his eternal reward.

¶ **Locust Grove,** 0.5 mile west on U.S. 42 to 561 Blankenbaker Lane.

This two-and-a-half-story brick Georgian house was built about 1790 by Major William Croghan for his bride, Lucy Clark, the sister of General George Rogers Clark, the famous military leader in the West during the Revolution. The house was originally part of a 693-acre tract which Croghan had acquired and was the birthplace of the Croghans' nine children. The house was host to John James Audubon, Aaron Burr, Cassius Clay, *Andrew Jackson, James and *Dolley Madison, James Monroe, and Zachary Taylor. In 1809 General Clark was brought to "Locust Grove" to recuperate after the amputation of his right leg. He died here nine years later.

Croghan was an Irish immigrant who had arrived in America in 1768 at the age of sixteen. He first lived with the famous frontiersman George Croghan – variously described as his father or uncle – from whom he purchased about 6,000 acres in the Pittsburgh area. Prior to the Revolution the younger Croghan was a planter in Virginia, but when war broke out he enlisted in a Virginia regiment and saw service at the battles of Brandywine, Germantown, Monmouth, and Yorktown, earning the honorary title "Major." After the war he headed west, first for Pittsburgh and then for the Falls of the Ohio, where his brother-in-law would soon found Louisville. He died in 1822.

§ Open Monday-Saturday 10-4:30, Sunday 1:30-4:30. Closed January 1, Easter, Derby Day, Thanksgiving, and December 24-25. Fee. Phone: 502-897-9845.

"Locust Grove," the home of Major William Croghan.

McAFEE

¶ James McAfee House, west on the Talmadge Pike. Private.

Built in 1790 by James McAfee, this two-story gable house was reputedly modeled after his home in Armagh, Ireland.

McAfee and his two brothers had come to this area from Virginia, after floating down the Ohio River and then up the Kentucky to the present site of Frankfort. En route they spent July 4, 1773, at Big Bone Lick in present-day Boone County, Kentucky. (See Covington and Harrodsburg, Kentucky.)

OWENSBORO

¶ Felix Grimes House, 1301 Leitchfield Road at the corner of Grimes Avenue. Private.

Constructed between 1867 and 1876, this was the home of Felix Grimes, an Irish immigrant, geologist, and proprietor of a local coal mine. The two-story house was a duplicate of the house in which Grimes' wife – Catherine Murphy – was raised in Providence, Rhode Island. (According to the 1880 census for Daviess County, Kentucky, Mrs. Grimes was also a native of Ireland.) The interior staircase from the hall to the second floor has fifteen steps, a number chosen to reflect Kentucky's admission to the Union as the fifteenth state. The two rooms in a wing at the back of the house were used as a schoolhouse, believed to be the first private school in this area. According to land deed records, Mrs. Grimes was the legal owner of the house and its surrounding property.

Felix Grimes was born in Ireland, most likely in 1826. By 1867 he had come to Daviess County, however, and three years later was listed in the county census as a collier with a wife and five children ranging in age from twelve to three years. The three oldest children (Frank, Anna, and Sarah) were born in Indiana, while the youngest (John) was born in Kentucky. (The fifth child – Felix – appears in the 1870 census but not in the subsequent count a decade later.) By 1876 Grimes had bettered his economic situation considerably, for in that year's census he was described as a farmer and the owner of a coal mine.

Mrs. Grimes died in 1888 and was buried in the Mater Dolorosa Cemetery in Owensboro. Her husband probably died soon later. (He is not listed in the 1900 census.)

RUSSELLVILLE

¶ James McGready House, west off U.S. 68. Private.

This was the residence of the Reverend James McGready, a Presbyterian minister of Scotch-Irish descent whose evangelical preaching helped set off the Great Revival of 1800.

McGready came to this area from North Carolina after the vehemence with which he denounced sin and hypocrisy had split his congregation there into two camps. (One of his enemies wrote to him in blood, insisting that he leave the area under threat of death.) Once reestablished in Kentucky, McGready ministered to three congregations in this region, each of which experienced a revival that resulted in many conversions and anticipated the Great Revival which swept over the western and southern states in 1800.

❡ Northeast of Adairville off State 663 is the site of the Red River Presbyterian Meetinghouse. A log church marks the spot where McGready held some of the first camp meetings in America. These revivalist gatherings of families from miles around lasted for several days and were accompanied by such physical manifestations of the Spirit as trances and visions.

WASHINGTON

❡ Simon Kenton House, Main Street (State 68).

This was once the home of Simon Kenton, the frontier scout who served with Daniel Boone and George Rogers Clark in several campaigns against the Indians.

Born in Virginia in 1755 to an Irish father and a Scotch mother, Kenton at age fifteen felt the sting of rejection when the young girl whose affections he had sought married another suitor. Kenton made the mistake of attending the wedding reception, possibly to stir up trouble, a goal he accomplished with consummate tactlessness. After seizing the new groom's lengthy locks, he wrapped them around a sapling and proceeded to beat him senseless.

Thinking that he had killed the man, Kenton fled across the Alleghenies, adopting the name "Simon Butler" as well as the life of a trapper, trader, hunter, and Indian fighter. For a time, as the unofficial guardian of white settlers coming into Kentucky via the Ohio River, he protected them against Indian attacks and provided them with food during sieges or harsh winters. During subsequent campaigns against the Indians, he was the friend and companion of Daniel Boone, whose life he saved during an Indian attack on Boonesborough. On several other occasions Kenton was in the service of General George Rogers Clark, either as a spy, as part of a force that captured Kaskaskia, Illinois, or as captain of a retaliatory force that burned Indian huts, forts, and crops.

In 1780, having learned that the rival suitor he thought he had killed was still alive, Kenton reverted to his real name and returned to Virginia to be reconciled with his family. After leading them into Kentucky, he recruited "Kenton's Boys," a group of scouts and spies who helped the militia carry out reprisals against the Indians. During the expedition of General Anthony Wayne against the native tribes in the Northwest in 1793-94, Kenton commanded a battalion of Kentucky volunteers. Two decades later, despite his fifty-eight years, he helped drive the British out of Detroit and fought at the battle of the Thames in 1814.

Although over the years Kenton had become the owner of vast tracts of land in the Northwest, his ignorance of the law, his failure to pay taxes, and the continual advance of settlers into the territory resulted in his dispossession. When he journeyed to Frankfort, Kentucky, in 1824 to petition the legislature to abandon the state's claim to some of his property, he was hailed as one of the West's great adventurers. The legislature complied with his request, and Congress granted him a pension of $240 a year. He died in 1836 at the age of eighty-one.

§ A map of the town's historic sites can be obtained from the visitor center on Main Street (State 68) March 15-December 31, Monday-Saturday 10-4:30, Sunday 1-4:30. Phone: 606-759-7411.

WINCHESTER

¶ **Site of Eskippakithiki,** 15 miles southeast on State 15.

From 1718 to 1754 this was the site of the village to which Shawnee Indians brought the Irish trader John Finley in 1752. It was near here that Finley built a cabin or trading post and where, according to one story, he scattered English Bluegrass seeds, the first in Kentucky. It was also to this area that Finley later led Daniel Boone.

Near the site of Eskippakithi is Lulbegrud Creek, beside which Finley, Boone, and their companions camped in 1769. Because they had been reading *Gulliver's Travels* by the campfire at night, one of the hunters referred to his visit to nearby Oil-Springs (where he had killed two buffalo) as a visit to Lorbrulgrud, the city in which Gulliver had killed two people. The name of the creek is a corruption of Swift's imaginary city. On another occasion, while Boone and the others were hunting, Finley set off in search of his trading post. When he returned in about ten days, he reported that some of the stockading and gate posts were intact, although the Indian huts had been burned. By June 7 the group had retraced Finley's steps to his old hunting grounds, where they remained until the end of December.

¶ Eight hundred feet above the plain is Pilot Knob, which Finley had told Boone was the traveler's landmark for the Kentucky plain and from which Boone first sighted the Bluegrass region in 1769.

LOUISIANA

ALGIERS

❡ John McDonogh Tomb, McDonoghville Cemetery.

Although the remains of John McDonogh now lie in Baltimore, his original tomb still stands as a reminder of the man who bequeathed more than $1 million to the public schools of Baltimore and New Orleans. The four sides of the sarcophagus are inscribed with his birth and death dates, his own epitaph, and his "Rules For My Guidance in Life – 1804":

"Remember always, that labor is one of the Conditions of our existence. Time is gold, throw not one minute away but place each one to account. Do unto all men as you would be done by. Never put off til tomorrow what you can do today. Never bid another do what you can do yourself. Never covet what is not your own. Never think any matter so trivial, as not to deserve notice. Never give out that which does not first come in. Never spend but to produce. Let the greatest order regulate the transactions of your life. Study in your course of life to do the greatest possible amount of good. Deprive yourself of nothing necessary to your comfort, but live in an honorable simplicity and frugality. Labor then to the last moment of your existence. Pursue strictly the above rules and the Divine blessing; and riches of every kind will flow upon you to your heart's content, but first of all remember that the chief and great study of our life should be, to tend by all means in our power, to the honor and glory of our Divine Creator. . . . The conclusion at which I have arrived, is that without temperance there is no health, without virtue no order, without religion no happiness; and that the sum of our being is, to live wisely, soberly, and righteously."

Born in Baltimore in 1779, McDonogh came to New Orleans twenty-two years later, expressly to take advantage of the economic possibilities which he had seen there on an earlier visit to the city. Within ten years his real estate interests had made him a fortune, much of which he spent, however, in a luxurious lifestyle. Apparently scarred by two unfortunate love affairs, he had become by middle age a miserly recluse, having abandoned the allure of New Orleans for the simplicity of his plantation at McDonoghville across the river. Although a slave owner, he was unusually solicitous about the well-being of his slaves and ultimately made arrangements for their emancipation. (McDonogh actually created this cemetery for his slaves, who, following his death in 1850, cared for their former master's grave until his remains were moved to Baltimore a decade later.)

BATON ROUGE

❡ Magnolia Mound Plantation, 2161 Nicholson Drive.

Named for a nearby magnolia grove, this plantation was acquired in 1791 by James Joyce, a native of County Cork, Ireland. The house which Joyce proceeded to build was constructed of materials found on the estate – cedar, cypress, mud, and moss. The structure stands on brick piers and has front and back galleries and an overhanging roof.

Prior to becoming the second owner of Magnolia Mound, Joyce had settled in Mobile, Alabama, where he became financially successful through land speculation and several commercial enterprises. While still in Mobile, he married Constance Rochon, a member of a family that had emigrated from Canada and had acquired its wealth through the provision of naval stores.

Attracted by the commercial prospects in what was then the Spanish possession of West Florida, Joyce and his partner, John Turnbull, moved into that area along the Mississippi River. There they engaged in trade with the Indians and gradually acquired extensive land holdings between New Orleans and Natchez. One of those properties was the 930-acre Magnolia Mound Plantation.

In May 1798 Joyce met an untimely death while returning to Mobile from the Baton Rouge area. While traveling aboard the schooner *Mobilian*, he insisted on sleeping on deck because of the unbearable heat below. The Irishman was washed overboard and drowned, however, when the vessel experienced rough seas and turbulent weather. Four years after Joyce's death, his widow married the Frenchman Armand Duplantier, who renovated the house in the Federalist style and furnished it with appointments from Europe, New York, and Philadelphia.

§ Open Tuesday-Saturday 10-4, Sunday 1-4. Closed major holidays and Mardi Gras Day. Fee. Phone: 504-343-4955.

BURAS

¶ Fort Jackson, 6 miles southeast on State 23.

Named for *General Andrew Jackson, this fort was constructed between 1822 and 1832 to defend the mouth of the Mississippi River from further encroachment by the Spanish. The fort continued to be used during the Civil War and World War II. A museum is on the premises.

§ Open daily 7-6. Phone: 504-657-7083.

BURNSIDE

¶ Houmas House, 942 River Road.

Although originally built in the late 1700s by a French planter, this French country house passed into the hands of the Revolutionary War general Wade Hampton in 1812. Wade's son-in-law purchased the house in the 1840s and added its Greek Revival features. In 1858 an Irishman

The Houmas House.

named John Burnside bought the 10,000-acre plantation. During the Civil War he successfully claimed British nationality in order to protect his property from seizure by Union troops. In recent times Houmas House and its surrounding live oaks have been the setting for several motion pictures, including *Hush, Hush, Sweet Charlotte* and *Moon of the Wolf.*

Born into poverty in Ireland around 1800, Burnside had enjoyed his first commercial success while operating a country store in Virginia. The great wealth which he later achieved as a partner in a large New Orleans firm was based on the importation of dry goods from Britain. After initial investments in sugar lands in 1832, he eventually owned ten of the finest sugar plantations in the state. His success in using free labor on his plantations was influential in reviving the economy of the South after the war and in obtaining badly needed credit for that part of the country. By 1880 Burnside had doubled the size of his estate at Houmas and had created one of the largest sugarcane operations in Louisiana, thereby earning the name the "Sugar Prince." At his death he was the largest sugar planter in the United States.

In addition to his ten plantations, Burnside owned the finest residence in New Orleans – a pallazo-style mansion which the banker James Robbs had built in the Garden District of the city. After Burnside's death in 1881 the house passed to two subsequent owners until it was razed in 1955.

§ Open February-October, daily 10-5; rest of the year, daily 10-4. Fee. Phone: 504-473-7841.

CHALMETTE NATIONAL HISTORICAL PARK

This 141-acre park occupies the site of *General Andrew Jackson's victory over the British on January 8, 1814. Although this battle of New Orleans was the climax of the War of 1812, the engagement ironically occurred after the British and the Americans had agreed to peace terms in Ghent.

At the end of the previous December, Jackson, the son of emigrants from County Antrim, Ireland, had retreated with his 2,000 men to Chalmette Plantation after an inconclusive battle against an equal number of British troops farther south along the Mississippi. Shortly after the Americans had thrown up defensive earthworks on the plantation, the British attacked, this time with almost 9,000 men under the command of General Edward Pakenham, a native of Westmeath, Ireland, of Anglo-Irish descent. The American force, in the meantime, had grown to almost 5,500, swelled by the addition of civilians from town, Jean Lafitte's pirates, and a force of free African Americans. When Pakenham was shot in the spine during the battle, Major General John Keane, an Anglo-Irishman from County Waterford, assumed command. His efforts to turn the tide were in vain, however, and the British ultimately suffered 2,000 casualties to the Americans' 13. (Pakenham was killed near Stop #6 on the battlefield tour.)

The fighting was not confined, however, to the Chalmette family's plantation. Some of the military action affected the property of Augustin François de Macarty, a descendant of an ancient and honorable family of Franco-Celtic roots. In fact, Macarty's estate was raked by rockets from the British batteries, not only because of its proximity to the battlefield but also because Jackson had established his field headquarters in the owner's plantation house. The galleried structure, built in the chateau style on brick pillars, was located just within the American line of entrenchment. (Before its destruction by fire in 1905, the Macarty house was located in what is now the Chalmette Slip to the west of the park.) It was from the gallery of the mansion that Old Hickory – on the day before the battle – had observed the movements of the British two miles down the river and had concluded that they were preparing to attack. At about one o'clock that night, Jackson and his staff were awakened by a messenger with news that "the British were coming." Luckily for the American high command, Jackson and his officers left the house just before a cannon ball crashed into the room where they had been sleeping.

Augustin François de Macarty was descended from Bartholomew Maccarthy-Mactaig, a seventeenth-century Irishman who had fled his native land because of political and religious persecution. After settling in France, he gallicized his name to Barthelmy Macarty, entered the French navy, and eventually rose to the rank of major general in charge of the department of Rochefort. He was also named a Chevalier de St. Louis.

While in France, Barthelmy married and had two sons, both of whom followed their father in military careers.

The brothers – Jean Jacques and Barthelmy Daniel – were French colonial officers when they were sent in 1732 to Louisiana, where they both married into prominent French families. Jean Jacques and his wife – the wealthy widow Françoise Barbe de Trépagnier – had five children. One of their sons – Augustin Guillaume – went on to serve in France with the King's Musketeers and was honored with the title Chevalier de St. Louis. Upon his return to New Orleans, he married and, like his parents, had two sons. It was the eldest son – Augustin François – who owned the Macarty plantation at the time of the battle of New Orleans.

At the beginning of the nineteenth century, Augustin Macarty had served as mayor of the Crescent City under the early American regime. As mayor he had ordered the destruction of the first shipment of ice to the city on the grounds that "cold drinks in summer would affect throats and lungs and make the whole population consumptive." A decade later, prior to the battle of New Orleans, he was appointed to the Committee for Public Defense and was among the citizens who contributed $10,000 toward preparing the city for an expected British attack.

§ Located at 8606 West Saint Bernard Highway. Park and visitor center open daily 8:30-5. Closed December 25. Phone: 504-589-4430.

¶ Chalmette Monument.

This 110-foot marble obelisk marks Andrew Jackson's defensive line during the battle of New Orleans. Although begun in 1855, construction was stopped during the Civil War and was not completed until 1908.

¶ Judge René Beauregard House.

Designed by *James Gallier Sr. in 1840, this Greek Revival house is one room deep, contains wide galleries on each of its two stories, and is faced with eight huge columns. The house was the centerpiece of Chalmette Plantation, named for its owner, Ignace de Lino de Chalmette.

CLOUTIERVILLE

¶ Bayou Folk Museum, 0.25 mile east of State 1 on State 495.

Named for a collection of short stories by Kate Chopin, this museum is the former home of the famous regionalist author and her husband. Among the museum's items of interest is a first edition of *Bayou Folk*. The house itself is a typical Louisiana residence of the early nineteenth century. While the first floor is constructed of brick, the upper story is made of cypress mortised with wooden pegs.

Chopin was the daughter of Thomas O'Flaherty, a native of Galway, Ireland, who had come to St. Louis at the age of eighteen. Kate often attributed her education more to her wide reading than to the formal instruction she received at the Sacred Heart Convent in St. Louis, where she was born. Two years after her graduation in 1868, she married Oscar Chopin, a cotton factor whom she accompanied to New Orleans. During the following decade, she and her husband had five sons and one daughter.

When her husband decided to personally manage his plantation in the Natchitoches area, the couple and their children moved to this house, where they lived from 1880 to 1883. The new surroundings introduced Mrs. Chopin to the Creole way of life which she later portrayed so accurately in *Bayou Folks*, *A Night in Acadie*, and *The Awakening*. In the last work she also offered her insights into female psychology by depicting a young mother's gradual awakening to her sexuality and artistic nature. Dismissing conventional expectations, Chopin declared about herself that she was not one of the "mother-women . . . who idolized their children, worshipped their husbands, and esteemed it a holy privilege to efface themselves as individuals and grow wings as ministering angels." When overseeing the estate after her husband's death proved more than she could handle, she sold the property and returned to St. Louis. She is buried in Calvary Cemetery in that city.

FRANKLIN

¶ **Donelson Caffery Statue,** on the front lawn of the Franklin Courthouse, Willow and Main streets.

This life-size statue is a representation of U.S. Senator Donelson Caffery (1835-1906), a prominent national politician of both Irish and Scotch-Irish descent. Caffery's grandfather, who was a relative of Andrew Jackson's wife, had become a planter in this area after migrating from Kentucky in 1811. While caught in a storm during a fishing trip in Vermilion Bay, the older Caffery was rescued by the smuggler Jean Lafitte, who supplied him with provisions and a barrel of rum.

During the Civil War Donelson Caffery fought for the Confederacy with the 13th Louisiana Regiment, although he had earlier opposed secession. After the conflict he returned to Franklin to practice law, resume his sugar planting operation, and help drive out carpetbaggers. In 1892 he was elected to the U.S. Senate, where he opposed free silver and the Spanish-American War. Four years later, after the Democratic party nominated *William Jennings Bryan on a free silver platform, Caffery helped form the National or "Gold" Democratic party. Although he received that party's presidential nomination in 1900, he declined the offer. He is buried in Franklin.

¶ **Oaklawn Manor,** west off State 182 via U.S. 90 exit 3211 to Irish Bend

Road.

Located at the center of a former sugar plantation, this three-story brick Greek Revival house is a reproduction of the mansion once owned by Alexander Porter, an Irish merchant who later became a U.S. senator. The façade of this 1926 reconstruction is adorned with wrought-iron balconies and six Doric columns. The mansion has a large number of prints and oil paintings by the naturalist John James Audubon, and its gardens are patterned after those at Versailles.

Born in County Donegal, Ireland, in 1785, Porter had emigrated to American as a child after his father was executed by the British for complicity in the rebellion of 1798. After working in his uncle's store in Nashville, Tennessee, the young Porter studied law and pursued a brief legal career before heading to Orleans Territory in 1809. There he seems to have been a conciliatory force between the French and American populations and consequently secured election to the state legislature and appointment to the state supreme court. Following his appointment to the U.S. Senate in 1833, Porter supported a national bank and blamed the policies of *President Andrew Jackson for the nation's economic ills.

Porter's own ill health forced him to resign from the Senate in 1837 and retire to his plantation at "Oak Lawn." By the end of the decade, he had increased his holdings to 2,000 acres, on which, with the help of 160 slaves, he raised cattle and sugar cane and maintained a racing track and a stable of horses. John Quincy Adams described Porter as "a man of fine talent, amiable disposition, pleasant temper, benevolent heart, elegant taste, and classical acquirements."

At the time of his death in 1844, Porter was eulogized by Senator Thomas Hart Benton on the floor of the U.S. Senate. Recalling their friendship of almost forty years, Benton explained that he had first met the young Irishman when the two belonged to a circle of young lawyers and law students. After referring to Porter's "mellifluous Irish accent," the Missouri senator confessed that "It was then that I became acquainted with Ireland and her children, read the ample story of her wrongs, learnt the long list of her martyred patriots' names, sympathized in their fate, and imbibed the feelings for a noble and oppressed people which the extinction of my own life can alone extinguish."

Benton continued his tribute with equal eloquence: "Our deceased brother was not an American citizen by accident of birth; he became so by the choice of his own will, and by the operation of our laws. . . . [W]e may say that our adopted citizen has repaid us for the liberality of our laws; that he has added to the stock of our national character by the contributions which he has brought to it in the purity of his private life, the eminence of his public services, the ardor of his patriotism, and the elegant productions of his mind."

§ Open daily 10-4. Closed major holidays. Fee. Phone: 318-828-0434.

HOMER

¶ Ford Museum, 519 Main Street.

This museum displays exhibits about Scotch-Irish and African-American history and culture in the region.

§ Phone: 318-927-3271.

LABADIEVILLE

¶ Old White Plantation House, 3 miles east on U.S. 1.

This one-and-a-half-story raised wooden cottage was the birthplace in 1845 of Edward Douglass White, chief justice of the U.S. Supreme Court from 1910 to 1921. The house was the centerpiece of a 1,600-acre plantation owned by White's father, a governor of Louisiana, a U.S. senator, and the grandson of an Irish immigrant.

The younger White attended Georgetown University in the District of Columbia until the outbreak of the Civil War, when he transferred to Jesuits' College in New Orleans. After serving in the Confederate army, he embarked on a legal career which by 1878 resulted in his appointment to the Louisiana Supreme Court. In 1890 he was elected to the U.S. Senate but four years later was appointed to the Supreme Court, where he served for twenty-seven years. In 1910 he became the second Southern Democratic Catholic to be named chief justice. While on the court, he generally opposed intrusions by the federal government on the power of the states to regulate their own economies. On the issue of federal taxing power, though, he dissented when the court overturned a congressional attempt to impose the first personal income tax.

NEW ORLEANS

¶ Beauregard-Keyes House, 1113 Chartres Street.

This was the birthplace in 1837 of *Paul Morphy, the internationally known chess player. (See Morphy Burial Site below.) For two years after the Civil War, the house was occupied by the Confederate general Pierre Beauregard. The Greek Revival house was restored by the novelist Frances Parkinson Keyes, whose apartment and study – like the general's bedroom – can be viewed.

§ Open Monday-Saturday 10-3. Fee. Phone: 504-523-7257.

¶ Beauregard Statue, at the Esplanade entrance to City Park.

Sculpted by *Alexander Doyle, this equestrian statue of the Confederate general was unveiled in 1913 by the general's granddaughter, Hilda Beauregard.

¶ Carrollton, at the uptown end of Saint Charles Avenue.

Once a separate municipality, Carrollton was originally the encampment of *General William Carroll while he and several hundred volunteers were en route to join Andrew Jackson in the defense of New Orleans against the British.

¶ Celtic Cross Monument, New Basin Canal Park, Pontchartrain Boulevard.

This impressive Celtic cross was erected in 1990 by the Irish Cultural Society of New Orleans to honor an estimated 3,000 to 30,000 Irishmen who perished while digging the New Basin Canal, a navigational outlet to Lake Pontchartrain, from 1832 to 1838. Almost a century after its completion, however, the canal was enclosed. The inscription on the base of the cross is written in both English and Gaelic.

Placement of the cross here grew out of protests from the Irish-American community in New Orleans against plans in the mid 1980s to construct low income housing on the forty-seven-acre tract where the New Basin Canal had been located and where many Irishmen were buried.

The original 136 Irish workers on the canal had been brought from Philadelphia under contract to the New Canal and Banking Company. Although the original terms were attractive – passage expenses, board and lodging, and $20 per month – the laborers soon discovered that they were virtually indentured servants, subject to the high prices of the company's store and at the mercy of an incompetent physician. While visiting New Orleans during the construction period, the Irish actor Tyrone Power complained that the workers were exploited by a contractor "who wrings profit from their blood" and who provided for the workers' families "worse than the cattle of the field."

Most of the workers who died during the five-year project succumbed

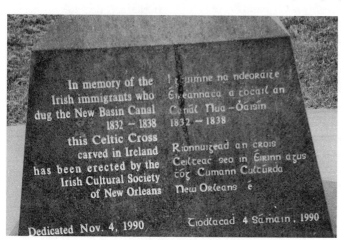

The English and Gaelic inscriptions on the Celtic Cross Monument.

to malaria, and many were buried along the banks of the canal. A song of the period perhaps best reflected the reality: "Ten thousand Micks, they swung their picks, / To dig the New Canal. / But the choleray was stronger 'n they. / An' twice it killed them awl."

¶ Confederate Memorial Museum, 929 Camp Street.

Dating from 1889, this museum features weapons, battle flags, portraits of Confederate leaders, and personal effects of Robert E. Lee and *Jefferson Davis. Following the death of the former Confederate president in 1893, his body lay in state here before it was transported to Richmond, Virginia, for burial.

¶ Daniel Clark House, 823 Royal Street.

Though now a commercial establishment, this was once the home of the Irishman Daniel Clark, a merchant and secret agent for the pirate Jean Lafitte. Clark is credited with first suggesting that the United States purchase the Louisiana Territory from France.

Born in Sligo, Ireland, in 1766, Clark attended Eton and other English schools before coming to New Orleans at the age of twenty. In association with an uncle there, he became part of a commercial network that reached to Philadelphia and the upper Ohio River. In addition, the pair owned properties in Natchez and Baton Rouge. The younger man also worked as a clerk in the office of the Spanish governor of Louisiana. When Philippe de Comines – the future King Louis Philippe of France – visited New Orleans in 1798, he and Clark became fast friends.

In 1801, soon after becoming an American citizen, Clark was appointed American consul in New Orleans by President Jefferson. In that capacity Clark used his influence to secure American control of the city, going so far as to suggest that the governor of neighboring Mississippi Territory use troops to seize New Orleans before the French arrived to take possession from Spain. In the end he broached with James Madison, the American secretary of state, the idea that the United States purchase the territory from France. Clark, in fact, assisted Jefferson in the negotiations which led to the American acquisition of the vast expanse and is often called the "Father of the Louisiana Purchase." Colonel Bellechasse, the Spanish commander in New Orleans at the time of the purchase, confirmed the Irish American's historic role by saying that "The United States owe the acquisition of Louisiana to Daniel Clark."

Clark's reputation came under a cloud, however, when his name began to be associated with the mysterious activities of Aaron Burr. Observers believed that two of Clark's commercial trips to Vera Cruz were somehow related to Burr's famous conspiracy. In addition, when Burr first visited New Orleans in 1805, he came with an introduction to Clark from General James Wilkinson, often regarded as a Burr confederate. To his credit, though, Clark warned Wilkinson about becoming too deeply involved with Burr. It was also at this time that Governor William Claiborne of Mississippi accused Clark of complicity with Burr. Although the governor later dropped his charge, continuing animosity between the two led to an unfortunate duel in 1807 in which Claiborne was seriously wounded in the leg. According to Clark, the governor challenged him to a duel because he was jealous of Clark's popularity and because he was "stung to the quick by the few words I said in Congress respecting his conduct to the militia."

In the meantime Clark had been secretly married by a Catholic priest in Philadelphia to Madame Zulime Des Granges. The later attempt of Myra Clark Gaines, one of the couple's two daughters, to obtain her inheritance resulted in fifty years of litigation. The case, begun in 1834, dragged on until 1868 with regard to the main issues and until 1890 on those of a collateral nature. The litigation found its way to the Louisiana Supreme Court five times and to the U.S. Supreme Court seventeen times.

¶ Donelson Caffery House, 1228 Race Street.

Built during the Civil War, this three-story stuccoed brick building was for a time the home of *Donelson Caffery, a well-known lawyer in the city. The house is notable for its mahogany spiral staircase, carved marble mantels, beautiful chandeliers, and sixteen-foot ceilings. (See Franklin, Louisiana.)

¶ Edward White Statue, in front of the new State Supreme Court Building, Duncan Plaza, 301 Loyola Avenue.

A bronze statue honors *Edward Douglass White, a native of Louisiana who served on the U.S. Supreme Court from 1894 to 1921, the last eleven years as chief justice. (See Labadieville, Louisiana.)

¶ Gallier Hall, 543 St. Charles Street, opposite Lafayette Square.

Considered the finest example of Greek Revival architecture in New Orleans, this former city hall was designed by James Gallier Sr., who also supervised its construction. The three-story building is ninety feet wide and 125 feet long and is faced on the St. Charles Street entrance with a portico containing ten Ionic columns. Bas-relief figures of Justice, Commerce, and Manufacturing adorn the pediment.

Gallier, whose original name was "Gallagher," was born in Ravensdale, County Louth, Ireland, in 1798, and attended the School of Fine Arts in Dublin. After coming to New York City in 1832, he worked as a draftsman in the architectural firm owned by Minard Lafever. While still in New York, Gallier gave lectures on the Greek style and published his *American Builder's Price Book*, a veritable encyclopedia on the building trades. Besides information on costs, materials, weights, measures, formulas, and architectural terms, the book gives handy practical advice, acquired, no doubt, from experience. His warning about "water closets" seems particularly universal: ". . . the greatest care should be observed in constructing water closets and laying pipes inside of houses; for if done imperfectly, or by persons unacquainted with the business, accidents may occur from imperfect joints, and other causes, by which the floors may be overflowed with water, and cause such injury to the ceilings and walls as will require much time and expense to repair. . . ." His later autobiography was an equally valuable source of information about antebellum construction practices in the United States.

By 1834, however, Gallier had moved to New Orleans, where he and his partner, Charles Dakin, established a successful business in commercial and residential design. Despite objections among Protestants in the city that the Gothic style was appropriate only to "the age of tyranny, of Baronial oppression, of monastic superstition, e.g., Catholicism," Gallier and Dakin designed many fine buildings in that style, including the Opera House and St. Charles Hotel (both since destroyed).

After 1840, however, Gallier worked alone. In this capacity he reconstructed St. Patrick's Church and the U.S. Mint and designed the Merchants' Exchange, City Hall, Christ Church, and many large residences in the city. He also won a competition with his design for the city hall in Mobile, Alabama, although the building was never constructed.

In the late 1840s Gallier's son, James, took over his father's firm under a succession of names. The son specialized in designing urban residences, most of which reflect the mixture of Italianate and Gothic that had become popular.

¶ **Gallier House,** 1118-1132 Royal Street.

This narrow Italianate townhouse was designed and constructed by James Gallier Jr., the son of New Orleans' famous Irish-born architect, for his Creole wife and their four daughters.

While the stuccoed exterior is stippled to resemble granite blocks and adorned with decorative wrought-iron, the interior combines Victorian and Rococo furnishings. The house is also noted for the latest in nineteenth-century amenities: a skylight, a ventilation system, built-in closets, a flush toilet, and a kitchen equipped with an iron range, hot running water, and an early type of linoleum.

§ Open Monday-Saturday 10-4:30. Fee. Phone: 504-523-6722.

¶ **Gallier Monument,** St. Louis Cemetery Number 3, 3421 Esplanade Avenue.

One of the prominent memorials in this cemetery is a monument designed by *James Gallier Jr. in honor of his parents. The monument is inscribed as follows: "This Monument Is Erected / To the Memory of James

Gallier / Architect of New Orleans / Born at Ravensdale, Ireland, July 24, 1795 / By his Son as a Tribute to his / Genius, Integrity and Virtue / and of / Catherine Maria Robinson / Born at Barre, Massachusetts / Wife of James Gallier / They Were Lost in the Steamer Evening Star Which Foundered / On the Voyage from New York to New Orleans / October 3, 1866."

The James Gallier Monument in honor of New Orleans' most famous architect.

❡ Greenwood Cemetery, City Park Avenue and West End Boulevard.

• At the entrance is a six-foot marble statue of a fireman, designed by *Alexander Doyle and erected in 1887 to honor the members of the Volunteer Fire Department who died in the line of duty.

• In the front left-hand corner of the cemetery is a monument "Erected in Memory of the Heroic Virtues of the Confederate Soldier." Around the four faces of the nine-foot marble shaft are life-size portrait busts of *Thomas "Stonewall" Jackson, *Leonidas Polk, Robert E. Lee, and Albert Sidney Johnston.

❡ Grinnan-Reilly House (formerly the Henderson House), 2221 Prytania Street.

Originally the home of an Englishman who had come to New Orleans before the mid 1800s, this two-story plaster and brick building in the Garden District was designed and constructed by *James Gallier Sr.

¶ **Irish Channel,** the area bounded by the Mississippi River, Louisiana Avenue, and Constance and St. Joseph streets.

This district received its name from the large number of Irish immigrants living in the area in the early part of the nineteenth century. The area was controlled by a variety of gangs (e.g, St. Mary's Gang and the Shot Tower Gang) and contained the city's most disreputable saloons and brothels.

¶ **Jackson Barracks,** facing Delery Street and the Mississippi River.

This military garrison was constructed during the presidency of *Andrew Jackson for the defense of New Orleans and as a base for troops rotated through the various forts along the river. At Jackson's urging, the barracks were constructed as a model of self-sufficiency so they could survive an attack by the townspeople. The eighty-four-acre garrison contains eighty buildings, some with eighteen- and twenty-two-inch-thick walls.

¶ **Jackson Square.**

Named for *Andrew Jackson, the "Hero of New Orleans," the square is dominated by the old St. Louis Cathedral, the Pontalba Buildings, and a bronze equestrian statue of the famous general. Annually on January 8, the square is the scene of ceremonies celebrating Jackson's defense of the city at the battle of New Orleans.

• The statue – whose horse and rider weigh ten tons – was constructed

Statue of Andrew Jackson, the "Hero of New Orleans."

in 1856 by Clark Mills and cost $30,000. The inscription on the pedestal – "The Union Must and Shall be Preserved" – was a toast which Jackson made during the nullification controversy with extreme states' rights supporters in the 1830s. The words were added to the monument by order of the Union general Benjamin Butler when he occupied New Orleans during the Civil War.

• The Pontalba Buildings, the two red-brick structures on St. Peter and St. Ann streets, were constructed in 1849 by the Baroness de Pontalba from designs prepared by *James Gallier Sr. Each building is four stories high and has wide galleries along the length of the second and third floors. In addition, each structure has three gables, brick chimneys, and black ironwork on the façade.

¶ **Jefferson Davis Monument,** Canal Street at Jefferson Davis Parkway.

Designed by Edward Valentine, this twenty-five-foot monument was dedicated in 1911, the fiftieth anniversary of *Jefferson Davis's inauguration as president of the Confederacy. The front side of the pedestal is decorated with the Confederate seal, while the back is engraved with these words: "His name is enshrined in the hearts of the people for whom he suffered, and his deeds are forever wedded to immortality."

¶ **Lee Monument,** Lee Circle, St. Charles and Howard avenues.

This 107-foot-high marble Doric column is surmounted by a fifteen-foot bronze statue of the famous Confederate general by *Alexander Doyle. The monument was dedicated in 1884.

¶ **Margaret Statue,** Camp and Prytania streets.

The first memorial erected to a woman in the United States, this statue of Margaret Haughery honors a New Orleans legend who dispensed more than $500,000 to various charitable institutions in the city. The statue, designed by *Alexander Doyle and carved from Carrara marble, portrays Mrs. Haughery seated outside her bakery, wearing her familiar shawl and calico dress and holding her arm around a child. The seven-foot pedestal bears the inscription "Margaret." The work was unveiled on July 9, 1884.

Margaret Gaffney Haughery was born near Killashandra, County Cavan, Ireland, in 1813, the daughter of the tenant farmer William Gaffney and his wife, Margaret O'Rourke. At the age of five Margaret accompanied her parents and two of her youngest siblings to Baltimore, where her father worked as a carter. Following the death of her parents from yellow fever in 1822, the young girl was raised by a Welsh Baptist neighbor, who, despite her good intentions, never saw to it that Margaret learned to read and write. After working as a domestic for a number of years, Margaret in 1835 married an Irishman named Charles Haughery and almost immediately moved with him to New Orleans, settling in the Irish Channel area. Within approximately a year, however, both her husband and her new-born daughter, Frances, had died.

Although this tragedy forced Margaret into habits of self-reliance, it also prompted her to generous acts of philanthropy. With the money she had saved while working as a laundress in one of the city's largest hotels, she started a dairy business, which within a few years counted forty cows among its assets. As the enterprise prospered, she helped the Sisters of Charity finance construction of the New Orleans Female Orphan Asylum, an orphanage which opened in 1840. In subsequent years she helped establish and maintain eleven such charitable institutions of various religious affiliations. Among the objects of her beneficence were St. Vincent's Infant Asylum, the Poydras Orphan Asylum, the German Protestant Asylum, the Seventh Street Protestant Asylum, the Widows and Orphans Jewish Asylum, and an asylum for working girls. Popularly hailed throughout the city simply as "Margaret," the energetic Irishwoman was also known for nursing yellow fever victims and caring for Mississippi flood victims.

In 1858 Margaret expanded her entrepreneurial efforts with the acquisition of the D'Aquin Bakery in payment for a debt. Although appar-

The Margaret Statue.
(Photo courtesy of The Historic
New Orleans Collection.)

ently still unable to read and write, she turned the enterprise into the city's largest export business, employing as many as forty men and earning the nickname "the Bread Woman of New Orleans." The creation of the first steam bakery in the South and the introduction of packaged crackers are generally attributed to her. Despite earning the respect of the business community for her business acumen, she continued to live a life of service and humility. She could usually be found sitting outside her bakery and dressed in her trademark shawl.

Although Margaret's reputation for charity was already secure, the Civil War and its aftermath offered her additional opportunities for beneficence. Besides feeding and caring for military prisoners on both sides of the conflict, she formed support groups of knitting and sewing women, helped with the "free markets" that provided food to the needy, and cared for many of the soldiers' families. She also regularly obtained permission to pass through the Union picket lines with supplies of bread and flour. In addition, during a three-year period after the war, she contributed $9,000 to a home for the aged staffed by the Little Sisters of the Poor.

Only with Margaret's death on February 9, 1882 and the publication of her will did her fellow citizens learn the full extent of her charity toward the city and people of New Orleans. Her demise was an occasion for public mourning, and her funeral cortege to St. Patrick's Church prompted an outpouring of citizenry along the route. Bernard Klotz, an orphan whom Margaret regarded as her foster son and whom she had prepared to assume the operation of her business enterprise, continued her bakery as well as her philanthropy.

Within two years of her death, the people of New Orleans had erected a statue in her honor in front of the New Orleans Female Orphan Asylum. Since 1948 a service organization named in her honor has carried on her charitable work by helping a different institution each year. And in a tradition that dates from 1958, the mayor of New Orleans annually designates February 9 as "Margaret Haughery Day," a fitting tribute to a woman about whom it was said that "the substance of her life was charity; the spirit of it, truth; the strength of it, religion; the end, peace – then fame and immortality."

❡ Margaret Haughery is buried in St. Louis Cemetery Number 2 (St. Louis and South Robertson streets).

❡ **McDonogh Monument,** Lafayette Square, St. Charles Avenue and South, Camp, and North streets.

This touching memorial depicts two small children presenting flowers to *John McDonogh, who at his death in 1850 bequeathed his fortune to the public schools of New Orleans and his native Baltimore. In return, he requested that "the children of the free schools be permitted to plant and water a few flowers around my grave." The schools of each city received approximately $750,000. (A bust of McDonogh was placed in each of the thirty-six school buildings constructed in New Orleans with the funds.)

Between 1892 and 1898, school children in the two cities contributed most of the $7,000 collected for the memorial in McDonogh's honor. For many years the school children of New Orleans visited the monument on the first Friday in May to leave their floral tributes.

❡ Metairie Cemetery, Pontchartrain Boulevard and Metairie Road.

Dedicated in the 1870s, this burial ground is filled with prominent pieces of statuary and memorial architecture, some of them in honor of well-known Confederates.

• The Army of Northern Virginia Monument was dedicated in 1881 to the memory of the Confederate general *Thomas "Stonewall" Jackson and the men of the Louisiana Division of the Army of Northern Virginia. The mausoleum, which contains the remains of 2,500 men, is surmounted by a thirty-two-foot granite shaft topped by a statue of Jackson. The pedestal is inscribed with the words "From Manassas to Appomattox, 1861 to 1865." For two years the mausoleum served as the tomb of *Jefferson Davis until his body was reinterred in Richmond, Virginia.

• The Louisiana Division of the Army of Tennessee Monument, the work of the sculptors *Alexander Doyle and Achille Perelli, was dedicated in 1887. Two statues stand outside the entrance to the mausoleum: a bronze equestrian statue of General Albert Sidney Johnston and a marble statue of a sergeant calling the roll of soldiers. The interior of the mausoleum contains the remains of General P. T. G. Beauregard and a memorial tablet in honor of Johnston.

• One of the cemetery's other outstanding memorials is the Moriarty Monument, a sixty-foot shaft erected by the Irish immigrant Daniel Moriarty in honor of his wife, Mary Farrell Moriarty. The granite monument is surrounded by female allegorical figures of Faith, Hope, Charity, and Memory. According to local lore, the Irishman erected the towering shaft so that the New Orleans snobs who had snubbed his wife in life would have to look up to her in death.

❡ The Montgomery-Hero House, 1213 3rd Street.

Originally owned by Archibald Montgomery, a native of Dublin, Ireland, this Garden District residence was designed by *James Gallier Jr.

❡ Morphy Burial Site, St. Louis Cemetery Number 1, Basin Street between St. Louis and Toulouse streets.

In addition to the tombs of many members of old Creole families, the cemetery contains the grave of Paul Charles Morphy, the famous chess player.

Although born in New Orleans in 1837, Morphy traced his Irish roots to a great-grandfather who had left Ireland in the early 1700s to begin a career in the Spanish army. Paul Morphy, meanwhile, early showed a talent for chess, and by age ten had beaten the city's best adult players. After futile attempts to avoid the spotlight, Morphy finally agreed to attend the Chess Congress in New York, where in 1857 he won 97 of 100 games. The reluctant celebrity duplicated his feats in various European competitions, twice playing – and winning – eights matches while blindfolded. By 1858 he had become the world champion and was hailed as a hero upon his return to the United States. (Oliver Wendell Holmes composed a poem in his honor.)

Still essentially shy and contemptuous of efforts to professionalize and commercialize the sport, Morphy declared in 1859: "Chess never has been and never can be aught but a recreation. . . . Unlike other games in which lucre is the end and aim of contestants, it commends itself to the wise by the fact that its mimic battles are fought for no prize or honor. It is eminently and emphatically the philosopher's game. Let the chessboard supersede the card table and a great improvement will be visible in the morals of the community."

❡ Morphy House, 604 Esplanade.

During the 1830s this large brick house was the home of *Judge Alonzo Morphy, whose son Charles was a renowned chess expert. (See entry above.)

❡ Old Absinthe House, 240 Bourbon Street.

Constructed between 1798 and 1806, this French Quarter bar room was for sixty years the favorite meeting place of New Orleans merchants, aristocrats, and buccaneers alike. According to tradition, *General Andrew Jackson and the smuggler Jean Lafitte met in a secret room on the second floor to plan the defense of the city against the British at the end of 1813. Today the building houses a restaurant.

§ Open daily 11 a.m.-2 a.m. Phone: 504-523-3181.

❡ Payne-Strachan House (formerly Forsyth House), 1134 First Street.

It was here that *Jefferson Davis, the former president of the Confederacy, died in 1889. At the time, the house was owned by Judge Charles Fenner, a close friend of Davis's and a man whom the Davis family visited whenever they came to New Orleans. After lying in state in City Hall, Davis's body was interred for two years in the mausoleum of the Army of Northern Virginia in Metairie Cemetery.

❡ St. Alphonsus Church, 2029 Constance Street.

This brick church was constructed in 1855 to serve the city's Irish Catholic population.

ℐ St. Patrick Cemeteries, Canal Street.

Following the plague epidemics of 1832 and 1833, the trustees of St. Patrick's Church purchased a fifteen-acre tract on land along Canal Street. The property was later divided into three plots.

The three cemeteries contain the graves of almost 8,000 Irish, many of them refugees from the Great Famine of 1846 who were felled by the cholera and yellow fever that regularly decimated the city. St. Patrick's Cemetery Number 1 contains the remains of 1,100 Irish immigrants who were struck down by those diseases in August 1853. The bodies were so numerous that they were buried in trenches, a fact that accounts for the irregularity of the graves. Even in the midst of the epidemic, a sectarian row threatened when the cemetery committee of the Board of Health appointed a Protestant Orangeman from Enniskillen, Ireland, to supervise the burials in this cemetery. Father James Mullon, the pastor of St. Patrick's Church and himself a native of Londonderry, Ireland, regarded the selection an insult to the Irish Catholic community and publicly protested the choice.

ℐ St. Patrick's Church, 724 Camp Street.

Modeled after York Minster in England, St. Patrick's was built in 1835-36 to replace an earlier wooden church erected to serve the Irish immigrants living in the American section of the city. The Gothic Revival structure was designed and erected by the architectural firm of Dakin and Dakin, but when the 185-foot tower began to lean while under construction, the Dakins were dismissed. Ten years later the tower was strengthened by *James Gallier Sr. The side altar in honor of St. Patrick is decorated with a view of the town of Armagh, Ireland. One of the large frescoes in the sanctuary is entitled "St. Patrick Baptizing the Kings and Queens of Ireland in Tara's Hall."

During the Civil War *Father James Mullon, the church's pastor, led his congregation in daily prayers for the success of the Confederate cause. When Benjamin Butler, the Union general in charge of the occupied city, ordered Mullon to stop such public prayers, the Irish priest asked his parishioners to pray for the Confederates in silence. Mullon was also accused of refusing to bury a dead soldier because he was a Yankee. When Butler ordered the priest to appear before him, Ryan defended himself. "Why, I was never asked to bury him and never refused," he said, adding gratuitously, "The fact is, General, it would give me great pleasure to bury the whole lot of you." (The same incident is related about *Father Abram Ryan. See Mobile, Alabama.)

ℐ Trinity Church, 1329 Jackson Avenue.

One of the many bishops attached to this church since its founding in 1847 was Leonidas Polk, the first Episcopal bishop of Louisiana and the "fighting bishop" of the Confederacy. Above and behind the altar is a stained-glass memorial dedicated to Bishop Polk and containing three scenes from the life of Christ.

Polk was a relative of the Scotch-Irish ancestors of President James K. Polk. Following his graduation from West Point, he entered the Virginia Theological Seminary and was ordained an Episcopal priest in 1831. Appointed bishop a decade later, he moved to Louisiana, where he was responsible for the creation of many Episcopal congregations. In the mid 1850s he assumed the rectorship of Trinity Church. He also helped establish the University of the South in Sewanee, Tennessee, an institution which he hoped would buttress the agrarian conservatism of the Southern aristocracy. During the Civil War Polk was commissioned a major general and saw action at Shiloh, Murfreesboro, Chickamauga, and Atlanta. He was killed during the battle of Pine Mountain, near Marietta, Georgia, in 1864.

❡ Polk is buried at Christ Church Cathedral on St. Charles Avenue.

❡ **Turpin House,** 2319 Magazine Street. Private.

This plastered brick residence was built in 1854 for John Turpin by *James Gallier Jr., his architectural firm partner. The house is generally regarded as the model for Gallier's own home in the French Quarter.

THIBODAUX

❡ **St. John's Episcopal Church,** Jackson Avenue and West 7th Street.

Dating from 1844, St. John's is known as "The Church of the Fighting Bishop" because the parish was founded by *Leonidas Polk, the first Episcopal bishop of Louisiana and one of the Confederacy's most famous generals.

MISSISSIPPI

BILOXI

¶ Beauvoir-Jefferson Davis Shrine, 2244 Beach Boulevard (U.S. 90).

This planter-style house was originally owned by Sarah Dorsey, a friend of *Jefferson Davis and his family. The basement in the main house displays memorabilia connected with Davis's tenure as president of the Confederacy as well as a congressional resolution restoring his United States citizenship.

In 1877 the former Confederate president rented a cottage on the property and proceeded to write *The Rise and Fall of the Confederate Government*. The following year he purchased the property from Mrs. Dorsey for $5,500, but she died before he finished paying for it. In her will she left the property to Davis. During the Confederate leader's final years, he was comforted by his daughter, Winnie (Varina Anne), who became his constant companion.

Besides presenting a half-hour historical film, the Confederate Museum on the property displays weapons, uniforms, medical instruments, and Confederate memorabilia. The cemetery contains the graves of more than 700 Confederates, including the Tomb of the Unknown Soldier of the Confederacy.

§ Open daily 9-5. Closed December 25. Fee. Phone: 601-388-1313.

¶ Church of the Redeemer, East Beach Boulevard (U.S. 90) and Bellman Street.

*Jefferson Davis worshipped in the original church on this site and served as its vestryman. The present church has four memorial windows in honor of the Davis family.

§ Phone: 601-436-3123.

¶ Father Ryan House, 1196 Beach Boulevard.

Now a bed and breakfast establishment, this was once the home of *Father Abram Ryan, the priest-poet of the Confederacy. While living here between 1865 and 1877, he made an acquaintance with *Jefferson Davis, the former Confederate president and a resident at nearby Beauvoir. Today the Ryan House exhibits a portrait of the priest, his writing desk, and some of his original works. (See Mobile, Alabama.)

§ Phone: 601-435-1189.

FAYETTE

¶ Springfield Plantation, 8 miles west on U.S. 61 or 1 mile west of the Natchez Trace Parkway on State 553.

Still a working plantation today, Springfield was the site of a famous invalid marriage. Here in August 1791 *Andrew Jackson married Rachel Donelson Robards after the bride-to-be learned that her first husband had obtained a divorce. Almost two and a half years later, however, the new couple's marital bliss was disturbed when they learned that the divorce had not been granted until September 1793, fully two years after Jackson's marriage to Rachel. Although the two were remarried in Nashville, they became the object of vilification during the 1828 presidential campaign: Jackson was called a "paramour husband" while his wife was branded a "convicted adulteress."

§ Open March to mid November, daily 9:30-dusk; rest of the year, daily 10-dusk. Closed December 25. Fee. Phone: 601-786-3802.

HATTIESBURG

¶ Sullivan-Kilrain Fight Marker, U.S. 11 and Richburg Road.

This historical marker commemorates the bout on July 8, 1889, in which John L. Sullivan went seventy-five rounds with Jake Kilrain in the last bareknuckle championship bout in America. Forbidden from holding the match in New Orleans, the bout's promoters had slipped the two boxers into Mississippi, set up a ring in a clearing three miles from here, and charged between $10 and $12 admission.

The bout, which lasted just over two hours in heat that topped 100 degrees, pitted an overweight Sullivan against the challenger Kilrain. Although the latter boxer hoped simply to wear down his opponent by delaying tactics, "Trip-Hammer Jack" Sullivan took the offensive and began laying into Kilrain with staggering blows, especially against his left side. The bout soon became so one sided that the attending physician warned that the challenger would die if the pounding was not stopped. Although Kilrain was still standing after the marathon battle, his seconds threw in the towel, thereby giving the victory to Sullivan. Years later the black poet Vachel Lindsay remembered witnessing the event, referring to it in his poem "John L. Sullivan, the Strong Boy of Boston."

The Boston-born Sullivan had inherited his size from his 180-pound mother and his pugnacity from his father, a short-tempered immigrant from Tralee, Ireland, and the champion hod-carrier in the Boston construction business. After a very brief attendance at Boston College, the young Sullivan became a plumber's apprentice but was dismissed when he broke his employer's nose during an argument. The youngster went on to knock out his first opponent in the ring at age nineteen, boasting afterwards that "I can lick any sonofabitch alive!" He soon become known for his ability to hit "hard enough to knock a horse down."

On February 7, 1882, Sullivan was matched with Paddy Ryan in the world champion bareknuckles contest in Gulfport, Mississippi. The bout, which took place under the live oaks at the intersection of Texas Street and U.S. 40, ended in the ninth round when Sullivan knocked out Ryan, the previous champion. "When Sullivan struck me," said Paddy, "I thought that a telegraph pole had been shoved against me endways."

By the mid 1880s Sullivan was approaching the zenith of his popularity. Nursing a particular animus for "foreign fighters," he gave the Englishman Charlie Mitchell such a trouncing in 1883 that the police stopped the fight to save the limey's life. In 1885 the Boston Strong Boy was the subject of a boozy ditty:

> You valiant Sons of Erin's Isle,
> And sweet Columbia too,
> Come gather 'round, and listen while
> I chant a stave for you.
> Oh! Fill your glasses up, every man,
> With Irish whiskey, stout;
> And drink to John L. Sullivan,
> The famous 'Knocker-out.'

On the eve of his departure for Europe two years later, Sullivan's fans gave him a $10,000 belt. Described as "the largest piece of flat gold ever seen in this country," the waist wear spelled out his name in diamonds and was adorned with emblems of Ireland and America. After a three-hour grudge match with Mitchell in France, the two pugilists were arrested, but Sullivan fled the country after posting a $1,600 bond. While in Great Britain, the "Knocker-out" met the Prince of Wales and broke all rules of protocol with his informality. "I'm proud to meet you," he said to the royal. "If you ever come to Boston he sure to look me up; I'll see that you're treated right." In Dublin, meanwhile, Sullivan was greeted by two brass bands playing "See, the Conquering Hero Comes" and after a week left with four jugs of whiskey and seventeen shillelaghs. At the height of his fame, he was the subject of a popular 1890 song:

> His colors are the Stars and Stripes, / He also wears the Green,
> And he's the grandest slugger that / The ring has ever seen.
> No fighter in the world can beat / Our true American,
> The Champion of all champions, / John L. Sullivan.

By 1892 "His Fistic Highness" had earned just over $1 million and knocked down an estimated 200 opponents. His drinking and riotous lifestyle, however, had brought him to the verge of bankruptcy. To pay off his debts, he was forced to sell his diamond belt and to accept a challenge from "Gentleman Jim" Corbett, one of ten children born to an Irish livery stable owner. By then Sullivan's love for excess had taken such a toll that he stood little chance against Corbett, eight years younger than his opponent. Knocked out in the twenty-first round of the only bout he ever lost, "the Boston Hercules" rose to his feet to deliver his valedictory address. "I fought once too often," he said through a broken nose. "But I am glad that it was an American who licked me and that the championship stays in this country."

With this loss the thirty-one-year-old Sullivan retired from the ring, his only future bouts to be with the bottle. At first he returned to the theatrical career that had earlier earned him $1,000 a week. For a while he toured the country in *Honest Hearts and Willing Hands* and played Simon Legree in *Uncle Tom's Cabin*. In 1905, however, he finally abandoned his liquor-loving ways for good and entered the lecture circuit as a temperance crusader. Three years later, the 335-pound Sullivan divorced his wife – from whom he had lived apart for almost a generation – and married Katherine Harkins, a native of County Derry, Ireland. The couple later moved to a farm in West Abington, Massachusetts. The property, which Sullivan named Donlee-Ross, was an abbreviated lesson in Irish geography, combining the names Donegal, Tralee, and Roscommon – the birthplaces, respectively, of his wife, father, and mother.

JACKSON

℥ Jefferson Davis Statue, Old Capitol, North State and Capitol streets.

This statue of *President Jefferson Davis originally stood in Confederate Park, where it was unveiled in 1891 before a crowd of 20,000 people.

§ Old Capitol open Monday-Friday 8-5, Saturday 9:30-4:30, Sunday 12:30-4:30. Closed major holidays. Phone: 601-359-6920.

℥ John Roy Lynch Burial Site, Greenwood Cemetery, North West Street at Davis Street.

In addition to two Confederate brigadier generals, four colonels, and more than 100 soldiers, John Roy Lynch, Mississippi's secretary of state immediately after the Civil War, lies buried here.

Lynch was born in 1847, the third son of Patrick Lynch, the Dublin-born manager of a Louisiana plantation, and Catherine White, a mulatto slave. Although the elder Lynch purchased his wife and their children with the intention of moving to New Orleans, his premature death ended such a possibility. In fact, the family was sold to the owner of a plantation near Natchez, Mississippi, where John Lynch remained a slave until Union troops liberated the property in 1863.

Although Lynch's formal education lasted no more than four months at the end of 1865, by reading and listening he transformed himself into an exceptionally literate public speaker. He also was quite successful in the photography business, using a skill he had learned while working in a studio in 1866. Taking advantage of the new political and social rights accorded blacks by the Republican party after the war, Lynch became involved with the party's activities in Natchez. As a result of this association, he was appointed justice of the peace by the Reconstruction governor. That same year – 1869 – the ambitious Lynch was elected by his black constituents to the state legislature, where in his second term he was elected Speaker of the House. Already viewed as one of the most influential political figures of the Reconstruction period, he was elected to the U.S. House of Representatives in 1872, serving three successive terms.

During a debate on a civil rights bill that would outlaw racial discrimination by public facilities, Lynch attempted to refute the charge that the bill would produce social equality between the races. "I can . . . assure that portion of my democratic friends on the other side of the House, whom I regard as my social inferiors," he proclaimed sarcastically, "that if at any time I should meet any one of you at a hotel and occupy a seat at the same table with you, . . . do not think that I have thereby accepted you as my social equal."

By the middle of the 1880s, Lynch had assumed national prominence. In the late 1890s and early 1900s, he received several presidential appointments. After passing the Mississippi bar in 1896, he practiced in the nation's capital for two years, until he joined the army as a major and paymaster of volunteers. When he retired from the regular army in 1911, he resumed his legal practice, but this time in Chicago.

It was during the remaining three decades of his life that he turned to writing seriously. In addition to monographs in the *Journal of Negro History*, he wrote *The Facts of Reconstruction*, an account of the African-American role during that postwar period. Written at a time when white historians argued that enfranchisement of freed blacks after the war had been a mistake, Lynch contended that black voters and black politicians had showed a high degree of civic responsibility. He also argued that the process of integrating blacks into the political system had been progressing well until the resurgence of the Democrats in the congressional election of 1874. That election, he contended, marked the seizure of political power by middle-class and poor whites, a development that prevented what he called the potential alliance of the old aristocracy and its new black allies in the Republican party. Lynch's autobiography – *Reminiscences of an Active Life* – was published posthumously in 1970.

MIZE

Located between the towns of Laurel and Magee, Mize is the acknowledged capital of "Sullivans' Hollow," reputedly first settled around 1810 by "Hog Tom" Sullivan and his eight brothers. Although they and their sons were successful farmers, their brawling and internecine feuds drove off their neighbors and caused the local sheriff to attempt to bring them to justice. "Wild Bill," the most notorious of them all, was crowned "King of the Hollow" because he had allegedly killed more Sullivans than any other member of the clan, yet he himself died peacefully in his bed. When the sheriff tried to arrest him, "Wild Bill" and a brother wedged the lawman's head between fence rails and left him there to starve. Following another murder several years later, "Wild Bill" remained in hiding for four years. Although he gave himself up for trial, a mysterious fire destroyed the courthouse and the records of indictment against him. As late as 1924 a disagreement over a call during a baseball game in Mize erupted into a melee that left two persons dead and six seriously wounded.

NATCHEZ

¶ **Briars Inn,** 31 Irving Lane, at the southeast end of the Mississippi River Bridge.

Erected between 1812 and 1815, Briars is an example of the Southern planter type of architecture. The house was later owned by William Howell, whose daughter Varina Howell married *Jefferson Davis here in 1845.

Mrs. Davis's maternal grandfather was James Kempe, a wealthy Irish nationalist from Castlefin, County Donegal, who had fled to Virginia after an unsuccessful uprising in Dublin in 1803.

§ Historic bed and breakfast inn. Phone: 601-446-9654.

¶ **Natchez State Park,** 10 miles north off U.S. 61.

Some of the horse trails in the park are thought to have been roads that led to Brandon Hall, the plantation home of *Gerard Chittocque Brandon II, the state's first native-born governor (1825-31).

Following his graduation from William and Mary College, Brandon began the practice of law in Washington, the capital of Mississippi Territory at the time. He later served in the territorial legislature before being successively elected Speaker of the House and governor. During his two administrations he opposed the further introduction of slavery into the state but aggressively promoted the opening up of Indian lands to white settlement. After he warned that the Native Americans might create an independent government "in defiance of the authority of the State," the Mississippi legislature abolished Indian sovereignty, subjected the tribes to state law, and extended citizenship to their members. Brandon was also an energetic proponent of a penitentiary system. "The object [of the justice system]," he wrote, "can be no other than to reform the offender, and at the same time to protect society from a repetition of the offense. These can be effectually accomplished only through the medium of a penitentiary [rather than] ignominious punishment. . . . In a well-regulated penitentiary the convicts have a full opportunity of reflecting upon the impropriety of crime, [and] they become accustomed to labour, and the means of which they can acquire a living by honest industry."

§ Fishing, boating, hiking trails, picnicking, camping.

¶ Stanton Hall, 401 High Street.

Regarded as one of the most palatial of all America's antebellum houses, Stanton Hall occupies an entire block. The white-painted brick house was constructed between 1851 and 1857 by Frederick Stanton, a wealthy cotton broker, as a replica of his Irish ancestral home. The mansion, which he christened "Belfast," is faced with a two-story Corinthian portico. Some of the ceilings are twenty-two feet high, and its main hallway measures seventy-two feet in length. The interior is decorated with mahogany doors, carved Carrara marble mantels, bronze gas-burning chandeliers from Philadelphia, gigantic French mirrors, and silver doorknobs and hinges from England.

By the 1850s seven separate households of Stantons lived in Natchez. Although originally a physician, Frederick Stanton went into the cotton commission business and later became a planter. At the time of his death, he owned 444 slaves and 15,000 acres. His six plantations in Louisiana and Mississippi produced more than 3,000 bales of cotton per year. He also had extensive real estate holdings in Concordia and Adams County. David Stanton, his brother, was also in cotton production and the cotton commission business. Besides his mansion "The Elms" and thirteen house slaves in Natchez, he owned $122,000 worth of property in Adams County.

§ Open daily 9-5 (except during pilgrimages). Closed December 25. Fee. Phone: 601-446-6631 or 800-647-6742.

"Stanton Hall," originally named "Belfast" after its builder's ancestral home.

¶ **Windy Hill Manor Site,** 4 miles east on Liberty Road.

The plantation house formerly on this site was sold in 1817 to Gerard Brandon I, an immigrant from County Donegal, Ireland, who later became a successful indigo and cotton planter.

Having been forced to flee Ireland during an abortive uprising, Brandon joined the Patriot cause during the American Revolution and served as a colonel under General Francis Marion in South Carolina. One of his proudest possessions was a rifle whose barrel was engraved with the words "Given For Valiant Conduct At King's Mountain." Sometime after the war he married Dorothy Nugent and received a Spanish land grant in the Natchez area. He is buried at Columbian Springs Plantation, sixteen miles from Woodville. His son, Gerard Chittocque Brandon II, was governor of the state from 1825 to 1831.

One of the former mistresses of Windy Hill was Elizabeth Brandon Stanton, the author of *Fata Morgana,* an historical novel about the Burr conspiracy. The author was Brandon's daughter and the wife of *William Stanton, a brother of the wealthy cotton broker Frederick Stanton, whose antebellum mansion is located on High Street in Natchez.

PORT GIBSON

¶ **Canemount,** 14 miles southwest on State 552 past the ruins of Windsor Manor House.

This one-and-a-half-story brick planter's house was built by John Murdock, a native of Ireland. Murdock settled in the area during the Spanish period, was financially successful, and played a considerable role during Mississippi's territorial period.

VICKSBURG NATIONAL MILITARY PARK

Throughout the park's 1,700 acres are more than 1,200 monuments, statues, memorials, and bronze markers honoring the troops who participated in the siege campaign which led to the capture of Vicksburg in July 1863. Recreations of the original trenches, forts, and artillery positions are visible along a sixteen-mile tour of the site.

§ Visitor center open daily 8-5. Phone: 601-636-0583.

¶ **General Grant Statue.**

An equestrian statue of *General Ulysses S. Grant marks the site of his headquarters during the battle of Vicksburg, a victory which effectively cut the Confederacy in two and assured Union control of the Mississippi.

Known as the "Gibraltar of the Confederacy" because of its impregnable eminence atop the bluffs, Vicksburg weathered a forty-seven-day siege before Grant's forces captured the city from the east rather than from the river.

Grant was born in Point Pleasant, Ohio, in 1822, the great-grandson of John Simpson, who came into this world near Dungannon, County Tyrone, Ireland, in 1738. After settling in Bucks County, Pennsylvania, Simpson married and had a son, who in turn headed west and took up residence in Ohio. Hannah, the daughter of this latter Simpson, married Jesse Grant and gave birth to their son – Ulysses S. Grant. Another Irish strain may have entered the famous general's pedigree through Rachel Kelley, his paternal grandmother.

In January 1879, after a long career in politics and the military, Grant arrived in Dublin during a two-year journey around the world. After visiting such landmarks as Trinity College, the Bank of Ireland, and the Royal Irish Academy, the former U.S. president was presented with the Freedom of the City by the Lord Mayor. In a speech outside City Hall, Grant acknowledged the honorary citizenship accorded him but boasted of America's Irishmen: "I am by birth a citizen of a country where there are more Irishmen, either native born or descendants of Irishmen, than you have in all Ireland. I have had the honor and pleasure, therefore, of representing more Irishmen and their descendants when in office than the Queen of England does."

General Grant Statue.

From Dublin Grant traveled to Dundalk, Omagh, and Strabane before arriving in Londonderry, that part of the Emerald Isle that he most likely had in mind when he referred to his visit to Ireland as "coming home." While in Londonderry, he gave an address in which he referred to his own Ulster roots and praised his host city, "whose history is so well known throughout America." He also expressed his hope that more Irish would immigrate to the United States when "you become more crowded and want more room," although he humorously warned his listeners that they would not be able to obtain American citizenship "as rapidly as you have made me a citizen here today."

After traveling by train to Belfast, Grant was greeted by thousands of linen mill workers let off work for the occasion. Again he emphasized the historic ties between America and Ulster in his talks but made no mention of the economic depression in the province, even though the situation had been brought to his attention earlier during a stop at Coleraine. In fact, Grant reported to a friend in the United States that "I have just had a delightful run through the North of Ireland. I saw no distress and no poverty."

¶ **General Lawler Memorial,** on Union Avenue, near the visitor center.

This memorial bust and bronze plaque honor Michael Kelly Lawler, whose assault on the Confederate position at Big Black River sparked a larger Union attack which forced the enemy to retreat to Vicksburg. During the initial assault Lawler's four regiments captured 1,100 prisoners and almost 1,500 muskets, at a loss of fourteen killed and 185 wounded.

Lawler, a native of County Kildare, Ireland, had come to America as a youngster in 1816. Within three years his father settled in Equality, Illinois, where the son early demonstrated an interest in all things military. In 1842, for instance, he served as captain of a military company which he had formed, and three years later he organized another unit for service in the Mexican War. During that conflict he also raised and commanded a cavalry company that was known as the Mamelukes, a reference to the members of the Egyptian military class.

Although the forty-six-year-old Lawler was back on the family farm in Equality when the Civil War began, he immediately recruited the 18th Illinois Volunteer Infantry. He and his unit fought in most of the early engagements in Tennessee and western Kentucky, and he himself was seriously wounded at the capture of Fort Donelson. (To recover from his wounds, he took a two-month leave of absence.)

After only months into the Civil War, Lawler came under fire for the alleged severity of his discipline. During his court martial in December 1861, the most serious charge was that he had allowed a soldier under his indirect command to be court-martialed for shooting and killing a civilian. In his defense he said that the civilian authorities to whom he had originally referred the case had refused to accept it out of fear that the soldiers who had witnessed the killing would no longer be in the area when the regular court sat several months from then. Rather than simply let the accused go free – Lawler argued – he remanded the soldier to his company commander for court martial. (The accused was found guilty and hanged.)

Although the other charges against Lawler were less serious, together they posed the possibility of his dismissal from the army. Besides being accused of causing his nephew Patrick to be commissioned a captain despite his incompetency, Lawler was charged with conduct unbecoming an officer and a gentlemen. The specific indictments included, among other things, knocking down and kicking a private and ordering two soldiers in his regiment to engage in a "most brutal and demoralizing fist fight." Although he was acquitted of some specific charges, the general verdict proclaimed him guilty and ordered that he be dismissed from service. This judgment was overturned, however, by General Henry Halleck.

For his brilliant assault against the Confederate position at Big Black River prior to the capture of Vicksburg, the Irishman received the personal thanks of *General Grant. "When it comes to just plain hard fighting, I would rather trust Old Mike Lawler than any of them," Grant proclaimed. In addition, Charles Dana, the assistant secretary of war, called the Irishman's assault "one of the most splendid exploits of the war." After the fall of Vicksburg, Lawler participated in the siege of Jackson, Mississippi, as well as in several campaigns in Texas.

Having drawn national attention for his part in the capture of Vicksburg, Lawler was the subject of a sketch in the *New York Tribune* on August 5, 1863. Described as standing almost six feet in height and weighing more than 200 pounds, the Irishman was known as the "Garibaldi of the West" and the "checkshirt general" for the informality of his dress. Wrote the *Tribune*: "He wears no insignia indicative of rank except a gilt cord on his hat. As a soldier he stands well, is a happy conversationalist and humorist, and as a disciplinarian is strict."

Some of Lawler's other traits were recorded in the writings of friends and diarists. One observer, for example, portrayed him as "a fine type of the generous, rollicking, fighting Irishman," adding that his "cherished maxim was the Tipperary one: 'If you see a head, hit it.'" A friend, meanwhile, recalled the officer's ironic humor: On hearing a member of his staff loudly cursing, the general said, "I am astonished to hear you praying at this time. I always say my prayers before going into battle." And a third acquaintance emphasized the general's Democratic politics and Catholic religion. (Lawler was once reprimanded for exposing himself to capture for passing within enemy lines on Sunday in order to hear mass.)

After the war Lawler returned to his farm near Equality, Illinois, but not before a brief career as a horse trader in the South. A monument in his honor stands in Equality, and he is buried in Hickory Hill Cemetery there.

¶ General Pemberton Statue, in the National Cemetery, Tour Stop 8.

This statue of the Confederate general John Pemberton is the work of Edmond Quinn, a native of Philadelphia of Irish descent. Pemberton made several unsuccessful attempts to stop the Union march toward Vicksburg. His defeat during the engagement at Big Black River was due in large measure to an initial attack by General Michael Lawler. (See above entry.)

Although Quinn first studied art under Thomas Eakins at the Pennsylvania Academy of Fine Arts, at age twenty-five he was able to spend a number of months in Spain, where he was influenced by the work of Velazquez. He later studied modeling and sculpting in Paris.

Among Quinn's other sculpted works are a statue of John Howard (Williamsport, Pa.), the reliefs on the battle monument at King's Mountain (South Carolina), a bust of *Edgar Allan Poe (Fordham, New York), a bronze statue of Edwin Booth as Hamlet (Gramercy Park, New York City), the female figure of "Victory" for the war memorial at New Rochelle (N.Y.), and busts of Henry Clay, Cass Gilbert, *Victor Herbert, Edwin Markham, and *Eugene O'Neill. His busts of Edwin Booth, Dr. Oliver Wendell Holmes, and *James McNeill Whistler are in the Hall of Fame of New York University. (See *Irish America, Volume 1.*)

¶ Great Redoubt, Tour Stop 11.

In May 1863 this defensive position was the scene of bloody fighting between Irish American soldiers on both sides of the Civil War. The massive earthwork, which came under attack by Union troops from the mostly Irish 7th Missouri Volunteers, was defended by members of the 21st and 22nd Louisiana, for the most part composed of Irish volunteers from New Orleans.

¶ Illinois Monument.

Designed by Charles Mulligan and modeled after the Pantheon in Rome, this memorial honors the 36,000 Illinois soldiers whose names are inscribed on the bronze plaques inside.

Mulligan left his native County Tyrone, Ireland, at age seventeen to become a stonecutter near Chicago, where he came under the tutelage of the sculptor Lorado Taft. The latter made the young Irishman his assistant in the sculpture department at the Art Institute of Chicago, where his enthusiasm infected the night students there. Even after succeeding Taft as chair of the department, Mulligan continued to carve his own designs rather than give his plaster models to someone else to be rendered in stone.

Among his other works are the *Home* (Chicago) and statues of George Rogers Clark (Quincy, Ill.), *John Finerty (Chicago), *William McKinley

(Chicago), and Abraham Lincoln (Chicago and Pana, Ill.). (See *Irish America, Volume 1.*)

¶ Jefferson Davis Statue.

A statue of the Confederate president *Jefferson Davis stands in front of the park museum.

WASHINGTON

¶ Brandon Hall, north on State 61 at Natchez Trace. Private.

Built in 1856 by *Gerard Chittocque Brandon III, this mansion is one of the largest in the state. Its front gallery is more than eighty feet long, while its huge dining room resembles an ancient Irish banquet hall. The property on which the house stands is known as Selma Plantation, originally settled by Brandon's Irish immigrant grandfather, Gerard Chittocque Brandon I. (See Windy Hill Manor Site, Natchez, Mississippi.)

WOODVILLE

¶ The Jefferson Davis Oak, in the courthouse square.

The tree honors the Confederate president *Jefferson Davis, whose boyhood home, Rosemont, is outside of town.

¶ Rosemont, 1 mile east of U.S. 61 on U.S. 24.

This typical planter's cottage was built in 1810 by Samuel Davis, who had arrived here from Kentucky with his wife, Jane Cook, and their ten children. (Mrs. Davis was of Scotch-Irish descent.) Here Jefferson Davis, the youngest of the brood, spent his childhood before going off to nearby Jefferson College and then to West Point.

After marrying Sarah Knox Taylor in 1835, Davis resigned from the army and moved to Vicksburg, where he lived the life of a Southern planter. Davis later served in the U.S. House of Representatives and fought in the Mexican War. When Mississippi seceded from the Union in 1861, he resigned from the Senate and was soon elected president of the Confederate States of America.

Rosemont's veranda is dominated by a Palladian window in the front gable, and a wide central hallway affords ventilation across the width of the house. Beyond the cottage are Mrs. Davis's rose garden and the Davis family cemetery, where five generations are buried, including Jefferson Davis's mother and his two sisters. (Davis himself is buried in Hollywood Cemetery in Richmond, Virginia.)

§ Open Monday-Friday 10-5. Fee. Phone: 601-888-6809.

MISSOURI

BELTON

❡ **Carry Nation Burial Site,** Belton Cemetery, Cambridge Road.

The grave of *Carry Nation, the fiery temperance advocate, remained unmarked until 1924, when members of the Woman's Christian Temperance Union erected a granite shaft inscribed with the words "Faithful to the Cause of Prohibition. 'She hath done what she could.'" (See Wichita, Kansas, and Bryantsville, Kentucky.)

BRANSON

❡ **Bonniebrook,** 9 miles north on U.S. 65.

This fourteen-room mansion is a reconstruction of the home in which Rose O'Neill, the creator of the Kewpie Doll, lived until her death in 1944. The original house was destroyed by fire three years later but was restored by the Bonniebrook Historical Society.

It was here at Bonniebrook, the family home, that the cherubic little figures later known as Kewpies appeared to O'Neill in a 1908 dream. The figures, she once explained, were intended to be "innocent, unsophisticated little souls perpetually amazed at their own exploits and discoveries." Although the Cupid-like figures at first appeared only as drawings, in 1913 they were transformed into dolls – originally manufactured in Germany from bisque but later mass produced in the United States from a variety of materials. Before O'Neill's retirement the Kewpies earned her $1.5 million.

Branson is the site of an annual "Kewpiesta," a four-day gathering each April at which Kewpie collectors from all over the world buy and trade the famous dolls.

CARROLLTON

❡ **General Shields Burial Site,** St. Mary's Cemetery, on U.S. 65 on the northeastern edge of town.

A colossal statue erected in 1910 marks the grave of James Shields, a native of County Tyrone, Ireland, who enjoyed a number of distinctions: He challenged Abraham Lincoln to a duel, served in three of the nation's wars, and was the only American to represent three states in the U.S. Senate.

While serving as auditor for the state of Illinois in the late 1830s, Shields was attacked in a letter submitted to the *Springfield Journal* by Abraham Lincoln. Using the pen name "Rebecca of the Lost Townships," Lincoln criticized Shields for requiring that taxes be paid in gold or silver. The letter, in the form of a dialogue between Rebecca and a farmer, called Shields "a fool, as well as a liar. With him truth is out of the question. . . . If I was deaf and dumb and blind I could tell him by the smell." A second letter, written in part by Mary Todd, Lincoln's future wife, playfully attempted a reconciliation with Shields: "I have long expected to die a widow, but as Mr. S is rather good looking than otherwise, I must say I don't care if we compromise the matter by – . . . maybe sorter let the old grudge drop if I was to consent to - be - be - h-i-s w-i-f-e? . . . . I never fight with anything but broomsticks or hot water, or a shovelful of coals or some such thing, the former of which, bein' somewhat like a shillalah, may not be very objectionable to him."

When Shields demanded to know the author of the letters, Lincoln accepted responsibility but failed to respond to the Irishman's demand for a retraction. Insulted by the silence, Shields challenged the lawyer to a duel. Only then did Lincoln offer his apologies: "I had no intention of injuring your personal or private character, or offending you as a man or a gentleman, and I did not then think . . . that that article could produce . . . that effect against you. . . . And I will add that your conduct toward me . . . had always been gentlemanly, and that I had no personal grudge against you and cause for any." Perhaps unexpectedly, Shields and the future president become lifelong friends.

A veteran of the earlier Black Hawk War, Shields went on to serve with extraordinary distinction in the conflict with Mexico. At the battle of Cerro Gordo, his right lung was pierced by a cannon grapeshot an inch and a third in diameter, although luckily the missile exited before hitting his spine. His life was saved when an Irish physician named McMillan removed the coagulated blood from the wound by forcing a bandaged ramrod through the general's body. On the field at Churubusco, Shields led the charge of New York Irish and South Carolina volunteers. Later at the battle of Chapultepec in September 1846, he fought on foot, with sword in hand, after his horse had been shot out from under him. Although he subsequently suffered a fractured arm during the assault on Mexico City, the men under his command were the first to plant the Stars and Stripes over the city. For his exploits he was honored by the states of Illinois and South Carolina. From the former he received a $3,000 sword, whose scabbard was engraved with the words: "Presented by the State of Illinois to General James Shields for gallant services at Vera Cruz, Cerro Gordo, Contreras, Churubusco, Chapultepec, and the Garita of Belen, City of Mexico." The diamond-studded sword presented by South Carolina was worth $5,000.

An example of James Shields' romantic daring was evident in an episode which occurred on the eve of the capture of Mexico City. That night an English boy entered the general's tent and informed him that his – the boy's – sister was being held captive in the city by a Mexican desperado.

Although Shields acknowledged that he had no authority to command any of his men to participate in a rescue attempt, more men volunteered than were needed. With Shields in the lead, he and his men stealthily followed the boy back into Mexico City, rescued the woman, and had almost returned to camp when the Mexicans opened fire on them, although without effect. The next morning when General Winfield Scott reprimanded Shields for his unauthorized expedition, the Englishwoman pleaded her rescuer's case. Scott was unyielding, however, and threatened the Irishman: "Shields, I shall court martial you; I shall have you dishonorably discharged, and disgrace you." Shields nobly replied: "General Scott, you can court martial me, you may have me dishonorably discharged, but no one, except myself, can disgrace me." The possibility of a court-martial disappeared the next day when his troops were the first to raise the American flag over the Mexican capital. Soon after her return to England, the object of the general's rescue sent him a diamond and emerald breastpin.

At the beginning of the 1850s, Shields represented Illinois in the U.S. Senate. His speech to that body in January 1850 on the bill to admit California is generally regarded as his most significant oration. Concerning the efforts of the South to force slavery upon California, he said: "Sir, [we] are laying the foundation of a great empire on the shore of the Pacific, . . . an empire that at some future day will carry your flag, your commerce, your arts and your arms into Asia, and through China, Hindustan, and Persia, into Western Europe. Talk about carrying slavery there, of imposing such a blight upon that people, of withering their strength and paralyzing their energies by such an institution! No, sir; such a things was never intended by God, and will never be permitted by man. It is sometimes urged here that our constitution carries slavery with it wherever it goes, unless positively excluded by law; in other words, that slavery is the normal law of this Republic. I think the principle is just the reverse. Slavery, being in violation of natural right, can only exist by positive enactment; and the constitution of the country only tolerates slavery where it exists, but neither extends [nor] establishes it anywhere."

After his defeat for reelection, the Mexican War veteran settled on his land grant in Minnesota Territory. While there, he became an energetic promoter of Irish colonization and was influential in establishing the townships of Erin, Kilkenny, Montgomery, and Shieldsville. By 1857 the last-named community had almost 300 residents, more than half of them natives of Ireland and most of the rest of Irish parentage. That same year he became one of Minnesota's first U.S. senators, drawing the short term, which lasted less than three years.

At news that Fort Sumter had been fired upon by the Confederates, Shields offered his services to Lincoln's war effort. At the time, Shields was married to the daughter of an old friend from Armagh, Ireland, and was manager and part owner of a mine in Mexico. As brigadier general of volunteers, he campaigned in the Shenandoah Valley, where he won recognition for his part in the battles of Winchester and Port Republic. Midway through the war, however, he resigned his commission and retired to San Francisco, later becoming the state railroad commissioner. He eventually settled in Missouri, again entering politics and winning election to the state legislature and then an appointment to an unexpired term in the U.S. Senate.

¶ **General Shields Monument,** on the east side of the Carroll County Courthouse.

This life-size bronze statue on a granite pedestal honors James Shields, the distinguished Irish-born soldier and senator from three states.

In 1893 the state of Illinois placed a statue of Shields in Statuary Hall in the nation's capitol building. For the occasion Charles J. Beattie composed the poem "The Shields Statue," which summarized the famous military leader's career. Portions of the work are quoted below:

> Unveil the statue! Let the bronze reveal
> The gallant soldier, true through woe and weal;
> Son of the island green, beyond the wave –
> Adopted by Columbia, free and brave;
> To her he gave his heart, and sword in strife.
> . . . .
>
> When fell marauders shed our soldiers' blood,
> And stained our soil by Rio Grande's flood,
> We saw the patriot host to battle throng,
> For our lov'd land – our country right or wrong –
> When soldiers mustered or for Aztec fields,
> First in the line was seen the gallant Shields.
>
> When the fierce storm of iron hail and rain
> At Vera Cruz swept over hill and plain,
> When Hell's red fires were hurled from fort and crag,
> He braved their furies and upheld our flag;
> In the wild cyclone's mass of wounds and death,
> He won the soldier's crown – the hero's wreath.
>
> In the advance on Cerro Gordo's height,
> He seemed the master-spirit of the fight;
> When the grim batteries from the ramparts frowned,
> He climbed the hill with all death's engines round,
> Leading the storm 'gainst embattl'd walls,
> With Spartan courage captured its high halls.
>
> Hero of heroes! in his bright career,
> He fought the post of danger, void of fear;

Foremost in fight – he led the crimson way –
Into the hottest of the bloody fray,
And proud as Mars amid the battle wreck,
Was hailed proud victor at Chapultepec.

Again war's sanguine sounds spread on the gale,
Fraternal strife convulsed the hill and vale,
Wild civil war with all its untold woes –
The North and South embattl'd – bitter foes;
Troops mustered past by field and ford,
Again the country claimed his trusty sword.

Again the hero led in war's red brunt –
The patriot men who mustered at the front
In battle's grand array, who nobly stood
Like living bulwarks 'gainst the crimson flood;
On Winchester's proud heights he led the free
And crown'd our flag with glorious victory.

Yet war was not his choice – his destined path –
He loved not bloodshed – and he sought not wrath,
His sphere was law – a Senator profound,
'Gainst slavery and injustice ever found,
Who represented 'mong our greatest – best –
Three sovereign states that gild the mighty West.

Hail, soldier of two wars! Hail, statesman true!
To-day we raise the cenotaph to you;
Though in our hearts your memory ever bright,
Outlasts the chaos of the field and fight –
And ever green be watered by our tears,
Through all the cycles of the coming years.

CONCEPTION

This small community was established in 1860 by the Reading Colony, a group of Irish Catholic railroad workers from Pennsylvania who had lost their jobs in the depression of 1857. The original fifty-eight members of the colony had been recruited through the efforts of Owen and Peter O'Reilly (contractors of the Lebanon Valley Railroad), William Brady (their paymaster), and Father James Power (the local priest). With a fund of $20,000 which the members had pooled, their leaders purchased a large tract of property near Conception. By 1869 the colony had grown to seventy-five families.

FLORIDA

❡ **Mark Twain Birthplace and Museum State Historic Park,** 0.5
mile south on State 107 in Mark Twain State Park.

The house in which Mark Twain – Samuel Langhorne Clemens – was
born in 1835 is preserved within a building constructed of stone, glass,
and steel. The museum on the property displays items associated with the
famous author's life as well as a handwritten manuscript of *The Adventures of Tom Sawyer*.

The famous author was descended through his mother from the
Irishman William Casey. Known as the Colonel, Casey was a buckskin
rifleman from the Logan's Fort area of Kentucky and the son of a Virginia
captain in the Revolutionary War. Although Twain never forgot that "my
maternal grandmother's maiden name was Margaret Casey," he generally lampooned genealogy. He once described heredity as "a procession
of ancestors that stretches back a billion years to the Adam-Clam or grasshopper or monkey from whom our race has been so tediously and ostentatiously and unprofitably developed." On another occasion, after coming across the Roman historian Suetonius's description of a certain Flavius
Clemens as "a man below contempt for his want of energy," Twain wrote
in the margin: "I guess this is where our line starts."

Twain continued his satire in an unpublished story that ridiculed the
pretensions of lineage. Casting his father as "Judge Carpenter," he makes
that character eager to "lie down in the peace and the quiet and be an
ancestor, I do get so tired of being posterity." The judge later expressed his
wish that he "would rather be a dog's ancestor than a lieutenant-governor's
posterity."

Sam Clemens' father had come to this part of Missouri from Tennessee in 1835. Once settled in the small village of Florida, he became a partner in a general store and opened a law practice. Four years after his son's
birth, the family moved to Hannibal, Missouri, which served as the model
for St. Petersburg, the home of his two most famous fictional characters –
Tom Sawyer and Huck Finn.

§ Open April-October, Monday-Saturday 10-4, Sunday noon-6; rest of
the year, Monday-Saturday 10-4, Sunday noon-5. Closed January 1, Easter, Thanksgiving, and December 25. Fee. Phone: 314-565-3449.

FLORISSANT

❡ **St. Ferdinand's Shrine,** at St. François and St. Charles streets.

Built in 1820, this unusual Federal-style church is the oldest Catholic
house of worship between the Mississippi River and the Rocky Mountains. Construction of the church was made possible largely through the
generosity of John Mullanphy, a native of Ireland and reputedly the first
millionaire west of the Mississippi. (See entry below.)

¶ **Taille de Noyer House,** 1 Taille de Noyer Drive, via a driveway on the McClure High School campus (1892 South Florissant Road).

The original part of this twenty-three-room frame house was a log cabin built in 1790 by a French fur trader. The larger main house was added about 1820 by John Mullanphy, who had purchased the property almost three decades before.

Born in County Fermanagh in 1758, Mullanphy had left his native Ireland as a young man to join the Irish Brigade in France. He eventually became an officer with that famous military unit and learned the language that would later serve him so well in St. Louis. After emigrating to America, Mullanphy and his wife lived for a time in Baltimore, where they became close friends with *Bishop John Carroll. In 1799 Mullanphy and his growing family headed west, operating a book store in Frankfort and later conducting trade with the West Indies, Natchez, and St. Louis. By 1804 Mullanphy had purchased a house in St. Louis and was serving on the Court of Common pleas, an appointment that was partially due to his fluency in French.

Much of the great wealth which the Irishman later acquired was the result of a wise business decision that he made after the War of 1812. Taking advantage of the prevailing economic depression, he bought up all the cotton in New Orleans at an average price of four cents per pound and sold it on the English market for thirty cents a pound. In this instance he seems to have followed the economic principle that served him so well: "When everybody wishes to sell, then I think it is a good time to buy, and when all have the buying craze, then it is my time to sell."

With money from his cornering of the cotton market, Mullanphy invested heavily in real estate. Besides buying the property on which Dubuque, Iowa, would later be founded, he attempted to establish an Irish colony on the rich farmland near Florissant, just north of St. Louis. In addition, from 1829 to 1833 he served as director of the St. Louis branch of the Bank of the United States. He was reputedly the first millionaire west of the Mississippi.

Mullanphy donated much of his wealth to charitable causes. Through his benefactions were established a home for boys, the first orphanage and academy for girls in St. Louis, and the first hospital west of the Mississippi River (staffed by Sisters of Charity, whom he had brought to the city). His charity was also evident in less conspicuous ways, as when he anonymously fed the poor and provided the sick with needed medicines. During a cholera epidemic in New Orleans, for example, he employed a physician to visit the afflicted in the surrounding areas. And in 1847 he allowed victims of the Irish famine to settle on his estate, a settlement that resulted in the creation of the Kerry Patch in St. Louis.

HANNIBAL

¶ Mark Twain's Boyhood Home and Museum, 208 Hill Street.

This restored house, where the famous author lived between the ages of seven and eighteen, was built by his father in 1843. Besides first editions of Twain's books and the desk on which he wrote *The Adventures of Tom Sawyer*, the museum contains photographs, original manuscripts, and sixteen oil paintings by Norman Rockwell used in the illustration of Clemens' two most famous books. (See Florida, Missouri.)

Although it is generally known that Twain modeled his famous character Huck Finn after the Hannibal scamp Tom Blankenship, that Huck's reprobate father was created in the image of another denizen of Hannibal is not so well appreciated. In Twain's most famous work, Pap Finn is an illiterate drunk who abuses his son and rails against mulattoes and free blacks. When Harold Beaver – in his critical analysis *Huckleberry Finn* – described Pap as an "Irish soaker," he most likely had in mind Jimmy Finn, the real-life resident of Hannibal upon whom Clemens based his character.

Twain on several occasions left descriptions of the presumably Irish Finn. In his autobiography he described Finn as one of Hannibal's two most notorious drunkards. (The author wrote that the pair "made as much trouble in that village as Christendom experienced in the fourteenth century, when there were two Popes at the same time.") And in 1877, more than forty years after Finn's death, Twain described the town legend as "a monument of rags and dirt; he was the profanest man in town; he had bleary eyes, and a nose like a mildewed cauliflower; he slept with the hogs in an abandoned tan-yard." The author also recalled how he and his youthful companions "stole [Finn's] dinner while he slept in the vat and fed it to the hogs in order to keep them still till we could mount them and have a ride." Although in *Huck Finn* Pap met a dramatic death – shot in the back and dumped into the Mississippi – Jimmy Finn died the death of a drunkard. According to Twain, the Irishman spent his last moments in a tan vat and died from delirium tremens combined with spontaneous combustion. In a final twist of sarcasm, Twain said that Finn's was a natural death – "I mean it was a natural death for Jimmy Finn to die."

§ Open January and February, daily 10-4; Memorial Day-Labor Day, daily 8-6; rest of the daily 8-5. Closed January 1, Thanksgiving, and December 25. Fee. Phone: 314-221-9010.

¶ Molly Brown Birthplace, Denkler Alley and Butler Street (U.S. 36).

Although this house is currently not open to the public, it was here that Margaret Tobin – the future "Unsinkable Molly" Brown – was born in 1867. Her father, John Tobin, a native of Ireland, had come to Hannibal after the death of his first wife, Catherine Pickett. Once settled in this small town along the mighty Mississippi, he found work at the Hannibal Gas Company and married Johanna Collins, with whom he had four children.

After attending the O'Leary private school, Margaret worked at a succession of jobs in town. At age thirteen, Maggie – as she was known in Hannibal – was employed at the Garth Tobacco Factory on what later became Mark Twain Avenue. She also waited on tables in the dining room of the Continental Hotel on Center Street and at the Park Hotel at 4th and Center streets. It was at the latter establishment that *Mark Twain told her about the riches to be found in the Rocky Mountains.

In 1886, at the invitation of her half-sister, Maggie and her brother Daniel traveled to Leadville, Colorado, by train, hoping to strike it rich in the silver mines. There Daniel found a job in the mines, while Maggie worked as a seamstress at the Daniels, Fisher and Smith Department Store before marrying J. J. Brown. (See Leadville and Denver, Colorado.)

¶ **Molly Brown Dinner Theater,** 200 North Main Street.

"Unsinkable Molly" Brown comes to life in lunch and dinner musical shows which also feature music from the 1920s, 1940s, and 1950s.

§ Dinner performances April-October, Monday-Saturday at 6:30 p.m. Fee. Reservations required. Phone: 314-221-8940.

¶ **Samuel Clemens Statue,** Riverside Park, at Inspiration Point, on the bluffs of the Mississippi River.

§ Park open daily 6 a.m.-10 p.m. Phone: 314-221-0154.

HOLDEN

¶ **Carry Nation House,** across from the Community Building. Private.

Following the marriage of Dr. Charles Gloyd to the twenty-one-year-old *Carry Moore, the couple moved into this house. Almost immediately, however, the marriage floundered when Gloyd's habitual drunkenness forced his young wife to roam the streets looking for him or trying to prevent local saloons from serving him. Gloyd died of drink in 1868, a year after their marriage and soon after the birth of their child. The widow subsequently prepared herself for a career in education and returned to Holden to teach school. She remained here until her marriage to David Nation, a minister and lawyer, four years later. (See Bryantsville, Kentucky, and Medicine Lodge, Kansas.)

KANSAS CITY

¶ **James Pendergast Statue,** Case Park, bounded by Interstate 85 and 8th, Jefferson, and 10th streets.

From 1911 to 1991, this ten-foot-high bronze statue stood in Mulkey Park, a tribute to the Irish-American political leader who laid the foundations of the city's powerful machine. The seated statue was moved to this site in 1992.

Pendergast was the son of Irish immigrants who had settled in St. Joseph, Missouri, in 1857. After moving to Kansas City, the young James worked first in a slaughterhouse and then at the Jarboe Iron Works, both in an ethnically mixed area known as the West Bottoms. In 1882, however, he bought a boarding house and saloon, which he promptly named "Climax" for the racehorse whose longshot win had enriched his pockets. After acquiring several more saloons, he was soon on his way to prosperity. The *Kansas City Star* later catalogued his assets: "A farm in Kansas, a farm near Lamar, Missouri; blooded stock, horses, cattle, swine and sheep; several pieces of real estate."

The story is told of the time that Fireman Jim Flynn – the only man to knock out *Jack Dempsey – sauntered one day into one of Pendergast's saloons. After more than drinking his fill, Flynn became belligerent when Pendergast denied him another draft and reminded him that there were 600 other saloons to which he could take his trade. Flynn refused to leave and shouted, "There's nobody big enough to put me out." The barkeep bested the braggart in a battle royal that lasted fifteen minutes.

Pendergast first took on political significance when the mayoral candidate he had touted to his saloon customers won easily over his opponent in the first ward. From then on, the tavernkeeper was known as the "King of the First." With this reputation he organized the city's first permanent Democratic club, which gradually gained control of the wards where his saloons were located. His election to the city council in 1892 marked the beginning of an eighteen-year career as "Alderman Jim."

Despite their growing influence, the Democrats were unable to dominate the city administration during most of the 1890s. This failure was due, in large part, to the rivalry between Pendergast and Joseph Shannon, the boss of the ninth ward. The two machines – popularly known as the Goats and the Rabbits – had received their nicknames from remarks made by two political writers of the period. While one journalist had claimed that Pendergast had obtained the vote of "everything in sight, including the goats on the hillsides," the other author had written that the Shannon men had "flocked to the polls like scared rabbits after hunters had beaten the brush."

In 1900 the *Star* captured the essence of the publican-politician in an editorial entitled "Pendergast at his Post." "What need, indeed, has he for halls or stages or rostrums?" the editor asked. "Here gather the candidates, to learn how the battle is waging. Here assemble the leaders to confer together. Here come the humble toilers of the Democratic vineyard to receive their instructions. . . ." Almost literally from behind the bar, Pendergast had created a benevolent machine which, through its patronage and care for the needy, had won the loyalty of the poor and the working class alike.

Yet Pendergast downplayed any suggestion that his position allowed him to wield great power. "You can't make 'em vote for you," he said. "I never coerced anybody in my life. Whenever you see a man bulldozing anybody, he don't last long. Still, I've been called a boss. All there is to it is having friends, doing things for people, and later they'll do things for you."

Following his premature death from Bright's disease in 1911, Pendergast was eulogized by the *Kansas City Journal*. "No deserving man, woman or child that appealed to 'Jim' Pendergast went away empty handed. . . . ," the paper recalled. "The extent of his bounty was never known, as he made it an inviolable rule that no publicity should be given his philanthropy. There never was a winter in the last twenty years that he did not circulate among the poor of the West Bottoms, ascertaining their needs, and after his visit there were no empty larders."

Two decades before, Pendergast had brought his younger brother Tom into his "operation." After serving an apprenticeship as a bookkeeper for his brother's saloons, Tom began his rise up the political ladder: from superintendent of streets (one of the city's richest patronage-dispensing posts) to city councilman. When the elder Pendergast retired from politics in 1910, he recommended his brother to his followers and – perhaps knowingly – wrote his own epitaph: "Take Brother Tom; he'll make a fine alderman, and he'll be good to the boys, just as I have been. Eighteen years of thankless work for the city, eighteen years of abuse; eighteen years of getting jobs for the push, is all the honor I want."

While retaining the loyalty of the city's working class, Tom Pendergast attempted to attract the support of middle-class voters. He succeeded in this effort by sponsoring various social events and by strategically awarding county and municipal contracts as well as franchises and tax deductions. The financial support which he received from cooperative businessmen and contractors helped build his personal fortune, due primarily to his Ready-Mixed Concrete Company, his wholesale liquor business, and a hotel that catered to prostitutes. After securing the election of a "pliant" Harry Truman to the Jackson County board in 1922, Pendergast established himself as the undisputed boss of the Democratic machine in the Kansas City area.

Pendergast enjoyed further opportunities to dispense patronage following the election of Franklin Roosevelt in 1932. Aware of his debt to the Kansas City boss for his support at the Democratic nominating convention that year, the president gave Pendergast control over many federal appointments under the Civil Works Administration and the Works Progress Administration. Pendergast's influence peaked when his machine helped elect Truman to the U.S. Senate, making the former haberdasher "the senator from Pendergast."

The boss's reputation for "cutting corners" finally caught up with him in the late 1930s. Never beneath bribing businessmen, stuffing ballot boxes, or protecting criminals, Pendergast was the target of a federal investigation into his income as well as into voting irregularities. As a result, he was convicted of income tax evasion and was sentenced to fifteen months in prison. Despite the obvious political dangers involved, Truman remained loyal to Pendergast. After hearing about the latter's conviction, the senator remarked, "Tom Pendergast has always been my friend and I don't desert a sinking ship." Later, as vice president, Truman attended his friend's funeral.

¶ **New York Life Building,** 20 West 9th Street.

The large bronze eagle that adorns the exterior of this brownstone structure was designed by Louis Saint-Gaudens and was cast in one piece. The two-ton eagle, which was placed in position in 1891, is poised with twelve-foot-long wings over a nest of eaglets. Saint-Gaudens was the brother of the more famous Irish-born sculptor Augustus Saint-Gaudens.

KEARNEY

¶ **Jesse James Birthplace,** 1.5 miles east on State 92 and then 1.5 miles on Jesse James Farm Road.

The notorious outlaw Jesse James was born in this log cabin in 1847, and it was here that he and his older brother Frank lived with their mother, Zerelda Cole James, a Catholic who traced her roots to Ireland. (Her husband, the Reverend Robert James, worked the surrounding farm until his death in California in 1850.) Jesse James's guns and personal effects, as well as his original tombstone, are on display in the adjoining museum.

In 1863 Union troops attacked the James home, beating Jesse and hanging his stepfather (who survived). Almost immediately Jesse and his brother joined the Confederate guerrilla force of the infamous William Quantrill. The following year the brothers were part of a band of approximately 200 guerrillas who looted Centralia, Missouri, held up a train, and killed twenty-five Union troops on board. That same day these raiders defeated an equal number of cavalrymen. In the last months of the Civil War, Frank James headed east with Quantrill's men in the hopes of assassinating President Lincoln. The scheme failed when the guerrilla leader was killed in Kentucky.

After the war the James brothers employed their guerrilla tactics in peacetime robbery. During the next fifteen years they ranged through eleven states and territories, carrying off an estimated twenty-five raids. After joining forces with the three Younger brothers, they terrorized the Midwest with their robberies. In retaliation, Pinkerton railroad detectives attacked the James house with a bomb, hoping to kill the outlaw brothers, who, it turned out, were not at home. Instead, the bomb tore off Zerelda's right arm and killed her eight-year-old son.

§ Open Memorial Day weekend-October 1, daily 9-4; rest of the year, Monday-Friday 9-4, Saturday-Sunday noon-4. Closed January 1, Thanksgiving, and December 25. Fee. Phone: 816-628-6065.

• The historical drama *The Life and Times of Jesse James* is presented on weekends from August through Labor Day.

¶ Near the James Home is the Claybrook House, an antebellum frame structure built in 1893 by Frank James. His brother's daughter Mary James Barr lived here between 1900 and 1921.

¶ Jesse James is buried in Mount Olivet Cemetery in Kearney, under a gravestone that reads, "Killed by a coward whose name isn't worthy to appear here." In July 1995 a team of scientists exhumed the bones in order to determine whether the remains in the grave are those of James. To help establish a definitive DNA link to the bank robber's bones, three of James's known descendants offered to provide genetic material to the forensic scientists working on the case.

LEBANON

¶ **McClurg Memorial,** Lebanon Cemetery, at the north end of town.

A granite shaft marks the grave of James McClurg, a congressman and governor of Missouri, whose grandfather had fled Ireland after the failed uprising of 1798.

After serving as deputy sheriff of St. Louis County in the first half of the 1840s, McClurg headed for the California gold mines as a caravan driver. After three years, however, he returned to Missouri, where he established a wholesale and retail mercantile business. A decade later he organized the Osage Volunteer Regiment at the beginning of the Civil War but left the fighting field when he was elected to Congress in 1862. There he became thoroughly identified with the Radical Republicans and their vindictive policy for the defeated South. After his election as governor, he successfully urged the establishment of the state agricultural college and the Missouri School of Mines and Metallurgy (now the University of Missouri at Rolla).

LEXINGTON

¶ **Battle of Lexington State Historic Site,** 4 miles off U.S. 24.

In September 1861 this was the site of a three-day engagement between Confederate and Union troops, the latter under the command of Colonel James Mulligan, an Irish politician from Chicago who commanded the 23rd Illinois, the "Irish Brigade."

After two days of intensive firing, the Confederates advanced behind hemp bales soaked with water to withstand the enemy's fire power and came within fifty yards of the Union position. The desperation of Mulligan's men is evident in his report that soldiers "dying from thirst [were] frenziedly wrestling for water in which the bleeding stumps of mangled limbs had been washed and drinking it with a horrid avidity." By the end of the day the Confederates had taken 3,000 prisoners, among them Mulligan himself.

Following his exchange two months later, he was wounded at Winchester. As his men carried him to safety, he noticed that the colors were about to be captured. "Lay me down and save the flag!" he cried. Although his men reluctantly obeyed, they returned to find that their commander had been captured.

§ Open April 15-October 31, Monday-Saturday 8:30-4:30, Sunday noon-5:30. Closed Easter. Phone: 816-259-4654.

ℐ Central College Park, 16th Street.

This was the original site of Masonic College, *Colonel James Mulligan's headquarters during the battle of Lexington in 1861. A scale model of the college is located in the park.

LIBERTY

ℐ Jesse James Bank Museum, 103 North Water Street.

In February 1866 this former bank was the scene of the first daylight bank robbery in the United States, at least outside of war time. The $60,000 heist – which resulted in the death of one bystander – was reputedly committed by the members of a gang led by *Jesse and *Frank James. Today the museum displays documents and pictures related to the gang. (See Kearney, Missouri.)

§ Open Monday-Saturday 9-4, Sunday noon-4. Fee. Phone: 816-781-4458.

PALMYRA

ℐ George Shannon Burial Site, in an old cemetery at the north end of town off U.S. 61 (Business Route).

A sign marks the grave of George Shannon, born in Pennsylvania to Irish Protestant parents and noteworthy as a member of the Lewis and Clark Expedition of 1804-06.

Shannon was only eighteen when he joined Captain Meriwether Lewis in 1803 and was listed as one of the "Nine young men from Kentucky." Although he was reputedly a good horseman and hunter, he frequently became lost during the expedition, but he was always able to rejoin the main party. (He once became lost when his companions reversed their course without his knowledge.) He is mentioned several times in Lewis and Clark's journal, once when he killed a deer, another time when he swam after some deer that his companions had wounded, and again as a member of a court-martial that found the accused guilty of sedition.

A year after returning from the famous trek west, Shannon was shot in the leg by Arikara Indians while he served with a force that tried to return Chief Shahaka to his home among the Mandans. The wound was so severe that his leg was amputated in St. Charles, Missouri. (He was known thereafter as "Peg-leg" and was lucky enough to obtain a pension from Congress for his injury.) While he recuperated, he helped Nicholas Biddle edit the famous Lewis and Clark journal. Although Captain Clark later proposed a partnership with him in the fur trading business – under the name "George Shannon & Company" – he declined, preferring instead to study law at Transylvania University in Kentucky. After briefly practicing in Lexington, Kentucky, he was elected to the state legislature in 1820 and 1822. After moving to Missouri, he continued his legal profession and served as U.S. senator and U.S. district attorney. He died while arguing a case in Palmyra at the age of forty-nine.

PLATTSBURG

¶ **Atchison Monument,** on the lawn of the Clinton County Courthouse.

This life-size metal figure on a granite base was erected in honor of David Rice Atchison, not usually listed among the presidents of the United States but nevertheless regarded by some as "president for a day."

Atchison, whose father was an emigrant from Ireland, was born near Lexington, Kentucky, in 1807. Forty-two years later, as the president *pro tempore* of the U.S. Senate, he was in the line of succession when the terms of *President James K. Polk and Vice President George Dallas expired at midnight on March 3. Because the following day was a Sunday, the president-elect, Zachary Taylor, chose not to take the oath of office until Monday. It was therefore asserted that the office of president devolved upon Atchison once Polk's term ended and before Taylor took the oath.

Atchison himself, however, denied that he had been president for that twenty-four-hour period. Years later he said that the office of president had been vacant during that brief time because his own term as president pro tem had ended with the adjournment of that session of Congress. According to this view, his occupancy of the office of president pro tem ended when his term as U.S. Senator ended, at midnight on March 3. Nevertheless, he good-naturedly recalled that some of his colleagues had asked him what his policies would be as president and had even sought positions in his cabinet. Atchison confessed that, after two or three busy nights finishing up the work of the Senate, he had slept "most of that Sunday" – the day he supposedly was chief executive.

REPUBLIC

¶ **General Sweeny's: A Museum of Civil War History,** 10 miles southwest via State 60, 0.75 mile southeast on Republic Road, and then 7 miles south on County ZZ.

Named for General Thomas William Sweeny, a Union officer and Fenian leader, this privately owned museum features a collection of Civil War memorabilia from the trans-Mississippi theater. In addition to weapons, photographs, flags, and uniforms, the collection contains personal effects belonging to Sweeny and his more famous fellow Irishman General Patrick Cleburne. (See Helena, Arkansas.) The museum is adjacent to Wilson Creek National Battlefield, where Sweeny was wounded on August 10, 1861.

Born in County Cork in 1820, Sweeny emigrated to America at the age of twelve. During the Mexican War he was second lieutenant of New York volunteers and served with General Winfield Scott from Vera Cruz to the capture of Churubusco. At the latter engagement, Sweeny was wounded in the right arm, although he continued to lead his troops until exhaustion forced him to be carried from the field. The limb was so severely damaged that it had to be amputated, an excruciatingly painful experience in the absence of anesthesia. From the end of the Mexican conflict to the eruption of the Civil War, he served as an infantry officer in several campaigns against Indian tribes in Nebraska and the Southwest.

By the beginning of 1862, Sweeny was colonel of the 52nd Illinois Volunteers. In rapid succession he aided in the capture of Fort Donelson and helped save the day at Shiloh. A captain in the regiment described the Irishman's remarkable composure under fire in that latter engagement: "The balls seemed to fill the air at this moment, the fire was so terrific, but our colonel coolly sat on his horse, quietly smoking a cigar, ever and anon removing it and puffing forth vast quantities of smoke. Presently a minié ball came cutting through the air, struck his cigar, and cut it off at his teeth, doing some slight injury to his moustache. Yet not a muscle moved. He quietly replaced the cigar with a fresh one and smoked away."

Under a subsequent barrage at Shiloh, however, Sweeny was not so lucky. Besides seeing his horse shot from under him (riddled with seven bullets), he was hit in the foot and in his remaining arm. Sweeny, in fact, was wounded so frequently during the war that after one engagement *General Ulysses S. Grant laughingly said to him: "How is it, Sweeny, that you have not been hit? There must be some mistake. This fight will hardly count unless you can show another wound."

Despite his long absence from Ireland, Sweeny still dreamed of independence for his native land. In 1856, while stationed at Fort Pierre in Nebraska, he alluded to the Emerald Isle in a letter to his family. "I see they are making another movement for Irish independence. . . , he wrote.

"We might accomplish great things – do deeds that our children could point at on the page of history with pride – perhaps help to pull a sinewy tyrant from his throne, and raise a prostrate people from chains to liberty."

Nine years later the Irishman appeared before the Fenian Congress in Philadelphia and submitted a plan for the conquest of Canada, a quixotic attempt to hold that British colony hostage for the liberation of Ireland. Subsequently elected secretary of war for the Irish "republic in exile," he orchestrated the ill-fated invasion of Canada from Vermont and New York State in 1866. The attempt was an unqualified failure, and Sweeny was among the Fenian leaders who were arrested by U.S. authorities at the border.

§ Open March-October, daily 10-5; February and November, Saturday-Sunday 10-5. Fee. Phone: 417-732-1224.

ROLLA

¶ **University of Missouri at Rolla,** North Pine Street.

Each year in the middle of March, students at Missouri's technological university honor St. Patrick, the patron saint of engineers, with a variety of special activities.

This annual tradition began on the Rolla campus in 1908, when the university was known as the Missouri School of Mines and Metallurgy. That year a student committee organized the first celebration of St. Patrick's Day, doing so secretly because classes were expected to be in session that day. When the unilaterally declared holiday arrived, the students on campus dressed in green sashes and carried shillelaghs as they greeted the arrival of St. Patrick. The Irish saint then proceeded to interpret the marks on a ready-made Blarney Stone, used a forked stick as a transit to survey a quadrangle, and knighted the members of the senior class (who were dressed in green robes and green mortar boards). Over the years since then, St. Patrick – dressed in his green and gold pontificals – has traditionally arrived on a railroad handcar and appeared in the annual parade on a manure spreader. (A snake-killing ritual was conducted some years.)

Today's activities last a week and typically include several contests: best beard, greenest person, leprechaun look-alike, walking stick and shillelagh competition, and best St. Patrick's jingle. Toward the end of the week, St. Patrick presides over the Honorary Knighting Ceremony and the coronation of the Queen of Love and Beauty. In 1994 the grand marshal of the annual parade was Missouri's first lady.

ST. JOSEPH

¶ **Jesse James Home,** 12th and Penn streets, on the grounds of the Patee

House Museum.

This simple frame building was the final home of *Jesse James, who lived here as a fugitive with his wife and children under the alias "Tom Howard." In April 1882 the house was the scene of James's death at the hands of Robert and Charles Ford, former confederates of James's who hoped to share a $10,000 reward from several railroad companies.

Although Robert Ford had originally intended only to turn James over to authorities, he shot James in the back of the head when the latter began to suspect Ford's treachery. According to Ford's account of the episode, he killed James while the famous outlaw straightened a picture on the wall: "As he stood there, unarmed, with his back to me, it came to me suddenly, 'Now or never is your chance. If you don't get him now he'll get you to-night.' Without further thought or a moment's delay, I pulled my revolver and levelled it as I sat. He heard the hammer click as I cocked it with my thumb and started to turn as I pulled the trigger. The ball struck him just behind the ear and he fell like a dog." (Ford was henceforth known as "that dirty little coward who shot Mister Howard.") Although the Fords were convicted of murder and were sentenced to be hanged, they were pardoned by the governor. Charles Ford later committed suicide, while Robert was shot in Colorado.

Fearing for his life following his brother's death, Frank James surrendered to the governor and was tried for murder and train robbery. In this and subsequent trials, however, the jury failed to convict, and within two years all charges were dropped. James died in 1915 after spending the rest of his life on the family farm. (See Kearney, Missouri.)

Today the Jesse James Home exhibits the famous bandit's rocking chair and shaving mug as well as the hole in the wall reputedly made by the bullet that killed him.

§ Open May-August, Monday-Saturday 10-5, Sunday 1-5; rest of the year, Monday-Saturday 10-4, Sunday 1-4. Fee. Phone: 816-232-8206.

ST. LOUIS

¶ **Bellefontaine Cemetery,** 4947 West Florissant Avenue.
• The Wainwright Tomb, located on Prospect Avenue in the southeast corner of the property, was designed in 1891 by *Louis Sullivan. Although the mausoleum was commissioned by Ellis Wainwright, the St. Louis entrepreneur, as the tomb of his wife, he was laid to rest there thirty-three years later. The tomb's low dome and the bands carved along the building's sides give it an Oriental flavor. (See Cedar Rapids, Iowa.)
• Among the others buried here are the Irish-Americans Francis Preston Blair, James Eads, and John O'Fallon. (See entries below.)

¶ **Calvary Cemetery,** 5239 West Florissant Avenue.

This spacious, parklike setting is dotted with the gravesites of many Irish-American figures from the city's past. Among the more well known are:

• Kate O'Flaherty Chopin, an author whose stories reflect the local color tradition and appreciatively depict the Creole culture of her day. (See Cloutierville, Louisiana.)

• Thomas Dooley III, a naval medical officer and physician who dedicated his short life to helping the people of Southeast Asia.

Dooley was the grandson of an Irish emigré from County Limerick who designed and built the first all-steel boxcar, while his father was an executive with the American Car and Foundry Company. Dooley himself, meanwhile, served as a medical corpsman in the U.S. Navy before graduating from Notre Dame University in 1948. After receiving a medical degree from St. Louis University Medical School, he reenlisted in the navy. In 1954 he served as medical officer aboard a rescue ship transporting refugees from North Vietnam to South Vietnam.

At a refugee camp which he established at Haiphong, Dooley and his fellow corpsmen treated 2,000 evacuees a day. "I was crowding more practice in malaria, yaws, beri-beri, leprosy and cholera into a month than most doctors see in a long lifetime," he later recalled. After helping treat and evacuate more than 600,000 refugees, he was honored by the South Vietnamese government and became the youngest U.S. naval officer to receive the Legion of Merit.

After resigning from the navy in 1965, Dooley joined three of his former corpsmen in resuming their medical work, this time in Laos. With medical supplies from U.S. manufacturers and financial support from the sale of *Deliver Us From Evil*, his best-selling account of his earlier work in Vietnam, he soon established three clinics in the country. Whether working in surgery or training the native people in better hygiene, he always reminded them that the source of their medical assistance was American good will.

To criticism that medical care would deteriorate when it was handed over to the Laotians, Dooley replied realistically. "In Asia I run a nineteenth-century hospital," he said. "Upon my departure the hospital may drop to the eighteenth century. That is fine, because previously the tribes in the high valleys lived, medically speaking, in the fifteenth century." He recorded his life in Laos in two additional best sellers: *The Edge of Tomorrow* and *The Night They Burned the Mountain*.

By 1959 Dooley had become so popular that a Gallup Poll that year listed him among the ten most admired men in the world. That same year Dooley suffered an injury to his chest after falling down a steep embankment in a Laotian village. When a malignant tumor developed, it was removed through surgery, but the cancer quickly reappeared and spread. On January 18, 1961, the day after his thirty-fourth birthday, this accomplished pianist, swimmer, and horseman fell victim to the disease. About a year and a half later, *President John F. Kennedy presented Dooley's mother with a congressional medal named in honor of her son.

• John Mullanphy, a native of County Fermanagh, Ireland, and reputedly the first millionaire west of the Mississippi. (See Florissant, Missouri.)

A circular plot known as "Exiles' Rest" is adorned with several Celtic crosses marking the burial place of many of the city's Catholic clergy, including Peter Richard Kenrick.

The first archbishop of St. Louis, Kenrick was born in Dublin in 1806 and completed his education at St. Patrick's College, Maynooth, Ireland. Following his ordination, he emigrated to Philadelphia at the request of his brother, the bishop of that diocese. While serving as rector of the cathedral and president of the seminary, the younger Kenrick published three books, most notably one entitled *The Validity of Anglican Orders*.

Kenrick was named archbishop of St. Louis in 1847 and enjoyed a tenure of almost fifty years. During that time the see experienced phenomenal growth, the Catholic population doubling to 200,000 and the number of priests increasing fivefold to 350. In several famous incidents, however, the archbishop came into conflict with the secular authorities. During the Civil War, for instance, when the provost marshal asked him to fly the Stars and Stripes over the cathedral, he refused. "No other banner may be placed there, for already there stands, and which alone shall stand, the banner of the Church," the archbishop defiantly said, pointing to the cross on the church spire. In fact, the Irishman's generally Southern sympathies caused William Seward, Lincoln's secretary of state, to broach with *Archbishop John Hughes of New York the possibility of Kenrick's removal by the Vatican. In another celebrated case after the war, Kenrick fought a Missouri statute which required all clergymen to take an oath of loyalty to the state before being allowed to preach or witness marriages. When one of his priests was imprisoned for failing to take the oath, the archbishop appealed the case to the U.S. Supreme Court, which ruled that the law was unconstitutional.

Kenrick also took a prominent contrarian position at Vatican Council I in 1870. As that ecumenical council in Rome prepared to define the dogma of papal infallibility, Kenrick became a leader of the minority opposed to such a formal declaration. He feared that such a pronouncement would not only alienate non-Catholics further but also pose the possibility of schism within the Church itself. He also argued that papal pronouncements on faith and morals were infallible only if the bishops throughout the world concurred with them, a position at odds with the notion promoted by the majority at the council.

ℐ Campbell House, 1508 Locust Street.

This three-story Greek Revival townhouse is the last of the residential mansions which adorned Lucas Place, the preserve of the city's affluent from 1850 to 1880. The house was purchased in 1854 by Robert Campbell, a native of County Tyrone, Ireland. Campbell and his wife, Virginia Kyle, lived in this house until he died in 1879. Of their thirteen children, only three survived the epidemics that regularly ravaged the city. The last of their two bachelor sons continued to reside here until his death in the 1938, maintaining it as it had appeared during his childhood. The house contains original furnishings, many of them acquired in Europe by Virginia Campbell.

A year after his arrival in St. Louis in 1824, Robert Campbell traveled west to the Rocky Mountains, primarily in search of a better climate for his weak lungs. There he became associated with William Ashley in the fur trade until the latter's retirement in 1830. Campbell was extremely successful as a trader and trapper, despite his dislike of life in the wilderness. His travels took him as far as the Great Salt Lake, and he was almost killed when his party was attacked by Blackfoot Indians. During those early years in the West, he formed close friendships with the other famous mountain men of the era: James Bridger, Kit Carson, William Sublette, Jedediah Smith, and fellow Irishman Thomas Fitzpatrick. Campbell even attracted the attention of Washington Irving, who said that the Irishman's "exploits partake of the wildest spirit of romance. No danger or difficulty can appall him."

The Campbell House.
(Photo courtesy of the
Robert Campbell House
Museum.)

At the end of 1832, Campbell and Sublette formed a partnership that became the source of their eventual great wealth. Supplied by provisions from Campbell's brother in Philadelphia, the resulting Rocky Mountain Fur Company established a post on the upper Missouri River with the intent of challenging the powerful American Fur Company. Although at first Campbell's enterprise profited from an arrangement that granted each company exclusive control over either the river or the mountain fur trade, his rival eventually won the contest. Even Fort Laramie – which Campbell had built in the southeastern corner of Wyoming – fell under his rival's control.

After ten years in the West, the Irishman returned permanently to St. Louis, where he oversaw his growing financial concerns. To his real estate holdings he added a dry-goods business and served as president of the Bank of Missouri and the Merchant's National Bank. In 1846, with the outbreak of war with Mexico, he recruited four regiments of Missouri volunteers and provided supplies for *General Stephen Kearny's expedition to California. Five years later Campbell served with the Jesuit missionary Father Pierre de Smet as a representative of the United States at a peace conference that attracted 10,000 Indians to Fort Laramie. Because of his reputation for dealing fairly with the Native Americans, Campbell was subsequently appointed to the Indian Commission.

§ Open March-December, Tuesday-Saturday 10-4, Sunday noon-5. Closed holidays. Fee. Phone: 314-421-0325.

√ Campbell's birthplace has been preserved and is on display at the Ulster Folk and Transport Museum near Bangor, County Down, in Northern Ireland.

¶ **Cupples House,** 3673 West Pine Boulevard on the campus of St. Louis University.

Although constructed in 1890 for Samuel Cupples, a St. Louis businessman and philanthropist, this $500,000 Romanesque residence is now a cultural center for St. Louis University. The forty-two-room mansion is noted for its ironwork, wood paneling, parquet floors, and Tiffany stained-glass windows. The former bowling alley in the mansion is now the McNamee Art Gallery.

Born in Harrisburg, Pennsylvania, Cupples was educated by his father, a teacher who had emigrated from County Down, Ireland, in 1814. By the age of twenty, the son had formed a business enterprise manufacturing and selling wooden-ware in St. Louis. To facilitate shipping, Cupples and a partner bought up property near the city's rail terminals and erected approximately fifty buildings, each with direct access to rail trackage.

As an outgrowth of his interest in education, Cupples helped establish two facilities at Washington University: the St. Louis Training School and the School of Engineering and Architecture. He later endowed the university with his railroad terminal property. His total bequests to educational institutions and the Southern Methodist Church amounted to almost $5 million.

§ Open Tuesday-Friday noon-4, Sunday 2-4. Fee. Phone: 314-658-3025.

¶ **Eads Bridge,** Washington Avenue, at the Mississippi River.

Hailed as the world's first steel-truss bridge, this St. Louis landmark was designed by Captain James Eads, under whose supervision it was constructed between 1867 and 1874. The bridge, whose three spans were – at the time of their construction – the longest fixed-end metal arches ever built, is 6,220 feet long. Construction of the bridge also involved use of the first pneumatic caissons in the United States.

Eads, whose maternal ancestors were from Ireland, gained international attention when he and 4,000 workers throughout the country constructed a fleet of seven steam-propelled, armor-plated gunboats for the Union navy during the Civil War. The first of the fleet – the *St. Louis* – was constructed in forty-five days. Eads later became a proponent of a ship railway across the Tehuantepec Isthmus in Mexico rather than a canal across Panama. He even proposed building the line at his own expense if the U.S. government would guarantee him a 6 percent return for fifteen years. Although a bill containing these terms passed the House, it was defeated in the Senate. In 1884 he became the first American to receive the Albert Award for services to the science of engineering from the British Society for the Encouragement of Art, Manufacture, and Commerce.

¶ **Forest Park,** bounded by Oakland Avenue and Lindell, Skinker, and Kingshighway boulevards.

This 1,000-acre expanse contains several attractions associated with figures in Irish-American history:

• The main entrance steps of the St. Louis Art Museum are flanked by two marble figures: *Painting* by *Louis Saint-Gaudens, and *Sculpture* by Daniel Chester French. The museum's American collection contains works by *John Singleton Copley, Thomas Hart Benton, George Caleb Bingham, Winslow Homer, and *Georgia O'Keeffe.

§ Museum open Wednesday-Sunday 10-5, Tuesday 1:30-8:30. Closed January 1, Thanksgiving, and December 25. Phone: 314-721-0072.

• At the northeast corner of the park stands a statue of Francis Preston Blair, the Unionist politician who was influential in preventing Missouri's secession in 1861. The people of the state later honored him by placing his likeness in Statuary Hall in the U.S. Capitol.

Blair, who was descended from a Scotch-Irish immigrant who had come to America in the eighteenth century, began his political career as a Free-Soiler, dedicated to stopping the spread of slavery into the western lands acquired from Mexico after 1848. Although he personally owned slaves, he opposed the spread of slavery for moral and economic reasons, believing that "the peculiar institution" would retard the West's economic development. After his election to Congress in 1856, he predicted the demise of slavery and encouraged Southern slave owners to support the colonization of African Americans outside the United States. Once war came, Blair helped lead a military force that captured Camp Jackson, a militia post in Missouri with strong Confederate leanings. Although this action caused thousands of his fellow Missourians to join the Confederate cause, the state ultimately remained in the Union, especially after the federal arsenal at St. Louis was saved from rebel hands. Following the war, during which he raised seven regiments and saw action at Vicksburg, he returned to state politics. There he found himself opposed to the punitive policies toward the South promoted by the Radical Republicans in Congress, particularly their efforts to enfranchise the newly freed slaves and disfranchise the whites. He preferred to allow the Southern states a greater degree of internal autonomy in return for swearing allegiance to the Constitution and accepting the abolition of slavery.

¶ **Grant's Farm,** 10501 Gravois (Route 30) at Grant Road, in southern St. Louis County.

After resigning from the U.S. Army in 1854, *Ulysses S. Grant lived and worked on a farm on this site, which he and his wife, Julia, had received from her father as a wedding gift. Julia regarded the large Southern-style log house which Grant built on the property as so unattractive that she called it "Hardscrabble." The Grants lived here until the beginning of the Civil War.

Grant continued to own the cabin and the farm until 1884, when they were repossessed by the mortgage holder. One subsequent buyer disassembled the structure, and another exhibited it at the 1904 St. Louis World's Fair. It was later purchased by Adolphus Busch, who removed it to his estate. In 1977 the cabin was again disassembled, but this time the deteriorated sections were replaced with new material. Today the farm and the Grants' house are part of Busch Gardens, a game preserve operated by Anheuser-Busch Company.

§ Open June-August, Tuesday-Sunday 9-3; April 15-May 31 and September 1-October 15, Thursday-Sunday 9-3. Reservations required for farm. Phone: 314-843-1700.

¶ **Grant Home at White Haven,** 7400 Grant Road.

"White Haven" was originally the residence and estate of Colonel Frederick Dent, the father-in-law of *Ulysses S. Grant. Here Grant met and married his wife, Julia, and it was here that their first child was born. After Grant resigned from the army in 1854, he and his wife lived here again, except for a brief stay at Hardscrabble. (See entry above.)

During his presidency Grant purchased White Haven from the Dent family. Although he never carried out his intention to retire on the property and raise horses, he held on to the estate until he lost it in payment for a debt. Today the property includes a two-story residence, slave quarters, a barn, a smoke house, and an ice house.

¶ **Grant Statue,** City Hall, Market Street and Tucker Boulevard.

A statue of *General Ulysses S. Grant stands atop a pedestal in front of the city hall, a sprawling Renaissance Revival structure modeled after the Hotel de Ville in Paris and built between 1891 and 1904.

¶ **Jefferson Barracks Historical Park,** Grant Road and Kingston, 10 miles south at Interstate 55 South Broadway exit.

Many famous military leaders have been stationed here since this garrison was established in 1826. Following his graduation from West Point two years later, *Lieutenant Jefferson Davis came to the barracks with an African-American slave as his valet; the future president of the Confederacy later returned from the West with the captive Chief Black Hawk. *Lieutenant Ulysses S. Grant was stationed here in 1843; he met his future wife, Julia Dent, at nearby "Whitehaven." The post's powder magazine is now a museum, while the national cemetery in the park contains the remains of 70,000 servicemen.

§ Museum open Wednesday-Saturday 9-5, Sunday noon-5. Closed January 1, Thanksgiving, and December 25. Phone: 314-544-5714.

¶ **Kate Chopin House,** 4232 McPherson Avenue. Private.

After the death of her husband in 1883, the famous regionalist author Kate Chopin moved to this house, where she wrote the last of almost a hundred short stories. A St. Louis newspaper which had earlier condemned her work lamented her death in 1904 by praising her as "the most brilliant, distinguished and interesting woman that has ever graced St. Louis." (See Cloutierville, Louisiana.)

¶ **Mullanphy Square Park,** bounded by Mullanphy Street and Cass Avenue between 11th and 12th streets.

This urban park near downtown St. Louis honors the memory of John Mullanphy, the Irish-born merchant and philanthropist. (See Florissant, Missouri.)

¶ **O'Fallon Park,** on West Florissant Avenue between Interstate 70 exits 245B and 246B.

This grassy oasis was named for John O'Fallon, the son of Dr. James O'Fallon, a native of Ireland, and Frances Eleanor Clark, the sister of two of the most famous brothers in American history (William Clark and

George Rogers Clark).

In a letter to the young O'Fallon, Uncle William advised: "I must recommend you to court the company of men of learning, sober, sedate and respectable characters. You will not only gain information from them but respectability and influence." In 1811, after deciding upon a military career, O'Fallon joined General William Henry Harrison's campaign against the Indians and was severely wounded at the battle of Tippecanoe. Later, during the War of 1812, he advanced rapidly to the rank of captain, eventually becoming Harrison's private secretary, deputy adjutant general, and aide-de-camp. Years later, when Harrison's role at Tippecanoe and the battle of the Thames was belittled by his political opponents, the beleaguered general asked his trusted subordinate to set the record straight. O'Fallon responded in an 1840 letter, in which he included the following laudatory remarks: "I can safely say that I never in my life saw a braver man in battle, one more collected, prompt, and full of resources than Gen. William Henry Harrison."

After the second war with the British, O'Fallon returned to St. Louis, where he quickly became one of Missouri's wealthiest and most influential citizens. Within a year he wrote that he was making $1,000 a month, a figure that was eclipsed by his later dealings as an Indian trader, an army contractor, a merchant capitalist, and a real estate speculator. With his wealth came appointment as president of the St. Louis branch of the Bank of the United States as well as president of two Midwestern railroads. The major objects of his philanthropy were the O'Fallon Polytechnic Institute, St. Louis University, Washington University, and the Methodist Episcopal Church South. His benefactions were so numerous that, according to a contemporary, "not a fire-company, not a library association, not a church, not anything but appeals to Col. O'Fallon in their hour of need."

¶ St. Patrick's Church, 800 Cherry Street.

This Italianate building was completed in 1875 to serve a parish that was predominantly Irish.

¶ St. John's Church, 16th and Chestnut streets.

A small Confederate flag in the stained-glass window in the choir loft recalls the role played by Father John Bannon, one of the church's pastors, as a Confederate chaplain during the Civil War.

Bannon was born in County Roscommon, Ireland, in 1829 and was educated at Maynooth College. Soon after his ordination in 1853, he came to St. Louis, where he served at the cathedral and at Immaculate Conception Church. Standing more than six feet in height, the young priest was described as having an "intellectual face, courteous manners, and . . . great personal magnetism" and quickly became a leading civic figure. Upon his appointment as pastor of St. John's Church, he began an ambitious program to build a new structure.

Almost as soon as the church was completed, however, the Civil War split the parish into rival factions. When many of the parishioners joined the Confederate forces under General Sterling Price, Bannon left his post at the church to serve as chaplain with the new enlistees in the 1st Missouri Brigade. Easily visible on the battlefield because of his slouch hat, butternut-colored uniform, and red cloth cross on his shoulder, he served with distinction at Pea Ridge, Corinth, Fort Gibson, and Vicksburg. Unlike other chaplains he placed himself in the front lines, ministering to the wounded and dying in the ferociousness of battle. His bravery won him accolades from Price himself: "The greatest soldier I ever saw was Father Bannon. In the midst of the fray he would step in and take up a fallen soldier."

In his own account of his experiences, Bannon described an encounter with a soldier who at first had tried to avoid the priest's ministrations. "Do you see how the devil deceives you; and how nearly he had you by the throat[?]" Bannon asked. "Indeed, I was a fool, Father; and I am sorry for it with all my heart." The chaplain continued his written account: "He made a good end, poor fellow: and I was careful to take down his name and the address of his family in Ireland, as I always did in similar cases; for I knew how great a consolation it is to Irish fathers and mothers to hear from a Priest that their child died well. He was the son of a small farmer in [County] Meath, and his family had heard nothing of him for several years."

After the fall of Vicksburg, Bannon was released from the army for an important diplomatic mission. Sent to Ireland by *President Jefferson Davis, the priest hoped to win support for the Confederacy and to stop the flow of Irish immigrants into the Union army. Like other agents sent from America with him, Bannon wrote articles and gave speeches emphasizing the intolerance and discrimination which the Catholic Irish faced in the northern states. Besides disseminating the familiar stories about the desecration of Catholic churches, he circulated thousands of handbills warning the Irish that the American nativists were the descendants of Cromwell. At the end of May 1864, Bannon summarized his work in a letter to the Confederate secretary of state: ". . . Priests and Bishops are instructed on the social and moral evils awaiting the emigrant in America, they are opposed to the emigration and [are] laboring to check it. They are informed of the mode of Federal enlistment and disgusted with the details, are warning and cautioning their people against the knavery of prigs [thieves] and primps. . . ." Although Bannon was moderately successful in explaining the Confederate cause to his Irish audiences, his visit to Rome with *Bishop Patrick Lynch of Charleston, South Carolina, failed to win papal recognition of the Confederacy.

Warned of the disabilities which ex-Confederates suffered after the

Civil War, Bannon returned to his native land rather than to St. Louis. In Ireland he entered the Society of Jesus and made his final vows in 1876. Until his death thirty-seven years later, he served at two Dublin churches: St. Ignatius and St. Francis Xavier.

¶ **St. Louis Cathedral,** Lindell Boulevard and Newstead Avenue.

This massive Byzantine and Romanesque structure stands as a fitting memorial to Cardinal John Glennon, who first envisioned a cathedral on this site and led the groundbreaking ceremonies in 1907. Although the cathedral was consecrated in 1926, decoration of the interior continued until 1988, four decades after Glennon's death. The mosaics covering the walls and the ceilings depict scenes from the Bible and local church history. The Blessed Mother's Chapel on the west side of the cathedral was constructed through the generosity of the Sheehan-Lamy family, while the high altar was a gift of Mr. and Mrs. William Cullen McBride. Cardinal Glennon is buried in the cathedral's Chapel of Holy Souls.

Glennon's birth in 1862 in County Meath, Ireland, brought him two unusual distinctions. He was the first American cardinal of Irish birth, and he acquired American citizenship at birth because of his father's previous residence in New Jersey. After completing his theological training at All Hallows College in Dublin, he attended the University of Bonn. The knowledge of German which he acquired there served him well in dealing with his German flock in Kansas City, Missouri, where he served as priest and later bishop.

As archbishop of St. Louis, Glennon organized the Colonization Realty Company to attract Catholic settlers from the urban centers of Europe and the United States to take up farming in Missouri. He also sponsored such charitable institutions as Father Dempsey's Hotel for the homeless and Father Dunne's Newsboys' Home and Protectorate. In addition, using gifts made to him personally, he erected two schools – Rosati-Kain High and McBride Memorial. He was equally well known for his oratorical skills, especially at eucharistic congresses throughout the world. Although St. Louis newspapers had speculated about his ascent to the cardinalate as early as 1912, it was not until 1945 that he was named to the College of Cardinals – at the age of eighty-five. During the trip to Rome to receive the "red hat," however, he was afflicted by bronchitis and died while visiting the home of Sean O' Kelly, the president of the Irish Republic, on his way back to the United States.

§ Open May-September, daily 6 a.m.-8 p.m.; rest of the year, daily 6-6. Phone: 314-533-2824 or 533-0544.

¶ **Union Trust Building,** 705 Olive Street.

This steel-frame skyscraper – the tallest building in St. Louis when it was completed in 1892 – was designed by the Chicago architectural firm of Dankmar Adler and *Louis Sullivan. Its terra-cotta floral and abstract designs reflect what became Sullivan's trademark ornamentation.

¶ **Wainwright Building,** 101 North 7th Street.

This prototype of the classic American skyscraper was designed in 1890-91 by Dankmar Adler and *Louis Sullivan. The structure reflects the latter's architectural ideals as expressed in his work *Tall Office Building Artistically Considered.* (See Cedar Rapids, Iowa.)

¶ **Wolfe House,** 5095 Cates Avenue.

In 1904, at the age of four, the future author *Thomas Wolfe moved here with his mother, who opened a boardinghouse – The North Carolina – at this location. Wolfe later incorporated some details from the house into his novel *Look Homeward, Angel* and into his short story "The Lost Boy." (See Asheville, North Carolina.)

STANTON

¶ **Jesse James Wax Museum,** at I44 exit 230.

Through wax figures of the famous outlaw and his brother Frank, the museum advances the claim that Jesse was not killed in 1882 but lived until the age of 103 under an assumed name. One of the wax figures is a likeness of J. Frank Dalton, the man who claimed to be James. The museum displays many of James's personal belongings as well as affidavits supporting the unusual theory about his advanced age.

§ Open June-August 31, daily 8-6; rest of the year, daily 9-5. Fee. Phone: 314-927-5233.

¶ **Meramec Caverns,** 3 miles south on County W from Interstate 44 exit 230.

In 1864 the Union gunpowder mill housed in this cave was seized by Quantrill's Raiders, a Confederate outlaw band that at the time included *Jesse James. The infamous outlaw was so impressed by the cave that he later used it as a hideout. In 1949, on the 102nd anniversary of James's birth, the cave was the scene of an outlaw reunion hosted by J. Frank Dalton, who claimed to be the centenarian James. (See Kearney, Missouri.)

§ Open May-August 31, daily 9-7; rest of the year, daily 9-5. Closed Thanksgiving and December 25. Fee. Phone: 314-468-3166.

MONTANA

ANACONDA

Although Anaconda's glory days are behind it, its name will always be associated with a shrewd and farsighted Irishman named Marcus Daly, the father of the state's copper industry.

Daly, who was born in Ballyjamesduff, County Cavan, Ireland, in 1841, arrived in New York at the age of fifteen, "with nothing in his pockets save his . . . Irish smile." Five years later he joined his sister in California, but he soon moved on to Virginia City, Nevada, where he worked in the Comstock Silver Mines. Some years later, while working in Utah for the Walker Brothers' mining company, he visited the Alice Mine in Butte, Montana. So confident was he of its possibilities that he persuaded the Walkers to buy it. The brothers put up $25,000 to Daly's $5,000 investment.

In 1881, with $30,000 he had saved while managing the Alice, Daly purchased the Anaconda Mine in Butte from a fellow Irishman named Edward Hickey. An ex-Union soldier, Hickey had gotten the name for his mine from an editorial in the *New York Tribune*. The editorial, written by *Horace Greeley, had stated that *General Ulysses S. Grant's army was "encircling Lee's forces like a giant anaconda." "That word struck me as a mighty good one," Hickey later said. "I always remembered it, and when I wanted a name for my mine I remembered Greeley's editorial and called it the 'Anaconda.'"

Although Daly expected the Anaconda to continue to produce silver, that precious metal was soon depleted. When the Irishman sank new shafts, he was at first disheartened to find copper, but he quickly realized his good fortune and bought up the mineral rights in the region. His find came at the most opportune of times, just as the metal began to be used in telegraph lines, electrical wires, and motors. During the next nine years, as president of the Anaconda Copper Mining Company, Daly extracted eighteen million tons of copper. By 1887 two of Butte's mines placed first and third in world production of copper, while eight years later the city was responsible for 25 percent of the world's copper production.

In the meantime, the "Copper King" had established the nearby town of Anaconda to support his mining operations. Although the Irishman had originally called the town "Copperopolis," the postmaster renamed it for Daly's Butte mine after learning that a Copperopolis already existed in the state. Daly's town was laid out according to its founder's command, issued from the top of a hill: "The main street will run north and south in a direct line from here to where that cow is standing." Before long, Daly had also constructed the Butte, Anaconda & Pacific Railway to transport the ore from his mines in Butte to Anaconda, where he had built a smelter.

According to the historian Clark Spence, the smelter's arsenic smoke "reportedly turned the wash green on the line and so impregnated the grass that local cattle had copper-plated teeth." The original stack was replaced in 1918 with the present one, which, at 585 feet, is the tallest freestanding brick structure in the world.

One reminder of Anaconda's peak years is the Montana Hotel (now known as Montana Square at Main and Park streets). Constructed by Marcus Daly and opened in 1889, the hotel was intended to accommodate the legislators who he believed would patronize it when Anaconda became the state capital. Although he spent more than $500,000 in his campaign to make his town the capital, he lost out, of course, to Helena, the choice of his archrival *William Clark, another Copper King of the era.

In addition to his entrepreneurial interests, Daly found time to foster Irish culture and promote Irish political interests. He was a member of the Ancient Order of Hibernians and was proposed for membership in the Robert Emmet Literary Society (Butte's chapter of the revolutionary Clanna-Gael). Besides hosting a visit of the Irish nationalist Michael Davitt in 1886, Daly was the honorary chairman of the Thomas Francis Meagher Memorial Association, responsible for erecting a statue of the Irish-born Civil War officer on the grounds of the state capitol in Helena.

BILLINGS

¶ *Range Rider of the Yellowstone*, on the Rimrock off the Chief Black Otter Trail north of the city.

The motion picture star William S. Hart and his horse, Paint, were the models for this bronze statue of a ranch hand and his horse. The life-size group was unveiled on July 4, 1927.

Hart, whose mother (Rose McCauley) was a native of northern Ireland, was born in Newburgh, New York, but became enamored of the West when his father took him along on business trips to that part of the country. While living near the Sioux in Minnesota and the Dakotas, the youngster even learned their language. Once returned to the East, however, he worked at odd jobs until in his twenties he became interested in acting. While part of a touring company, he appeared in various Shakespearean plays as well as *The Man in the Iron Mask* and *Ben Hur*. After acting in such Western dramas as *The Squaw Man*, *The Virginian*, and *The Trail of the Lonesome Pine*, however, Hart became thoroughly identified with that genre and was hailed as the quintessential cowboy of the American theater.

Hart made the transition to motion pictures almost out a sense of obligation, believing that his knowledge of the West made him a perfect candidate for such films. In his autobiography *My Life East and West*, he related the incident that decided his fate: "While playing in Cleveland, I attended a picture show. I saw a Western picture. It was awful!" Although in his early fifties by then, he was a neophyte when it came to the film industry. When other actors with similar experience were earning $2,000 a week, he signed his first contract for $125 a week. Nevertheless, his debut as a villain in a 1914 film began the use of a winning formula: realistic action and the creation of sympathy for an outlaw character whose criminal career never completely obscured his inherent goodness and whose final heroic act assured a happy ending.

With the money he earned from his films, Hart bought a large estate in West Hollywood, California, and an eight-acre ranch in Newhall, just north of Los Angeles. He bequeathed each of these properties for public use: his Hollywood estate as a park, and his ranch as a public park and museum. (See Santa Clarita, California.)

¶ "Yellowstone Kelly" Burial Site, 27th Street to Highway 3 east and then right onto Chief Black Otter Trail.

Although eclipsed by the more famous Irish-American scouts Thomas Fitzpatrick and "Wild Bill" Cody, Luther "Yellowstone" Kelly played a significant role in the exploration of the Missouri and Yellowstone rivers.

A sign at the gravesite reads: "A long breach-loading Springfield rifle covered from muzzle to stock with the skin of a huge bullsnake was carried by Major Luther Sage 'Yellowstone' Kelly, Shakespeare-quoting Indian fighter and scout. Kelly, a New Yorker born April 19, 1849, and Civil War veteran, guided government expeditions in the 1870s and '80s in the Yellowstone River Valley. He later served with the military in Alaska and the Philippines and then retired to California before his death December 17, 1928. He asked to be buried on this point overlooking the area he had scouted. . . . Yellowstone Kelly was the little big man with a big heart."

Kelly traced his ancestry to John Kelly, who had died in Massachusetts almost 200 years before the famous explorer's birth. According to Joshua Coffin, an eighteenth-century chronicler of Newbury, Massachusetts, the earlier Kelly was an Irishman who had made his way to Newbury, England, where he found employment in the household of a gentleman. There Kelly reputedly won the hand of the gentleman's daughter after courageously defending the man's home from robbers. However, a nineteenth-century account by another Newbury historian rejects this claim that Kelly was of Irish ancestry.

Whatever the case, Luther Kelly attended Geneva College in Lima, New York, for a year before succumbing to his "roving disposition" by enlisting in the 10th Infantry in the final months of the Civil War. After the conflict he was sent west and was in Dakota Territory when he was discharged in 1868. In his new role of trapper and hunter, he was known to the Indians as "the lone wolf" and "The man who never lays down his gun." He later served as the chief guide for General Miles' expedition to the upper Missouri and Yellowstone rivers. An 1877 article in the *Bismark Tri-Weekly Tribune* described this mysterious man of the West: "Accompanying Gen. Miles on his victorious return is a strange, brave man, known as 'Yellowstone Kelly' . . . Gen. Miles recognizes him as the best, the truest, and the most resolute scout in the army. . . . Although a good talker under rare influences and circumstances, he is to the crowd and to the curious the most reticent man known to the service. . . . He is a gentleman all over, extremely polite and choice in his language." Kelly's acquaintance with the Sioux language and the information he acquired while with the expedition proved helpful to the U.S. military in the subsequent Indian wars. During the late 1870s and the early 1880s he served as chief army scout for several important campaigns, the most significant being those against Sitting Bull and the Sioux.

Following his service for the military in the West and a brief tenure as a clerk for the War Department, Kelly was selected to head two successive expeditions to Alaska. On the basis of his explorations, he wrote a report urging adoption of a particular route for a railroad between Portage Bay and Krik Arm. During the Spanish-American War he was sent to the Philippines, where he first saw combat as captain of a volunteer company and later served as a provincial official of the occupying forces. *President Theodore Roosevelt later commended him for defending the Filipinos under his charge from an attack by outlaws and escaped prisoners. Once returned to the United States, the former officer was named Indian agent at the San Carlos Reservation in Arizona.

BUTTE

ℐ Arts Chateau, 321 West Broadway.

This twenty-six-room mansion was designed in the style of a French chateau for Charles Clark, the son of "copper king" *William Clark. The house is noted for its stained-glass windows, Louis XV salon, wood paneling, and spiral four-story staircase. The chateau is now an art gallery and a museum. (See Copper King Mansion below.)

§ Open Memorial Day-Labor Day, Tuesday-Saturday 10-6, Sunday noon-5; rest of the year, Tuesday-Saturday 11-4, Sunday noon-5. Fee. Phone: 406-723-7600.

ℐ Columbia Gardens, Park Street.

This extensive recreation park was donated to the city in 1898 by *William Clark, who spent $1 million to develop it from a barren expanse on the outskirts of the city.

ℐ Copper King Mansion, 219 West Granite Street.

This thirty-two-room Victorian mansion was built in 1884 by William Clark, the "copper king" whose political and mining rivalry with *Marcus Daly was legendary. The three-story red brick house boasts a chapel, a sixty-two-foot-long ballroom, a billiard room, Tiffany windows, marquetry floors, frescoed ceilings, and an 850-pipe organ. (The Leonard Hotel next door was constructed by Daly, reputedly to obstruct Clark's view.)

Clark was born in Pennsylvania to parents of Scotch-Irish ancestry. By the time he was twenty, however, he had driven a team to Colorado and was working the gold quartz mines there. With the $1,500 worth of gold which he later discovered in Montana, he opened the first of several general stores that catered to miners in Virginia City, Helena, and Elk City. (After finding a tobacco supplier in Idaho, he hauled a thousand pounds of the weed to Helena and made a handsome profit from selling the highly prized commodity.) A contract to carry the mails from Missoula to Walla Walla rounded out his early enterprises.

With his newly acquired wealth, Clark sought additional types of investment. After forming a banking and wholesale merchandising partnership, he bought up half a dozen mining claims in Butte, Montana. (To prepare himself for his new role as a miner, he attended the School of Mines at Columbia University for a year.) He subsequently rivaled Marcus Daly in developing silver and copper mining in Butte, forming the Colorado and Montana Smelting Company and building the city's first electric plant and water system. Besides constructing the San Pedro, Los Angeles & Salt Lake City Railroad, he owned a sugar plantation and refinery in California and a copper company in Arizona. It was not without reason that he was called one of the 100 men who ruled America.

Clark's mineralogical rivalry with Daly spilled over into the political arena, as each tried to control the Democratic party in the state. The contest apparently began when Daly successfully used his influence to defeat Clark's bid to be elected the territorial delegate to Congress in 1888. Much of Clark's energy thereafter was exerted in trying to win election to the U.S. Senate. Although he was chosen for that post by the state's first legislature, the U.S. Senate sat his Republican rival instead. When Clark announced his candidacy again in 1893, accusations of fraud – brought naturally by Daly's forces – caused the legislature to adjourn without selecting a senator. A similar deadlock occurred in 1899 amid all too familiar charges of bribery. Clark was finally elected when eleven Republicans threw their votes behind him. The victory was short-lived, however, since a Senate investigative committee ruled that he had not been "duly and legally elected." After his undisputed election to the Senate two years later, Clark became an early "sage brush" rebel, opposing *President Theodore Roosevelt's conservation policies and insisting that the federal government relinquish its control of state forests.

§ Open May-October, daily 9-4. Fee. Phone: 406-782-7580.

¶ **Marcus Daly Statue,** West Park Street, at the entrance to the University of Montana campus.

Erected by popular subscription in 1907, this bronze statue by *Augustus Saint-Gaudens depicts the Montana copper king in a leisurely stance, holding his coat on his arm and his rumpled hat in his hand. In sculpting the statue, Saint-Gaudens worked from photographs of Daly as well as the subject's clothing and death mask.

When the statue was unveiled, an old-timer – undoubtedly Irish – remarked: "Arrah, they should have put him astride a big, phite harse. Marcus Daly was always wild about horses!" (See Hamilton, Montana.)

At the time of Daly's death in 1900, the headlines in a Butte newspaper attested to the Irishman's influence on the state:

A MIGHTY OAK HAS FALLEN
The Architect of Montana's Greatness Is Gone
Marcus Daly Is Dead
His Name and Works Held Sacred in Montana
Love That Was His Due in Life Now Made Manifest
Marcus Daly Was a Gift of Nature
Greater Than Napoleon – A Leader of Men
Died Amid the Mountains of His Glory
All Montana Mourns His Death

By the year 1900 Butte was one of the most overwhelmingly Irish cities in the country. Of the community's 30,000 inhabitants, 8,000 of them – or 26 percent – were of Irish birth or descent. (In 1894, 40 percent of the miners in Daly's own Anaconda Mine were Irish-born.) Many of these residents had come from copper mines in Michigan, anthracite coalfields in Pennsylvania, and gold, silver, and quartz mines in the West.

But whatever their immediate source prior to the turn of the century, almost 48 percent of them had come ultimately from six counties in western Ireland. That the six most common surnames in Butte were Sullivan, Harrington, Murphy, Kelly, Shea, and O'Neill attests to the predominance of Corkonians among them. In fact, over the years more than 6,000 men and women came from one parish — Eyeries in Castletownbarre Township in the westernmost section of County Cork. Fr. Patrick Brosnan of Butte wrote in 1917 that "Everyone here is from Castletownbarre. . . . Butte is a great city. We have seven fine Catholic parishes, all Irish." Other parts of Ireland, however, were mentioned in a miner's song, which identifies "two of [the men] from Mizen Head, / Two more of them from Clare, / Two of them from Dingle Town, / the place of great renown."

The overwhelmingly Irish character of Butte was due, in large part, to Marcus Daly himself. The Irish flocked to the town primarily because of his high wages. At a time when other industrial workers in the United States made less that $600 a year, the Copper King paid his miners twice as much – $3.50 per eight-hour day, or $100 a month. The Irish were also

Statue of Marcus Daly by the Irish-born sculptor Augustus Saint-Gaudens. (Photo by Dennis Grose and courtesy of Montana Tech, Butte, Montana.)

attracted by Daly's investments in the region, each of which held out new opportunities for employment: irrigation systems, power plants, lumber mills, and railroads. And, finally, as Father Brosnan expressed it, Daly preferred his own: "Marcus Daly was the man who made Butte an Irish town. . . . He did not care for any man but an Irishman and . . . did not give a job to anyone else."

Butte's predominantly Celtic influence was evident in its churches and even in the names of its mines. The town's first two houses of worship bore the names of those "most Irish" of saints – Patrick and Lawrence O'Toole. With 10,000 parishioners, St. Patrick's was the largest of the town's seven parishes, while St. Lawrence's – just north of Butte – enjoyed the benefactions of Marcus Daly himself. That Butte was the West's *Nova Hibernia* was confirmed in the nostalgic associations of its mines: Exile of Erin, Michael Davitt, Druid, Hibernia, Dublin Gulch, St. Lawrence O'Toole, Parnell, and Robert Emmet.

Once in their new American home, however, many of the Irish replicated the filthy conditions in which they had lived in Ireland. The inadequate sanitation and ventilation in the overwhelmingly Irish areas of Butte – Dublin Gulch and Corktown – frequently came under the inspection of the county board of health. Some blocks and streets were described as "very dirty, many people, hogs and cows, slops and refuse thrown into alley" and "would require a boat to get through" and "piles of decayed meat in the alley; manure is very much in evidence," and "so much refuse in the alley that it is almost impossible to drive through."

To ameliorate these conditions – at least for his miners – Daly established a first-class hotel near the Anaconda Mine. The Florence, as it was known, had accommodations for 600 men and was described as "the zenith of service for working men in America." Its appointments included a library, a gym, a billiard room, a lobby, a reading room, a bathroom, and a changing room for miners. Despite its modernity the hotel had only eight toilets, all in the basement. All the help, including the manager, were Irish, mostly natives of Ireland and many of them Gaelic speakers. In 1900, 54 percent of the hotel's 377 residents were Irish.

DEER LODGE

¶ Towe Ford Museum, Interstate 90 exit 184 or 187 at 1106 Main Street.

The museum's collection includes more than eighty vintage Fords and Lincolns built between 1903 and the 1950s. One of the cars is a camper which belonged to the industrialist *Henry Ford and which he outfitted like a chuck wagon. Ford used the unusual automobile – built on a 1922 Lincoln chassis – when he went traveling and camping with Harvey Firestone, John Burroughs, and Thomas Edison. (See Fort Meyers, Florida.)

§ Open June-August, daily 8 a.m.-9 p.m.; rest of the year, time varies. Closed Thanksgiving. Fee. Phone: 406-846-3111.

GLENDIVE

The name of this small community is derived from the word "Glendale," which the famous Irish sports hunter Sir George Gore gave to a nearby creek. Gore passed this way in 1846 while on a hunting expedition led by Jim Bridger. Besides a few accompanying hunters, the Irishman brought in tow 40 servants, 14 hunting dogs, 112 horses, 12 yoke of oxen, a huge supply of weapons and ammunition, and 25 wagons full of "creature comforts." After scandalizing the local Indians by the number of animals that he and his companions slaughtered, the gory Irishman moved on to Fort Union, where he burned his equipment and supplies rather than pay to transport them to St. Louis.

HAMILTON

¶ Marcus Daly Mansion, 2 miles northeast at 251 Eastside Highway (County 269).

This forty-two-room mansion was the summer home of *Marcus Daly, the Anaconda "Copper King." Constructed in 1890, this three-story Georgian Revival house has twenty-four bedrooms, fifteen bathrooms, and seven Italian-marble fireplaces. Known originally as "Riverside," the mansion was the centerpiece of Daly's 22,000-acre stock farm.

Daly first established Hamilton in 1887 as a source of the timber he needed to extend his Anaconda Mine. (The mine was so cavernous that it required 40,000 board feet of timber a day in its continued construction.) In his effort to develop the town, he built a number of houses and stores and gave two lots to each of Hamilton's religious congregations. In 1890 he purchased 22,000 acres for what became known as Bitter Root Stock Farm. Here he trained and bred thoroughbred racehorses and created a racing center that boasted a one-mile race course, a grandstand for 1,000 spectators, and stables that could accommodate up to 130 horses. His racing colors – appropriately – were copper and green, and on racing days he gave his miners a holiday with pay.

§ Open April 15-October 15, daily 11-4; rest of the year, by appointment. Fee. Phone: 406-363-6004.

HARDIN

¶ **Little Bighorn Battlefield National Monument,** 15 miles southeast via Interstate 90 exit 510 to U.S. 212.

This memorial park commemorates the battle which occurred here in June 1876 between several thousand Sioux and Cheyenne and the 7th U.S. Cavalry Regiment under George Armstrong Custer. By the end of the battle, the 7th Cavalry was annihilated, almost all of its 210 soldiers stripped naked and mutilated and dismembered. Among the dead were thirty-two Irish born, including Myles Keogh, the captain of Company I.

The battlefield today includes a national cemetery, a historical museum, several memorials and monuments, and a visitor center.

§ Open Memorial Day-Labor Day, daily 8-8; day after Labor Day-October 31, daily 8-6; rest of the year, 8-4:30. Closed January 1, Thanksgiving, and December 25. Fee. Phone: 406-638-2621.

¶ One of the many memorials on the battlefield tour is a plaque marking the spot where Captain Myles Keogh fell and died during the battle.

If, as Dr. John Langellier maintains, Custer was among the first killed at the Little Bighorn, Keogh was the ranking officer during the battle. Whatever the case, his body and Custer's were among the few which escaped mutilation. Langellier theorizes that Keogh's corpse may have been spared either because the Indians respected his fighting skills or because they regarded the religious medal which they found around his neck as an amulet that would inflict harm on a future wearer. Although the Indians refrained from taking the medal, they did steal the photograph of Keogh which he carried on his person.

The neckpiece which the Indians found may have been the *Pro Petri Sede* ("For the See of Peter") medal, one of two which Keogh had received during his service in the papal army. The photograph of Keogh, meanwhile, had been taken soon after his promotion to lieutenant in the papal guards. About a year after the battle, the photograph was recovered from a Sioux Indian by Henry Nolan, a former comrade of Keogh's in the papal troops and later a captain in the 7th Cavalry.

Although the Irishman was buried on the battlefield, a month after the disastrous engagement his corpse was exhumed for interment in Fort Hill Cemetery in Auburn, New York. The poetic inscription on his funeral monument reads:

> Sleep soldier! Still in honored rest
> Your truth and valor wearing
> The Bravest are the tenderest
> The loving are the daring.

Despite the massacre, Keogh's horse, Comanche, survived, its saddle twisted under its belly. One Indian was apparently tempted to take the saddle blanket but changed his mind when he saw that it was heavily stained with blood. When another Indian yelled at the horse and threw a clod of dirt at it, the horse refused to move.

Keogh had bought his famous mount at Ellis Station, Kansas, in 1868. The $90 horse stood fifteen hands in height and weighed 925 pounds. When Comanche died in 1891 at the age of twenty-nine, it was rendered almost immortal by the skillful hands of a taxidermist. Today the horse is on display at the University of Kansas in Lawrence [*q.v.*].

Some of Keogh's personal belongings are among the exhibits at the Gene Autry Western Heritage Museum in Los Angeles [*q.v.*]. A stained-glass window in his honor is located in St. Joseph's Church at Tinryland, County Carlow, Ireland.

• Myles Keogh was born in County Carlow, Ireland, in 1840 or 1842, one of thirteen children. His father was an officer in the 5th Royal Irish Lancers stationed in a suburb of Limerick known as Garryowen, from which came the name of the unit's drinking song. Myles's sister, meanwhile, later became the grandmother of *Cardinal Francis Spellman, archbishop of New York City.

Apparently attracted by the prospect of a military career, the young Keogh traveled to Italy to enlist in the papal army, which in 1860 was waging war against the Italian nationalists who hoped to incorporate the Papal States into a unified Italy. The Irishman served with distinction and rose through the ranks to become second lieutenant in the Battalion of St. Patrick and then lieutenant in the Papal Guards. He was a member of the garrison which surrendered at Ancona. Although like the other Irish soldiers be was offered the chance to return to his native land after the surrender, he chose to stay in Italy until the end of that war. Before leaving

Rome in 1862, he was awarded the *Pro Petri Sede* ("For the See of Peter") medal and the Cross of the Order of St. Gregory the Great.

After immigrating to New York City in 1862, Keogh continued his military career, but now with the U.S. Army. He joined the Union forces as a cavalry captain and went on to see action in more than a hundred battles. For his bravery and good conduct during the war, he was breveted lieutenant colonel in the volunteers, while his services at Gettysburg earned him the rank of major. Within weeks after Lee's surrender, Keogh transferred to the 7th Cavalry and was quickly commissioned captain. For a time after the war, he was stationed in Kentucky, where his cavalry unit crushed several uprisings by the Ku Klux Klan. Later, in Kansas, he and his men were employed to protect railroad workers laying track toward the west.

In a memoir published in 1890, George Custer's widow, Elizabeth, recounted an incident in which she and her husband visited Keogh during one of his tours of duty, probably in 1870. After mentioning that the Irish officer had "turned himself over to his man [valet] for safe-keeping," she went on: "Literally, he had given himself up to be directed as Finnigan [the valet] willed – not, of course, in official affairs, but in every-day doings. He even enjoyed declaring that he had no further responsibility in life. Finnigan kept track of his purse, his clothes, his outfit, his debts. [Keogh] did not know where anything was, and he did not propose to inquire. Wishing to show us some decorations he had received in foreign service, he called to his man. Finnigan, clean, respectful, unspoiled by the familiarity and dependence of his master, produced the [decorations] from his own little 'A' tent at the rear. This captain [Keogh] . . . became so hopelessly boozy, [that] the man concluded that the safest place for the valuables and the family funds was in his own quarters. As we held these precious possessions, admiring their beauty, and drawing their owner out to tell us of the fields on which they were won, the subject turned upon the Pope. Finnigan visibly swelled with pride to think his master had once been in the service of that magnate. . . ." At this point in the episode, Finnigan's demeanor suddenly changed. Mrs. Custer continued: "In trying to account for this change, I attributed it to the conversation. It was, if I am not mistaken, the summer when the doctrine of infallibility of the Pope was agitated. The captain was a Romanist, but not an ultra one, and Finnigan had looked remonstrance when the laughing officer said to us, 'Why, I have had so many notices of excommunication I feel strange if I waken and don't find one waiting for me every morning now."

In May 1876 Keogh was at Fort Abraham Lincoln in Dakota Territory, preparing to lead Company I of the 7th Cavalry in Custer's disastrous expedition against the Sioux. As the cavalry marched off to its fate the following month, it did so to the strains of "Garry Owen," the famous Irish air that Keogh as a youngster had often heard sung by his father's lancer unit near Limerick. In fact, Keogh himself may have introduced the song to the 7th's regimental band. Such a possibility is suggested in the remark by Custer's widow that she first heard her husband whistle the tune shortly after the 7th Cavalry was organized at Fort Riley, Kansas, and that she thought Keogh was in some way connected with introducing the song to the regiment.

Whatever the case, a survivor of the Little Bighorn massacre later described that poignant scene in a letter to George McMurry, the 7th Cavalry's chaplain: "On the day we moved out from Powder River with the pack train, the Band was posted on a knoll overlooking the river, where they played merrily while we were fording the river. After all were crossed and the six troops formed we took up the march towards Tongue River and the Rosebud, the Band broke into the rollicking strains of 'Garry Owen' which as usual brought a hearty cheer, and its notes were still ringing in our ears as we left the river bottoms and the Band was lost to sight as we wound up a wide ravine. The strains of the old Regimental Air were the last notes from the old Band that fell on the ears of General Custer, the staff and many officers and men of the old Regiment."

HELENA

J Carroll College, Benton Avenue between Leslie and Peosta streets.

Originally known as Mount St. Charles College when it was established in 1909, this Catholic institution was renamed in 1932 for its founder, *Bishop John P. Carroll. In 1910 and 1912 Carroll, the second bishop of Helena, had served as the national chaplain of the Ancient Order of Hibernians.

J General Meagher Statue, State Capitol, 6th Avenue and Montana Street.

Outside the west entrance of the capitol is a bronze equestrian statue of General Thomas Meagher (pronounced MAH-r), the famous commander of the Irish Brigade during the Civil War and the acting territorial governor of Montana. The statue, sculpted by *Charles J. Mulligan and unveiled in 1905, was erected through the efforts of the Meagher Memorial Association chaired by Marcus Daly, the Irish-born "Copper King" of Butte, Montana.

One of the bronze plaques on the base of the statue summarizes Meagher's career: "American soldier and statesman; Brigadier General United States Army; raised and organized the Irish Brigade in the Army of the Potomac, and personally commanded it in the battles of Fair Oaks, Mechanicsville, Caine's Mill, White Oak Swamp, Malvern Hill, Fredericksburg, Antietam and Chancellorsville; appointed to the command of the Etowah District as acting Major General in November, 1864; acting

General Meagher Statue.
(Photo courtesy of the
Montana Historical Society.)

governor of Montana from September 1865 to July 1, 1867, when he was drowned in the Missouri River, at Fort Benton, Montana."

Two other plaques contain excerpts from his speeches:

"My heart, my arm, my life are pledged to the National cause, and to the last it shall be my highest pride, as I conceive it to be my holiest duty and obligation to share its fortunes." Jones Woods, New York, 1861.

"The true American knows, feels, and with enthusiasm declares, that of all human emotions, of all human passions, there is not one more pure, more noble, more conducive to good and great and glorious deeds, than that which bears us back to the spot that was the cradle of our childhood, the playground of our boyhood, the theater of our manhood." Virginia City, Montana, March 17, 1866.

• Meagher was born in Waterford, Ireland, in 1823, the son of a prominent merchant who for a time was a member of the British Parliament. The younger Meagher attended the Jesuit college at Clongowes-Wood in Kildare and the English college at Stonyhurst. At the age of twenty-three, a year after joining the Young Ireland party, he made his debut as an orator at the "monster rally" at Kilkenny attended by Daniel O'Connell. A year later, however, Meagher made his break with O'Connell's constitutionalist approach to political change and adopted a more militant nationalist position, thereby earning the nickname "Meagher of the Sword." In

1848 he traveled to Paris to promote the possibility of French assistance for an Irish uprising and returned to Dublin with an Irish tricolor. Following a speech in which he made incendiary remarks, he was arrested for sedition. Several months later he was tried and condemned to death for high treason, although that sentence was soon commuted to banishment to a penal colony. After about thirty months in Tasmania, however, the Irish nationalist escaped and arrived in New York City in May 1852.

Almost from the moment of his arrival in America, Meagher became the darling of the New York Irish. After a period of time on the lecture circuit, he undertook the study of law and was admitted to the bar in 1855, thereafter combining a legal career with the editorship of the *Irish News*. At the onset of the Civil War, Meagher organized a company of Zouaves, which was later incorporated into the Irish 69th Volunteers. In the winter of 1861-62, he organized and commanded the Irish Brigade, whose banner boasted an Irish harp, a wreath of shamrocks, and the Gaelic motto "They shall never retreat from the charge of lances." The brigade fought at Bull Run, Fair Oaks, the Seven Days, Antietam, Fredericksburg, Chancellorsville, and the siege of Yorktown.

When the Irish Brigade became so decimated that its continued existence seemed doubtful, Meagher sought permission to recruit replacements. When he was denied this request, however, he resigned his commission. In taking leave of his men on May 19, 1863, he shook the hands of his officers and many of his men. Like his, many of their faces were covered in tears. His parting address ended with both a tribute and a promise: "The graves of many hundreds of brave and devoted soldiers who went to death with all the radiance and enthusiasm of the noblest chivalry, are so many guarantees and pledges that, as long as there remains one officer or soldier of the Irish Brigade, so long shall there be found for him, for his family and little ones, if any there be, a devoted friend in Thomas Francis Meagher."

In 1865 Meagher was named secretary of Montana Territory, although after his arrival in the West he served as acting governor for a year. On July 1, 1867, he was in Fort Benton, Montana, waiting to board a steamboat that would take him down the Missouri River to pick up weapons for a campaign against the Indians. Late that night, after a visit to a tavern, he boarded the vessel and went to his stateroom but was never seen again. Some of the subsequent rumors claimed that he had been pushed into the river as he boarded the steamboat, although this theory was denied by people who had accompanied him to his stateroom. Other speculation that he had been forcibly removed and thrown overboard without provoking a commotion was discounted by his large size and irascibility. Nevertheless, even the contemporaries who dismissed this latter theory admitted that Meagher had made decisions as acting governor which were unpopular and might have caused a political enemy to kill him.

¶ **Hill Park,** Neill Avenue between Main Street and Park Avenue.

This seven-acre greensward was donated to the city of Helena in 1912 by the Great Northern Railway. The park was named for the railroad's founder, James J. Hill whose grandparents had emigrated from Ireland to Canada in 1829. (His grandfather was from Mars Hill, County Armagh, while his grandmother was from Newry, County Down.)

Although as a youngster Hill had intended to become a doctor, he abandoned such plans when an accident with an arrow caused the loss of sight in one eye. After arriving in St. Paul at the age of seventeen, he found work as a clerk for a steam packet line and soon learned all aspects of the freight business. By 1867 he had contracted to supply the St. Paul & Pacific Railroad with fuel. Realizing that coal would soon replace wood as the railroad's chief source of energy, he completed a survey of the nation's coal sources and markets and formed the Northwestern Fuel Company. Through his subsequent development of the Great Northern Railroad system between St. Paul and Puget Sound, he was soon on his way to gaining monopoly control of the rail freight between Chicago and the Pacific Northwest. (Between 1891 and 1906 the G.N.R. network constructed an average of one mile of railroad per day.) By 1901 Hill and his associates had secured controlling interest in both the Northern Pacific and the Chicago, Burlington & Quincy lines.

In the administration of his railways, Hill insisted that his officers follow a simple maxim: "Intelligent management of railroads must be based on exact knowledge of facts. Guesswork will not do." While at the height of his railroad career, he was also a director of several banks, including Chase National. In the last year of his life, his friends honored him with the endowment of the James J. Hill Professorship of Transportation at Harvard University.

Hill left an eyewitness account of the ill-fated Fenian incursion into Manitoba, Canada, on October 5, 1871. Undertaken in an effort to seize Canadian territory and thereby force Britain to grant Irish independence, the attack by thirty Fenians succeeded in capturing the Hudson Bay trading post at North Pembina. Distracted by their plunder of the post, however, the Fenians were surprised by a force of American troops from nearby Fort Pembina. Although the Fenians fled, within twenty minutes the American soldiers had rounded up three of the four Fenian "generals" and ten of their followers. "General" O'Donahue, however, escaped into Manitoba with some of the half-breeds who had joined his cause.

Hill recorded his amused reaction to witnessing the farcical episode: "It certainly looked as if the [Fenian] leaders would have been very much disappointed if they had not been kindly taken charge of by the United States troops and in that way kept out of harm's way. The whole thing was laughable in the extreme. . . . About five o'clock the same evening a French half-breed named Gordon rode though Pembina to the United States fort on a gallop, and it proved later that he was [bringing] news of the capture of Mr. O'Donahue. It seems that O'Donahue got hungry or dry and went into a half-breed's house and was there taken prisoner by the breeds, but not until he had made them pledge him that they would not deliver him to any but the United States authorities."

¶ **St. Helena Cathedral,** Warren Street and East Lawrence Street.

The construction of this $1 million neo-Gothic structure was financed primarily by the gold miner Thomas Cruse and his heirs. The church, which is modeled after Cologne Cathedral in Germany, was constructed between 1908 and 1924 and is adorned with stained-glass windows from Munich. The cathedral's roof, like its 218-foot spires, is covered with red tiles. The north spire is named for Cruse and contains a set of sixteen chimes.

Cruse, a native of Drumlummon, Ireland, had made his fortune after striking gold in 1876 near what is now Marysville, Montana. The mine, which he named for his birthplace, was so rich in gold and silver that Cruse sold it to English investors for $1.5 million in cash and another $1 milllion in the stock of the corporation which they formed to develop it. It is estimated that between 1885 and 1895 the mine produced $20 million of precious metals. (The gold and silver later recovered from the Drumlummon's tailings brought the production total to $50 million.) Cruse, meanwhile, later developed the Bald Mountain and West Belmont mines, which reputedly yielded $3 million in precious metals.

¶ **William Clark Memorial,** State Capitol, 6th and Montana streets.

A bronze bas-relief depicting the shaggy head of *William Clark is located in the rotunda and is inscribed with the following words:

"WILLIAM ANDREWS CLARK
Pioneer Prospector and Miner
Merchant Banker Railroad Builder
Benefactor of Children and Philanthropist
This Memorial is Erected by
The Society of Montana and Other Friends
As a Tribute to his Great Achievements
And to perpetuate His Memory"

§ Open daily 8-5. Closed holidays. Phone: 406-444-4789.

MILES CITY

¶ **Fort Keogh,** 2 miles southwest off U.S. 12.

When established by Colonel Nelson Miles in 1877, this frontier outpost was intended as a military base from which to force the Sioux and Cheyenne back onto their reservations after the battle of the Little Bighorn. The fort was named for *Captain Myles Keogh, one of the officers who were killed with General Custer at the disastrous battle only a year before. (See Hardin, Montana.)

FALLON

Located in the eastern part of the state, this town of 125 inhabitants was named for the Indian agent and trader Benjamin O'Fallon. Nearby O'Fallon Creek is also named for the famous western figure, the son of an Irish-born physician and his wife (a sister of William and George Rogers Clark).

Benjamin and his more famous brother, John, were only infants when, about 1793, their mother separated from their father after the latter's involvement with an unsavory and treasonous scheme. As general agent for the South Carolina Yazoo Company, the elder O'Fallon had expressed to the Spanish governor at New Orleans the company's intention to separate its colony in Georgia from the United States and to form an independent government allied with Spain. O'Fallon's disgrace was complete when President Washington issued a proclamation against him and his purported plan.

Under the circumstances the young Benjamin O'Fallon was raised by his uncle, William Clark, in St. Louis. (During the subsequent Lewis and Clark Expedition, Clark immortalized his nephew by naming a Montana creek after him.) By his mid twenties O'Fallon had become an Indian agent, and he subsequently helped negotiate treaties between the United States and the Ponca and Oto tribes. Although he later joined the Yellowstone Expedition led by Major Stephen Long, insufficient appropriations from Congress prevented the party from achieving its goals: to pacify the Indians, protect the fur trade, and counter British influence in the region.

Long's accounts of O'Fallon's speeches at the Indian councils demonstrated the Irish-American's keen knowledge of the Indians and his unusual oratorical skills. "How long, how long Saukees, will you continue to disturb the repose of other nations?" O'Fallon asked a deputation from the Saukee nation on April 3, 1821, using a Ciceronian flourish. "How long will you (like the serpent creeping through the grass) continue to disturb the unsuspecting stranger passing through your country?. . . . Saukees, be cautious; you live in the woods, and the game of your country is nearly exhausted. You will soon have to desert those woods in which the red skins of Missouri cannot find you, and follow the buffalo in the plains, where the red-skins are not less brave than you, and as numerous as the buffalo. . . . I know that your guns are better than those of Missouri, and you shoot them well: but when you reach the prairies, they will avail you nothing against the Otoes, Missouris, Omawhaws, and Pawnees." Four years later, in one of his last acts as Indian agent, O'Fallon signed fifteen treaties between the United States and the tribes of the upper regions of the Missouri River.

SHELBY

¶ **Marias Museum of History and Art,** 4 blocks south of U.S. 2 at 206 12th Avenue North.

Along with exhibits on dinosaur fossils, barbed wire, and the oil industry, this small museum displays memorabilia connected with the 1923 Jack Dempsey-Tommy Gibbons prizefight.

The championship heavyweight fight was intended as a public relations stunt to attract attention to this small town of only 500 residents. The fight's promoters suffered a major financial reversal, however, when only 7,000 paying customers showed up at the arena – built especially for the event and boasting a capacity of 40,000. (See Manassa, Colorado.)

§ Open Memorial Day-Labor Day, Monday-Friday 1-5 and 7-9, Saturday 1-4; rest of the year, Tuesday 1-5. Closed major holidays. Phone: 406-434-2551.

NEBRASKA

CRAWFORD

¶ Fort Robinson State Park, 3.5 miles west on U.S. 20.

Fort Robinson was established in 1874 to provide a military presence for the Red Cloud Indian Agency (two miles east), a government outpost that supplied rations to as many as 13,000 Sioux in the area. Although no structures from the agency remain, a monument and several historical plaques mark the site.

In 1876, not long after General George Custer's disastrous defeat at the battle of the Little Bighorn, about 800 Indians fled the agency. With *William "Buffalo Bill" Cody as chief scout, the 5th Cavalry pursued the natives and drove them back to the government post. According to tradition, Cody fought a duel with a warrior named Yellow Hand during that pursuit. (See Van Tassell, Wyoming.)

§ Park open daily 24 hours. Visitor center open Memorial Day-Labor Day, daily 7-6. Fee. Phone: 308-665-2660.

FAIRBURY

¶ Rock Creek Station State Historical Park, 6 miles south off Route 36.

Rock Creek Station was established in 1857 as a stop for travelers along the Oregon Trail. Within a few years the buildings on either side of the creek came to be known as East Ranch and West Ranch and were connected by a toll bridge. East Ranch was eventually leased to a freight company for use as a stagecoach stop and a remounting station for the Pony Express. Today the park features reconstructions of the toll bridge and the ranch buildings.

In 1861, while working here as a stable hand, the twenty-three-year-old *James Butler Hickok was involved in an episode that became part of the growing folk lore surrounding "Wild Bill." After agreeing to buy the station from David McCanles, the agents of the freight company attempted to delay payment. When McCanles showed up to press the point, Hickok invited him into one of the buildings and offered him a drink. As the aggrieved party became suspicious of Hickok's intention, he attempted to leave the building. In the gunplay that followed, Hickok killed McCanles and wounded the latter's two companions. (Both died from additional wounds at the hands of Hickok's assistants.) Although the assailants were prosecuted for murder, they were acquitted on the grounds of self-defense. From this unfortunate episode came reports that Hickok had single-handedly killed ten men with a gun and a Bowie knife. (See Abilene, Kansas.)

§ Grounds open daily 8-dusk. Visitor center open Memorial Day-Labor Day, daily 9-5; mid April-late October, Saturday 9-5, Sunday 1-5. Fee. Phone: 402-729-5777.

HOMER

¶ **O'Connor House,** 2 miles east on U.S. 77 to signs.

This fourteen-room brick Italianate mansion was the home of Cornelius O'Connor, a member of the Irish colony which was established in old St. John's in 1856. Examples of O'Connor's carpentry can be found throughout the house: the double front door, the curving staircase in the front hall, and the walnut sideboard in the dining room. In 1969 the Dakota County Historical Society purchased the house from O'Connor's great-grandson, J. Colin Green.

O'Connor and his wife, Catherine Duggan, came to old St. John's in May 1857 after arriving by steamer from Omaha. Catherine, a native of Canavee, County Cork, had immigrated to New York in 1849. Three years later she married O'Connor, a carpenter who had left County Cork with his parents when he was eight years old. During his early twenties he had participated in the war with Mexico.

A year before the O'Connors arrived in the St. Johns area, Catherine's brother Daniel and his family had been among the Irish colonists who gathered near Garryowen, Iowa, to begin the trek by covered wagon to

The O'Connor House. (Photo courtesy of the Dakota County Historical Society.)

Dakota County, Nebraska. The following winter proved to be one of the century's most severe and portended the failure of the St. Patrick's Colony at that location. For six weeks the temperature remained below freezing. According to Father Henry Casper, a chronicler of the Catholic Church in Nebraska, "The Duggans . . . could make their way from the dugout to the stock shelter only by the means of a clothesline hung from one point to the other, since snow drifts frequently obliterated all traces of a dugout." Although the colony's two dozen families survived that terrible winter, within a few years they experienced tornadoes, floods, prairie fires, and grasshopper plagues. As a result, the families moved to nearby farms or to Jackson two miles away.

Whether O'Connor and his wife knew of the hardships which Catherine's family had suffered that first winter is unknown, but it was to that area that they came in 1857. They first settled in Elk Creek but by 1863 had moved to Homer. O'Connor, who was known as "Captain" after the governor appointed him to head a company of soldiers to defend against Indian attacks, soon became a leading figure in the community. He was among the founders of the county's first school, of the Farmers' Institute (dedicated to the promotion of scientific agriculture), and of the Dakota County Pioneers Association. He also represented the county in the legislature in 1861 and again four years later. During twenty-five years in Homer, the O'Connors increased their holdings from an original 160 acres to more than 1,300.

In an unusual statistic for that time, all ten of the O'Connors' children reached adulthood, but seven of them were cut down by consumption between 1887 and 1898. When Charlotte, the last victim, died, her parents received a letter of condolence from Jeremiah O'Donovan Rossa, a founder of the Fenain Brotherhood and a fiery opponent of British rule in Ireland.

Meanwhile, O'Connor's eldest son, C. J. O'Connor, became president of the Homer State Bank. (His mother was a director.) The younger O'Connor also owned a ballroom and a grain elevator and was something of a railroad entrepreneur. In 1904 he purchased the Sioux City, Homer & Southern Railway for $4,500. Although the line had not yet been built, O'Connor assumed its $22,000 debt and announced his intention to construct the railroad as originally intended. O'Connor lost his investment, however, when the Burlington Railroad ran its line from Sioux City to Lincoln by way of Homer, a decision that obviated his plan.

§ Open every Sunday, June-August. Fee. Phone: 402-698-2288. The house sponsors a Christmas tour on the last two weekends in November.

JACKSON

¶ St. Patrick's Church, U.S. 20.

A historical marker in front of the church sketches the history of St.

John's, the first Catholic parish in Nebraska: "About 1.5 miles north of this spot is the abandoned site of 'Old St. John's,' one of the first towns established in Dakota County. The townsite was settled on June 2, 1856, by the Father Trecy Colony – sixty people, with eighteen ox-drawn covered wagons. The site was surveyed and platted June 24, 1856, and the town was named St. John's, in honor of St. John the Baptist. The Colony was led by Father Jeremiah Trecy, a young Catholic Priest from the Garryowen Parish near Dubuque, Iowa. [He was a native of County Louth, Ireland.] Consisting mostly of Irish immigrants, it constituted the first Catholic parish in Nebraska. The town of St. John's grew rapidly and by 1858 it had two hundred inhabitants. In 1860 Father Trecy went to Washington seeking permission to establish a mission among the Ponca Indians. Meanwhile the Civil War began. Father Trecy became an army chaplain, and never returned to his beloved Colony. In the early sixties, the Missouri River began to threaten St. John's. The people began moving their buildings to the new town of Jackson. By 1866 all buildings were gone and the townsite was abandoned. The site of St. John's still exists as a symbol of courage and hope and of the religious faith of a dedicated peope." During its heyday St. John's boasted a church, a log school, a hotel, fifty dwellings, a sawmill, a grist mill, a store, and two doctors.

KEARNEY

¶ Fort Kearny State Historical Park, 2 miles south on State 44 from Interstate 80 and then 4 miles east on County L-50A.

Unlike the nearby town of Kearney, Fort Kearny incorporates the correct spelling of its namesake, *General Stephen Watts Kearny, the leader of the expedition which helped wrest control of California from Mexico. (See Escondido, California.)

This post was built in 1841 to protect caravans and mail coaches along the Oregon and Mormon trails. In the mid 1860s the troops stationed at the fort were used to protect the work crews laying track for the Union Pacific Railroad. Although the fort had between thirty and thirty-five buildings when it was abandoned in 1871, today only replicas greet the visitor: a sod-roofed blacksmith-carpenter shop, the powder magazine, and one of the three original stockades.

§ Open Memorial Day-Labor Day, daily 9-5. Fee. Phone: 308-234-9513.

LINCOLN

¶ Fairview, 900 Sumner Street.

This brick Queen Anne and Greek Revival house was built in 1902 by William Jennings Bryan as a country home on an estate that eventually grew to 300 acres. Here Bryan and his wife raised their three children.

Described as a radical Democrat in a conservative town, Bryan adorned his driveway with two stone lions: one with mouth open and fangs threatening (called Radicalism), and the other with its mouth shut (Conservatism). The first floor of the house contains Bryan furnishings and memorabilia. A statue of Bryan stands opposite Fairview.

Bryan, whose first Scotch-Irish ancestor in America arrived in 1650, had come to Lincoln in 1887, eager to practice law but quickly attracted by the lure of politics. After two terms in the House of Representatives, he accepted a position as editor-in-chief of the *Omaha World Herald* and began a career as a public lecturer on the Chatauqua circuit. At the Democratic national convention in 1896, Bryan's dramatic denunciation of the gold standard in his "Cross of Gold Speech" led to his selection as the party's presidential candidate. Although he crisscrossed the country on an 18,000-mile campaign swing, he was defeated by *William McKinley, the Republican candidate. Bryan again lost to McKinley four years later.

Following this second electoral defeat, Bryan began to publish the *Commoner*, a weekly newspaper which he used to attack the influence of money in the political process. After another failed presidential bid – against William Howard Taft – in 1908, the "Great Commoner" was instrumental in securing the nomination of *Woodrow Wilson for the presidency in 1912. He served for two years as Wilson's secretary of state until he resigned in disagreement with the president's policy toward Germany prior to World War I. As an early advocate of the idea that a declaration of war should be ratified in a national referendum, Bryan declared: "I so believe in the right of the people to have what they want that I admit the right of the people to go to war if they really want it. There should be a referendum vote about it, however, and those who voted for war should enlist first, together with the jingo newspaper editors."

§ Open Memorial Day-Labor Day, Saturday-Sunday 1:30-5. Fee. Phone: 402-471-4764.

McCOOK

¶ George Norris House, 706 Norris Avenue.

Constructed in 1886, this was the home of George Norris, the Nebraska senator who advocated creation of the Tennessee Valley Authority and who authored the amendment to the U.S. Constitution which eliminated the lame-duck session of Congress.

Norris, whose father was of Scotch-Irish descent, began his forty-year career in the national legislature in 1902, originally as a Republican but increasingly as a progressive. Allied with the insurgents in the House who were determined to restrain the power of the Speaker, Norris in 1910 maneuvered the passage of a bill creating an elected rules committee from which the Speaker would be excluded. Although in the Senate he sup-

ported *President Wilson's fiscal reform measures, he opposed his jingo-
istic policy toward Mexico and was one of only six senators who voted
against America's entry into war in April 1917.

During the "Republican Ascendancy" of the following decade, Norris
criticized his party's corruption and intimate relationship with corporate
interests. He was also an early advocate of granting diplomatic recognition to the Soviet Union. From 1925 on, he became the leader of the congressional liberals, calling for labor and farm relief, the direct election of
the president, and better management of the country's natural resources.
Known as the "Gentle Knight of Progressive Ideals," he also successfully
offered legislation to continue government ownership and development
of the Muscle Shoals hydroelectric facilities and to develop the Tennessee
River Valley.

By 1928 his break with the Republicans was virtually complete, and
in subsequent campaigns he successively supported *Alfred Smith and
Franklin Roosevelt. Ever the independent, though, he attacked Roosevelt's
plan to "pack" the Supreme Court, proposing instead a measure to limit
federal judges to a single nine-year term and to require a two-thirds majority before the Supreme Court could overturn acts of Congress.

§ Open Wednesday-Saturday 10-noon and 1-5, Tuesday and Sunday
1:30-5. Fee. Phone: 308-345-5293/7134.

¶ Norris is buried in Memorial Park Cemetery.

NORTH PLATTE

¶ **Buffalo Bill Cody Ranch State Historical Park,** 3.5 miles northwest on U.S. 30 and Buffalo Bill Avenue.

This historical park occupies the site of Scout's Rest Ranch, the 4,000-
acre spread of *William "Buffalo Bill" Cody, the legendary frontier scout,
buffalo hunter, and Wild West Show promoter.

Cody lived in the Victorian ranch house on the property during the
1880s and 1890s, during intermittent visits between tours of his Wild West
Show. After moving in 1902 to Cody, Wyoming, a town of his own creation, he was beset by financial problems that forced him to sell his ranch.
Today the property includes a log cabin and a horse barn brought here
from Cody's ranch on the Dismal River. The buildings contain displays
on Cody's life and his famous Wild West Show. The main house is noted
for its cone-shaped lightning rods, stained-glass windows, eave supports
in the shape of gunstocks, and wallpaper designed by Cody to depict scenes
from his life.

§ Open Memorial Day weekend-Labor Day, daily 10-8; other times in
September, October, and May, Monday-Saturday 9-5, Sunday 1-5; April,
Monday-Friday 9-5. Fee. Phone: 308-535-8035.

• Each June North Platte celebrates Nebraskaland Days with the four-day Buffalo Bill Rodeo.

¶ Cody Park, 0.5 mile north of Rodeo Road on U.S. 83.

This ninety-acre expanse along the North Platte River was named for *William Frederick Cody. "Buffalo Bill" lived in North Platte for thirty years, having arrived with his family in 1870, at the peak of his fame as a frontier scout, guide, and buffalo hunter.

§ Swimming pool, children's rides, and train depot open daily, Memorial Day-Labor Day. Fee. Phone: 308-534-7611.

¶ Fort McPherson National Cemetery, 13 miles east via Interstate 80 to Maxwell and then 4 miles south on N-56A.

Established in 1873, the cemetery is located on the former grounds of Fort McPherson, a military post that was used from 1863 to 1887. One of the fort's frequent visitors was *William "Buffalo Bill" Cody.

In 1872 Cody was in charge of a buffalo hunting expedition that included Grand Duke Alexis of Russia, *General Philip Sheridan, and army officers from the fort. After leading the group to a bend of the Red Willow Creek, Cody set up camp and persuaded a hundred Sioux warriors encamped nearby to perform a war dance and to accompany the white men on the hunt. With Cody at the head of the carefully planned maneuver, the Grand Duke succeeded in killing several buffalo.

OMAHA

¶ Boys Town, 2.5 miles west of Interstate 680 on Dodge Street.

The story of Boys Town begins in 1917, when Father Edward Flanagan provided shelter for three boys placed in his care by the Omaha juvenile court system. The Irish-born priest had to borrow $90 from a friend to pay the rent on the midtown house, and his first Christmas dinner with the boys featured a donated barrel of sauerkraut.

Today Boys Town serves more than 550 abused or abandoned boys and girls. The famous campus boasts three schools, two churches, a post office, a music hall, farmlands, a horse farm, athletic fields, and a field house (with an indoor track, swimming pool, and basketball, handball, and tennis courts). Since its founding, Boys Town has served almost 14,000 young people.

From the first, Flanagan employed an educational system built upon trust between himself and his charges. Eschewing corporal punishment, he promoted athletics, music, hobbies, and moral values. His philosophy was best summed up in these words: "Boys are better capable of governing themselves than of submitting to government by adults. Don't repress a boy, give him outlets for his energies. Don't preach at him, give him the example you want him to follow. Make him responsible. Remember, there are no bad boys."

The Irish priest accepted boys of all religious denominations and counted among his benefactors several Protestant ministers and Jewish merchants. Out of necessity he became skilled at public relations, hoping to draw attention to his efforts by letting his athletic teams compete in the area, entering his boys' band in Omaha parades, and raising money through the boys' "traveling circus."

After moving his home for boys to the 160-acre Overlook Farm west of Omaha, he expanded his program to provide elementary, secondary, and vocational education. In 1936 Boys Town was incorporated as a village, with its own mayor, police chief, fire chief, parks commissioner, and two sanitation commissioners. (Its first mayor, the seventeen-year-old Dan Kampan, visited New York City as the guest of Mayor LaGuardia.) Two years later the institution gained national attention with the release of the motion picture *Boys Town*, starring Mickey Rooney and Spencer Tracy (as Father Flanagan). The fame which Hollywood conferred upon his work allowed him to expand his facility to accommodate 500 boys.

Following a visit to his native Ireland, Flanagan in 1946 wrote to an official at the Irish Legation in Washington, D.C. "I have always been proud of my Irish heritage," he began, "and I am proud to be a son of this great land of saints and scholars which has been so truly blessed in the nobility and character of its people. On many occasions . . . I have spoken in high-

*Father Flanagan
Memorial.
(Photo courtesy
of Boys Town,
Omaha, Nebraska)*

est praise of Ireland and its people, of the great work which is being done there by the Gaelic Athletic Association, and of the great advantage the people of Ireland have above all others, because the nation has the gift of faith . . . ."

¶ Other major points of interest are located on the 1,300-acre facility:

• The original sandstone "Two Brothers" statue – "He ain't heavy, Father, he's m' brother" – stands inside the Boys Town Center building. Three modern castings of the statue are located on the campus: one near Dowd Chapel on Flanagan Drive, another at the Boys Town Center, and the third at the Pacific Street entrance.

• The Hall of History chronicles the story of Boys Town from 1917 to 1946 through a variety of exhibits and audiovisual displays. Among the exhibits are the "Juvenile Entertainers" show wagon, a statuary group of Father Flanagan and one of his young charges, and the Oscar which Spencer Tracy won for his portrayal of the Irish priest in the film *Boys Town*.

• The Father Flanagan Statue on Heroes Boulevard features a seated figure of the priest surrounded by four young boys. The seven-and-a-half-foot statue was presented to Boys Town in 1948 by the Variety Club International. At the dedication, R. J. O'Donnell, the organization's chief barker, commented: "It is our hope that this statue of Father Flanagan, surrounded by his boys and placed in the spot he loved, will serve as a constant inspiration – a shrine to the memory of a man who gave eagerly and unselfishly of his time and talents in order that the boys of America – boys who would not have had these advantages – might through proper guidance and instruction become upright citizens of our country." Flanagan was the first recipient of the Variety Club's annual humanitarian award.

• The Father Flanagan Home was the residence of the Boys Town founder from 1927 to 1941. One of the most interesting items on display is the priest's inlaid wood desk, completed in three years by twenty boys and containing thirty-nine different kinds of wood.

• The Dowd Memorial Chapel, which was dedicated in 1941, was a gift of Mary Dowd of New York City in honor of her parents, brothers, and sister. Many of the chapel's interior decorations emphasize young people. Some of the stained-glass windows, for example, highlight young martyrs as well as saints who dedicated their lives to youth.

• Father Flanagan is buried in an octagonal shrine connected to the Dowd Memorial Chapel. The priest's bronze sarcophagus is decorated with Celtic ornamentation and eight panels depicting scenes from his life, including the original Boys Town building in downtown Omaha. Two of the panels depict the priest with two young boys and include two of his most famous comments: "This work will continue because God provides" and "There are no bad boys. There is only bad environment, bad example, bad thinking." The tomb also bears the words, "Father Flanagan, Founder of Boys' Town, Lover of Christ and Men."

- The Chambers Protestant Chapel was erected in honor of Herbert Chambers, a longtime benefactor of Boys Town.
- The Alumni Armed Services Memorial honors the more than 2,100 alumni who served in the nation's armed forces.
- The Leon Myers Stamp Center features an audiovisual display on commemorative stamps and the famous 600-pound ball of stamps created by Boys Town youngsters in the 1950s.
- The Garden of the Bible contains 150 plants mentioned in the Bible.

§ Visitor center open May-August, daily 9-5:30; rest of the year, daily 9-4. Guided tours available June-August, daily 9-4. Closed January 1, Thanksgiving, and December 25. Phone: 402-498-1140.

¶ **Creighton University,** 24th Street between California and Burt streets.

This Jesuit institution – Omaha's first university – was established with a bequest of $100,000 from the will of Mary Lucretia Creighton upon her death in 1876. In making the bequest, Mrs. Creighton was carrying out the wish of her husband, Edward Creighton, to establish a free Catholic institution of higher learning.

The fifth of nine children born to Irish immigrants, Edward Creighton early became fascinated with the possibilities of the newly invented magnetic telegraph. After a number of years contracting to build telegraph lines in the Midwest and the Southwest, he brought his brother John into the business in 1854. Two years later the pair extended the lines from St. Joseph, Missouri, to Omaha City.

In the meantime, Edward had come into contact with Hiram Sibley, one of the telegraph magnates of the day and the force behind the concept of a transcontinental telegraph. Now in Sibley's employ, Creighton proceeded to seek a telegraph route from Omaha City to San Francisco. Braving the elements in the winter of 1861, he covered the entire stretch on muleback, going by way of Fort Kearny, Laramie, and South Pass, and over the Sierras to Sacramento. After receiving financial assurances from Congress for the undertaking, Sibley chartered the Pacific Telegraph Company. During the ensuing extension of the lines, Creighton and his brother supervised the work from Julesburg, Colorado, to Salt Lake City. The entire distance to the West Coast was "lined" in only four months and eleven days. As one of the largest shareholders in Sibley's company, Creighton eventually amassed a fortune, a financial coup that was complemented by successful investments in cattle-raising and gold and silver mining.

Creighton's brother John, who inherited much of the former's property, later gave between $1 million and $2 million to the university which his sister-in-law had originally endowed. For this and his many other benefactions, Creighton was made a knight in the Order of St. Gregory and a count of the papal court by Pope Leo XIII. Thereafter known as "Count Creighton," the silver-haired philanthropist was posthumously honored when Creighton University celebrated the anniversary of his death as Founder's Day.

O'NEILL

Now the seat of Holt County, this town of about 5,000 residents was named for General John O'Neill, one of the foremost promoters of Irish colonization in the area. His question to the Irish in coal mines and the large eastern cities expressed his high expectations: "Why are you content to work on public projects and at coal mining when you might, in a few years, own farms of your own and become wealthy and influential people?" Between 1874 and 1877 he personally escorted to this site four contingents totaling approximately 200 men, a small number of whom had families.

The first group to arrive at the originally 160-acre site was composed of twenty-two settlers – all men except for two women and five children. The surnames of these pioneers illustrate the Celtic nature of the experiment: Alworth, Brennan, Cain, Henry Carey, Connolley, Curry, Dempsey, Haynes, Patrick Hughes, Kelly, McGrath, McKarney, O'Connor, and Sullivan.

This initial contingent was greeted by the starkness of the Plains, so strikingly in contrast to the lushness of Ireland. Faced with the reality that no timber grew in that part of the county, the settlers resorted to building a large sod house, thirty-six by eighteen feet in size. To provide roofing for the structure, a half dozen of the men headed for a timbered area of the county known as the Redbird. Employing a variation on the string used by Theseus, the Irishmen marked their trail with willow sticks, driven into the ground at intervals to guide their footsteps back. Once the sod house was completed, it served as a suitably cozy home for all the members of the colony. Within a year, however, the sod house gave way to log houses, built on the settlers' individual claims and constructed of timber hauled a distance of eighteen miles. Each of the subsequent waves of colonists first lived in the sod house, which quickly became known as the "Grand Central Hotel," a name that led the unsuspecting newcomers to expect accommodations on a truly grander scale.

John O'Neill had been born in County Monaghan, Ireland, in 1854. Although his widowed mother preceded him to America, he later joined her in Elizabeth, New Jersey. A clerking job in a store frustrated his natural wanderlust, however, until a publishing house hired him as a traveling agent for the mid-Atlantic states. Although this employment was considerably successful, he settled in Richmond, Virginia, to open a Catholic bookstore, a venture that failed because of the city's small Catholic population.

In 1857 O'Neill made a major career change by joining the army. While serving with the 2nd U.S. Dragoons in Utah, however, he deserted and made his way to California, where he joined the 1st Cavalry. When the Civil War broke out, he returned with this regiment to the East and joined the Union army. He subsequently fought in the Peninsular campaign and at various battles in Kentucky, Indiana, and Ohio. Although by the spring of 1864 he had risen to the rank of first lieutenant, he felt that he had been overlooked for further promotion. As a result, he volunteered to captain the 17th U.S. Colored Infantry, although injuries from an earlier wound forced him to resign after only six months.

After the war O'Neill became interested in the Fenian Brotherhood, an organization that hoped to establish an Irish Republic, chiefly by force of arms against the British. Until that day should arrive, the Fenians operated an "Irish Republic" in America, a shadow government in exile that expected someday to assume constitutional authority in Ireland. When the Fenians proposed to invade Canada in order to hold that country hostage until Britain granted Irish independence, O'Neill became an enthusiastic leader in the quixotic scheme. In May 1866 he led a detachment of Fenian recruits from Tennessee to the staging point in Buffalo, New York. Unexpectedly finding himself in command of the invasion, he led 600 men across the Niagara River and seized the Canadian village of Fort Erie. The following day he and his men defeated a small Canadian force near Ridgeway but were forced to flee before British troops could surround them. Although the members of the Fenian force were arrested, they were released a few days later. O'Neill himself was charged with violating American neutrality laws, but the charge was soon dropped.

Within a short time O'Neill was appointed "inspector-general of the Irish Republican Army." Although his preparations for a second invasion prompted intense opposition from most members of the Fenian leadership, the Irishman went ahead with a raid along the Vermont border in May 1870. When the Canadians opened fire, however, his 200 men fled, and he himself was arrested by a U.S. marshal sent to enforce the neutrality laws. Although sentenced this time to two years' imprisonment, O'Neill was released in three months after obtaining a pardon from *President Ulysses S. Grant. (During a visit to St. Louis, the president had received a ten-foot-long petition with two columns of signatures seeking O'Neill's release from prison.)

Despite the folly of the Fenians' efforts, O'Neill attempted another invasion of Canada. In September 1871, without the support of the Fenian council, he and a few followers seized the Hudson's Bay post in what is now Manitoba before being arrested by American troops. Again he escaped penalty when an American court released him. (See Hill Park, Helena, Montana.)

NEVADA

CARSON CITY

¶ Orion Clemens House, 502 North Division Street. Private.

This stucco-covered house was constructed in 1864 by Orion Clemens, the first and only territorial secretary of Nevada. The residence was originally built with wood siding.

Clemens, whose ancestors included Irish Caseys, brought his brother Samuel – the future Mark Twain – with him as his private secretary when he took up his post in Nevada. The brothers first lived at a boardinghouse run by a Mrs. Murphy, who later achieved immortality as the character Mrs. O'Flannigan in Twain's semi-autobiographical *Roughing It*.

In that work the famous author described one of his brother's experiences with the federal bureaucracy in Washington. At first the territorial secretary thought that U.S. Treasury officials would appreciate his frugality in getting an Indian to saw up a load of office wood for $1.50 rather than the $3 which white men usually charged. Clemens accordingly submitted the usual invoice but appended a note explaining that it was unsigned because the Indian was unable to write his name. When the Treasury Department replied that Clemens would have to pay the $1.50 bill, Twain was prompted to consider larceny: "But the next time the Indian sawed wood for us I taught him to make a cross at the bottom of the voucher ... and I 'witnessed' it and it went through all right. The United States never said a word. I was sorry I had not made the voucher for a thousand loads of wood instead of one. The government of my country snubs honest simplicity but fondles artistic villainy, and I think I might have developed into a very capable pickpocket if I had remained in the public service a year or two."

LAUGHLIN

As recently as 1970, what is now Nevada's third largest gambling mecca boasted not much more than a run-down motel and a tackle shop on the Colorado River. Today the town of 3,000 permanent residents swells to 20,000 on a given weekend – its visitors drawn by the hope of easy winnings. Above Casino Drive, Laughlin's main street, tower at least a half dozen luxury hotels up to twenty-six stories in height and with as many as 1,900 rooms.

This wagering capital traces its origins to the dreams of an Irish-American visionary named Don Laughlin. As a youngster in Michigan, Laughlin was fascinated by the gambling business and enjoyed a reputation as a supplier of legal gaming equipment. When he was old enough to legally play the numbers himself, he headed for Las Vegas, where he mixed drinks behind the bar. With the money he saved from this kind of work, he bought a small gambling establishment. The venture was so successful that with the profit from its sale he acquired the dilapidated motel and tackle shop that became the nucleus of the community which he created – and named for himself – on the banks of the Colorado.

RENO

¶ Mackay School of Mines, University of Nevada, 9th and North Virginia streets.

Named for the Irish-born miner-capitalist John Mackay, this famous Nevada institution was founded by his widow, Louise Mackay, and their son, Clarence. Mother and son also honored the "Silver King" with a memorial statue in his honor as well as several other major benefactions to the school: Mackay Athletic Field, Mackay Quadrangle, and Mackay Science Hall.

• The Mackay Memorial, a heroic-size bronze statue of John Mackay by Gutzon Borglum, the sculptor of Mount Rushmore, stands in front of the school. In 1992 a team of artists made a rubber mold of the statue so it could be reproduced for the museum at the Rushmore-Borglum Story Museum in Keystone, South Dakota.

John Mackay Statue.
(Photo courtesy of the
University of Nevada, Reno.)

• The Mackay Museum of Mines in Room 112 displays exhibits about the history of mining in the state, including photographs, mineral samples, and Mackay's own vault. (See Mackay Mansion, Virginia City, Nevada.)

¶ **Patrick McCarran Ranch,** 20 miles east on Interstate 80 to Patrick Turnoff. Private.

Noted for the shamrock woodcarvings that originally adorned its façade, this five-room frame structure was the home of "Old Pat" McCarran and his son Patrick, Nevada's powerful U.S. senator during the 1930s and 1940s.

The elder McCarran was a native of Ireland who had come to America about 1848, having sailed from Londonderry as a teenage stowaway. He subsequently settled in Nevada, where he fought the Paiute Indians while serving with the United States cavalry. After becoming a sheep rancher, he met and married Margaret Shea, an emigrant from County Cork. Their son, Patrick, attended the University of Nevada but was forced to quit the school during his senior year in order to take over his father's sheep ranch after the elder man suffered a crippling injury. The university later awarded honorary master's and doctorate degrees to their most famous "would-have-been" alumnus.

The younger Patrick McCarran initially supported his wife and the first of their five children by farming and sheep-raising, but in 1902 he was elected to the Nevada legislature. For the next thirty years, he enjoyed a career that included private legal practice, a term as a state district attorney, and five years on the Nevada supreme court. His successful handling of a Nevada divorce for the film star Mary Pickford merited a footnote in the legal history of the state.

After two unsuccessful attempts at election to the U.S. Senate, McCarran was swept into Congress on the coattails of Franklin Roosevelt's Democratic victory in 1932. Although technically a Democrat, the new senator showed a strong independent streak that allowed him to join conservatives who opposed the major thrust of the New Deal. In fact, in 1937 he became a leading opponent of Roosevelt's attempt to change the conservative composition of the Supreme Court by enlarging its membership. In the midst of the controversy, the former jurist upheld the principle of an independent judiciary. The ultimate operation of the president's plan, he charged, "would be to make this Government one of men rather than one of law, and its practical operation would be to make the Constitution what the executive or legislative branches of the Government choose to say it is – an interpretation to be changed with each change of administration." In describing his political leanings, he frequently used a metaphor from the days when he played football at the University of Nevada. "My first year, I was left tackle," he said. "The next year they moved me to right guard, and I have never been left of center since."

McCarran served a total of twenty-two years in the Senate and died in 1954, midway through his fourth term. By that time he was one of the most powerful members of the Senate, chiefly because of his chairmanship of the Judiciary Committee, a post that controlled approximately 40 percent of congressional legislation. He used his influence, for example, to press for the creation of a separate U.S. air force, and he was the chief sponsor of a bill creating the Civil Aeronautics Board to regulate commercial airline routes, rates, and safety. In addition, he was responsible for the appropriation of $500 million for the construction of municipal airports throughout the nation, one of which became McCarran International Airport in Las Vegas, Nevada. As a senator from a "silver state," he fought for the Nevada mining interests and endorsed the remonetization of silver at 16 to 1. For his silver-throated oratory on behalf of the precious metal, he was nicknamed the "silver-haired, silver-tongued, and silver-minded" senator from the Silver State. The people of Nevada rewarded his memory by placing a statue of their native son in Statuary Hall in the U.S. Capitol.

The senator's conservatism was most evident in his anti-Communism. During the Truman administration, for example, he urged support of the Franco regime in Spain and was successful in obtaining congressional approval for the construction of American naval and air bases in that country. Although a consistent supporter of the Nationalist Chinese under Chiang Kai-shek, he failed to win a $1.5 billion loan for that leader's struggle against the Communist Mao Tse-tung. When China fell to the Communists in 1949, McCarran blamed the Truman administration for abandoning the Nationalists.

On the domestic front, McCarran lent his considerable support to efforts to ferret out homegrown Communists and their sympathizers. The chairman supported Senator Joseph McCarthy in his campaign against what the latter alleged was Communist influence in the State Department, for instance, and helped obtain passage of the Internal Security Act of 1950. This particular piece of legislation required that individual Communists and their organizations register with the U.S. government and strengthened laws against sedition and espionage.

In line with his efforts to monitor what he regarded as un-American activities, McCarran supported keeping tough immigration restrictions. Through the help of like-minded congressmen, his efforts were rewarded with passage of the Immigration and Nationality Act of 1952, a bill which gave preference to immigrants from western and northern Europe and which required more effective screening of aliens. This legislation was the cornerstone of American immigration policy until 1965, when Congress radically changed the ethnic balance of the immigration flow in favor of South Americans and Asians.

VIRGINIA CITY

Although now only a small town with a population of about 1,500, Virginia City in the 1870s was the mining capital of the West, boasting more than 100 saloons, fifty dry goods stores, five newspapers, seven churches, and a population of 30,000. In addition, the $234 million in ore extracted from its largest mine – the Consolidated Virginia – helped build San Francisco and win the Civil War.

Virginia City's phenomenal growth began inauspiciously enough in 1859. While two Irish immigrant miners – Patrick McLaughlin and Peter O'Reilly – were working their claim above Six Mile Canyon, they discovered gold at the edge of what turned out to be one of the richest lodes in history. Almost out of the blue, however, a loudmouthed Canadian named Henry Comstock asserted a previous claim to the area, insisting – falsely – that he and a partner owned the land on which the Irishmen's discovery had occurred. Although McLaughlin and O'Reilly were aware that they were being taken in, they acquiesced out of fear that Comstock and his associate would use violence against them. As a result, the Irishmen formed an unholy partnership with the deceivers and named their discovery the Ophir Mine – for the fabled source of King Solomon's wealth. At first the four partners were perplexed and annoyed by the blue-black sand which contaminated the extracted gold ore. But when an assayer tested a sample of the "blue stuff," he was amazed to find that it assayed out to be $3,000 in *silver* as well as almost $900 in gold a ton.

Despite the unimaginable potential which the Ophir held, each of its owners sold out prematurely. McLaughlin accepted only $3,500 for his share, selling it to a group of investors headed by George Hearst, the father of the famous newspaper publisher. The first thirty-eight tons of high-grade silver ore which Hearst and his companions extracted from the Ophir yielded them $3,000 a ton, netting them a profit in excess of $90,000. Although O'Reilly held out for $45,000 before selling, he suffered some kind of mental breakdown soon later. After hearing voices telling him to dig in a nearby mountain, he was sent to a hospital for the insane, where he died a year or two later.

When McLaughlin and O'Reilly muffed their chance to become known as the "Silver Kings," that argentiferous title fell to four other argonauts of Irish descent. Three of them were Irish natives – John Mackay, James Flood, and William O'Brien – while the fourth (James Fair) was born in New York to Irish immigrant parents. By 1868 the four had individually arrived in Virginia City, where they enjoyed varying degrees of success in the mines. After forming a partnership, they paid $100,000 for a controlling interest in a mine which the seller though was worthless. (More than a $1 million had already been expended in unprofitable exploration.) The Irishmen had the last laugh, however. Between 1873 and 1882 the mine –

located at the heart of the Comstock Lode – yielded $65 million in gold and silver.

The Comstock yielded up its guts – so to speak – in other ways also, less remuneratively to miners, certainly, but quite handsomely for historians. In 1867 the Comstock's Savage Mine became immortalized when the Irish-American photographer Timothy O'Sullivan took the first underground photographs of a mine. Because he realized that candles could not provide light sufficient for proper exposure in such subterranean conditions, he carried a variety of reflective and illuminating materials when he descended into the mine. The miners must have thought him merely odd as he surrounded them with his tin reflectors, but when he lit a load of magnesium to provide sight for his camera's eye they must have regarded him as a potential arsonist.

For the next three years O'Sullivan served as official photographer with two surveying expeditions. The first was with the U.S. Geological Service team when it explored the fortieth parallel. In a life-threatening episode on the Truckee River, rapids forced the surveyors' boat between two rocks. Although O'Sullivan jumped overboard to swim to shore, he was swept downstream 200 feet before reaching an embankment. After walking back to where the boat was snagged, he was thrown a line by a member of the crew. The latter, unfortunately, had weighted the line with the photographer's wallet, which contained $300 in twenty-dollar gold-pieces. Although the Irishman caught the line, his wallet fell into the river. "That was rough," he recalled, "for I never found that wallet again, although I prospected a long time, barefooted, for it." With the rope, O'Sullivan managed to dislodge the boat. Luckily, his camera and chemicals remained unharmed in their watertight bags. After entering Pyramid Lake the next day, O'Sullivan spent several more days photographing the area's pyramid-like rocks, some 500 feet in height. As he clambered up one of the formations to take a panoramic shot, he found himself in the midst of a circle of hissing rattlesnakes. Only a hasty retreat and the bullets of the sure-shots in his party saved him.

In 1870 O'Sullivan accompanied an expedition to the Isthmus of Darien and later superintended the photography on the U.S. Geographic Survey west of the one hundredth meridian. Although the San Blas Indians in Panama were intrigued by the American's camera, their chief – known as "Shoemaker" because of his fondness for shoes – refused to pose for photographs until he received several pairs of footwear.

¶ **Mackay Mansion,** 129 South D Street.

Built in 1861, this ten-room structure was originally the headquarters of the Gould and Curry Mine Company. Its first resident was George Hearst, whose later enormous wealth was derived from the original Comstock find. The mansion was subsequently the home of John Mackay, one of the famous "Silver Kings" whose fortune was also derived from the fabulous riches of the Comstock Lode.

Born in Dublin, Ireland, in 1831, Mackay had come to America with his parents and three siblings nine years later. The death of his father forced the youngster to take employment as an apprentice with a New York ship-builder. At the age of twenty, however, he joined the rush to the California gold fields, where for the next seven years he worked the mines. Later, while earning $6 a day as a timber man in Virginia City, he acquired expert skill in timbering.

After saving a small amount of his wages, Mackay headed off on his own and enjoyed middling success at Gold Hill, Nevada. In 1864 he and his partner joined forces with James Flood and William O'Brien, two Irish-born saloon keepers from San Francisco who had been lured to the mine country by the tales of their customers. Four years later the trio was joined by James Flair, the son of Irish immigrants to New York. After acquiring control of the Hale and Norcross Mine, this "Irish quartet" struck pay dirt and rolled their $500,000 in profits into the Virginia Consolidated Mine. The resulting "Big Bonanza" strike in 1873 opened the floodgates to more than $1 million in gold and silver.

Finding himself a millionaire overnight, Mackay tried to adjust to his new role as miner-capitalist. Such a role was initially difficult, for after his first big strike in the Mother Lode had netted him $200,000 he said that

John Mackay Mansion. (Photo by Robert C. Gray and courtesy of Robert C. Gray and the Virginia & Truckee Railroad.)

this was enough money for any man and that "the man who wanted more was a fool." At the risk of appearing foolish, however, he invested heavily in real estate in San Francisco and in other parts of the West. He later became a director of the Southern Pacific Railroad and a cofounder of the Bank of Nevada in San Francisco.

In the meantime Mackay had married a New York widow. When he had proposed to her, he cautioned her to make her decision not on the basis of his wealth but on his personal qualities. In doing so he warned her that "Circumstances in the mining business change quickly" but that he could "always dig a living" with his bare hands if misfortune should ever strike. In any event he promised to protect her "with my fists, if need be." Twenty-five years later, at the age of sixty, the Irishman had reason to remember this particular promise when a newspaper reporter stated that Mrs. Mackay had once been a washerwoman and had later sunk "even lower than that." After searching out the writer of the slanderous remarks, Mackay hit him in the left eye. "Then I hit him again," he boasted. ". . . I'm not so handy with my fists as I used to be twenty-five years ago on the Comstock, but I have a little fight in me yet, and will allow no man to malign me or mine."

After briefly taking up residence in San Francisco, Mackay and his wife moved to New York in 1874. Stung by the snubbing they received there, however, they sailed for Europe, where they spent most of their remaining years and where the Prince of Wales called Mackay "the most unassuming American I have ever met." Mackay's extravagant wife, meanwhile, maintained splendid mansions in Paris and London. In the late 1870s when she commissioned a 1,200-piece silver service from Tiffany & Company, the job cost him a minor fortune: $100,000 in wages to 200 silversmiths and $17,000 for almost 15,000 ounces of silver.

After selling his interest in the Comstock in 1883, Mackay went into the expanding cable communications industry. His first major undertaking was to lay his own line from New York to London and Europe. When the Western Union Telegraph Company refused to send his cable company's messages throughout the United States, he formed the rival Postal Telegraph Company.

Despite his immense wealth, Mackay found no great comfort in it, a feeling that may have been the basis of his philanthropy. At a time when he was earning $800,000 a month, he confessed that his great wealth had deprived him of his former interest in gambling. "I don't care whether I win or lose," he once said after throwing down his cards during a game in Virginia City. "When you can't enjoy winning at poker, there's no fun left in anything."

Before his death he distributed more than $5 million to various charities and private individuals. So many people besieged him as he walked from his hotel to his office each day that he estimated his alms to be $50 a block. His workmen had always regarded him as a fair and honest employer, although many of them were unaware of his charities (e.g., paying as much as $3,000 a month toward his miners' grocery bills when the men were out of work). Yet he was the object of an unsuccessful assassination attempt in 1895 by a speculator who blamed him for his mining reverses. At his death Mackay's assets were valued at $50 million.

§ Open April-November, daily 9-7; rest of the year, 11-5. Fee. Phone: 702-847-0173.

¶ **Mark Twain Museum,** in the *Territorial Enterprise* Building, C Street between Union and Taylor streets.

This unusual printing museum is located in the newspaper office where the young Samuel Clemens worked as a reporter and first used his famous pen name (the steamboating term "Mark Twain"). The museum displays antique printing presses and type fonts.

Twain, who was proud of his maternal Irish ancestry, referred to the *Territorial Enterprise* in his semi-autobiographical work *Roughing It*, published during the "flush times" in Virginia City. At the time, the paper was clearing from $6,000 to $10,000 a month and had a staff of five editors and twenty-three compositors.

The famous humorist also expressed the frustration he experienced while serving as chief editor of the *Enterprise* for a week: "It destroyed me. The first day, I wrote my 'leader' in the forenoon. The second day, I had no subject and put it off till the afternoon. The third day I put if off till evening, and then copied an elaborate editorial out of the 'American Cyclopedia,' that steadfast friend of the editor, all over this land. The fourth day I 'fooled around' till midnight, and then fell back on the Cyclopedia again. The fifth day I cudgeled my brain until midnight, and then kept the press waiting while I penned some bitter personalities on six different people. The sixth day I labored in anguish till far into the night and brought forth – nothing. . . . The seventh day I resigned. . . . [I]t is unspeakable hardship to write editorials. *Subjects* are the trouble – the dreary lack of them, I mean."

§ Phone: 702-847-0525.

¶ **St. Mary's in the Mountains,** E and Taylor streets.

In 1875, when a large portion of Virginia City was swept by fire, St. Mary's was caught in the path of the flames. When one of the parishioners ran to the Comstock mine to implore *John Mackay to help save the church, the Irish-born "Silver King" promised that he would rebuild the structure if the parishioners helped him save his mine. ("Damn the church!" he cried. "We'll build another one, if we can keep the fire from going down these shafts.") Mackay kept his word and helped rebuild the house of worship.

The first Catholic church on this site was built in 1860 but was blown down by a Washoe "zephyr," like the one described so hyperbolically by Mark Twain in Chapter 21 of *Roughing It*. The second church was erected in 1863 under the direction of Father Patrick Manogue, the Kilkenny-born curate who was later known as the "Apostle of the Mother Lode." Most of the $12,000 cost of construction was raised from contributions which the miners made to "Manogue's kitty," the name given to the collection boxes which were placed in every saloon in town. This frame structure was succeeded by a brick one which cost $65,000 and which succumbed to the 1875 fire. The present church is a red brick building whose façade is adorned with two pinnacles, a rose window, and three pointed-arch doorways. It is noted for its redwood columns, arches, and trusses as well as the silver bell from the earlier church.

Manogue had first come west to restore his health after a cholera epidemic forced the closure of the seminary he attended in Chicago. He soon adopted the harsh life of a miner in the Nevada gold fields, not necessarily in hopes of striking it rich but rather of earning and saving enough money to continue his studies for the priesthood. As one of his pick-and-shovel partners explained, the Irishman "worked tirelessly from morning till night, drilling, blasting, and shoveling as hard as any."

Despite his studious nature and reputation as a peacemaker among the miners, Manogue was capable of throwing a few punches when he thought it was necessary. On one occasion, when two bandits thought they could intimidate him into abandoning his cabin to them, Manogue's Irish temper came to the fore. Before the conniving pair knew what they were up against, the brawny miner grabbed one of them by the neck, hurled him into the underbrush, and disarmed him of his pistol. "I've heard of claim-jumping," Manogue said wryly, "but this is the first I've heard of cabin-jumping!" (Even after his ordination he once struck a gun-toting husband in the jaw for trying to prevent him from entering his house to give his wife the last rites.)

By about 1857, at the age of twenty-six, Manogue had saved enough money to return to his theological studies. En route to the Continent to fulfill his dream of studying at the Sulpician seminary in Paris, he visited relatives in Ireland. Four years later, following his ordination in the French capital, Father Manogue returned to his beloved miners in Nevada. After finding temporary lodging with an Irish landlady in Virginia City, he celebrated the first mass ever said in that part of the territory.

The new curate was undaunted by the vast expanse of his parish, however, as two episodes clearly illustrate. Once while riding circuit from camp to camp, the priest was approached by a few riders who recognized him from the description they had been given: "as tall as a steeple when he stands up." The riders informed Manogue that they came on behalf of Mike McClellan, who, in his dying hours, had asked them to fetch a priest. After traveling more than 300 miles, the priest comforted McClellan with the last rites. On another occasion Manogue rode more than 100 miles to attend to another dying man, this time a poor wretch about to be hanged for a crime he claimed he had not committed. After being convinced that the condemned was telling the truth, the priest retraced his 100-mile route, but this time to the home of the territorial governor, from whom he obtained a reprieve for the hapless prisoner.

By the end of the 1880s, Manogue had presided over the growth of a thriving parish. He had seen the construction not only of St. Mary's Church but also of two schools, an orphanage, a convent, and a hospital, the last primarily with the financial backing of John Mackay. It was naturally with great sorrow that he left Virginia City to take his place among the episcopacy, first as coadjutor bishop of Grass Valley and then as the first bishop of Sacramento, California. Under his direction the cathedral of the Blessed Sacrament was constructed, a magnificent structure which still stands in the California capital and which at the time of its dedication in 1889 was the largest church west of the Mississippi.

NEW MEXICO

ABIQUIU

¶ **Georgia O'Keeffe House and Studio,** about 50 miles from Santa Fe.

Although Georgia O'Keeffe first came to New Mexico in 1917 – as one of the artists, musicians, and writers "collected" by the art patron Mabel Dodge – it was not until 1945 that the famous artist bought the house and studio on this site. The structures, parts of which date from the early eighteenth century, had belonged to the Catholic Church.

Following a three-year restoration program, the buildings were ready for occupancy, and the famous artist took up permanent residence on the site, one of two properties which she maintained in northern New Mexico. She remained at Abiquiu until her death in 1986, just two years shy of her one hundredth birthday. Many of her works were inspired by the house and its surroundings, including its patio and the local cottonwood trees.

O'Keeffe was the daughter of Francis Calyxtus O'Keeffe, a native of Ireland whose parents had fled oppressive taxation of their prosperous woolen business in County Cork. At the insistence of his Hungarian wife, Ida Totto, Frank abandoned Catholicism and allowed his children to be raised as Protestants. Nevertheless, Georgia was permitted to attend Sacred Heart School in Sun Prairie, Wisconsin. In contrast to the starkness of the Congregational church which she usually attended with her family, the art and ritual which she found when she occasionally attended Catholic services with her uncle hit a responsive chord in her artistic nature. In addition, her desire to be like her paternal grandmother – Mary Catherine O'Keeffe – may have made the older woman's Catholicism all the more attractive to the young girl. At the very least Georgia wished that she had been given her grandmother's name and later said, "I love the Irish [in me]." Although the artist never converted to the religion of her father's family, she remained influenced by its imagery and even dressed like a nun, a habit which caused her to be mistaken for a Catholic sister one time during a visit to Vienna.

After studying at the Chicago Art Institute and Columbia University in New York, O'Keeffe intermittently tried her hand at painting and drawing and found that she could "say things that I couldn't say in any other way – things that I had no words for." The artist first drew serious critical attention when Alfred Stieglitz, a pioneer in photography and her future husband, included some of her charcoal drawings in a show at his New York studio. Through these and other works she soon became known for her experimentation in subject matter and technique. (Some of her most famous paintings depict gigantic flower blossoms or bleached animal bones and skulls.) Despite the acclaim which her work received, she was distressed that some critics saw symbols of feminine sexuality in her designs, although she once said that her paintings were her children. By 1939 she was being hailed by the New York World's Fair Tomorrow Committee as one of the twelve most outstanding women of the previous fifty years.

Long before settling permanently at Abiquiu, O'Keeffe had spent many winters there. She was equally familiar with her summer house and studio at Ghost Ranch, a property now closed to the public about a mile and a half from the Ghost Ranch Museum in Abiquiu. The almost hypnotic effect which the ranch had on her can be glimpsed in a letter to her husband in 1937: "At 5:30 I went out and walked – just over the queer colored land – such ups and downs – so much variety in such a small space . . . I've been up on the roof watching the moon come up – the sky very dark – the moon large and lopsided – and very soft . . . ."

Today the Abiquiu house is administered by the Georgia O'Keeffe Foundation, established in 1989 to perpetuate the legacy of the famous artist.

§ Indoor tours are available by reservation on Tuesday, Thursday, and Friday but are limited to six participants per tour. Exterior tours are limited to twenty people. No photography is permitted on the property.

Reservations should be made as far in advance as possible through the Georgia O'Keeffe Foundation, P. O. Box 40, Abiquiu, New Mexico 87510. Phone: 505-685-4539. Fax: 505-685-4428.

FORT SUMNER

¶ Fort Sumner State Monument, 3 miles east on U.S. 60 and then 3 miles south on Billy the Kid Road.

The fort formerly on this site was built in 1862 by General James Carleton as a resettlement area for Apache and Navajo. The only remaining portion of the fort is the officers' quarters, turned into a twenty-room mansion in 1875 by a former owner. Six years later Billy the Kid – the Irish-American Henry McCarty – was shot and killed in the house by Sheriff Pat Garrett. (See Lincoln, New Mexico.)

In July 1881, McCarty had returned to Old Fort Sumner to visit a ladyfriend, Celsa Gutiérrez. During the night he left her room in search of some food. Entering the suite of rooms which his friend Peter Maxwell had made out of the former officers' quarters, McCarty asked in Spanish "¿Quien es?" but was surprised to see Garrett waiting for him in the dark. A bullet from the lawman's gun struck McCarty in the heart and instantly killed him. The Kid was buried the next day in the fort's military cemetery, at age twenty-one the victim of his own notoriety.

§ Monument open May-September 15, daily 9:30-5:30; rest of the year, daily 8:30-5:30. Fee. Phone: 505-355-2573.

¶ Old Fort Sumner Museum, 0.25 mile east of the monument.

This small museum displays photographs and memorabilia associated with the history of the fort and the life of Billy the Kid (Henry McCarty).

Born about 1860 in the Irish slums of Brooklyn, McCarty was one of America's most notorious outlaws. Reputedly the son of Irish immigrants, McCarty followed his family to Kansas and then to New Mexico, where his widowed mother, Catherine – described as a "jolly Irishwoman" – married William Antrim in the First Presbyterian Church in Santa Fe. Antrim's name was presumably Irish and provided Henry with a variety of pseudonyms ("Henry Antrim," "Kid Antrim," and "William Antrim").

In 1877, after having spent two years working as a cowboy, a teamster, and a general laborer in eastern Arizona, McCarty killed an Irish blacksmith named Frank Cahill after the latter had thrown him to the floor. Although indicted for murder, McCarty (now using the alias William Bonney) escaped and headed for New Mexico, where he later worked as a ranch-hand for an Englishman named John Tunstall, a man who seems to have been a substitute father for McCarty. In addition to his ranch, Tunstall operated a bank and general store in Lincoln. Unfortunately for Tunstall, though, this new enterprise competed with a similar store owned by James Dolan and Laurence Murphy, natives, respectively, of County Wexford and County Galway, Ireland. The commercial rivalry reached a climax when Tunstall was killed by members of the Murphy-Dolan gang. Enraged by the murder, McCarty swore vengeance on "every son of a bitch who helped kill John."

During the spring of 1878, the young McCarty and his confederates tracked down Tunstall's killers. Among the five members of the Dolan-Murphy gang who fell victim to the avengers was Sheriff William Brady, who had led the posse that killed the Englishman. During the better part of 1880, McCarty was on the run for killing a would-be assassin at Fort Sumner, New Mexico. Returning to the fort later that year, the Kid and his followers ran into a posse led by Sheriff Pat Garrett. In the gunfire that ensued, McCarty escaped but surrendered a week later when cornered in Stinking Springs.

The following spring, while awaiting execution in the Lincoln County Courthouse for the murder of Sheriff Brady, McCarty again escaped. This time the young outlaw slipped out of his handcuffs (while on a visit to the privy), grabbed a six-gun (despite his leg irons), and killed his two guards. As he calmly rode out of town, he shouted, "You won't follow me any more with that gun."

§ Open May-September 15, daily 9:30-5:30; rest of the year, daily 8:30-4:30. Closed winter holidays. Fee. Phone: 505-355-2942.

¶ Billy the Kid's grave is located behind the museum. The inscription on his tombstone reads: "The Boy Bandit King – He Died as He Had Lived."

Because in the past Billy's headstone was frequently the object of thefts, it is now surrounded by a chain-link fence. These attempts at theft are memorialized in the Billy the Kid Tombstone Race, held during Old Fort Days each June.

The Fort Sumner cemetery is also the final resting place of Tom O'Folliard, the son of an Irish immigrant and an outlaw confederate of Billy the Kid. Born in Uvalde, Texas, in 1858, O'Folliard gravitated to New Mexico, where he became a horse thief, one of the Kid's band of rustlers, and a partisan in the Lincoln County War. On December 19, 1880, while he and Billy the Kid rode into Fort Sumner, they were unexpectedly greeted by Sheriff Pat Garrett and his posse. When O'Folliard reached for his gun, he was struck in the chest just below the heart, presumably by one of the posse. Although the wounded outlaw tried to flee, he quickly gave himself up, calling out, "Don't shoot, Garrett. I'm killed" and telling the lawman that if he were a friend he would put him out of his misery. The sheriff replied that he was no friend to the likes of O'Folliard. After asking one of the deputies to inform his grandmother of his death, the wounded outlaw moaned, "Oh, my God, is it possible I must die?" and answered himself: "The sooner the better. I will be out of pain."

LAS VEGAS

¶ Old Town Plaza Park.

On August 15, 1846, spectators in the town plaza in Las Vegas watched as *Stephen Watts Kearny, the commander of the U.S. Army in the West, claimed New Mexico for the United States. From the roof of one of the buildings in the plaza, Kearny issued a proclamation promising the Mexicans that their fields and crops would be protected and their religion respected if they stayed peaceably at home. After posting sentries to guard the fields, he warned his own men against looting. (See Escondido, California.)

LINCOLN

¶ Lincoln State Monument, 30 miles east of Ruidoso on U.S. 70 and then 10 miles west on U.S. 380.

This historic district contains several preserved or reconstructed buildings associated with the 1878 Lincoln County War, a series of bloody skirmishes between rival landowners and business factions for control of the local economy. Some of the participants had such Irish names as Brady, Dolan, McCarty, McCloskey, Murphy, and O'Keefe.

One of the preserved structures is the Lincoln County Courthouse, which at one time served as the Dolan-Murphy store and from which *Henry McCarty ("Billy the Kid") made a daring escape. Now a museum, the building displays the wooden marker from the grave of Billy the Kid's mother as well as personal effects belonging to Sheriff Pat Garrett, who killed the Kid on July 14, 1881.

§ Tours of the structures are available May-September, daily 10:30 and 2:30; self-guiding tours daily 9-5, rest of the year. Closed January 1, Easter, Thanksgiving, and December 25. Fee. Phone: 505-653-4372 or 505-653-4025.

• On the last weekend in August, the Last Escape of Billy the Kid Annual Pageant includes a reenactment of the famous outlaw's escape from the county courthouse as well as a parade, a fiddlers' contest, and arts and crafts demonstrations.

ROSWELL

¶ Roswell Museum and Art Center, 11th and Main Streets.

Although the museum houses exhibits on space science and rocketry, the art gallery includes works by the Southwestern artists *Georgia O'Keeffe, Ernest Blumenschein, Andrew Dasburg, Stuart Davis, Marsden Hartley, and John Martin.

§ Open Monday-Saturday 9-5, Sunday and holidays 1-5. Closed Thanksgiving and December 25. Phone: 505-624-6744.

SHAKESPEARE

This well-preserved ghost town was originally known as Ralston, named for *William Ralston, the town's founder and the president of the Bank of California. (See Belmont, California.) During the early 1870s the banking magnate platted the land and staked all claims. After the mines' silver was quickly depleted, some of Ralston's associates unsuccessfully tried to contrive another boom by scattering the landscape with diamonds. Today Shakespeare boasts a saloon, a general store, and the Stratford Hotel, where *Henry McCarty ("Billy the Kid") is believed to have been employed as a dishwasher.

§ Tours of the site are available only on the second weekend of each month or by advance reservation. Phone: 505-542-9864.

SILVER CITY

During the early 1870s, Henry McCarty ("Billy the Kid") lived here with his mother, brother, and stepfather. (See Lincoln, New Mexico.) One of his school teachers recalled that he was "a scrawny little fellow with delicate hands (he supposedly loved to play the piano) and an artistic nature, always willing to help with the chores around the schoolhouse."

Despite such a positive characterization, one legend maintains that McCarty committed his first murder at the age of twelve, when he killed a man in a barroom brawl for insulting his mother. According to more accurate accounts, though, he was fifteen when he first ran afoul of the law and was arrested for stealing clothing from a Chinese laundry in town. (He escaped from jail by climbing up the chimney.) Even at his worst, however, the five-foot seven-inch, 135-pound "Kid" never smoked, drank, or frequented prostitutes.

Today visitors can take a self-guided Billy the Kid tour past the site of McCarty's boyhood home, the Star Hotel (where he worked as a waiter), his mother's grave, and the site of the jail where he effected his first escape from the law.

NORTH CAROLINA

ASHEVILLE

❡ Thomas Wolfe Memorial State Historic Site, 48 Spruce Street.

Known as "Old Kentucky Home," this twenty-nine-room boarding-house was where the future author *Thomas Wolfe lived from age six to about sixteen, when he left to attend the University of North Carolina. (Wolfe's father refused to move from the family residence two blocks away.) The boardinghouse was operated by Thomas's mother, whose Scotch-Irish ancestors had settled in the state in the late eighteenth century.

The author's life at the boardinghouse figures prominently in his first novel, the autobiographical *Look Homeward, Angel.* The work is set in Altamont, Catawba, the fictional name which Wolfe gave to Asheville. Eugene Grant, the protagonist in the novel, lives in Dixieland, a boarding-house run by his mother. Wolfe described his own mother's renovations to the house as "made after her own plans, and of the cheapest material. It never lost the smell of raw wood, cheap varnish, and flimsy rough plastering."

The residents of Asheville were so angered by their portrayal in *Look Homeward, Angel* that the book was banned from the local Pack Memorial Public Library until *F. Scott Fitzgerald donated two copies of the work in 1935.

§ Open April-October, Monday-Saturday 9-5, Sunday 1-5; rest of the year, Tuesday-Saturday 10-4, Sunday 1-4. Closed Thanksgiving and December 24-25. Fee. Phone: 704-253-8304.

❡ A marker on College Street notes Wolfe's birthplace on Woodfin Street.

❡ Wolfe is buried in Riverside Cemetery, at 53 Birch Street, off Pearson Drive. His tombstone bears inscriptions from two of his works (*Look Homeward, Angel* and *The Web and the Rock*).

CARTHAGE

❡ Moore County Courthouse, Courthouse Square, Madison Street.

• On the lawn is a marker honoring *President Andrew Johnson, who once worked as a tailor in Carthage.

• West of the courthouse is a monument to James McConnell, a member of the French Flying Corps who died in 1917. Part of the inscription on the memorial reads: "He fought for Humanity, Liberty and Democracy, lighted the way for his countrymen and showed all men how to dare nobly and to die gloriously."

Named for an Irish immigrant grandfather who had come to New

York about 1812, James McConnell was born in Chicago but moved with his parents to Carthage. After attending the University of Virginia from 1808 to 1810, he entered its law school but dropped out to return to Carthage. There he worked as an agent for the Seaboard Air Line Railway until the outbreak of World War I, when he joined the American Ambulance Corps and went to France. Although he won the *Croix de Guerre* for various acts of courage, he felt that both he and the United States should do more in the war against Germany.

As a result, he entered an aviation training program in France and was one of the thirty-eight pilots who formed the Lafayette Escadrille. In 1916 he was injured in a crash when his plane experienced engine trouble. His description of the crash was later published in *Flying for France with the American Escadrille at Verdun*, a personal narrative of his wartime experiences published the next year. "I was skimming the ground at a hundred miles an hour and heading for the trees . . . ," he wrote, "and thought to myself that Jim's hash was cooked, but I went between two trees and ended head-on against the opposite bank of the road . . . . I was n't even bruised."

Despite this boast, McConnell in fact suffered a severe back injury that grew only worse, until his inability to walk forced him to be hospitalized. Nevertheless, at the beginning of March he persuaded the authorities to let him in the air again. On March 19, while flying one of the squadron's famous biplanes, he was shot down by two German pilots. One of the last entries in his diary seemed prophetic: "This war may kill me, but I have it to thank for much."

A visitor to his grave near the French village of Jussy later wrote: "At the foot was his battered machine-gun, while, on either side, were pieces of his aeroplane, including a blade from the propeller. Forget-me-nots and other fresh flowers were blooming, and American and French flags were waving, on the wooden cross that marks the grave. There is no fear that the site will be disturbed. The place is sacred, for that is a hero's grave." (See the University of Virginia, Charlottesville, Virginia.)

CHARLOTTE

¶ **Hezekiah Alexander House,** three miles east at 3420 Shamrock Drive.

Known for its two-feet-thick walls, this stone structure was built by Hezekiah Alexander, one of the drafters and signers of the Mecklenburg Declaration in 1774. The site also includes a two-story springhouse, a log kitchen, and a museum.

Of Scotch-Irish ancestry, Alexander was born in Cecil County, Maryland, in 1728. After learning the blacksmith's trade, he moved to western Pennsylvania but was forced to flee that area when the frontier came under attack during the French and Indian War. After settling in North Carolina, where many of his relatives were already living, he became one of the most influential men in Mecklenburg County. Appointed county magistrate by the governor, Alexander was also an elder in the local Presbyterian church and played a major role in the creation of Queens College, the only Presbyterian seminary south of New Jersey.

Like his coreligionists Alexander objected to various policies of the British government. The most egregious were the imposition of taxes to support the Anglican Church and the royal veto of the Queens College charter. By the mid 1770s Alexander had become a member of the Mecklenburg Committee of Safety and played a major role in securing the adoption of the Mecklenburg Resolves, which declared all British laws and authority in the colony to be null and void. He later outfitted and supplied the expedition which crushed the Tories in the western region of South Carolina. As a member of an executive committee entrusted with almost dictatorial powers, he helped set military policies for the province, primarily in the raising of a patriot force that crushed the Tory threat in the east and the Cherokees in the west.

Following the declaration of American independence by the Continental Congress, Alexander was elected to the convention which established a new state government. In that capacity he helped draft the North Carolina constitution, an instrument which, second to Pennsylvania's, was the most democratic of those adopted during the revolutionary period.

§ Museum and grounds open Tuesday-Friday 10-5, Saturday-Sunday 2-5. Guided house tours Tuesday-Friday at 1:15 and 3:15, Saturday-Sunday 2:15 and 3:15. Fee for house. Phone: 704-568-1774.

¶ **White House Site,** Independence Square, on the northeast corner of Trade and Tyron streets.

The site now marked by a plaque, the White House was the home of *Colonel Thomas Polk, the leader of the county militia, a member of the general assembly, and a great-uncle of President James K. Polk. (See Pineville, North Carolina.)

Following news of the battles of Lexington and Concord in the spring of 1775, Colonel Polk convened an assembly of twenty-seven representatives to respond to the first engagements of the Revolutionary War. On May 20 of that year, the extralegal group adopted twenty resolutions challenging the legitimacy of all royal and parliamentary authority. Polk publicly read the resolutions – known as the Mecklenburg Declaration of Independence – for the first time in this square.

¶ Thomas Polk is buried in the Old Cemetery, at the rear of the First Presbyterian Church on West Trade Street.

CLINTON

¶ Moore Birthplace Marker, northeast on State 403.

A historical marker notes that Thomas Overton Moore, the secessionist leader and wartime governor of Louisiana, was born about 4.5 miles northwest of this site.

Through his paternal ancestors Moore was descended from James Moore, a governor of South Carolina who had emigrated from Ireland in the seventeenth century. At the age of twenty-five, the latter-day Moore moved to Rapides Parish, Louisiana, to manage his uncle's sugar plantation. In time, the younger man acquired his own plantation and became one of the state's most influential planters. In 1848 he began a political career that took him to both houses of the state legislature and, in 1859, to the governor's mansion.

With the election of Lincoln the following year, Moore issued a message to the people of the state: "I do not think it comports with the honor and respect of Louisiana, as a slave-holding state, to live under the government of a Black Republican President." Responding to his wishes, the legislature called a special convention to decide the issue. Moore, meanwhile, accurately anticipating that the convention would vote to secede, ordered the seizure of several federal garrisons throughout Louisiana. Once the state had joined the Confederacy, the governor actively used his authority to raise troops and supply them with provisions.

Following the capture of New Orleans by federal troops in June 1862, however, Moore found his effectiveness severely curtailed, although he continued to govern the central and northern portions of the state. In addition, disaster struck closer to home when Union soldiers confiscated his plantation and burned his home and mill. Fleeing arrest, he escaped to Havana, Cuba. Through the good graces of friends, he was later allowed to return to the United States with a full pardon. He spent the rest of his life trying to rebuild his plantation and recover from his earlier financial losses.

CONCORD

This town of 27,000 residents was founded as part of a compromise between Scotch-Irish and German-Dutch settlers who had tired of fighting over the site of the county seat. To commemorate their forced harmony, they gave the respective names of Concord and Union to their new town and its main street.

¶ Poplar Tent Presbyterian Church, 8 miles west on Poplar Tent Road.

This church was formed sometime before 1770 by Scotch-Irish settlers from Maryland and Pennsylvania. The church building received its name from the large tent in which the members of the congregation worshipped after they first arrived here.

CURRIE

¶ **Moore's Creek National Battlefield,** 20 miles northwest of Wilmington and 4 miles west of U.S. 421 on State 210.

This ninety-acre site commemorates a major American victory after a series of maneuvers orchestrated by Colonel James Moore against a force of Scottish Highlander loyalists in February 1776. The final brief battle at Moore's Creek broke the power of North Carolina's loyalists and prevented the British conquest of the southern colonies.

Moore was descended from Roger Moore, a leader of the 1641 Irish uprising who had immigrated to Charleston, South Carolina, about 1675. The latter-day Moore served in the French and Indian War and later sat in the North Carolina House of Commons. During the escalating political dispute with Great Britain, he was one of the leaders of a mob which prevented enforcement of the Stamp Act. His activities with the Sons of Liberty led him to press for the convening of a revolutionary provincial congress. It was this assembly which in the fall of 1775 appointed him colonel of the 1st North Carolina Continental Regiment.

The following January the royal governor, Josiah Martin, issued a proclamation calling upon Scottish Highlanders in the colony to assemble at Brunswick to augment the forces of the expected British regulars. After learning that more than 1,400 Highland loyalists had assembled at Cross Creek, Colonel Moore deployed his 650 troops so as to cut off the enemy's direct route to the coast. The loyalist commander maneuvered his troops around Moore's, however, and succeeded in crossing the creek. Although Moore ordered Richard Caswell, one of his officers, to station 600 militia at the next probable crossing, the Highlanders again escaped and forded the Black River on bridges of their own construction. At Moore's orders Caswell led his men to Widow Moore's Creek Bridge, where he waited with an enlarged militia force of 950 men.

When the Highlanders arrived within six miles of Caswell's position, they decided to make their way through the intervening swamp preparatory to a daring attack. At dawn on February 27, the Highlanders rushed Moore's Bridge, shouting their trademark "King George and Broad Sword." When they arrived at the bridge, however, they found that half of the flooring had been removed and the remaining girders greased with soap and tallow. Although a few Highlanders succeeding in crossing the bridge, they were killed before reaching the nearby earthworks. By the end of the brief engagement, the Highlanders had lost thirty killed and 850 captured, while the Patriots had suffered the loss of only one man.

Although Moore and his troops did not participate in the culminating battle at the widow's bridge, for his direction of the successful campaign the Continental Congress appointed him brigadier general of its forces in North Carolina. A year later Congress ordered him and his troops to join General Washington in the north. While preparing for the march, however, Moore died from "a fit of Gout in his stomach."

DURHAM

¶ **O'Kelly Church,** near the junction of State 54 and State 55.

A monument in front of this white clapboard building with a small steeple marks the grave of James O'Kelly, the founder of a sect which broke away from the Methodist Episcopal Church in 1793.

After joining the Methodists in 1755, O'Kelly became a circuit preacher or evangelist. Although he tried to remain neutral during the Revolution, he became a passionate patriot after he was robbed, captured, half-starved, and slandered by British troops. When the Methodist Episcopal Church was first organized in the United States in 1784, O'Kelly was ordained in the new denomination. He was described by a contemporary as "laborious in the ministry, a man of zeal and usefulness, an advocate for holiness, given to prayer and fasting, an able defender of the Methodist doctrine and faith, and hard against negro slavery, in private and from the press and pulpit." (A year after his ordination he freed his one slave.)

O'Kelly soon became embroiled, however, in a dispute about the nature of episcopal authority in the new church. When he was not supported in his claim that ministers should be free to accept or refuse assignments by their bishop, he and several other ministers left the Church in 1793 and formed what they first called the Republican Methodist Church to point out their opposition to an episcopal polity. The name of the offshoot was later changed to the Christian Church.

EDENTON

¶ **Bandon Site,** 6 miles north on State 32 and then left on Rockyhock Road to the entrance to the Arrowhead Beach subdivision.

The plantation formerly on this site was bought in 1769 by the Reverend Daniel Earl, who had resigned from the British Army to seek ordination in the Anglican Church. He renamed the property "Bandon" for the village in County Cork, Ireland, where he had been born. An advocate of advanced agricultural techniques, he introduced his neighbors to the latest methods of preparing and weaving flax. He was also a pioneer in the local fishing economy. After his retirement from the active ministry, he spent the last twelve years of his life at his plantation, where he conducted a classical school for boys. He is buried on his estate. A plaque on one of the ruins commemorates the site of the plantation.

¶ **St. Paul's Episcopal Church,** on the northwest corner of Broad and Church streets.

The *Reverend Daniel Earl served as the rector of this church from 1759 to 1778. During the Revolution he actively supported the Patriot cause, although he refused to leave the service of the Anglican Church. He once wrote that he had avoided becoming embroiled in the political events around him by never introducing "any Topic into the Pulpit except exhortations and prayers for peace, good order and a speedy reconciliation with Great Britain." Nevertheless, his involvement with revolutionary activities must have been considerable, because authorities in the Anglican Church prevented him from holding services in the church.

Although the date of a poem found attached to the church door one morning is unknown, it may suggest the writer's opinion about "Parson Earl" and the state of his parish: "A half-built church, / A broken-down steeple, / A herring-catching parson, / And a damn set of people."

FAYETTEVILLE

¶ **Fort Bragg,** off Interstate 95 exit 52 (State 24) northwest to Bragg Boulevard.

• John F. Kennedy Special Warfare Museum, at Ardennes Marion streets, serves as headquarters for the Special Forces Training Group for the Green Berets.

§ Open Tuesday-Sunday 11:30-4. Phone: 910-432-1533.

GREENSBORO

¶ **Greensboro Historical Museum,** 130 Summit Avenue.

In the museum's Dolley Madison Room are gowns and other personal effects of *Dolley Payne Todd Madison, the wife of the fourth president of the United States.

§ Open Tuesday-Saturday 10-5, Sunday 2-5. Closed city holidays. Phone: 910-373-2043.

¶ The site of Dolley Madison's birth in 1768 is near the town of Guilford College, about seven miles west of Greensboro on U.S. 421. The site is marked by the Dolley Madison Well. The year after Dolley's birth, her parents – John and Mary (Coles) Payne – moved to Virginia. Dolley's maternal grandfather was William Coles, born about 1703 in Enniscorthy, Ireland, while her paternal grandmother was Ann Fleming, born in Ireland in 1712.

HILLSBOROUGH

¶ Archibald Murphey Monument, Presbyterian Church, Queen Street.

This monument marks the grave of Archibald Murphey (1777-1832), an attorney whose 2,000-acre plantation included a sawmill, a gristmill, an eighty-gallon distillery, and a large number of slaves.

Murphey was the grandson of Alexander Murphey of York, Pennsylvania, who probably came from the north of Ireland during the Scotch-Irish emigration of the early eighteenth century. Although Archibald Murphey was a noted North Carolina jurist, his primary interest was improving the social and economic conditions of his native state. His belief that the state's economic retardation was due to its lack of transportation facilities prompted him to advocate legislative appropriations for a sweeping internal improvements program.

With regard to public education, Murphey offered the first comprehensive plan ever proposed in the state, calling for the creation of primary schools and increased support for the University of North Carolina. On this front his efforts were in vain, however, at least during his lifetime. His attention was also directed toward such issues as mitigating the severity of the criminal law, colonizing free blacks, and abolishing imprisonment for debt. Although he succeeded in achieving the last item on this agenda, imprisonment for debt was soon restored and he was forced to endure the experience during a bankruptcy procedure.

¶ Hearttsease, Queen Street off Churton Street.

This frame structure was originally the residence of Thomas Burke, the governor of North Carolina during the last two years of the Revolutionary War. It received its name from a later resident – Dennis Heartt, the publisher of Hillsborough's first newspaper.

Born about 1747 in County Galway, Ireland, Burke studied medicine, probably in Dublin, before coming to Virginia. He soon abandoned medicine, however, for the study and practice of law and the writing of poetry. Among his compositions were "Hymn to Spring by a Physician" and poems celebrating the repeal of the Stamp Act and the British defeat at Yorktown.

After his arrival in Hillsborough in 1771, Burke continued to practice law and became active in the revolutionary struggle against British rule. He was elected as a delegate to three provincial or state congresses and was a member of the committee which recommended that North Carolina's delegates to the Continental Congress join with the other delegates in declaring independence from Britain. In the debates surrounding the drafting of the state's new constitution and bill of rights, he advocated popular sovereignty, separation of powers, annual elections, and separation of Church and State – concepts that were eventually incorporated into the state's organic law.

From 1776 to 1781 Burke represented his adopted state in the Continental Congress. There he generally opposed the secrecy which surrounded that body's proceedings. He also vigorously attacked the proposed Articles of Confederation but was partially mollified when the final document explicitly guaranteed that the states would retain all powers not specifically granted to Congress.

Following his election in 1781 as North Carolina's third governor, Burke took vigorous action to defend the state against the recent British invasion. He was so successful in recruiting and provisioning Patriot troops that the state's Tories hoped to blunt his influence through a daring gamble. During a raid on Hillsborough, the British loyalists kidnapped the governor and subsequently imprisoned him – first in Wilmington, North Carolina, and then in Charleston, South Carolina.

Although he was soon paroled to an island in Charleston Harbor, he came to believe that his life was in danger. When he asked to be paroled to the American lines, he was informed that he was being held as a hostage to obtain the release of a notorious Tory. Believing that his captors had violated the terms of the earlier parole, he effected his own escape and took refuge at the headquarters of General Nathanael Greene. The governor eventually returned to North Carolina to resume his gubernatorial duties, but his weakened condition led to his death soon afterwards.

❡ Two miles northeast of Hillsborough is the site of "Tyaquin," Burke's estate, apparently named after the family's ancestral seat in Ireland. His grave in Mars Hill Churchyard – 0.75 mile east of State 57 – is marked by a large granite stone.

JAMES CITY

❡ **Spaight Burial Site,** Madame Moore's Lane.
Among the members of the Spaight and Moore families laid to rest here are Richard Dobbs Spaight, the first native-born governor of North Carolina, and Richard Dobbs Spaight Jr., the last governor elected by the state legislature. According to tradition, when Federal troops burned the Moore family mansion on this property during the Civil War, the soldiers stole the skeleton of the elder Spaight from its tomb and displayed the skull on a pole.

Despite such an undignified fate, Richard Dobbs Spaight had been a political force in his native North Carolina and in the new national government which he helped create. The son of an Irishman who had married the daughter of one of the colony's royal governors, Spaight was orphaned at the age of eight. After returning to Ireland for his early education, he continued his studies at the University of Glasgow. Once back in North Carolina, he was immediately elected to the House of Commons and became its Speaker at the age of twenty-seven. As a democrat he opposed the claim by the North Carolina courts to possess the authority to declare acts of the legislature unconstitutional. While a delegate to the Constitutional Convention of 1787, he supported efforts to create a strong central government. Five years later he was elected to the first of three terms as governor of North Carolina. During his single term in Congress, he cast his ballot for Thomas Jefferson when the results of the election of 1800 were decided by the House of Representatives.

KENANSVILLE

This town is named after the Kenan family, whose original American ancestor arrived from Ireland in 1730 and developed a plantation called "The Lilacs" in Turkey, North Carolina. Thirty-five years later his son General James Kenan led a force of volunteers from here to Brunswick to block enforcement of the Stamp Act. The son later served for many years in the North Carolina legislature, including ten terms in the state senate.

¶ **Liberty Hall,** State 11/24/50/903 (South Main Street).

This Greek Revival house was built in the early 1800s by Thomas Kenan II, a son of General James Kenan. The builder's motto was "He who enters these open gates, never comes too early, never leaves too late."

The younger Kenan served in both branches of the state legislature before serving in the U.S. House of Representatives from 1805 to 1811. Although he owned the 5,000-acre Laughlin Plantation in North Carolina, in 1833 he moved to Selma, Alabama, to engage in planting. After several

Liberty Hall. (Photo by Henry S. Fullerton.)

years in the lower house of that state's legislature, he died in 1843 and is buried in Valley Creek Cemetery, near Selma.

When possession of Liberty Hall passed from the Kenan family in 1964, a successful restoration effort was headed by Thomas Kenan III, the great-great-great-grandson of the family's Irish ancestor. Today the property includes a smokehouse, a wash shed, a carriage house, and a privy. The visitor center presents historical exhibits and twelve-minute film.

§ Open Tuesday-Saturday 10-4, Sunday 2-4. Closed January 1, Thanksgiving, and December 25. Fee. Phone: 910-296-2175. Reservations are required for the Candlelight Christmas Tour on the second weekend in December.

MANTEO

¶ **Fort Raleigh National Historic Site,** 3 miles north of Manteo off U.S. 64.

An earthen fort today marks the approximate site of Fort Raleigh, built in 1585 as part of the first attempted English colony in what is now the eastern United States.

Several Irishmen were among the 108 colonists who accompanied Sir Richard Grenville's expedition to Puerto Rico, Hispaniola, and what is now North Carolina in 1585-86. One of those sons of Erin was a man by the name of Kelly, while at least two others – probably Edward Nugent and Darby Glande (or Glavin) – had served in Ireland with Ralph Lane, the governor of the proposed colony at Roanoke Island. Glande later claimed that he had been forced to join the Roanoke colony after his impressment from a French ship captured by Grenville.

After initially good relations with the Native Americans, the English at Roanoke soon provoked their animosity and became the object of a planned attack by the Algonquin chief Wingina. To gain the upper hand, Lane decided on a preemptive strike, attacking the chief's village at night in June 1586. Wingina at first played dead but soon ran for his life, until he was shot "through the buttocks" with a cavalry pistol by either Kelly or Glande. After a chase through the woods, the chief was killed and beheaded by Thomas Hariot and Edward Nugent. Lane later wrote that Nugent had "volunteered to kill Pemisapan, King of the Indians. We met him returning out of the woods with Pemisapan's head in his hands, and the Indians ceased their raids against the English camp," at what is now Edenton, North Carolina.

The next year Glande seems to have been an unwilling member of Captain John White's attempt to establish a colony in Virginia. During White's fourth voyage to Virginia, his ship sailed from St. Croix to Puerto Rico to take on fresh water. While on the latter island, Glande and his fellow Irish colonist Dennis Carrell either deserted or were left behind.

Glande may have been deserting not only White's colony but also his own wife, since one of the female colonists was listed as "Elizabeth Glane." Although Glande warned the governor of Puerto Rico of an impending attack by English privateers, he was forced into service in the Spanish galleys.

§ In addition to a film about English colonization in the New World, the visitor center displays manuscripts and artifacts associated with the colony's first years. Open mid June-Labor Day, Monday-Saturday 9-8, Sunday 9-6; rest of the year, daily 9-5. Closed December 25. Phone: 919-473-5772.

MARION

¶ **John Carson House,** on U.S. 70 between Marion and Pleasant Gardens.

The original portion of this large clapboard house was a walnut log cabin constructed about 1790 by Colonel John Carson, an Irish immigrant and a leader in the local militia.

Born in Ireland in March 1752, Carson settled in Burke County, North Carolina, about twenty years later. He and his first wife, Rachel MacDowell, the daughter of another Irish native, had seven children. He had five additional children with his second wife, Mary Moffitt. As a result of his successful land speculation, Carson was able to enlarge the residence with a second log cabin, which he connected to the first with an open breezeway. He eventually acquired an estate of 8,000 acres of fertile bottomland, on which he raised cattle and grew corn. The Irishman was a representative to the state convention which ratified the federal constitution in 1789. He later served in the North Carolina Assembly and participated in county government until his death in 1841.

Like his father, Carson's son Samuel followed a political career. Following two terms in the state senate in the mid 1820s, he served for eight years (1825-1833) in the U.S. House of Representatives. While on Capitol Hill, he became friends with *Sam Houston and *James K. Polk and was known as the best impromptu speaker in Congress. He was a staunch defender of states' rights and strict interpretation of the Constitution and an equally strong opponent of tariffs, a national bank, and federally-funded internal improvements. During the nullification controversy in the early 1830s, he had a falling out with *President Andrew Jackson and Daniel Webster over the issue of states' rights. As a result of supporting *John C. Calhoun during the nullification crisis in 1832, Carson was defeated for reelection to the House. In 1834, however, he was returned to the North Carolina senate and served in the state constitutional convention. During that body's deliberations, he supported popular election of the governor, opposed granting the franchise to free blacks, and opposed continued restrictions on the right of Catholics to hold office.

Carson's political career was marred by his participation in a duel that resulted in the death of Dr. Robert Vance, his opponent in the 1827 congressional election. Vance, it seems, had accused Carson's father of disloyalty to the Patriot cause during the Revolutionary War. To defend his father's reputation, Carson challenged his opponent to a duel, which took place across the border in Saluda Gap, South Carolina. Once on the "field of honor," Carson confided to his seconds that he intended only to wound Vance rather than kill him. The seconds, however, insisted that Vance had come to kill Carson and that if the duel failed to result in the death of one of the antagonists a second duel would be necessary. The seconds also announced his intention to resign if Carson did not promise to try to kill Vance.

In 1835, at the suggestion of his friends *David Crockett and *Sam Houston, Carson migrated to Texas with his wife, Catherine Wilson. In the spring of that year he purchased property on the west side of the Red River and on the Arkansas side of the border with Texas. As a delegate to the convention which met at Washington-on-the-Brazos a year later, he signed the Texas declaration of independence and was elected the new republic's first secretary of state. On a visit to Washington, D.C., in his official capacity, he successfully sought support for congressional recognition of the Texas Republic.

The family home near Marion was eventually inherited by Samuel Carson's brother Jonathan. It was he who covered the log walls with clapboard, added paneling to most of the interior, and installed the fluted front door and window facings. It was probably at this time also that an ell was built at the rear of the house in order to accommodate travelers along the old stage road. (The ell no longer exists.) One of the famous visitors to the inn was *Andrew Jackson, who enjoyed the horse racing which took place on the Carson plantation. When McDowell County was created in 1843, the house served as the seat of government until a courthouse could be constructed in nearby Marion.

§ Open May-October, Tuesday-Saturday 10-5, Sunday 2-5. Open November-April by appointment. Phone: 704-724-4640.

NEW BERN

¶ **Governors' Marker,** Courthouse Lawn, on the west side of Craven Street between New and Broad streets.

On the lawn is a marker in honor of three New Bern natives who went on to become governors of North Carolina. Two of them were *Richard Dobbs Spaight and his son of the same name. (See James City, North Carolina.)

¶ **Spaight-Stanly Duel Site,** Hancock and Johnston streets.

At the rear of the Masonic Theater is the site of the duel which occurred on September 5, 1802, between *Governor Richard Dobbs Spaight Sr. and John Stanly Jr. As respective leaders of the Republican and Federalist parties, they continually clashed on political issues. The governor died of injuries suffered from the duel.

¶ **William Gaston House,** 421 Craven Street.

Beginning in 1818, this eighteenth-century Georgian structure was the home of William Gaston, a justice of the North Carolina Supreme Court. Three years later the first recorded Catholic mass in New Bern was celebrated in this house by *Bishop John England. Gaston was one of five laymen selected by the bishop to conduct religious services every Sunday in the absence of a priest. He later donated $1,200 for the construction of St. Paul's Church in New Bern, the oldest Catholic house of worship in North Carolina.

Born in New Bern in 1778, Gaston was the son of an Irish native of Huguenot descent. The young Gaston was the first student to enroll in Georgetown College, recently founded by *John Carroll, the nation's first Catholic bishop. When illness forced Gaston to withdraw from Georgetown, he transferred to the College of New Jersey (now Princeton). Upon graduation he returned to New Bern to take up the study of law and to commence a political career that spanned three decades.

Beginning in 1800, Gaston served four terms in the state senate and house and two more in the U.S. House of Representatives. In Congress he used his considerable oratorical skills to support the Bank of the United States and to oppose an appropriation of $25 million for the conquest of Canada during the War of 1812. When this opposition caused some people to question his patriotism, he reminded them that as a youngster he had seen his father, an ardent supporter of the Revolutionary cause, murdered by a band of Tories: "I was baptized an American in the blood of a murdered father."

In 1832 Gaston was elected to the state supreme court, in which position he attempted to lessen the harshness of slavery in the state. In one case, in fact, he ruled that a freed slave was a citizen of North Carolina. Later at the state constitutional convention, he was among those attempting to democratize the political system further. Although he was unsuccessful in opposing an amendment that deprived freed blacks of the vote, he was instrumental in securing a change that allowed Catholics to hold civil office in the state.

Much in demand as a commencement speaker, Gaston gave an address at the University of North Carolina in June 1832 at the height of the nullification controversy. In his remarks he pleaded with the people of the state to uphold the Constitution and preserve the Union. He also condemned slavery and urged its abolition, even though at the time of his death he owned 200 slaves.

❡ Gaston's Grave is in Cedar Grove Cemetery, on the northeast corner of Queen and George streets. The desk and the chair which he used in his legal practice were reputedly buried with him.

❡ Gaston's Law Office is next to City Hall, on the northwest corner of Craven and Pollock streets. Built in 1792, it is noted for its interior woodwork.

PINEVILLE

❡ James K. Polk Birthplace State Historic Site, 0.5 mile south on U.S. 521.

A stone pyramid and a reconstructed log cabin mark the site of the cabin in which James K. Polk, the eleventh president of the United States, was born in 1795. A visitor center on the site exhibits items connected with Polk's presidency and presents a film about his life.

The future president was the son of Samuel Polk, a farmer and surveyor of Scotch-Irish descent. James K. Polk's great-great-great-grandfather was Robert Pollock (pronounced "Poke" or "Polk"), who had left County Donegal, Ireland, for Maryland's Eastern Shore late in the seventeenth century. The president's maternal great-grandparents – Thomas and Naomi Gillespie of Rowan County, North Carolina – also may have had roots in northern Ireland.

At age eleven James K. Polk moved with his family to Tennessee but returned to attend the University of North Carolina. There the young student excelled in mathematics and the classics and delivered the Latin oration for his graduating class. He was later so renowned for his oratory that he was dubbed the "Napoleon of the Stump."

Polk began his political career as a protégé of Andrew Jackson, another Scotch-Irishman who was born in the Carolinas. In 1824 the young lawyer was elected to the first of seven terms in the House of Representatives, over whose proceedings he presided as Speaker for four years. After completing one term as governor of Tennessee, he was selected in 1844 as the dark horse presidential candidate on the Democratic ticket. He ran on a platform that emphasized the nation's "manifest destiny" to advance across the continent to the Pacific.

Despite his relative obscurity to many Americans, Polk is generally regarded by many historians as one of the country's most effective presidents. During his single term he successfully pursued policies which rivaled the Louisiana Purchase for increasing the territorial size of the nation. Through annexation he extended American sovereignty to Texas, for example, while his bluster toward the British resulted in the acquisition of the Oregon Territory. In turn, the annexation of Texas led to a war with

Mexico which resulted in the sale of California and the vast reaches of "New Mexico" to the Northern Colossus.

§ Open April-October, Monday-Saturday 9-5, Sunday 1-5; rest of the year, Tuesday-Saturday 10-4, Sunday 1-4. Closed Thanksgiving and December 25. Phone: 704-889-7145.

RALEIGH

¶ **Andrew Johnson Birthplace,** Mordecai Historic Park, north on Person Street to the junction of Wake Forest Road and Mimosa Street.

Among several eighteenth- and nineteenth-century buildings in the park is the 200-year-old frame house in which *President Andrew Johnson was born in 1808 and where he lived until 1824. The house was originally located in the courtyard of Casso's Inn just south of the State House. (The site is indicated by a granite marker at 123 Fayettesville Street.) Johnson's father operated the inn and was the town constable and a caretaker at the capitol, while the future president's mother, Mary ("Polly the Weaver"), worked at the inn.

Johnson's paternal grandfather had immigrated to America from Ballyeaston, County Antrim, Ireland, about 1750. The president's maternal grandfather was Andrew McDonough of Beaufort County, North Carolina, and was most likely of northern Irish descent.

§ Open March to mid December, Monday-Friday 10-3, Saturday and Sunday 1:30-3:30. Fee. Phone: 919-834-4844.

¶ **Elmwood,** 16 North Boylan Avenue.

For a time this antebellum house was the home of *William Gaston, who later became a justice of the state supreme court. A bronze tablet marks the site of the nearby office in which in 1840 he composed the words and adapted the music for "The Old North State," selected as North Carolina's official song in 1927. (See New Bern, North Carolina.)

¶ **North Carolina Museum of Art,** off Interstate 40 at Wade Avenue exit and then to 2110 Blue Ridge Road.

In addition to paintings by Thomas Hart Benton, Botticelli, Winslow Homer, Monet, Raphael, Rubens, Van Dyck, and Andrew Wyeth, the museum displays works by the Irish-American artist Georgia O'Keefe. (See Abiquiu, New Mexico.)

§ Open Tuesday-Saturday 9-5, Friday 9-9, Sunday 11-6. Closed January 1, July 4, Thanksgiving, and December 25. Phone: 919-833-1935.

¶ **Three Presidents Statue,** State Capitol, Capitol Square.

This bronze statue by Charles Keck on the capitol lawn portrays three U.S. presidents of Scotch-Irish ancestry: Andrew Jackson, James K. Polk,

Three Presidents Statue.
(Photo courtesy of the
State Capitol, North Carolina
Division of Archives and History.)

and Andrew Johnson. Although the three men were natives of North Carolina, they lived in Tennessee at the time of their election to the presidency.

SALISBURY

¶ Samuel McCorkle Burial Site, Thyatira Presbyterian Church, 9 miles west on State 150.

"The tall, the wise, the reverend head must lie as low as ours" is the self-written epitaph which adorns the grave of the Reverend Samuel McCorkle, a pioneer educator in the state.

McCorkle's parents, who were natives of northern Ireland, began to attend Thyatira Church soon after settling on a 300-acre farm about fifteen miles from Salisbury. In 1776 their son Samuel became the pastor here, having studied for the ministry at the College of New Jersey under the venerable divine John Witherspoon.

Because McCorkle believed that education helped promote individual happiness and the well being of society, he established two short-lived academies in which he prepared students for education at the university level. One of his schools – Zion Parnassus – took its name from the two historical hills that reflected his dual objective: one hill was associated with religion, and the other with learning. In 1784 he proposed the creation of a state university, and when one was chartered five years later he was actively involved in developing its curriculum and establishing the regulations which governed discipline and attendance at religious services. Although he delivered the address when the institution's cornerstone was laid in 1793, within six years he had withdrawn his affiliation with the school because he felt that its administrators were improperly influenced by Deism. By that time, however, he had trained forty-five men for the Presbyterian ministry.

WAXHAW

¶ Andrew Jackson Monument, off Rehobeth Road.

This stone monument marks the alleged site of the farmhouse in which the seventh president of the United States was born in 1767. The farmhouse belonged to Thomas McKemey (or McCamie), one of Jackson's uncles.

Andrew Jackson was of Scotch-Irish descent, his ancestors having emigrated from Scotland to northern Ireland sometime after 1690. His parents – Andrew and Elizabeth – were weavers from Carrickfergus, County Antrim, and had emigrated from Ireland about 1765, bringing with them two young sons, Robert and Hugh. (Elizabeth's maiden name was Hutchinson, the anglicized form of the old Gaelic McCutcheon.)

Only two years after settling in the Waxhaw region of the Carolinas, however, the elder Jackson suffered an injury that quickly proved fatal. Widowed and virtually penniless, Elizabeth sought the help of Thomas McKemey, in whose farmhouse she gave birth to her third son, whom she named for her deceased husband. Before her death from yellow fever in 1781, Elizabeth mourned the death of two of her sons. Hugh was killed in 1779, and Robert died while he and Andrew languished in a British prison during the Revolution. (This latter tragedy may have been one reason for Jackson's proverbial hatred of the British.)

Orphaned at fifteen, Jackson worked as a saddler for two or three years, but not before squandering a £350 bequest from his grandfather on gambling and "carousing" in Charleston. The young Jackson eventually turned to the study of law and was admitted to the bar at the age of twenty.

At the time of Jackson's birth, the McKemey farmhouse was close to the old boundary line between North and South Carolina. After Jackson became famous, both states claimed him as their native son. Although "Old Hickory" referred to himself as a South Carolinian, partisans continue to claim that he was born in North Carolina. South Carolina historians, however, point out that the putative birthplace in the Tarheel State was part of South Carolina at the time of Jackson's birth.

Nevertheless, the controversy continues. Lancaster County, South

Carolina, and Union County, North Carolina, both claim to be Jackson's birthplace. In 1979 the officials in both counties agreed that high school football teams from the two counties would compete each year in the Old Hickory Football Classic. The victorious county wins the right to claim Jackson as its native son and display a seventeen-inch bust of him in its courthouse for a year.

• The history of Jackson's family and the early members of the Old Waxhaw Settlement is depicted in the drama *Listen and Remember*, performed in an outdoor amphitheater in Waxhaw every Friday and Saturday night in June. Phone: 704-843-5598 (Tuesday and Friday 9-1).

√ The Andrew Jackson Centre outside Carrickfergus, Northern Ireland, is a seventeenth-century cottage near the site of the Jacksons' ancestral home. The restored building contains furnishings from the 1850s as well as displays about the life of Andrew Jackson and the Ulster-American connection.

WILMINGTON

¶ Brunswick Town State Historic Site, 19 miles south on U.S. 17 and State 133.

Among the ruins on the site are those of St. Philip's Anglican Church, built in the 1750s by Arthur Dobbs, the royal governor of North Carolina from 1754 to 1765. His grave is located within the church precincts.

Born at Castle Dobbs, County Antrim, Ireland, in 1689, Dobbs inherited his father's estate at the age of twenty-two and became high sheriff of Antrim nine years later. His interests were of a scientific bent, as is evident in his promotion of efforts to find a northwest passage to India and in his publication of *An Account of Aurora Borealis, Seen in Ireland*.

After his election to the Irish Parliament in 1727, Dobbs showed unusual interest in the economic and political improvement of his native land. He did extensive studies into the commercial and agricultural condition of the country and published his findings in several pamphlets. His ideas attracted the attention of the British prime minister Robert Walpole, who appointed him engineer-in-chief and surveyor-general of Ireland. From these positions Dobbs successfully urged parliamentary approval of measures to increase tillage and land reclamation, although he failed in his larger attempt to reform the Irish land tenure system in favor of the small farmer. Despite his generally anti-Catholic bias, he called for the relaxation of the penal laws so as to allow Catholics to purchase land.

At the same time, Dobbs concluded that the Irish Parliament was an obstacle to the economic and social development of the country. Such development, he believed, could be achieved only by Ireland's political union with Great Britain through the Parliament at Westminster. Only in this way could the Protestant ascendancy in Ireland be maintained while allowing some degree of liberalization in the treatment of Irish Catholics.

In 1745 Dobbs turned his attention to North Carolina. Nine years after purchasing 400,000 acres in what is now Mecklenburg and Cabarrus counties, he was appointed the colony's royal governor. Although he generally labored for the well being of North Carolina, he immediately found himself at odds with the colonial assembly over such issues as his own authority, the power of the purse, political representation, and support of the established church.

Sometime in the 1750s Dobbs encouraged the construction of St. Philip's Church in Brunswick, at that time a relatively important seaport. The structure, which he intended to be the province's royal chapel, was built of English bricks and was partially financed with the proceeds of a captured Spanish privateer. In 1758, to escape the humidity of the capital at New Bern, Dobbs himself moved to Brunswick, where he purchased a "shell of a house." In no time the governor had renovated the two-story structure and added stables, coach houses, and a fruit garden to the sixty-acre estate. Here he died in 1765, survived by his second wife, whom he had married when he was seventy-three years old and she but in her teens.

§ Open April-October, Monday-Saturday 9-5, Sunday 1-5; rest of the year, Tuesday-Saturday 10-4, Sunday 1-4. Closed Martin Luther King Jr.'s Birthday, Veterans Day, Thanksgiving (and the day after), and December 24-25. Phone: 910-371-6613.

¶ **First Presbyterian Church,** on the northeast corner of 3rd and Orange streets.

The present structure occupies the site of a church whose pastor was the *Reverend Joseph Ruggles Wilson, the father of Woodrow Wilson. A plaque in the church commemorates the president, who, as a youngster, was a member of the congregation.

¶ **Rose Greenhow Burial Site,** Oakdale Cemetery, at the north end of 15th Street.

Rose O'Neal was the daughter of the wealthy Maryland planter John O'Neale, who was presumably a descendant of a seventeenth-century Irish settler on the state's Western Shore. In 1835 Rose O'Neal married Robert Greenhow, a librarian and translator for the U.S. State Department. Through this political connection, the couple developed friendships with such prominent figures as *James Buchanan, *John C. Calhoun, and William Seward.

With the outbreak of the Civil War, Mrs. Greenhow was recruited into a Confederate espionage ring. So successful were her efforts that in July 1861 she was able to supply the Confederates with information that allowed them to prepare for the first battle of Bull Run. She continued to operate unhindered from her house in Washington, D.C., until a counterespionage agent arrested her at her front door as she attempted to swallow a coded message. Despite this awkward situation, she did not feel compromised. She later expressed her defiant attitude in her book, *My Imprisonment and the First Year of Abolition Rule at Washington*: "I had as yet no fear of consequences from the papers which had as yet fallen into their hands. I had a right to my own political opinions. . . . I am a Southern woman, born with revolutionary blood in my veins, and my first crude ideas on State and Federal matters received consistency and shape from the best and wisest man of this century, John C. Calhoun."

Nevertheless, Greenhow was forced to endure a thorough search of her house, something she described in her book. "For seven days my house remained in charge of detective police," she wrote, "the search continuing throughout all that time, as also the examination of my papers and correspondence. The books in the library were taken down and examined leaf by leaf. . . . Several large boxes, containing books, china, and glass, which had been packed for several months, were subjected to like ordeal. Finally, portions of the furniture were taken apart, and even the pictures on the wall received their share of attention also." Despite the search, her home remained – according to detective Allan Pinkerton – a "rendezvous for the most violent enemies of the Government."

Even when she was imprisoned, the wily Greenhow continued to foil the efforts of her captors. Not only did she still funnel information to her contacts but on at least one occasion she displayed a Confederate flag from her window. According to her book, one of her jailers was "a burly Irishman, with a smooth tongue, professing the religion of my ancestors, that of the Holy Catholic faith. He marveled that so noble a lady should have been taken as a common malefactor; and, by way of still further showing his sympathy, he set himself to the task of making love to my maid, hoping by this means to possess himself of the important State secrets of which he believed her to be the repository. Sentimental walks, and treats at confectioneries at Uncle Sam's expense, were a part of the programme. She, Lizzy Fitzgerald, a quick-witted Irish girl, warmly attached to me as a kind mistress, and knowing nothing which the severest scrutiny could elicit from my disadvantage, entered keenly into the sport, and, to use her own expressive words, 'led Pat a dance,' and, under these new auspices, performed some very important missions for me."

Following her release in the spring of 1862, Greenhow was sent south on condition that she not return to the North while the war continued. In Richmond she was welcomed by *President Jefferson Davis, who awarded her $2,500 for her services to the Confederacy, while in Charleston she was received by General Pierre Beauregard. In August 1863 she visited France and Britain as an unofficial agent for the Confederate government. On her return voyage a year later, however, her ship ran aground near Wilmington, North Carolina. When her small lifeboat overturned, she immediately drowned, pulled down by the weight of a purse filled with gold coins – royalties from her book.

℧ St. Thomas Church, Dock Street.

Between 1868 and 1872 this church served as the cathedral of James Gibbons, the Catholic bishop of North Carolina and, at the time of his appointment, the youngest of the 1,200 Catholic bishops throughout the world. It was in a room behind the altar in this church that he began his most famous work, *The Faith of Our Fathers*, an exposition of Catholic teaching that sold two million copies during his lifetime and brought him national recognition.

While ministering to North Carolina's 800 Catholics (out of a population of one million), this son of immigrants from County Mayo came in contact with large numbers of non-Catholics. Through his intelligence, liberalmindedness, and warm personality, he established such good will in this traditionally anti-Catholic area that he was offered the use of courthouses, Masonic halls, and Protestant churches where no Catholic church could be found.

In a St. Patrick's Day sermon in 1870, Gibbons acknowledged the tremendous debt which the Catholic Church in America owned the Irish. "Is not this country chiefly indebted to her [Ireland] for its faith?" he asked. "There are few churches erected from Maine to California, from Canada to Mexico which Irish hands have not helped to build, which Irish purses have not supported, and in which Irish hearts are not found worshipping. She contributes not only to the materiel but also to the personnel of the Church in this country. A large proportion of our Bishops and clergy are of Irish origin or descent."

Gibbons also proffered salutary advice to the newcomers from Ireland who flocked to America's shores. The Irish immigrant, he wrote, must "adapt himself to the land in which he seeks a refuge, and he must remember that he owes a debt of gratitude to that country which opens wide its doors to him, and places within easy reach what is today the greatest of civil privileges, American citizenship. He leaves a land where as yet he is debarred, directly or indirectly, from many things that his heart desires, but that his race or religion, or both, prevent him from enjoying. He comes into the chief state of the New World, and in five years he walks a king among men, clothed with the panoply of free citizenship, with the right of suffrage, active and passive, eligible to every office but the highest, from which, however, his children are not debarred. The very magnificence of this American political generosity makes many foreigners forget that it is a boon pure and simple, to which they have no right, and which may be curtailed or denied as easily as it has been lavished."

Following his consecration as archbishop of Baltimore in 1877, Gibbons banished from the public mind the belief that Catholicism was incompatible with American institutions. Since the nation's capital was at that time within his archdiocese, he made the acquaintance of each president from Jackson to Harding and developed strong friendships with *Grover Cleveland, *Theodore Roosevelt, and William Howard Taft. He was also perhaps the first Catholic prelate in America to throw his influence behind observance of Thanksgiving Day by the Catholic community.

Gibbons' subsequent appointment as the nation's second cardinal drew enthusiastic public praise because of his thorough identification with American ideals. He, in turn, attributed the success of the Catholic Church in America to the liberty found in a country "where the civil government holds over us the aegis of its protection, without interfering with us in the legitimate exercise of our sublime mission as ministers of the gospel of Christ." He later drew additional support from the Catholic working classes of America when he intervened to prevent the Vatican from condemning the fledgling Knights of Labor on the erroneous grounds that this early labor union was a secret organization that required its members to take an oath.

In 1911, on the twenty-fifth anniversary of his elevation to the cardinalate, Gibbons was feted at public ceremonies in Baltimore and eulogized by President Taft and *Theodore Roosevelt, both of whom praised his patriotism and civic virtue. Upon the cardinal's death in 1921, former president Taft remarked: "He did not belong to the Catholic Church alone, but he belonged to the country at large. He was a Catholic not only in the religious sense, but in the secular sense."

NORTH DAKOTA

BOTTINEAU

❡ **Chaplains' Memorial,** in front of the rectory, St. Mark's Catholic Church, 322 Sinclair Street.

This concrete obelisk honors the four chaplains – one Catholic, one Jewish, and two Protestant – who gave up their life jackets to soldiers aboard the sinking U.S.S. *Dorchester* in 1943. The four clergymen were Father John Patrick Washington, Rabbi Alexander Goode, Reverend Clark Poling, and Reverend George Fox. The monument, which was erected by Monsignor Joseph Andrieux in 1956, contains a plaque describing the heroism of the four men.

Born in Newark, New Jersey, in 1908, Washington was the oldest of either seven or nine children born to Irish immigrant parents. Although blessed with a love for music and a beautiful singing voice, as the leader of the 12th Street gang he never shied away from a good fight. At the age of twelve, however, he was stricken by a throat infection which was so severe that he was given the last rites by his parish priest. After a remarkable recovery, the youngster said to his sister Anna that "God must have something special he wants me to do."

Following his graduation in 1931 from Seton Hall College in South Orange, New Jersey, Washington pursued his studies for the priesthood at Immaculate Conception Seminary in Darlington, New Jersey. Ordained in 1935, he subsequently served in three parishes in his native state: St. Genevieve (Elizabeth), St. Venantius (Orange), and St. Stephen (Arlington).

After five years of pastoral work, however, Washington decided to enlist in the nation's war effort as a chaplain. Although he was rejected by the navy because of his poor eyesight, the army accepted the young priest into its chaplain corps. While undergoing preliminary training at Fort Benjamin Harrison, Indiana, he developed an aversion for the army's insistence upon saluting. "The only pain in the neck is that saluting business," he complained in a letter to one of his brothers. "When I go to town I always turn my back and look in the store windows whenever I see a gang of soldiers coming by." He was later stationed at Fort Meade, Maryland, and Camp Miles Standish in Taunton, Massachusetts.

At the end of January 1943, Washington found himself aboard the *Dorchester*, originally a passenger liner but then an Army troop ship recently out of New York. As the ship approached Torpedo Junction, an area off Newfoundland where dozens of ships had been victims of German U-boat attacks, the men became somber and fearful. A raging storm added seasickness to the men's list of discomforts. When Father Washington tried to ease the situation with humor and dry crackers, one sufferer said to him: "Listen, Father, if you really want to do good, get me out on deck so I can jump overboard." The priest quickly changed the subject, urging him into a game of poker and joking that God would understand if the players raised the stakes from pennies to quarters. When one soldier asked the priest to bless his cards, Washington looked at his hand and joked, "What? Me bless a measly pair of deuces?"

Disaster struck on February 3, when the ship was torpedoed 150 miles off Greenland. As the ship began to sink, one of the soldiers told Washington that he didn't know how to swim and that he didn't have a life jacket. Without hesitation the Irish-American priest removed his own life preserver and wrapped it around the soldier, an act of generosity that was repeated when the other chaplains on board gave up their only chance of survival to three other soldiers. As the last of the lifeboats pulled away from the sinking wreckage, the chaplains linked arms and prayed – in a babel of English, Latin, and Hebrew – as they went down with the ship.

Since their sacrificial deaths, the four chaplains have been honored in a number of ways. Besides awarding them the Purple Heart and the Distinguished Service Cross, the United States government in 1948 issued a three-cent stamp to celebrate their heroism. The commemorative stamp contains four oval portraits of the clergymen above the sinking ship, all enclosed within the words "These Immortal Chaplains" and "Interfaith in Action." Three years later an interfaith shrine known as the Chapel of the Four Chaplains was dedicated on the campus of Temple University in Philadelphia. In addition, Congress in 1961 posthumously awarded the chaplains a Special Medal of Heroism, the only one ever given.

Because structural damage required closure of the Chaplains' Chapel at Temple University in 1990, efforts are under way to erect another memorial on a site near Valley Forge, Pennsylvania. The four clergymen are also honored by the Four Chaplains Memorial Viaduct in Massillon, Ohio, and by a monument in National Memorial Park in Falls Church, Virginia [q.v.].

MANDAN

¶ **Roosevelt Equestrian Statue,** in the railway depot park.

This small bronze statue of *Theodore Roosevelt is a copy of the larger monument to the famous Rough Rider in Minot, North Dakota. One of Roosevelt's ancestors was *John Barnwell, who came to South Carolina from Ireland in 1701. (See Beaufort, South Carolina.)

MINOT

¶ **Roosevelt Equestrian Statue,** Roosevelt Park, at the east end of 4th Avenue S.E.

This bronze equestrian statue, which depicts *Theodore Roosevelt as a Rough Rider, was presented to the city in 1924 by Dr. Henry Waldo Coe, a lifelong friend of the president. The pedestal on which the statue stands simulates the formations to be found in the Badlands along the Little Missouri River where Roosevelt once lived.

THEODORE ROOSEVELT NATIONAL PARK

This 70,000-acre park is located in a portion of the Badlands where the twenty-sixth president hunted big game, studied natural history, engaged in ranching, and wrote articles and part of a book. The park consists of three tracts of land in the western end of the state: the North Unit (south of Watford City), the South Unit (north of Medora), and Elkhorn Ranch (thirty-five miles north of Medora).

¶ **Medora Visitor Center,** South Unit, off Interstate 90, north Medora.
Just behind the visitor center stands the Maltese Cross Cabin, the restored log building in which *Theodore Roosevelt lived from 1883 to 1885. (The cabin was originally located on the Maltese Cross Ranch, about seven miles south of Medora.) The three-room pine cabin has two doors, mortar chinking, several glass-pane windows, and a high-pitched shingle roof.
Between 1883 and 1889 Roosevelt worked the ranch in a partnership

The Maltese Cross Cabin. (Photo by Bruce M. Kaye and courtesy of the National Park Service, Theodore Roosevelt National Park.)

venture with two other men. (He renamed it for Chimney Butte nearby.) In 1884 the future president also began an open-range ranch of his own, calling it the Elkhorn. Today only a few foundation stones mark the site of Roosevelt's cabin on his Elkhorn Ranch, which he used as headquarters for hunting expeditions. (He shot his first grizzly bear and his first buffalo at two sites not far from Marmarth.) Over the years, however, his ranching operations were not financially successful, partly because he ran small herds and had other interests. When the severe winter of 1886-87 decimated his herd, he sold his ranches.

The Maltese Cross Cabin was purchased in 1904 by the North Dakota Commission, which sent it to the St. Louis World's Fair that year, to the Lewis and Clark Centennial Exposition in Portland, Oregon, in 1905, and finally to the grounds of the state capitol in Bismarck, North Dakota.

Roosevelt had first come to the Badlands in 1883, hoping to improve his health and forget the deaths of his mother and his wife. Because of his thick eye glasses, the twenty-five-year-old Easterner was known as "the four-eyed dude from New York" until he knocked out a bully. From then on, Roosevelt was called "Old Four-eyes." After fully adopting a western lifestyle, Roosevelt won many friends. He helped organize the Little Missouri River Stockmen's Association, serving as its chairman and delivering the principal address at a 4th of July celebration in 1884. After 1887, however, Roosevelt's visits to the Badlands were shorter and less frequent, although he renewed acquaintances when many of his western friends served under him in the Rough Riders during the Spanish-American War. In 1900 he visited Medora on a campaign tour and returned three years later.

§ Visitor center open early June-Labor Day, daily 8-8; May 1-early June and the day after Labor Day-September 30, daily 8-5; rest of the year, daily 8-4:30. Closed January 1, Thanksgiving, and December 25. Phone: 701-624-4466. The center's museum displays Roosevelt memorabilia and features an orientation film.

§ From mid June-Labor Day the nearby town of Medora presents two dramatic productions in honor of Theodore Roosevelt:

• *Bully*, a dramatization of Roosevelt's life (held in the community center) and

• *Medora Musical*, a blend of music, comedy, and Dakota history in honor of the famous president.

OKLAHOMA

CLAREMORE

¶ **Will Rogers Birthplace,** 12 miles northwest and then 1.5 mile north of State 88 on an unmarked road in Oologah.

Despite his later "poorboy persona," the famous cowboy humorist William Penn Adair Rogers was born in this rather substantial house, the son of a successful rancher and banker. His father was of mixed Irish and Cherokee ancestry and held a prominent position in the Cherokee Nation. Proud of his Indian blood, Will Rogers once boasted to a Boston audience: "My ancestors didn't come over on the Mayflower – they met the boat." About his Irish ancestry he quipped: "These Irish, you got to watch 'em. There was a few of 'em sneaked into Oklahoma and got mixed up with the Rogerses and the Cherokees, and I am a sort of an offshoot – an Irish Indian." After the famous Florenz Ziegfeld said that he thought Rogers had a touch of Jewish blood, the humorist described a possible family crest: "a shillelagh with a tomahawk on one end, and a percent sign on the other." Rogers later joked that "The English should give Ireland home rule – and reserve the motion picture rights."

The fact that Rogers' birthplace was built of both logs and frame additions allowed him – and his mother – to claim that he was born in a log house. "Just before my birth," explained the humorist, "my mother, being in one of these frame rooms, had them remove her into the log part of the house. She wanted me to be born in a log house. She had just read the life of Lincoln. So I got the log-house end of it okay; all I need now is the other qualifications."

As a youngster, Rogers' favorite sport was roping calves, a skill which he continued to perfect on his classmates, cajoling them to "stoop over, run down the hall, and beller like a calf." After leaving high school, he became known as "The Cherokee Kid," a rope artist and rough rider with Texas Jack's Wild West Circus. (His most famous rope trick was lassoing a horse and its rider simultaneously with two ropes.) While touring the country with this troupe and others, he began to exploit the amusement which his drawl elicited by engaging in self-deprecating banter with the audiences. After making the switch to vaudeville, he quickly became a Broadway star with his intermittent appearance in the Ziegfeld Follies between 1916 and 1925.

In the meantime Rogers had begun what developed into a promising journalistic career. Beginning with a series of weekly articles for the *New York Times*, he gradually went on to attract an audience of 40 million readers with his "daily telegram," a short paragraph that became syndicated in 350 newspapers. After touring Europe as President Coolidge's "ambassador of good will" and as a correspondent for the *Saturday Evening Post*,

Rogers wrote *Letters of a Self-Made Diplomat to His President*, the first of several longer volumes in a humorous style.

Because of his later popularity as a lecturer and radio speaker, it was probably only natural that Rogers should make the transition to motion pictures. By 1919 he and his family had moved to California, where he was named honorary mayor of Beverly Hills and where he reached the pinnacle of his acting career between 1929 and 1935. (He made a total of seventy films.) In the midst of the Depression, he was earning $200,000 per motion picture. His annual income as an actor, writer, lecturer, and radio personality was estimated at $600,000, a figure that made him the highest paid entertainer of his era. He was generous in his charity, however, especially to the Red Cross during World War I and the Depression. He was also an outspoken champion of commercial aviation, although ironically he was killed in a plane accident near Point Barrow, Alaska [*q.v.*].

§ Grounds open daily dawn-dusk. Tours of the house depart daily at 10 and 2. Closed Thanksgiving and December 25. Phone: 918-275-4201 or 341-0719.

¶ **Will Rogers Memorial,** 1 mile west on State 88 (West Will Rogers Boulevard).

This ranch-style museum is located on the site where Will Rogers planned to build a house. His tomb – in a small garden in front of the memorial – is marked by a huge bronze sculpture of Rogers by Jo Davidson (inscribed with his self-selected epitaph: "I never met a man I didn't like"). Besides his personal saddles and riding paraphernalia, the museum displays his joke book and the typewriter on which he pounded out two million words. His life as a rodeo performer, vaudeville entertainer, columnist, author, and movie star is chronicled through documentary films and thirteen dioramas.

§ Open daily 8-5. Closed Thanksgiving and December 25. Phone: 918-341-0719.

• Every August the nearby town of Vinita, where Rogers went to elementary school, celebrates the Will Rogers Memorial Rodeo. The event has been held yearly since his death in 1935.

Will Rogers Statue.

LAWTON

¶ Fort Sill Military Reservation and National Historic Landmark, 5 miles north on U.S. 62/277/281.

Although now the headquarters of the U.S. Army Field Artillery, the original fort on this present 100,000-acre site was known as Camp Wichita after its creation by *General Philip Sheridan in 1869. Soon renamed Fort Sill, the post succeeded in pacifying the local Indian tribes, including the Apache, who were imprisoned here between 1894 and 1913. (Geronimo is buried on the east range.) Today the "Old Post" museum includes twenty-three buildings open to the public, including the guardhouse, commissary, stone corral, and chapel.

§ Open daily 8:30-4:30. Closed January 1-2 and December 25-26. Phone: 405-442-5123.

LINDSAY

¶ Murray-Lindsay Mansion, 2 miles south on State 76 and then 0.5 mile west on Erin Springs Road.

This renovated three-story stone and stucco house was originally the home of Frank Murray, a native of Ireland who lived here with his Choctaw wife and their eight children. The original house, erected in 1883, was a two-story square faced by a wooden veranda and containing fifteen rooms, four fireplaces, and two baths. The present appearance of the house dates from 1902, when Murray's wife added a story and a Greek Revival portico. Today the house contains photographs and mementos associated with the family.

Born in Ireland in 1832, Frank Murray had come to America at the age of eighteen. From New Orleans, his port of entry, he traveled to Sherman, Texas, and then to Fort Washita, Oklahoma, where he found employment as a mail carrier between there and Fort Arbuckle in the 1850s. During the Civil War he served as foragemaster in the Union army.

In April 1871 Murray married Alzira McCaughey Powell, the daughter of John McCaughey, a native of Ireland, and his wife, a woman of Choctaw descent. Alzira had attended the Mississippi Female Seminary in that state and at the age of eighteen had married Captain William Powell, another native of Ireland. At the time of her marriage to Murray, Alzira was Powell's widow, with whom she had had a daughter, Anita.

At first Murray and his wife and his stepdaughter lived in Paul's Valley, Oklahoma, to the west of the Chickasaw Nation. They soon moved, however, to a site near the Washita River which became known as Erin Springs, named after the couple's daughter Erin. There they went into the ranching and farming business, eventually acquiring more than 20,000 acres, chiefly through their ability as an interracial couple to acquire Indian land. At the height of his prosperity, Murray owned more than 26,000 head of cattle and in one record year harvested 400,000 bushels of corn.

In 1883 Erin Springs was visited by Father Hilary Cassal, a Catholic priest riding circuit in the western Indian territory. In a diary entry he recorded the details of his pastoral visit to Murray's home: "Some of his renters being Catholic I stayed there two days to celebrate Mass and to administer the Sacraments. I heard six confessions, baptised two children and preached. The step-daughter of Mr. Murray (Anita) received the Sacraments but Mrs. Murray could not, being still a Gentile. She received instructions however, and a year later, baptism. Ever since she had proven herself to be a sincere and practical member of our church. One of her sons, Frank, a pupil of our school, was baptized and made his first Communion at Sacred Heart. The other son, John, died unfortunately after being thrown from his horse. I met at Erin Springs two daughters of Dr. Shirley of Anadark." (Shirley was also a native of Ireland.)

By the time of Murray's death in 1892, his operation was in decline. Although Alzira took steps to put the business on a sounder financial footing, she was ultimately forced to diversify into banking and sawmill operations. In the meantime her daughter Anita married Lewis Lindsay, after whom Lindsay, Oklahoma, was named.

§ Open Tuesday-Sunday 1-5. Closed Thanksgiving and December 25. Donations. Phone: 405-756-2121 or 756-2019.

OKLAHOMA CITY

℩ International Photography Hall of Fame and Museum, Kirkpatrick Center, 2100 Northeast 52nd Street and Martin Luther King Jr. Avenue.

One of several galleries and educational facilities at the Kirkpatrick Center, this museum features works by photographers from around the world, including the famous *Mathew Brady, whose photographs of the Civil War captured the horror of that fratricidal conflict. One of the main attractions in the hall is a 360-degree laserscape of the Grand Canyon, the world's largest photographic mural.

Some of Brady's photographic assistants were fellow Irish Americans. One of them, T. C. Roche, went on to develop bromide photographic papers, while another, Stephen Horgan, invented a procedure that allowed photographs to be printed on paper from copper and zinc plates. Some of the other men – D. F. Barry, Alexander Gardner, T. J. Hines, V. T. McGillycuddy, John Moran, and Timothy O'Sullivan – served as photographic chroniclers of America's westward expansion by participating in various military and scientific expeditions. (See Virginia City, Nevada.)

§ Open Memorial Day-Labor Day, Monday-Saturday 9-6, Sunday noon-6; rest of the year, Monday-Friday 9:30-5, Saturday 9-6, Sunday noon-

6. Fee. Phone: 405-424-4055.

¶ National Cowboy Hall of Fame and Western Heritage Museum,
1700 Northeast 63rd Street, 0.5 mile west of Interstate 35 on Interstate 44.

Constructed as a memorial to the pioneers who conquered and settled
the West, this complex contains a thirty-three-foot statue of *William "Buffalo Bill" Cody, the Rodeo Hall of Fame, a $50 million Western art collec-
tion, and a reconstruction of a typical Western town. The Western Per-
formers Hall of Fame honors such entertainers as Gene Autry, Tom Mix,
Roy Rogers, Dale Evans, and *John Wayne. A special gallery displays
Wayne memorabilia as well as his collections of guns, knives, and kachina
dolls.

§ Open end of May-Labor Day, daily 8:30-6; rest of the year, daily 9-5.
Closed January 1, Thanksgiving, and December 25. Fee. Phone: 405-478-
2250.

SHAMROCK

An oil boom in the first decade of the twentieth century caused
Shamrock's population to swell to 10,000, although today this town between Tulsa and Oklahoma City has only 200 residents. The town, which
was founded by Edwin Dunn, a real estate agent, still boasts of its St.
Patrick's Day parade and of street names like Tipperary and Cork. Its early
newspapers were known as the *Brogue* and the *Blarney*.

TULSA

¶ Thomas Gilcrease Museum, off U.S. 64/State 51 at 1400 Gilcrease
Museum Road.

In addition to a collection of more than 300,000 Indian artifacts and
art pieces, this museum displays maps, sculpture, manuscripts, and paintings about the American West. The museum has works by Frederic
Remington and Charles Russell as well as 60 paintings, 500 etchings, and
1,200 sketches by Thomas Moran, the single largest collection of his art.

Moran was born in England in 1837 to an Irish father and an English
mother. After coming to America with his parents and brothers in 1844, he
served an apprenticeship with a wood engraver in Philadelphia but gravitated toward painting, eventually in oils. During the first of two sojourns
in Europe, he was captivated by the work of Turner in the National Gallery in London, and on a subsequent visit to France and Italy he tried his
hand at copying works by the old masters.

During the three years following his return to the United States in
1871, Moran ventured into the West on several expeditions. The first two
explored various reaches of the Grand Canyon and resulted in his famous

paintings *The Grand Canyon of the Yellowstone* and the *Chasm of the Colorado*. Both works were later purchased by Congress for $10,000 each and were hung in the Capitol. Between these two trips he visited Yosemite Valley in California. (A small and frail man, Moran had never ridden a horse prior to this first expedition, and he was forced to place a pillow between his saddle and his bony posterior.) In 1873, meanwhile, he accompanied Major John Wesley Powell in southern Utah and Arizona and in 1874 sought the Mountain of the Holy Cross in central Colorado. His *Mountain of the Holy Cross* was awarded a medal at the Centennial Exposition in 1876. (See the Gene Autry Western Heritage Museum, Los Angeles, California.)

The art which Moran produced after returning from these expeditions played a significant role in preserving portions of the West for future generations to enjoy. A series of his Yellowstone watercolors, for example, caused officials in the federal government to set aside that region of the country as a national park in 1872. During his lifetime other parts of the West which he had captured on canvas were declared national parks or monuments, and he was regarded by the National Park Service as a major pioneer in the conservation movement. His name is preserved in Moran Point, Arizona, and in Mount Moran, in the Teton Range in Wyoming.

Although in executing his work Moran insisted on absolute fidelity in depicting the details of nature, such honesty was but a means of conveying an impression. "What I ask is to see a man's brains as evidenced in his work," he wrote. "I want to know what his opinions are. He is the arbiter of his pictures and nature. Zola's defintion of art exactly fills my demands when he said, 'Art is nature seen through a temperament.' . . . An artist's business is to produce for the spectator of his pictures the impression produced by nature on himself."

Although later in life Moran and his wife, who was also an artist, established a studio on Long Island, he continued to travel extensively. Between trips to Maine and Florida, he journeyed to his beloved West as well as to Italy, Mexico, England, and Scotland. At the time of his death he was a member of the National Academy and a fellow of the British Society of Painter-Etchers and was regarded as the dean of America's landscape painters.

§ Open Monday-Saturday 9-5, Sunday and holidays 1-5. Closed December 25. Donations. Phone: 918-596-2700.

TUSKAHOMA

¶ **Choctaw Nation Museum,** north of U.S. 271 on a county road, about 30 miles east of the Indian Nation Turnpike.

Among the museum's exhibits are several which describe the Choctaws' assistance to the suffering people of Ireland during the Great

Famine. The Indians' generous gift of $170 in 1847 came only sixteen years after their own 500-mile genocidal march from their ancestral home in Mississippi to Oklahoma.

As a result of the U.S. government's policy of Indian removal, the Choctaw had been the first of the Five Civilized Tribes forced to leave their lands for the Oklahoma Territory. Generally unprepared for the grueling journey during one of the worst winters in the South, more than half of the Choctaw died of exposure, starvation, dysentery, cholera, and smallpox. Along the way they were victimized by soldiers and government contractors who charged them exorbitant prices for liquor and spoiled food supplies.

Once resettled on the Oklahoma plains, the Choctaw learned of the suffering of the Irish during the Great Famine. At a meeting held in Skullyville, the capital of the Choctaw Nation in Oklahoma, the Indians contributed an amount variously given as either $170 or $710. Whatever the amount, it was a gracious gesture of solidarity from a people whose recent history had been filled with suffering of their own.

The first reference to the Choctaws' generosity appeared in the *Arkansas Intelligencer* on April 3, 1847. Although the article contained patronizing remarks about the Choctaw, it at least acknowledged the Indians' generosity "to their White Brethren of Ireland." "A meeting for the relief of the starving poor of Ireland," the article began, "was held at the Choctaw Agency . . . after which the meeting contributed $170. All subscribed, Agents, Missionaries, Traders and Indians, a considerable portion of which fund was made up by the latter. The 'poor Indian' sending his mite to the poor Irish . . . . What an agreeable reflection it must give the Christian and philanthropist to witness this evidence of civilization and Christian spirit among our red neighbors. They are repaying the Christian world for bringing them out of benighted ignorance and heathen barbarism . . . ."

The only other reference to the Choctaws' gift to the Irish to appear in the nineteenth century is contained in *The Voyage of the Naparima*. This work is based on the diary of Gerald Keegan, an Irish schoolteacher from County Sligo, who fled Ireland in 1847 aboard the *Naparima*. In a diary entry he acknowledged the assistance given the starving Irish by Jews in New York City, the working people of England, and the rulers of Turkey, Russia, and China. His most lengthy remarks, however, were reserved for the Choctaws: "Among the donations from various parts of the world there is one that is singularly appreciated. It comes from a small tribe of native North American Indians, the Choctaw tribe from central western United States. These noble-minded people, sometimes called savages by those who wantonly released death and destruction among them, raised money from their meagre resources to help the starving in this country. This is indeed the most touching of all the acts of generosity that our condition has inspired among the nations."

Even almost 150 years later, relations between the Choctaw and the Irish continue to be strong. In 1992 the mayor of London unveiled a plaque in Dublin Mansion House to commemorate the generosity which the Choctaw and Canadian Indians showed to the Irish during the terrible years of the famine. In May 1995 Mary Robinson, the president of Ireland, visited the Choctaw Nation in Oklahoma and recalled the historic relationship between the two peoples: "The pain and suffering and loss caused by the dreadful famine in Ireland nearly a century and a half ago, have created an indelible record in the fond memory of our nation. We will always remember with gratitude, however, the compassion and concern displayed by the Choctaw Nation who, from their distant lands, sent assistance to the Irish people at that sad time. It has been my great privilege to be made an honorary chief of the Choctaw Nation [the only women ever to be so honored] and I am conscious that the honor bestowed on me will help to keep alive, in your country and in mine, the memory of their noble deed. . . ."

§ Open Monday-Friday 8-4. Closed holidays. Phone: 918-569-4465.

YALE

¶ Jim Thorpe House, 706 East Boston.

This five-room clapboard bungalow was the home of Olympic champion Jim Thorpe from 1917 to 1923. The house is furnished with pieces that belonged to the family and displays awards which he received as an All-American halfback at the Indian school in Carlisle, Pennsylvania.

Born in Indian Territory in 1887, Thorpe was five-eights Indian (mostly Fox and Sac) and three-eights Irish and French. During the 1912 Olympics in Stockholm, he became the first athlete to win both the pentathlon and the decathlon in the same year. Although he was called the "World's Greatest Athlete" by the king of Sweden, Thorpe was later stripped of his medals when it was learned that he had unconsciously broken the Olympic rules by playing semiprofessional baseball prior to the Stockholm games.

§ Phone: 918-387-2815.

OREGON

DAYTON

¶ Fort Yamhill Blockhouse, Dayton City Park.

Construction of this two-story structure was begun by Lieutenant William Hazen and completed by *Lieutenant Philip Sheridan in 1855-56. The blockhouse was one of three constructed in this area to house troops needed to protect settlers from the Indians whom the government was trying to confine on the Grand Ronde Reservation. Like the barracks, the officers' quarters, the barns, and the work shops at the fort, the block-house is made of logs and rough-hewn wood. The structure was moved here from its original site in 1911.

In his memoirs Sheridan mentioned the conditions which prevailed during the fort's construction: "In those days the Government did not pro-vide very liberally for sheltering its soldiers and officers, and men were frequently forced to eke out parsimonious appropriations by toilsome work, or go without shelter in most inhospitable regions. Of course this post was no exception to the general rule, and as all hands were occupied in its construction, and I the only officer present, I was kept busily em-ployed in supervising matters, both as commandant and quartermaster until July, when Captain D. A. Russell . . . was ordered to take command, and I was relieved from the first part of my duties."

Sheridan served at Fort Yamhill, under Captain Russell, until the lat-ter was reassigned early in 1861, when Sheridan assumed command. He expressed his impatience at being in the West when he preferred a chance to participate in the civil war that had so recently erupted: "On the day of the week that our courier, or messenger, was expected back from Port-land, I would go out early in the morning to a commanding point above the post, from which I could see a long distance down the road as it ran through the valley of the Yamhill, and there I could watch with anxiety for his coming, longing for good news." When he was finally called east, he departed from his men with these words: "I am going into this war to win a captain's spurs, or die with my boots on. Goodbye, boys, I may never see you again."

OREGON CITY

¶ McLoughlin House National Historic Site, 7th and Center streets.

This restored residence dates from 1846, when it was built by Dr. John McLoughlin, the representative of the Hudson's Bay Company in the re-gion for the previous twenty years and a major figure in the development of the Oregon territory. The doors and windows used in building the hip-roofed clapboard house were shipped around the Horn from the East.

Born in Riviere du Loup, Quebec province, in 1784, McLoughlin was the son of John McLoughlin, a native of County Derry, Ireland, and his wife, Angelique Fraser, born in Canada to Scottish parents. Though baptized a Catholic, the youngster was not raised in the faith of his father after the latter's untimely death by drowning. (His uncle insisted that the boy and his brothers and sisters be raised Protestant.) The young McLoughlin was subsequently prepared for a career in medicine by his maternal grandfather and then received his formal training in Scotland.

After completing his medical studies, McLoughlin returned to Canada but did not take up the practice of medicine. Instead he became a partner in the North West Fur Company. In 1824, soon after the company had merged with the larger Hudson's Bay Company, he was named its chief representative in the Columbia River region. Within a year he had erected a fort on the site of present-day Vancouver, Washington, as the company's primary trading post in the region. (See Vancouver, Washington.)

As subsequent events were to prove, carrying out his official mandate for the Hudson's Bay Company was extremely difficult. Although his chief goal of monopolizing and maximizing the fur trade in the region seemed straightforward enough, the steps necessary to achieve this objective presented major problems. His efforts to pacify the Indians, train them in efficient trapping practices, exclude rival traders, and prevent the development of agriculture sometimes conflicted with his own moral sensibilities – the tide of history – and brought him into conflict with his superiors.

The John McLoughlin House.
(Photo courtesy of Smith-Western, Inc., Portland, Oregon.)

Although the six-foot-four-inch McLoughlin generally succeeded in maintaining peace between the Indian tribes and encroaching whites, he was sometimes criticized for his methods. Such was the case when he inflicted punishment upon an Indian village when some members of the tribe were suspected of murdering the crew of a shipwrecked British vessel. When McLoughlin ordered the Indians to return the goods which they had presumably stolen from the ship, they responded by sending him only a broom and a tin dipper. In response he sent a schooner to bombard the Indians' village. In another instance he was correctly accused of exceeding his power when he carried out the execution of an Indian found guilty of killing an employee of the Hudson's Bay Company.

In addition, McLoughlin was sometimes accused of exploiting the Indians under his charge, even though his long snow-white hair had prompted the natives to affectionately call him the "White-Headed Eagle." In 1837, for instance, he was forced to defend himself to the company's governor: "Though we cannot prevent Indians having slaves, we tell the masters it is very improper to keep their fellow beings in slavery. Moreover we have redeemed several and sent them back to their own company this very season."

Although in his official capacity McLoughlin did what he could to frustrate the efforts of rival American traders in the region, his personal behavior toward them was always gracious and generous. He often provided them with supplies, offered them lodging at Fort Vancouver, and assisted them in other ways. He was equally supportive of Protestant and Catholic missionaries who began to move into Oregon from the United States after 1834. Such acts, of course, ran counter to his responsibilities as an agent for the Hudson's Bay Company and facilitated the gradual Americanization of the region.

In the meantime McLoughlin had taken steps to establish a settlement at the falls of the Willamette River. Although Indians burned the three log cabins which he ordered built there in 1828-29, he continued his efforts, first by building a sawmill and a flour mill and then by laying out a town – which he named Oregon City – and selling lots. In 1843 some of the American settlers formed a provisional government, a move which perhaps helped prompt the British to abandon the Oregon Territory south of the Columbia River three years later. This development – as well as criticism of his stewardship – led to his retirement from the Hudson's Bay Company that same year. When he subsequently filed a claim with the provisional government for the site that he had earlier developed, some of the Americans in the region objected to this move. The lengthy legal battle that followed was not concluded until 1850, when Congress invalidated his claim. This setback – combined with the failure of many settlers to pay him for the supplies he had earlier provided them on credit – contributed to his financial reversal. Not until 1862 – seven years after his death – did the state of Oregon recognize his claim to his property and hand it over to his heirs.

In his private life, however, McLoughlin seems to have enjoyed some degree of compensation for the misfortunes which he suffered in his official capacity. His marriage to Margaret McKay, a half-breed Chippewa (or Cree) and the widow of a Scottish trader, seems to have been a consolation. (He always treated her with great respect and insisted that male visitors remove their hats in her presence.) In 1842, meanwhile, he professed the Catholic faith of his infancy, made confession to the French missionary Father François Blanchet, and regularized his marriage in the eyes of the Church. Five years later, as a fitting tribute to a man whose humane and civilizing instincts had helped tame a wilderness, he was created a papal knight by Pope Gregory XVI. In granting him this honor, the pope said: "We have been informed on the highest authority that you are esteemed by all for your upright life, correct morals and zeal for religion and that you are conspicuous for your allegiance to ourselves and to the Chair of Peter."

Although the "White-Headed Eagle" was first buried in St. John the Evangelist Church in Oregon City, in 1970 his body was reinterred near the home that he had built after his retirement. A stained-glass window donated to the church in his honor was inscribed with the words: "In Memoriam / Dr. John McLoughlin / Knight of St. Gregory / Father of Oregon & Father of this City." The window was later given to the Clackmas County Historical Society. For his numerous contributions to the development of Oregon, he was selected to represent that state in Statuary Hall in the nation's Capitol, where a full-size likeness of him now stands.

§ Open February-December, Tuesday-Saturday 10-4, Sunday 1-4. Closed holidays. Fee. Phone: 503-656-5146.

¶ The White-Headed Eagle is commemorated in Mount McLoughlin, a 9,495-foot volcanic cone in the eastern unit of Rogue River National Forest.

PORTLAND

¶ **Sister Miriam Theresa Lounge,** Shoen Library, Marylhurst College, 5 miles south on State 43 between Lake Oswego and West Linn.

This quiet reading area is named for a nun who as a young woman helped secure passage of the first state legislation designed to protect working women and minors.

Born Caroline Gleason in Milwaukee, Wisconsin, in 1886, she was the daughter of an Irish father (John Gleason) and a French-Canadian mother (Fidelia Maria Lucia). A graduate of the University of Minnesota, the young Gleason championed the working women of Portland while she was on the faculty of St. Mary's Academy and College in Portland. In 1912, at the age of twenty-six, she was asked by the Oregon Consumers League to compile data about the wages and working conditions of women in the state. In the process she interviewed thousands of women, worked in factories and laundries, lobbied the state legislature, and endured the insults of employers. (While working in a shoe factory, she earned fifty-two cents for a ten-hour day.) The poor pay and the unsanitary and dangerous conditions which her survey uncovered led the legislature to pass the Wage and Hour Law in 1913. The statute was the model on which the later federal Fair Labor Standards Act was patterned.

In 1915 Gleason joined the Sisters of the Holy Names of Jesus and Mary, taking the religious name "Sister Miriam Theresa." In her desire to obtain a doctoral degree from the Catholic University of America during the 1920s, she met the determined opposition of the sociology department to the admission of a woman to its program. Sister Miriam was equally persevering in her determination, however, and was finally granted the degree. It was published at government expense as a history of the minimum wage legislation in Oregon.

In 1930 Sister Miriam accepted the position of chair of the sociology department at Marylhurst College, where she trained 116 sociology students over the next three decades. During the 1950s she was recognized in several ways: as one of Oregon's greatest women (1951), as a Woman of Achievement (1956), and as a recipient of a brotherhood citation from the National Council of Christians and Jews (1958). In March 1962, while doing research for a history of Oregon's Wage and Hour Law, she suffered a stroke. She died two months later.

An editorial in the *Oregon Journal* eulogized the state's most important champion of labor: "It is not enough to say that Sister Miriam Theresa of the Holy Names order . . . was a dedicated woman. She was that, of course, but also she was a brilliant teacher and a guiding hand in much of the best in Oregon's welfare programs, private and public. . . . She was founder of the Oregon State Conference of Social Work and an authority on labor legislation. Her life, dedicated to God, was for other people – in His Name."

SALEM

¶ **State Capitol,** Court, State, and 12th streets.

The upper walls of the rotunda are adorned with four large murals depicting episodes in the history of the state. The two by Barry Faulkner show Captain Robert Gray landing at the mouth of the Columbia River and *Dr. John McLoughlin welcoming settlers at Fort Vancouver; those by Frank Schwartz depict the Lewis and Clark expedition at Celilo Falls and a wagon train of 1843.

§ Open Monday-Friday 8-5, Saturday 9-4, Sunday noon-4.

PUERTO RICO

One of the earliest Irishmen to arrive in Puerto Rico was Manuel Gilligan, a late seventeenth-century trader who most likely had commercial and familial connections in Spain. In the middle of the next century, the Irish-born general Alejandro O'Reilly was sent to the island by the Spanish king in order to report on its economy and defense system. In his subsequent report the general recommended steps to increase the island's population and to promote economic growth. Among the colonists of Irish ancestry who came to the island at the end of the 1700s were Miguel Conboy, a Caribbean tobacco merchant; Juan Kennedy, the operator of San Juan's major slave market; and various members of the commercially influential O'Neill family. San Juan commemorates its Irish heritage with an annual St. Patrick's Day parade.

LOIZA VIEJA

¶ **Holy Spirit and San Patricio Church,** on the north side of the plaza.

Originally known simply as San Patricio, this church is regarded by some authorities as the oldest in continuous use in Puerto Rico. It is also the first house of worship in the New World to be named for the patron saint of Ireland. The main altar boasts a statuette of a red-bearded St. Patrick.

As early as 1645 a hermitage under the patronage of St. Patrick existed at the mouth of the Loiza River. (That chapel is reputedly the nucleus of the present church.) According to a mid-seventeenth-century account, the name of the Irish saint had become associated with the area almost a century before – after a plague of ants began to destroy the local yucca. When the inhabitants petitioned their priest to select a saint as protector against the pestilence, they placed the names of various *santos* into a box and began to choose one by lot. The name of St. Patrick was the first drawn but, because the townspeople knew nothing about him, they drew again. To their surprise, the name reappeared, but they again rejected it. When the Irish saint's name was drawn a third time, however, the people accepted the choice and proceeded to make a novena to their new patron. After their prayers brought an end to the plague, the people proclaimed St. Patrick the protector of the yucca.

SAN JUAN

¶ **El Castillo de San Cristóbal,** at the eastern end of Old San Juan, north of Avenida Muñoz Rivera.

Although construction of the original fort on this site was begun in

1631, it was not completed until 150 years later. At that time, however, the belief that the fortress was vulnerable to attack resulted in the dispatch in 1776 of *Colonel Tomás O'Daly of the Spanish Royal Engineers to improve the city's defenses. As part of that effort, he and *General Alejandro O'Reilly enlarged the fortifications by building a system of battlements and outworks that made capture of the fortress impossible without first taking all its ramparts. So massive was the project that it was not finished until 1783. When a British force bombarded the fortress fourteen years later, the strengthened defenses were powerful enough to resist. In the nineteenth century *Demetrio O'Daly, one of Tomás O'Daly's relatives and a general in the Spanish army, represented Puerto Rico in the parliament at Madrid.

    • General Alejandro O'Reilly was born in Baltrasna, County Meath, Ireland, in 1722. After accompanying his parents to Spain, he became at age ten a cadet in the Hibernia Regiment of the Spanish army. Although he suffered a crippling wound while fighting in Italy during the War of the Austrian Succession, he enjoyed rapid promotion. In fact, his knowledge of modern warfare made him a leader in the effort to modernize the Spanish army. He was rewarded with the rank of lieutenant general for his services in the war with Portugal and for his reorganization of the defenses in Cuba and Puerto Rico.

    O'Reilly's later actions in Louisiana led to his further advancement. Following a successful uprising in 1768 against the first Spanish governor of Louisiana, the Irishman was sent with a force of 3,000 troops to crush the rebellion. Although he pardoned most of the leaders in the uprising, he earned the sobriquet "Bloody O'Reilly" for his execution of five of the ring leaders. Two years later he was appointed inspector-general of infantry and placed in command of an officers' training school. The next year he received the title of count.

    Beginning in 1775, however, O'Reilly experienced a fall from grace. For the failure of his expedition against Algeria, he was demoted from the military governorship of Madrid to that of Cadiz. His later intrigues led to his banishment to the province of Galicia.

¶ Hugh O'Neill Memorial Presbyterian Church, 61 Fortaleza Street, Old San Juan.

¶ San Patricio District.
    This area of the city received its name from Hacienda San Patricio, *Tomás O'Daly's family estate, which was originally on the outskirts of the city.

SOUTH CAROLINA

ABBEVILLE

¶ **Calhoun Family Cemetery,** 9 miles south on State 823.

Tombstones mark the graves of approximately thirty members of the family of Patrick Calhoun, who at the age of five had emigrated with his parents from County Donegal, Ireland, in 1733. The obelisk monument was erected in Calhoun's honor by his son, John C. Calhoun.

Proceeding from Philadelphia, the family had made its way through the Shenandoah Valley to the Waxhaws in the Carolinas and finally to the Ninety-Six district of South Carolina. It was there that Patrick built a house for his third wife, Martha Caldwell, the daughter of an Irish Presbyterian immigrant. It was also there that their five children were born, including their most famous son, John C. Calhoun, a future vice president of the United States.

As a youngster, John Calhoun was nurtured on tales of the Indian frontier. He knew, for instance, that his father had survived the Long Cane Massacre of 1760 only to bury the bodies of its twenty victims, among them Patrick's brother and mother, "most inhumanely butchered." He was also aware that his father was one of fifteen men who had held off forty Cherokee, killing twenty-three Indians but losing seven of their own.

Patrick Calhoun had also been an outspoken advocate for the rights of back-country settlers. Whether it was to argue for representation in the Assembly or to plead for roads, schools, and courts for the up-country, Calhoun was always in the forefront of the effort. In 1769, in fact, he led his neighbors 200 miles on foot down to the polling booths, within twenty-three miles of Charleston. There, in what must have been a very dramatic scene, the back-country men held the election officials at gunpoint, seized their rightful ballots, and voted Calhoun into the colonial assembly. He served in the legislature until his death almost thirty years later. Once during debate in the Assembly, a member spoke in favor of a bill to place a bounty of so many shillings on each wolf's scalp. Calhoun replied that he would rather see a law which placed the bounty at one pound – but for each lawyer's scalp.

It was this same radically independent strain that forced the elder Calhoun to vote against the federal constitution in 1788 on the ground that it permitted other people to tax South Carolinians. Many years later John Calhoun recalled his father's saying that the best government was one which allowed the citizen the most liberty "compatible with order and tranquility" and that the purpose of all government should be to "throw off needless restraints."

¶ Twelve miles from Abbeyville and 0.75 mile beyond Patterson's Bridge over Long Cane Creek is a memorial stone which Patrick Calhoun erected to his brother James, his mother, Catherine, and the twenty-two others killed in the Long Cane Massacre of 1760.

BEAUFORT

¶ Edward Barnwell House, 1405 Bay Street.
This porticoed frame structure was built in 1785 by Edward Barnwell, a great-grandson of the famous Indian fighter John Barnwell, a native of County Meath, Ireland. The latter-day Barnwell had seventeen children. (See below.)

¶ Elizabeth Barnwell Gough House, 705 Washington Street.
Constructed about 1789, this tabby building was home to Elizabeth Barnwell Gough, a granddaughter of *John Barnwell. Elizabeth returned here with her sixteen-year-old daughter following a quarrel with her husband, Richard Gough, whom she had married against her family's wishes.

¶ John Barnwell Burial Site, St. Helena Episcopal Church, Church Street, between North and King streets.
John Barnwell came to South Carolina from Ireland in 1701 and subsequently became known as "Tuscarora Jack" for his part in avenging a massacre of settlers by Tuscarora Indians in 1711. He variously served the colony as its secretary and as a member of the Assembly and the Governor's Council. In 1720, after South Carolina had cast off the government of the Proprietors, he was sent to England as the official agent of the temporary government. During that visit he urged the Board of Trade and Plantations to take steps to protect the colonials from pirates, Spaniards, and Indians. Upon his return to South Carolina the following year, he built Fort King George on the Altahama River as a bulwark against further Spanish encroachment. Barnwell was the first Irish ancestor of Theodore Roosevelt to come to America.

BELTON

Belton was named for John Belton O'Neall, civic leader, historian, and chief justice of South Carolina. He was of Irish ancestry on both sides, being the son of Quakers Anne Kelly and Hugh O'Neall. (His earliest American ancestor had deserted a British ship in the Delaware River about 1730.)

After graduating from South Carolina College, O'Neall served in the state legislature, two years as Speaker. During the nullification controversy of the 1830s, he opposed talk of disunion and secession, although his advanced age prevented him from actively opposing secession when the issue reached crisis proportions in 1860.

In his later life O'Neall exerted his considerable influence in the state for the cause of temperance. Even as a youngster selling rum at his father's grocery store, he had developed a dislike for the liquor traffic. This aversion turned to hatred when his father's frequent intoxication led to bankruptcy and the loss of his mind. Nevertheless, it was not until he was in his forties that the younger O'Neall threw himself into the cause, swearing off liquor first and then tobacco. In this new role he was elected to the presidency of several temperance organizations.

CAMDEN

¶ Hampton Park, Lyttleton Street near U.S. 1.

Named for *Wade Hampton, the park was the scene of a rally for the former Civil War general during his successful gubernatorial campaign in 1876. Although many of Hampton's Democratic supporters used terrorism to prevent newly enfranchised black voters from casting their ballots for the Republican candidate, Hampton himself gave no support to their efforts. In fact, at rallies throughout the state, he assuaged black fears that he would use his influence to deprive them of their rights, reminding them that he had supported a limited degree of black suffrage as far back as 1865. He also promised that, as governor, "the colored people . . . shall be equals under the law of any man in South Carolina." (See Marion Square, Charleston, South Carolina.)

CHARLESTON

¶ Aiken House, 456 King Street.

This house was the residence of William Aiken Sr., a native of County Antrim, Ireland, and the first president of the South Carolina Canal and Railroad Company. The company's line between Charleston and Hamburg, South Carolina, was the first in the nation to carry the U.S. mail and to use a steam engine to pull a passenger train. The house is one of several structures in a complex which includes a train depot and a warehouse.

¶ Aiken-Rhett Mansion, 48 Elizabeth Street.

Although built in 1817 in the late Federal style, this large residence was remodeled with Greek Revival features by Governor William Aiken Jr., who lived here from 1833 to 1887. Many of the furnishings, including the chandeliers, were selected by Aiken during a three-year sojourn in Europe. *Jefferson Davis and General Pierre Beauregard were guests here during the Civil War. The Confederate general used the mansion as his headquarters for a time.

The son of the Irish immigrant William Aiken (mentioned in the previous entry), the younger Aiken was born in Charleston and was graduated from South Carolina College. At the death of his father, a successful merchant, Aiken inherited a fortune and major commercial responsibilities. More interested in agriculture than business, he developed a model rice plantation on Jehossee Island, near Charleston.

Aiken began his political career in 1838 with the first of two terms in the state assembly. While later serving in the state senate, he was elected governor and used his position to promote the state's economic interests. At the beginning of the 1850s, he served two terms in the U.S. House of Representatives. Although he had always opposed disunion and secession, he supported the Southern cause with supplies and loans once the Civil War began. At the end of the conflict, he was arrested by federal authorities and taken to Washington but was paroled soon afterwards. When he was subsequently elected to Congress, the Radical Reconstructionists in that body refused to let him take his seat.

§ Open daily 10-5. Fee. Phone: 803-723-1159.

¶ Calhoun Mansion, 16 Meeting Street.

Built in 1876 by banker George W. Williams, this thirty-five-room mansion passed to his son-in-law, *Patrick Calhoun, the grandson of the prominent national political figure John C. Calhoun. The house is noted for its 300-pound walnut front doors and a glass skylight above the ballroom. Each of the rooms features a different type of wood.

§ Open Wednesday-Sunday 10-4. Fee. Phone: 803-722-8205

¶ Charleston County Courthouse, Broad and Meeting streets.

This building incorporates the walls of the original Provincial State House, which was constructed about 1760 and rebuilt after a fire in 1788. It is possible that the rebuilt structure was designed by James Hoban, the Irish-born architect of the White House in the nation's capital. Hoban had come to America in 1785 and for a time worked as a "house carpenter" in Charleston. He may have designed other buildings in the city that reflect a distinctly Irish Georgian style.

¶ City Hall, Broad and Meeting streets.

Constructed in 1801 as a branch of the Bank of the United States, this municipal building displays a 1791 portrait of George Washington by John Trumbull. The gallery also contains a painting of *John C. Calhoun addressing the U.S. Senate, the work of the Irish-American artist George Healy. (See *Irish America, Volume 1*.)

§ Open Monday-Friday 9-5. Phone: 803-577-6970.

¶ Edward Rutledge House, 117 Broad Street. Private.

This was formerly the residence of Edward Rutledge, a signer of the Declaration of Independence, a delegate to the Continental Congress, and the tenth governor of South Carolina.

Rutledge was born in Charleston in 1749, the son of a physician who had emigrated from Longford, Ireland, fourteen years before. After studying at the Middle Temple in London, the young Rutledge returned to Charleston to begin practice of the law. Although he voted for independence from Britain at the Second Continental Congress, he believed that the states should have formed some kind of confederation before cutting the final tie with the mother country. During the Revolutionary War he commanded an artillery company and was captured when Charleston fell to the enemy in 1780. For the next eleven months he was imprisoned in St. Augustine, Florida. While serving in the South Carolina legislature after the war, he opposed reopening the African slave trade and authored the bills which abolished primogeniture and confiscated the property of Loyalists. He died in 1800 while serving as the state's governor.

¶ **General Wagner Statue,** Bethany Cemetery, Cunnington Street, off Meeting Street.

This statue of the Confederate general John Wagner was sculpted by William O'Donovan.

O'Donovan was born in 1844 in what is now West Virginia and enlisted in the Confederate army at the age of eighteen. In the 1870s, after establishing a studio in New York City, he achieved recognition for his bas-reliefs and portrait busts of well known Americans, among them the bust of *Archbishop John Hughes at St. John's College, Fordham, New York. O'Donovan's many military works include equestrian reliefs of Lincoln and Grant for the Soldiers' and Sailors' Arch (Brooklyn, N.Y.), a monument to the captors of Major André (Tarrytown, N.Y.), a statue of General Daniel Morgan (Schuylerville, N.Y.), and additional statues of Washington in Newburgh, New York, and Caracas, Venezuela.

¶ **Hibernian Hall,** 105 Meeting Street.

This two-story Greek Revival structure was built in 1840 by the Hibernian Society, an Irish fraternal organization established on March 17, 1799, by eight Irish newcomers to the state. Under the portico is a piece of the Giant's Causeway, brought here from County Antrim, Ireland, in 1851. The hall is still the headquarters of the society and the scene of its annual St. Patrick's Day banquet as well as of the St. Cecilia Society Ball, one of the city's most prestigious social events.

Long before the creation of the Hibernian Society, however, St. Patrick's Day was celebrated in Charleston. On March 19, 1777, the *South Carolina Gazette and Country Journal* reported: "Sunday being St. Patrick's Day, the tutelar Saint of Ireland, the same was celebrated here yesterday by a number of Gentlemen who met on the occasion, and after partaking of a sumptuous dinner, spent the evening with the mirth and jollity ever conspicu-

ous to the natives of that country." The following year the same paper
mentioned that St. Patrick's Day was ushered in by the ringing of bells,
and in 1773 the newspaper described a public dinner hosted by the Friendly
Brothers of St. Patrick.

Before the Hibernian Society was organized in 1799, its founders had
met at one another's residence every second Tuesday to contribute toward a fund for the relief of Irish emigrants and on every fourth Thursday
to engage in "Sentiment, Song and Supper." About six months after the
founding, the group adopted a constitution which formalized these objec-
tives, "thus blending the happiness of assisting others, with the promotion of their own felicity." It was probably at that time that the society also
adopted its official badge: a green ribbon stamped with a gold harp surrounded with the words "Hibernian Society, Charleston, S.C." and to be
worn on the left breast.

When Hibernian Hall was officially opened in January 1841, approximately 2,500 people attended the festivities, more than the building's
eighty-foot-long ballroom could accommodate. In a memorial address
*Bishop John England emphasized the goals of the Hibernian Society and
stressed that its charitable work was one "in which not only native descendants of Irishmen, but South Carolinians and natives of every clime,
who had gathered under the wings of the Bird of Liberty, had cheerfully
united."

Today the Hibernian Society numbers 400 members, many of differ-

Hibernian Hall.

ent nationalities and religious persuasions. The presidency of the organization is annually alternated between a Protestant and a Catholic. On January 1 each year, the members gather to wish one another a happy and
prosperous new year and to partake of the traditional Charleston dish
known as Hoppin' John, a sign of health and good fortune.

The society's St. Patrick's Day celebrations begin with a business meeting at noon followed by lunch. At the evening banquet for the members
and their guests, three toasts are traditionally given: to St. Patrick's Day
itself, to South Carolina, and to the United States. The respective toasts
are responded to by a member of the clergy, a prominent South Carolinian, and an outstanding American.

¶ One of the items of interest inside Hibernian Hall is a portrait painting of Aedanus Burke, a congressman and jurist known for his wit and
irascible temper.

Born in 1743 in Galway, Ireland, he attended the Jesuit seminary in St.
Omer, France. Of his ancestors he knew little, an ignorance that he said
was due to "a want of Spirit of inquiring into my Origins in my youth,
which seems natural to a more advanced age." He was aware, however,
that his grandfather, a native of Connaught, had settled in County Kilkenny
after serving under James II in that monarch's unsuccessful Irish campaign against William of Orange during the Jacobite war of 1689-91.

After immigrating to South Carolina by way of the West Indies in the
1760s, Burke studied law in Virginia. He later fought in the Revolution
with the 2nd South Carolina Continental Regiment. In 1778, as one of the
state's associate judges, he extolled the virtues of South Carolina's new
constitution, particularly its abolition of what he called the "unnatural
distinctions of nobleman and commons." During most of the 1780s, he
served in the state legislature, at a time when the foremost issue in the
state was the treatment of the Loyalists. In a pamphlet entitled *An Address
to the Freemen of South Carolina*, he argued that humanity and legal principle demanded amnesty for the former partisans of the British cause. In a
more famous work, he warned against the dangers of nobility posed by
the nascent Order of the Cincinnati, a hereditary fraternal organization of
officers who had served in the Revolutionary War. "[H]owever pious or
patriotic the pretence, yet any political combination of military commanders, is, in a Republican government, extremely hazardous and censurable,"
he wrote, "and a fatal stab to that principle of equality, which forms the
basis of our government."

Despite his disdain for a native aristocracy, Burke apparently had no
objection against that most aristocratic of rituals – the duel. Once while
serving as the second for Colonel Aaron Burr, he was unable to ram the
bullet tightly into the pistol. Because Burr's pistol ball was unusually small,
it would fit snugly into the weapon only if encased in a leather patch. In
his haste, however, Burke had failed to grease the leather, an omission

that made loading the weapon difficult. When Burr complained of this irregularity, the judge replied: "I forgot to grease the leather; but you see [your opponent] is ready, don't keep him waiting. Just take a crack as it is, and I'll grease the next."

While serving in the state convention called to debate the new federal Constitution, Burke voted against its adoption. He was especially concerned that the document's failure to deny the president a second term would prove dangerous to republican liberties. Despite his negative vote, he was elected to the first Congress, where he tried his best to restrict the federal government to its delegated powers so as to keep "our liberties from being fooled away." In this attempt he opposed the excise tax and the creation of a national bank, although he supported the plan to allow the federal government to assume state debts incurred during the Revolution. He also proposed a constitutional amendment that forbade the creation of a standing army in time of peace without a two-thirds vote of Congress. To the end, though, he was a strong proponent of slavery.

Following his retirement from political life, Burke devoted his energies to his judicial duties. In 1785, however, he was part of a commission charged with the responsibility of revising the state's statutes. Although the revision was not adopted *in toto*, portions of it found their way into subsequent pieces of legislature. At the end of 1799 he was elected chancellor of the court of equity.

Just before Burke died in 1802, his physician told him that he would have to tap him for the dropsy. Witty even to the end, the judge replied: "Before God, then, my days are numbered, for nothing was ever tapped in this house that lasted long." Burke died a bachelor and left in his will a bequest of £600 to Ruth Savage, an unmarried woman in Charleston. In leaving this legacy he explained that "I have been for some years back engaged to Miss Savage by ties of great esteem" and that just before he was taken ill they had "engaged to be married." (According to another version, Burke said that he had courted the woman for ten years and that, "if he had persevered, she would have had him.")

❡ Burke is buried in the Episcopal cemetery in St. Bartholomew's Parish near Jacksonborough, South Carolina.

❡ **Irish Volunteers Memorial,** St. Lawrence Cemetery, 60 Hughuenin Avenue at Meeting Street, next to Magnolia Cemetery.

The obelisk inside the main gate commemorates the South Carolina militia company known as the Irish Volunteers. Officially designated as the 2nd Company, 1st Battalion, 28th South Carolina Volunteers, the unit was most likely founded in Charleston soon before 1798, since numerous notices of its meetings appear in the *City Gazette and Daily Advertiser* after that date.

One of the Irish Volunteers' many social events in Charleston was described in the *Truth Teller* of April 1, 1826. An article in that New York newspaper reported that the unit's new banner was consecrated during a solemn religious ceremony in the Cathedral of St. Finbar in Charleston. After sprinkling the banner with holy water, Bishop John England, himself a native of Ireland, presented the standard to the Irish Volunteers' captain. The banner was described as follows: "Field – Emerald green, bound with gold fringe; on one side the Harp of Erin, richly gilt, supported by the arms of the State – the American Eagle descends, holding a ribbon in his beak and talons (uniting the Arm of the State with the Harp), on which is inscribed, 'Where Liberty Dwells There is One Country.' On the foreground are trophies of war, the American and Irish standards entwined; the whole surrounded by a brilliant wreath of Shamrock; above the Eagle in large characters is written, 'Erin go Bragh.' On the Reverse: the Irish Harp between a figure of Hibernia holding the pole and Cup of Liberty; and the genius of America, holding the standard of the United States; immediately over the Harp is the Irish Wolf Dog with the motto – 'Gentle when soothed, fierce when provoked.' The foreground and Shamrock the same as the other side; the whole crowned with 'Erin go Bragh' in large characters."

Although the Irish Volunteers offered their services during the War of 1812 and the nullification crisis of 1832-33, they were not activated. They did, however, serve in the Seminole War during the mid 1830s, losing, according to one source, many of their members. In a public letter calling attention to the Irish Volunteers on the eve of their departure for the war in Florida, Bishop England described the men as "prompted by zeal and patriotism [who] devoted themselves to the praiseworthy service of protecting the settlers on the frontier from the horrors of savage aggression."

¶ **John Mitchel Burial Site,** Magnolia Cemetery, Old Meeting Road and Cunnington Street.

The small monument over this grave commemorates Captain John Mitchel, a casualty of the Union bombardment of Fort Sumter in July 1864. The memorial was erected fourteen years later by Mitchel's former comrades. The curbstones around the grave represent Fort Sumter's ramparts and were added in 1914. The tomb is inscribed with the words: "I could not fight for Ireland, so I chose to fight for the South."

Mitchel was born in Newry, County Down, Ireland, in 1838, the son of a leader of the anti-British United Irishman movement. When the older Mitchel was banished to a penal colony in Tasmania for his seditious writing, the son shared his father's exile until they both escaped to America in 1853. After several years in San Francisco, where he founded a newspaper, the elder Mitchel moved with his wife and children to Richmond, Virginia. There he assumed the editorship of the *Enquirer*, whose pro-Confederate policy he continued in his editorials. (See Hampton, Virginia.)

In the meantime the younger Mitchel had settled in South Carolina, where he enlisted in the Confederate army. As a newly commissioned lieutenant in the 1st South Carolina Artillery Regiment, he assisted in the successful attack on Fort Sumter on April 12-13, 1861. He later helped capture the federal gunboat *Isaac Smith*, one of several that had blockaded Charleston harbor. By July 1863 Mitchel was in command of the Confederate defensive works on the south end of Morris Island, a steppingstone in the Union's planned attack on Charleston. When the Irishman and his troops failed to prevent a combined Union force from landing on the island, it was only a matter of time before the Federals captured Battery Wagner, from which they intended to launch their bombardment of Fort Sumter. Despite these setbacks, Mitchel still expected to be promoted to major, in accordance with an earlier recommendation.

Instead, however, Mitchel received command of Fort Sumter in May 1864. Bracing for the bombardments that were daily expected, the twenty-five-year-old officer strengthened the fort's defenses and readied his men. As the second week of the Union barrage began, Sumter came under attack from 200-pound rifles and 13-inch howitzers, a blitz that averaged 500 shots a day. By the end of the week the garrison had suffered substantial casualties: six killed and twenty-six wounded.

It was at this juncture – on July 20 – that Mitchel was killed. As was his custom, the young officer had climbed the fort's ramparts at about 1 p.m. to observe the movements of the Union fleet. While stationed behind a breast-high shelter within the parapets, Mitchel heard the burst of a mortar shell eighty feet above the surrounding water. Apparently undisturbed by the explosion, he continued to observe the enemy through his eyeglass until a falling piece of shell knocked him down, causing a large laceration on his left hip. Although bleeding, he was mentally lucid and spoke calmly about his wound. To Captain John Johnson, an engineer at the fort, he alluded to his unfulfilled ambition: "They have killed me, captain, but I ought to have been a major, though." By the time Mitchel was moved to the surgeon's table in the garrison hospital, however, he had to be revived with stimulants. Almost immediately the physician ruled out surgery, realizing that the wound was fatal. When the dying officer was later asked what could be done for him, he replied, "Nothing, except pray for me." Mitchel died after lingering for four hours.

In his definitive work *The Defense of Charleston Harbor*, Captain Johnson eulogized his comrade. "The death of Captain John C. Mitchel," he wrote, "greatly deplored by the many friends he had made in his adopted country, was the closing of a brief career which gave promise of undoubted distinction in military service. He commanded Fort Sumter for two weeks of its third and last grand bombardment. In that time the fears for its safety, which at first he felt, were completely dissipated. Injuries had been repaired, loss of material had been met with new supplies, and precautions against assault had been increased to perfection."

¶ John Rutledge House, 116 Broad Street.

Now an inn, this restored 1763 structure was once the town house of John Rutledge, delegate to the Continental Congress and the Constitutional Convention, governor of the state, and chief justice of the U.S. Supreme Court.

Rutledge was born in Charleston in 1739, the son of a Scotch-Irish physician from Longford, Ireland. The future South Carolina governor began his varied political career in 1761, when he was elected to the colony's House of Commons. He subsequently represented the colony in both continental congresses and was a member of the committee which in 1776 wrote the constitution of the newly independent state. Although he was immediately elected South Carolina's first president, he soon came into conflict with those who wanted to democratize the state constitution further. He later resigned after vetoing revisions to the state constitution that disestablished the Anglican Church and created a senate elected by the people.

Yet when the state was threatened by invasion in January 1779, Rutledge accepted election as governor and was entrusted with almost dictatorial power "to do everything necessary for the public good, except the taking away the life of a citizen without a legal trial." After Charleston fell to the British, Rutledge encouraged militia leaders to carry on resistance with guerrilla warfare and raised money for badly needed war materiel by confiscating and selling a large quantity of indigo. He was famous for his remark that "I would rather lose my all, than retain it subject to British authority."

§ Open daily 10-4. Phone: 803-723-7999.

¶ Lining House, 106 Broad Street. Private.

Between 1782 and 1790 this residence was where Ann Donovan Timothy and her son Benjamin Franklin Timothy published the *South Carolina Gazette*. When Benjamin retired from the printing business in 1802, the paper's sixty-nine-year old history came to an end.

The story of the *Gazette* began in 1733, when Benjamin's grandfather Lewis Timothy formed a partnership with America's premier printer – Benjamin Franklin – to establish the colony's first permanent newspaper. By 1745 control of the paper had fallen to Timothy's son Peter, who that same year married Ann Donovan, most likely a descendant of an immigrant named Daniel Donovan.

During most of her years of marriage, Ann was preoccupied with bearing the couple's fifteen children and raising the seven who survived infancy. Following her husband's death in 1782, however, the widow resumed publication of the *Gazette*, recently suspended because of the British occupation of Charleston at the end of the Revolutionary War. With the help of E. Walsh, she published the paper until her death a decade later. During that time she also served as South Carolina's official printer.

¶ A plaque in honor of Ann Donovan Timothy is located at Vendue Range and East Bay Street, the former site of the offices occupied by the *Gazette*. The marker was dedicated in 1981 by Sigma Delta Chi, the Society of Professional Journalists.

¶ **Marion Square,** Calhoun Street, between King and Meeting streets.

• On the south side of this pleasant urban oasis stands a statue of *John C. Calhoun, the South Carolina native who was a prominent national political leader for forty years. During his career as a U.S. senator and representative, secretary of war, vice president, and secretary of state, he was a consistent defender of states' rights. His views about the nature of the federal union prompted the nullification crisis in the 1830s and served as the rationale for secession prior to the Civil War. (See Clemson, South Carolina.)

• A shaft in honor of General Wade Hampton is located on the east side of the square. Of direct Irish ancestry on his maternal side, Hampton threw in his lot with the Confederacy once civil war commenced, although he had earlier opposed secession. Besides offering his sizeable cotton crop to be exchanged in Europe for armaments, he raised a combined infantry, cavalry, and artillery regiment known as the Hampton Legion. He was in command of a brigade during most of the Peninsular campaign and participated in almost all of J. E. B. Stuart's major operations, including the battle of Gettysburg, where he received his third wound.

Following Stuart's death in May 1864, Hampton was placed in command of the cavalry corps. His effectiveness in this new command was hindered, however, by the lack of sufficient remounts, a problem which ultimately forced him to deploy some of his men in the search for fresh horses. In the final weeks of the war, he was ordered to evacuate Columbia, lying as it did in the path of Sherman's "March to the Sea." (Sherman unsuccessfully tried to blame Hampton for the fire which engulfed the city.) Hampton subsequently offered to accompany *President Jefferson Davis to Texas, where they would continue resistance against the Union army. He abandoned this plan, however, and returned to his native state.

After the war Hampton used his influence to effect the reconstruction policy advocated by *President Andrew Johnson. When the president's congressional critics countered with a more punitive policy of their own, Hampton joined the resistance to these Radical Republicans but was unsuccessful in defeating their candidates in the 1868 elections. In the last year of the state's military occupation by U.S. troops, Hampton was elected the state's first Democratic governor since the war. Although he himself had appealed for the votes of the newly enfranchised blacks, his supporters guaranteed his election by keeping large numbers of these Republican voters from the polls. He was subsequently elected to the U.S. Senate. In 1899, when his residence in Columbia was destroyed by fire, he moved into an outbuilding, taking with him only his dog, his gun, and his fishing tackle. (He lamented that he had not saved his army tent.)

¶ O'Donnell House, 21 King Street. Private.

This Italianate-style residence was built in the 1850s by Patrick O'Donnell for his fiancée. The Irish-born master builder took so long in finishing the gift house, however, that his fiancée lost patience and married someone else.

¶ Old Exchange Building, 122 East Bay Street.

Off the lobby is a room named for *John Rutledge, known as "Dictator Rutledge" because he wielded so much political and military power as chief executive of South Carolina during the Revolutionary War. He was also a member of the Hibernian Society and the Friendly Brothers of St. Patrick. After the British seized the Exchange Building during the Revolution, his brother *Edward Rutledge was one of the three signers of the Declaration of Independence to be imprisoned in the dungeon.

§ Open daily 9-5. Closed major holidays. Fee. Phone: 803-727-2165.

¶ Old Slave Mart, 6 Chalmers Street.

When built in 1853 by *Thomas Ryan, this was known as Ryan's Auction Mart and was one of several such markets in the city. Although Ryan originally did not sell slaves here, he began to do so after 1856, when the city of Charleston forbade the sale of slaves near the customary venue at the docks.

¶ St. John the Baptist Church, 120 Broad Street.

Among the early leaders of the Catholic Church who were laid to rest in the cathedral crypt are John England and Patrick Lynch, both natives of Ireland and the respective first and third bishops of Charleston. England's youngest sister, Joanna Monica, who had accompanied him to America in 1820, is reputedly buried in her brother's casket.

• Although born to Catholic parents in Cork, Ireland, in 1786, John England attended a school conducted by the Church of Ireland, a circumstance that made him and his Catholicism the object of insults from both teachers and fellow students. After flirting with a career in law, he studied for the priesthood and was ordained in 1808. During his subsequent chaplaincy positions in Cork, he became an outspoken critic of the conditions surrounding the transportation of convict labor to Australia. His campaign finally prompted the government to reform the prison ships and to allow Catholic clergy to carry out their ministry in the penal colonies. (One Australian authority described England as the founder of the Catholic Church in Australia.) England was no less tactful in his support for the nationalist cause in Ireland, a fact that prompted the archbishop of Armagh to describe him as lacking in "sacerdotal meekness, and prudence" and not acting with "sufficient caution" in political matters. His elevation to the episcopacy and assignment to Charleston in 1820 were looked upon by many as the penalty for his outspokenness.

Once in his new diocese, Bishop England labored to remedy the deplorable state of the Church there. Because he had only five missionary priests for the 5,000 Catholics nominally under his care, he himself rode circuit, preaching in churches placed at his disposal by friendly Protestant ministers. Remarkably democratic in his views, he immediately applied for American citizenship and met President Monroe and John Quincy Adams within a year of his arrival. Although he generally accepted American slavery – which he described as less severe than the existence of Irish peasants – he insisted upon the humane treatment of its victims. He welcomed Africans to the cathedral and instructed them himself, but he was forced to abandon the school which he had opened for them when its presence caused rioting and destruction of church property by opponents. One of his most lasting creations, however, was the *United States Catholic Miscellany*, the first distinctly Catholic newspaper in the country. In managing the paper, he was helped by his sister, on whom he also depended for assistance in administering the diocese. Following her death from yellow fever in 1827, England acknowledged her influence upon him in a letter to Dr. Bruté: "She was a sensible companion, a great literary aid, the gentle monitor, who pointed out my faults, who checked my vanity, who taught me that what was done was the work of God and not that of the miserable and frail instrument which He used. She did more by the sacrifice of her money and her comfort to establish the Diocese than was done by any other means I know."

A year before his sister's death, England became the first Catholic priest invited to address the House of Representatives as a guest. In a letter to *Judge William Gaston of North Carolina, he mentioned that the House was so thronged that day that President John Quincy Adams had difficulty finding a seat. The bishop also confessed his mixed feelings at hearing his own name proclaimed as he entered the House chamber: embarrassment tinged with "some unwonted glow in my cheek and on my forehead." His two-hour speech was singularly theological, covering such topics as the obligations of religion, the role of reason and revelation in the search for God, and the nature of papal authority. In that same letter to Gaston, England expressed his belief that his predominantly Protestant fellow-citizens "are not obstinate heretics – they are an enquiring, thinking, reasoning, well-disposed . . . pious people, – & God will bless them & bring them to truth."

• Patrick Lynch, meanwhile, had come to the United States at the age of two, emigrating from County Monaghan with his parents and settling in Cheraw, South Carolina, in 1819. After attending the Seminary of St. John the Baptist in Charleston, the young cleric continued his education at the College of the Propaganda in Rome. There he earned recognition as a polyglot, on one occasion preaching in Hebrew before Pope Gregory XVI.

After returning to Charleston following his ordination in 1840, Lynch assumed a variety of responsibilities. While serving as curate at the cathedral, he edited the diocesan newspaper and taught at the diocesan seminary. His tenure as pastor of St. Mary's Church was followed by his appointment to the rectorship of the cathedral and of the seminary. He also defused widespread opposition to the creation of an Ursuline convent in the city and supervised the completion of the Cathedral of St. John and St. Finbar. In 1858, he was consecrated the see's third bishop.

Lynch's appointment to the episcopacy occurred as political events in the nation were reaching the explosive point. Undoubtedly crushed by the destruction of the new cathedral in a fire that swept the city in 1861, the bishop weathered the additional ravages of the Civil War, particularly the siege of Charleston and Sherman's brutal march through the state. In 1863 the pro-Southern bishop agreed to act as special commissioner for the Confederacy at the papal court, believing that such a mission might result in an end to the conflict. While the message which the bishop carried to the pope expressed *President Jefferson Davis's desire for peace, it unrealistically asked the pontiff to use his influence to prevent the use of Irish recruits for the Northern cause. The letter also tacitly hinted at diplomatic recognition by the Holy See. When Lynch arrived in Rome, however, the fate of the Confederacy seemed sealed; he accordingly paid his respects to the pope simply as a bishop rather than as a Confederate emissary. Nevertheless, his mission to Rome was mistaken for papal support of the Southern cause and prompted a disavowal by the Vatican.

On the same trip to Europe, the bishop visited his native land, hoping to counter the efforts of Northern agents who were enlisting Irishmen in the Union army. He hoped to "educate" the Irish by reminding them of the indignities which his fellow emigrants had often experienced in the North before the war and by informing them of Union acts of destruction against Catholic churches in the South. Despite his obvious support for the Confederacy – he had celebrated the dissolution of the Union with a special mass in the Charleston cathedral – Lynch received a pardon from *President Andrew Johnson in August 1865.

¶ St. Philip's Episcopal Church, 146 Church Street.

In the churchyard, which extends across the street, are the graves of three famous South Carolinians of Irish ancestry: John C. Calhoun, Edward Rutledge, and Edward McCrady.

¶ **Sullivan's Island,** reached from Charleston via U.S. 17 and State 703.

The island was named for Florence O'Sullivan, the captain of the *Carolina*, one of the first English ships that transported colonists to the Charleston area in 1669. After leaving England, the ships stopped at Kinsale, Ireland, where they picked up additional passengers. Besides O'Sullivan, the known Irish on board his ship were Joseph Dalton, Priscilla Burke, and Teigue Shuegeron. In subsequent years O'Sullivan was named an officer of the Charleston militia, received a land grant along the Cooper River, and was the colony's first surveyor-general.

• On the island is Fort Moultrie, constructed in 1776 of palmetto logs. Although its garrison was outnumbered, it survived an offshore British naval bombardment in June of that year because the fort's sand and spongy palmetto logs blunted the force of the incoming shells. When the fort's blue flag was shot down during the firing, *Sergeant William Jasper leaped over the walls, retrieved the banner, tied it to a stick, and implanted it on the side of the fort closest to the British. Although *Governor John Rutledge offered him a lieutenant's commission for his bravery, Jasper modestly replied: "I cannot mingle with those who are superior to me in education and manners without exposing myself to deserved contempt. Let me alone; let me serve my country in the way that suits me best, as an humble and devoted laborer in the cause of freedom." (See next entry.)

• *Edgar Allan Poe wrote his poem "Israfel" while he was a soldier stationed here in 1828 and used the island as the setting of his later story "The Gold Bug." (The gold bug is a type of beetle found on the island.)

¶ **William Jasper Statue,** at the east end of the Battery.

More formally known as the Defenders of Fort Moultrie Monument, this memorial is noted for its statue of Sergeant William Jasper, who retrieved the fort's blue flag after it was shot down during the British attack. (See Sullivan's Island above.) The monument was unveiled on Carolina Day, June 28, 1876, the centenary of the successful American defense of Fort Moultrie. (See William Jasper Statue, Savannah, Georgia.)

CLEMSON

¶ **Clemson University,** 11 miles west of Interstate 85 exit 19B, on U.S. 76.

Originally founded in 1889 as Clemson College, this institution is located on the former 1,100-acre plantation of *John C. Calhoun, who served as vice president under John Quincy Adams and *Andrew Jackson. Calhoun willed the property to his son-in-law, Thomas Green Clemson, who in turn offered it for "the establishment of the Agricultural College which will afford useful information to the farmers and mechanics."

• The James F. Byrnes Room in the Robert Muldrow Cooper Library displays a collection of manuscripts and other memorabilia that once belonged to Byrnes, secretary of state under President Harry Truman. (See Columbia, South Carolina.).

§ Library open Monday-Friday 7:45 a.m.-1 a.m., Saturday 10-6, Sunday 1 p.m.-1 a.m. during the school year; abbreviated schedule during the rest of the year. Closed holidays. Phone: 803-656-3024.

¶ **Fort Hill,** Clemson University campus.

The oldest part of this two-story Doric-columned residence was built in 1803 by Dr. James McElhenny, the pastor of the Old Stone Church. Known at that time as Old Clergy Hall, it was used as a parsonage by McElhenny and his son-in-law, the Reverend James Archibald Murphy.

Between 1825 and 1850 the structure was the home of *John C. Calhoun, who renamed it "Fort Hill" and added the present wings. Among the many Calhoun family furnishings in the fourteen-room house is a sideboard made from the mahogany paneling of the officers' quarters on the U.S.S. *Constitution*. A springhouse, a kitchen, and a library and office are on the grounds.

While living here, Calhoun followed an accustomed schedule. He invariably rose at dawn, walked over the hills on his estate, and returned to the house at 7:30 to breakfast. He then usually worked in his office until 3

"Fort Hill," the home of John C. Calhoun.

p.m. and after dinner entertained visitors or read history or travel books.

Although during his early political career Calhoun had been an ardent nationalist, he later became a spokesman for the uniquely sectional interests of the South. From 1810, the year of his election to the House of Representatives, until approximately 1825, he had supported those policies that were intended to transform a gaggle of states into a nation: internal improvements, a federal army, a national bank, and a high tariff. By the mid 1820s, however, he had come to understand the pernicious effect which the protective tariffs favored by Northern manufacturing interests were having on the South's plantation economy. In essence, he concluded, the issue came down to whether the political majority should have the right to effect policies which were harmful to a minority.

In his search for some constitutional means to resist the majority and thereby protect Southern interests, Calhoun at first developed the theory of nullification. According to this concept, the individual states had the right to judge whether the federal government exceeded the powers granted it by the Constitution. If a formal state convention decided that Congress had indeed acted beyond the scope of its powers with the passage of a particular statute, the state had the right to declare the offending law null and void within its boundaries and refuse to permit its enforcement there. When in 1830 the issue of nullification was confronted in the famous Webster-Hayne debates, Calhoun – then vice president – found himself at odds with *President Andrew Jackson. At the annual Jefferson birthday dinner, Jackson left no doubt about his position, as he rose and made a toast to "Our Federal Union. It must be preserved." Two years later, when South Carolina proceeded to declare the tariff acts of 1828 and 1832 null and void, the nation was faced with a constitutional crisis that carried within it the seeds of civil war. Jackson was even more forceful in demonstrating his intention to uphold the authority of the federal government and to enforce acts of Congress.

Following the war with Mexico in the 1840s, Calhoun again championed the rights of the South. This time, though, he argued that Southern slaveholders must be free to introduce their "peculiar institution" into the vast western territories acquired from Mexico. Otherwise, he insisted, the future western states would enter the Union as free states, a prospect that would forever consign the South to minority status politically and constitutionally. In particular he warned that the free states might someday be numerous enough to pass a constitutional amendment to abolish slavery. In this regard he saw the vital nexus between the earlier protective tariff issue and the later slavery issue and the need to protect Southern interests: "While the tariff takes from us the proceeds of our labor, abolition strikes at the labor itself."

Although Calhoun had earlier proposed his constitutional remedy for the South's status as a minority, he repeated it in his final speech to the

Senate in 1850. In short, the remedy was an amendment to the Constitution which would guarantee to the South a "concurrent majority." According to this constitutional device, both the majority and the minority interests in the nation would be granted "either a concurrent voice in making and executing the laws or a veto on their execution." In Calhoun's view, the best way to implement the concurrent majority in the United States would be to create a dual executive. In other words, the nation would have two presidents, each representing one of its two great sections and enjoying the right to veto legislation passed by Congress. "Is it then, not certain that if something decisive is not now done to arrest it," he asked, almost rhetorically, "the South will be forced to choose between abolition and secession?"

§ Open Monday-Saturday 10-5, Sunday 2-5. Closed holidays. Donations. Phone: 803-656-4789.

COLUMBIA

¶ First Presbyterian Church, 1324 Marion Street.

*Dr. Joseph Ruggles Wilson and his wife, the parents of President Woodrow Wilson, are buried in the churchyard.

§ Open daily. Phone: 803-799-9062.

¶ Hampton-Preston Mansion and Garden, 1615 Blanding Street.

This restored antebellum house was constructed in 1818 for a wealthy merchant who later sold the mansion to General Wade Hampton. This veteran of the Revolutionary War and the War of 1812 was the first of three successive Wade Hamptons to occupy the house between 1823 and 1873.

Through his marriage in 1801 to Mary Cantey – a fourth-generation descendant of Teige Cantey – Hampton had introduced an Irish element into his family's lineage. This element was strengthened by the marriage of his namesake son to Ann FtizSimons, the daughter of a well-to-do merchant from Dundalk, Ireland. Wade Hampton III, meanwhile, married Margaret Preston, a member of a prestigious family of Irish ancestry. This Hampton was the famous Civil War general who later served as a South Carolina governor and a U.S. senator.

The family's two-and-a-half-story mansion passed into the possession of John Preston when he married Caroline Hampton, a daughter of Wade Hampton I. In the 1840s the couple added a suite of twenty-four rooms to the house and stuccoed the red brick. The mansion's Doric portico has a full entablature. Today the house is furnished with items from the three plantations once owned by the Hampton and Preston families, including Wade Hampton I's ivory and ebony dominoes and his son's gold-handled umbrella.

John Preston, whose grandfather William had come to Virginia from Ireland about 1740, attended the University of Virginia and later studied law at Harvard. He managed his large sugar plantation in Louisiana so well that it was the source of his great wealth, a portion of which he used in the collection of paintings and sculpture. He was also an early patron of the sculptor Hiram Powers.

During his career in the state senate from 1848 to 1856, Preston became known as an exceptional public speaker and as a supporter of an extreme states' rights position. In 1860, following four years' residence in Europe, where his children were educated, he was the chairman of the state convention which voted in favor of secession.

During the Civil War Preston saw action in the Manassas campaign and was commissioned assistant adjutant general. After briefly serving in Charleston, where he was in charge of mustering troops into the Confederate army, he was assigned to Columbia, South Carolina, to command the prison camp and the conscript camp there. He concluded his service with the Confederacy as the superintendent of the government's bureau of conscription in Richmond.

After the war Preston used his oratorical skills to oppose the North's reconstruction policies. He remained an outspoken defender of secession and argued against reconciliation. His last public address was delivered at the unveiling of the Confederate monument in Columbia in 1880.

§ Tours are given at quarter past the hour, Tuesday-Saturday 10:15-3:15, Sunday 1:15-4:15. Closed major holidays. Fee. Phone: 803-252-1770.

¶ A plaque outside the Hampton-Preston Mansion commemorates a series of events involving Sister Baptista Lynch and General William Sherman, whose army had already burned Atlanta and in February 1865 occupied Columbia.

Sister Baptista was born in Cheraw, South Carolina, in 1823, the daughter of Conlaw and Eleanor Lynch, immigrants from Clones, Ireland. After attending the Ursuline Academy in Charleston, South Carolina, she joined the Ursuline order of nuns at its novitiate in Cincinnati, Ohio. When her brother, Bishop Patrick Lynch, invited the Ursulines to South Carolina in 1858, she led a group of sisters to Columbia to take over the Immaculate Conception Academy and Convent.

Seven years later, however, as General Sherman completed his plans to capture the city, Sister Baptista took steps to protect her community of nuns and the sixty young schoolgirls at their academy. In a note that reminded the general of her earlier acquaintance with his sister and his daughter, Sister Baptista pleaded for his protection. In response Sherman ordered Colonel Charles Ewing, his brother-in-law, to "tell her we'll destroy no private property."

As federal troops marched into Columbia on February 17 – at each step getting closer to the Ursuline convent – Sister Baptista sent Sherman two more pleas for help. Each time, the general replied with his assurance that the convent would be protected. Between these reassurances, however, Major Thomas Fitzgibbon, a young cavalry officer, had called on Sister Baptista. Although he had come in a private capacity to help protect the convent, his warning – "This is a doomed city. . . . I doubt that a house will be left standing" – terrified the nuns and their charges, many of whom were younger than ten years of age.

In the meantime fire had broken out again in the city and Union troops had broken into a local distillery. As the flames inched closer to the convent, the mother superior appealed to Sherman again, this time reminding him of her "personal as well as religious claim" upon his assistance. For the fourth time Sherman – himself raised a Catholic – gave his assurances.

As the fires drew closer and closer to the convent, a local priest, Father O'Connell, urged the sisters to prepare to abandon the building. After the nuns and the schoolgirls had bundled up their clothing, the priest led the community in prayer in the chapel. As the women and girls were reciting the rosary, the door came crashing down, felled by "the most unearthly battering . . . like the crash of doom. Drunken soldiers piled over each other, rushing for the sacred gold vessels of the altar, not knowing they were safe in the keeping of one blessed of God."

Sara Aldrich, one of the girls, later described the surreal scene which followed. "We marched through the blazing streets with the precision of a military band," she recalled. "It was our safety. Not a cry, not a moan. The roaring of the fires, the scorching flames on either side . . . did not create the least disorder. That majestic figure of the Mother Superior in the graceful black habit of the Ursuline order . . . The long line of anxious, white young faces of the schoolgirls."

After taking refuge in a nearby church, Father O'Connell and his companions watched in anguish as the burning convent roof collapsed. They were soon greeted by new terrors, however, as taunting soldiers cried out: "Oh, holy! Yes, holy! We're just as holy as you are! . . . Now, what do you think of God? Ain't Sherman greater?" And when a group of soldiers burst into the church shouting that they were going to blow up the building, the terrified girls fled into the graveyard and sought safety behind the bushes. Soon after dawn, however, Union officers arrived and dispersed the unruly soldiers.

The subsequent arrival of General Sherman only added to the high drama of the scene. Although, as Sarah Aldrich recorded, Sister Baptista looked like "an injured empress dethroned," she held her ground. To the general's pious remark that "there are times when one must practice patience and Christian endurance," she replied wittily: "You have prepared for us one of those moments, General." When the conqueror lamely explained that the fire "got beyond control, from buildings I had to burn," she played with his conscience: "General, this is how you kept your promise to me, a cloistered nun." And when the general offered her any house in the city for a convent, she replied by saying, "I do not think the houses left are yours to give . . . ."

Later in the day Sister Baptista successfully requested from Sherman permission to occupy the Hampton-Preston mansion. She most likely selected this house because of her friendship with the two families, both of which had Irish ancestry. At the time, however, the mansion was the headquarters of the Union general John Logan and was slated to be razed the following morning. In fact, when the nuns and their schoolgirls arrived at the house, Logan himself was preparing to torch the building by igniting barrels of pitch in the cellar. When the mother superior presented him with Sherman's order to spare the structure, Logan cursed "mightily" but removed the barrels and left.

The nuns and their pupils lived in the Hampton-Preston mansion only temporarily, before moving to a farm outside the city. In 1887 the community returned to the house, where they remained for the next three years.

❡ James F. Byrnes House, 12 Heathwood Circle. Private.

Now owned by the McKissick Museum, this was once the residence of James F. Byrnes, known most notably as an associate justice of the Supreme Court and secretary of state under President Truman. Byrnes bought the house in 1955, soon after serving a single term as governor of South Carolina.

A native of Charleston, Byrnes was the son of Irish immigrants. His father's death in 1879, a few months before the child's birth, forced his mother, Elizabeth McSweeney Byrnes, to earn a living as a dressmaker. When he was older, the youngster found employment as a stenographer in a Charleston law office until he was offered a similar position with a state circuit court in Aiken, South Carolina. There he studied law with a local judge and was admitted to the bar in 1903. For the next four years he was also the editor and one of the owners of the *Aiken Journal & Review*.

Byrnes was first introduced to politics with his election as local district attorney in 1908. Two years later he was elected to the first of seven terms in the U.S. House of Representatives. Following a five-year hiatus during which he practiced law in Spartanburg, South Carolina, he was elected to the U.S. Senate. There he was a strong advocate for the legislative agenda of his friend, President Roosevelt, and helped guide the New Deal legislation through the Senate. While serving briefly on the U.S. Supreme Court, Byrnes generally exercised "judicial restraint," although he wrote the majority opinion using the commerce clause to strike down a California law to prevent the transportation of indigents into the state.

After only sixteen months on the court, however, the sixty-three-year-old Byrnes resigned, prompted by a desire to assist the nation's war effort. Roosevelt accordingly appointed him to head the Office of Economic Stabilization. In this position the former justice administered a national economic policy intended to enlist the nation's productivity in the war effort without stimulating inflation. Armed with power second only to the president's, the "assistant president," as Byrnes was known, could issue directives to a multitude of federal agencies. (His zeal led to the suppression of horse racing.)

At the end of World War II, Byrnes was appointed secretary of state by President Harry Truman. One of the most pressing issues which faced the new secretary was the postwar peace settlement. While the United States, Britain, France, and China favored broader involvement in the process, the Soviet Union hoped to limit the treaty making to itself, the United States, and Britain. In a subsequent move that portended the coming Cold War, Byrnes warned the Soviets against coercive action against its weaker neighbors.

When the Paris peace conference was finally held in the spring of 1946, the American secretary of state proposed that the United States, Britain, France, and the Soviet Union guarantee the disarmament of Germany for the next quarter century. In outlining the American policy toward that defeated nation, he insisted that the Germans be entrusted with the operation of their internal affairs, including industrialization and the formation of a democratic state. And with a ringing declaration he declared an end to American isolation: "We intend to continue our interest in the affairs of Europe and of the world. . . ."

¶ **Millwood,** 4 miles out of town on U.S. 76 to Garner's Ferry Road.

Although reduced to five columns on brick bases, this once-proud Greek Revival mansion was the home of *Colonel Wade Hampton II and his son and namesake, the famous Confederate general. The house was destroyed by fire during Columbia's occupation by the Union general William T. Sherman. (See Columbia, South Carolina.)

During the War of 1812, Colonel Hampton participated in the battle of New Orleans. He achieved fame less as a combatant in that crucial engagement than as a messenger selected by *Andrew Jackson to deliver news of the victory to the president. Hampton covered the distance to Washington, D.C., in only ten days, using but one steed and a single pack horse. After the war Hampton assumed management of his father's plantation. In addition to breeding thoroughbred horses, he opened Millwood to numerous guests, among them George Bancroft and Henry Clay.

The colonel's son, Wade Hampton III, spent much of his boyhood here, learning to hunt and to ride. After graduating from South Carolina College, he married into the illustrious Preston family. Although he had studied the law, he decided upon a career as a planter instead, interesting himself chiefly in developing and expanding his plantations in Mississippi. During the 1850s, as a member of the state legislature, he began to question the economic viability of slavery. Although he regarded secession as constitutional, he believed that South Carolina's departure from the Union was inexpedient and without sufficient justification. Nevertheless, he wholeheartedly supported the Confederacy once war erupted. (See Marion Square, Charleston, South Carolina.)

¶ Richard Manning Burial Site, Trinity Episcopal Cathedral, 11 Sumter Street.

Among those buried in the churchyard here is South Carolina governor Richard Irvine Manning, the son of an Irish immigrant who had served under "Light-Horse Harry" Lee during the Revolution. Through his mother Manning was descended from Richard Richardson, the common ancestor for five other South Carolina chief executives.

In 1814 Manning married his cousin, Elizabeth Peyer Richardson, a woman who was variously niece, wife, sister, mother, aunt, and grandmother to the governors mentioned above. Manning, meanwhile, served as governor from 1824 to 1826 and had the honor of hosting the Marquis de Lafayette when the famous French general of the Revolutionary War visited South Carolina in 1825. During the nullification controversy with the federal government in the 1830s, Manning opposed the extreme states' rights position. In 1832 he was one of a handful of unionists elected to the state convention, where he voted against the Ordinance of Nullification.

§ Tours of church mid March-mid May and mid September-mid November, Monday-Friday 10-2; rest of the year, by appointment. Phone: 803-791-9146.

¶ State House, Gervais Street, between Assembly and Sumter streets.

• In a niche in the lobby of the capitol is a life-size plaster statue of *John C. Calhoun. The figure was used as the model for the marble statue of Calhoun which represents South Carolina in Statuary Hall in Washington, D.C.

• South Carolina's signers of the Constitution and the Declaration of Independence are honored by two bronze plaques on the first-floor staircase landings. Among the seven signers honored are Irishman Pierce Butler and Irish Americans Thomas Lynch Jr., Edward Rutledge, and John Rutledge.

§ Open Monday-Friday 9-12 and 1-4. Phone: 803-734-2430.

¶ The State House grounds contain several monuments associated with figures in Irish-American history.

• West of the capitol is a granite monument marking the site of the first state house built after the capital was moved from Charleston to Columbia. That earlier structure was designed by *James Hoban and was completed in 1791, although fire destroyed it in 1865.

• On the state house grounds is an equestrian statue of the Confederate general *Wade Hampton by F. W. Ruckstuhl.

• On the grounds facing Sumter Street is the Monument to South Carolina Partisans. Topped by a bronze figure, the granite shaft is adorned with bas-relief medallions of three of the state's most famous Revolutionary War leaders: Thomas Sumter, Francis Marion, and *Andrew Pickens. (See Old Stone Church, Pendleton, South Carolina.)

• On the southeast corner of the grounds is a bronze bust of J. Marion Sims, the "Father of Gynecology," by the Irish-American sculptor Edmond Quinn. (See the General Pemberton Statue, Vicksburg National Military Park, Mississippi.)

¶ Woodrow Wilson Boyhood Home, 1705 Hampton Street.

Constructed in the style of a Tuscan villa, this 1872 residence belonged to the *Reverend Joseph Ruggles Wilson and his wife, Jessie Woodrow. Here their teenage son, Thomas Woodrow Wilson, lived while his father was the minister at the First Presbyterian Church in the city and a professor at the Columbia Theological Seminary. One of the period pieces on display in the house is the bed in which "Tommy" – as people here called the future president – was born in Virginia.

§ Tours are offered at quarter past the hour, Tuesday-Saturday 10:15-13:15, Sunday 1:15-4:15. Closed major holidays. Fee. Phone: 803-252-1770.

GEORGETOWN

¶ Hampton Plantation State Park, 16 miles south on U.S. 17 and then 2 miles west on Rutledge Road to 1950 Rutledge Road.

The centerpiece of this former 1,300-acre rice plantation is a two-and-a-half-story mansion that once belonged to Frederick Rutledge and his wife. The nucleus of the mansion was a six-room farmhouse erected about 1730 by Rutledge's mother-in-law.

The mansion's Adam-style portico, which is framed with black cypress and contains yellow pine columns, is one of the best and earliest examples of its kind in North America. To highlight the mansion's architectural detail, restorers have left the structure unfurnished and some of the interior walls cut away.

Frederick Rutledge was born in South Carolina in 1768, the grandson of an Irish-born physician and the son of South Carolina's first governor after independence. (See the John Rutledge House, Charleston, South Carolina.) In 1797 he married Harriet Pinckney Horry, the daughter of Harriet Pinckney and Daniel Horry, the grandson of a French Huguenot who had come to America in 1686. The couple had eight children.

One of their descendants was Archibald Rutledge, the last resident of the plantation house. In 1931 Rutledge was named South Carolina's first poet laureate. His major prose works were *Tom and I on the Old Plantation*, *Old Plantation Days*, *Plantation Game Trails*, and *Home by the River*, each of which centers on the ancestral home.

§ Park open Thursday-Monday 9-6. Mansion open April 1-Labor Day, Thursday-Sunday 1-4; rest of the year, Saturday-Sunday 1-4. Fee for mansion. Phone: 803-546-9361 (Thursday-Monday 11-noon).

¶ **Hopsewee Plantation,** 12 miles south on U.S. 17.

Built about 1740, the house on this former rice plantation was the home of Thomas Lynch, a South Carolina delegate to the Continental Congress, and the birthplace of Thomas Lynch Jr., a signer of the Declaration of Independence. Constructed of black cypress, the house has a Georgian staircase, two central chimneys serving eight fireplaces, and a two-tiered piazza.

The Lynches were descendants of Jonack Lynch, who had emigrated from Connaught, Ireland, at the beginning of the eighteenth century. Thomas Lynch Jr. was educated at Eton and Cambridge, England, and studied law at the Middle Temple, although he soon abandoned its practice upon returning to South Carolina. After his marriage he assumed the responsibilities of a planter, including election to the first and second provincial congresses, the first state assembly, and the Second Continental Congress. While serving in the Revolution as a captain of the 1st South Carolina Regiment, he contracted bilious fever, which left him partially incapacitated for the rest of his life. Hoping to restore his health in the south of France, he and his wife sailed for the West Indies in 1779, but their ship was never heard of again.

§ Open March-October, Tuesday-Friday 10-4. Fee. Phone: 803-546-7891.

GREENVILLE

¶ **Greenville County Museum of Art,** 420 College Street.

In addition to the world's largest collection of works by Andrew Wyeth, the museum has paintings by Washington Allston, Jasper Johns, and the Irish Americans George Healy and Georgia O'Keeffe.

§ Open Tuesday-Saturday 10-5, Sunday 1-5. Closed major holidays. Phone: 803-271-7570.

GREENWOOD

¶ **Stony Point,** north at the junction of State 246 and State 39. Private.

Beginning in 1858, this was the home of David Wyatt Aiken, whose parents were both natives of County Antrim, Ireland. During the Civil

War he was wounded at Antietam and saw action at Gettysburg. After the war he became an advocate of the South's economic rehabilitation and discussed the issue in the *Rural Carolinian,* a monthly agricultural magazine of which he was eventually the editor and sole owner. In 1872 he was named a Southern delegate to the National Grange of the Patrons of Husbandry and later that year established the first grange in South Carolina. During the last decade of his life, he was a forceful spokesman for agricultural interests in the U.S. House of Representatives.

KINGS MOUNTAIN

¶ **Kings Mountain National Military Park,** south off Interstate 85.
     In October 1780 this 4,000-acre site was the scene of an engagement between Loyalists and American militia and frontiersmen from Virginia and the Carolinas. The object of the outnumbered Americans – many of them Irish and Scotch Irish – was Kings Mountain, a narrow ridge about 1,800 feet long. After repeated charges up the sixty-foot incline, the Americans captured the summit.
     • The American victory is commemorated by the U.S. Monument on the Battlefield Trail. The base of this eighty-three-foot obelisk is adorned with four bronze tablets by *Edmond Quinn. The tablets list the names of the American commanders during the battle as well as the names of the men who were killed here.
     Of the eight American colonels who held command during the engagement, four were of Irish birth or descent, William Campbell playing the most important role during the battle. Campbell's Scottish ancestors had immigrated to Ireland about 1600, living in their new home for several generations until John Campbell moved to America with his ten or twelve children a century and a quarter later. Although Campbell and his family first lived in Donegal, Pennsylvania, his son eventually moved to Augusta County, Virginia, where his grandson William was born in 1745.
     The American victory at Kings Mountain reversed a long string of demoralizing defeats for the Patriot cause in the South. By the fall of 1780 the British had captured Charleston, defeated the colonials at Camden, and almost extinguished the hope for independence in Georgia and South Carolina. Emboldened by this turn of events, Major Patrick Ferguson, a native Scot and an officer under Lord Cornwallis's command, roamed at will through the Carolinas. While carrying out his promise "to lay their country waste with fire and sword," he terrorized the Patriots, gave hope to the Tories, and enlisted Loyalist recruits.
     Hoping to take the offensive against Ferguson, a group of militia officers gathered a small army of backwoodsmen. From a nucleus of 400 Virginians under the command of Colonel Campbell, the patriot force grew to 1,800 under several militia officers. After Campbell was elected officer

of the day, a force of 900 Americans began their march to a ridge known as Kings Mountain, where Ferguson was ensconced with a force of 1,100 men, mostly Tory militiamen. "I hold a position on the King's Mountain that all the rebels out of hell cannot drive me from," boasted Ferguson.

Nevertheless, the American backwoodsmen launched a surprise attack against the sixty-foot ridge on October 7. (One of the attackers was David Crockett's father, whose Norman-French and Irish ancestors had migrated to America at the beginning of the eighteenth century.) Ferguson's men at first were able to repulse the colonials with repeated bayonet charges, but the hill was so steep that, as more Americans wended their way up its sides, his men had to expose themselves to the fire of their attackers. One of the colonials later summed up the British dilemma: "They overshot us altogether, scarcely touching a man, except those on horseback, while every rifle from below seemed to have the desired effect.... " Ferguson himself was finally shot down from his horse, his body riddled with eight bullets that broke both his arms and left "his hat and clothing ... literally shot to pieces." (An inscribed monument to Ferguson stands at the western edge of the ridge.)

During the repeated assaults, Campbell was in the thick of the fighting, exhausting two horses and leading his men on foot with cries of "Shout like hell and fight like devils." After the Tories surrendered, he helped put a stop to the indiscriminate shooting of prisoners by the victors. The Marquis de Lafayette later asserted that Campbell's services at Kings Mountain that day and at Guilford Courthouse six months later would "do his memory everlasting honor and insure him a high rank among the defenders of liberty in the American cause."

The victory of a spontaneously created Patriot army over one of the best Loyalist units in the British army seemed incredible. The Americans had lost only twenty-eight killed, while the Tories had suffered severe losses: 157 killed, 163 wounded, and 689 taken prisoner. When a French officer in Rochambeau's army heard about Campbell's victory, he commented, "We cannot conceive how regular troops and they superior in numbers allowed themselves to be beaten by peasants.... " In the long run the victory stiffened the spine of lukewarm patriots and helped stem the flow of recruits to the British armies. It also caused the British to abandon their offensive through the Carolinas and was what Sir Henry Clinton called "the first link of a chain of evils that followed each other in regular succession until they at last ended in the total loss of America."

§ Open Memorial Day-Labor Day, daily 9-6; rest of the year, 9-5. Closed January 1, Thanksgiving, and December 25. Phone: 803-936-7921.

KINGSTREE

This oldest inland settlement in South Carolina dates from 1732 when "poor

Calvinists" from Ireland sailed up the Black River to build their shelters around the "King's Tree" (marked with an arrow to set it aside as a mast for a royal ship). These Irish settlers named the surrounding area Williamsburg Township for William III, the Presbyterian king of England.

LANCASTER

¶ **Andrew Jackson State Park,** 8 miles north on U.S. 521.

Believed by *Andrew Jackson to be the site of his birth in 1767, this 360-acre park features a five-room reconstructed log house similar to Jackson's first house on the farm of his uncle, James Crawford. The park also contains a log schoolhouse, a museum of Waxhaw frontier furnishings and artifacts, and a life-size equestrian statue of Jackson called *Boy of the Waxhaws*.

Although there is still disagreement between South Carolina and her neighbor to the north about the birthplace of the seventh president, Jackson once wrote in a letter that he had been born on the James Crawford Plantation "about one mile from the Carolina road-crossing of Waxhaw creek." A five-foot granite monument marks the reputed site. To partisans who claim that "Old Hickory" was born in North Carolina, local historians point out that the putative birthplace in the Tarheel State was part of South Carolina at the time of his birth.

Even as a youngster the future hero of the battle of New Orleans demonstrated the principled stubbornness that became his trademark. On one occasion during the Revolutionary War, when a British officer tried to force him to polish the Redcoat's boots, the young patriot refused. For his insubordination Jackson received a saber lashing that left scars on his body the rest of his life.

§ Park open daily 9-9 early April-early October; 9-6 the rest of the year; Museum open Saturday-Sunday 1-5, other days by appointment. Phone: 803-285-3344.

¶ **Waxhaw Presbyterian Church,** 8 miles north off U.S. 521.

The original church here was built about 1755 and served the Scotch-Irish settlement in the Waxhaws. The family of Andrew Jackson was among the emigrants from northern Ireland who settled here, as were the Crawfords, Dunlaps, McCalls, and Pikenses. Jackson's father and brothers are buried in the adjacent cemetery.

According to tradition, Jackson's father was lost somewhere between his deathbed and the grave. After his demise in 1767 – so the story goes – a sled bearing his coffin was dragged from house to house during a two-day version of an Irish wake, at each stop attracting more mourners. When the members of the entourage reached the cemetery, however, they noticed that the coffin was missing, apparently knocked off the sled by drooping tree limbs somewhere along the cortege route. When the missing coffin was found, it was buried with due decorum.

McCONNELLS

¶ **Historic Brattonsville,** 4 miles east on State 322 and Brattonsville Road.

This historic village comprises twenty-four restored structures, among them a pioneer cabin, a girls' academy, the Scotch-Irish McConnell House, and three residences owned by various members of the Bratton family. The buildings are furnished to illustrate the way of life experienced in the Piedmont area during the late eighteenth and mid-nineteenth centuries.

The oldest Bratton house is a log structure with clapboard siding and probably dates from the early 1770s. It was the home of William Bratton, one of four brothers who emigrated from Ireland in 1733. During the French and Indian War, he was a member of Braddock's ill-fated command. Bratton lived here with his wife, Martha, and their eight children.

The house was the scene of an ugly incident when plundering Tories and British regulars swarmed into the area in July 1780. Because Bratton was away at the time, the Tories demanded that his wife reveal his whereabouts and persuade him to join their cause. When Mrs. Bratton refused to comply with either demand, a British soldier attacked her, pinning her head to the porch rail with a reaping hook over her neck. She was released, however, when a more gentlemanly officer came to her rescue. The next day, when the British and their allies were defeated by a small band of Patriots, the "gentlemanly officer" was among those captured. His life was saved when Mrs. Bratton interceded on his behalf.

The Brattons' son Dr. John Simpson Bratton (1789-1843) significantly increased the family acreage as well as its slave population and production of cotton, grains, and livestock. The two-story colonnaded structure which he constructed is a typical antebellum plantation residence. The third Bratton house belonged to Dr. Bratton's son John and dates from the 1850s.

§ Open from the first Sunday in March to the Sunday before Thanksgiving, Tuesday-Thursday 10-4, Saturday-Sunday 2-5. Open for the Christmas Tour the first Friday-Sunday in December, Friday-Saturday 6:30-9, Sunday 3-7. Fee. Phone: 803-684-2327.

PENDLETON

¶ **Old Stone Church,** Tiger Boulevard (U.S. 76).

Completed in 1802 for the Hopewell Presbyterian congregation, the church was designed and built by John Rusk, an Irish stonemason who had settled on land belonging to *John C. Calhoun, the future senator and champion of states' rights. (Rusk's son, Thomas Jefferson Rusk, was a signer of the Texas declaration of independence from Mexico and one of the first U.S. senators from Texas.) The elder Rusk is buried in the church cemetery.

One of the founders and elders of this church was Andrew Pickens, whose Huguenot ancestors had emigrated from France to Ireland in the last quarter of the seventeenth century. His Irish-born parents subsequently immigrated to Pennsylvania, where their son was born in 1739. By the early 1750s the family had moved to South Carolina, and it was there that Pickens married into the Calhoun family, taking as his wife a first cousin of the famous congressional leader. Pickens took up farming and was a justice of the peace on the eve of the Revolution. Perhaps because of his strict Presbyterian upbringing, he never laughed and seldom smiled and was so prudent in his speech that "he would first take the words out of his mouth, between his fingers, and examine them before he uttered them."

At the outbreak of the Revolution, Pickens threw in his lot with the Patriot cause, eventually becoming with Marion and Sumter one of its three great leaders in the colony. Many of his fellow Scotch-Irish parishioners followed him into the battles of Ninety Six, Cowpens, Eutaw Springs, and Kettle Creek. His victory at the last site is regarded as the most serious defeat which the Loyalists ever suffered in South Carolina. After Charleston surrendered to the British in 1780, Pickens and his 300 men returned home on parole, although he returned to the field after the en-

Old Stone Church, the center of Pendelton's Scotch-Irish community.

emy plundered his plantation. For his subsequent efforts at Cowpens, he was promoted to brigadier general. (See Spartanburg, South Carolina.) In the last months of the Revolution, he raised a regiment that was compensated with plunder and slaves seized from Loyalists.

His tombstone in the church cemetery here is engraved with the following tribute: "General Andrew Pickens was born 13th, September, 1739, and died 11th August 1817. He was a Christian, a Patriot and Soldier. His character and action were incorporated with the history of his country. Filial affection and respect raises this stone to his memory." Pickens' son Andrew – who served as governor of the state from 1816 to 1818 – is also buried here.

¶ **Pickens House,** on the shore of Lake Hartwell on State 149. Private.

Known as "Hopewell" and "Cherry Place," this two-story white frame house was the home of Andrew Pickens, the famous Revolutionary War general. For fifteen years after the conflict, he was empowered by Congress to deal with various Indian tribes and to negotiate treaties with them. After his election to the state legislature in 1782, he raised and commanded a company of 500 men to subdue the warring Cherokee. Three years later he negotiated a treaty by which several tribes surrendered claim to western North Carolina, approximately one third of Georgia and Tennessee, and several counties in South Carolina. As many as thirty-seven chiefs and a thousand Indians attended the ten-day conference on Pickens' property at Hopewell. The treaty also provided for the release of Anna Calhoun, a member of the famous South Carolina family and a former prisoner of the Indians. The tree under which the treaty was signed at Hopewell stood for a century after the peace conference. Today a historical marker indicates the site of the "Treaty Oak."

¶ To the northwest of Pendleton, the town of Tamassee has two sites associated with Andrew Pickens. A small stone on State 95 (about a mile from its junction with State 375) marks the location of "Red House," the residence which he built on Tamassee Creek. A second stone marks Pickens' victory over the Cherokee in July 1779. While the militia from this region were at the eastern end of the colony supporting the Patriot military operation, the Cherokee took advantage of the situation to attack settlements on the frontier. When Colonel Pickens and his militia returned, they launched a punitive expedition against the marauders. Although the colonials were at first surrounded by the Cherokee, Pickens saved his troops by setting fire to a cane brake, a diversion that caused loud popping sounds when the joints of cane exploded from the heat. Thinking that the noise was the gunfire of reinforcements, the Cherokee fled.

¶ **St. Paul's Episcopal Church,** Queen's Street.

The register of those interred in the church graveyard includes Floride

Colhoun, the daughter of John Ewing Colhoun (who spelled his surname with an "o" instead of an "a"). She was the cousin and wife of *John C. Calhoun. Most of the Calhouns' children are buried here also, including Anna Maria Calhoun and her husband, Thomas Clemson.

SPARTANBURG

¶ **Cowpens National Battlefield,** 18 miles northeast and 0.25 mile east of the junction of State 11 and State 110.

This 845-acre site preserves the battlefield on which Patriot troops under General Daniel Morgan defeated a more experienced British force under Lieutenant Colonel Banastre Tarleton in January 1781. The major battlefield sites are marked along a three-mile auto tour and a 1.5-mile walking tour. The visitor center offers a slide presentation about the battle and contains a lighted map outlining the troop movements that day.

At the time of the engagement, the Americans were outnumbered by British dragoons and infantry. The Patriots counted among their ranks regular army troops from Delaware and Maryland as well as militia units from Georgia, Virginia, and the Carolinas. Among the Carolinians was a crack corps of riflemen commanded by Andrew Pickens, a native of northern Ireland who later handed the Loyalists in South Carolina their most serious defeat.

Before the battle in the cowpens pasture, Morgan divided his troops into three consecutive lines. The first two – including Pickens' riflemen – were to meet and slow the enemy's advance before finally falling back, thereby forcing the British to engage the more experienced troops under Morgan himself. Prior to the battle Pickens gave precise orders to his men: "Do not shoot until the enemy is within thirty paces, then aim low and fire in relays, picking off the officers first; every third man fire, while the others hold their fire in reserve."

When the British attacked the American position, Pickens waited until Tarleton's men were within fifty yards of his line before ordering his men to fire. The Carolina riflemen held their ground and continued to fire into the enemy's ranks, but when the British charged with bayonets, Pickens gave the order to withdraw. In turn, other American units began to fall back until they learned that Pickens' men had inflicted such casualties on the enemy's officers that the British right flank was exposed and in a state of confusion. In the meantime Pickens had reestablished his broken line and led his men to Tarleton's left, where the British advance threatened to outflank the Maryland-Virginia troops, Morgan's third line of defense. With their steady fire Pickens' militia unit was able to stop the enemy onslaught.

The four-hour morning battle was a complete American victory, resulting in the loss of 800 British soldiers, about 75 percent of Tarleton's force. The victory effectively deprived General Charles Cornwallis of a third of his army.

§ Battlefield and visitor center open daily 9-5. Closed January 1, Thanksgiving, and December 25. Phone: 803-461-2828.

¶ **Walnut Grove Plantation,** 9 miles south on U.S. 221 to Still House Road and then to 1200 Otts Shoals Road.

The ancestral home of the Moore family lies on land granted by the royal governor to Charles Moore in 1763. In addition to the main house, the plantation contains the family's original log cabin, a kitchen, a smokehouse, a blacksmith's forge, a school, a doctor's office, and barns. The family burial ground is also on the property. The walnut trees that give their name to the plantation were planted by Moore's daughter about 1800.

Charles Moore, who may have been born in Ireland, had first come to this area in the company of fourteen other Scotch-Irish Presbyterian families from Pennsylvania. Subsequent land grants brought his holdings to 3,000 acres. He and his wife, Mary, had ten children, the first of whom was Margaret Catherine (Kate) Moore, born in 1752 most likely in North Carolina, although family traditions claim both Ireland and Pennsylvania as her birthplace. At age fifteen she married Andrew Barry, the first physician in the county and a captain and sharpshooter in *General Andrew Pickens' brigade.

Walnut Grove plantation house.

During the Revolution Kate was a volunteer scout and the local Paul Revere, riding through the neighborhood announcing impending Tory attacks. On one occasion, when Tories came to her house demanding to know the whereabouts of her husband's unit, she refused to give them any information. For her obstinacy she was struck three times with a leash. On another occasion, after hearing a Tory raiding party across the river from Walnut Grove, she rounded up her husband's troops and sent them off to join General Daniel Morgan. (Before mounting her steed, however, she took care that her young daughter would not wander away from home in her absence. She tied the little girl to a bedpost.) For her part in the ensuing Tory defeat, Kate received the title "Heroine of the Battle of Cowpens."

• On the property is a reconstruction of Dr. Andrew Barry Moore's office. Moore, who was born in 1771, four years after his sister Kate's marriage to Andrew Barry, was apparently named for his brother-in-law. The office displays many early medical instruments as well as medical records from Dr. Moore's forty-eight-year practice.

• Special signs in the family cemetery point out the graves of Charles and Mary Moore and those of three of their children: Kate Moore Barry, Dr. Andrew Barry Moore, and General Thomas Moore. The last-named child had fought at the battle of Cowpens when he was only seventeen and later represented this district in Congress almost continuously from 1800 to 1820. During the War of 1812 he was charged with defending the city of Charleston.

§ Open April-October 31, Tuesday-Saturday 11-5, Sunday 2-5; rest of the year, Sunday 2-5. Closed holidays. Fee. Phone: 803-576-6546.

SOUTH DAKOTA

ABERDEEN

¶ Hamlin Garland Homestead Site, north on U.S. 281 and then east on County 11.

A twelve-ton boulder marks the site of the homestead where Hamlin Garland began his career as an author and where he lived intermittently from 1881 to 1884.

Garland, whose maternal grandfather (Hugh McClintock) was of Scotch-Irish descent, was early attracted to the prospect of writing fiction which mirrored the harsh conditions experienced by his parents and other farmers in this part of the country. His first stories in this vein were published in 1891 under the title *Main Travelled Roads*, praised by William Dean Howells as an advance in American literary realism. Although Garland subsequently attempted to wed realism in fiction to the advocacy of social and economic reform, his four novels in this genre lacked convincing characterization and eventually alienated many readers because of their emphasis on the grimmer side of life.

Garland finally achieved a measure of the recognition he sought, however, with the publication in 1917 of *A Son of the Middle Border*, an autobiographical account of his youth on which he had worked for the previous fifteen years. In the book Garland explained that his desire to pursue a writing career had emerged while he was stacking wheat in a field next to the homestead. The farm featured prominently in his subsequent poem "The Color in the Wheat." In 1921 he received the Pulitzer Prize for *A Daughter of the Middle Border*, judged that year's best biography.

BROOKINGS

¶ The Coughlin Campanile, South Dakota State University.

Known locally as the "Singing Silo" because of its chimes, the 165-foot-high Coughlin Campanile dominates not only the campus but the entire community. The unusual structure was a gift to the school from *Charles Coughlin, a farm boy from Carthage, South Dakota, who graduated from the college in 1910 and went on to become a prominent Milwaukee manufacturer. The tower, which was erected in 1930 to mark the twentieth anniversary of Coughlin's graduation, measures thirty feet square at the base. Built at a cost of approximately $75,000, it is constructed of white limestone, red brick, and concrete. The balcony floor, which visitors can reach by climbing 180 steps, is 112 feet above the ground.

CANTON

ℐ Newton Hills State Park.

Local tradition claims that this area was a frequent hideout for out-laws, including the *James brothers after their robbery of a bank in Northfield, Minnesota, in 1876. Here Frank and Jesse reputedly picked up fresh horses, after exhausting the mounts they had stolen from Nils Nelson in Minnehaha County. (See Kearney, Missouri.)

DEADWOOD

ℐ Number 10 Saloon, 657 Main Street.

This is a replica of the barroom in which *James "Wild Bill" Hickok was shot by Jack McCall while playing cards on August 2, 1876.

Hickok had come to Deadwood earlier that summer in search of gold, but the lawless element in town feared that they would be driven out if he was appointed marshal. After McCall was promised $300 for Hickok's death, the assassin sought out his victim and found him at the poker table in the Number 10 Saloon, his back to the open door. McCall shot Hickok in the head. (The combination of aces and eights in Hickok's hands gave rise to the phrase "dead man's hand.")

Although the murderer was apprehended soon after fleeing the scene, he was acquitted and later bragged of the killing. While living in Wyo-ming, however, he was arrested by a U.S. marshal and tried in the district court in Yankton. The court dismissed his claim of double jeopardy on the ground that the miners' court in Deadwood had been incompetent to hear the original case. In short order McCall was convicted and hanged.

• Between the end of May and the end of August the "Trial of Jack McCall" is staged in Old Towne Hall on Lee Street, Monday-Saturday and holidays at 8 p.m. Fee. Reservations are recommended. Phone: 605-578-3583 or 578-2510.

ℐ Theodore Roosevelt Monument, at the summit of Mt. Roosevelt, 4.5 miles west off U.S. 85.

A thirty-five-foot circular tower honors *President Theodore Roosevelt, whose love for the surrounding Black Hills was the subject of some of his best prose. The tower bears a bronze tablet inscribed "In Memory of Theodore Roosevelt 'The American.'" The monument was conceived by Seth Bullock, a close friend of the president and a captain in his famous Rough Riders. The tower was erected in 1919 by the Society of Black Hills Pioneers.

ℐ "Wild Bill" Hickok Burial Site, Mt. Moriah ("Boot Hill") Cemetery, 5 blocks from town.

A life-size statue marks the grave of *James "Wild Bill" Hickok, the "Prince of Pistoleers." The adjoining grave is that of Calamity Jane (Canary) Burke, who claimed that she was Hickok's secret wife.

¶ **"Wild Bill" Hickok Bust,** on Sherman Street.

KEYSTONE

¶ **Mount Rushmore National Memorial,** 2 miles southwest via U.S. 16A and State 244.

The largest sculpture undertaken since the time of the ancient Egyptians, the memorial on the side of 6,000-foot Mount Rushmore commemorates the role of four U.S. presidents in some of the nation's major achievements: George Washington (the creation of the nation), Thomas Jefferson (the Declaration of Independence and the Louisiana Purchase), Abraham Lincoln (the preservation of the Union), and *Theodore Roosevelt (the nation's expansion and preservation of its natural resources).

In size, the gigantic faces are proportional to men standing 465 feet tall: Washington's face is sixty feet in length, while Lincoln's forehead is seventeen feet high. Beginning in 1930, a staff of thirty-six men – of whom twenty operated the carving drills – worked under the direction of the famous sculptor Gutzon Borglum. As the features of Jefferson's face took shape, a deep fissure appeared in the rock, a development that caused the workers to blast out the third president's face and recarve it on Washington's left and deeper into the mountain side. When Borglum died in 1941, Roosevelt's face was just emerging from the rock. The sculptor's son, Lincoln, assumed direction of the huge project and saw it through to completion.

§ The memorial and the visitor center are open Memorial Day-Labor Day, daily 8 a.m.-10 p.m.; rest of the year, daily 10-5. Phone: 605-574-2523.

¶ **Parade of Presidents Wax Museum,** 0.25 mile southwest on U.S. 16A.

In addition to life-size figures of the U.S. presidents, this museum near Mount Rushmore features representations of many statesmen and First Ladies as well.

§ Open June-August, daily 9-7; May and September, daily 9-5. Fee. Phone: 605-666-4455.

LEAD

¶ **Homestake Gold Mine,** on U.S. 14A/85.

The Homestake Mine is the largest gold mine in the United States and the largest producer of gold in the Western Hemisphere. The town of Lead (pronounced "Leed") was named for the mine's "lead" (vein or lode). Visitors can view an audiovisual presentation about the techniques used in mining and refining gold.

In 1877 the Homestake Mine was purchased by *George Hearst and a group of investors who bought it for $77,000. The success of the resulting Homestake Mining Company was the basis of the family fortune inherited by Hearst's son, William Randolph Hearst, the famous newspaper and magazine publisher. Between 1876 and 1970 the mine produced almost 31 million ounces of gold, extracted from 107 million tons of ore. The mine was the source of most of the $500 million produced in the Black Hills since 1875. (See Berkeley, California.)

§ Open June-August, Monday-Friday 8-5, Saturday-Sunday 10-5; rest of the year, Monday-Friday 8-4. Closed major holidays. Fee. Phone: 605-584-3110.

MITCHELL

¶ Friends of the Middle Border Museum, 1311 South Duff Street.

This museum of upper-Midwestern history and culture was founded in 1939 by a group of incorporators that included the authors *Hamlin Garland and Steward Edward White, the historian James Truslow Adams, the educational philosopher John Dewey, the sculptor Gutzon Borglum, and Secretary of Agriculture Clinton Anderson. The museum takes its name from the "middle border" country that was the subject of Garland's books. (See Aberdeen, South Dakota.)

Today the museum includes the Case Art Gallery, the American Indian Gallery, several restored late nineteenth- and early twentieth-century buildings, and other artifacts of pioneer life.

§ Open June-August, Monday-Saturday 8-6, Sunday 10-6; May and September, Monday-Friday 9-5, Saturday-Sunday 1-5; rest of the year, by appointment. Fee. Phone: 605-996-2122.

PIERRE

¶ Fort Sully Site, Farm Island State Park, 3 miles east on State 34.

Only a marker stands to remind visitors of the fort where Fanny Wiggins Kelly escaped to freedom after being held in captivity by the Sioux for six months in 1864.

Born in Ontario, Canada, Fanny Wiggins was the second daughter of James Wiggins and his Irish-born wife. In July 1864 Fanny and her husband, Josiah Kelly, were among the eleven members of a wagon train on its way from Kansas to Idaho Territory. About eighty miles beyond Fort Laramie, however, the party was stopped by 250 mounted Ogala Sioux. After killing all but two of the men, the Indians took the two women and the two children in the party as captives. Fanny eventually became the property and servant of Chief Ottawa and was lodged with his six wives and three sisters. Although the nineteen-year-old often suffered from hunger and was sometimes pinched black and blue by her captors, she was generally well treated. In a remarkably short time she became fluent in the Sioux language and even nursed the tribe's wounded warriors.

A long-shot opportunity to escape presented itself when Fanny was borrowed by a band of Blackfeet Sioux. These Indians hoped to use her in a ruse to gain entrance to Fort Sully in order to overcome the garrison. When Fanny heard of this planned attack, she sent a warning to the fort via an Indian who had shown some affection for her. The message apparently served its purpose, because when more than 1,000 Sioux approached the fort on December 12, the Americans wisely opened the gates only long enough to admit the leading chiefs and Fanny, their hostage.

The young woman gradually regained her strength and within two months was reunited with her husband, one of the two men who survived the initial Indian raid. When her husband died two years later, she sought compensation for her losses from the government. Congress obliged by awarding her $5,000 for her services in saving the garrison at Fort Sully. In 1871 she published an account of her captivity, a work which provided much information about the beliefs and customs of the Sioux and which remained popular with readers for the next two decades.

STURGIS

¶ Fort Meade Cavalry Museum, 2 miles east on State 34.

The museum features a film and exhibits on Fort Meade, the cavalry post which was laid out here in 1878 to prevent conflict between local prospectors and the Cheyenne and Lakota Indians. The site was selected by *General Philip Sheridan, who pointed out where he wanted each building erected by galloping across the prairie. The fort was named in honor of *General George Gordon Meade, the Union commander at the battle of Gettysburg. Some of the fort's original buildings still stand on the site.

§ Open Memorial Day weekend through Labor Day, daily 8-7; May 1 to day before Memorial Day weekend and day after Labor Day to September 30, 9-5; rest of the year, by appointment. Fee. Phone: 605-347-9822.

WALL

¶ Wild West Historical Wax Museum, Main Street (across from Wall Drug Store).

Among the famous figures associated with the "Wild West" on display here are Wyatt Earp, Clint Eastwood, and Irish Americans James "Wild Bill" Hickok, Jesse James, and John Wayne.

§ Open May-October, daily 8 a.m.-9 p.m. Fee. Phone: 605-279-2915.

TENNESSEE

BOLIVAR

❡ **Polk Cemetery,** Union Street.

Among those buried here is *Colonel Ezekiel Polk, the grandfather of President James K. Polk. (See Pineville, North Carolina.) Three years before he died, the colonel wrote his epitaph, an unusual anticlerical warning against the entanglement of politics and religion:

Here lies the dust of old E. P. / One instance of mortality,
Pennsylvania born, Car'lina bred; / In Tennessee died on his bed,
His youthful years he spent in pleasure, / His later years in
      gathering treasure.
From superstitions liv'd quite free, / And practiced strict morality.
To holy cheats was never willing, / To give one solitary shilling;
He can foresee and foreseeing. / He equals most in being.
That church and state will join their pow'r, / And misery on this
      country show'r,
And Methodists with their camp bawling / Will be the cause
      of this down falling;
An era not destined to see, / It waits for poor posterity;
First fruits and tenths are odious things, / So are bishops, priests
      and kings.

Portions of this epitaph were used against Polk's grandson during the latter's presidential campaign in 1845.

CHATTANOOGA

❡ **Alexander Stewart Monument,** Hamilton County Courthouse, Fountain Square Plaza, Georgia Avenue.

Erected by the United Daughters of the Confederacy, this memorial statue honors *Lieutenant General Alexander Peter Stewart.

Of Scotch-Irish ancestry, Stewart was born in Tennessee in 1821. After his graduation from the U.S. Military Academy in 1842, he was commissioned second lieutenant in the 3rd Artillery. For about a year he was an assistant professor of mathematics at the academy before resigning to teach mathematics and natural and experimental philosophy at Cumberland and Nashville universities.

Although he had voted against secession, Stewart joined the Confederate army as a major when war finally came. During the conflict, he participated in numerous engagements, among them the battles of Shiloh and Chattanooga and Chickamauga. At the end of the war, he was in North Carolina, in command of the Army of the Tennessee.

After the Confederate defeat, Stewart returned to Cumberland University, but in 1874 he was chosen chancellor of the University of Mississippi. During his twelve-year tenure there, he was privately referred to as "Old Straight," a nickname first used by his soldiers because of his military bearing and impartial adherence to regulations. When Congress created the Chickamauga and Chattanooga National Military Park in 1890, Stewart was selected by President Harrison as the Confederate on the three-member commission charged with transforming the site into a national memorial. Even though he was in his early seventies at the time, the former professor moved to the site and supervised the creation of roads and the placement of monuments.

COLUMBIA

¶ **James K. Polk Ancestral Home,** 301 West 7th Street (U.S. 43).

Constructed in 1816 by *Samuel Polk, the father of President James K. Polk, this brick structure was where the future president spent his boyhood from 1820 to 1824. The house contains the president's library and furnishings from his other residences. One of the items is a circular marble table inlaid with an eagle and thirty white stars.

• Adjacent to the house is an almost identical one built by Samuel Polk for his daughters. Now a museum, it features exhibits and a film on the life and career of James K. Polk.

§ Both houses are open April-October, Monday-Saturday 9-5, Sunday 1-5; rest of the year, Monday-Saturday 9-4, Sunday 1-5. Closed January 1, Thanksgiving, and December 25. Fee. Phone: 615-388-2354.

¶ **James K. Polk Home,** 318 West 7th Street (U.S. 43). Private.

This two-story residence was built by *James K. Polk in the 1820s. Here he entertained *Andrew Jackson and Martin Van Buren during his successful presidential campaign of 1845.

¶ **Rattle and Snap,** south on State 43. Private.

This two-story Greek Revival mansion was constructed in 1845 by George Polk, whose brother Leonidas Polk was a bishop in the Episcopal Church and a Confederate general during the Civil War. The property on which the house was built originally belonged to Colonel William Polk, who reputedly won the 5,000-acre estate while playing a game of "beans" with the governor of North Carolina. The members of this Polk family were of the same Scotch-Irish stock as their collateral relative President James K. Polk.

¶ **St. John's Episcopal Church,** west on U.S. 43.

This Greek Revival plantation church was constructed in 1841 by Bishop Leonidas Polk and his younger brother, George Polk. The bricks for the church were made by the Polk family slaves. The churchyard contains the graves of various members of the Scotch-Irish Polk family. (See Trinity Church, New Orleans, Louisiana.)

DAYTON

¶ Hiwassee Island.

The island contains mounds and village sites of a band of about 300 Cherokee Indians who lived here in the nineteenth century. It was to this island that young *Sam Houston, tiring of life in Maryville, fled in 1809. For three years he lived with the Indians, learning their language, hunting with them, and developing an appreciation for their way of life. The Indians called him "The Raven" and assigned him the eagle as his totem or guardian. His experiences with the tribe caused him to believe that the American settlers were to blame for much of the conflict between the two races on the frontier. He eventually became the adopted son of Chief Oo-loo-te-ka ("He Who Puts the Drum Away," meaning "Peace lover").

¶ Rhea County Courthouse and Museum, North Market Street.

This courthouse preserves the courtroom where in July 1925 *William Jennings Bryan successfully prosecuted John Scopes, the high school teacher accused of violating a Tennessee statute forbidding the teaching of biological evolution. The courtroom has been restored to its 1925 appearance, and a museum displays memorabilia connected with the trial.

Here Bryan proclaimed his belief in the literal interpretation of the Bible against the ridicule of the defense attorney, Clarence Darrow. The famous "monkey trial" daily attracted 10,000 spectators and 200 reporters. Bryan, who had unsuccessfully run for president three times, died here just five days after the trial.

§ Open Monday-Thursday 8-4, Friday 8-5:30. Closed holidays. Phone: 615-775-7801.

DOVER

¶ Fort Donelson National Battlefield, on U.S. 79, 1.5 miles west of the Cumberland Bridge.

This 554-acre park is the site of the first major Union victory during the Civil War. The original fort and its defenses were constructed in the summer of 1861 by Randal William McGavock and the members of his 10th Tennessee Volunteer Infantry Regiment, a mostly Irish unit. According to Pat Griffin, the regiment's drummer, McGavock's men called the redheaded officer "God's own gentleman." Griffin himself remembered the colonel as "a clean, strong, brave man, a noble soldier, a loyal friend," who worked hard and overlooked the men's off-duty diversions.

By the middle of February 1862, *General Ulysses S. Grant had assembled 27,000 men at this point along the Tennessee River. During initial skirmishes, the 10th Tennessee was stationed on the Confederate right, in an area along the defenses known, oddly enough, as Erin Hollow. (The 10th, popularly called the "Sons of Erin," boasted a green company flag emblazoned with the motto, "Sons of Erin, Go Where Glory Waits You.") When Union troops directed a full-blown attack against this position, the Irish regiment was able to drive them back, at the same time inflicting heavy casualties. Despite this cause for celebration, most of the Confederate forces feared that they would be encircled and cut off from escape. As a result, Confederate officers ordered the retreat of about 2,000 troops, a number that appeared minor compared to the 13,000 men who were captured the next day when Grant demanded immediate and unconditional surrender. Grant's victory virtually delivered Kentucky and western Tennessee into the Union column.

Randal McGavock was the grandson of James McGavock, an immigrant from County Antrim, Ireland, who had sailed from Londonderry to Philadelphia in the middle of the eighteenth century. While attending Columbia College (now the University of Tennessee), the young Randal was a member of the debate team. (He once had to defend the resolution that foreign immigration to the United States should be prohibited.) After his graduation in 1844, he entered Harvard Law School, where he was honored with the title of Chief Marshal. He served in this capacity during the procession to Faneuil Hall when the president of Harvard delivered his eulogy on John Quincy Adams.

While touring Europe in the early 1850s, McGavock visited the land of his ancestors. Although he was unable to find any members of the McGavock clan in northern Ireland, his visit to the troubled island raised his consciousness as an Irish American. In his famous journal of his European travels, he described Ireland as the "land of potatoes and poverty" and contrasted the generally impoverished south with more prosperous Ulster, the birthplace of his ancestors. About County Cork he wrote that "the dwellings of the peasantry are miserable hovels, far inferior in point of comfort and cleanliness to our negro cabins." His most depressing descriptions, though, were of Cork city, whose "streets are narrow and filthy, the houses look old and dilapidated, and the population the worst I ever saw. The streets are filled with men, women, and children almost in a state of nudity – and the most filthy beings in the world." While in Killarney he recorded that he had met "four stout Irish boys, all of whom told me they were going to America, which seems to be like the Promised Land to all Irishmen." In the north, though, he saw "comparatively no beggary or misery," a circumstance which he attributed to the Scottish ancestry of many inhabitants of that part of Ireland. Although he described Belfast as the most attractive place in Ireland (clean, decent, and blessed with wide streets), he advised visitors to the Giants' Causeway "to take a stick or horsewhip along to keep off the swarms of human insects that infest the region about."

After returning to Nashville, McGavock settled down to the routine of domestic life. His marriage to Seraphine Deery, a descendant of an immigrant from County Down, was followed by increasing involvement with politics. Although he worked for the election of *President James Buchanan, he was disappointed in his quest for a foreign post in Europe. McGavock was popular with the city's new immigrants, especially the Irish who had flocked to the city to work on the region's railroads and who dubbed him a son of Erin. He helped the Irish through the naturalization process and encouraged them to exercise their new franchise, a right which redounded to his benefit when he decided to run for mayor in 1858. During one particular campaign rally, he was introduced by a long-winded speaker who carried on about McGavock's qualifications and achievements, even pointing out that in Italy McGavock had been taken for Christ. Suddenly a drunken supporter of McGavock's opponent cried out, "If this man be the Christ, let him be crucified on election day." McGavock was handily elected.

By 1860 McGavock had achieved considerable financial and political standing. Besides owning real estate valued at $50,000 and personal property worth $20,000, he was a member of the state Democratic central committee. In this capacity he attended the disastrous Democratic national convention at Charleston that year and witnessed the breakup of the party over the slavery issue. He ultimately supported John Breckenridge, the most strongly pro-slavery candidate in the presidential race. With the election of Lincoln, McGavock openly called for a state convention to consider secession, and with the fall of Fort Sumter he resolved to take up arms against the United States.

In preparing to defend the state against an expected Union advance, McGavock helped recruit young Irish workers in Nashville for the 10th Tennessee Volunteers, his so-called "Sons of Erin Company." Although he and his men repulsed a federal attack at Fort Donelson, the battle was a disastrous Confederate defeat. While later imprisoned at Fort Warren in Boston Harbor, he learned that Nashville had been captured by federal troops and that his beloved green company flag had been delivered as a trophy to the 69th New York Regiment, the North's most famous Irish unit. McGavock was later killed while leading a charge of his 400 men at the battle of Raymond, where he was shot in the left breast, a casualty of the eight bullets that ripped through his coat.

§ Visitor center open daily 8-4:30. Closed December 25. Phone: 615-232-5706.

FRANKLIN

℘ Carnton Plantation House and Confederate Cemetery.

This two-and-a-half-story brick house was completed in 1824 by Randal McGavock, who named his 1,000-acre estate after his family's ancestral home in County Antrim, Ireland. McGavock was the great-uncle of the commander of the 10th Tennessee Volunteers during the battle of Fort Donelson. (See above entry.)

Prior to the battle of Franklin in November 1864, Confederate troops gathered on McGavock's property, and after the disastrous Confederate defeat the house was crowded with dead and wounded. Among the dead were five Confederate generals, including Patrick Cleburne and John Adams. (Cleburne was a native of County Cork, Ireland, while Adams was the son of immigrants from Ulster.) About two years after the battle, McGavock set aside two acres next to his family burial plot as a Confederate cemetery, where 1,500 soldiers were reinterred. (See Helena, Arkansas.)

McGavock was the son of an Irish immigrant who about 1750 had sailed from Londonderry to Philadelphia, where he initially worked as a ditch-digger. The younger McGavock was educated in Carlisle, Pennsylvania, and came to Tennessee in 1796. After serving clerkships in various state courts (including the Supreme Court of Errors and Appeals), he was elected mayor of Nashville in 1824.

§ Take Interstate 65 exit 65, go 1.5 miles west to Mack Hatcher Bypass, and then drive 1.25 miles south to State 431. Open April-October, Monday-Saturday 9-5, Sunday and holidays 1-5; rest of the year, Monday-Saturday 1-4, Sunday and holidays 1-4. Closed January 1, Thanksgiving, and December 25. Fee. Phone: 615-794-0903.

℘ Carter House, on U.S. 31.

Now a Civil War museum, this 1830 brick farmhouse features exhibits and a videotape about the battle of Franklin, where the Irish-born Confederate generals Patrick Cleburne and John Adams were killed. (See above entry.)

§ Open Monday-Saturday 9-4, Sunday 1-4 (until 5 during daylight savings time). Closed major holidays. Fee. Phone: 615-791-1861.

℘ Eaton House, 125 Third Avenue North. Private.

This was the home of John Eaton and his wife, Peggy O'Neale Eaton, the daughter of an Irish tavern keeper in Washington, D.C.

Eaton, who was secretary of war under *President Andrew Jackson, became the object of a power play by *John C. Calhoun, who hoped to cause Eaton's resignation. When rumors arose that Eaton and his wife had been living together prior to her husband's death, the wives of some of Jackson's cabinet members refused her entry into Washington's social life and boycotted functions which she attended. Although one diarist described Mrs. Eaton as "ambitious, violent, malignant, yet silly," Jackson stood by her and her husband, threatening to dismiss any cabinet member whose wife continued to ostracize the woman. Despite Jackson's support Eaton ultimately resigned. Following her husband's death in 1856, Mrs. Eaton married an Italian dancing master, who soon defrauded her of her property and eloped with her granddaughter.

¶ **Maury House Marker,** on U.S. 431, on the north edge of town.

A historical marker notes that the home of *Matthew Fontaine Maury, the famous oceanographer, was located a mile and a half west. (See Virginia Military Institute, Lexington, Virginia.)

GATLINBURG

¶ **John Reagan Birthplace Marker,** on U.S. 441.

The marker indicates that *John Reagan, the postmaster general of the Confederacy, was born near here in October 1818. (See Palestine, Texas.)

GALLATIN

¶ **Trousdale Place,** east on U.S. 25E to 183 West Main Street.

This two-story brick structure was the home of William Trousdale, a veteran of four wars and the governor of Tennessee from 1849 to 1851.

The son of Presbyterian parents of Scotch-Irish descent, Trousdale was born in Orange County, North Carolina, in 1790. Six years later, his father moved the family to Tennessee, where the son joined the state militia at the start of the Creek War in 1813. During the nation's second conflict with Britain, he helped *Andrew Jackson capture Pensacola from Britain's Spanish allies. Although Jackson's troops succeeded in gaining control of the town, they continued to face relentless bombardment from the Spanish garrison at the fort. So formidable was the barrage that, when Jackson called for volunteers to storm the fortress, his men uncharacteristically made no response.

It was at this juncture that Trousdale intervened with his persuasive powers. After proclaiming his own willingness to participate in the assault, he reminded the troops of the relevant facts: that they were duty bound to carry out Jackson's wishes, that the British had recently torched the American capital, and that the Spanish continued to pound their position with firepower. For good measure he added that the Americans would suffer disgrace if they failed to join the assault. Within seconds a storming detail was formed and the attack set for two o'clock in the morning. About his own readiness, Trousdale explained: "I had my scaling ladder prepared and leaned it against a pine tree close to my tent and then laid down to sleep. On the following morning we were on the eve of moving in the execution of the scheme when the fort surrendered." He distinguished himself further in Jackson's eyes at the subsequent battle of New Orleans.

After a term in the state senate, Trousdale again took to the field of Mars. He first served as major general of volunteers in the 1836 campaign against the Seminoles in Florida. A decade later he participated in the Mexican War, leading his troops at Contreras, Churubusco, and Molino del Rey. At the battle of Chapultepec, however, he was twice wounded in the arm. For his bravery in this last engagement, he was breveted brigadier general in the regular army. He declined the promotion, though, saying that he had no interest in the military except during wartime.

After a term as governor, Trousdale hoped that a change of climate would alleviate his chronic rheumatism. As a result, he gladly accepted an appointment from President Franklin Pierce to serve as U.S. minister to Brazil. Despite temporary improvement, his health continued to decline until in the last four years of his life he rarely left Trousdale Place in Gallatin. Following his death in 1872, he was buried in the city cemetery there.

§ Open Tuesday-Saturday 9-4:30, Sunday and holidays 12:30-5:30. Closed January 1, Easter, Thanksgiving, and December 25. Fee. Phone: 615-452-5648.

GREENEVILLE

¶ Andrew Johnson National Historic Site, College and Depot streets.

This seventeen-acre tract contains three structures associated with *Andrew Johnson, who assumed the presidency after Lincoln's assassination: the Johnson Tailor Shop, the wooden clapboard building where he worked at his first trade; the Johnson House, his home from 1831 to 1851; and the Johnson Homestead, where he lived from 1851 until his death in 1875. (See Raleigh, North Carolina.)

§ Open daily 9-5. Closed January 1, Thanksgiving, and December 25. Fee. Phone: 615-638-3551.

¶ Andrew Johnson National Cemetery, Monument Avenue.

*President Andrew Johnson, his wife and children, and other members of his family are buried here. The twenty-six-foot monument over his grave is carved with an American eagle, a scroll, a hand placed on a Bible (representing the constitutional oath of office), and the words "His faith in the people never wavered." In accordance with Johnson's request, his remains were buried with a copy of the Constitution as a pillow and an American flag as a blanket.

§ Open daily 9-5. Closed December 25.

¶ **David Crockett Birthplace State Park,** 15 miles northeast on U.S. 11E.

The park features a replica of the cabin in which *David Crockett was born in 1786 as well as the limestone doorstep of the original cabin. The park was formerly a Cherokee Indian camp site. (See Morristown, Tennessee.)

§ Park open daily. Visitor center open Memorial Day weekend-Labor Day, daily 8-4:30; rest of the year, Monday-Friday 8-4:30; closed January 1, Thanksgiving, and December 25. Phone: 615-257-2167.

KNOXVILLE

¶ **James White's Fort,** 205 East Hill Avenue, between Neyland Drive and Mulvaney Street.

The reconstructed fort on this site commemorates the first settlement in this area by Captain James White and some other families in 1786. After establishing themselves on White's Creek, the group cleared a tract of land, built a log cabin, planted turnips, and constructed a fort. Today's reconstruction includes seven log cabins (one of them White's), each of which displays pioneer furnishings and tools.

White, whose mother (Mary McConnell) was probably of Scotch-Irish ancestry, was born in North Carolina and during the Revolution was a captain of that state's militia. By 1785 he had moved across the Alleghenies with his wife and children to what is now Knox County and was a member of the legislature of the State of Franklin. Three years after establishing White's Fort, he was again in his native state, where he served in the state legislature and in the state convention that ratified the U.S. Constitution.

After Tennessee Territory was organized in anticipation of its admission to the Union, White successively held a variety of positions there: major and lieutenant colonel in the militia, justice of the peace, chairman of the court of pleas and quarter sessions, and member of the territorial house of representatives. After serving as a delegate to the state convention which drew up Tennessee's constitution, he was elected to the new state's general assembly and later became Speaker of the state senate. He was also a trustee of Blount College and an elder of Lebanon Presbyterian Church. He is buried in the churchyard of the First Presbyterian Church in Knoxville.

§ Open March 1-mid December, Monday-Saturday 9:30-4:30. Closed major holidays. Fee. Phone: 615-525-6514.

LAWRENCEBURG

¶ **David Crockett State Park,** 1 mile west on U.S. 64.

This 1,000-acre park is located on Shoal Creek, the site of the grist mill, powder mill, and distillery owned by *David Crockett. The park features a reconstructed grist mill like that operated by Crockett between 1817 and 1822.

§ Open daily. Camping, picnicking, hiking, boat rentals, fishing, swimming, bicycle trails, tennis, restaurant, visitor center. Phone: 615-762-9408.

MARYVILLE

¶ **Sam Houston Schoolhouse,** 3 miles north on State 33 and then 2 miles east on Sam Houston Schoolhouse Road.

This 1794 rebuilt log structure is the schoolhouse where *Sam Houston, the future president of the Texas Republic, taught for one term in 1812. Although he was only eighteen years old and lacked much formal education himself, the young teacher was a voracious reader. He charged $8 tuition, payable in corn, cash, or calico.

Houston had come to this area in 1807 with his widowed mother and eight brothers. A few years after the family opened a store in Maryville, the wild Sam ran away to Cherokee territory, explaining that he preferred "measuring deer tracks to tape." (See Huntsville, Texas.)

§ Open Monday-Saturday 10-5, Sunday 1-5. Closed January 1, Thanksgiving, and December 25. Fee. Phone: 615-983-1550.

MEMPHIS

¶ **Jefferson Davis House,** 129 Court Avenue.

A plaque marks the site where former Confederate president *Jefferson Davis lived from 1867 to 1875.

¶ **Jefferson Davis Statue,** Confederate Park, Front Street and Madison Avenue.

Within the ramparts used to defend the city against federal gunboats in 1862 stands a statue of the former Confederate president, who lived in Memphis following his release from prison after the Civil War.

¶ **Magevney House,** 198 Adams Avenue.

This frame house, the oldest surviving residence in the city, originally belonged to the McKeon family but was purchased in 1837 by Eugene Magevney, an Irish immigrant who was the city's first schoolmaster.

Born near the village of Arney in County Fermanagh, Magevney had studied for the Catholic priesthood but instead chose a career as a teacher. After immigrating to the United States in 1828, he worked as a bookkeeper in Pennsylvania before moving to Memphis, Tennessee. From 1833 to 1840 he taught in a log cabin on Court Square and helped create the city's public school system. In the latter year he married Mary Smythe, also a native of County Fermanagh and a former student of his in Ireland. The first Catholic mass, christening, and wedding performed in the city took place in the couple's house until nearby St. Peter's Church was erected.

Soon after his marriage Magevney retired from teaching to manage his real estate holdings. One of his most foresighted investments was his purchase of a cow pasture in South Memphis – now the corner of Main and Union streets. Between 1842 and 1847 he served as alderman of the fourth ward and later was the official historian of the Old Folks Society, an organization devoted to recording the history of the local area.

A particularly interesting fact about Magevney is that he owned five or six African Americans, presumably as slaves. In 1848, for instance, he purchased a young black woman named Hannah. In addition, a census twelve years later lists five African Americans living on his property: a couple (John and Leah), their two small children (George and Elizabeth), and an unnamed thirteen-year-old girl. The Irishman had each of his slaves baptized at St. Peter's Church.

During the Civil War Magevney's family was one of ten to be banished from Memphis by the Union general Stephen Hurlbut in retaliation for a Confederate attack on a train near Moscow, Tennessee. After the war Magevney was influential in founding the Christian Brothers College in Memphis. Following his death in 1873, Kate Magevney, one of his daughters, managed his estate so well that she tripled its value to $3.5 million.

The Eugene Magevney House.

Her generosity made possible the establishment of St. Joseph's Hospital and the Lourdes Grotto at St. Mary's Church in Memphis.

The Magevneys' other daughter, Mary, became a Dominican nun in 1863 and was thereafter known as Sister Mary Agnes. Sixteen years later she and her sister jointly adopted a three-year-old orphan named Blanche Madaline. The child apparently accompanied Sister Mary Agnes to Galveston, Texas, when the bishop there asked the Dominicans to establish a school in that city. Sister Mary Agnes served as superior of Sacred Heart Convent and Academy until her death in 1891. It was then that Blanche moved to Memphis permanently and eventually inherited the Magevney House, which she presented to the city of Memphis in 1941.

Among the family furnishings on display in the house are the trunk which Mrs. Magevney brought from Ireland, the bureau used for the first Catholic mass in Memphis, and portrait paintings of Eugene Magevney and his wife.

§ Open June-August, Tuesday-Saturday 10-4; September-December and March-May, Tuesday-Friday 10-2, Saturday 10-4. Closed January, February, Thanksgiving, and December 24-25. Fee. Phone: 901-526-4464.

¶ **Mallory-Neely House,** 652 Adams Avenue.

Constructed in 1852, this twenty-five room Italianate mansion was purchased in 1883 by James Columbus Neely, who added the third story, the tower, and the Tiffany stained-glass windows.

Neely, who was born in North Carolina in 1826 to parents of Scotch-Irish descent, had come to Shelby County, Tennessee, with his parents at the age of thirteen. In 1854 he moved to Memphis, where he engaged in the grocery and provision business in partnership with William Goyer. Although the business was a profitable one, it was cut short by uncertainties caused by the Civil War. Following the national conflict, Neely established the firm of Brooks, Neely & Company, a cotton factoring business that sold supplies to planters on credit and then sold their crops on commission. The enterprise was so successful that it became one of the largest business concerns in the South and brought Neely appointment to directorships of several railroad companies, banks, and insurance companies.

The best known of Neely's children was Frances, familiarly known as Daisy. After marrying Barton Lee Mallory in 1900, she and her new husband moved into the ancestral home, where she lived until her death at the age of ninety-eight.

§ Open March-December, Tuesday-Saturday 10-4, Sunday 1-4. Closed Thanksgiving and December 24-25. Fee. Phone: 901-523-1484.

¶ **President's Island.**

Named for *President Andrew Jackson, the island is the largest in the Mississippi River's 2,500-mile course. Jackson's name became associated with the island after he bought a farm here and placed it under the direction of the Irishman Paddy Meagher, one of the first six settlers in what is now Memphis.

Meagher, who claimed to be a close friend of Jackson's, operated the Old Bell Tavern in Memphis. The future president made Paddy's public house his headquarters when in was in the city, as did *David Crockett and Thomas Hart Benton. After Meagher's death the tavern fell on hard times and became a magnet for the city's gamblers, flatboatmen, and prostitutes. During the severe winter of 1831-32, the tavern was partially torn down by poor people seeking fuel.

MORRISTOWN

¶ **Crockett Tavern and Museum,** 2002 Morningside Drive.

This structure is a replica of the six-room tavern which John Crockett built along the main road between Knoxville and Abingdon. The log structure features two open fireplaces, pioneer furnishings, and a collection of items pertaining to the Crocketts.

John Crockett, the father of the famous "Davy, King of the Wild Frontier," was of Norman-French and Irish ancestry on his paternal side. His great-great-great-grandfather Antoine de Crocketagne was an agent for various wine and salt merchants in southern France in the late seventeenth century. Sometime before 1675 de Crocketagne converted to Protestantism, a decision that proved personally costly when, a decade later, King Louis XIV expelled the Huguenots from the country. With his family Antoine fled abroad, first to England and then to Bantry Bay on the west coast of Ireland. There his third son – Joseph Louis – married Sarah Stewart, presumably of Scotch-Irish ancestry, and soon joined the Irish migration to America. Either on the voyage or soon after the couple's arrival in New Rochelle, New York, in 1709, Sarah gave birth to a son. A century and a half later, the frontiersman David Crockett confused this ancestor – his great-grandfather – with his own father, John, whom he claimed had been born either in Ireland or on the voyage across the Atlantic. By 1718 Joseph Louis and his son, William, had left New Rochelle (named for the famous Huguenot stronghold in France) for the back country of Virginia.

The Crocketts arrived in Tennessee in the next generation, when William's son David – the frontiersman's grandfather – crossed the Appalachian Mountains in 1775. Two years later the elder David and his wife were killed when Creek and Cherokee Indians attacked their settlement at what is now Rogersville. (A historical marker near the site reads: "Here lies the bodies of David Crockett and his wife, Grandparents of 'Davy Crockett,' who were massacred near this spot by Indians in 1777.")

At the time of the attack, David Crockett's son John was away from home, serving as a ranger along the frontier. Two of John's brothers, however, were not so lucky: a rifle bullet broke Joseph's arm, while James (a deaf mute) was kidnapped and held in captivity for twenty years until his brothers rescued him.

In 1780 John Crockett was among the many Irish and Scotch-Irish who fought at Kings Mountain. It was probably in that same year that he married Rebecca Hawkins and moved to North Carolina. During that decade he served several terms as constable of Greene County and bought a total of 500 acres there. Although he later sold a portion of that property – a 200-acre homestead – at a hefty profit, the other 300 acres were sold at a sheriff's auction to settle a $400 debt that Crockett could not pay.

Crockett's chronic flirtation with bankruptcy was complete when a flood destroyed a grist mill which he and a partner had built on Cove Creek. No doubt beaten and perhaps embittered by this string of bad luck, Crockett returned with his family to Tennessee. Finding a well traveled spot along the road between Knoxville and Abington, Virginia, he and his wife established an inn, which they operated for two decades.

To reduce his expenses by decreasing the number of mouths he had to feed, Crockett sought to bind his sons to some of the wagoners who frequented his tavern and inn. It was thus that at the age of twelve Davy was taken into the employ of a teamster named Jacob Siler. For the trouble of herding a large stock of cattle to Rockbridge County, Virginia, the youngster was paid five or six dollars and received the praise of his employer.

Despite this exploitation, Davy agreed to remain as Siler's indentured servant. Crockett later revealed a psyche torn by conflicted feelings toward parental authority: "I had been taught so many lessons of obedience by my father that I at first supposed I was bound to obey this man [Siler], or at least I was afraid openly to disobey him; and I therefore staid with him, and tried to put on a look of perfect contentment until I got the family all to believe I was fully satisfied."

Before too long, however, the youngster escaped by joining three other wagoners who agreed to protect him from a pursuing Siler. In an episode that presaged the more heroic deeds that were attributed to Crockett, the boy found his rescuers by trudging seven miles in the dead of night through a blizzard – in snow which was so deep, he later wrote, that it came up to his knees and which fell so rapidly that it covered his tracks.

Although the young Crockett soon returned to his father's tavern, he ran away less than a year later. In this case the reason for the boy's truancy was his refusal to obey his father's wish that he return to school. Nevertheless, at eighteen Davy attended school for six months, primarily to impress a young lady, but when she jilted him he never darkened the door of a schoolhouse again. Even in later life Crockett was proud of his lack of education, regarding correct spelling as something "contrary to nature" and grammar as "nothing at all," despite "the fuss that is made about it."

Following his election in 1833 to a third term in Congress, Crockett was mentioned by the French observer de Tocqueville in his classic description of American democracy. After repeating the usual slanders against the Tennessean – that he owned no property, lived most of the time in the woods, was uneducated and almost totally illiterate – the French aristocrat cited Crockett's career as a reason for opposing universal suffrage. (See Rutherford, Tennessee, and Crockett, Texas.)

§ Open May-October, Tuesday-Saturday 11-4. Fee. Phone: 615-587-9900.

NASHVILLE

¶ The Hermitage, 12 miles east off Interstate 40 to Old Hickory Boulevard/Hermitage exit.

In 1804 *Andrew Jackson bought a 625-acre tract on this site, where he built a two-story log cabin and subsequently hosted such visitors as Aaron Burr, President James Monroe, and *Jefferson Davis. In 1819 Jackson constructed a two-story brick house for his wife, Rachel, and a decade later he added one-story wings. In 1834, however, most of the interior was gutted by fire; during the reconstruction, front and back porticoes were added. The former president retired here in 1837. The mansion preserves almost all of Jackson's known personal effects.

One of the Jackson memorabilia is a certificate proclaiming his mem-

Grave of Andrew Jackson
and his wife at the Hermitage.

bership in the Philadelphia branch of the Hibernian Society for the Relief of Emigrants from Ireland. Jackson proudly alluded to his Irish blood during a speech to the Charitable Irish Society in Boston: "It is with great pleasure that I see so many of the countrymen of my father assembled on this occasion. I have always been proud of my ancestry and of being descended from that noble race, and rejoice that I am so nearly allied to a country which has so much to recommend it to the good wishes of the world. Would to God, sir, that Ireland on the other side of the great water enjoyed the comfort, contentment, happiness and liberty that they enjoy here. I am well aware, sir, that Irishmen have never been backward in giving their support to the cause of liberty. They have fought, sir, for this country valiantly, and I have no doubt, would fight again were it necessary. But I hope it will be long before the institutions of our country need support of that kind."

On the grounds of the former plantation are original log houses, a smokehouse, a springhouse, several slave quarters, and "Rachel's Garden." In the far corner of the garden is the tomb of Rachel and Andrew Jackson, a circular Doric structure covering a small obelisk.

§ Open daily 9-5. Closed the third week of January, Thanksgiving, and December 25. Fee. Phone: 615-889-2941.

❡ Near the Hermitage is Old Hermitage Church, which Jackson built at the request of his wife. The story is told of the time when the local clergyman called on the former president to request a contribution for a new church roof. Noticing that Jackson was preparing to watch a cock fight, the minister pointed to one of the birds and said to Jackson, "I'll bet a church roof that this cock wins." Ever ready for a wager, Jackson accepted the challenge – and paid up when his rooster lost.

❡ **St. Patrick's Church,** 1219 Second Avenue South.

This church continues to be the gathering place each spring and fall for the Irish Nomads, the descendants of several Irish families of horse traders who came to the United States in 1875.

For many years this church was the site of a funeral mass held every May 1 for those among the Irish Nomads who had died during the previous year. In the past, as many as 3,000 people attended this annual reunion, parking their trailers or pitching camp in the open fields near the city. These Irish Horse Traders, as they are also called, were known for their skill in healing horses and for the depots in which the animals were collected and auctioned off. Many of the mules which the Italian army used to transport artillery during its invasion of Ethiopia in 1935 were obtained through the Irish Nomads. (See Atlanta, Georgia.)

§ Phone: 615-256-6498.

❡ Mt. Calvary Cemetery in Nashville is the burial place for the Irish Horse Traders from west of the Alleghenies.

❡ **State Capitol,** Capitol Plaza, Charlotte Avenue.

On the grounds of the capitol are memorials to Tennessee's two U.S. presidents:

• Although *President James K. Polk and his wife were first buried in the garden of their Nashville estate, their bodies were reinterred here in the Polk Tomb after the house came into the possession of another family.

• The equestrian statue of *President Andrew Jackson is the work of Clark Mills and is identical to his statues of "Old Hickory" in New Orleans and Washington, D.C.

The rotunda of the capitol contains busts of the Irish Americans Matthew Fontaine Maury (the "Pathfinder of the Seas") and presidents Andrew Jackson, James K. Polk, and Andrew Johnson.

§ Open daily 8-5. Phone: 615-741-2692.

Grave of James K. Polk and his wife.

❡ **Tennessee Performing Arts Center,** 505 Deaderick Street.

The arts center contains three theaters named in honor of Irish-American presidents Andrew Jackson (concert hall), Andrew Johnson (theater in the round), and James K. Polk (drama/musical/dance theater).

§ Phone: 615-741-2787.

ROGERSVILLE

❡ **Amis Stone House (Rogers Inn),** 3 miles northeast on Berum Road.

This house was built about 1780 by Thomas Amis, who later established a store, a distillery, a gristmill, a hotel, and a blacksmith shop. In 1785, when his daughter married Joseph Rogers, an Irishman working for him as a shopkeeper, Amis gave the couple the property on which Rogersville was established the following year. The Rogers Inn was known as one of the best public houses between the Cumberland and Allegheny mountains and was frequented by *Andrew Jackson while he was practicing law in this part of Tennessee.

ℐ Hale Springs Inn, 110 West Main Street.

This recently restored building was constructed in 1824 by John McKinney, an Irish-born lawyer who designed several of the town's finest structures. It was used as federal headquarters during the Civil War and is the oldest continuously operating inn in Tennessee.

ℐ Three Oaks, 306 Colonial Road. Private.

Constructed in 1815, this was the home and law office of *John McKinney. "Three Oaks" is noted for the brickwork of its twelve chimneys.

ℐ Rosemont, 500 East Main Street. Private.

This 1842 structure was the home of *John McKinney's daughter Susan and her husband, John Netherland.

RUTHERFORD

ℐ David Crockett Cabin, Rutherford Elementary School, off State 45.

Built partially of logs from a cabin owned by *Davy Crockett, this reconstruction features a rocking chair built by the famous frontiersman. Near the cabin are the graves of his mother and one of his children.

Crockett's cabin was originally located four miles east of town, along the Rutherford fork of the Obion River. When a northern visitor once asked him for directions to his cabin, Crockett said, "Why, sir, run down the Mississippi till you come to the Obion River, run a small streak up that, jump ashore anywhere, and inquire for me." While living in this area, Crockett hunted bear with his famous long rifle, "Old Betsy."

Always known for his "tall tales," Crockett told of how, when caught in a hollow tree by a mother bear, he held on to the animal's tail and jabbed her with his knife until she pulled him out. Another story related how he had fought hand to claw with a vicious black bear until he stabbed it to death. According to his own count, he killed 105 bears during a nine-month period. He was also known for participating in local shooting matches, which went on during the day and into the night.

Crockett later went into politics when someone jokingly suggested to him that he run for Congress. After his election to the House of Representatives in 1826, the young Tennessean caught the attention of official Washington with his frontier dress and speech. When he lost his seat in 1835, he moved to Texas, where he was killed the next year while defending the Alamo from a Mexican army.

TEXAS

AUSTIN

¶ **St. Edward's University,** 3001 South Congress Avenue.

The main building on this 180-acre campus was originally constructed in 1887 according to the design of Nicholas Clayton, a native of Ireland and a renowned Galveston architect. (See Galveston, Texas.)

¶ **St. Mary's Cathedral,** 201-207 East 10th Street.

This High Victorian Gothic structure was designed by the Irish-born architect Nicholas Clayton.

¶ **State Capitol,** 100 East 11th Street at the north end of Congress Street.

• Near the entrance to the capitol is a monument to the defenders of the Alamo. The structure was erected in 1891 and consists of four seven-foot columns supporting arches topped by a dome. On the columns are inscribed the 187 names of those who died during the siege of the Alamo, thirty-eight of them either Irish natives or men with traditional Irish surnames.

Atop the whole thirty-five-foot memorial stands a bronze figure of a Texan soldier holding a long-barreled muzzle-loader. On the west lintel are engraved the words "Heroes of the Alamo"; on the east, "God and Texas, Liberty or Death"; on the south, "I shall never surrender or retreat"; and on the north pediment and lintel, "Thermopylae had her messenger of defeat, the Alamo had none."

• On the center walk is the Confederate Dead Monument, designed by Pompeo Coppini and erected in 1901. The dominant bronze figure is that of *President Jefferson Davis; four other figures represent a Confederate sailor and three Confederate soldiers (infantry, cavalry, and artillery).

• In the Senate chamber hang the paintings *Dawn at the Alamo* and *The Battle of San Jacinto*, both by the Irish-born painter Harry McArdle (1836-1908). After immigrating to the United States at the age of fourteen, the youngster continued the art studies which he had begun in Dublin. In 1860 he won the Peabody Prize at the Maryland Academy of Design. After the Civil War, during which he served on the engineering staff of General Robert E. Lee, McArdle migrated to Texas. Within a few years he was offered a professorship of art at Baylor Female College.

§ Open Monday-Friday 7 a.m.-10 p.m., Saturday 9-5, Sunday noon-5. Closed January 1, Thanksgiving, and December 25. Phone: 512-463-0063.

¶ **Texas State Library,** Brazos Street between 12th and 13th streets.

The library building displays some of the major documents connected with the history of Texas, including facsimiles of the Texas Declaration of Independence and the letter which *William Travis issued from the Alamo "To the People of Texas & all Americans in the World." A forty-five-foot mural depicting the history of Texas includes the figures of Stephen Austin; James Bowie, *David Crockett, and *William Travis (heroes of the Alamo); and *Sam Houston, Mirabeau Lamar, and Anson Jones (presidents of the Texas Republic).

¶ **University of Texas,** centering at University Avenue and West 21st Street.

The double walkway to the main administration building of the university is flanked by statues of Albert Sidney Johnston, Robert E. Lee, and the Irish-Americans Jefferson Davis, James Stephen Hogg, John Reagan, and Woodrow Wilson. Each of the statues was sculpted by Pompeo Coppini.

BEAUMONT

¶ **The *Clifton* Walking Beam,** Riverfront Park, off Main Street behind City Hall.

This walking beam is a relic of the U.S.S. *Clifton*, one of the three federal gunboats captured by Dick Dowling and his detachment of fellow Irish soldiers during a heroic stand at Sabine Pass on September 8, 1863. (See Sabine Pass, Texas.)

BRACKETTVILLE

¶ **Alamo Village Movie Location,** 7 miles north of U.S. 90 on FM 674.

This movie production site includes a replica of the Alamo, erected for the filming of the 1959 motion picture *The Alamo*, starring the Irish-American John Wayne.

Financing for the film – the story of the heroic stand for Texan independence – included $1 million of Wayne's own money. The famous actor, who played the role of David Crockett, another Irish American, said about the film: "We wanted to recreate a moment in history that will show this generation of Americans what their country stands for . . . what some of their forebears went through to win what they had to have or die – liberty and freedom." (See Winterset, Iowa.)

§ Open Memorial Day-Labor Day, daily 9-6; rest of the year, daily 9-5. Closed December 21-26. Fee. Phone: 210-563-2580.

BURTON

¶ **Leander McNelly Burial Site,** Mt. Zion Cemetery.

A white stone monument marks the grave of Leander McNelly, the son of Irish immigrants and one of the most famous members of the Texas Rangers. The burial memorial was erected by Captain Richard King and is adorned with bas-reliefs of a cannon and a Masonic emblem.

Born in what is now West Virginia in 1844, the future Ranger was the son of P. J. and Mary (Downey) McNelly, emigrants from County Down. By 1860 the family had moved to this part of Washington County, where the father took up sheep ranching. The son, meanwhile, worked as a sheepherder for a local rancher but enlisted in a regiment of the Texas Mounted Volunteers soon after the Civil War commenced. For his valor at the battle of Val Verde, he was made a member of the regimental staff, and he later fought in the New Mexico campaign and at Galveston.

At the end of 1863 McNelly was commissioned captain of scouts to raise a company of mounted troops. After recruiting most of his men from Washington County, he and his command participated in several engagements until he was wounded in the spring of 1864. As the conflict came to a close, McNelly was transferred from military duty to police work. After helping round up deserters in Louisiana, he and his scouts were ordered to Washington County, where they made camp and continued to track down deserters.

Immediately after the war, McNelly took up farming, but in 1870 he accepted a commission in the recently formed State Police. Most Texans hated this policing agency because it had been created by the Republican "carpetbagger" government. Yet even a loyal Southerner like McNelly – he named his only son "Rebel" – realized the need to restore the rule of law. He therefore had no quarrel with hunting down those who used violence against freed blacks. In one celebrated instance, he was seriously wounded by gunshot while escorting to jail three white men suspected of killing an African-American who had testified against them in court.

When the Texas State Police was disbanded after only three years, McNelly joined the Texas Rangers, recently reestablished by the state legislature. As a newly appointed captain, he was assigned the task of crushing the rival factions that had contributed to the breakdown of law enforcement in DeWitt County. At the head of a volunteer militia unit, he succeeded in protecting prisoners from lynching parties, guaranteed that judicial sessions could proceed without intimidation, and even organized a network of spies who informed him about criminal activities. One of his most effective techniques was the blitzkrieg raid on saloons and other usual meeting places for the criminally inclined. "I find," he said "that it does a great deal of good to disperse congregations that usually meet at grogshops to . . . concoct devilment; most of them, being under indictment in some part of the State, are in constant expectation of the approach of an officer and when they hear of my men coming, they scatter."

McNelly and his men gained even more renown for successfully suppressing cattle stealing along the Rio Grande border. By 1875 rustlers were stealing an estimated 200,000 head of cattle from the sprawling and thinly protected ranches between the Rio Grande and the Nueces rivers. As part of his crackdown, McNelly decided to make an example of the cattle rustlers by capturing one of their most notorious Mexican leaders. After learning that General Juan Cortinas planned to steal several hundred cattle and transport them to Cuba on a steamer waiting off Brownsville, the lawman took the offensive. In a skirmish that resulted in the death of all twelve bandits, McNelly lost but a single man and captured 265 head of cattle stolen from the vicinity of King's Ranch. As a warning to other cattle thieves, he deposited the bodies of the dead bandits in the Brownsville public square.

McNelly's most daring raid, however, occurred later in 1875 when he and thirty of his fellow Rangers crossed into Mexico and attacked Las Cuevas, the heavily fortified headquarters of the thieves. After General Juan Flores, the patron of the Rio Grande bandits, was killed in the attack, McNelly proceeded to threaten the Mexicans with a second assault if they did not return the stolen animals. The Mexicans responded positively, apparently intimidated by the U.S. troops along the border. (McNelly had hoped to exploit these troops even more by drawing them into combat with the Mexican bandits.) These returned cattle were the first stolen herds ever to retrace their steps across the Rio Grande – an event that added luster to the legend of the Texas Rangers.

CASTROVILLE

¶ **Landmark Inn State Historic Site,** Florence and Fiorella streets.

The first floor of this two-story structure was built in 1849 by a French immigrant named Cesar Monod. Four years later the Irish immigrant John Vance purchased the property and added the second floor and the double galleries. Known as the Vance Hotel, the inn was a familiar stopping place for travelers between El Paso and San Antonio. The property still serves as an inn, but it is now administered by the Texas Parks and Wildlife Department.

Born in Strabane, Ireland, in 1819, Vance had first lived in New York City before moving to Little Rock, Arkansas, where he and his two brothers established a general store. By 1843, however, he was operating his own retail store in San Antonio, Texas. Continuing his itinerant ways, he moved to Castroville a decade later, purchasing the Monod property as a home for his wife, Rowena Baldwin. Vance subsequently enlarged the structure by building a gabled wing sixty-four feet in length. For the next four decades the structure served a variety of purposes: family home, general store, post office, and hotel.

During the Civil War, the inn suffered depredations from both sides.

Union troops raided the structure, seizing and destroying merchandise with impunity, while Confederate soldiers reputedly melted the lead tank in the bath house in order to make bullets. Despite this pillaging, the evidence points to Vance's continued prosperity. According to the 1870 census, for instance, his real property was valued at $20,000 and his personal wealth at $10,000, figures that a decade before were only $4,000 each.

Although little specific information is known about Vance's business activities during the 1870s, he most likely continued to operate a general store in the new wing of his combined home and hotel. Besides mentioning the usual inventory of groceries, hardware, hats, boots, books, and clothing, an advertisement in the *San Antonio Express* in April 1870 announced that Vance's store "will pay cash for country Produce such as Corn, Wheat, Dried Beef, Hides, Dressed Deer Skins, Sheep and Goat Skins; also for Wool, Bacon, Lard, Pecans, Honey, Bees-Wax, etc." Most likely in a effort to diversify his merchandise, the Irishman set up a manual wool press in the basement of the house. There his four employees baled wool into 200-pound sacks for sale in his store upstairs.

John Vance died in 1890 while visiting his daughter in St. Louis. In its eulogy the *Castroville Quill* wrote: "Vance was a man of sterling worth, and was held in universal esteem. In his death, Medina County loses an esteemed and valuable citizen."

§ Open Thursday-Monday 8-5. Reservations required. Phone: 210-931-2133.

CORPUS CHRISTI

❡ **McCampbell House,** 1501 North Chaparral Drive and Fitzgerald Street.

This two-and-a-half-story Southern Greek Revival structure is one of several former private residences in Heritage Park, each representing the contribution of a particular ethnic group to the city's history.

Now Corpus Christi's Irish cultural center, the McCampbell House was formerly the home of Mary Alice Ward McCampbell. The widow of William Berry McCampbell, she built the house on property she had purchased in 1908 at 1421 Water Street, in the old Irishtown section of the city.

During the hurricane of 1919, the widow and her three sons watched from their second-story porch as floodwaters from the nearby sea rose to cover the first floor of the structure. Although the house survived the storm, Mrs. McCampbell allegedly contracted pneumonia while watching the storm and died early the next year.

Although the three sons subsequently left Corpus Christi to attend military schools, they all returned to the city. The house remained in the family until 1945 and was eventually acquired by the city and removed to Heritage Park in 1984.

§ Open daily 10-4:30. Phone: 512-883-9662.

CROCKETT

¶ **David Crockett Memorial Park,** 5th Street and Anson Jones Avenue.

The park honors the famous frontiersman-politician who made camp near here on his way to the Alamo in San Antonio in the late winter of 1836.

Although the death of *David Crockett at the Alamo for the cause of Texan independence assured him a place in the pantheon of the new republic's heroes, the process of deification had actually begun in his own lifetime. As early as the 1820s, when he was a young state legislator, Crockett had been invested with larger-than-life stature. He first drew truly national attention, however, with the appearance in 1830 of a biographical play entitled *The Lion of the West*. This was followed three years later by a spurious biography known by its clumsy title: *The Life and Adventures of Colonel David Crockett of West Tennessee*. It was this work that included the most famous of Crockett's reputed self-introductions: "I'm that same David Crockett, fresh from the backwoods, half-horse, half-alligator, a little touched with the snapping-turtle; can wade the Mississippi, leap the Ohio, ride upon a streak of lightning, and slip without a scratch down a honey locust; can whip my weight in wild cats, – and if any gentleman pleases, for a ten dollar bill, he may throw in a panther, – hug a bear too close for comfort, and eat any man opposed to Jackson." The young symbol of America's boastfulness was also mentioned in the titles of reels and marches named in his honor. The symbol himself wrote an autobiography under the title *A Narrative of the Life of David Crockett of the State of Tennessee*.

Crockett's death brought an additional flood of bogus biographies, melodramas, comic almanacs, and dime novels. In elaborating on the Tennessean's alleged powers over nature, one almanac wrote that he had wrung the tail of Halley's Comet, freed the earth from its frozen axis with a swift kick and a bit of bear grease, and drained the Gulf of Mexico in order to bring Texas and the United States closer together. Some of these accounts, however, tended to justify the prejudices of the day by imputing them to Crockett. In one episode, for instance, after being attacked by Indians, Crockett says that he will never be revenged until "I extinctified the whole race of varmints."

In more modern times the popularity of the "King of the Wild Frontier" hit record heights during the 1950s and 1960s. Spurred by its desire for equal footing with the other two national broadcasting systems, ABC aired three programs that glorified Crockett's major *personae*: as Indian fighter, congressman, and martyr. Walt Disney later released the three programs as the motion picture *King of the Wild Frontier*, and ABC repeated the winning strategy with two new television episodes.

In 1955 Fess Parker, who played Crockett on TV and in the films, toured forty-two American cities and thirteen foreign countries promoting the ABC program, the film, and America's latest hero. Besides catapulting Parker into instant celebrity status, the public relations and sales blitz helped move him into the higher tax brackets. (He earned a 10 percent royalty on the sale of all the attendant Disney/Crockett paraphernalia.)

The spin-offs from the craze must have broken all previous marketing records. "The Ballad of Davy Crockett," which Tom Blackburn wrote in twenty minutes, sold 18 million copies and topped the musical charts in 1955. Crockett-related books sold 14 million copies, a related comic strip was syndicated in 200 newspapers, and the demand for coonskin caps drove the price of pelts from 25 cents to $6 a pound.

The national phenomenon even took on political significance. Afraid that the Republicans would adopt Crockett and his coonskin cap as their symbols during the 1955 presidential campaign, liberal Democrats countered with a campaign to debunk the famous hero. The editor of *Harper's*, for instance, declared that Crockett "was never king of anything, except maybe the Tennessee Tall Tales and Bourbon Samples Association." The education director for the United Auto Workers in Detroit, meanwhile, charged that Crockett was "a drunk and brawler, a wife beater, hireling of big business, and shiftless no-account." (See Morristown and Rutherford, Tennessee.)

¶ **David Crockett Spring,** on West Goliad Street at State 7/21.

The spring marks the site of the frontiersman's encampment under a large oak tree. Crockett and a small detachment of men stopped here on their way to the Alamo in 1836. A historical plaque indicating the spot is inscribed with Crockett's motto, "Be sure you are right, then go ahead."

DALLAS

¶ **Dealey Plaza,** Houston and Elm streets.

A bronze plaque in the plaza recounts the assassination of *President John F. Kennedy: "On November 22, 1963, John Fitzgerald Kennedy, thirty-fifth president of the United States, visited Dallas. A presidential parade traveled north on Houston Street to Elm Street and west on Elm Street. As the parade continued on Elm Street, at 12:30 p.m. rifle shots wounded the president and Texas governor John Connally. Findings of the Warren Commission indicated that the rifle shots were fired from a sixth floor window near the southeast corner of the Texas School Book Depository Building, Elm and Houston, a block north of this marker. President Kennedy expired at Parkland Memorial Hospital at 1 p.m."

¶ **Hall of State,** State Fair Park, 2 miles east on U.S. 67/80, 3 blocks east of Interstate 30.

The Hall of Heroes, the curved vestibule foyer inside the Hall of State, is lined with statues of several heroic figures from the Texas Revolution: Stephen Austin, James Fannin, Mirabeau Lamar, and the Irish-Americans David Crockett, Sam Houston, Thomas Rusk, and William Travis. A memorial plaque recounts the latter men's achievements:

"Sam Houston 1793-1863, soldier under Andrew Jackson, signer of the Texas Declaration of Independence, hero of San Jacinto, president of the Republic of Texas, governor of Tennessee and of Texas, United States senator, the guiding spirit of political life in Texas 1836-1860."

"Thomas Jefferson Rusk 1803-1857, signer of the Texas Declaration of Independence, secretary of war at San Jacinto, brigadier general of the army, chief justice of the supreme court, United States senator. Soldier, statesman, jurist of the Republic and State."

"William Barrett Travis 1809-1836, valiant soldier in the Texas Revolution. Commander of the Alamo when it was stormed and taken by General Santa Anna on March 6, 1836, he fell leading its defenders. 'Victory or Death!' 'I shall never surrender or retreat.'"

§ Open Tuesday-Saturday 9-5, Sunday and holidays 1-5. Closed Thanksgiving and December 25. Fee. Phone: 214-421-4500.

¶ **John F. Kennedy Memorial,** Main and Market streets.

This unusual thirty-foot-square monument in honor of the slain presi-

The John F. Kennedy Memorial.

dent was erected in 1970 by Philip Johnson, an architect and friend of the Kennedy family. The walls of the open-style white memorial were designed to block out traffic noise, thus allowing the structure to be used as a place of meditation.

¶ The Sixth Floor, 411 Elm Street.

This 9,000-square-foot exhibit space is located on the sixth floor of the former Texas School Book Depository. It was from here that Lee Harvey Oswald assassinated *John F. Kennedy and severely wounded *Governor John Connally as their motorcade passed the "grassy knoll" and the triple underpass below.

The exhibit includes six films, almost 400 photographs, and various artifacts that chronicle Kennedy's administration, his death, and the findings of the Warren Commission concerning the assassination.

§ Open Sunday-Friday and holidays 10-6, Saturday 10-7. Closed December 25. Fee. Phone: 214-653-6666.

EL PASO

¶ Magoffin House, 1120 Magoffin Avenue.

This large one-story house was designed and built in 1875 by Joseph Magoffin as an almost perfect replica of his father's home, erected in 1849 but destroyed when the Rio Grande flooded almost twenty years later. The building's thirty-inch-thick adobe walls are scored to look like blocks of stone, while its fourteen-foot ceilings are supported by wooden rafters. These Southwestern features are complemented by such classical architectural adornments as pediments and pilasters around its doors and windows, a combination known as the Territorial style.

Magoffin's father, James Wiley Magoffin, was born at Harrodsburg, Kentucky, in 1799, the son of an immigrant from County Down, Ireland. Beginning in the 1820s, James began a long association with Mexico, both through trading expeditions into the country and later as U.S. consul at Saltillo. At the outbreak of the Mexican War, "Don Santiago" – as he was known by then – was appointed by *President James K. Polk to assist *General Stephen Watts Kearny in his conquest of the Southwest. Magoffin was so successful in his negotiations with General Manuel Armijo that the latter allowed Kearny and his troops to enter Santa Fe, thus giving the Americans access to the Southwest without firing a shot. While performing similar services for American forces in Chihuahua, however, Magoffin was arrested as a spy and escaped execution only because of his popularity with Mexican officers. After the war, with the $30,000 he received for his services to the U.S. government, he settled in western Texas, where he constructed an adobe house and became legendary for his hospitality and lavish entertainment. The house, along with a store and various warehouses which he built, became known as Magoffinsville, one of several settlements that developed into El Paso.

When Texas seceded from the Union, Magoffin's son Joseph enlisted in the Confederate army and saw action in New Mexico and Virginia. After the war he returned to El Paso to assert his claim to his father's estate, confiscated during the early years of the Radical Republican regime. After reestablishing title to the family's property, he replicated his father's earlier home. The Magoffin family lived in this new house until 1986.

The younger Magoffin subsequently became one of the city's prominent political leaders, serving as justice of the peace and county judge and winning election to the mayoralty four times. He was also the director of the State National Bank and helped organize the Street Railway Company to unite El Paso and Juarez.

Today the Magoffin House contains many of the family's Victorian furnishings, including a full-length pier glass mirrored wardrobe and a thirteen-foot-high canopied bed.

§ Open Wednesday-Sunday 9-4. Closed January 1, Thanksgiving, and December 25. Fee. Phone: 915-533-5147.

FORT DAVIS

¶ **Fort Davis National Historic Site,** north near Limpia Canyon off State 17 and 118.

Built in 1854 and named for *Jefferson Davis, the U.S. secretary of war at the time, the fort protected travelers and the mail route along the San Antonio-El Paso Road. Although the fort had more than seventy buildings between 1867 and 1891, today only the restored barracks, officers' quarters, kitchen, commissary, and hospital remain. The fort's modern facilities include a visitor center, museum, and auditorium.

§ Open Memorial Day-Labor Day, daily 8-6; rest of the year, daily 8-5. Closed December 25. Fee. Phone: 915-426-3224.

FORT WORTH

¶ **Will Rogers Memorial Center,** Lancaster Avenue and University Drive.

Named for the famous cowboy-humorist *Will Rogers, this complex contains a coliseum, an auditorium, and an equestrian center. A bust of Rogers is located in the shared lobby of the auditorium and the coliseum, while an equestrian statue of him stands in front of the complex. The statue – Riding into the Sunset – was sculpted by Electra Waggoner and was dedicated by Dwight D. Eisenhower in 1947. (See Claremore, Oklahoma.)

GALVESTON

Few architects have had such a profound influence on the complexion of any city as Nicholas Clayton had on Galveston between 1870 and 1900. Born in Cork, Ireland, in 1840, Clayton accompanied his mother to America two years later – following the death of his father. Once in the United States, mother and son made their way to Cincinnati, Ohio, to live with a relative, who made shoe buckles. It was there that the young Clayton received his early parochial school education, and it may have been in Cincinnati that he spent a year as an apprentice to a stonemason.

After serving in the Union navy during the Civil War, Clayton studied architecture in Memphis with the firm of Jones & Baldwin. He arrived in Galveston at the end of 1872 to supervise construction of the First Presbyterian Church for Jones & Baldwin. The cottage into which he and his mother moved in 1874 is today a private residence at 36th and L streets. The ambitious Clayton soon established a partnership with two other architects, although he continued to do most of his work alone. Before his death in 1917 he designed more than 200 churches, convents, residences, and civic and commercial buildings in the city. All but fifty of them, however, were destroyed by fire or storms. He was known for his eclecticism, favoring elements from the Romanesque, the Queen Anne, the Second Empire, and the Victorian styles.

Clayton stood five feet ten inches tall, had brown hair, blue eyes, and a ruddy complexion, and in his younger days wore a bow-tie with his well-tailored suits. In 1892, now past fifty, he married Mary Lorena Ducie, a young woman half his age. The couple had five children. Perhaps to keep up with his young children, the middle-aged father exercised every day and taught Nicholas Jr. and his friends how to swim. The Irishman was also a faithful Catholic and attended mass almost every day.

Clayton died of pneumonia in 1916 after suffering severe burns while investigating a crack in the chimney in an upstairs bedroom. When his widow inquired of friends about a fitting memorial for her husband, Rabbi Henry Cohen of Temple B'Nai Israel replied: "Oh, you don't need one, my dear Mary Lorena. He's got them all over town. Just go around and read some cornerstones." The most significant structures which Clayton designed, built, or modified are listed below.

¶ Ashbel Smith Building, University of Texas Medical Branch.

Known locally as "Old Red" because of the red pressed brick used in its construction, this Romanesque Revival building was designed by Clayton to house classrooms, laboratories, and medical amphitheaters.

¶ The Bishop's Palace (Gresham House), 1402 Broadway.

Completed in 1893 for Colonel Walter Gresham at a cost of $250,000, Clayton's design for this outstanding example of Victorian residential architecture called for limestone, granite, and sandstone. The house's exterior sculpted elements, meanwhile, reflect Romanesque, French Renais-

The Bishop's Palace.

sance, Moorish, and Tudor styles. Ornamental chimneys rise from its pitched tiled and dormered roof, and wrought iron balconies project from the third floor.

Clayton's influence is also evident in the interior features. In addition to hand-carved paneling in mahogany, rosewood, and satinwood, the house boasts sliding glass doors, folding interior shutters, and a gas-burning fireplace in the first floor hall. The fireplace in the music room is a $10,000 Mexican onyx piece from the 1886 New Orleans World Fair. The mansion is listed by the American Institute of Architects as among the 100 outstanding buildings in the country.

The Gresham House passed into the possession of the Catholic diocese of Galveston-Houston in 1923. For the next twenty-seven years it was the residence of Bishop Christopher Byrne, a native of Missouri and the son of Irish immigrants who had settled in St. Louis about 1857. After his ordination Byrne did pastoral work in several parishes in Missouri before being named bishop of Galveston in 1918. During his administration the diocese experienced phenomenal growth. The Catholic population tripled, the number of children in the diocesan schools more than quadrupled (to 33,000), and the number of priests and churches doubled (to approximately 200 each).

§ Open Memorial Day weekend-Labor Day, Monday-Saturday 10-5, Sunday noon-5; rest of the year, Wednesday-Monday noon-4. Closed January 1, Easter, Thanksgiving, and December 25. Fee. Phone: 409-762-2475.

¶ Burr-Avery House, 1228 Sealy. Private.

This 1876 structure by Clayton is a mix of Classic Revival and Victorian Gothic. Regarded as one of the most elaborate frame structures in Galveston, it was constructed for a cotton broker.

¶ Eaton Memorial Chapel, Trinity Episcopal Church, 2216 Ball Street.

A fine example of the Gothic Revival style, this Galveston landmark was designed and constructed by Clayton in 1882.

¶ First Presbyterian Church, 1903 Church Street.

Designed by the Memphis architectural firm of Jones & Baldwin, this church was constructed under Clayton's supervision. The Irish-born architect had come to Texas expressly to oversee construction of this Romanesque Revival edifice.

¶ Garten Verein Dancing Pavilion, Kempner Park, Avenue O and 27th Street.

Now more than 120 years old, this massive wooden structure is one of several which Clayton designed. It is currently used as a recreation building.

¶ Grace Episcopal Church, 1115 36th Street.

This Gothic Revival white-limestone house of worship was built by Clayton in 1894-95.

¶ Sacred Heart Church, Broadway and 14th streets.

After a storm which hit the city in 1915, Clayton supervised construction of the new dome on the present building. (Despite his seventy-five years, he climbed over the roof to inspect the damage caused by the storm.) Today's structure was erected on the site of an earlier French Romanesque church designed by Clayton but destroyed in a storm in 1900.

¶ St. Mary's Cathedral, 2011 Church Street.

Originally constructed in the late 1840s with a half million bricks donated by Belgium, this Gothic Revival building was altered by Clayton in the 1870s and 1880s with the addition of a central tower and the heightening of the two front towers.

¶ St. Patrick's Church, 1010 35th Street

¶ Temple B'Nai Israel, 3006 Avenue O.

¶ Trueheart-Adriance Building, 210 22nd Street.

One of many commercial buildings designed by Clayton, this three-story structure was erected for the first chartered real estate firm in the state. Carved-stone bases and capitals accent the pressed bricks used in its construction.

Some of the other commercial buildings which Clayton designed are:

• The Greenleve, Block and Company Building (2120-2128 Strand), noteworthy because its four stories are equal in height to a modern seven-story building;

• The Hutchings, Sealy and Company Building (2326 Strand), a bank building constructed in the Classic Revival style in 1895-97; and

• The *Galveston News* Building (2108-2116 Mechanic Street), built with white and pink marble and pressed red and yellow brick.

Several equally famous structures which Nicholas Clayton designed during his career in Galveston are no longer in existence, the victims of either fire or hurricane Carla: St. Mary's College; the Electric Pavilion (1881-1883), the first building in Texas outfitted with electricity and formerly located on the site of the present Moody Civic Center; the Beach Hotel (1883-1898); and the Ursuline Academy, Convent, and Chapel (1891-1961).

¶ The site of the former Ursuline Academy is today occupied by an Ursuline convent and the Galveston Catholic School (2601 Ursuline Street/ Avenue N, between Rosenberg Avenue and 27th Street).

Among the nuns buried in the convent cemetery is *Mother St. Pierre Harrington, the religious superior of the convent during the Civil War. When federal troops attacked the city, she converted the convent into a hospital for wounded soldiers from both sides. Because the Union forces thought that the convent was a Confederate stronghold, however, gunboats off the coast began to fire on the building. Following a suggestion that the sisters fly a yellow flag – the signal for quarantine – they desperately hunted for a bit of yellow cloth. According to tradition, the nuns found a yellow skirt in a student's trunk and a soldier unfurled it from the belfry. The gunboats immediately ceased their shelling. For many years after Mother St. Pierre's death, representatives of both the Union and the Confederate armies gathered here to decorate her grave.

GOLIAD

¶ **Bahia Presidio,** 1 mile south on U.S. 77A/183.

Established in 1749 to protect Mission Espiritu Santo de Zuniga, the presidio has been restored to its appearance in 1836. Visitors can see the barracks, officers' quarters, guardhouse, and Our Lady of Loreto Chapel.

The presidio was the scene of two major events during the Texas Revolution. On October 9, 1835, the fort was seized from its Mexican garrison by a group of Texans – most of them Irish Catholics. The following December 20 the presidio was the scene of an even more historic event when ninety-one Texas colonists signed the Goliad Declaration of Independence from Mexico. Of the signers, at least twenty-six had recognizably Irish surnames and probably hailed from the Irish colonies at Refugio, Victoria, and San Patricio. To mark the occasion, Philip Dimmit, one of the two men who drafted the declaration and one of the Irish-American signers, created a flag emblazoned with a red arm holding an unsheathed sword, undoubtedly reminiscent of the red flag of Ulster.

The other signers with recognizably Irish surnames were Jeremiah Day, Andrew Devereaux, Spirse Dooley, John Dunn, Nicholas Fagan, E. B. W. Fitzgerald, Timothy Hart, Thomas Hanron, Michael Kelly, J. D. Kilpatrick, Martin Lawler, Alexander Lynch, Charles Malone, Edward McDonough, Morgan O'Brien, Thomas O'Brien, C. J. O'Connor, James O'Connor, Thomas O'Connor, Michael O'Donnell, Patrick O'Leary, Patrick Quinn, William Quinn, Edmond (or Edward) Quirk, and Michael Riley.

Various authorities claim that the following signers were also of Irish descent: John Bower, Elkanah Brush, Morgan Bryan, James Duncan, James Elder, John Fagan, Thomas Hansom, John James, Timothy Hart, Peter Hynes, Walter Lambert, Victor Loupy, Robert McClure, Edward McDonald, George McKnight, Hugh McMinn, John Pollan, Edward Quirk, John Shelly, Edward St. John, James St. John, and John W. Welsh.

§ Open daily 9-4:45. Closed January 1, Easter, Thanksgiving, and December 25. Fee. Phone: 512-645-3752.

⚓ Fannin Battleground State Historic Site, 9 miles east on U.S. 59.

In the months following the Goliad Declaration of Independence, the Bahia Presido was occupied by Colonel James Walker Fannin and between 400 and 500 Texan and American troops. In mid March 1836, hearing that a 1,600-man Mexican army was on its way to La Bahia, Fannin and his men fled the presidio. After stopping to rest at Coleto Creek, however, he and his troops were surrounded by the Mexicans and after a day and a half of fighting surrendered. This historic site commemorates the battle, fought just three weeks after the fall of the Alamo.

⚓ Fannin Burial Site, 2 miles south off U.S. 183.

After the battle of Coleto Creek in mid March 1836, James Fannin and his 407 remaining troops returned to La Bahia Presidio as prisoners. A week later, however, most of them were executed, a massacre that only strengthened the Texans' determination to achieve independence. Colonel Fannin and his men are buried at this site.

Among the dead were forty-seven Irish natives or men with Irish surnames. The following twenty soldiers were from the Irish colonies at Refugio and San Patricio: Matthew Byrne, Daniel Buckley, George Cash, Alfred Dorsey, Matthew Eddy, John Fadden, Edward Garner, Lewis Gates, John Gleason, John James, John Kelly, John McGloin, Dennis McGowan, Dennis Mahoney, Patrick Nevin, Thomas Quinn, William Quinn, Thomas Quirk, Edward Ryan, and Captain Ira Westover.

That all of Fannin's men were not executed was due to the fact that twenty-eight escaped and another twenty were saved from the firing squad for various reasons. Eight (including William Brennan and Thomas Cantwell) were spared because they spoke Spanish, and John Fagan and John McGloin were rescued by their Mexican neighbors. Andrew Boyle, meanwhile, was saved by a Mexican captain named Carlos de la Garza, who had been entertained at the home of the Irishman's brother and sister in San Patricio only a few days before. Among the other Irish spared were James Byrnes, Edward Perry, Nicholas Fagan, and Anthony and John Sidick. (Fagan escaped death by obscuring his face with a side of beef hoisted onto his shoulders.)

Located a few hundred yards from La Bahia Presidio, the Goliad Memorial Shaft marks the graves of Colonel Fannin and the other victims of the Goliad Massacre. The remains of the victims, which were left unburied for three months, were gathered up and carried in procession to the grave site. There they received a full military burial conducted by Texas general *Thomas Rusk on June 3, 1836.

¶ Goliad State Historical Park, 1 mile south on U.S. 77A/183.

This 184-acre site commemorates the Texans who were killed during the battle of Goliad on March 27, 1836. (See previous two entries.) Visitors to the park headquarters can see artifacts and a multimedia presentation about the massacre.

§ Open daily 8-5. Fee. Phone: 512-645-3405.

GREENVILLE

¶ Audie Murphy Exhibit, W. Walworth Harrison Public Library, 3716 Lee Street.

In addition to extensive files on Murphy's life, the library displays a first edition of his memoir (*To Hell and Back*), posters advertising his movies, replicas of his many medals, and an oil portrait of the country's most highly decorated veteran.

Murphy traced his paternal roots in America to a great-grandfather who had arrived from Ireland by way of New Orleans and whose son, George Washington Murphy, had fought for the Confederacy during the Civil War. Audie's father, Emmet ("Pat"), was a Texas sharecropper who deserted his wife and their eleven children when the future hero was only a boy.

For a number of years Audie helped his mother raise his siblings. About this early period in his life, he later confessed: "God knows where my pride came from. But I had it. And it was constantly getting me into trouble. My temper was explosive and my moods, typically Irish, swung from the heights to the depths. At school I fought a great deal. Perhaps I was trying to level with my fists what I assumed fate had put above me." Ruth Rutherford, one of his elementary school teachers, confirmed his self-impression: "'My Little Pat' . . . seemed to carry a chip on his shoulder. I always thought of him as my 'Fighting Irishman,' and many, many times I had to be referee. After I had learned of his home situation, I could more easily understand his feelings and attitude."

In 1942 the young Murphy tried to enlist in America's war effort. Although he succeeded in lying about his age – he was only sixteeen – he was turned down because he failed to meet the height requirement. After rejection by the Marines and the Paratroopers, he was finally accepted by the Army Infantry.

By the end of January 1945, Murphy had participated in the Allied invasions of Italy and France and was with the 3rd Infantry Division as it closed in on the German army. He had already won the Purple Heart, the Distinguished Service Cross, and the silver and bronze stars when he found himself in perhaps the most desperate situation of his military career. When Second Lieutenant Murphy realized that he and his men faced almost 600 German troops and a half dozen tanks, he ordered his men into the surrounding woods. Murphy, however, mounted one of his own burning tanks and let loose against the Germans with deadly machine gun fire. During a half-hour barrage, he single-handedly held off the Germans' infantry and Panzer attack, thereby forcing the enemy to pull back and allowing his own men to mount a successful counterattack.

For this act of courage Murphy was awarded the Medal of Honor, the final recognition which the nation could give him. Not yet twenty-one, he had been wounded three times and had received twenty-four medals from the United States, three from France, and one from Belgium.

Upon his return to the United States, Murphy was accorded a hero's welcome and was featured on the cover of *LIFE* magazine. He subsequently began an acting career that counted more than forty films to his credit, including *Red Badge of Courage* and the 1955 movie version of his autobiography, *To Hell and Back*.

For all his fame, though, Murphy seems to have been possessed by some personal demon. His survival only highlighted for him the wartime deaths of so many of his friends, and he once threw away the many decorations he had received. He later succumbed to excessive gambling and experienced several unhappy marriages. He died – anticlimactically – in a 1971 plane crash in North Carolina. (See Brush Mountain, Virginia.) He was buried in Arlington National Cemetery. (See Arlington, Virginia.)

¶ **Old Post Office,** Lee Street.

A historical marker in front of the post office identifies this as the building in which Audie Murphy enlisted in the U.S. Army on his eighteenth birthday, June 20, 1942.

¶ Three other sites associated with Audie Murphy are found in the vicinity of Greenville:

• A historical marker on U.S. 69 eight miles north of Greenville identifies the site of Murphy's birthplace in 1924.

• A historical marker on U.S. 69 on the eastern edge of Celeste (12
miles northwest of Greenville) identifies where he lived for four years
and received most of his schooling.

• The Audie Murphy Memorial Plaza in Farmersville (15 miles west
of Greenville) contains a marble tablet dedicated to the World War II hero
and all Americans who served their country. The monument is inscribed
with a verse from Murphy's poem "Dusty Old Helmet, Rusty Old Gun."

HENDERSON

¶ **Thomas Rusk Statue,** North Main between Fordall and Charlevoix
streets

This bronze statue was erected in 1936 to honor Thomas Rusk, one of
the Irish-American signers of the 1836 Texas Declaration of Independence.
The base of the statue is inscribed with the following tribute: "Soldier,
Patriot, Jurist, Statesman. Bold, intrepid and daring on the field of battle
he is yet more honored for his forbearance and sound judgement. His able
counsel as secretary of war materially assisted in the winning of freedom
for Texas. He signed the Declaration of Independence and helped draft
the Constitution. To a large degree he devised the court system and served
as the chief justice of the Republic of Texas. Strong advocate for annexation he presided over the convention of 1845 which framed the first state
constitution and as United States Senator he was foremost in the settlement of the Rio Grande as the boundary of Texas."

The son of an Irish stonemason who had worked on the estate of
*John C. Calhoun in South Carolina, Rusk played a prominent role in
achieving and maintaining Texas independence. At the 1836 convention
he helped draft and adopt a constitution for the Texas Republic and was
elected secretary of war in the newly created government. Rusk fought
gallantly during the battle of San Jacinto and led several successful charges
after *General Sam Houston was wounded. For several months after the
battle, which effectively achieved Texas independence, he was in command of the infant republic's army. He later served Texas as a member of
its second congress and chief justice of its supreme court.

During the 1840s Rusk advocated American annexation of Texas. In
July 1845 he was president of the convention which considered the offer
of annexation made by the U.S. Congress. On assuming the presidency of
the convention, Rusk said: "Our duties here, although important, are plain
and easy of performance. . . . [W]e have one grand object in view, and that
is to enter the great American Confederacy with becoming dignity and
self-respect. Let us, then, lay aside all minor considerations, and avoid all
subjects calculated to divide us in opinion." His words had their intended

effect, because the convention approved annexation by a 55-1 vote and went on to adopt a constitution for the newest state in the Union.

Three years later, as a member of the U.S. Senate, Rusk expressed his views about the territory recently acquired by conquest and treaty from Mexico: "It is said, Mr. President, that it would be robbery to take away their country from the Mexicans. On this point, I would ask whether the principles of our Government do not guaranty to all of our citizens the full enjoyment of life, liberty, and property? If so, would not the extension of our Government throughout Mexico give perfect security to the inhabitants, who would, in that event, be entitled to the protection of our laws? . . . It would take from the tyrannical military chiefs the power of oppressing the people. It would deprive foreigners of their power and privilege to make use of the Government for their own purposes, in effecting their own aggrandizement and enriching themselves. It would afford the country an opportunity to develop its mighty resources, and prevent them from being monopolized by a few foreign capitalists, whose interests are in conflict with those of the United States. . . . I would not be willing to vote for a treaty of peace that would not secure to us the territory as far as the Sierra Madre, including the Californias."

HILLSBORO

¶ Harold B. Simpson Confederate Research Center and Audie Murphy Gun Museum, in the Hill College history complex.

Besides numerous Civil War photographs and documents, this museum displays the guns and army uniform of Audie Murphy, the country's most highly decorated serviceman. (See Greenville, Texas.)

§ Open Monday-Friday 8-noon and 1-4. Closed college holidays. Phone: 617-582-2555, ext. 242.

HOUSTON

¶ Annunciation Church, 1618 Texas Avenue.

In about 1880 the serious structural defects in this Catholic church were eliminated by *Nicholas Clayton. In remodeling the church along Romanesque-Revival lines, he added a new roof, buttresses, and a 175-foot tower between the spires. He also stuccoed the exterior of the building and added brown marble trim.

¶ Bayou Bend, 4.5 miles west via Memorial Drive and then 0.5 mile south on Wescott Street.

This twenty-eight-room mansion was built in 1827 for the children of James Stephen Hogg, the first native-born governor of Texas and the son of a prominent planter of Scotch-Irish descent. (See Rusk, Texas.)

In the mid 1950s Hogg's daughter, Ima, coordinated the house's conversion into the Bayou Bend Collection of the Museum of Fine Arts. The collection's 4,700 art objects range from the seventeenth to the nineteenth century and include furniture, Paul Revere silver, and art work by *John Singleton Copley, Edward Hicks, Charles Willson Peale, Gilbert Stuart, and Benjamin West. The fourteen-acre estate also has a number of cultivated formal gardens.

§ House open Tuesday-Friday 1-4, Saturday 10-12:45. Gardens open Tuesday-Saturday 10-5, Sunday 1-5. Closed major holidays. Fee. Phone: 713-520-2600.

§ **Hermann Park,** South Main Street between Hermann Avenue and Marlborough Drive.

• At the main entrance to this 545-acre park is a bronze equestrian statue of *General Sam Houston by Enrico Cerracchio. Although Houston's son objected that the statue was a very poor likeness of his father and even tried to prevent its unveiling, the statue was publicly dedicated in 1924.

• At the south entrance to the park is a statue of *Dick Dowling, the hero of the battle of Sabine Pass. The life-size statue of the Confederate officer is part of a granite memorial inscribed with the names of the Davis Guards, the all-Irish unit which repulsed a planned Union attack on Fort Griffin in the Sabine Pass. (See Sabine Pass, Texas.)

The statue was erected in 1905 by the Ancient Order of Hibernians and the Dick Dowling Company of United Confederate Veterans. For many years the memorial was kept clean by Tom Needham Sr., who once quipped that "St. Patrick ran the snakes out of Ireland. And Dick Dowling ran the Yankees out of Texas."

On March 6, 1889, the city of Houston presented Dowling's daughter Annie with a diamond-studded gold medal in recognition of his services to the Confederacy, especially to saving Texas from a Union invasion in 1863.

§ **John Connally Statue,** outside the Heritage Gallery, The Heritage Society, 1100 Bagby Street.

This life-size standing statue depicts Governor John Connally, who was wounded in the sniper attack which killed *President John F. Kennedy in Dallas on November 22, 1963.

The governor, whose great-grandfather Charles Connally emigrated from Ireland to escape the Great Famine, enjoyed a varied career in law, business, and politics. While still a law student, he began a lengthy political association with Lyndon Johnson, initially as the latter's campaign aide and then as a strategist and administrative assistant while Johnson served in the Senate. In addition, Connally was a founder and manager of radio station KVET in Austin and later served as attorney for – and officer of – the far-flung interests of the Texas oil magnate Sid Richardson.

When President-elect Kennedy nominated Connally as secretary of the navy, concern was expressed about a conflict of interest between the nominee's earlier role as a lobbyist for various oil and gas companies and the navy's status as the largest oil purchaser in the world. Although confirmed as navy secretary, Connally served less than a year before going on to win the first of three terms as governor of Texas. He subsequently served in the Nixon administration as secretary of defense and special presidential advisor. His reputation was tarnished, however, when he was later accused of accepting gifts illegally during the 1972 presidential campaign, although he was acquitted of the charges.

¶ **Kennedy Trading Post,** 813 Congress Street.

This Creole-style building was erected about 1845 by John Kennedy, an Irish immigrant who made a name for himself in America as a miller, merchant, planter, baker, and Indian trader. His two-story shop – adorned with wrought-iron grillwork – is Houston's oldest commercial structure on its original site and remained in his family until 1970.

Besides operating the general merchandise store at this location, Kennedy regularly sold supplies to a group of Alabama-Coushatti Indians who lived north of Houston. Every Saturday the Native Americans came to the Irishman's store to exchange their venison, turkeys, and other game for calico, lead, powder, and whiskey. During the Civil War the Irishman supplied the Confederates with hardtack.

According to the 1860 census, Kennedy was the seventh richest man in Houston. Since the previous census a decade earlier, the value of his industrial investments had grown to $13,000 and his real property had increased in value to $100,000 – from respective amounts of $5,000 and $10,000.

¶ **St. Vincent's Cemetery,** adjacent to Our Lady of Guadalupe Church, 2405 Navigation Boulevard.

The city's oldest Catholic graveyard contains the remains of *Dick Dowling and some members of the Davis Guards, the unit which thwarted a Union attempt to capture Houston by way of the Sabine Pass.

When the exact location of Dowling's grave was still unknown, a granite monument to his memory was erected in the cemetery. The pyramid-shaped memorial was unveiled in 1935 by his only surviving daughter, Annie Dowling Robertson. In 1988, after Dowling's grave had been positively identified, a tombstone and an engraved marker were placed on the site by his descendants. (See Sabine Pass, Texas.)

¶ **San Jacinto Battleground State Historical Complex,** 21 miles east via State 225 and then 3 miles north on State 134.

This 1,000-acre park marks the site of the battle of San Jacinto on April 21, 1836, a victory for the Texans which effectively achieved their independence from Mexico. Ironically, the battlefield was owned by Peggy McCormick, an Irish-born widow whose husband had purchased the property sometime after 1822.

The final phase of the Texas Revolution began when Santa Anna's armies burned the Irish colonies of Refugio, San Patricio, and Victoria. This outrage caused more men from these colonies to rally to the Texan cause against the Mexican dictator. Approximately 100 Irish-born – or one-eighth of the Texas army – participated in the subsequent battle of San Jacinto. There, in a contest that lasted only eighteen minutes, *Sam Houston's 800-man army defeated a Mexican force of between 1,100 and 1,400 soldiers. Santa Anna suffered the loss of 630 men and the capture of 730 prisoners, while the Texan loss was only two killed and thirty wounded (seven fatally).

Among those who fought at San Jacinto were forty-one Catholics with what William Ryan in *Shamrock and Cactus* calls recognizably Irish surnames: William Boyles, William Brennan, Patrick Bryody [Brody?], James Burch, Valentine Burch, George Casey, John Cassidy, James Connor, Patrick Curneal, Matthew Dunn, Thomas Farley, Thomas Flynn, S. T. Foley, James Freele, Edward Gallagher, Michael Goheen, James Hogan, Thomas Hogan, John Karner, C. O'Donnell Kelly, William Kenkennon, Walter Lambert, Walter Lane, Nicholas Lynch, Charles Malone, John McCrabb, Joseph McCrabb, Joseph McGee, Robert McLaughlin, Stephen McLaughlin, Samuel McNeely, Andrew McStea, Daniel Murphy, Patrick O'Connor, Thomas O'Connor, Daniel O'Driscoll, John O'Neill, John Plunkett, Dennis Sullivan, and Patrick Usher.

After the battle Mrs. McCormick surveyed the bloody field, strewn with Mexican dead, and demanded to know who was going to remove the corpses. "Madam," said the victorious Houston, "do you not know your land will be famed in history?" The chagrined widow reputedly replied, "To the devil with your glorious history!"

As if reinforce the general's prediction, the famous battlefield is today dominated by the San Jacinto Monument, a 570-foot obelisk surmounted by a 35-foot-high Star of Texas. The base of the monument is covered with eight panels with scenes from the Texas Revolution, while the frieze above the panels depicts episodes in the American colonization of Texas. The San Jacinto Museum of History, located inside the base of the monument, traces the history of Texas from the beginning of Spanish exploration and displays memorabilia connected with the men who fought here. An elevator takes visitors to an observation level near the top, and a multi-image slide show "reenacts" events during the Texas Revolution.

§ Monument open daily 9-6. Closed December 24-25. Fee for elevator and slide show. Phone: 713-479-2421.

HUNTSVILLE

❡ Sam Houston Burial Site, Oakwood Cemetery, 9th Street and Avenue I.

The grave of *Sam Houston is marked by a granite monument with a bas-relief depicting the first president of the Texas Republic seated on a horse. Erected on 1911, the memorial is inscribed with the words of *Andrew Jackson: "The World Will Take Care of Houston's Fame." A nearby historical marker gives a summary of Houston's life:

"Born March 2, 1793, in Rockbridge County Va.; son of Samuel and Elizabeth Houston. Moved to Tennessee in 1807 with widowed mother and her family. In 1813 joined U.S. Army under General Andrew Jackson, with whom he formed lifelong friendship and political ties. In Tennessee, taught school, kept a store, served in U.S. Congress, was state governor. In 1829, after his young bride left him, resigned as governor and went westward. Settling in 1833 in Nacogdoches, became a leader in cause of Texas independence from Mexico. Elected March 4, 1836, to command the Army of the Republic, engineered retrograde movement that led to victory of San Jacinto, which won Texas independence. President of the Republic, 1836-1838 and 1841-1844, he was senator after annexation. In 1859 he was elected governor and served until secession. In 1861 he declined to

Sam Houston Burial Site.

take oath of office in Confederacy, retiring instead after a quarter-century of service to his state. However, he did not oppose Confederate Army enlistment of his young son, Sam Houston, Jr. While the Civil War continued, he died on July 26, 1863, at his home, "Steamboat House," Huntsville. With him was his family, to hear his last words to his wife: 'Texas–, Margaret, Texas–.'"

¶ **Sam Houston Memorial Museum Complex,** 0.5 mile south on State 75 (Business) at 1836 Sam Houston Avenue.

This fifteen-acre museum complex contains seven structures, among them a museum, an exhibit hall, Houston's law office, two of his homes, and three reconstructed outbuildings.

• The Woodland Home is a dogtrot house which Houston built when he and his wife, Margaret, moved to Huntsville in 1847, while he was a U.S. senator. The house was constructed of squared logs covered with hand-hewn, whitewashed boards. The detached kitchen and law office were built of unfinished squared logs. In a letter to a friend, Houston described his new home as a "bang up place."

Because of his determined opposition to secession, Houston was later removed from the governorship and was henceforth regarded as a traitor. Prior to his dismissal, however, he made an eloquent plea for American nationhood: "Men who never endured the privation, the toil, the peril that I have for my country call me a traitor because I am willing to yield obedience to the Constitution and the constituted authorities. Let them suffer what I have for this Union, and they will feel it entwining so closely around their hearts that it will be like snapping the cords of life to give it up. . . ."

When Houston and his wife attempted to rent or repurchase the Woodland Home in 1862, they were refused. He eventually succeeded in renting the nearby Steamboat House, where he died the next year.

• The museum contains many Houston memorabilia, including his sword and dueling pistol and some of his letters to his wife. One of the most interesting items in the museum's collection is General Santa Anna's gold, brass, and leather saddle.

• Houston's law office is outfitted with his bookcase and desk.

§ Open Tuesday-Sunday 9-5. Closed January 1, Thanksgiving, and December 24-25. Donations. Phone: 409-295-7824.

¶ **Sam Houston Statue,** on the upper campus of Sam Houston State University (opposite the Sam Houston Memorial Museum Complex).

¶ **Sam Houston Statue,** 34000 State 75 at Interstate 45 exit 109 (north) or Interstate 45 exit 112 (south).

Known as "A Tribute to Courage," this 67-foot-high statue is the world's tallest in honor of an American hero. "Big Sam" was created in the mid 1990s by David Adickes and consists of five layers of concrete poured over steel mesh attached to a welded steel framework. The colossal statue is visible from the south for six miles and is the highest point between Dallas and Houston.

KINGSVILLE

¶ King Ranch, west off Route 141.

Although today the King Ranch sprawls over 826,000 acres and is larger than Rhode Island, it began as a much more modest tract of 75,000 acres purchased in 1853 by Captain Richard King and known as the Santa Gertrudis Ranch. Seven years later King formed a cattle ranching partnership with Mifflin Kenedy, like himself a former riverboat captain. They continued to acquire additional property until the ranch included more than a quarter of a million acres – almost 2,000 square miles.

Mifflin Kenedy had been born in Pennsylvania in 1818, a descendant of Irish immigrants who had come to Maryland with Lord Baltimore in 1634. From a devout and well established Quaker family in Chester County, Pennsylvania, Kenedy was educated at a boarding school run by the Quaker scholar Jonathan Gouse. At about the age of twenty, Kenedy began a career as a clerk and captain in the steamboat trade, traversing the "Father of Waters" as well as the Apalachee and Chattahooche rivers in Florida. As an enlistee during the Mexican War, he was responsible for transporting troops and supplies along the Rio Grande. He converted to Catholicism when he married Petra Vela de Vidal, the widow of a colonel in the Mexican army.

After the conflict Kenedy and three partners – one of them Richard King – developed a profitable merchandising traffic along the Rio Grande, owning a fleet of twenty-seven vessels at the height of their prosperity. While still in partnership with King, Kenedy acquired half interest in the former's Santa Gertrudis Ranch. (They soon became the first Texas ranchers to fence in their huge holdings.) When they dissolved their ranching partnership in 1868, they divided the property equally.

To his vast holdings from Santa Gertrudis, Kenedy added the 132,000 acres of the Laurelos ranch. He later sold his combined 242,000 acres – with 50,000 head of cattle – for $1 million. In the meantime he became involved in railroad construction. In 1876 he and King built a narrow-gauge line from Corpus Christi to Laredo (163 miles), while nine years later he financed the construction of the San Antonio & Arkansas Pass Railroad (700 miles).

§ Loop Road open daily 9-5. Phone: 512-592-8516.

¶ Mifflin Pens, about twenty miles from Kingsville, is located at the approximate center of the Kenedy Ranch, which today includes more than 500,000 acres. The nearby town of Sarita, the seat of Kenedy County, was named for Mifflin Kenedy's granddaughter.

LA GRANGE

¶ **Father Muldoon Monument,** south on U.S. 77 just north of the intersection with FM Road 2436.

This six-foot-high rough hewn granite marker is inscribed with the following dedication: "In Memory / of the forgotten man of Texas history / Father Miguel Muldoon / resident priest of Austin's colony / true friend of Stephen F. Austin and his people / 1823-1842 / contributed much towards the success of Austin's colonial venture."

Although it is known that Muldoon was descended from prosperous farmers in northern County Meath, Ireland, some question remains about the place of his birth. Family tradition claims that he was born in that part of Ireland, while at least one other source says that he was born about 1780 in Spain, where his Dublin-born father had married a "señorita." (The elder Muldoon had fled Ireland after a quarrel with British soldiers there.) Whatever the case, Muldoon appears to have received a hedge school education in Ireland before deciding – somewhat reluctantly – to

Father Muldoon Monument.

prepare for the priesthood. According to tradition, he was educated at the Irish College of Seville in Spain, where he seems to have achieved fluency in Spanish.

By 1831 Muldoon was living in Texas, where he had become a creditor to Stephen Austin. To pay off his debt, Austin helped Muldoon secure legal title to 48,000 acres, more than 20 percent of it in the La Grange area. Muldoon subsequently served as pastor to the members of the colony which Austin created on additional land granted him by Mexico.

At the time of his arrival in Texas from Mexico, Muldoon seems to have enjoyed extensive authority. An article in a Mexican publication of the time described him in grandiloquent terms: "The Reverend Doctor Muldoon, Parish Priest of Austin and Vicar General of All the Foreign Colonies, Already Existing, Or That May Be Hereafter Established In His Times, Invested With Plenipotentiary Papal and Episcopal Powers In Order To Dispensations. . . ." The newspaper also recounted that on his journey from Monterey he had baptized "upwards of a hundred persons" at two dollars apiece. In a firsthand account a Texan described Muldoon's early relations with the colonists in somewhat ambiguous terms: "His sage appearance and seemingly good manners caused him to be kindly received by the colonists, as a kind of necessary evil, which they could not well avoid. Every courtesy and attention was paid to him, and for a time, him and his parishioners got on very well together; he never troubled them with church services, but confined himself in his duties to baptism and marriage ceremonies. . . ."

Austin had sought a priest for his colony not only to minister to the Catholics already among its number but also to carry out the conversion of Protestant Texans who wished to become eligible for land grants from the Mexican government. Because many of these Protestants adopted Catholicism only superficially, however, they were known as "Muldoon Catholics." That the Mexican requirement about conversion was often ignored is evident in the account of a young German girl about how her father received title to land from Austin. "My father had to kiss the Bible," she wrote, "and promise, as soon as the priest should arrive, to become a Catholic. People were married by the alcalde, also, on the promise that they would have themselves reunited on the arrival of the priest. But no one ever became Catholic, though the priest, Father Muldoon, arrived promptly. The people of San Felipe made him drunk and sent him back home."

Despite such abuse, Muldoon remained on friendly terms with Austin himself. At a New Year's Day banquet in Anahuac in 1832, for example, the priest offered this toast to his patron:

> May plow and harrow, spake and fack
> Remain the arms of Anahuac
> So that her rich and boundless plains

May yearly yield all sorts of grains.
May all religious discord fall
And friendship be the creed of all.
With tolerance your pastor views
All sects of Christians, Turks and Jews.
We now demand three rousing cheers
Great Austin's health and pioneers.

In addition, two years later Muldoon visited Austin while the American was imprisoned by Mexican authorities. In a diary entry for February 23, 1834, Austin wrote: "I was visited by Padre Muldoon, who had with great difficulty obtained this privilege. He was allowed to speak to me only in Spanish in the presence of the Commandant of the prison, manifesting his friendship &c. I permitted him to make a bargain with some Tavern keeper for my meals, which he did, & sent me wine and cheese, he promised to send me books." And when Muldoon decided to sell his property in the La Grange area, Austin bought it from the priest. (Unfortunately for Austin, various members of Muldoon's family brought suit to obtain the land. Some of the claimants were reputed cousins in St. Louis, Belfast, and Dublin.)

Although additional information about "Paddy" Muldoon is sketchy, he did figure prominently in an episode which occurred in 1837. In that year William Wharton, who represented the Texas Republic in Washington, D.C., resigned his position. En route home, however, he was captured by two Mexican gunboats. While imprisoned in Mexico, he was visited by Father Muldoon, who offered the diplomat a chance to escape: "Mr. Wharton, the next time I come to see you I will bring the garb of a Catholic priest with me. In this you must dress yourself – and simply walk out of prison. There will be no questions asked. If you are accosted, simply extend your right hand with the first two fingers elevated and say, 'Pax vobiscum' and remember that you are a Catholic priest until you reach Texas." For his part in Wharton's escape, the Irishman was reputedly imprisoned by General Santa Anna five years later.

NACOGDOCHES

¶ **Stone Fort Museum,** on the campus of Stephen Austin University at Clark and Griffith boulevards.

Nine flags have flown over this historic building, where Mexican authorities administered the oath of allegiance to such early Texas pioneers as James Bowie and Irish-Americans David Crockett, Sam Houston, and Thomas Rusk.

§ Open Tuesday-Saturday 9-5, Sunday 1-5. Donations. Phone: 409-568-2408

§ Thomas Rusk Burial Site, Oak Grove Cemetery, at the east end of Hospital Street at North Lanana.

A granite monument erected by the state of Texas marks the grave of *Thomas Rusk, one of the most prominent leaders of the Texas Republic. Three other signers of the Texas Declaration of Independence are also buried here.

While serving in the U.S. Senate, Rusk became reacquainted with *John C. Calhoun, on whose estate in South Carolina he had grow up in the early 1800s. The transplanted Texan was also a consistent champion of government support for construction of a southern railroad line to the Pacific. Following the death of his wife in 1856, Rusk fell into despondency and committed suicide at his home in Nacogdoches. (See Henderson, Texas.)

ODESSA

§ The Presidential Museum, 622 North Lee Street.

Although originally intended to be a memorial to *President John F. Kennedy, this museum evolved into the only one in the United States devoted to the office of the presidency. The facility offers exhibits and educational programs designed to enhance the understanding of the American presidency, presidential campaigns, and the electoral process. The museum features campaign memorabilia, portraits, documents, medals, cartoons, signatures, and commemorative items associated with the nation's presidents, vice presidents, first ladies, and unsuccessful presidential candidates, as well as the presidents of the Texas Republic.

§ Open Tuesday-Saturday 10-5. Closed major holidays. Phone: 915-332-7123.

OZONA

§ David Crockett Monument, in the city park on the town square.

A ten-foot-high bas-relief statue of *David Crockett is part of an impressive stone memorial to the famous frontiersman. The base of the monument is inscribed with Crockett's advice: "Be sure you are right. Then go ahead."

PALESTINE

§ John Reagan Statue, Reagan Park, Crockett Road and Reagan Street.

This memorial statue by Pompeo Coppini honors John Henninger Reagan, the postmaster general of the Confederacy. According to the sculptor, the standing figure represents Reagan as a modern Roman tribune in the act of delivering a speech in the U.S. Senate. At the base of the statue is

Statue of John Reagan, a member of the Confederate cabinet.

a seated, nude male figure representing the "Lost Cause" of the Confederacy. The bronze tablet at the back of the monument summarizes Reagan's political career and concludes with his words: "The old Roman's highest ambition was to do his full duty: consciousness of having done it was his ample reward. A good name is rather to be chosen than great riches, and loving favor rather than silver and gold."

Born in Tennessee in 1818, Reagan was of Irish, English, Welsh, and German stock. Both a grandfather and a great-grandfather had served in the Continental Army during the Revolutionary War, the former as a surgeon and the latter (Timothy Reagan) as a soldier wounded at the battle of Brandywine.

As a youngster, John Reagan worked in his father's tannery, but at age fifteen or sixteen he went off to seek his own fortune. After working on a farm for $9 a month, he found employment as the manager of several flour and saw mills, eventually earning enough money to attend a college in Maryville, Tennessee. He remained at the school for only a year, however, before heading to Texas, intent upon a career as a salesman.

When the prospect of a commercial career faded, however, Reagan joined the Texas army, at the time engaged in a campaign against the Cherokee. The gallantry which he showed during a battle in July 1839 resulted in an offer of appointment as a junior second lieutenant, but he declined the promotion to take up surveying instead. A year later he was appointed surveyor-general for the Republic of Texas. During one of the first surveying expeditions to the Upper Trinity country, he and his party were attacked by Indians. Although some of the Texans were wounded, they succeeded in capturing eight of the Indians' packhorses. He was one of only six men who persevered to reach the banks of the Trinity River.

Between 1842 and 1844, Reagan continued his peripatetic ways. After brief stints fighting Indians, doing farm work, and driving oxen, he settled down on a farm in Palestine, where he raised cattle and horses. He soon succumbed to the lure of politics, however, and in rapid succession was elected to the Texas legislature, a district judgeship, and finally Congress. In the meantime he had been admitted to the practice of the law.

As was to be expected, Reagan's congressional career was dominated by the slavery issue. Although he opposed reopening the slave trade and regarded slavery as immoral, he recognized that the latter was constitutionally protected. When the national debate turned into armed conflict, he sided with his state and the Confederacy. In a speech at the beginning of 1861, he explained why he could not remain in Congress: "Up to this time, I had been an ardent Unionist, denouncing all schemes and views favoring its disruption, whether they came from the North or the South. But when we were told that we must submit to the violation of the Constitution, the overthrow of the rights of the States and the destruction of three thousand million dollars worth of property in slaves – property recognized by the Constitution, Federal and State laws, and by the decisions of the Supreme Court of the United States, – I could no longer agree to such a Union, and determined to join in any measure which might defeat it."

In March 1861 Reagan was appointed postmaster general of the new Confederate government by *President Jefferson Davis. Despite Reagan's best efforts, the postal service was never satisfactory to the public, primarily because the government insisted that the service be self-sufficient, a demand that forced Reagan to eliminate routes and accept inferior service from contractors with the lowest bids. When he persuaded the Confederate Congress to double the postal rates on printed materials, he was denounced by the press. The *Richmond Daily Examiner*, for instance, cried that he had converted his department into "an engine for the suppression of intelligence," adding that he was forcing soldiers to pay dearly for the luxury of reading the news.

During the last month of the Confederacy, Reagan was captured by Union troops and, with Davis, was imprisoned – first in Hampton Roads, Virginia, and then at Fort Warren in Boston. From the latter prison Reagan wrote to the people of Texas, urging them to accept the Union victory, lest they be punished further with the "twin disasters" of military occupation and universal black suffrage. He went on to urge Texans to accept the authority of the United States, renounce secession and slavery, and grant suffrage to former slaves if demanded to do so by the federal government. Only then, he believed, could the people of the state reestablish a government and elect congressmen to their liking. With regard to the former slaves, he believed that they could be accorded the constitutional protections demanded by the North but that those not ready to exercise the duties of citizenship could be kept from the polls by literacy and property qualifications. For such advice, however, he was later regarded as disloyal to Texas. As a result, when he returned to the state following his release from prison in October 1865, he withdrew from public life to his farm in Palestine.

After the postwar situation had stabilized, Reagan returned to the practice of law and in 1874 was elected to the first of seven terms in the House of Representatives. During a subsequent term in the U.S. Senate, he resigned to become chairman of the Texas state railroad commission, doing so, as he said, "both from a sense of duty to the state and of gratitude to the people who have honored and trusted me so long and in so many ways."

¶ A historical marker in nearby Fort Houston Park notes that the park was a gift of Reagan's descendants and is located on the site of his former farm.

¶ A bust of Reagan is located in the front lobby of the Palestine Public Library, 1101 North Cedar Street.

QUITMAN

¶ Governor Hogg Shrine State Historical Park, Route 37 South.

The main attraction on the property is the Honeymoon Cottage, built in 1952 to replicate the first home of *Governor James Stephen Hogg and his wife, Sarah Ann Stinson Hogg. The house, which was furnished by the Hoggs' daughter, features memorabilia and family photographs.

• The Miss Ima Hogg Museum on the property was named for the Hoggs' daughter, a philanthropist and expert in the decorative arts. Among its displays are decorative arts and Indian artifacts.

§ Open Wednesday-Sunday 8-noon and 1-5. Fee. Phone: 214-763-2701.

REFUGIO

Beginning in the early 1830s, Refugio became the site of an Irish colony founded as the result of a contract between the Mexican government and Irishmen James Hewetson of Kilkenny and James Power of Wexford. Hewetson, who had been part of Stephen Austin's original band of immigrants to Texas, used agents to recruit settlers from southeastern Ireland, while Power returned to County Wexford to successfully recruit 250 families.

The two Irishmen had achieved title to this tract of land under a contract system designed to encourage the settlement of Mexico's northern province of Texas. In exchange for a promise to bring to the province an agreed upon number of settlers within a certain length of time, contractors known as *empresarios* would receive from the Mexican government a tract of land equal to approximately 67,000 acres. In addition, the head of each migrating family which engaged in agriculture was granted 177 acres of farming land and 4,428 acres of grazing land. Both the immigrants and the *empresarios* were required to pledge allegiance to the Mexican government and to profess the Roman Catholic faith.

Despite the optimism which characterized this early attempt at colonization, disaster dealt the effort a crippling blow. Although Power's recruits safely weathered the Atlantic and arrived in New Orleans, there many of the them contracted cholera and died. Power's desperate attempt to transport his colonists to Texas before they were further decimated met with further misfortune, however, when their ships ran aground on the coast of Texas and cholera again broke out. In the end, more than 200 of these colonists died before finally finding refuge at the appropriately named Refugio.

Although the Irish colony at Refugio was ultimately successful, the political issues which buffeted Texas at this time caused a rupture between Power and Hewetson. Power was in favor of independence for Texas and actively supported the Texas Revolution. He was a signer of the Texas Declaration of Independence on March 2, 1836, later served as a member of the General Council of the provisional government, and represented Refugio County in the Congress of the Republic of Texas. He later became an ardent supporter of annexation by the United States and was a delegate to the state Constitutional Convention in 1845. Hewetson, on the other hand, opposed annexation and returned to Mexico, where he acquired about 642,000 acres of land before his death in the 1870s.

¶ **Ballygarrett,** in the 200 block of Purisima Street (opposite King Park). Private.

This large Victorian structure was constructed at the beginning of the twentieth century by Mary Power Woodworth, a granddaughter of Refugio's original colonizer, James Power.

Called "Ballygarrett" for the town in County Wexford, Ireland, from which many of Refugio's Irish colonists came, this huge wooden edifice has always been painted yellow. The original structure was only one story in height, but a second floor was added in 1907. The sun parlor is octagonal in shape, while two other rooms have seven sides each and an entrance foyer has twelve sides and eight doorways. Several rooms are adorned with Italian crystal chandeliers and stained-glass windows.

¶ **Irish Colonists Memorial,** King Park, Commerce and Purisima streets.

This historical plaque on a granite base traces the influence of Irish settlers in this part of Texas and was dedicated on March 17, 1996, in the presence of a delegation from Ballygarrett, Ireland. The text of the plaque reads:

"The history of settlement in Refugio is closely associated with Ballygarrett, County Wexford, Ireland. Irish natives James Power (c. 1788-1832) and James Hewetson (1796-1870), both of whom immigrated to the United States in the early 19th century and later became citizens of Mexico, obtained permission from the Mexican government to oversee the immigration of more than 200 Irish families to Texas in the 1830s.

The first group of Irish settlers arrived on the Texas Gulf coast in 1834. A cholera epidemic and the loss of provisions and equipment in rough waters as the immigrants reached the shore delayed their arrival in Refugio, where they were to settle near the former Spanish mission of Nuestra Señora del Refugio. The colony soon was established, however, and almost immediately the new settlers were embroiled in the cause of Texas independence from Mexico. Many Irishmen fought in the Texas army and later served in the Republic of Texas Congress.

The Irish people established a lasting presence in the Refugio area. Many descendants of the early immigrants still reside in the area, some on land granted to their ancestors in the 1830s."

¶ **James Power Burial Site,** Mount Calvary Catholic Cemetery, Pecan and West Santiago streets.

When James Power died in 1852, he was buried on a bluff overlooking Copano Bay, where his Wexford colonists had first landed. Sometime in the 1870s, however, when his grave was vandalized, his remains were reburied at this site.

The monument over his grave reads: "James Power. Born Wexford Co., Ireland 1789. Died Live Oak Point, Tex. 1852. 1827 he came to Texas. Served under three Flags. As empresario, soldier, signer of the Constitution and Senator, he was always a loyal son to Texas. The sunset of his life was crowned by his name being enrolled in the Declaration of the Republic which he so honorably served. Pioneer, Statesman."

¶ **James Power Memorial,** in front of the Refugio County Courthouse, Commerce and Purisima streets.

A historical marker summarizes James Power's role in the history of Texas and Refugio County: "Born in Ireland, Colonel James Power came to New Orleans in 1809 and to Texas in 1823. With fellow Irish empresario James Hewetson (1796-1870), he was awarded contracts to settle Irish Catholic and Mexican families between the Guadalupe and Lavaca rivers.

The memorial marker at James Power's Gravesite.

Their territory was extended in 1830 to the Nueces. Power went to Ireland to recruit colonists. On the return voyage sickness and shipwreck tragically reduced their numbers. In 1835 he urged his colonists to garrison Goliad, and battled staunchly against hostile Indians. He was a fine diplomat and helped secure Indian neutrality during the Texas Revolution. A close friend of *General Sam Houston, Power signed both the Texas Declaration of Independence and the Constitution. In 1838 he was commissioned to conclude a treaty with the Lipan Indians. In 1842 he was briefly imprisoned by a Mexican invasion force. He represented Refugio in the Republic of Texas Senate and at the annexation convention of 1845. Power married twice, to Dolores (d. 1836) and later Tomasa Portilla, a Spanish-born daughter of empresario Felipe Portilla, and had seven children. He died at Live Oak Point, his principal home, in 1852, and was reinterred at Mount Calvary Cemetery, Refugio, about 1872."

¶ **Refugio County Museum,** 102 West West Street.

Among the museum's exhibits are displays about the history of the town's Irish colony.

§ Open Tuesday-Friday 9-5, Saturday 1-5. Phone: 512-526-5555.

RUSK

¶ **Jim Hogg State Historical Park,** on U.S. 84, 2 miles east off Park

Road.

This 177-acre park was originally part of "Mountain Home," the estate of Joseph Lewis Hogg, a prominent planter of Scotch-Irish descent and a member of the state legislature. The museum in the park is a one-third-scale replica of the plantation house which the Hogg family built in 1846. Hogg's son James Stephen Hogg was born here five years later and went on to become the state's first native-born governor.

Following his parents' death, the younger Hogg provided for himself by working as a farm hand, a typesetter, and a country editor before pursuing the study of the law. In rapid succession he was elected county attorney, district attorney, and state attorney general, primarily because of his reputation as a determined prosecutor. As attorney general he battled fraudulent insurance companies and advocated the regulation of railway rates in the state. Later as governor (1891-95) he saw the passage of the "Hogg Laws," which created the Railroad Commission, with authority over the oil industry, transportation, and utilities in the state. He was also influential in obtaining passage of legislation to end stock-watering, limit municipal expenditures, and prevent creation of giant landholding companies. Although when he retired from office he said that he possessed only fifty dollars in cash, his subsequent law practice and the discovery of oil on his property assured him a substantial fortune.

§ Park open September-May, Thursday-Monday 8-5; June-August, Thursday-Monday 8 a.m.-9 p.m. Museum open Thursday-Monday 10-4. Phone: 214-683-4850.

SABINE PASS

¶ **Sabine Pass Battleground State Historic Park,** 15 miles south of Port Arthur on State 87.

The centerpiece of this historic park is a nine-foot-tall bronze statue of *Lieutenant Richard ("Dick") Dowling, the commander of a Confederate force which repulsed a Union attempt to seize Sabine Pass in September 1863. The statue, which depicts Dowling naked to the waist, stands on a granite pedestal engraved with Dowling's account of the battle and the names of the forty-seven members of his unit – all Irish natives. The monument was dedicated in 1936.

Richard Dowling was born in Tuam, County Galway, Ireland, in 1838 and at the age of ten had come to New Orleans with his sister. After moving to Houston, he opened a tavern named "The Finish" and married Anne Odlum. (His father-in-law had emigrated from County Kildare and settled in the Texas colony of San Patricio de Hibernia in the early 1830s.) On the eve of the Civil War, Dowling was part-owner of a liquor-importing business in Galveston and the owner of "The Bank of Bacchus," a saloon and billiard parlor formerly at Main Street and Congress Avenue in Houston.

(The bar's specialty was a drink called "Kiss Me Quick and Go.")

During the Civil War, Dowling volunteered for the Confederate army. He quickly advanced to the rank of lieutenant and helped recapture Galveston on New Year's Day 1863. Three weeks later he and his Davis Guards – an all-Irish unit of Company F, Texas Heavy Artillery – received an order from General John Magruder to spike the cannon at Fort Sabine, a defensive position guarding a six-mile-long pass on the boundary of Texas and Louisiana. (Magruder, who had gotten word of a planned Union attack involving 5,000 troops, believed that the pass was indefensible.) When Dowling's more immediate commanding officer, however, advised him to use his own discretion, the Davis Guards – like Leonidas and his 300 Spartans at Thermopylae – choose to defend the pass.

By the beginning of September, the Guards had constructed Fort Griffin, an earthwork for their six guns, and were awaiting the Union advance. Before the three federal gunboats off the coast opened fire to cover the landing of their 1,200 troops, however, the Davis Guards fired off 137 shots, never even stopping to swab the guns. A shot fired by gunner Michael McKernan tore a hole through the boiler of the gunboat *Sachem*, causing the vessel's crew to jump overboard to escape the steam and boiling water. The Irish gunners then turned their fire on the *Clifton*, making its way up the channel with a complement of seventy-seven sharpshooters. When

*The Dick Dowling Monument
at Sabine Pass.*

a shot from Fort Griffin broke the gunboat's wheel rope, the vessel went out of control and crashed into the banks of the channel. Dowling himself – stripped to the waist and covered with gunpowder – boarded the *Clifton* and identified himself as the lieutenant in command of the Confederate position. Although the Irish unit killed fifty Union soldiers and captured 350 others as well as two gunboats, it suffered no losses during the forty-five-minute battle.

For this victory – the most spectacular engagement in Texas during the war – Dowling and his men were accorded heroes' welcomes. Besides receiving the only silver medals struck by the Confederacy, they shared in the proceeds of a benefit performance in Houston which raised $3,000. *President Jefferson Davis, for whom the Guards were named, described the battle as "the Thermopylae of the Civil War" – although this time the defenders were victorious. In his volume *The Rise and Fall of the Confederacy*, Davis later wrote: "There is no parallel in ancient or modern warfare to the victory of Dowling and his men at Sabine Pass, considering the great odds against which they had to contend." (This comment is inscribed on the back of the monument.) Two weeks after the battle, the *Houston Telegraph* editorialized: "Let no one hereafter cast any imputations on the honest Irish soldier. . . . The noble men belonging to the Davis Guards, who are all natives of the green Emerald Isle, deserve well of the nation. . . . Inured to hard labor, nobly did they stand by the guns and fight to the last." Dowling himself reported that "All my men behaved like heroes. Not a man flinched from his post. Our motto was 'Victory or Death.'"

The members of the Davis Guards were Patrick Abbott, Michael Carr, Abner Carter, Pat Clair, James Corcoran, Thomas Daugherty, Hugh Deagan, Michael Delaney, Dan Donovan, Jonathan Drummond, Michael Egan, Pat Fitzgerald, James Fleming, John Flood, William Gleason, Tom Hagerty, William Hardy, John Hassett, John Hennessey, James Higgins, Tim Huggins, Tim Hurley, William Jett, Pat Malone, Alex McCabe, Pat McDonnell, Tim McDonough, John McGrath, John McKeever, Michael McKernan, Dan McMurray, Jonathan McNealis, Michael Monoghan, Peter O'Hara, Lawrence Plunkett, Maurice Powers, Edward Pritchard, Charles Rheins, Michael Sullivan, Pat Sullivan, Thomas Sullivan, Mathew Walsh, John Westley, John White, Joseph Wilson, Dr. George Bailey, and Lieutenant N. H. Smith.

After the war Dowling returned to Houston to operate his tavern and billiard parlor. He also organized the first oil company in Texas and was the first Houstonian to replace lard oil lamps and candles with gas light. He died of yellow fever in 1867, just shy of his thirtieth birthday.

J Sabine Pass Battle Monument, in the town of Sabine Pass.

Until 1936 this was the only monument commemorating the battle and Dick Dowling and his men. The large stone marker is located about a mile from the site of Fort Griffin. The stone is inscribed as follows: "Commemorating the feat of Dick Dowling and his forty two Irish patriots, Sabine Pass, Texas. 1861 C.S.A. 1865. September the 8th 1863, an army of fifteen thousand [actually 1,200] Federals attacked the small fort at the pass. The brave little garrison under Lieut. Dick Dowling, without the loss of a man, disabled and captured three of the gunboats and three hundred and fifty soldiers."

SAN ANTONIO

¶ **The Alamo,** 100 Alamo Plaza.

The Alamo was destined to become the focal point of the Texan Revolution when, in February 1836, the Mexican dictator General Santa Anna led 5,000 troops north across the Rio Grande in an attempt to crush the Texans' struggle for independence. The previous month the frontiersman Jim Bowie had arrived in San Antonio with orders from *General Sam Houston to evacuate the town after destroying the Alamo, formerly a mission but at that time a military depot and storehouse. Bowie and the eighty Texans he found at the Alamo decided to defend the fort, however, hoping that reinforcements would arrive to help in the struggle.

During the first two weeks of February, the Texans were joined by Colonel William Barrett Travis, one of thirty-seven men of Irish ancestry who would make the supreme sacrifice. (Travis's grandmother was Jemima McNamara.) Travis was soon followed by the more famous *David Crockett, who arrived with fifteen fellow Tennesseans. Following the Mexicans' arrival at San Antonio on February 23, Travis ordered his garrison of 150 men into the Alamo. On March 1 reinforcements arrived in the form of thirty-two men from the town of Gonzales. One of the newcomers was Thomas Jackson, whose arrival brought to a dozen the number of Irish-born defenders in the makeshift fort.

Despite the reinforcements, the number of Texans and Americans was desperately inadequate to protect the Alamo, an establishment which at that time covered two and a half acres and included a chapel, a large walled plaza, a convent, several stone rooms, and a corral. As a result, on March 2 Travis wrote to Governor Henry Smith urgently requesting assistance. The next day the colonel sent a message addressed "To the people of Texas and all Americans in the world": "I am besieged by a thousand or more of the Mexicans under Santa Anna – I have sustained a continual Bombardment and cannonade for 24 hours & have not lost a man – the enemy has demanded a surrender at discretion, otherwise the garrison are to be put to the sword if the Fort is taken – I have answered the demand with a cannon shot, & our Flag still waves proudly from the walls – I shall never surrender or retreat. Then, I call on you in the name of Liberty, of patriotism and everything dear to the American character to come to our aid with all dispatch – the enemy is receiving reinforcements daily and will no doubt increase to three or four thousand in four or five days. If this call is neglected, I am determined to sustain myself as long as possible & die like a soldier who never forgets what is due to his own honor & that of his country. – Victory or Death!"

By March 5, however, the defenders had exhausted their ammunition, but not before their superior marksmanship had exacted heavy casualties upon the Mexicans. Realizing the hopelessness of their situation, Travis offered his men three choices: surrender, retreat, or fight. According to tradition, the American commander used his sword to draw a line in the dirt and invited those who intended to stay to cross it. All did so except a Frenchman, who promptly escaped over the wall.

The next morning the Mexican troops stormed the Alamo, although they were twice repulsed. In the third assault, however, they breached the walls. As the Mexicans came over the walls or through the breaches, Travis – who had earlier been hit by a bullet in his temple – cried out to his men, "Don't surrender!" Just then, however, General Mora discovered Travis on the ground and tried to run him through with his sword. Travis parried the blow and instead killed the Mexican leader. In the meantime the Irishman Robert Evans attempted to fulfill the agreement which the defenders had made before the assault. Seizing a torch, he tried to ignite several hundred pounds of powder that were stored in a room off the chapel. Within a foot of the powder, however, he was killed by a Mexican officer. Santa Anna ordered that the other survivors be shot and that their bodies be cremated.

Of the 187 men who gave their lives during the siege of the Alamo, thirty-seven were either Irish natives or men with traditional Irish surnames.

• The known Irish natives were thirteen: Samuel Burns, Andrew Duvalt, Robert Evans, Joseph Hawkins, Thomas Jackson, William Daniel Jackson, Edward McCafferty, James McGee, Robert McKinney, James Nowlan (or Nolan), John (or Jackson) Rusk, Burke Trammel, and William Ward.

• Another three were from the Irish colonies in eastern Texas and for that reason were most likely Irish-born: Samuel Blair, James Brown, and James Hannon.

• Five others had Irish-American ancestry: Peter James Bailey, Daniel William Cloud, David Crockett, William Fontleroy, and William Travis himself.

• Another sixteen casualties were men with Irish surnames: John Blair, Daniel Bourne, John Cane, William Carey, Robert Cochrane, George Washington Cottle, James Girard Garrett, John Garvin, James Gwin, William Hersee (or Hersey), James Kenny, William Malone, Albert Martin, James McCoy, John Purdy Reynolds, and Isaac Ryan.

Ironically, Crockett had written his last letter to his wife and daughter just two months before he died at the Alamo. In a letter dated January 9 from St. Augustine, Texas, he spoke expectantly of the prosperity and good fortune which he felt awaited him in an independent Texas: ". . . as to What I have seen of Texas, it is the garden spot of the world, the best land & best prospects for health I ever saw is here, and I do believe it is a fortune to any man to come here; . . . every man is entitled to his headright of 4438 [acres] and they may make the money to pay for it off the land. . . . I have but little doubt of being elected a member to form the Const[itution] for the Provence. . . . I am in great hopes of making a fortune for myself and family bad as has been my prospects."

• In the center of the former Alamo fortress stands the Heroes of the Alamo Cenotaph, sculpted by Pompeo Coppini and erected in 1939. The shaft rises from a sarcophagus whose south side bears the figure of a male (representing the Spirit of Sacrifice rising from the funeral pyre of the cremated defenders) and whose north face bears a female figure (symbolizing the Spirit of Texas) holding under her arms shields that represent Texas and the United States. The other two sides of the sarcophagus depict groups of soldiers – the foremost being Jim Bowie and the Irish-Americans William Barrett Travis and David Crockett.

The Irishmen who died at the Alamo are honored each St. Patrick's Day with a memorial wreath placed near this historic shrine by members

The most prominent reliefs on the west side of the Alamo Cenotaph are those of William Travis and David Crockett, both of Irish ancestry.

of the Harp and Shamrock Society of Texas.

§ Two museums and a videotape presentation describe the significance of the Alamo in the history of Texas. Open Monday-Saturday 9-5:30, Sunday and holidays 10-5:30. Closed December 24-25. Phone: 210-225-1391.

¶ **Audie Murphy Statue,** Audie Murphy Memorial Veterans Hospital, South Texas Medical Center.

In 1973 this $47 million, 720-bed complex was named for the nation's most highly decorated military hero. It is the only hospital in the Veterans Administration system which was named after a soldier "for being a soldier." Two years later an eight-foot-high bronze statue of Murphy in battle dress was erected on the grounds of the hospital. The $75,000 artwork was sculpted by Jimilu Mason, who prepared herself for the task by examining hundreds of wartime photographs and watching Murphy's autobiographical film *To Hell and Back* three times.

¶ **The Crockett Block,** 317-323 Alamo Plaza.

Named for *David Crockett, one of the martyrs in the defense of the Alamo, this block contains four three-story buildings built in the mid 1880s in an Italianate style.

¶ **Fort Sam Houston,** 2 miles north between Harry Wurzbach Highway and Interstate 35.

Named for *Sam Houston, the first president of the Texas Republic, this active military post was created in 1845, although its was moved to this site thirty years later. A 550-acre portion of the post is a National Historic District. The Fort Sam Houston Museum chronicles the history of the fort and displays uniforms and equipment used since its creation.

§ Quadrangle open daily 6 a.m.-9 p.m. Museum open Wednesday-Sunday 10-4; closed holidays; fee; phone: 512-221-1886.

¶ **Healy-Murphy Center,** 618 Live Oak Street (at Nolan).

Although today the center is an alternative high school, it was founded in 1888 as St. Peter Claver School, dedicated to the education of black students and appropriately named for the Jesuit who devoted his life to helping slaves. The original school was founded by Margaret (Healy) Murphy, a widow who founded the Sisters of the Holy Spirit. Since 1970 the center has been nondenominational and open to pregnant teenagers, dropouts, and other young people unable to function in traditional school settings.

A native of Ireland, Margaret Healy had come to Virginia at the age of twelve with her widowed father. Soon after they settled in New Orleans, however, the death of her father left the young girl an orphan. It was at this time that she and some of her relatives moved to Matamoros, Mexico, where at the age of sixteen she married John Bernard Murphy, a native of

Cork, Ireland. The next year, 1850, the couple moved to Murphy's 4,000-acre ranch in the San Patricio area outside Corpus Christi.

Despite the admission of Texas to the Union, freebooters operated with almost complete impunity in the region of the Nueces River. Acting on her charitable instincts, Mrs. Murphy – who was an excellent horsewoman, by the way – assisted the victims of the local violence as best she could. When the Murphy ranch itself became the object of plunder, the couple moved to a house in Corpus Christi at Williams and Water streets. Later, during the Civil War and the yellow fever epidemic of 1867, Mrs. Murphy operated a clinic and soup kitchen in her home. When a hurricane struck the city in 1875, she helped relieve the suffering of the homeless by distributing food and clothing. She also sheltered the homeless in the buildings on a piece of property she owned on Antelope Street.

Until his death in 1884, John Murphy played a prominent role in the history of Corpus Christi. Besides practicing law and engaging in his commercial business, he was a delegate to the state constitutional convention in 1875 and later served as a district judge. In 1880 he was elected mayor of Corpus Christi. Murphy and his wife had no children of their own but adopted two girls – Minnie Delaney and Elizabeth Murphy – both of whom became nuns.

Following the death of her husband, Mrs. Murphy turned her attention to the education of African-American children. Despite an unsuccessful first attempt, her enthusiasm for the project was revived in 1887 when she heard Father John Maloney exhort his parishioners at St. Mary's Church in San Antonio to help create schools for the black students in the city. Taking the challenge to heart, Mrs. Murphy confided to a friend: "This will be my work someday; it is the great need of this time. The Holy Spirit has helped me to make this decision."

After selling off a portion of her husband's San Patricio ranch, Mrs. Murphy purchased property on the corner of Live Oak and Nolan streets for her intended school. By the beginning of 1889 the new St. Peter Claver School had sixty students. Although financial support for the facility remained adequate – even when enrollment exploded to 200 students within three years – the widow had difficulty staffing the academy. It was at this juncture that she decided to form a religious congregation of women dedicated to the needs of youth in crisis – specifically the education of black children excluded from the Texas public schools. It was thus that three teachers joined with Mrs. Murphy to form the Sisters of the Holy Spirit in 1892. The foundress became the superior of the congregation as Mother Margaret Mary Healy-Murphy, and the four made public profession of their vows four years later.

In an effort to recruit new members for the Sisters of the Holy Spirit, Mother Margaret Mary visited her native Ireland four times during the next decade. She returned to Texas each time with young postulants eager to participate in her noble work. Her efforts in Ireland were so successful that as late as 1980 about 90 percent of the congregation's members were Irish born. By the time of the foundress's death in 1907, the Sisters of the Holy Spirit had established schools in Laredo, Texas, and Oaxaca, Mexico.

❡ A Calvary statuary group in the cemetery of the Sisters of the Holy Spirit (301 Yucca Street, San Antonio) honors the memory of Mother Margaret Mary. She is buried with her husband in Corpus Christi (Holy Cross Cemetery, 3025 Upper River Road).

❡ **John Twohig House,** Witte Museum, 3801 Broadway.

This imposing two-story structure was built in 1841 for the Irish merchant John Twohig. A plaque on the outside front wall summarizes the history of the building, which now houses museum offices:

"In 1841 John Twohig – a San Antonio pioneer, Texas patriot and prosperous merchant – erected this house on a site which was part of the garden of the Veramendi Palace within a curving bend of the San Antonio River at St. Mary's and Commerce Streets. Mr. Twohig's house was unique in the community since few buildings in this area at that time could boast a second floor. In 1853 John Twohig surrounded his home with a beautiful garden for his bride, Elizabeth Priscilla Calvert, and later with smaller guest houses for his important friends. The Twohigs were famous for their hospitality! The property eventually passed into the ownership of the San Antonio Public Service Company and finally, in 1941, was moved to the grounds of the Witte Museum. The building as it now stands was restored as authentically as possible to John Twohig's original house. Built entirely of local limestone, each stone was carefully numbered and replaced in its proper position. The original fireplace mantle and doors were installed, the outside stairway replaced, and details, such as lamps, were reproduced. Even the bend in the river is strongly reminiscent of the landscape which surrounded the house downtown."

Twohig, who was born in County Cork in 1806, ran away from home at the age of fifteen to serve an apprenticeship on a British merchant ship. After later engaging in the coastal trade between Boston and New York, he journeyed to San Antonio, where in 1830 he established a general store on the Main Plaza. During his residence in San Antonio, he was known for his "burial club." It seems that, when a prominent figure came to town, Twohig invited him to join the club by paying a $1 fee. In return, the Irishman agreed to attend the new subscriber's funeral, send flowers for the service, and hire a carriage to convey his body to the cemetery. The only proviso to this arrangement, however, was that the member had to die in San Antonio. In reality, Twohig donated the dues to St. Joseph's Orphans Asylum in the member's name.

During the struggle for Texan independence, the Irishman sided with the rebels against the Mexican government. Arrested by the Mexican general Martín Cos for allegedly communicating with the Texan army besieging San Antonio, he was sentenced to be executed. He escaped death, however, during the confusion that followed the Texans' attack on the town.

Even after the victorious Texans established an independent republic, Mexican troops twice invaded San Antonio. As the first army approached, Twohig expected that the invaders would loot his store, primarily for its ammunition. As a result, after allowing the town's poor to help themselves to his provisions, he blew up his establishment. During the second invasion, he was one of the fifteen San Antonians who were captured and held in Perote Prison in Mexico.

Since Twohig refused to engage in hard labor as his captors demanded, he was forced to remain in his cell all day. He used his idle time profitably, though, by digging a tunnel under the walls of the fortress. When the prisoners tried to make their escape, however, Major Colquhoun – the portliest one among them – was unable to fit through the passage. Twohig accordingly returned to his work, widening the tunnel and thereby allowing the men to escape on July 2, 1843.

Although six of the prisoners were recaptured, Twohig successfully eluded the Mexicans. According to one story, he escaped detection in two ways – first by joining a band of guerrillas and then by disguising himself as a peddler carrying a tray of sugar cones on his head. The Irishmen eventually made his way by ship to New Orleans and from there to San Antonio.

From 1869 until his death twenty-two years later, Twohig was engaged in the banking business. Despite the international character of his operation – with branches in New York, St. Louis, New Orleans, San Francisco, and London – he was known locally as the "bread banker" for his distribution of bread to needy women each Saturday morning. When he died in 1891, he left an estate valued at almost $500,000, much of which he bequeathed to the Catholic Church.

§ Open June-August, Monday-Saturday 10-6, Sunday noon-6; rest of the year, Monday-Saturday 10-5, also Tuesday 5-9), Sunday noon-5. Fee. Phone: 210-820-2111 or 820-2166.

¶ **Institute of Texas Cultures,** 801 South Bowie Street.

Located in the former Texas Pavilion of the 1969 World's Fair, this research and educational center is dedicated to preserving and recreating the life-styles of the native and immigrant groups who populated the state. A series of interactive exhibits chronicles the history of twenty-seven different ethnic groups – including the Irish. The center also features a multiscreen audiovisual presentation.

§ Open Tuesday-Sunday 9-5. Closed Thanksgiving and December 25. Donations. Parking fee. Phone: 210-558-2300.

J Menger Hotel, 204 Alamo Plaza.

Built in 1859 as an early example of a hotel whose rooms had adjoining baths, the Menger became the most famous and popular establishment in the Southwest. During the winter of 1872-73, the author *Sidney Lanier was a guest while he wrote a story called "San Antonio de Bexar." (The hotel has several Lanier tablets and exhibits.) At the onset of the Spanish-American War, the hotel hosted *Theodore Roosevelt, who set up headquarters here while he recruited ranchers for his soon-to-be-famous Rough Riders. The Menger's taproom – modeled after the luxuriant watering hole in the House of Lords – later became known as the Roosevelt Bar. The hotel's present Renaissance Revival appearance dates from 1909.

J Milam Park, between North Santa Rosa Avenue and West Commerce, West Houston, and North San Saba streets.

Formerly the cemetery of San Fernando Cathedral, this present-day park contains a monument with a plaque listing the names of those buried here. Among them is John McMullen, a native of County Donegal, Ireland, who in 1829 helped *James McGloin establish a colony of Irish settlers in San Patricio, thirty miles from Corpus Christi.

On January 20, 1853, McMullen was the victim of foul play. On that night the Irishman was killed in his home in San Antonio – apparently during a robbery attempt – by a Mexican boy whom he had adopted. According to a legend, McMullen's ghost appeared to McGloin in San Patricio and greeted him with the words "Hello, Jack!" before disappearing. When McGloin saw the ghostly figure – blood streaming from a neck wound – he cried out, "Something has happened to John" and set out on horseback for San Antonio, where he found his dead fellow *empresario*. (See San Patricio, Texas.)

J San Fernando Cathedral, 115 Main Plaza.

This Gothic Revival structure was built between 1868 and 1873 as an addition to an earlier mid-eighteenth-century Spanish church. A white marble sarcophagus inside the cathedral is adorned with photographs of the three most famous defenders of the Alamo: James Bowie and Irish Americans David Crockett and William Travis. Following the fall of the Alamo to Mexican troops in 1836, the bodies of the American defenders were burned on a funeral pyre. Their bones were later rescued and buried in the church.

§ Open daily 6:15 a.m.-6 p.m. Phone: 210-227-1297.

J Travis Park, between Pecan, Travis, Navarro, and Jefferson streets.

This downtown park was named for *William Barrett Travis, the commander of the defenders of the Alamo in March 1836.

SAN PATRICIO

¶ **James McGloin House,** at Round Lake, about 2 miles down Nopal Road off State 666 (Main Street).

A monument erected in front of the house in 1936 reads: "James McGloin / Born in County Sligo, Ireland / With John McMullen he secured a contract to settle 200 families / August 17, 1828 / Landed his colonists at El Copano 1830 / In 1834 laid out the town of San Patricio / His house on this site was built in 1855 / Died here 1856."

The James McGloin House.

¶ **James McKeown House,** about 0.5 mile north along State 666.

Now restored and used as a museum, this one-story cottage dates from the late 1860s and was purchased by James McKeown Sr. in 1875.

Born in Raleigh, North Carolina, in 1823, McKeown was the son of emigrants from northern Ireland. After his father's early death, the son and his widowed mother made their way west, living for a time in Mobile, Alabama, before settling in Bedias, Texas. Like many young men at that time, McKeown was lured to California by tales of the Gold Rush. On the way, however, he met and married Anne Mulholland, a native of Athlone, Ireland, and a recent postulant at the Ursuline convent in New Orleans. Rather than continue on their way to the West Coast, the couple returned to Bedias. During the Civil War McKeown threw in his lot with the Confederacy and became a riverboat sailor on the Mississippi.

After the war McKeown and his wife settled in Bee County, where they tended to the raising of their growing family. Although their son Tom was killed in an accident and the twins died within six months, Esasmus and James Jr. survived to carry on the family name. (About Esasmus it was said: "Old Zoz knew all the words in the dictionary. When books were scarce, Zoz studied the dictionary.")

In the meantime James Sr. had bought a house in San Patricio and was operating a store which he had built there. Besides serving as county treasurer until 1893, he was well known as a fiddler and frequently played for dances in the community. His son James took over the house and continued to operate the store until 1917.

❡ James McKeown Sr. and his wife are buried in the cemetery next to St. Patrick's Catholic Church.

❡ Old Cemetery on the Hill, 0.5 mile off County Road 21 (Fitzgerald Street).

• A granite memorial erected in recent years commemorates James McGloin, who cofounded the Irish colony at San Patricio and who is buried in this cemetery. The marker contains an engraved inscription: "Empresario James McGloin, born about 1799 in Castlegal, County Sligo, Ireland. Died June 19, 1856 at his home on Round Lake. McGloin and John McMullen secured a grant from the Mexican government to bring colonists to Texas and founded the colony of San Patricio de Hibernia and the city of San Patricio in 1830, the first Irish colony in Texas. Faithful friend and leader, may he rest in eternal peace." Various descendants of McGloin are buried in marked graves in the family plot at the center of the graveyard.

The first large influx of Irish into Texas occurred as the result of a contract granted by the Mexican government to McGloin and his partner, John McMullen of County Donegal. The two *empresarios* recruited Irish newly arrived at the ports of Philadelphia and New York as well as Irish who were already living in Kentucky and Louisiana. The first two shiploads arrived in Texas in October 1829 and settled in San Patricio de Hibernia on the Nueces River about thirty miles from what later became Corpus Christi. Unfortunately, few of the colonists were farmers; many, in fact, were engineers, teachers, contractors, lawyers, and other professionals unsuited for colonization.

Patrick Burke, a member of a group which arrived from Ireland in 1834, remembered that "these colonists [had] left their homes in Tipperary County, Ireland, under contract with the Mexican government, and were required to come equipped with supplies enough, including arms and ammunition, to last them two years. The Mexican government agreed to furnish the head of each family with ten milch cows, one cart and a yoke of oxen, and a garrison of soldiers to guard and protect the colonists against incursions of hostile Indians. . . . The cowardly soldiers were a nuisance. They lived upon the provisions of the colonists and were afraid to show their heads outside of the house when danger from Indian raids seemed imminent. . . . Camp was placed about one mile back from the water's edge on a treeless prairie. The weather was intensely hot, and the campers had to stretch quilts and blankets for awnings to protect the women and children from the scorching rays of the vertical summer's sun. . . ." By 1836 the population of the colony had grown to 600, although today San Patricio has only a little more than half that number.

• A bronze plaque next to the McGloin memorial contains the names of the San Patricio residents who either were killed in the Goliad Massacre of March 27, 1836, or escaped through the intervention of Colonel Francisco Garay. The San Patricio dead were Sergeant John McGloin, Mathew Byrne, John Fadden, Edward Garner, Patrick Niven, Edward Ryan, while Andrew M. O'Boyle and George Pittock (or Pettick) were spared. (See Goliad, Texas.)

¶ Old Dougherty House Site, at State 666 and Nopal Road.

A historical plaque points out the "location of noted St. Paul's Academy for boys. Home of school owner Robert Dougherty (1827-1881), refugee from 1840s Irish famine. Educated at St. Mary's College, Kentucky, Dougherty worked as a journalist and merchant before settling in Texas, here marrying Rachel Sullivan. In 1867-1874, he was principal, Hidalgo Seminary, Corpus Christi. Built his school here on Round Lake, near wife's family, 1876. He taught geography, history, mathematics, Latin, Greek, classical literature and Gaelic – subjects rare in that era. His seven children all began their careers as teachers."

¶ Old San Patricio Memorial, in front of the old county courthouse, State 666 and McGloin Avenue.

A large bronze plaque adorned with the Texas Lone Star and an image of St. Patrick commemorates the major events and figures in the history of San Patricio, now a community of less than 400 people. The text of the memorial reads as follows:

"San Patricio de Hibernia, founded in 1830 by John McMullen and James McGloin as the seat of their Irish colony under an empresario contract dated August 17, 1828, which was fulfilled by the empresarios 1830-1835. Named in honor of Saint Patrick, the patron saint of Ireland.

As the frontier outpost of Texas when the Revolution began, San Patricio 1835-1845 suffered all the miseries of that conflict with no compensating returns.

At and near San Patricio, on February 27, 1836, General Jose Urrea's division of Santa Anna's army surprised and overwhelmed Johnson's Texan party of 35 men: 9 or 10 Texans were killed, 6 or 7 escaped, and 20 were sent to Matamoros as prisoners. After San Jacinto the town was destroyed and its inhabitants driven away.

In memory of Rev. Henry Doyle, Rev. T. I. Molloy, Wm. O'Docharty, Geo. O'Docharty, Walter Henry, Patrick Henry, John Hart, Michael Haley, Mark Killalea, Wm. Hefferman, Oceola Archer, Lewis Ayers, Catherine Hoye, Owen Gaffney, John Ross, Wm. Pugh, early settlers of San Patricio.

John McMullen, delegate to the Consultation, 1835.

John Turner, John White Bower, signers of the Texas Declaration of Independence.

John McGloin, John Fadden, Dennis McGowan, Andrew M. O'Boyle, Geo. Pettick, Mathew Byrne, Patrick Nevin, Edward Garner, Edward Ryan, Dennis Mahoney, Miles Andross, Wm. Quinn, soldiers in the Texas Revolution.

San Patricio has contributed the following distinguished citizens: Patrick O'Docharty, Susanna O'Docharty, Thomas O'Callaghan, Patrick McGloin, Chris Sullivan, Rose K. Mahoney, John Ryan, Geo. McCowan, Catherine Ryan, James McKeown, Patrick McMurray, Thomas Magowan, Wm. P. Allen, Mary Ann Collins, Hubert Timon, David Odem, John Timon, Andrew Jackson Brown, John Donahue, Mary E. McCloin, Margaret Hart McFall, Patrick Brennan, Margaret Baldesch Wiler, John Corrigan, Margaret Q. James, Andrew Gerhardt, Mathew Kivlin, James Grover, Robert Weir, Eliza A. Sullivan, J. Chrys Dougherty, Steve J. Lewis, Joe E. Sullivan, Hugh Touhy, John Dee."

¶ **Old San Patricio Museum,** State 666.

¶ **St. Patrick's Church,** State 666.

A plaque near the church details the history of San Patricio's Irish Catholic community:

"Empresarios John McMullen and James McGloin brought Irish Catholic immigrant families to Texas about 1829 to form a new colony, San Patricio de Hibernia. Under the direction of the Rev. Henry Doyle, the colonists established Saint Patrick's Catholic Church about 1830. A fire in 1858 destroyed the original frame church building and all church records. The Rt. Rev. Jean Marie Odin, first bishop of Texas, dedicated a replacement church building about 1859.

Local citizens built a two-and-a-half-story building for a convent and school on the grounds of Saint Patrick's Church. After an 1875 hurricane destroyed facilities at Indianola, nuns from the Order of Sisters of Mercy relocated in San Patricio and operated Saint Joseph's Convent and School from 1876 until 1884.

After a 1919 hurricane completely demolished the church facilities, the congregation rebuilt in 1922. A need for a larger facility led the congregation to build a fourth structure in 1961. Through the years Saint

Patrick's Catholic Church has served the community with Sunday mass and the sacraments and missions given by visiting priests."

SHAMROCK

This small town of 2,000 people developed from a post office created in 1890 in the dugout home of George Nichels, an Irish sheep rancher. A fragment of the famous Blarney Stone – from the ruins of Blarney Castle in County Cork, Ireland – is located in Elmore Park.

TIVOLI

¶ **Peter Fagan Mausoleum,** on the Fagan Ranch.

Located on a knoll between the Fagan house and the San Antonio River, this massive mausoleum was erected by Peter Fagan six years prior to his death in 1929. Fagan constructed the marble memorial on the original homesite of Nicholas Fagan, an ancestor who was one of the first Irish settlers in this region. When asked why he preferred to be buried on the ancestral ranch rather than in the family cemetery, he replied, "Here I was born; here I have lived; here will I die; and here I want to remain forever." Fagan selected the inscription that is engraved on the front door of the mausoleum: "After all when a man comes to die, all that he will have left, is what he has given away."

Fagan's ancestor Nicholas was born in Wexford County, Ireland, and was a cousin of Sir Edward Pakenham, the British commander at the battle of New Orleans. At the age of fifteen, Nicholas Fagan ran away from home, bent on boarding a man o' war in the Royal Navy. Because he was almost penniless, the lad failed to find lodgings for himself in Dublin. He soon returned to his parents after one landlady advised him to abandon his quest for fame "before the mast."

By 1816, however, Fagan had left Ireland for New York City, this time with a wife and three children and apparently in search of religious liberty and political freedom. After four years in New York, the family moved west – sojourning briefly in Philadelphia, Pittsburgh, Cincinnati, and St. Louis. Life in an area north of St. Louis at first looked promising, but the cold, threats of Indian attacks, the sparse white population, and the absence of a Catholic church caused the family to move to New Orleans. Their arrival there, however, was marred by the death of Fagan's wife, Kate Connally, from yellow fever. When the children were likewise stricken, they were cared for by a kindly woman in the Crescent City until their father married a second time. His new wife – Catherine Hausellman-Balch – was a Lutheran, whom he later converted to Catholicism.

In the meantime Fagan had become interested in the colonization plans of the Irishman James Power. (See Refugio, Texas.) In 1829, finally reunited with his children, Fagan moved into Texas and acquired title to a portion of the land granted Power by the Mexican government. Fagan and his son John later joined the army of Texas in its struggle against the Mexican dictator General Santa Anna. The elder Fagan signed the Texas Declaration of Independence at Goliad and was one of the few who escaped the subsequent slaughter there. (See Goliad, Texas.) After this massacre Fagan threw himself into the cause of Texan independence even more energetically, supplying the Texas army with beef and horses from his own ranch and sending cartloads of corn and provisions to the suffering civilians at Refugio.

VICTORIA

¶ McNamara House Museum, 502 North Liberty Street.

Formerly the home of William McNamara, this 1876 Victorian house uses the history of the McNamara family to interpret the region's social, cultural, and economic history at the turn of the century. The museum has an extensive collection of photographs, architectural drawings, furniture, and historical documents pertaining to the McNamaras and local history.

A native of County Cork, Ireland, McNamara came to America sometime in the early 1850s. According to a family tradition, he and his future wife – Mary Ann Buckley, also of County Cork – sailed aboard the same ship, although they did not become acquainted until several years later.

The McNamara House Museum.

McNamara initially lived with the Madigan family in New York City, while Buckley moved on to Pittsburgh, Pennsylvania, to live with her brother. In time McNamara also made his way to Pittsburgh, for it was there in 1866 that he married Mary Ann. At the end of the decade, however, the couple moved to Port Lavaca, Texas, bringing with them their two children, Mary Ellen and Elizabeth. Following the birth of two more daughters (Margaret and Catherine), the growing family settled in Victoria.

Before long, McNamara was on his way to becoming one of Victoria's most prosperous and influential citizens. To complement his growing cotton and wool interests, he established a hide business in the city, an operation that eventually extended to Austin, Dallas, and San Antonio. He also had interests in the Texas Continental Meat Company, whose packinghouses in Victoria and Fort Worth were the first in Texas. Besides serving for three years on the city council, he helped finance Victoria's first electric lighting system and took a leading role in creating the city's municipal water plant. Records indicate that he paid $1,000 for three lots in town.

By 1900, however, McNamara had suffered a major financial disaster. As the result of a hurricane which sources say occurred either in that year or in 1886, he lost a shipment of cotton destined for New Orleans. Because of the loss, he was forced to mortgage his house to his son-in-law, T. M. O'Connor, an arrangement that was never disclosed to the McNamara children.

Of the four girls, Elizabeth, Margaret, and Catherine attended St. Mary's of the Woods College in Indiana, where they studied music, art, literature, history and needlework. (Catherine died in her thirties, a victim of tuberculosis.) Mary Ellen (Molly), meanwhile, was a pianist who was trained at a music conservatory in the East and was the only daughter to marry. She and her husband had one daughter (Helen) and three sons (William, James, and Lawrence). Following her husband's death in 1910, Molly and her daughter moved to San Antonio, presumably because better treatment for Molly's diabetes was available there. In their mother's absence, William and James lived in the McNamara House, under the care of their maiden aunts, Elizabeth and Margaret.

§ Open Tuesday-Sunday 1-5. Closed major holidays. Fee. Phone: 512-575-8227

¶ **St. Mary's Church,** 101 West Church Street.

This Gothic Revival church was built in 1904 according to the designs of *Nicholas Clayton, the famous Galveston architect.

WACO

¶ **Texas Rangers Hall of Fame and Museum,** Fort Fisher Park, at the junction of Interstate 35 and the Fort Fisher exit.

This Waco attraction pays tribute to twenty-six members of the Texas Rangers, an elite group of lawmen originally created in 1823. The museum features exhibits and a slide presentation on the history of the famous corps. One of the most illustrious Rangers in the Hall of Fame is *Leander McNelly. (See Burton, Texas.)

§ Open daily 9-5. Fee. Phone: 817-750-5986.

WEST COLUMBIA

¶ Varner-Hogg Plantation State Historical Park, 1 mile northeast off State 35 at 1702 North 17th Street.

The two-story Plantation House Museum dates from 1836 and was formerly the home of *Governor James Stephen Hogg. (See Rusk, Texas.)

Although the former governor had for several years unsuccessfully drilled for oil on this property, he remained optimistic about future prospects and begged his four children not to sell the plantation after his death. A dozen years after his demise in 1906, his children's efforts resulted in the discovery of the West Columbia Field. The resulting "black gold" made the siblings – Ima, Mike, Tom, and Will – among the richest family members in Texas.

Ima subsequently used her wealth to renovate the house in the Greek Revival style and decorate it with furniture and art objects from the early American and postbellum Texas periods.

§ Open Wednesday-Saturday 9-11 and 1-4; Sunday 1-4. Fee. Phone: 409-345-4656.

UTAH

BRIGHAM CITY

¶ **Golden Spike National Historic Site,** 32 miles west off Interstate 15 and Interstate 84.

This historic site commemorates the completion of the transcontinental railroad and marks the spot where the Central Pacific and the Union Pacific rails met on May 10, 1869. The last spike driven was a golden one now in the possession of Stanford University. Among the dignitaries who witnessed the event was John Conness, the Irish-born U.S. senator who first proposed a railroad that would span the nation. (See Mount Conness, Yosemite, California.)

Large numbers of Irish laborers were involved in constructing the transcontinental lines, more so along the Central Pacific route from California, however, than on the Union Pacific route from the east. Along the latter line the Irish and the Chinese workers were often at odds, although many of the stories about the degree of their animosity may not be true. While some stories relate how members of each ethnic group sneaked into the other's camp at night and set off sticks of blasting powder, another tale relates what obviously happened when the Irish uncoupled a rail car loaded with Chinese workers ascending a steep hillside.

Even the Chinese working for the other rail company became the object of life-threatening "pranks." "Our Irishmen," wrote General Dodge of the Union Pacific, "were in the habit of firing their blasts in the cuts without giving warning to the Chinamen on the Central Pacific working right above them. From this cause, several Chinamen were severely hurt. Complaint was made to me by the Central Pacific people, and I endeavored to have the contractors bring hostilities to a close but . . . they failed to do so. One day the Chinamen . . . put in what is called a 'grave' on their work, and when the Irishmen right under them were all at work let go their blast and buried several of our men. This brought about a truce at once. From that time on the Irish laborers showed due respect for the Chinamen, and there was no further trouble."

§ Visitor center open Memorial Day-Labor Day, daily 8-6; rest of the year, 8-4:30. Fee. Phone: 801-471-2209.

¶ Four miles from the visitor center is a replica of the original sign commemorating the laying of ten miles of track in one twelve-hour day, an accomplishment that still stands as a record. (The original sign is in the visitor center museum.)

This remarkable feat was achieved by a team of eight Irishmen on April 28, 1869, just days before the transcontinental line was completed. At the rate of about 240 feet per eighty seconds, these "Iron Men" – Thomas Dailey, Patrick Joyce, Michael Kennedy, Edward Kioleen, Fred McNamara, Michael Shay, Michael Sullivan, and George Wyatt – laid track a distance of ten miles and 200 feet. During the grueling task they lifted and placed a total of 4.3 million pounds in the form of about 26,000 ties, 3,500 rails, 55,000 spikes, 7,000 poles, and 14,000 bolts. The rails – each weighing 560 pounds (or fifty-six pounds to the yard) – accounted for approximately half the 4.3 million pounds.

GRANTSVILLE

¶ Donner-Reed Memorial Museum, 90 North Cooley Street.

A plaque on the building at 87 North Cooley describes the area's association with the Donner party: "In 1846 they stopped at nearby Twenty Wells to let their animals rest and gain strength before continuing their ill-fated trip. While crossing the Salt Desert they lost many wagons and other belongings on the mud flats east of Pilot Mountain. The hardships suffered in Utah delayed their journey. Winter overtook them in the Sierra Nevada Mountains, resulting in their well known catastrophe. Some of the articles left by the Donner-Reed Party are displayed in this museum, along with other pioneer and Indian relics." (See Knolls, Utah.)

§ Open by appointment. Phone: 801-884-3348.

KNOLLS

¶ Donner-Reed Trail Monument, Interstate 8 rest area at mile marker 54.

This roadside marker honors the eighty-one emigrants who, on September 10, 1846, passed here and continued to the northwest, attempting to follow the Hastings Cutoff across the Great Salt Lake to California. Almost 35 percent of the group had Irish surnames – among them Breen, Dolan, Halloran, McCutchen, Murphy, and Reed.

The emigrants, under the leadership of Jacob Donner and *James Reed, had broken off from the original party that had set out from Fort Bridger. Misinformed about the distances and the conditions on the desert, the smaller group endured unimaginable hardships. They exhausted their food and fuel, thirty-six of their oxen died, and several of their wagons had to be abandoned. Although they successfully reached the Sierra Nevadas, their arrival was late in the season and heavy snows prevented their crossing. Trapped during the savage winter that followed, thirty-six of the eighty-one members perished. (See Truckee, California.)

MONUMENT VALLEY

¶ Goulding's Trading Post & Lodge, 2 miles west of U.S. 163, just north of the Arizona border.

Located near the 30,000-acre Navajo tribal park, this famous lodge was established in 1923 by Harry Goulding, the sheep rancher who convinced the Irish-born filmmaker John Ford that the locale's rugged terrain of cliffs, gullies, and mesas was the perfect setting for western movies.

The famous director brought his film crew to this valley almost a dozen times, first to shoot *Stagecoach* in 1938 and then to make *Fort Apache, She Wore a Yellow Rose, Wagon Master, Rio Grande, The Searchers,* and *The Man Who Shot Liberty Valance.*

A museum connected with the trading post displays exhibits on Ford's life and film career. Open daily 7:30 p.m.-9 p.m. Phone: 801-727-3231.

• The famous film director was born in 1894 in Cape Elizabeth, Maine, the son of Sean and Abby Feeney, emigrants from County Galway who had arrived in America in 1872. The child's name was officially registered as John Martin Feeney, although throughout his youth he called himself John Augustine Feeney. (Even after he changed his surname to Ford, he continued to claim that his name was Sean Aloysius O'Feeney.) His mother was a Gaelic speaker from the Aran Islands who could neither read nor write English, while his father was a ward heeler in Portland, Maine.

After graduating from high school in 1914, young Jack Feeney decided to follow in the footsteps of his brother, a film star and director in California known in the business as Francis Ford. (Jack later confessed his own early love affair with celluloid: "As a kid I was fascinated by the nickelodeon of that period. Any time I got a nickel or dime I would go to the movies.") Once in Hollywood, the newly christened John Ford got a job at Universal Studios, initially as an extra, a bit actor, and a prop man, but by 1923 he had directed thirty-nine films. Ford achieved international recognition with *The Iron Horse*, one of the top-grossing films of the decade and an extravaganza that boasted 116 locomotives, 1,300 buffalo, 5,000 extras, and 10,000 head of cattle.

In the meantime Ford had visited Ireland in 1921, in the midst of the revolution by Sinn Fein nationalists against the British. In a letter to his wife, Ford wrote that he had had difficulty finding his father's family in Spiddal ("There are so many Feeneys out there") and that in fact the town was "all shot to pieces. Most of the houses have been burned down by the Black and Tans . . . ." Unknown to his wife, though, Ford also went into the Connemara Mountains in search of a cousin, a member of the Irish Republican Army with a price on his head. When the British learned that Ford had provided the cousin with food and money, they roughed him up "pretty well" before putting him on a ship with the warning that he would be jailed if he ever set foot in Ireland again. When he returned in 1952 to make *The Quiet Man*, Ireland was, of course, an independent republic.

Ford's concern for the underdog was again evident in his relations with the Navajo in Monument Valley. When he was there with his film crew, he paid the Indians union wages, studied their language, and was even adopted into the tribe (with the name *Natani Nez* – "Tall Soldier"). He also used his influence to get army planes to drop food and supplies onto the reservation when a blizzard made the valley inaccessible.

Stung by criticism that he "took pleasure in killing Indians in the movies," Ford responded by referring to the work he had given the Navajo and claiming that his adoption into the tribe meant more to him than winning his Oscars. He later asked: "Who better than an Irishman could understand the Indians, while still being stirred by the tales of the U.S. Cavalry? We [Irish] were on both sides of the epic." On another occasion he wrote in a similar vein but with more understanding of the complexity of history: "My sympathy was always with the Indians. Do you consider the invasion of the Black and Tan into Ireland a blot on English history? It's the same thing, all countries do the same thing. . . . Genocide seems to be a commonplace in our lives. But it was not a systematic destruction of the Indians. All I know is that the cavalry got the hell kicked out of them, and the Indians practically destroyed themselves. It was the loss of the buffalo that wiped them out."

Although only five of Ford's films received an Academy Award for best picture, most of them became cinematic classics. His first Oscar winner was *The Informer*, a film based on a novella by Liam O'Flaherty and revolving around a perennial Irish weakness: the betrayal of a friend to the British. (*The Informer* became the most censored film in British history. All references to the I.R.A., the "Irish Republic," the Troubles, and the Black and Tans were excised.) Some of his other well known classics are *Mary of Scotland, The Plough and the Stars, Young Mr. Lincoln, Drums Along the Mohawk, The Grapes of Wrath, The Long Voyage Home,* and *The Last Hurrah.*

Even his wartime work with a special photographic unit of the navy produced some of the best documentaries ever made, most notably *The Battle of Midway.* Ford, who was with the fleet during the epic contest, was apologetic about the Oscar-winning footage: "The image jumps a lot because the grenades were exploding right next to me."

In 1973 *President Richard Nixon presented Ford with the Medal of Freedom. "In the annals of American film," the commendation read, "no name shines more brightly than that of John Ford. Director and filmmaker for more than half a century, he stands preeminent in his craft – not only as a creator of individual films of surpassing excellence, but as a master among those who transformed the early motion pictures into a compelling new art form that developed in America and swept the world. As an interpreter of the Nation's heritage, he left his personal stamp indelibly printed on the consciousness of whole generations both here and abroad. In his life and in his work, John Ford represents the best in American films and the best in America."

SALT LAKE CITY

℔ Cathedral of the Madeleine, 331 East South Temple Street.

This Roman-Gothic structure was constructed in 1900 by Lawrence Scanlon, the first Catholic bishop of Salt Lake City, and was dedicated nine years later by *Cardinal James Gibbons. The church's two towers are 220 feet high, while its interior is decorated with Venetian mosaics. Bishop Scanlon is buried in the crypt.

A native of Ballytarsha, County Tipperary, Ireland, Scanlon attended All Hallow's Seminary in Dublin, where he was ordained in 1868. He immediately departed for California to serve the increasing numbers of Irish immigrants to that state. After successive tenures as assistant pastor of St. Patrick's Church and St. Mary's Cathedral in San Francisco, he headed for Pioche, Nevada, where miners and railroad workers helped him establish a church and a hospital. In 1873, however, he was sent to Utah, at first the only priest in an 85,000-square-mile parish. He eventually established more than thirty churches in the state and with his later assistant, the famous Jesuit missionary Father Pierre De Smet, enjoyed friendly relations with the Mormons. Under Scanlon's direction, All Hallows College, Holy Cross Hospital, and St. Anne's Orphanage were founded in Salt Lake City, while a school and a hospital were established in Silver Reef.

An aspect of early Catholic-Mormon relations is evident in an incident which occurred after Father Scanlon's arrival in the mining town of Silver Reef in 1877. Before the Catholic church could be built, Mormon authorities in nearby St. George invited the priest to celebrate high mass in their tabernacle. Although at first it was feared that the Kyrie, the Gloria, and the Credo could not be sung during the liturgy because the tabernacle choir did not know Latin, the choir director took up the challenge. After being provided with the musical setting for Peter's Mass, he and his choir were ready to sing the Latin mass within two weeks, "the Mormon choir executing it with great credit to themselves, rendering the Gloria and Hosanna in clear, sweet tones."

℔ Donner Trail Monument, Fairgrounds, 155 North 1000 West Street.

A five-foot-high granite monument marks the route used by the ill-fated Donner party during its trek to California. A plaque on the memorial reads: "The Donner Party led by George and Jack Donner and James F. Reed passed here and crossed Jordan River nearby about September 2, 1846. This party, consisting of 81 persons, 35 of them children, was delayed two weeks building a road via Emigration Canyon, lost some wagons and many animals crossing Great Salt Lake Desert, and became snowbound in the Sierra Nevada Mountains, where 36 of them perished this winter." (See Knolls, Utah.)

❡ **Governor's Mansion,** 603 East South Temple Street. Private.

This three-story residence – built in 1904 along French Renaissance designs – was originally the home of Senator Thomas Kearns. His widow presented the thirty-six-room house to the state of Utah in 1939.

Kearns was born in 1862 to Irish immigrant parents living in Ontario, Canada. While he was still a child, his parents moved to the Irish colony of O'Neill, Nebraska, where he worked on a farm and attended school until he was seventeen. The youngster was irresistibly draw to the West, however, and for the next four years he worked as a freighter hauling provisions and equipment to miners in the Black Hills of South Dakota and in Tombstone, Arizona.

In 1883 Kearns moved to Park City, Utah, where he finally struck it rich. For the first six years he was employed as a laborer with the Ontario Mining Company and prospected in his free time – usually without significant success. While timbering a tunnel in a mine owned by another company, however, he noticed that the main ore vein led toward an undeveloped property known as the Mayflower. After acquiring a lease on this mine, he and his partners discovered ore at 200 feet and shared in the $80,000 which the mine's first shipment of ore yielded. (The Mayflower ultimately produced ore worth $1.6 million.) With his newfound wealth, Kearns and several new partners bought the Silver King Mine for $67,000. When the ore from this investment yielded approximately 45 percent lead,

The Governor's Mansion (The Thomas Kearns Residence).

60 ounces of silver, and a by-product of gold, Kearns' fortune was made. (By 1907 the Silver King Mine had paid out about $10.75 million in dividends.) Kearns was later a member of a consortium which built the railroad between Salt Lake City and Los Angeles, California.

Beginning in 1892, the Utah "Silver King" became the major political and philanthropic leader in the state. A term on the Park City municipal council led to his selection as a delegate to the state constitutional convention in 1894 and to the Republican national conventions in 1896 and 1900. The next year he was elected to the U.S. Senate and acquired ownership of the *Salt Lake Tribune*. He and his wife, Jennie Judge – whose father was a native of Ireland – traveled widely and were received by Pope Leo XIII at the Vatican. The couple made many charitable bequests, chief among them a $100,000 endowment for the creation of St. Anne's Orphanage and a $10,000 gift toward the construction of the Cathedral of the Madeleine, both in Salt Lake City. In addition, for his high wages and efforts to help destitute miners and their widows, Kearns was held in the highest esteem by his workers.

At the time of his death, an editorial expressed the general sentiment about a man who had done so much for Salt Lake City and Utah: "Now that he has gone to his reward he will be sincerely mourned by a large circle of devoted friends and acquaintances throughout the country, among them the revered Cardinal Gibbons and others who hold or have held the highest positions within the gift of the people. They loved and admired him for his sterling worth as a man among men, one who held stoutly to his own opinions, but always accorded the same right to others. He was large in stature and great in soul. He carved out a fortune in the world for himself by indomitable pluck and energy. Wealth and political honors came to him comparatively early in life, but they did not spoil him or cause him to hold himself aloof from old-time friends upon whom fortune never smiled. He loved Salt Lake and was proud of the fact that he had been an important factor in its upbuilding. He was charitable to a marked degree and the orphanage he founded will stand as a monument to his memory."

¶ **Patrick Connor Burial Site,** on Chiapeta Way (in the middle of a complex of buildings known as South Research Park).

A large stone in the Fort Douglas Cemetery marks the grave of Patrick Edward Connor, the Irish-born army officer who founded Fort Douglas in 1862. The plaque on the stone summarizes his career: "Patrick Edward Connor / Brigadier General and Brevet Major-General / U.S. Volunteers / Born March 17, 1820, Died December 17, 1891 / Camped in this vicinity with his California volunteers October 20, 1862 / Established Camp Douglas, Utah, October 26, 1862 / Participated in the Battles of Buena Vista, Bear River and Tongue River / The Father of Utah Mining."

¶ Patrick Connor Statue, Cannon Park, on the east side of the Fort Douglas Military Museum.

A life-size statue of Patrick Edward Connor stands near the museum, which displays exhibits about the Irishman and the history of the 9,000-acre former military installation.

Born Patrick Edward O'Connor in County Kerry, Ireland, in 1820, he had come to New York with his parents when he was only a child. Upon enlisting in the army at the age of nineteen, however, he registered as "P. E. Connor," using that name in order to conceal his Irish identity. After fighting in the Seminole War, he left military service in 1844. Two years later he moved his New York mercantile business to Texas but almost immediately enlisted for service in the recently declared war between the United States and Mexico. During that conflict he saw action at Palo Alto, Resaca de la Palma, and Buena Vista before resigning with the rank of captain. Like thousands of other "Forty Niners" after the war, he headed for California, where he engaged in mining and operated a general store. It was there that he married Johana Connor, also of County Kerry.

Still attracted by military life, Connor enlisted once again at the outbreak of the Civil War. Named colonel of the 3rd California Infantry, he was ordered to Salt Lake City to take command of the Military District of Utah and Nevada. From his base at Fort Douglas, which he had estab-

Statue of Patrick Connor.

lished on an eminence overlooking the Mormon capital, he and his 700 men guarded the mail routes and the transcontinental telegraph from Indian incursions.

To the Mormons' complaint that his arrival was an intrusion, Connor showed open contempt. Reflecting his suspicions about the Mormons' loyalties during the war, he described them as "a community of traitors, murderers, fanatics and whores" and deliberately named Fort Douglas after the extremely anti-Mormon senator from Illinois. Connor also frequently threatened the use of force to settle conflicts between the Latter Day Saints and the government which he represented. Even in creating the *Union Vidette*, the first daily newspaper in Utah, he was remarkably anti-Mormon in his goal: "the education of the Mormon people up to American views." As a result, his relations with the inhabitants of Deseret were cool at best and openly hostile at worst.

Connor's relations with the Mormon leader Brigham Young were equally strained, especially after the Irishman trained one of the cannon at Fort Douglas at Young's house. In 1863 the Mormon feared that Connor would take him prisoner after Congress passed laws against polygamy. The Mormons consequently kept Fort Douglas under surveillance with a telescope at Beehive House. One night when the sound of cannon fire from the military camp shattered the night silence, the Mormon militia quickly mobilized. They were relieved to learn that the cannon had been fired to celebrate Connor's promotion to brigadier general. Yet, despite these unpleasant relations with Young, the Irishman in 1871 offered to pay the Mormon leader's bail when he was charged with polygamy or, as the grand jury indictment expressed it, with "lewd and lascivious cohabitation."

Connor's ultimate solution to the "Mormon problem" was to influence historical events in such a way that the power of the "Saints" would gradually diminish. He accordingly encouraged his soldiers to look for precious metals in the Utah mountains in the hope that a major discovery would attract a flood of "Gentile" settlers. Connor himself built Utah's first large smelter in 1864 and led his soldiers on prospecting expeditions. In 1869 three of his men found an outcrop of quartz just south of Park City. The assay of a chunk which they broke off disclosed 96 ounces of silver, one-tenth ounce of gold, and 54 percent lead. Several other men named the town of Ophir after the legendary mines of King Solomon.

§ Fort Douglas is located east of the University of Utah campus on East Wasatch Drive. The fort's military museum is open Tuesday-Saturday 10-12 and 1-4. Closed federal holidays. Phone: 801-588-5188.

VIRGINIA

ALDIE

❡ Aldie Historic District.

This area contains an early nineteenth-century mill complex built by Charles Fenton Mercer, the grandson of an Irish immigrant who had come to Virginia in 1720 and made a fortune as a businessman and a lawyer. The complex includes a manor house, a miller's residence, and a mill that is still in operating condition.

After graduating from the College of New Jersey (now Princeton), Mercer studied law and was elected to the Virginia House of Delegates for the first time in 1810. There he promoted internal improvements, the colonization of free blacks to Africa, and a comprehensive system of public education, all with varying degrees of success. Later in the U.S. House of Representatives, he continued to espouse the first two proposals, to which he added attempts to abolish the slave trade and opposition to increasing presidential authority as exercised by *Andrew Jackson. He promoted the construction of the Chesapeake and Ohio Canal and for five years was its president. Back in Virginia he supported efforts to democratize the state constitution, calling for equal representation, universal manhood suffrage, and popular election. In 1845 he published a work which examined the weakness and inefficiency of the United States government.

ALEXANDRIA

❡ John Fitzgerald Plaque, King and Union streets.

A plaque on the former colonial warehouse on the corner commemorates its owner: "This building was the warehouse of John Fitzgerald, Alexandria merchant and officer of the Third Virginia Regiment of the Continental Line. Colonel Fitzgerald was a close friend of General George Washington and was his secretary and aide-de-camp during the American Revolution. After the war Colonel Fitzgerald served as mayor of the City of Alexandria (1787) and collector of the port (1798). He was a founder of St. Mary's Roman Catholic Church."

A native of Wicklow, Ireland, Fitzgerald had immigrated to America in 1769 and settled in Alexandria, where he entered into a partnership with Valentine Piers to become "wheat purchasers." Said to have been the finest horseman in the American army, Fitzgerald was wounded at the battle of Monmouth on June 28, 1778. As Washington's aide-de-camp, he was the first to inform the commander-in-chief of a plot by generals Horatio Gates, Thomas Mifflin, and *Thomas Conway to supersede him as head of the Continental Army. Fitzgerald was also one of the most active promoters of the Potomac Company, which promoted "the Potomack River and its tributaries as the safest, most direct and cheapest route from the Western country for its produce to the sea, and being about the centre of the Union, offers the most eligible site, somewhere on its banks, for the permanent seat of the Federal Government."

¶ Fitzgerald is buried in St. Mary's Catholic Cemetery, at the southeast corner of Washington and South streets.

¶ **Woodlawn Plantation,** 7.5 miles south on U.S. 1.

Originally a part of Mount Vernon, this property was a wedding gift from George Washington to his nephew Lawrence Lewis and his wife, Eleanor Parke Custis, Martha Washington's granddaughter. Eleanor was a seventh-generation descendant of John Custis of Baltimore, County Cork, Ireland. (See Arlington House, Arlington, Virginia.)

The Georgian mansion at Woodlawn was designed by Dr. William Thornton, the first architect of the U.S. Capitol, and was constructed between 1800 and 1805.

§ Open daily 9:30-4:30. Closed January 1, Thanksgiving, and December 25. Fee. Phone: 703-780-4000.

¶ **Woodrow Wilson Memorial Bridge,** spanning the Potomac River between Alexandria, Virginia, and Oxon Hill, Maryland.

This bridge in honor of *President Woodrow Wilson was dedicated in 1961. On both sides of the traffic tower are aluminum medallions measuring five feet across and containing the profile of the president.

ALTAVISTA

¶ **Avoca,** 1514 Main Street.

Recently restored by the town of Altavista, "Avoca" is the third house to stand on this site, originally the property of Colonel Charles Lynch, whose Irish-born father had settled in this area in the early 1700s.

The first residence at this location was "Green Level," the home of Colonel Lynch and the scene of extralegal court proceedings which gave rise to the term "Lynch law." That house was destroyed by fire in 1878; its successor was a victim of another blaze twenty-two years later. The present structure was named for the lush valley on the east coast of Ireland, the subject of "The Meetings of the Waters" by the nineteenth-century Irish composer Thomas Moore.

According to family lore, the colonel's father – also named Charles – had come to America as a youngster fleeing the disgrace of a punishment he had received at school. After taking passage on a ship leaving northern Ireland, though, he changed his mind and jumped overboard, intending to swim back to shore. His purpose was frustrated, however, when he was fished out of the ocean and returned to the ship.

Arrived in Louisa County, Virginia, the young Lynch entered an indenture with Christopher Clark, for whom he worked and by whom, in effect, he was raised. It was probably at the time of his marriage to Clark's daughter Sarah that he received from his father-in-law a parcel of land later known as Chestnut Hill, near the present site of Lynchburg. He later represented Bedford and Campbell counties in the House of Burgesses.

It was at Chestnut Hill that Lynch's wife gave birth to their son Charles Jr. in 1736. Because of his father's premature death, the son was educated by his mother, a Quaker. After marrying Anna Terrell at the age of nineteen or twenty, Charles settled on the land he had inherited from his father in Bedford County. There he was installed as justice of the peace in 1766, although he was soon disowned by the Quakers for taking the oath required of the position. (A decade later he was expelled from the pacifist sect for taking up arms.)

Beginning with his election to the Burgesses in 1769, Lynch became a prominent leader in the political affairs of the colony. He signed the Williamsburg protests against British taxation and attended the state constitutional convention in 1776. Two years later he assumed command of a volunteer regiment of 200 riflemen, who served with particular distinction under General Nathanael Greene at the battle of Guilford Court House.

During the last years of the war, when military events had disrupted the workings of the regular courts in Bedford County, Lynch served as the judge of an extralegal court. A former justice of the peace, he became known for his summary judgments, especially against criminals and Tories who had conspired to sabotage production at local lead mines. In this role he gave his name to the terms "Lynch Law" and "lynching," although the punishments which he dispensed were usually no more severe than whipping. After the Revolution he was exonerated by the Assembly on the ground that his actions, though not "strictly warranted by law" were "justifiable from the imminence of danger."

The nearby city of Lynchburg was named for Charles Lynch's brother, John, who at the age of seventeen established a ferry there in 1757.

§ Open June-August, Thursday-Saturday 11-3, Sunday 1:30-4:30. Fee. Phone: 804-369-1076.

APPOMATTOX

¶ Appomattox Court House National Historical Park.

These historic grounds contain a village of twenty-seven structures restored to their Civil War appearance. One of them, the McLean House, was where *General Ulysses S. Grant accepted the surrender of Confederate general Robert E. Lee on April 9, 1865. According to Grant's generous terms of surrender, Lee's men were to be paroled and his officers were allowed to keep their horses and side arms. After further ordering that

Lee and his troops be supplied with 25,000 rations, Grant apologized to the Confederate general for his unkempt appearance.

• One of the other structures in the village is the Kelly House, restored in the 1960s to its appearance a century before. The house was first built in 1855 by Lorenzo D. Kelly, a wheelwright who died in 1862 at the age of thirty-seven. Possibly of Irish extraction, he was survived by his mother, one sister, and one brother, all of whom were probably living in the house when the surrender ceremony took place opposite the house – in the triangular plot of land which Kelly had bought in 1855.

§ Park is open June-August, daily 9-5:50; rest of the year, daily 8:30-5. Closed January 1, Martin Luther King Jr.'s Birthday, Presidents' Day, Thanksgiving, and December 25. Fee. Phone: 804-352-8987.

ARLINGTON

¶ Arlington House.

Situated on an eminence commanding a view of the Arlington Cemetery and the Lincoln Memorial, this Greek Revival mansion was built between 1802 and 1804 by George Washington Parke Custis, the grandson of Martha Washington.

The 1,100 acres on which the house originally stood were purchased in 1778 by John Parke Custis, Martha Washington's son and her famous husband's stepson. Martha was the widow of Daniel Park Custis, a fifth-generation descendant of John Custis of Baltimore, County Cork, Ireland. This Irish-born Custis had arrived in Virginia about 1640 from Holland, which, with France and Ireland, formed the triangle within which he conducted his mercantile business. In making the trans-Atlantic voyage, he brought three of his six sons with him. Custis later was appointed customs collector for the Eastern Shore of Virginia.

Following the death of John Parke Custis in 1781, the property passed to his son, George Washington Parke Custis, generally known simply as Washington. Although his famous adoptive step-grandfather – George Washington – loved him, the first president bemoaned the younger man's lack of ambition, at least once referring to him as "inert." The step-grandson, however, idolized the "Father of His Country" and built the Arlington House as a memorial to him, making sure that it could be seen from almost every part of the national capital. The mansion achieved its later association with Robert E. Lee when the future Civil War general married Custis's daughter, Mary Anna Randolph Custis, in 1831. It was here – exactly thirty years later – that Lee agonized over his decision to resign from the U.S. Army and throw in his lot with the Confederacy and the native state which he said he could never abandon.

George Washington Parke Custis was born in Maryland in 1781, a descendant – as has been mentioned above – of an Irishman from Baltimore, Ireland. Custis's mother, in turn, was descended from Cecil Calvert, the second Lord Baltimore, whose English title of nobility, ironically, was derived from that same Irish village.

Young "Washington" received his formal education at St. John's College in Annapolis and at the College of New Jersey. After receiving a commission in the army, he served briefly as aide-de-camp to General Charles Pinckney. In 1824, when Lafayette visited the United States in triumph, Custis escorted the famous Frenchman to his step-grandfather's grave at Mount Vernon. Although the American suggested that Lafayette be buried next to his old comrade in arms, the Gallic general politely declined. Two years later Custis began a thirty-year serialization in the newspapers of his recollections of the first president as well as of life at Mount Vernon.

Custis achieved additional renown as a dramatist and a painter. Among the half dozen plays for which he is best known, *Pocahontas, or the Settlers of Virginia* was his most successful, although, like Walt Disney Studios, he took liberties with history to heighten the dramatic climax. Meanwhile, his play *The Railroad* was apparently the first to produce a real "locomotive steam carriage" on stage. As a painter he is known for four large canvasses depicting General Washington at Yorktown and scenes from the battles of Germantown, Princeton, and Trenton.

Beginning in the 1820s, Custis employed his considerable oratorical skills on behalf of political and religious liberty. He championed the aspirations of such diverse peoples as South Americans, Poles, Greeks, and Irish to be free from the empires which ruled them. He readily acknowledged the support which his step-grandfather had received from the Irish during the Revolution, and in 1826 he helped organize a rally in the nation's capital "to express . . . sympathy for the people of Ireland and an earnest desire and hope for a speedy amelioration of their condition." During his address to a St. Patrick's Day gathering in 1844, he expressed his hope that, "after my mortal body shall have been laid in the bosom of our common mother, some Irish heart may come and, dropping a shamrock on my grave, cry, 'God bless him.'"

¶ Custis's grave is located near the obelisk at the rear of Arlington House. Since 1954 this site has been the scene of a ritual that fulfills the Hibernophile's wish. Each March 17, officials from the Irish Embassy join members of the Ancient Order of Hibernians and the Friendly Sons of St. Patrick to place a shamrock on the grave.

§ Open April–September, daily 9:30-6; rest of the year, daily 9:30-4:30. Closed January 1 and December 25. Phone: 703-557-0613.

¶ **Arlington National Cemetery,** across the Memorial Bridge from Washington, D.C.

Above the entrance to the cemetery are four lines from the famous ode "The Bivouac of the Dead" by *Theodore O'Hara: "On Fame's eternal camping-ground / Their silent tents are spread, / And Glory guards, with solemn round, / The Bivouac of the dead." In the Trophy Room is the bronze and gold-leaf figure of "Victory" by *Augustus Saint-Gaudens.

§ Open April-September, daily 8-7; rest of the year, daily 8-5. Phone: 703-692-0931.

❡ The following persons of Irish birth or descent are buried in the cemetery:

• William Jennings Bryan (beyond the Fort McPherson earthworks), *President Woodrow Wilson's secretary of state and a three-time presidential candidate.

• Sir John Dill, chief liaison between the British and the American general staffs during World War II.

Born in Lurgan, northern Ireland, Dill was educated at Sandhurst, England, and saw service in South Africa, France, India, and Palestine with the British army. During the Second World War he was the senior British representative on the Combined Chiefs of Staff. After his death he was awarded the Distinguished Service Cross by Congress and was granted the extraordinary honor – for a foreign soldier – of being buried in Arlington National Cemetery. The monument over his grave is one of only two equestrian statues in the cemetery.

• William Joseph "Wild Bill" Donovan, World War I hero, the father of the U.S. intelligence network, and the first American to receive his country's four highest decorations.

The son of Irish immigrants, Donovan formed a New York cavalry troop which served under General John Pershing, first on the Mexican border in 1916 and then in France in the last months of World War I. During his service in Europe, he was colonel of the 165th Infantry (formerly known as the "Fighting 69th") and was wounded three times. According to one account, Donovan received his nickname during a workout with his men. "I have fifty pounds on my back, the same as you," he said challengingly, "and I'm twenty years older than any of you boys." Anonymously from within the ranks came the response, "Yeah, but we ain't no wild man like you, Bill."

With the outbreak of World War II in Europe, Donovan pressed the U.S. government to create an intelligence network for the nation. In 1942, when the Office of Strategic Service was established as a result of Donovan's efforts, he was named its director. In that capacity he oversaw the agency's efforts at intelligence gathering, counterintelligence, underground activities, psychological warfare, propaganda, and sabotage.

In 1957, when Donovan was awarded the National Security Medal, he became the first American to receive the nation's top four decorations. (He had already received the Medal of Honor, the Distinguished Service Cross, and the Distinguished Service Medal.)

• General Philip Kearny, the Union cavalry officer who lost his left arm as the result of a wound received during the Mexican War.

Kearny's earliest paternal ancestor in America was Michael Kearny, an Irish emigrant who had settled in Perth Amboy, New Jersey, sometime after 1704. The latter-day Kearny was trained at the French Cavalry School in Saumur, France, and later enlisted in the U.S. Army for duty on the western frontier. In 1847, while leading an attack on Churubusco, Mexico, he sustained a hit that resulted in the amputation of his left arm. After the Mexican War he returned to France to fight for Napoleon III in the Franco-Italian conflict. With the outbreak of the American Civil War, he returned to his native land and was given command of the 1st New Jersey Brigade in the Union army. Seemingly unhindered by his earlier injury, he was often seen holding the reins of his horse in his teeth as he directed his men with his right arm. Just before the Second Battle of Bull Run, however, he was fired upon and killed after unwittingly crossing the Confederate lines. So highly was he regarded by General Robert E. Lee that the latter ordered the return of Kearny's body as well as of his horse and sword.

When the fallen leader's men wanted to pay him special tribute, they created the Cross of Honor, to be awarded to noncommissioned soldiers for exceptional valor in battle. That award later evolved into the Medal of Honor, the nation's highest military award. In 1912 Kearny's body was exhumed from Trinity Churchyard in New York City and interred at Arlington. Two years later his grave was adorned with a life-size equestrian statue of the "little general."

• John Fitzgerald Kennedy and Jacqueline Bouvier Kennedy Onassis
Following a grave-side service conducted by *Cardinal Richard Cushing of Boston, the slain president was buried with full military honors. After the ceremony his widow lighted an eternal flame over the grave, which is marked by a black granite slab inscribed with the words "John Fitzgerald Kennedy 1917-1963." The slab is surrounded by a concrete pavement in the shape of a Greek cross. The esplanade portion of the memorial is elliptical in shape and is rimmed by concrete and granite blocks inscribed with quotes from Kennedy's inaugural speech.

Despite the French blood which Jacqueline Bouvier inherited from her father, her mother was 100 percent Irish, the family's first American ancestor having come from Ireland to New York City in the 1840s. Jacqueline's grandfather – James Thomas Lee – was vice president of Chase Manhattan Bank and president and chairman of the board of New York Central Savings Bank. When he died at the age of ninety-five, he left a $12 million estate.

• Robert F. Kennedy, U.S. senator and victim of an assassin's bullet in Los Angeles in 1968.
The seventh of the nine children born to Joseph and Rose Kennedy, Robert was a graduate of Harvard College and the University of Virginia Law School. His first work as an attorney was with the Justice Depart-

ment, prosecuting graft and income-tax cases. He later served as counsel on a Senate committee investigating labor racketeering. As attorney general for his brother, Kennedy prosecuted school desegregation cases and threw his support behind the 1964 Civil Rights Act.

When it became clear that he would not be Lyndon Johnson's vice presidential running mate, Kennedy successfully ran for the U.S. Senate from New York. In Congress he supported the expansion of the federal welfare system and denounced the Vietnam War. After declaring his candidacy for the presidency, he rolled to five victories in the six primaries that he entered, until he was gunned down by Sirhan Sirhan, an Arab immigrant.

• William Daniel Leahy, recipient of the highest rank ever conferred on a U.S. naval officer. (See Hampton, Iowa.)

• Audie Murphy, the most highly decorated American of World War II. (See Greenville, Texas.) His simple tombstone, just across Memorial Drive from the Memorial Amphitheater, is approached by a flagstone walkway.

• Joseph Patrick O'Neil, the leader of an 1890 expedition which explored the Olympic Mountains in the Pacific Northwest. (See Olympic National Park, Washington.)

• William "Buckey" O'Neill, one of the organizers of the famous Rough Rider cavalry unit during the Spanish-American War. (See Prescott, Arizona.)

• General Philip Sheridan, generally regarded as the third most important Civil War Union general (after *Ulysses S. Grant and William T. Sherman).

The son of immigrants from County Cavan, Ireland, Sheridan attended the U.S. Military Academy but was suspended for a year for lunging at a cadet-officer with a bayonetted rifle. During the Civil War he practically saved the army of General William Rosecrans by holding off a Confederate advance. Later, in command of the 20th Corps of the Army of the Cumberland, he contributed to General Grant's victory at Chattanooga. As a result, the Union commander placed him in charge of the 10,000-man cavalry corps of the Army of the Potomac.

In the last year of the war, Sheridan carried out a series of raids that prepared the way for major Union victories. In an attempt to break the Confederate communications line around Richmond, his men destroyed ten miles of railroad track, cut off telegraph communication to the city, and captured many supply trains. As commander of the Army of the Shenandoah, Sheridan later laid waste to the Shenandoah Valley, which had long sustained successful guerrilla campaigns against Union lines. In the spring of 1865, "Little Phil" carried out one final raid, destroying Confederate supply depots and leaving General Robert E. Lee with only one railroad line of communication with the South. Sheridan's final strategic action during the war forced Lee's evacuation of Petersburg and his retreat to Appomattox.

Philip Sheridan Gravesite.
(Photo by William A. Miller.
Library of Congress, LC-M6-26.)

❡ The mast of the battleship *Maine*, which was sunk in Havana Harbor in 1898, is surrounded by the graves of the 62 known and 167 unknown Americans killed in the explosion. The numerous Irish surnames among the casualties prompted Joseph I. C. Clarke to compose the "The Fighting Race" in their honor. The first two of the poem's five stanzas follow:

> Read out the names!" and Burke sat back,
>   And Kelly drooped his head.
> While Shea – they called him Scholar Jack –
>   Went down the list of the dead.
> Officers, seamen, gunners, marines,
>   The crews of the gig and yawl,
> The bearded man and the lad in his teens,
>   Carpenters, coal passers – all.
> Then, knocking the ashes from out his pipe,
>   Said Burke in an offhand way:
> "We're all in that dead man's list, by Cripe!
>   Kelly and Burke and Shea."

"Well, here's to the Maine, and I'm sorry for Spain,"
　　Said Kelly and Burke and Shea.

"Wherever there's Kellys there's trouble," said Burke,
　　"Wherever fighting's the game,
Or a spice of danger in grown man's work,"
　　Said Kelly, "you'll find my name,"
"And do we fall short," said Burke, getting mad,
　　"When it's touch and go for life?"
Said Shea, "It's thirty-odd years, bedad,
　　Since I charged to drum and fife
Up Marye's Heights, and my old canteen
　　Stopped a rebel ball on its way.
There were blossoms of blood on our sprigs of green –
　　Kelly and Burke and Shea –
And the dead didn't brag." "Well, here's to the flag!"
　　Said Kelly and Burke and Shea.

Clarke, a journalist, playwright, and former Fenian, was born in Kingstown (now Dun Laoghaire), Ireland, in 1846. Following the death of his father, the boy's widowed mother moved with her children to London, where the youngster found work in the printing trade. At the age of sixteen, however, he obtained a position as a clerk in the Home Office. Although this sinecure guaranteed him security, he jeopardized his position through involvement with the Irish Republican Brotherhood. Just as the police were about to discover his subversive activities, he escaped to Paris.

After immigrating to New York in 1868, Clarke began a career in journalism. At first he worked for the *Irish Republic* but soon moved on to the staff of the *New York Herald*. For the latter paper he served in a wide variety of editorial positions (e.g., sports, drama, music, and literature). He subsequently manned the editorial desk at Pulitzer's *Morning Journal*, the *Criterion*, and the Sunday *Herald* and was publicity director of the Standard Oil Company.

In the meantime Clarke's literary output took new directions. As a playwright he was the author of seven stage plays, among them *Lady Godiva*, *For Bonnie Prince Charlie*, and *The Prince of India*. In addition to poems and ballads, he wrote *Robert Emmet: A Tragedy*, *Malmorda: A Metrical Romance*, *Japan at First Hand*, and the autobiographical *My Life and Memories*. In the last work he recounted his meeting with Eamon De Valera and expressed an opinion that may yet contain the key to a united Ireland: "There will be no Republic in Ireland until there is a Republic in England." In his "Requiem of Michael Collins," Clarke lauded the assassinated Irish revolutionary leader: "Sleep, darling son, upon our mother's breast, / In wisdom and in valor who had borne his part, / Her bold, brave Michael of the lion heart." During the last decade of his life, Clarke served as president of the American Irish Historical Society.

ASHLAND

¶ Scotchtown National Historic Landmark, about 9 miles northeast on State 685.

One of the largest houses in colonial Virginia, this 94-by-36-foot structure was for a time the home of young *Dorothea Payne (later known as Dolley Madison). The girl lived here with her parents while they leased the 960-acre property from Patrick Henry between 1777 and 1783. (See Greensboro, North Carolina.)

§ Open April, Saturday 10-4:30, Sunday 1:30-4:30; May-October, Tuesday-Saturday 10-4:30, Sunday 1:30-4:30. Fee. Phone: 703-227-3500.

BRUSH MOUNTAIN

¶ Audie Murphy Monument.

A monument erected by the Veterans of Foreign Wars commemorates *Audie Murphy, the nation's most decorated hero of World War II, who was killed when his private plane crashed near Roanoke, Virginia, on May 28, 1971. He was only forty-six.

The monument is inscribed with the following words: "Audie Leon Murphy / June 20, 1942 / May 28, 1974. Born in Kingston, Texas, died near this site in an airplane crash. America's most decorated veteran of World War II. He served in the European Theatre – 15th Infantry Regiment – 3rd Infantry Division and earned 24 decorations, including the Medal of Honor, Legion of Merit, Distinguished Service Cross and three Purple Hearts. He was survived by his wife, Pamela, and two sons, Terry Michael and James Shannon." (See Greenville, Texas.)

CHANCELLORSVILLE

¶ Chancellorsville Battlefield Visitor Center.

The Irish Brigade was still suffering from its decimation at Fredericksburg when it was almost annihilated at the battle of Chancellorsville on May 2-4, 1863. So serious had the situation become that its commander, *Thomas Meagher, sought permission to recruit more Irish soldiers from New York. When he was denied permission, he resigned, primarily because he suspected that his superiors were planning to disband the brigade.

On May 19, 1863, Meagher wept openly as he bade his men adieu. After shaking the hands of many of them, he pledged that "as long as there remains one officer or soldier of the Irish Brigade, so long shall there be found for him, for his family and little ones, if any there be, a devoted friend in Thomas Francis Meagher." (See Helena, Montana.)

One of the sons of Ireland who distinguished himself at Chancellorsville was St. Clair Mulholland, who received the Congressional Medal of Honor for covering the withdrawal of the Union army across the Rappahannock River. At the start of the war, he had helped organize the 116th Pennsylvania Volunteers and received the first of four wartime wounds while charging with the Irish Brigade at Fredericksburg. He later led the 140th Pennsylvania Volunteers at Gettysburg.

§ Visitor center open mid June-Labor Day, daily 8:30-6:30; rest of the year, daily 9-5. Closed January 1 and December 25. Phone: 703-371-0802.

¶ **"Stonewall" Jackson Monument,** Chancellorsville Battlefield.

This memorial marks the spot where *Thomas "Stonewall" Jackson was accidentally shot by Confederate pickets soon after returning to his lines to announce his victory against the right wing of the Union line. Jackson was hit twice in the left arm and once in the right hand. After his shattered arm was amputated the next morning, General Robert E. Lee said: "He has lost his left arm, but I have lost my right." Fearing that Jackson might be captured, Lee ordered his removal to Fairfield plantation at Guinea Station.

CHARLOTTESVILLE

¶ **"Stonewall" Jackson Monument,** on the northeast corner of Jefferson and East 4th streets.

This equestrian statue of *Thomas "Stonewall" Jackson bending forward astride his horse, Little Sorrell, was unveiled in 1921.

¶ **University of Virginia,** on U.S. 29/250.

• In the west range of the original academic buildings is Room 13, where *Edgar Allan Poe lived while he attended the university. The bronze tablet above the door describes the room as *domus parva magni poetae* ("the small home of a great poet"). The Wilson Room (Number 31) was the quarters of *Woodrow Wilson in 1879-80.

• A bronze bust of *Edgar Allan Poe is on display in the Taylor Room on the third floor of Alderman Library.

• A memorial in honor of *James Rogers McConnell by Gutzon Borglum stands in a triangular plot bounded by Alderman Library, Miller Hall, and Clemons Hall. Dedicated in 1919, the statue is a memorial to the University of Virginia graduate who was shot down in France while flying with the Lafayette Escadrille during World War I. Known as the *Winged Aviator*, the Icarus-like figure is said to have been the first attempt by a sculptor to depict an airplane pilot. While at the university, McConnell

Memorial in honor of
James Rogers McConnell
by Gutzon Borglum.

founded the Aero Club and was an assistant cheerleader and a member of two fraternities. He was so famous for his pranks that he was elected "King of the Hot-Foot." (While a pilot in France, he painted a red foot on the side of his plane.) (See Carthage, North Carolina.)

DANVILLE

❡ Danville Museum of Fine Arts and History, 975 Main Street.

Formerly the Sutherlin House, this mansion became the "Last Capitol of the Confederacy" when *President Jefferson Davis fled to Danville with the members of his cabinet after learning of General Lee's retreat from Richmond. Visitors can view the museum's permanent collection as well as the living quarters, including Davis's bedroom.

§ Open Tuesday-Friday 10-5, Saturday and Sunday 2-5. Closed holidays. Phone: 804-793-5644.

FAIRFIELD

❡ Sam Houston Birthplace Site, Timber Ridge Plantation, south of the Presbyterian church.

A monument and tablet mark the spot where Sam Houston was born in 1793, a descendant of Irish-born emigrants from northern Ireland. Both his grandfather and great-grandfather had immigrated to Philadelphia in 1735, and his father, Major Samuel Houston, had been a member of Daniel Morgan's rifle corps during the Revolution. The younger Houston went on to serve as a congressman, the governor of Tennessee, the Texan commander at the battle of San Jacinto, the president of the Texas Republic, and the first governor of Texas.

FALLS CHURCH

¶ **Chaplains' Memorial,** National Memorial Park.
The memorial honors four chaplains – one Catholic, one Jewish, and two Protestant – who gave up their life jackets to soldiers aboard the sinking U.S.S. *Dorchester* in 1943. The four clergymen were *Father John Washington, Rabbi Alexander Goode, Reverend Clark Poling, and Reverend George Fox. (See Bottineau, North Dakota.)

FREDERICKSBURG

¶ **Fredericksburg Battlefield Visitor Center,** Lafayette Boulevard (U.S. 1) and Sunken Road.
The Irish Brigade suffered its most devastating losses when it was ordered by the Union general John Pope to storm Marye's Heights during the battle of Fredericksburg in December 1862. Before the brigade's commander, *Thomas Meagher, led his men in six heroic but suicidal charges, he told them to adorn their caps with sprigs of boxwood to take the place of their tattered banners. Some of the Confederates wore their own emblems of green, for sons of Erin were to be found in both of the contending armies that day.
The gallant deeds of these Irishmen were recorded in these lines from the poem "At Fredericksburg" by *John Boyle O'Reilly:
> Their foemen are proud of the country that bore them,
> But Irish in love, they are enemies still.
> Out rang the fierce word, "Let them have it!" The rifles
> Are emptied point-blank in the hearts of the foe;
> It is green against green, but a principle stifles
> The Irishman's love in the Georgian's blow. . . .
> The lesson it brought we should evermore heed:
> Who loveth the Flag is a man and a brother,
> No matter what birth or what race or what creed.
A Confederate gunner on Marye's Heights that bloody day described one of several Union assaults. "With them were the Zouaves and the Irish Brigade . . . bearing aloft the green flag with the golden harp of Ireland," he wrote. "The brave fellows came within five and twenty paces of the

stone wall [at the bottom of the heights], but encountered such a fire of shot, canister, and musketry as no command was ever known to live through. The result was that two-thirds of this splendid and gallant brigade was left on the field."

Although the Irish Brigade's average loss per regiment that day was almost 41 percent, one regiment suffered a 78-percent casualty rate. During the course of the war, 7,000 men enlisted in the brigade, although it probably numbered no more than 5,000 at any one time; at war's end fewer than 1,000 were alive. Overall, the Irish Brigade lost about 500 men in the Peninsular campaign and an equal number each time at Antietam and Fredericksburg.

§ Open mid June-Labor Day, daily 8:30-6:30; April to mid June, and the day after Labor Day-October 31, Monday-Friday 9-5, Saturday and Sunday 9-6; rest of the year, daily 9-5. Closed January 1 and December 25. Phone: 703-371-0802.

¶ Matthew Maury Monument, State 3 to Catherine Furnace Road.

This monument is located near the birthplace of *Matthew Fontaine Maury, the pioneer oceanographer who was born in 1806. He was of Irish and French Huguenot descent. (See Virginia Military Institute, Lexington, Virginia.)

¶ "Stonewall" Jackson Memorial Shrine National Historic Landmark, 15 miles south via Interstate 95, U.S. 1, or State 2 and then on State 606 to Guinea.

This restored 1828 plantation house was where *Thomas "Stonewall" Jackson was brought after the amputation of his shattered arm and where he died on May 10, 1863. In the rear room is the bed in which he died, just after uttering his famous last words: "Let us cross over the river, and rest under the shade of the trees."

§ Open April to mid June, and the day after Labor Day-October 31, Friday-Tuesday 9-5; mid June-Labor Day, daily 9-5; November-March, Saturday-Monday 9-5. Closed January 1 and December 25.

HAMPTON

¶ Fort Monroe National Historic Landmark.

The present fortification on this site was built between 1819 and 1847 and shares several Irish or Irish-American associations.

Among the soldiers stationed here in 1828-29 was *Edgar Allan Poe, who had enlisted in Boston under the name of Edgar A. Perry. *Jefferson Davis was a prisoner here following his capture at the end of the Civil War, as was *John Reagan, the postmaster general of the Confederacy. (See Palestine, Texas.) In addition, the fortress held the poet *Sidney Lanier as well as John Mitchel, the Irish nationalist and outspoken journalist who was imprisoned for criticizing the North's policy toward the defeated Confederacy. Items relating to Poe and Davis are on display in the Casemate Museum, while plaques mark the cells occupied by Mitchel and the former Confederate president.

Although Davis was at first imprisoned in a wall chamber (Casemate #2), his rapidly failing health resulted in his transfer to Carroll Hall elsewhere in the fortress. Later in his life Davis said that his imprisonment at Fort Monroe had allowed him time to read Macaulay's *History of England*. The former Confederate president likened the system of settlement and confiscations under Cromwell in Ireland to what he expected to happen to the people of the defeated South. "There was no excuse for it here; there had been some in Ireland," Davis wrote. "Between the conquering forces of Cromwell and the Irish there were essential differences of race, religion, habits, laws, and hopes. There had been war for centuries, and no promise of future tranquility on less rigorous terms." Davis saw "the further parallel that both countries suffered for loyalty to what each regarded as the rightful government; Ireland, for devotion to the Royal Family of the Stuarts; and the South, for its fidelity to the principles defined by the Constitution of 1787."

Oddly enough, Davis's neighboring cellmate was John Mitchel, a native of County Londonderry, the area of Ireland which had suffered the most from Cromwell's depredations. Like many of the illustrious Irish nationalists who had preceded him, Mitchel was a Protestant, the son, in fact, of a Presbyterian minister. After graduating from Trinity College, Dublin, in 1834, the younger Mitchel studied law. Before setting up practice in a town near Newry, however, he eloped with a schoolgirl of sixteen, but the pair was captured in Chester, England. Although Mitchel served a brief jail sentence before being released on bond, he and his beloved made a second attempt at elopement, this time successfully.

At age thirty Mitchel abandoned his legal career for one as a revolutionary. Disenchanted with the nonviolent and constitutional approach taken by Daniel O'Connell to achieve an independent Irish parliament, Mitchel joined the Young Ireland movement. Although at first he wrote for the *Nation*, that group's mouthpiece, he later founded his own political organ, the *United Irishman*. From its pages he openly preached armed resistance to Britain and repeal of the constitutional union of that country and Ireland. Within six months, however, he was arrested and convicted of treason and condemned to fourteen years imprisonment, most of which was to be spent in Van Dieman's Land (Tasmania). His family later joined him there, and it was with them that he escaped in 1853, after serving only five years.

Mitchel was treated to enthusiastic welcomes from the Irish in San Francisco and New York. Buoyed by this experience, he established the

Citizen, which he dedicated to the cause of Irish independence and which quickly came to enjoy a circulation of 50,000. His newfound status in New York soon dimmed, though, when he attacked the temporal power of the papacy and became an outspoken defender of slavery, the latter an extremely odd position for a champion of Irish liberty.

Seeking more congenial pastures in the South, Mitchel took up farming near Knoxville, Tennessee. Within two years, however, he began to publish the *Southern Citizen*, an extremist newspaper subservient to the slavery interests. On the eve of the Civil War, he and his family traveled to Paris, where for eighteen months he was a correspondent for several American newspapers.

Upon the family's return to America, Mitchel's three sons enlisted in the Confederate army. After his own rejection because of poor eyesight, he accepted a position as editor of the *Richmond Enquirer*. As in the past, he used his pen to justify the Southern cause and to argue the states' rights position. In addition, as a member of a Confederate ambulance committee, he helped evacuate the wounded from the battlefields of Spotsylvania and the Wilderness. Within two years two of his sons had made the supreme sacrifice – John a casualty of the Union shelling of Fort Sumter, and Willy killed in Pickett's Charge at Gettysburg. His third son lost an arm during an engagement near Richmond. (See Magnolia Cemetery, Charleston, South Carolina.)

By the spring of 1864, Mitchel had turned against *President Jefferson Davis, apparently because of the latter's failure to prosecute the war more aggressively. From his new editorial position at the New York *Daily News*, a notoriously pro-Southern publication, the Irishman continued that paper's violent opposition to *President Andrew Johnson's reconstruction policies. For his fulminations in the press, Mitchel was arrested by the military authorities and was confined to Fortress Monroe in Virginia. He never recovered physically and mentally from the four-month imprisonment.

In the journal which he kept while in prison, Mitchel included an episode that brought tears to his eyes. While in his cell, he was quietly approached by one of his guards, who proceeded to speak to him through the grating. "'I wanted to tell you,' [the soldier] said, still whispering, 'that my name's Mike Sullivan, from Fetrhard, in the County Tipperary, and there's but one company of Irish in all this big regiment, ... and we feel badly about you and the way you're used here. ... I know these divils brought you away from home without letting you get a change of clothes or any little conveniences that you're used to; and so, as I was to be on guard to-night, I just took the liberty to go to the store, and to buy you a comb and a tooth-brush, and – and here they are."

After his release Mitchel continued his opposition to the North's reconstruction policies, this time as editor of the *Irish Citizen* in New York.

In 1875 he returned to his native land and was elected to the British parliament as a member from Tipperary. However, the British prime minister invalidated the result (on the ground that Mitchel was a convicted felon) and ordered a new election. The Irishman again won but immediately declared his intention not to assume his seat, thereby hoping to expose "the fraudulent practice of Irish representation" in the British parliament. His death a week later shattered his supporters' jubilation. He was buried in Newry, where his widow raised a monument to his memory.

In 1951 the Virginia Press Association honored Mitchel by dedicating a plaque outside his prison cell at Fort Monroe. On that occasion Raymond Bottoms, himself a Richmond newspaperman, pronounced a fitting eulogy for his professional colleague: "Freedom of the press is a shining light in a world darkened now by the notions of many who like no opposition to their ways. Upon this freedom the liberties of the people rest more now, perhaps than ever before in history. . . . Mitchel's world was one of controversy, too, but he dared speak and write his mind . . . . This example of unquenchable determination beckons us in our duty, strengthens us in our own determination. Mitchel did not win the battle; the contest still rages. Let this modest marker attest forever the respect in which we hold such a high expression of faithfulness to a trust and commend again to us, in these present days, the worth of its emulation."

§ Open daily, 10:30-4:30. Closed January 1, Thanksgiving, and December 25. Phone: 804-727-3391.

HARRISONBURG

¶ Shenandoah Valley Heritage Museum, 115 Bowman Road.

Among the displays in the museum is a twelve-foot vertical relief map that depicts the 1862 valley campaign of *General Thomas "Stonewall" Jackson.

§ Open May-October, Monday-Saturday and Sunday afternoon; rest of the year, Friday, Saturday, and Sunday afternoon. Closed holidays. Fee. Phone: 703-879-2626.

HOPEWELL

¶ Grant Headquarters and Home, City Point Unit, Pecan Avenue and Cedar Lane.

This 25-by-27-foot log cabin was built for *Ulysses S. Grant as his residence and headquarters during the siege of Petersburg in 1864-65. The cabin is on the property of Appomattox Manor, a large frame house used as Union army headquarters.

Three weeks before the end of the war and his own assassination, President Lincoln visited Grant and General William T. Sherman here. Their strategy meeting aboard the *River Queen* is the subject of *The Peacemakers*, a painting by the Irish-American artist George Healy now in the White House. Between 1868 and 1981 Grant's cabin was on exhibit in Philadelphia's Fairmount Park.

§ Open daily 9-5. Closed January 1 and December 25. Phone: 804-458-9504.

LEXINGTON

¶ Cyrus McCormick Statue, Washington and Lee University campus.

This standing statue honors the famous inventor *Cyrus McCormick, who was born in the nearby town of Steeles Tavern, where he perfected the first mechanical grain reaper.

¶ Lee Memorial Chapel, Washington and Lee University, at the west end of Henry Street.

More well known as the burial place of the Confederate general Robert E. Lee, this national historic landmark is also the final resting place of his wife, Mary Custis, the great-granddaughter of Martha Custis Washington. Through her paternal ancestors, Lee's wife was descended from John Custis of Baltimore, County Cork, Ireland. (See Arlington House, Arlington, Virginia.)

¶ Matthew Maury Memorial, Goshen Pass, 19 miles northwest on State 39.

A memorial to *Matthew Fontaine Maury, a pioneer in oceanography, is located at this gorge formed by the Maury River. The granite memorial shaft has a large iron anchor propped against it.

While teaching at the Virginia Military Institute in Lexington, Maury became enamored of the scenery in Goshen Pass. On his deathbed he requested that his body be taken through the gap on its way to Richmond for burial in Hollywood Cemetery.

¶ "Stonewall" Jackson Burial Site, Stonewall Jackson Memorial Cemetery, on the east side of Main Street, next to Lexington Presbyterian Church.

The grave of *Thomas "Stonewall" Jackson is marked by an eight-foot-high bronze statue of the Confederate general atop a pedestal ten feet in height. The standing figure by Edward Valentine holds a pair of field-glasses in its right hand, while the left rests on the hilt of a sheathed sword.

In an address in Richmond in 1897, *Dr. Hunter McGuire, Jackson's corps surgeon, eulogized his former commander. "[I]t is with swelling heart and deep thankfulness," he said, "that I recently heard some of the first soldiers and military students of England declare that within the past

two hundred years the English-speaking race had produced but five soldiers of the first rank – Marlborough, Washington, Wellington, Robert Lee,
and Stonewall Jackson. I heard them declare that Jackson's campaign in
the Shenandoah Valley, in which you [and I] followed this immortal, was
the finest specimen of strategy and tactics of which the world has any
record; that in this series of marches and battles there was never a blunder
committed by Jackson; that his campaign in the Valley was superior to
either of those made by Napoleon in Italy."

ℑ **"Stonewall" Jackson House,** 8 East Washington Street.

Beginning in 1858, this brick house was the residence of *Thomas
Jonathan (later "Stonewall") Jackson while he taught at the nearby Virginia Military Institute. His wife expressed what the house meant to her
husband: "[I]t was genuine happiness to him to have a home of his own: it
was the first one he had ever possessed, and it was truly his castle. He lost
no time in going to work to repair it and make it comfortable and attractive . . . but he liked to have everything in perfect order – every door 'on
golden hinges softly turning' as he expressed it . . . ."

While living here, Jackson followed a strict routine that reflected his
military training. He rose at six in the morning, took a cold bath (no matter what the weather), led family prayers at seven, ate breakfast, and
headed off to V.M.I. by eight. His wife recorded the remainder of his daily
schedule: "He was engaged in teaching only three hours a day, except for
a few weeks before the close of the session, when the artillery practice
demanded an additional hour in the afternoon. Upon his return home at
eleven o'clock, he devoted himself to study until one. The first book he
took up daily was his Bible, which he read with a commentary, and the
many pencil-marks upon it showed with what care he bent over its pages.
From his Bible he turned to his text-books, which engaged him until dinner, at one o'clock."

Jackson was a professor at the school for ten years, teaching natural
philosophy, optics, acoustics, astronomy, and analytical mechanics. Because he knew almost nothing about most of these subjects when he was
hired to teach, he had to spend long hours preparing, a task made more
difficult because of his badly weakened eyes. As an instructor, he was
known as a humorless martinet. One cadet referred to him in a poem:
"The V.M.I., O what a spot, / In winter cold, in summer hot. / Great Lord
Al . . . . , what a wonder / *Major Jackson, Hell & Thunder*."

§ Open Monday-Saturday 9-5, Sunday 1-5 (until 6, June-August).
Closed January 1, Easter, Thanksgiving, and December 25. Fee. Phone:
703-463-2552.

ℑ **Virginia Military Institute.**

• The statue of *Thomas "Stonewall" Jackson in front of Cadet Battery depicts the illustrious Civil War general as he surveyed the field at Chancellorsville before he was accidentally shot by his own men in 1863.

• Jackson Memorial Hall displays a heroic oil painting depicting the charge of V.M.I. cadets at the battle of New Market in 1864.

• Among the items on display in the V.M.I. Museum are Little Sorrel ("Stonewall" Jackson's war horse) and a bronze statue of the general like that in front of Cadet Battery. The museum also contains items pertaining to *Matthew Fontaine Maury, a naval officer of Irish and French Huguenot descent who taught physics, astronomy, and meteorology at the school from 1868 to 1872. For his innovations in the field of oceanography, he was dubbed the "Pathfinder of the Seas."

During his thirty-six-year career in the U.S. Navy, Maury conceived the idea of an Atlantic cable and was instrumental in founding the U.S. Naval Observatory, the Hydrographic Office, and the Weather Bureau. He first received major recognition from the navy with a published work on navigation. Later as superintendent of the Naval Observatory in Washington, D.C., he published his research on winds and currents and accompanying sailing directions. In the mid 1850s he published the first textbook on modern oceanography and was consulted about both the route and the best time for laying the Atlantic cable.

Maury's fame was assured when he accurately predicted that use of his charts and directions would reduce sailing time appreciably. Ten to fifteen days were shaved off a voyage from New York to Rio de Janeiro, for example, while the average New York-San Francisco run was reduced by an incredible forty-five days. Faced with such impressive results, the world's navies and merchant marines adopted the uniform system of recording oceanographic data which Maury advocated.

With the outbreak of the Civil War, Maury resigned his naval office and accepted a commission in the Confederate navy. During the war he served as the Confederacy's special agent to Britain, where he helped obtain ships for the Southern cause. When he was excluded from the postwar amnesty, he proposed to the Mexican government a plan to colonize former Confederates and their families in that country, a scheme that came to nothing, however. After two years in England, he returned to Lexington to accept the professorship of meteorology at the V.M.I.

Thoroughly modern in his educational views, Maury advocated replacing the traditional classical curriculum based on the study of Latin and Greek with courses in mathematics and science. He regarded the military academy at West Point as "the only tolerable institution in the United States because of the absence there of the humbuggery of the Learned Languages."

❡ On display in Preston Library are a bust and a portrait painting of *General "Stonewall" Jackson as well as a heroic statue of *Matthew Fontaine Maury. This last work is by F. William Sievers and depicts its subject seated on a dais, under which swim numerous creatures of the sea.

§ V.M.I. is open March-October, Monday-Saturday 9-5, Sunday 2-5; rest of the year, Monday-Saturday 9-4, Sunday 2-4. Closed January 1, Thanksgiving, and December 25. Phone: 703-463-7103.

§ Jackson Memorial Hall and the V.M.I. Museum are open Monday-Saturday 9-5, Sunday 2-5. Closed Thanksgiving and December 24-January 1.

LYNCHBURG

¶ **Maier Museum of Art,** Randolph-Macon Woman's College, 2500 Rivermont Avenue.

The museum's collection includes works by the American artists Thomas Hart Benton, Mary Cassatt, Edward Hicks, Winslow Homer, *Georgia O'Keeffe, and *James McNeill Whistler.

§ Open late August-late May, Tuesday-Sunday 1-5. Closed holidays and Christmas vacation. Phone: 804-947-8136.

¶ **Packet Boat *Marshall*,** Riverside Park, Rivermont Avenue.

Now mounted on a stone base, this vessel was used to transport the body of *Thomas "Stonewall" Jackson to Lexington, where he is buried.

§ Open daily.

¶ **South River Meeting House,** 5810 Fort Avenue.

The cemetery next to the church contains the grave site of *John Lynch, regarded as the founder of Lynchburg. The brother of the more famous Colonel Charles Lynch of Altavista, John first came to this area in 1757, when at the age of seventeen he established a ferry here. (See Altavista, Virginia.)

At the time of his death in 1821, John Lynch was eulogized in the following obituary: "He lived to see those lands which he acquired for little more than the fees and expenses of location, advance in value, so as to constitute immense fortunes for all his descendants. He witnessed the rise and progress of the town of Lynchburg, from the period when the site was a howling wilderness – to its present size and grandeur; and such was the veneration which the inhabitants of the town entertained for him, that he might be regarded as standing amongst them very much in the light of the patriarchs of old."

§ Open daily except major holidays. Phone: 804-239-2548.

MANASSAS

¶ **Manassas National Battlefield Visitor Center,** State 234 between

Interstate 66 and U.S. 29.

• On July 21, 1861, the poorly trained Union troops who converged at this important railroad junction were under the command of *General Irwin McDowell. After ten hours of fighting, the federal troops fell back in retreat, bested by Confederate forces under generals Joseph Johnston and Pierre Beauregard.

• During the Union defeat at this first battle of Manassas, the "Fighting 69th" New York State Militia was commanded by Colonel Michael Corcoran.

Corcoran was born in Sligo, Ireland, into a family whose estates had been confiscated by the British in the seventeenth century. Although as a young man he entered the Irish constabulary, he soon resigned in protest against British mistreatment of his native land. Once in America, he enlisted in the 69th and rapidly rose up the ranks. When he refused to parade his regiment for the visiting Prince of Wales, he became the darling of the New York Irish – but the object of a court-martial. The charges were dropped, however, when he offered his services and those of his men to the newly forming Union army.

The young colonel was captured at Manassas and remained a Confederate prisoner for thirteen months because he refused to agree that he would never again take up arms. (See Libby Prison Site, Richmond, Virginia.) After his release he made a triumphal return to New York, passing through the major cities on the East Coast and enjoying "a perfect ovation, perhaps never surpassed since the days of the immortal Washington." Corcoran later organized and led the Irish Legion until he was killed in an accidental fall from the horse of *General Thomas Meagher in 1863. Corcoran is buried in Calvary Cemetery in New York City.

¶ The equestrian statue of *Thomas "Stonewall" Jackson on Henry Hill commemorates the episode during the battle when the famous Confederate officer received his nickname. As Jackson and his men awaited attack behind Henry House Hill, General Barnard Bee tried to rally his men by pointing out Jackson: "Look! There stands Jackson like a stone wall! Rally behind the Virginians!"

§ Open mid June-Labor Day, daily 8:30-6; rest of the year, daily 8:30-5. Closed December 25. Phone: 704-361-1339.

McLEAN

¶ **Hickory Hill,** 1147 Chain Bridge Road. Private.

This Georgian mansion on five acres of rolling terrain was the home of Senator John F. Kennedy from 1954 to 1957. Kennedy sold the house to his brother Robert, who lived here until his assassination in 1968. During the Civil War the house had been the headquarters of General George McClellan.

MIDDLETOWN

❡ **Belle Grove,** 1 mile south on U.S. 11 and then 0.5 mile west on County 727.

Built about 1794 – reputedly according to a design by Thomas Jefferson – this Classical Revival mansion was the home of Major Isaac Hite Jr. and his wife, a sister of James Madison. Madison and his famous wife – *Dolley Payne Todd – spent part of their honeymoon here. Seventy years later, during the battle of Cedar Creek, *General Philip Sheridan used the mansion as his headquarters. The house is now a museum and an educational center, while the 100-acre estate surrounding it is a working farm.

On the morning of October 19, 1864, Sheridan's troops were encamped at nearby Cedar Creek, although Sheridan himself was in Winchester to the north, returning from a military conference in Washington. Sheridan's absence provided the Confederate general Jubal Early with the perfect opportunity for a lightning attack. Within minutes the Confederates had captured more than 1,000 prisoners, and fleeing Union soldiers clogged the road north from Middletown.

Sheridan, meanwhile, alarmed by the gunfire he could hear in the distance, hastened from Winchester to rally his men. Although standing only 5'5" and weighing but 130 pounds, "Little Phil" struck awe into his troops when they saw him mounted on his horse, Rienzi, ordering them to regroup and counterattack. When his men began to chant his name, he cried, "Don't cheer me. Fight, damn you, fight!" Sheridan and his men turned disaster into victory by killing or capturing a large portion of Early's command. He renamed his horse "Winchester" in honor of his victory.

The poet Thomas Buchanan Read later memorialized the victor – and his horse – in "Sheridan's Ride," excerpted here:

> The first that the general saw were the groups
> Of stragglers, and then the retreating troops.
>
> What was done! what to do? a glance told him both;
> Then, striking his spurs, with a terrible oath,
> He dashed down the line, 'mid a storm of huzzas,
> And the wave of retreat checked its course there because
> The sight of the master compelled it to pause.
> With foam and with dust, the black charger was gray;
>
> By the flash of his eye, and the red nostril's play,
> He seemed to the whole great army to say,
> "I have brought you Sheridan all the way
> From Winchester, down to save the day!"

Sheridan's success at Cedar Creek was the final major victory in his campaign to clear Confederate troops from the Shenandoah Valley. The statistics that he soon dispatched to *General Ulysses S. Grant showed that he had more than fulfilled his order to "eat out Virginia clear and clean, so that crows flying over it for the balance of the season will have to carry their own provender with them." His report portrayed an appalling litany: the seizure or destruction of 425,000 bushels of wheat, 77,000 bushels of corn, 20,000 tons of hay, 15,000 swine, 12,000 sheep, 11,000 cattle, and 4,500 horses and mules. For his pains Sheridan was promoted to major general, thereafter to be ranked the third most important Union general of the Civil War (after Grant and William T. Sherman).

§ Open March 15-November 15, Monday-Saturday 10-4, Sunday 1-5. Fee. Phone: 703-869-2028.

¶ Cedar Creek Battlefield is located near the intersection of Interstate 81 and Interstate 66. Although the battlefield is not a protected park, the Cedar Creek Battlefield Foundation provides a tour map of the site and annually sponsors a reenactment of the battle.

MOUNT VERNON

¶ **Mount Vernon,** at the southern end of the George Washington Memorial Parkway.

Beginning in 1754, this plantation was the home of George Washington until his death in 1799. Washington's diaries contain the names of numerous Irish or Irish Americans who visited his plantation either as guests, neighbors, or workmen. The following were among the visitors whom Washington invited to dine or spend the night at his famous estate:

• Charles Carroll, a senator from Maryland whom *Secretary of War James McHenry suggested for president if George Washington declined a second term;

• John Carroll, the first Catholic bishop of the United States;

• John Fitzgerald, a native of County Wicklow and Washington's secretary and aide-de-camp;

• Andrew Lewis, a soldier whom Washington regarded as the best military tactician in America and whom he suggested as commander-in-chief of the Continental Army in 1775;

• Father Anthony McCaffrey, the pastor of St. Patrick's Catholic Church in the District of Columbia;

• James Mease, one of the founders of the Friendly Sons of St. Patrick, the paymaster and treasurer of the Continental Army, and a subscriber of £1,500 to provision the American army;

• John O'Donnell, Baltimore's leading merchant and shipowner, the president of the Fire Insurance Company of that city, a member of the Hibernian Benevolent Society of Baltimore, and the owner of the first American vessel to fly the new nation's flag in India;

• Oliver Pollock, a native of Coleraine, County Antrim, the American commercial agent at New Orleans during the Revolution and a merchant who advanced $300,000 to the American war effort;

• Walter Stewart, a native of Donegal who accompanied Washington on his expedition to the Ohio River in 1754 and who commanded a Pennsylvania infantry regiment during the Revolution;

• Charles Thompson, the secretary of the Continental Congress and the man chosen to visit Mount Vernon to officially inform Washington of his election as first president of the United States; and

• Pierce Butler, Thomas FitzSimons, Thomas Lynch, and Thomas McKean – all signers of the Declaration of Independence.

§ Open April-August, daily 8-5; March and September-October, daily 9-5; rest of the year, daily 9-4. Fee. Phone: 703-780-2000.

NEWPORT NEWS

In 1621 Thomas Newce and his brother, Sir William Newce, both from Ireland, patented land in what is now Newport News. Soon later Daniel Gookin, an Englishman from Port Newce in County Cork, Ireland, arrived in this area with eighty other settlers. Gookin most likely named the region either for his home in Ireland or for the Newce brothers who had preceded him.

NORFOLK

¶ **Father Ryan House Site,** Lafayette Boulevard and Cottage Toll Road.

A marker denotes the site of a house once occupied by *Father Abram Ryan, the poet-priest of the Confederacy. (See Mobile, Alabama.)

ORANGE

¶ **Montpelier National Historic Landmark,** 4 miles southwest on State 20.

The original two-story brick house on this site was begun in 1760 by James Madison's father. When the future president inherited the 5,000-acre estate, he enlarged the house to its present size.

Madison lived here with his wife, *Dolley Payne Todd Madison, from 1817 until his death is 1836. During that time Dolley cared for Madison's aged mother, read to her husband, served as his secretary, and carried on her tradition of hospitality as best she could. A visiting Englishwoman described Dolley as "a strong-minded woman, fully capable of entering into her husband's occupations and cares, and there is little doubt that he owed much to her intellectual companionship, as well as to her ability in sustaining the outward dignity of his office."

Although Mrs. Madison later benefited financially from the posthumous sale to Congress of her husband's famous notes on the Constitutional Convention, continued financial problems eventually caused her to sell Montpelier as well as other manuscripts of her husband's.

Madison and his wife are buried in the cemetery on the property. The president's grave is marked by a monolith; his wife's, by a smaller stone. Mrs. Madison was originally buried in the Congressional Cemetery in Washington, D.C., but was reinterred here in 1858.

§ Open March-December, daily 10-4; rest of the year, Saturday and Sunday 10-4. Closed January 1, Thanksgiving, and December 25. Fee. Phone: 703-672-2728.

PETERSBURG

¶ **Old Blandford Cemetery,** Old Blandford Cemetery, 319 South Crater Road.

Made famous as the site of the first Memorial Day ceremony, this cemetery contains the gravesites of John Daly Burk, an Irish refugee and historian, and General William Mahone, who helped achieve the Confederate victory at Petersburg in 1864.

• Burk was born in Ireland about 1775 and was a student at Trinity College in Dublin when he became involved in an episode that caused him to flee to America. While attempting to help rescue a political prisoner about to be executed, he himself was pursued by the police, but he was able to elude them by dashing into a shop. There he disguised himself in a dress provided by a Miss Daly and prudently left the country, still wearing his female costume. Out of gratitude he subsequently added his rescuer's name to his.

After his arrival in Boston in 1796, Burk tried to launch a career in journalism. Although his newspaper – *The Polestar and Boston Daily Advertiser* – failed within six months, an editorial in the second issue is typical of his attachment to republican ideals. In referring to the upcoming election for a successor to President Washington, Burk expressed his realization of its immense significance: "[W]e hope the future president may be as good a republican as Washington. . . . People of America! with this great example of genius and patriotism before your eyes, you will be without excuse, if you err. Let the man of your choice be a man of talent, information, integrity and republican modesty; . . . He ought to be a friend of the revolutions of Holland and of France; he ought to be a hater of monarchy, not only on account of the danger, but the absurdity of it; he ought not to be willing to divide people by any distinctions. Americans should have but one denomination – the people."

After a second publishing venture failed in New York City, Burk turned his attention to the writing of history. While living in Petersburg, Virginia, he completed *A History of the Late War in Ireland,* a treatise on Irish music, and the first three volumes of the four-volume *History of Virginia.*

It was as a dramatist, though, that Burk achieved considerable fame during his lifetime. In 1796 he saw the successful production of *Bunker Hill, or the Death of General Warren,* one of the first dramas to stage a battle scene in front of the footlights. After seeing the play, President Adams remarked to the manager: "My friend Mr. Warren was a scholar and a gentleman, but your author has made him a bully and a blackguard." Despite this charge and although the play is too full of bombast for modern audiences, it remained a Fourth of July favorite for half a century. Two of Burk's other major dramas had a mortuary air about them: *Female Patriotism, or the Death of Joan d'Arc* and *The Death of General Montgomery in Storming the City of Quebec.* (Montgomery, by the way, was the first Irish-born general in the American revolutionary army.) Burk rounded out his career with *Bethlem Gabor, Lord of Transylvania, or the Man-hating Palatine.*

Burk's promising career was cut short, however, by his death in 1808 during a duel with the Frenchman Felix Coquebert. A Richmond newspaper described the unfortunate episode: "The causes which led to misunderstanding between Mr. Coquebert and the deceased, and which finally produced so distressing a catastrophe, were of a political nature. In a conversation, at a public table, sometime during the last week . . . the deceased expressed himself with considerable warmth, reprobated the conduct of the French government towards the United States; . . . Mr. C. being a native of France, conceived himself individually assailed, by the words uttered, as well as insulted by the epithets applied to his nation and government: he demanded an explanation of the object of the speaker. Very few words, however, passed between Mr. C. and the deceased: the explanation required was not given, and the former, in a few moments, left the room. Soon after a challenge was sent by Mr. C., which was accepted, and early, on Monday morning, the parties, with their seconds, met in a field adjoining town. On the first fire Mr. C's pistol snapped and the contents of Mr. B's were discharged ineffectually. The second fire proved decisive. Mr. C's ball passed through the heart of his antagonist, who expired without a word or a groan."

• William Mahone, whose paternal ancestors were Irish, was graduated from the Virginia Military Institute in 1847. After teaching for two years at the Rappahannock Military Academy, he studied civil engineering and became chief engineer and constructor of the Norfolk and Petersburg Railroad.

When civil war rent the nation, he joined the Confederate army, advancing to the rank of colonel of the 6th Virginia Infantry. He was present at the capture of the Norfolk Navy Yard in 1861 and participated in most of the battles of the peninsular campaign, including Fredericksburg, Chancellorsville, Gettysburg, Spotsylvania, and Cold Harbor. When his wife learned that he had suffered a flesh wound at Second Manassas, she knew that even a superficial wound could be serious for a man who weighed less than a hundred pounds. "The General hasn't any flesh!" she replied to the news.

Later at Petersburg, when Union troops exploded the tunnel they had built under the Confederate lines, Mahone led two of his brigades to the edge of the huge hole and kept up a merciless barrage of fire until the Yankees caught in the cavity surrendered. For his efforts in what was a stupendous failure for the Union, he was lauded with the title "Hero of the Crater" and was promoted to major general.

After the war Mahone became president of the Norfolk and Tennessee Railroad. Although he unsuccessfully sought the nomination for governor of Virginia in 1878, he was elected to the U.S. Senate two years later.

¶ **Trapezium,** 244 North Market Street.

This three-story red brick house is a curiosity because it has no parallel walls or exterior ninety-degree angles. It was built in 1815 by Charles O'Hara, an Irishman who apparently had followed the advice of a West Indian servant that evil spirits would be kept away by the use of such architectural features. O'Hara was nicknamed "the General" because of his custom of dressing in a British uniform on the Queen's birthday. Because of the pet rats which the eccentric O'Hara kept here, the house was known as "Rat Castle."

§ Tours begin at the Siege Museum (15 West Bank Street) April-October, daily 10-5. Fee. Phone: 804-733-2402 or 800-368-3595.

¶ **William McKenney Library,** South Sycamore Street.

A portion of this public library was formerly known as the Mahone House because of its association with *William Mahone. (See Old Blandford Cemetery above.) The Confederate general lived here for approximately a year, in 1867 playing host to Robert E. Lee and his son.

¶ Although a house which Mahone built three blocks away no longer exists, some of the furniture from that residence is now in the Centre Hill Mansion off Franklin Street. Among the items are a bookcase, a sofa, two chairs, and a piano which Mahone gave his daughter.

§ Mansion open daily 10-5. Closed January 1, Thanksgiving, and December 24-25. Fee. Phone: 804-733-2400 or 800-368-3595.

¶ **Five Forks Unit,** 6 miles southwest via State 613 to the junction of State 627 and State 645.

Here at the battle of Five Forks on April 1, 1865, *General Philip Sheridan and his Union troops smashed the Confederate lines to gain access to the South Side Railroad, the last supply line into Petersburg.

RAPIDAN

¶ Waddel Memorial Presbyterian Church, southeast on State 615.

This late eighteenth-century Gothic Revival church was built in honor of the Reverend James Waddel, a famous orator and a teacher of the explorer Meriwether Lewis.

After emigrating with his parents from Newry, Ireland, in 1739, Waddel attended the "log college" of *Samuel Finley at Nottingham, Pennsylvania. Following his ordination as a Presbyterian minister in 1762, he served various congregations in the Northern Neck of Virginia and then in the Shenandoah Valley. In 1785 he moved to "Belle Grove," a plantation east of the Blue Ridge Mountains. He subsequently established churches in the western end of the state and became an outspoken opponent of deism, a philosophy which held sway among the Southern aristocracy and which undermined traditional Christian beliefs. Although he staunchly defended Calvinist orthodoxy, he allowed his daughter to learn the minuet. In 1787 his eyesight failed him, although he temporarily regained his sight after a cataract operation eleven years later.

RICHMOND

¶ The Capitol, Capitol Square.

Several famous Confederates are represented with busts in the Old Hall of the House of Delegates: *Matthew Fontaine Maury, *President Jefferson Davis, and generals *Thomas "Stonewall" Jackson, Fitzhugh Lee, Joseph Johnston, and J. E. B. Stuart. A bust of *Woodrow Wilson was unveiled in the new House of Delegates in 1931 by the former president's widow.

§ Open April-November, daily 9-5; rest of the year, Monday-Saturday 9-5, Sunday 1-5. Closed January 1, Thanksgiving, and December 25. Phone: 804-786-4344.

¶ Capitol Square, between 9th & Governor streets and Capitol & Bank streets.

• On the northwest corner of the square is a sixty-foot monument to George Washington and other famous Virginians. The equestrian statue of the first president was designed in 1849 by Thomas Crawford, a New Yorker of Scotch-Irish descent also known for his work on the U.S. Capitol building. At the base of the monument are bronze statues of Patrick Henry, Thomas Jefferson, *Andrew Lewis, John Marshall, and Thomas Nelson. Lewis's military prowess was so well known that Washington suggested him as commander-in-chief of the Continental Army.

Crawford modeled the equestrian statue of Washington in Rome and had it cast in bronze in Munich. While it was still in the Italian capital, it attracted the attention of Nathaniel Hawthorne, who described it as a "foolish and illogical piece of work – Washington mounted on a very uneasy steed, on a very narrow space." The smaller statues, Hawthorne continued, were "not looking up to wonder at his predicament, but each intent on manifesting his own personality to the world around."

Statue of Andrew Lewis on the Washington Monument in Richmond's Capitol Square.

• Along the north side of the square are statues of *General Thomas "Stonewall" Jackson and *Dr. Hunter McGuire.

McGuire, whose father was a physician and surgeon, was descended from an emigrant from County Kerry, Ireland, who had come to Virginia in 1747. Following his attendance at the University of Pennsylvania and Jefferson Medical College, Hunter McGuire served briefly as professor of anatomy at the Virginia Medical College.

So strong were McGuire's sympathies for the South that, after John Brown's raid on Harpers Ferry in 1859, he persuaded 300 other Southern medical students attending universities in Pennsylvania to transfer to medical schools in the South. (He personally defrayed the expenses of those unable to pay their own way to Richmond.)

Once civil war broke out, McGuire was commissioned a medical officer in the Confederate army. He later served as medical director under a variety of commands throughout Virginia. Besides acting as "Stonewall"

Jackson's personal physician, he accepted that officer's appointment as surgeon of the 1st Virginia Brigade. According to some sources, McGuire organized the Reserve Corps Hospitals of the Confederacy and turned the Ambulance Corps into a more effective force. His touching and sympathetic account of Jackson's death appeared in the *American Medical Weekly* on January 6, 1883.

After the war the former medical director continued to enjoy a prestigious career. Not only was he appointed professor of surgery at the Virginia Medical College, but he was also influential in establishing the College of Physicians and Surgeons in Richmond. Besides serving as president and professor of surgery at the latter institution, he established St. Luke's Home for the Sick. Although most of his medical treatises were on the subject of surgery, they include an article entitled "Sexual Crimes among the Southern Negroes, Scientifically Considered."

McGuire's medical career is recalled in the inscription on the pedestal of his statue: "President of the American Medical and of the American Surgical Associations; founder of the University College of Medicine; Medical Director of Jackson's Corps, Army of Northern Virginia. An eminent civil and military surgeon, a beloved physician, an able teacher and vigorous writer, a useful citizen and broad humanitarian, gifted in mind and generous in heart."

• On the west side of the square is a seated statue of *Edgar Allan Poe.

¶ Matthew Maury Bust, Virginia State Library, on the east side of Capitol Square.

Among the library's collections is a bronze bust of *Matthew Fontaine Maury, the "Pathfinder of the Seas," by Edward Valentine. (See Virginia Military Institute, Lexington, Virginia.)

¶ Hollywood Cemetery, on the southwest corner of Cherry and Albemarle streets.

Two of the famous Confederates buried here are *Jefferson Davis and *Matthew Fontaine Maury.

Davis's grave is marked by a life-size statue of the president of the Confederacy standing atop a pedestal inscribed with the following words: "Jefferson Davis at Rest. An American soldier and Defender of the Constitution. Born in Christian Co. Kentucky June 3, 1808. Died at New Orleans Louisiana Dec. 8, 1889. West Point Class 1828. Member of House of Representatives from Mississippi 1845-1846. Col. 1st Miss. Rifles Mexican War 1846-1847. Brigadier Genl. U.S. Army May 17, 1847. U.S. Senate 1847-1851. Secretary of War 1853-1857. U.S. Senate 1857-1861"

¶ Libby Prison Site, Carey and 20th streets.

The site of the infamous Confederate prison is now occupied by a flood control wall built by the Army Corps of Engineers. The prison's history is commemorated by two plaques erected on 20th Street by various Union and Confederate veterans' groups.

The prison's most famous inmate was Colonel Michael Corcoran, a native of Ireland and the commander of the mostly Irish 69th New York militia regiment. Corcoran had been captured at the battle of Manassas in July 1861 and was one of fourteen Union officers sent to the Richmond prison to be held in exchange for an equal number of Confederate sailors. During a trial in Philadelphia, the Southerners had been condemned to death for piracy because of their part in the seizure of $13,000 worth of cargo from a Union ship off the coast of Delaware. In the end, the prisoners on both sides were released in less than a month, and Corcoran was promoted to the rank of brigadier general. (See Manassas, Virginia.)

¶ Maupin-Maury House, 1105 East Clay Street. Private.

At one time this three-story brick building was occupied by *Matthew Fontaine Maury, the famous oceanographer. The house had come into the possession of Robert Maury, the oceanographer's cousin, in 1853. Here it was during the summer of 1861 that Matthew Maury lived after arriving in Richmond to offer his services to the Confederacy.

Maury's stay here was brief, however, because the Confederate government sent him on diplomatic missions to Cuba and Europe. Nevertheless, he was here long enough to conduct experiments on a submarine torpedo. Robert Maury's daughter remembered seeing servants carry tubs of water upstairs to her cousin's room for the experiments, which the inventor's son described as efforts "to explode nitrate charges of powder under water."

¶ Maymont Park and Mansion, Hampton Street and Pennsylvania Avenue.

This 100-acre park with its accompanying neo-Romanesque mansion was formerly the estate of Major James Dooley, the son of an Irish immigrant. The property also includes a carriage house, Italian and Japanese gardens, a children's farm, and a nature center.

Dooley was born in 1841 in Richmond, where his parents, natives of Limerick, Ireland, had settled after moving here from Alexandria, Virginia. At the age of eight the youngster came under the tutelage of Dr. Socrates Maupin – many years later a professor at the University of Virginia – who prepared him for entrance to Georgetown College in the nation's capital. The young man was graduated in 1861 with the highest honors in his class.

At the onset of the Civil War, Dooley enlisted in the 1st Virginia Regiment, at the time under the command of his father. At the battle of

Williamsburg in 1862, however, the young soldier was shot through the wrist and captured. Following his release from prison at Hampton Roads four months later, he was appointed lieutenant of ordnance in the Confederate government. In

After the war Dooley enjoyed a successful legal and business career. He engaged in the practice of law and was a member of the Virginia legislature during the mid 1870s. As his vast business interests grew, he served as either president or director of a wide array of enterprises, including the Richmond & Danville Railroad, the Richmond and St. Paul Land Improvement Company, the North Birmingham Street Railway Company, and the Merchants National Bank of Richmond.

When asked what he had to say to young Americans, Dooley replied with this advice: "Let them avoid loafers, and associate with earnest people who have high ideals and aspirations. Let them do each day, with all their might, the work which comes to hand. Let them not be content to do only as much work as they are obliged to do, but so much more as to attract the attention of those above them, and compel their approbation. Let them tell the truth, and be honest under all circumstances. Let them avoid speculation, and live within their means. If they follow these precepts they will be successful and honorable men."

Dooley lived in Maymont Mansion with his wife, Sallie May, until his death in 1922. Because Mrs. Dooley was fascinated by swans, she decorated her bedroom with appropriate furnishings, among them a swan bed and a swan rocker. Her obsession was so great that she named her summer home "Swannanoa." (See Waynesboro, Virginia.) At his death Dooley left $3 million in trust for the establishment of three charitable institutions.

§ Grounds open April-October, daily 10-7; rest of the year, daily 10-5. Mansion open June 1-Labor Day, Tuesday-Saturday 10-5, Sunday noon-5; rest of the year, Tuesday-Sunday, noon-5. Fee for carriage and tram rides. Phone 804-358-7166.

¶ Monument Avenue.

Between Belmont and Lombard Streets, Monument Avenue is lined with equestrian statues of Robert E. Lee, J. E. B. Stuart, and Irish Americans Jefferson Davis, Thomas "Stonewall" Jackson, and Matthew Fontaine Maury.

• Jefferson Davis Monument, at Davis Avenue. This bronze statue by Edward Valentine depicts the Confederate president in front of a semicircular colonnade and a classical column supporting an allegorical female figure. The former president is depicted in a speaking pose, with his right hand and foot extended and his left hand on the open book of history. The colonnade is inscribed with an excerpt from Davis's farewell address at the time of his resignation from the U.S. Senate: "Not in hostility to others, not to injure any section of the country, not even for our own pecuniary benefit; but from the high and solemn motive of defending and protecting the rights we inherited and which it is our duty to transmit unshorn to our children."

• Thomas "Stonewall" Jackson Monument, at Boulevard. This bronze statue portrays the Confederate general riding his horse, Little Sorrel.

• Matthew Fontaine Maury Monument, at Belmont Avenue. This memorial consists of a bronze statue of the famous oceanographer seated in a chair below a huge bronze globe.

¶ Museum of the Confederacy, 1201 West Clay Street.

The museum displays numerous Civil War relics, including items associated with *Jefferson Davis and *Thomas "Stonewall" Jackson.

§ Open Monday-Saturday 10-5, Sunday noon-5. Closed January 1, Thanksgiving, and December 25. Fee. Phone: 804-649-1861.

¶ Poe Museum, 1914 East Main Street.

Housed in the Memorial Building next to the oldest house in Richmond, the Poe Museum gives a slide presentation about Edgar Allan Poe's life in the capital area and displays some of the possessions he left at his death.

Poe's grandfather, David Poe, was an emigrant from Londonderry, northern Ireland. After settling about 1748 in Pennsylvania, he married Elizabeth Cairnes, also of an Irish family. Although born in Boston, Edgar Allan Poe regarded himself as a Virginian. Following the death of his widowed mother when he was almost three years old, he became a ward of the Allan family. The young Poe spent five years in England with the Allans before returning to Richmond, where he lived and worked for more than thirteen years, until he left to attend the University of Virginia in 1826.

§ Open Tuesday-Saturday 10-4, Sunday-Monday 1-4. Closed December 25. Fee. Phone: 804-648-5523.

¶ St. Paul's Episcopal Church, 9th and Grace streets.

While attending services here on Sunday, April 2, 1865, the Confederate president, *Jefferson Davis, was informed that Union troops had smashed through General Lee's line at Petersburg and that Richmond could no longer be defended.

The church is a veritable memorial to the Confederacy, containing several Tiffany stained-glass windows in honor of Robert E. Lee, *Matthew Fontaine Maury, and *Jefferson Davis. The Confederate president is memorialized by two windows—"Paul Before Herod Agrippa" (in the lower west wall) and "Angels of Goodness and Mercy" (in the upper west wall). "Christ on the Way to Emmaus" (in the lower west wall) is a tribute to Maury, known as the "Pathfinder of the Seas" because of his pioneering work in oceanography.

§ Open Monday-Saturday 10-4, Sunday 8-3. Closed holidays. Phone: 804-643-3589.

¶ **Thomas Crawford Statue,** Virginia Museum of Fine Arts, 2800 Grove Avenue and North Boulevard.

This outdoor standing statue honors *Thomas Crawford, who designed the Washington Monument near the capitol building in Richmond as well as some of the ornamentation on the U.S. Capitol, including the statue of "Freedom" on the dome.

¶ **White House of the Confederacy,** next to the Museum of the Confederacy.

Following the transfer of the Confederate capital to Richmond, *President Jefferson Davis and his wife took up residence in the new executive mansion. The Davises' daughter, Winnie, the "Daughter of the Confederacy," was born here, while their five-year-old son, Joseph, died here after falling from a railing. Mrs. Davis recalled the latter episode: "I left my child quite well, playing in my room, . . . when a servant came for me. The most beautiful and brightest of my children, Joseph Emory, had, in play, climbed over the connecting angle of a bannister and fallen to the brick pavement below. He died a few minutes after we reached his side. The child was Mr. Davis's hope, and greatest joy in life."

§ Open Monday-Saturday 10-5, Sunday noon-5. Closed January 1, Thanksgiving, and December 25. Fee. Phone: 804-649-1861.

STAUNTON

¶ **Augusta Church,** 7 miles north on U.S. 11 in Fort Defiance.

Although the Irish-Presbyterians in this area welcomed their first minister in 1740, this stone church was not built until eight years later. It is the oldest Presbyterian house of worship in continuous use in Virginia.

The church's first pastor was the Reverend John Craig, who was born in County Antrim, Ireland, in 1709 and who was educated in Edinburgh. After arriving in Augusta, he confided his first impressions to his journal: "The place was a new settlement, without a place of worship, or any church order . . . and a few Christian settlers in it with numbers of the heathens traveling among us, but generally civil, though some persons were murdered by them about that time. [The Indians] march about in small companies from fifteen to twenty, sometimes more or less. They must be supplied at any house they call at, with victuals, or they become their own stewards and cooks, and spare nothing they choose to eat and drink."

Because Craig's parish encompassed 6,000 square miles, the settlers decided to erect two churches. The families in one part of the parish were extremely uncooperative in this effort, although the settlers in the Augusta neighborhood were, according to Craig, "a good-natured, prudent, governable people, and liberally bestowed a part of what God gave them for religious and pious uses . . . ."

Craig was noted for his energy and apostolic zeal. His Sunday service lasted from 10 a.m. until noon, followed by afternoon worship from one o'clock until sunset (when it was so dark that the clerk had difficulty reading the final psalm). After ordaining an unusually large number of elders throughout his mission area, Craig was asked how he had found so many qualified men. "Where I cudna get hewn stanes," he replied, "I took dornacks."

§ Open by appointment. Phone: 703-248-2634.

¶ Museum of American Frontier Culture, Interstate 81 exit 222 and then 5 miles west on U.S. 250.

This living-history museum allows visitors to experience working farms of the eighteenth and nineteenth centuries in England, Germany, northern Ireland, and the Shenandoah Valley. Besides a German farmhouse and an English cottage, the museum features mid-nineteenth-century farm buildings from Drumquin, County Tyrone, Ireland. The visitor center presents a film on the development of the living-history project.

§ Open mid March-November, daily 9-5; rest of the year, daily 10-4. Closed January 1, Thanksgiving, and December 25. Fee. Phone: 703-332-7850.

¶ Woodrow Wilson Birthplace, 24 North Coalter Street.

In 1856 Woodrow Wilson was born in this two-story columned house, which served as a parsonage for his father, a Presbyterian minister. The house contains Wilson furnishings, while the museum chronicles the president's career through photographs and memorabilia. The carriage house features Wilson's 1919 Pierce-Arrow sedan.

President Wilson's paternal grandfather, James Wilson, was a native of Strabane, County Tyrone, northern Ireland, and had immigrated to Philadelphia in 1807. Aboard the ship which brought him to America was his future wife, Amy Adams, an Irish native who liked to say that she lived so close to Scotland that she could see the linen flying on the clotheslines across the Northern Channel. In Philadelphia Wilson found employment with the *Aurora*, a newspaper which was edited by William Duane and which generally supported the views of Thomas Jefferson. To express their admiration for Duane – one of the first victims of the Sedition Act – the Wilsons named their first child in his honor.

Although James Wilson eventually succeeded to the management of the *Aurora*, he later moved to Pittsburgh and then to Ohio, where he founded the *Steubenville Western Herald*. Each of his seven sons served an apprenticeship on the *Herald* and became expert compositors. In 1832 he and four of his sons established the *Pennsylvania Advocate* in Pittsburgh.

James Wilson's youngest son – Joseph Ruggles Wilson – went on to attend Jefferson College in Canonsburg, Pennsylvania, and later followed a call to the Presbyterian ministry. He was ordained in 1849, shortly after his marriage to Janet Woodrow, a member of a 600-year-old Scottish family. The young minister taught chemistry and natural sciences at Hampden-Sydney Presbyterian College prior to accepting the pastorate of the Presbyterian Church in Staunton.

§ Open April-November, daily 9-5; December and March, daily 10-4; rest of the year, Monday-Saturday 10-4. Closed January 1, Thanksgiving, and December 25. Fee. Phone: 703-885-0897.

Woodrow Wilson Birthplace.

√ The home in which Woodrow Wilson's paternal grandfather lived until he left for America is still located in the village of Dergalt, near Strabane, Northern Ireland. The whitewashed thatched cottage contains some of the original furniture: a cupboard bed in the kitchen and curtained beds in the main bedroom. Wilsons still live in the modern farmhouse nearby.

STEELES TAVERN

J **Walnut Grove,** Interstate 81 exit 205 to State 606.

Encompassing a large brick residence and a blacksmith shop, this is the restored homestead of Cyrus McCormick, who perfected the first mechanical grain reaper.

The famous inventor was the great-grandson of Thomas McCormick, an emigrant from Ulster, Ireland, who settled in Pennsylvania sometime after 1734. The inventor's mother was the daughter of Patrick Hall, a Virginia farmer whose ancestors had been driven out of Armagh, Ireland, after the massacre of 1641.

It was in the primitive workshops at Walnut Grove that McCormick perfected his reaper, a device that allowed a farmer to cut his crop whenever it was ready and to do so five times more quickly. For several years McCormick, his father, and his two brothers manufactured the device on the homestead, turning out between two and fifty machines a year. By 1847 the inventor had sold 778 of the new devices. In commercially marketing his "Virginia Reaper," the inventor was among the first to use deferred payment plans and testimonials in advertising. An original reaper is on view in the homestead's blacksmith shop.

McCormick was subsequently honored at competitions in major European cities and was elected to the French Academy of Sciences for having done more for agriculture than any other living man. William Seward summed up the historical significance of the famous reaper with the remark that "owing to Mr McCormick's invention the line of civilization moves westward thirty miles each year." In 1861 the commissioner of pat-

Cyrus McCormick's workshop at Walnut Grove.

ents paid a backhanded tribute to McCormick by refusing to extend the inventor's original patent on the ground that "the reaper was of too great value to the public to be controlled by any individual."

§ Open April-December, daily 8-5; rest of the year, Monday-Friday 8-5. Phone: 703-377-2255.

TAZEWELL

¶ **Burke's Garden,** 15 miles southwest from Tazewell on State 623.

This ten-mile-long valley, now part of the Virginia Scenic Byway, was discovered in 1749 by James Burke, most likely one of the Irish redemptioners brought to the colonies by Colonel James Patton, himself a native of Ireland.

At various times in the 1740s and 1750s, Burke was a member of the Augusta County militia. In 1746 he was part of a work crew that cut roads through the Blue Ridge in present-day Roanoke County. Two years later he was granted 400 acres in that same area. In 1748 Burke seems again to have been part of a road surveying team, as a later account by Colonel Thomas Preston indicates: "It was late in the fall, and the next morning, after reaching the Garden, a heavy snow had fallen, and they determined to suspend their surveying until the next year. After cooking their breakfast, a man named Burke, who was with the party as an axeman or chain-carrier, cleared away the place where the fire had been made, and planted a lot of potato peelings, covering them lightly with brush. The following Spring or Summer, [a party] returned to survey lands, and found a large bed of potatoes where Burke had planted the peelings, and they gave it the name 'Burke's Garden.'"

By 1755 Burke was living in this area but was driven out during an Indian attack. It may have been during this episode that he was captured by Native Americans, although he was later able to escape. Whatever the case, he was again living at Burke's Garden in 1756 when Captain William Preston and his troops arrived in the area to seek out and punish the Indians. Burke and his wife were killed during another Indian raid eighteen years later.

TEMPERANCEVILLE

¶ **Makemie Monument,** Makemie Park, south on State 288/695.

This monument is a stone statue of the Reverend Francis Makemie, the founder of the first presbytery in America, and is located near the site of his house

Makemie was born in County Donegal, Ireland, most likely in 1658. Following his graduation from the University of Glasgow, he was ordained by the presbytery in Laggan, Ulster. Between 1683 and 1698, he served as a missionary in the American colonies – originally in North Carolina, Virginia, and Maryland but later in Barbados. During his ministry he was a well known controversialist, defending with his pen Presbyterian practices and beliefs against the attacks of Quakers and Anglicans. After settling in Accomac, Virginia, he acquired property and married the daughter of a wealthy merchant.

While visiting England in 1704-05, Makemie laid the foundation for the Presbyterian Church in America by persuading the Presbyterian and Independent ministers of London to send two of their number to America. The following year these two joined Makemie and four other ministers to form the first American presbytery, a move generally ascribed to Makemie's leadership. The church which he erected at Westover, Maryland, in 1705 is the oldest Presbyterian house of worship in the United States.

At the beginning of 1707, Makemie was arrested in New York for preaching without a license from the royal governor, Lord Cornbury. After having been denied permission to preach publicly in the Dutch Church in New York City, Makemie had responded by preaching instead in a private house "though in a public manner, and with open doors." In the ensuing controversy, Cornbury called Makemie a "Jack of all Trades . . . a Preacher, a Doctor of Physick, a Merchant, an Attorney, or Counsellor at Law, and which is worse of all, a Disturber of Governments."

The Puritan ministers of New England banded together in support of Makemie and requested their agents in London to "humbly petition the Queen's Majesty on this occasion, and represent the sufferings of the Dissenters in those parts of America which are carried on in so direct violation of her Majesty's commands, of the laws of the nation, and the common rights of Englishmen."

At his trial the embattled minister argued that "if our liberty . . . depended upon [either] a license or certificate from the Bishops of England, or the Governors of America, we should soon be deprived of our liberty of conscience secured to us [nonconformists] by [the Toleration Act]." The jury apparently agreed with Makemie's logic and acquitted him.

WATERFORD

¶ **Waterford Historic District,** northeast of Leesburg on State 662.

Waterford was first settled in 1733 by Quakers from Pennsylvania, although the area later received many English, German, and Scotch-Irish settlers. The most well known of the Irish immigrants was Thomas Moore, who, according to tradition, named Waterford for his birthplace in the Old Country. Many structures in the town, including the grain mill and several residences, date from pre-Revolutionary times. Three of the houses belonged to various members of the Moore family:

• The Thomas Moore House, on Bond Street, across from the John

Wesley Church. The earliest portion of this structure – the frame section with the bay window – was originally a small log house built about 1780 for Thomas Moore Jr., the son of the Irishman who reputedly gave Waterford its name. In the early 1800s the owner built the two-story Federal-style addition.

• The James Moore House, on the Big Hill just above the center of town. This large brick residence was constructed about 1805 by James Moore, another son of the Irish family's founder in America. Originally, the first floor contained a kitchen and a root cellar and the two floors above each had two rooms. On the street level the original kitchen has brick floors, a walk-in fireplace, and a ceiling beamed with logs. A bedroom, a dining room, and a new kitchen take up the remainder of the street-level story. The third floor, meanwhile, contains a parlor and a master bedroom.

• The Samuel Means House, on Bond Street, across from the John Wesley Church. The stone portion of this double-fronted house was reputedly built by Mahlon Janney about 1762. The brick wing was added about forty years later by Asa Moore, the third son of the Irish immigrant Thomas Moore. Asa Moore was a major force in developing Waterford and was one of its most educated inhabitants; his personal library included many volumes on science, literature, and religion. The house remained in the Moore family until it was purchased by Samuel Means in 1850.

WAYNESBORO

¶ **Swannanoa,** off Interstate 69 exit 99 to County 610 at the junction of U.S. 250 and Skyline Drive.

This marble Florentine villa was completed in 1912 by *Major James Dooley for his wife, a woman obsessed by the use of swans as a decorative motif. Construction of the fifty-two-room palace took eight years and the efforts of 300 master artisans. Paintings and sculpture adorn the central baronial hall, the gold-tapestried ballroom, the library, and the oak-paneled dining room. A large Tiffany stained-glass window stands at the head of the marble double staircase. The terraced grounds are decorated with balustraded gardens. (See Maymont Park and Mansion, Richmond, Virginia.)

§ Open daily 9-5. Fee. Phone: 540-942-5161.

WINCHESTER

¶ **Sheridan House,** on the southwest corner of Braddock and Piccadilly streets. Private.

During the last year of the Civil War, this house was the headquarters of the Union general *Philip Sheridan. From here he set out on his famous fourteen-mile ride to rally his men at the battle of Cedar Creek on October

19, 1864. (See Belle Grove, Middletown, Virginia.)

¶ **"Stonewall" Jackson Headquarters,** south on U.S. 11 at 415 North Braddock Street.

This brick home was the residence of *Thomas "Stonewall" Jackson during the winter of 1861-62. The house exhibits a large collection of Jackson memorabilia.

§ Open April-October, daily 9-5; March, November, and December, Friday-Sunday 9-5. Fee. Phone: 703-667-3242.

YORKTOWN

¶ **Yorktown Monument to Alliance and Victory,** Comte de Grasse Street.

The statue of "Peace" atop this memorial to the American alliance with France and the victory against Great Britain is the work of the sculptor *Alexander Doyle.

¶ **Yorktown Victory Center,** on State 238 near U.S. 17 and the Colonial Parkway.

The film *The Road to Yorktown* chronicles the final days of the American Revolution and the surrender of the British under Lord Cornwallis to General George Washington in October 1781. Contrary to popular belief, though, the British surrender was made not by Cornwallis but by his second in command, Major General Charles O'Hara, the scion of an illustrious Irish military family from County Mayo.

After serving with British forces in Gibraltar, Portugal, and Africa, O'Hara had come to America to help prosecute the war against the colonials. By August 1781 he was serving with Cornwallis at Yorktown but was aware that the British had no hope of surviving the American siege of their position. Cornwallis, refusing personally to demean himself by participating in a surrender ceremony with his colonial "inferiors," feigned illness and sent O'Hara to suffer the embarrassment. The latter, whom the French aide-de-camp described as the "dark, ruddy-faced Irishman," attempted to make his formal surrender to the French commander rather than to the Americans. When Rochambeau directed O'Hara to General Washington, the American commander indicated that the surrender should be made to General Lincoln, his second in command. Like the other British officers, O'Hara was paroled.

§ Open daily 9-5. Closed January 1 and December 25. Fee. Phone: 804-887-1776.

WASHINGTON

OLYMPIC NATIONAL PARK

This scenic wilderness of 923,000 acres stands as a monument to Joseph Patrick O'Neil, the leader of an 1890 expedition which explored the Olympic Mountains and cut a trail over the almost impenetrable range. The little-known explorer is immortalized in O'Neil Pass and Mount O'Neil, both located in the Mount Olympus Range.

O'Neil was born in New York in 1862, the son of Major Joseph O'Neill, an Irish immigrant who had left his native land a dozen years before, at the age of eighteen. (The younger O'Neil explained how he came to change the spelling of his surname: "My father's name was O'Neill. In 1885 I had so many papers to sign, carelessly dropped one 'l' and have since then signed O'Neil.") At the outbreak of the Civil War, the older O'Neill helped organize the 63rd New York Volunteers, one of the regiments that made up the Irish Brigade. Dangerously wounded at the battle of Fredericksburg in 1862, he never completely recovered and died five years later.

O'Neill's son attended St. Mary's College, a Jesuit institution in St. Mary's, Kansas. Joseph Patrick later completed a bachelor's degree in science at the University of Notre Dame. While a student there, he served as a cadet officer and made a name for himself as a talented athlete. (During his senior year he won the running jump with a leap of 17' 2".)

Following his graduation in 1883, O'Neil was commissioned a second lieutenant in the regular army and was assigned to the 14th Infantry. Except for a two-year stint at the Infantry and Cavalry School in Fort Leavenworth, Kansas, he served tours of duty at posts in Nebraska and the Pacific Northwest. Authorized by Brigadier General Nelson Miles to reconnoitre the Olympic Mountain Range in Washington State, O'Neil in 1890 led a group of handpicked men that literally blazed a trail through unexplored territory.

Although five years earlier he had led an expedition into the northeastern part of the Olympic Peninsula, this second adventure took him from Hoodsport up past Lake Cushman and on up the North Fork of the Skokomish River to the East Fork of the Quinault. By revealing the mountains' topography, geology, and flora and fauna, the expedition surpassed in scope the collective contributions of all earlier exploration into the region. Almost immediately after returning from this second expedition, O'Neil suggested that the wilderness be preserved as a national park, a wish that was granted when Congress passed the necessary legislation in 1938, only a month before his death.

The year after his remarkable expedition, O'Neil, now a first lieutenant, was transferred to the 25th Infantry, a Black regiment stationed at Fort Custer, Montana. It was during this service in Cheyenne country that the Indians gave him the nickname which stayed with him the rest of his life. Having noticed that O'Neil's white fellow officers called him "Pat" and that he frequently found himself in a fight, the Indians began to call him "Fighting Patsy."

At the beginning of the Spanish-American War, O'Neil accompanied the 25th Infantry to Cuba. There they helped capture El Caney, supplied support for the troops who stormed San Juan Hill, and participated in the siege of Santiago. (During the war he was dubbed "the wild Irishman" by General Arthur MacArthur.) O'Neil later boasted that he had survived the rigorous campaign only because of the "spartan athletic training" he had received at Notre Dame. In 1899 he and his regiment were transferred to the Philippines to help put down the insurgency against American rule there. For the gallantry he demonstrated in several skirmishes and one "prolonged and severe" battle, he received the Silver Star.

O'Neil's dashing wartime career was followed by more routine garrison duty at a succession of posts. After six months in the Philippines in 1907, he served at the Presidio in San Francisco and at a post in Alaska, where he also did some surveying and exploring. His tour of duty in the frozen north was interrupted when he attended the Army War College in Washington, D.C., for two years. He later accompanied the 30th Infantry to Texas, where it did border patrol duty.

The outbreak of World War I presented O'Neil with a chance to exchange routine service for the challenge of actual combat. As a newly appointed brigadier general, he organized and trained the 179th Infantry Brigade, which sailed to Europe as part of the American Expeditionary Force. For a wound which he received during the St. Mihiel and Meuse-Argonne campaigns, he was awarded the Purple Heart. He also received the Croix de Guerre from the French government. He is buried in Arlington National Cemetery.

O'Neil's nephew, Frank Keller Jr., left an appreciative description of his inadequately heralded uncle: "I can think of one word which my memory uses to tabulate my uncle, and that is 'cocky.' I mean the ready to go, go to Hell sort of attitude that stands there ready and eager to back up his views. . . . He was short, active, loved to tease, and never in all the time I knew him gave an equivocal answer. He said 'yes' or 'no' with no attempt to hide his opinions, which were generally strong. His living room was lined with pictures, all autographed, of ball players, actresses, boxers, priests and ministers, politicians, and old Army friends. I sensed at the time that he was a real live character, and a story teller of great fame."

ORCAS ISLAND

¶ **Moran State Park,** on the east side of the island, 8 miles southeast of Eastsound.

This 5,000-acre park, which includes mountain lakes and hiking trails, was donated to the state in 1926 by Robert Moran, a former mayor of Seattle and a famous shipbuilding magnate. A fifty-foot lookout tower at the top of Mount Constitution is reached by a steep six-mile road.

Moran, the grandson of an Irish immigrant who had settled in New York in 1826, was born in that city thirty-one years later. By the age of eighteen, the grandson had learned the basics of the machinist's trade and, with $50 in his pockets, had journeyed to California by sea. Finding prospects for his trade in San Francisco nonexistent, he proceeded to Seattle, where he landed with only a dime to his name.

Again Moran could find no work in the machinist's trade, since the town's 1,500 inhabitants could support no more than the one machinist there already. As a result, he was forced to accept employment loading coal into a ship's hold, a job that was followed by a succession of others (including one as a cook in a logging camp). Finally seduced by the magnificent sea around him, he accepted a position as a fireman on a steamer that plied Puget Sound. After advancing to the engine room, he remained in constant demand in the steamer trade in the waters of the Sound as well as in those off Alaska and British Columbia.

In 1882 Moran was joined in the West by his mother and his brothers and sisters. Abandoning the steamship trade, he invested $1,500 in a small machine shop that was subsequently known as Moran Brothers and specialized in the repair of steamboat and sawmill machinery. Seven years later, however, while Moran was serving his first term as mayor of Seattle – by then a city of 40,000 – fire destroyed most of the city, including the Morans' enterprise. During the chaos that engulfed the city, Moran personally assumed the direction of affairs and prevented looting through the prompt use of the police and the militia.

Although Moran Brothers had suffered $40,000 worth of destruction in the conflagration, the family decided to rebuild. This time, however, they chose to construct not only another machine shop but also a shipbuilding facility. In 1897-98, anticipating the rush of miners to the newly discovered Klondike Mines in Alaska, the company completed twelve river steamers and ten barges with which to transport food and supplies along the Yukon River. Moran himself captained the flotilla of vessels as they made the 3,000-mile voyage toward the Arctic. The shipbuilding enterprise was so prosperous that in 1902 it contracted to construct the hull and the engine of the *Nebraska*, a 15,000-ton battleship.

During his lifetime Moran was a member of numerous associations, including the Northwest Society of Engineers, the American Shipmasters' Association, the Institute of Naval Architects (London), and the American Society of Naval Engineers. When his health failed him in 1905, his brothers decided to sell the family business.

§ Open daily 6 a.m.-dusk. Phone: 360-376-2326.

SEATTLE

¶ John Leary House, 1551 10th Avenue East.

This is the former home of John Leary, a pioneer lawyer in the Pacific Northwest, an early Seattle mayor, and an entrepreneur whose business activities had a far-reaching effect upon his adopted city. The stone mansion's vaulted baronial hall was carved by a team of Belgian artisans. During World War I the residence was given to the American Red Cross; in 1948 it became the headquarters of the Episcopal diocese of Seattle.

Most likely of Irish ancestry, Leary was born in St. John, New Brunswick, Canada, in 1837. Beginning at the age of seventeen, he was engaged in the lumber trade, eventually becoming a manufacturer and a shipper. During this first phase of his life he also conducted an extensive mercantile establishment in St. John and in Woodstock, New Brunswick. He later operated a lumber business in Houlton, Maine, before succumbing to the possibilities of a prosperous future in the Pacific Northwest.

Arriving in Seattle in 1869, Leary found a frontier village of about 1,000 inhabitants. Despite his earlier intention to enter the lumber trade, he studied the law instead and was admitted to the bar two years later. For the next decade he was associated as a partner with two legal firms in the growing town. In the meantime he served several terms on the city council, and in 1884 he was elected mayor, becoming the town's first chief executive to keep regular business hours. An indication of the primitive state of Seattle at the time can be seen in the fact that First Avenue – formerly a mud hole – was improved and planked during his administration.

Leary was farsighted enough to realize that Seattle's strategic location was the key to its future greatness. Like his contemporary Thomas Burke, he championed construction of a railroad that would assure the city's future. A contemporary historian described Leary's role in this regard in the following terms: "A pioneer among pioneers, it fell to his lot to blaze the way for what time has proven to have been a wise and well directed move. When the Northern Pacific Railroad Company sought to ignore and possibly to commercially destroy Seattle, Mr. Leary became a leader of resolute men who heroically undertook to build up the city independently of the opposition of this powerful corporation. To this end the Seattle & Walla Walla Railroad was built, an enterprise which at that time served a most useful purpose in restoring confidence in the business future of the city, and which has ever since been a source of large revenue to the place."

Leary's interests led him to engage in a variety of other pursuits. In 1872 he opened and operated the Talbot coal mine, the first in a series of endeavors which proved that the western part of the state was rich in coal and iron. Besides forming a company which supplied Seattle with gas, he was active in establishing the Alaska Mail service and became the principal owner of the *Seattle Post*. He also organized the Columbia River & Puget Sound Navigation Company, having put up 20 percent of its $500,000 capitalization. Leary also served as either president or director of numerous other enterprises, chief among them the Seattle Warehouse and Elevator Company, the Seattle National Bank, two land development companies, and two railroads. At his death in 1905 he left an estate valued at about $2 million.

A biographer explained the civic-minded principle which motivated Leary: "He had ever recognized and acted upon the principle that property has its duties as well as rights, and that one of its prime duties is to aid and build up the community where the possessor has made his wealth. There are few men in the city, therefore, who, in the course of the last twenty years, have aided in giving employment to a larger number of men than Mr. Leary, or whose individual efforts have contributed more of good to the general prosperity of Seattle."

§ Open Monday-Friday 9-5.

¶ **Thomas Burke Memorial,** Volunteer Park, in the Capitol Hill district, at 1400 East Galer Street.

This stone monument was erected in honor of Thomas Burke, the Irish-American lawyer, jurist, and railroad promoter who is known as the man who built Seattle.

The inscription on the front side of the pedestal is as follows: "Patriot Jurist / Orator Friend / Patron of Education / First in Every Movement for the Advancement of the City and the State. Seattle's Foremost and Best Beloved Citizen." The base of the pedestal bears the legend "Champion of Law and Order / Unselfish Leader in the City's Early Struggle for Existence." The stone seat located near the statue is inscribed with these words: "Faithful unto death in the promotion of understanding and amity among nations."

Burke was born in Clinton County, New York, in 1849, the son of the Irish immigrant James Burke and his second wife, Delia Bridget Ryan Burke. After studying law and being admitted to the bar in 1873, the younger Burke moved to Seattle to begin a distinguished legal and judicial career in the territorial government of Washington. He first served as judge of the probate court and then as chief justice of the supreme court. He was unsuccessful, however, in his efforts to win election to Congress.

But it was his promotion of his adopted city as a major Pacific port that earned him the title "the man who built Seattle." He energetically supported construction of the Seattle, Lakeshore and Eastern Railway in 1885, and after fire destroyed the city four years later he tried to restore confidence by constructing the largest office building that the city had ever seen. Although he has been credited with persuading *James J. Hill

Thomas Burke Memorial.

to extend his Great Northern Railway into Seattle, the judge's role was actually less dramatic but no less important. As Hill's agent and legal counsel, he helped implement the railroad magnate's decision to build his lines to the Pacific by facilitating the merger of several small railroads in the Puget Sound area. Burke was also active in promoting apple growing and land development in the Wenatchee valley.

During one of the anti-Chinese demonstrations which periodically swept through Seattle, Burke came to the Asians' defense. He had always had a number of Chinese of all classes among his clients, although his critics claimed that his empathy for these Asians stemmed from his ties with the railroads and their desire to have a source of cheap labor. Whatever the case, in a speech before 700 workers gathered at the opera house in 1886, the judge warned against attempts to pit class against class, adding that in a frontier society like Seattle's the only classes were workers and neighbors. He reminded the audience that the Chinese were entitled to protection by the government and that riots and lawlessness would be especially detrimental to the workers, white and Asian. He particularly singled out the Irish in the audience, alluding to the oppressive conditions in his parents' native land with the opportunity which awaited the Irish in America. He expressed his belief that any Irishman who resorted to violence against the authorities in his adopted country would be guilty of gross ingratitude. He then criticized the mob of 300 men in Tacoma who had recently dispossessed the Chinese in that city and sent them out into the prairie to freeze or starve. In making his point, however, he showed some prejudice of his own: "The Mayor of Tacoma is a foreigner, and can hardly speak the English language. I have read how the Germans rose against the Jews and drove them from their homes. . . . [W]hat am I to think that only thirty miles from where I stand, in the Republic of the United States, such atrocities have been committed. It could not be done under an American. It was done under a German."

¶ **Thomas Burke Memorial Washington State Museum,** 17th Avenue N.E. and Northeast 45th Street (in the northwest corner of the University of Washington campus).

This institution, the state's official scientific and historical museum, is named for Thomas Burke, popularly known as the man who built Seattle. (See above entry.)

The museum, which has been affiliated with the university since 1880, developed from the efforts of the Young Naturalists' Society and was endowed by Burke's widow. Its exhibits feature artifacts from various Pacific Rim cultures, including canoes and twenty-five-foot totem poles.

§ Open daily 10-5. Closed January 1, July 4, Thanksgiving, and December 25. Fee. Phone: 206-543-5590.

SPOKANE

¶ **Crosby Student Center,** East 502 Boone Avenue, on the Gonzaga University campus.

A gift from Bing Crosby, perhaps Gonzaga's most famous student, the center contains a collection of the famous crooner's records and other memorabilia, including his trophies and pipes.

Born Harry Lillis Crosby in Tacoma, Washington, in 1904, the future singer was the fourth of the seven children of Harry Crosby and his wife, Catherine Harrigan. The moniker "Bing" most likely came from the name "Bingo," given to him by his schoolmates when they learned that he was a great fan of "The Bingville Bugle," a column in a Spokane newspaper.

Bing's mother boasted a long Irish ancestry and a strong Catholic faith. Her great-grandparents had been married in County Cork, Ireland, in the 1770s and her grandparents had settled in New Brunswick, Canada, in 1831. Her father – Dennis Harrigan Jr. – was the youngest of eleven children and came to Tacoma with his wife (Catherine Ahearn) in 1888 or 1889. The younger Catherine married Harry Crosby, a Tacoma bookkeeper, in 1894, following his conversion to Catholicism.

Although young Harry Lillis attended Gonzaga University with the intention of becoming a lawyer, he abandoned that plan and left school to become a vocalist with a dance orchestra. Not much more than a year later, he signed a contract to appear in a trio that sang with Paul Whiteman's dance band. This move eventually led to a successful career as a radio crooner during the 1930s and 1940s and later as a recording artist.

By the time of his death in 1977, Crosby had recorded about 600 songs, and more than 300 million copies of his records had been sold. About 200 million of them were "White Christmas," a phenomenally popular song that he had recorded in only eighteen minutes. On his overseas Christmas trips during World War II, he found that that song was the most requested. "So many young people were away and they'd hear the song at that time of year and it would really affect them," he wrote in his autobiography. "I sang it many times in the field in Europe for the soldiers. They'd holler for it, they'd demand it, and I'd sing it and they'd all cry. It was really sad."

Crosby's acting career paralleled his popularity as a singer and made him one of Hollywood's greatest box-office draws. Most of his 100 films were musicals, including the "Road" pictures with Bob Hope. Probably believing that his talent as an actor was limited, Bing insisted that he never be starred alone: "If I let them put 'Bing Crosby' over whatever the name of the picture is, and the rest of the cast in small type, people would say, 'Well, he certainly thinks he's a big shot.' They'd expect greater things from a big shot than I'm able to deliver." He must have been shocked, therefore, when he won the Oscar for Best Actor in 1944 for his role as a young priest in *Going My Way*. About the award, he said: "This is the only country where an old broken-down crooner can win an Oscar for acting. It shows that everybody in this country has a chance to succeed. I was just lucky enough to have Leo McCarey take me by the hand and lead me through the picture."

Indeed it was McCarey, an eccentric Irishman, who had talked Crosby into the role of Father O'Malley and who had directed the motion picture. During filming, Crosby and his costar Barry Fitzgerald often arrived on the set only to find McCarey plunking away at a piano until he came up with an idea for the next scene. McCarey's mother said about him and his brother: "Leo drinks between making pictures and Ray makes pictures between drinks."

In between drinking and filming, Leo McCarey enjoyed playing practical jokes. He maneuvered an especially cheeky one against Father Devlin, the film's technical advisor. One day while rehearsing a scene between Crosby (Father O'Malley) and Ingrid Bergman (Sister Benedict), Bing slipped his arm around her and gave the "nun" a passionate kiss until the director cried "Cut!" As the scandalized Devlin watched in horror, the entire cast and crew broke out in laughter, betraying the fact that the scene had been staged for the real priest's "benefit." "You've just removed five years from my life," said Devlin.

One of Crosby's lesser known films with an Irish theme was *Top o' the*

Morning. In this 1949 movie he played the role of an insurance investigator who travels to Ireland in search of the stolen Blarney Stone and, while there, falls in love with an Irish lass.

§ Open September-April, Monday-Friday 8:30-4:30, Saturday-Sunday 11:30-4:30; rest of the year, Monday-Friday 9-4:30. Phone: 509-328-4220, ext. 4297.

¶ Patsy Clark's Mansion, West 2208 2nd Avenue.

Noted for its horseshoe arches and round tower, this Moorish-looking structure was once the home of Patrick Clark, an Irish-born millionaire whose wealth was derived from his many successful mining interests. This turn-of-the-century mansion has twenty-six rooms and nine fireplaces and cost $1 million to construct. Since its sale seventy years ago by Clark's widow, the mansion has been used as a private home, a boarding house, an inn, and, currently, a restaurant.

"Patsy" Clark was born in Ireland on that most Irish of feasts – St. Patrick's Day – in 1850 and by the age of twenty had come to America. After minor mining success in California, Virginia City (Nevada), and Utah, he headed for Butte, Montana, at the time well on its way to becoming one of the most overwhelmingly Irish cities in the country. There he became associated with fellow Irishman Marcus Daly, serving first as foreman of the latter's Alice Mine and then of his more famous Anaconda Mine. While participating in the battle of Big Hole against the Nez Percé Indians, "Patsy" served under *William Clark, the major in command and Daly's longtime political and mining rival.

In 1887, however, Patrick Clark ventured off on his own to begin the even more profitable second phase of his mining career. After moving to Spokane, he opened up the Poor Man Mine in the Coeur d'Alene district, serving as part owner and general manager. Before long his mining interests stretched from Mexico to British Columbia and included the War Eagle and the Republic mines in that Canadian province.

Clark's son, Patrick, was born in Butte and attended Georgetown College (now University) in the nation's capital and studied engineering in New York. Like his father, he also pursued a career in mining, variously superintending his father's interests in Nevada and Mexico. After becoming a resident of Spokane in 1908, he traveled throughout the country seeking additional opportunities for mining investments. He eventually formed a partnership that oversaw his extensive real estate holdings in the state.

§ Open weekdays 11:30-1:45 and 5-9; till 10 Fridays and Saturdays; Sundays 10-1:30. Phone: 509-838-8300.

TUMWATER

¶ Crosby House, at Grant and Deschutes Way.

This structure was built in 1860 by Bing Crosby's paternal grandfather, Nathaniel Crosby III, a Massachusetts sea captain who traded in the Far East before coming to the Pacific Northwest in 1847. There he was among the founders of Portland, Oregon, and Olympia, Washington.

In addition to Bing Crosby's undisputed Irish ancestry through his mother (Catherine Harrigan), he may have inherited some Irish blood from his paternal forebears. According to Bing's brother Larry, the Crosbys may have been descended from Vikings who settled in Ireland sometime between A.D. 900 and 1100. Supporters of the proposition point out the existence of an ancient House of Crosby in County Kerry and of a knight by the name of Pierce Crosby in Ulster.

§ Open Thursday 2-4 and by appointment. Phone: 360-753-8583.

VANCOUVER

¶ **Fort Vancouver National Historic Site,** East Evergreen Boulevard, 0.5 mile east off Interstate 5 exit I1C at Mill Plain Boulevard .

The stockade and five major buildings on this 165-acre site are reconstructions of the fort constructed here in 1824 under the direction of *John McLoughlin, the newly appointed chief factor of the Hudson's Bay Company. The original fort's extensive garden has also been reconstructed as well as archival research will allow. A visitor center offers living history

The Chief Factor's House at Fort Vancouver.
(Photo by Rick Edwards and courtesy of Fort Vancouver National Historic Site.)

programs and slide shows on the history of the fort and contains a museum with artifacts recovered from the site.

McLoughlin, known among the Indians as the "White-Headed Eagle" because of his prematurely white hair, was entrusted with virtual palatine powers over the Pacific Northwest. As the so-called "despot west of the Rockies," he tried to maintain British dominance in the region, pacify the Indians, and prevent Americans from intruding on the fur trading monopoly which the Hudson's Bay Company enjoyed.

Within two years of his appointment, McLoughlin and his employees had constructed a wooden stockade with a stone powder magazine and forty log buildings, including warehouses, workshops, a chaplain's residence, the chief factor's house, and seventeen hive-like cells called the Bachelor's Range. In addition, the workers had cleared a considerable area around the fort, had built a forge and a sawmill, and were grazing 700 head of cattle. At the height of its influence, the fort employed between 400 and 500 people from all over the world in its various trapping, trading, and transportation enterprises.

The most important reconstructed structure in the fort is the chief factor's residence, where McLoughlin himself lived. Like the original, the house is constructed of white clapboard siding and has a large front veranda. It was also here that the company's clerks and officers dined and enjoyed the few social amenities that the frontier offered. McLoughlin described the house as "very handsome" and "commodious and elegant."

For eight years McLoughlin, who had been trained as a physician in Scotland, was the only doctor at the fort to care for the company's employees and local Indians. He also opened at the fort the first school west of the Rockies, hiring John Ball, a graduate of Dartmouth College, as its first teacher.

In 1846 Britain abandoned its joint occupation of the Oregon Territory with the United States and retreated north of the 49th parallel. With the future states of Oregon and Washington now under American control, McLoughlin retired from the Hudson's Bay Company and moved to Oregon City, which he had established in the 1830s and where he now built a house. (See Oregon City, Oregon.)

§ Open day after Memorial Day to Labor Day, daily 9-5; rest of the year, daily 9-4. Closed January 1, Thanksgiving, and December 25. Fee. Phone: 360-696-7655.

¶ **Officers' Row,** east of Interstate 5 on East Evergreen Boulevard.

Now housing various retail establishments, Officers' Row preserves twenty-one Victorian structures built between 1849 and 1906 to house the U.S. Army officers stationed here.

Following American occupation of the Oregon territory in 1848, the U.S. government established a military reservation on this site. From here expeditions were sent out to subdue the local tribes, and young *Ulysses S. Grant and *Phil Sheridan were stationed for brief periods. While serving as a brevet captain here in 1852-53, Grant lived in the two-story log cabin still on this site.

§ Open Monday-Friday 9-5. Closed holidays. Donations. Phone: 360-693-3103.

¶ Nearby at 5th Street is the Grant Memorial, erected in 1927 to commemorate *Ulysses S. Grant and his potato patch.

In his memoirs Grant described how he hoped to earn extra money by planting potatoes on land near the military reservation, enticed, no doubt, by the prospects of selling them at the exorbitant going rate of $45 per hundred weight. So many other people in the area had the same idea, however, that by 1853 the market was glutted with the vegetable. "Luckily for us," Grant wrote, "the Columbia River rose to a great height from the melting of the snow in the mountains in June, and overflowed and killed most of our crop. This saved digging it up, for everybody on the Pacific Coast seemed to have come to the conclusion at the same time that agriculture would be profitable. In 1853 more than three-quarters of the potatoes raised were permitted to rot in the ground or were thrown away. . . ."

YAKIMA

¶ **Carbonneau Castle,** 620 South 48th Avenue. Private.

Notable because of its turrets, ballroom, and sweeping staircases, this fourteen-room three-story mansion was built in 1910 with money from the gold mining fortune of Belinda Mulrooney Carbonneau. The Irish-born entrepreneur was the wife of Charles Eugene Carbonneau, a charming figure variously described as a "phony count," a champagne salesman for a French firm, and a barber, waiter, and restaurateur from Montreal.

Belinda had first shown her entrepreneurial spirit in 1892, when, at the age of eighteen, she went to Chicago in hopes of earning some money during the World's Fair. While the exposition was in the construction phase, she bought a piece of property on the grounds and proceeded to lease part of it to a ferris-wheel concession. From that lease and her operation of a food booth during the fair, she made $6,000. Armed with her profit, she traveled to San Francisco, where she found work in several hotels and restaurants.

The catalyst for Mulrooney's real fortune, however, was the Yukon Gold Rush. After working as a stewardess on a steamship that plied between Seattle and Skagway, she decided to join the argonauts on their way to the gold fields. She had no intention of wielding a pick axe, though, but instead hoped to engage in the fur trade. She accordingly crossed the

Chilkoot Pass with $5,000 worth of cotton goods, silk underwear, and hot water bottles.

With the proceeds from this unusual commerce and a small restaurant in Dawson City, Mulrooney erected in 1898 a luxury hotel called "The Fairview." The three-story establishment boasted baths, linen tablecloths, cut-glass chandeliers, and twenty-two steam-heated bedrooms. (During its first twenty-four hours in operation, the hotel's bar took in $6,000.) One of its many famous visitors was Jack London, who used Mulrooney's St. Bernard – Nero – as the inspiration for Buck in his famous novel *Call of the Wild*. Because of her highly regarded business acumen, Mulrooney was asked to assume management of the Gold Run Mine, at the time in a serious state of decline. Under her direction the mine yielded $1.5 million in gold dust in only a year and a half.

In 1900 Mulrooney met and married "Count" Charles Carbonneau. After a honeymoon in Paris, the couple spent the next decade traveling on business between Dawson City, Seattle, and the "City of Lights." While visiting Seattle in 1910, the unlikely pair purchased twenty acres in the Yakima Valley as the site of their future mansion. (According to R. N. DeArmond of Juneau, Alaska, the marriage collapsed long before 1910. In this interpretation Mulrooney left her husband in 1903 or 1904 after he had spent all of her money. He later stole her furs and jewelry and kidnapped her sister in Philadelphia.)

Other sources, however, claim that the Charbonneaus were still together as late as 1914. When World War I erupted in Europe, the couple invested in a steamship line and the count became a purchasing agent for the Allies. When the war disrupted shipping, the Charbonneaus lost almost everything. In addition, the count was killed while on an inspection trip to the front. Although Mulrooney lived in her Yakima castle until 1930, her unrefined manners and sharp tongue kept her from being accepted by polite society. The former Midas of the gold fields spent the last years of her life in a home for the aged, where she died at the age of ninety-five.

(An alternative version says that Charbonneau was not killed but checked into a New York hotel in 1915 suffering from "nervous exhaustion." He claimed that he had been a lieutenant in the French army and that he had escaped after being captured on a battlefield.)

WEST VIRGINIA

BERKELEY SPRINGS

¶ O'Farrell House Site, Fairfax Street, facing the park.

Now occupied by a restaurant, this was once the site of the O'Farrell House, established in 1840 by John O'Farrell and since then known by a variety of names. During the Civil War O'Farrell's widow operated the tavern. A woman of decidedly Southern sympathies, she used her charm to gather information from a Union soldier and passed it along to the Confederates.

¶ Flagg House Site, on the corner of Wilkes and Congress streets.

An inn known as the "Sign of General Washington" was operated on this site in 1783 by John Hunter, an Irish immigrant. Tradition says that George Washington was a guest at the inn during his last visit to Berkeley Springs in 1794. The house eventually passed into the hands of John Flagg, Hunter's son-in-law. The large red brick building currently on this site was built in the 1930s and now houses a law office.

BETHANY

¶ Alexander Campbell Mansion, 1 mile east on State 67.

This twenty-four-room mansion was the home of Alexander Campbell, a native of County Antrim, Ireland, who became the leader of a local religious revival. Here he played host to such visitors as Henry Clay, *Jefferson Davis, and James Garfield.

A small octagonal brick building in the front yard is the study in which Campbell composed his sermons. His books and bookcases are on display there. Behind the residence is the schoolhouse which his fourteen children attended. The Campbell family cemetery is nearby.

Following his arrival in America in 1809, Campbell set for himself the lofty goal of reforming religion. Through daily study of the Bible and the classical languages, he prepared himself for a ministry that saw him preach more than a hundred times that first year. He was particularly concerned about effecting a reformation in the manners and morals of young people, a theme he expressed in articles to the local press.

The birth of his first child caused Campbell to question his acceptance of infant baptism, an issue of some controversy among various sects at the time. After deciding against it and concluding that his own baptism had been invalid, he underwent immersion by a Baptist minister. In 1823 Campbell started the *Christian Baptist*, the beginning of a printing ministry which he continued for forty years. During that time he broke with the Baptists, having come to the conclusion that baptism was necessary for the remission of sins and not merely a symbol of a new life already completed.

§ Open April-October 31, Tuesday-Saturday 10-12 and 1-4, Sunday 1-4; rest of the year, by appointment. Closed commencement day and July 4. Fee. Phone: 304-829-7285/4258.

¶ Nearby is the Brush Run Meeting House, brought here from Pennsylvania, where it had served as the house of worship for a congregation gathered in 1811 by Campbell's father, Thomas.

The elder Campbell had been a Presbyterian minister but joined the Baptists before forming the Disciples of Christ. Alexander Campbell was the first preacher at the Brush Run church and moved the congregation to Bethany in 1827. Beginning in the 1830s, he was the leader of a religious revival which gave birth to the Church of Christ and the Christian Church.

¶ Bethany College, State 67.

This institution of higher learning was chartered in 1840 by *Alexander Campbell to replace Buffalo Academy, which he had conducted from 1818 to 1823. Bethany College and Marshall College, which Campbell founded in Huntington in 1837, were the only two colleges in West Virginia when it became a state.

BIG CHIMNEY

¶ Simon Kenton Marker, Elk Memorial Gardens, on U.S. 119.

This marker commemorates the adventurous life of *Simon Kenton, the scout, spy, and Indian fighter who helped consolidate American control over Kentucky and Ohio. (See Washington, Kentucky.)

While making camp in this area in the 1770s, Kenton and a companion were attacked by Indians. Although he was wounded and his comrade was killed, Kenton was able to escape.

CHARLESTON

¶ "Stonewall" Jackson Statue, on the lawn of the State Capitol.

This memorial to *Thomas "Stonewall" Jackson is the work of Sir Moses Ezekial and honors not only the famous Confederate general but also all Confederate soldiers. A bust of Jackson is located in the capitol rotunda.

¶ Sunrise Museums, 746 Myrtle Road.

The museums on this sixteen-acre property are located in two historic houses associated with members of the MacCorkle family, regarded as one of the state's most prominent and descended from both Scottish and

Irish ancestors.

Science Hall, located in Sunrise Mansion, features hands-on exhibits, Playscape, a nature center, a planetarium, and a nature trail. The art museum, meanwhile, is housed in the Torquilstone Mansion.

Sunrise Mansion was originally the home of William MacCorkle, the ninth governor of West Virginia. Constructed in 1905, the thirty-six-room house symbolized its owner's prosperity and belied his humble beginnings. MacCorkle later wrote about an early experience in the house: "I slept on a bare table for one whole winter. What was the use of telling people about it? I knew I would sooner or later have a bed!" Torquilstone Mansion was built in 1828 for MacCorkle's son.

The first of MacCorkle's Scottish and Irish ancestors in America had arrived about 1630. Both his paternal great-grandfathers were killed at the battle of Cowpens in South Carolina in 1781. After graduating from Washington and Lee University in Lexington, Virginia, in 1879, MacCorkle came to Charleston, where he eventually made a name for himself in law, business, and politics. Between 1880 and 1889 he was the state's prosecuting attorney, while during his tenure as governor in the mid 1890s he urged banking and insurance reform. While a member of the state senate, he championed the development of the Kanawha Valley. Before his death in 1930, he authored four books, among them two on the Monroe Doctrine and one entitled *Recollection of Fifty Years of West Virginia*.

§ Open Tuesday-Saturday 10-5, Sunday 2-5. Closed holidays. Fee. Phone: 304-344-8035.

CHARLES TOWN

¶ **Carriage House,** 417 East Washington Street.

This colonial-style inn was the site of a strategy session in 1864 between the Union generals *Ulysses S. Grant and *Philip Sheridan.

¶ **Cassilis.** Private.

This large yellow brick house was built about 1835 by *Andrew Kennedy, a successful lawyer whose father was a native of northern Ireland of Scottish descent. Over the years, Cassilis hosted such prominent visitors as Washington Irving and William Makepeace Thackeray. As a result of these visits, the latter author wrote *The Virginians* rather than a proposed book on California. At Kennedy's death in 1858, he was survived by his wife, their six children, and his brother (John Pendleton Kennedy, President Fillmore's secretary of the navy).

¶ **Harewood,** 3 miles west on State 51. Private.

This two-story limestone house was built about 1770 for George Washington's brother Samuel. George Steptoe Washington later inherited the property, where he lived with his wife, Lucy Payne, the sister of Dolley Payne Todd. (Two of the sisters' four grandparents were natives of Ireland.) (See Greensboro, North Carolina.)

It was at Harewood in 1794 that Dolley married James Madison. The bridegroom was so idolized by the young ladies at the reception that they tore the lace ruffles off his shirt and cut them up into pieces for souvenirs. Dolley and her sister – both Quakers – were later "read out" of the Society of Friends because they had married men of a different religious persuasion.

CLARKSBURG

¶ Jackson Cemetery, East Pike Street between Cherry Street and Charleston Avenue.

The Jackson family plot in this public cemetery contains the graves of *Thomas "Stonewall" Jackson's great-grandparents (John Jackson and Elizabeth Cummins), his father (Jonathan), and his sister (Elizabeth). *Dolly Madison's mother (Mary Coles Payne) and her sister (Mary Payne Jackson) are also buried here.

¶ "Stonewall" Jackson Birthplace Site, 326-328 West Main Street.

A bronze plaque marks the site of the small brick house in which *Thomas Jonathan Jackson was born in 1824. His Scotch-Irish ancestors haled from a parish near Londonderry, northern Ireland. His first American ancestor probably arrived in Maryland in 1748.

One of four children, the future "Stonewall" Jackson was three years old when his father died. His widowed mother did sewing and conducted a school in order to support her children. When she remarried in 1830, the young Jackson went to live on his grandfather's farm, now Jackson's Mill in Weston, West Virginia [q.v.].

¶ "Stonewall" Jackson Equestrian Statue, on the northeast corner of Court House Plaza.

FALLING WATERS

¶ "Stonewall" Jackson Memorial, on U.S. 11.

A marker denotes the site where *General "Stonewall" Jackson was sitting under an oak tree on July 2, 1861, when Union troops fired upon him. Although a limb of the tree was shot away, the general escaped unharmed.

HARPERS FERRY

On the night of October 16, 1859, the federal arsenal in this pictur-
esque town at the confluence of the Shenandoah and Potomac rivers was
captured by a band of insurgents led by John Brown. The notorious abolitionist hoped that the attack would led to an armed uprising of black slaves.

The first casualty in the attack was an Irishman named Patrick Higgins,
the night watchman at the railroad bridge into Maryland. For refusing to
halt and surrender his post when ordered to do so – and for striking Oliver
Brown, the abolitionist's son – Higgins was shot, the bullet making a fur-
row in his scalp. He later explained about the incident: "Now, I didn't
know what 'Holt' mint then any more than a hog knows about a holiday."

Despite his injury, Higgins was able to take himself to safety at the
Wagner House and helped sound the alarm throughout the town. Later
that night, as an incoming Baltimore & Ohio train approached the bridge,
he informed the conductor about the earlier attack. Higgins also helped
care for Hayward Shepherd, a free black who was shot through the heart
as he approached the bridge in search of the missing watchman.

JUNCTION

¶ **Sloan-Parker House,** east on U.S. 50. Private.

This fieldstone house, with its log smokehouse and barn, was built
about 1803 for Richard Sloan, a Scotch-Irish immigrant who conducted a
weaving business here. From 1860 to 1910 the house was a stage stop along
the Northern Turnpike.

LEWISBURG

This town of 3,600 inhabitants was named for *Andrew Lewis, who camped
here in 1751 while surveying the area for the Greenbrier Land Company.
Four years later he constructed Fort Savannah for the protection of settlers coming into the region.

¶ **Andrew Lewis Park,** North Jefferson Street.

Originally called Camp Union, this site was the staging area for the
1,000 militiamen under *Andrew Lewis who in 1774 set off from here in a
successful campaign against the Indians. After marching the 160 miles to
Point Pleasant, West Virginia, in nineteen days, the troops defeated a combined force of Ottawa and Shawnee. This victory is often referred to as the
first battle of the American Revolution.

¶ **Old Stone Church,** Church Street, 2 blocks southwest of U.S. 219 and
U.S. 60.

This stone church was constructed in 1796 by Scotch-Irish settlers to
replace an earlier log building. It is the oldest house of worship in con-

tinuous use west of the Alleghenies.
    § Open daily 9-4. Phone: 304-645-2676.

The Old Stone Church, built in 1796 by Scotch-Irish settlers.

MIDDLEWAY

¶ Priest's Field Chapel.

Although this chapel was built about 1925, the history surrounding it dates from some unsettling events which, according to local legends, occurred in Middleway more than a century and a quarter earlier.

The tale began in 1790 when a traveler whom Adam Livingston had allowed into his house grew alarmingly ill and called for a Catholic priest. Adamant against allowing a priest into his home, the Lutheran Livingston refused, adding, truthfully, that there was no priest in the neighborhood.

Shortly after the stranger's death and burial, however, Livingston's home and property became the objects of some inexplicable power. The mysterious manifestations included the following unnatural occurrences: hot coals from his fireplace began to jump around on his floor, his ducks were decapitated by invisible but audible shears, his money disappeared from a locked chest, and his and his neighbors' clothing was cut to shreds. In a dream Livingston saw a man dressed like a priest offering to help him. At the advice of a friend, the bewildered settler went to Shepherdstown, West Virginia, to consult Father Dennis Cahill, who returned with him to Middleway. After the Irish priest said mass in

Livingston's house, the mysterious happenings no longer occurred.

In gratitude for his deliverance, Livingston deeded thirty-four acres of his property to the Catholic Church, stipulating that a chapel be built on the site. Because of legal obstructions put up by his heirs, however, the church was not erected until the 1920s.

MORGANTOWN

¶ **William McCleery House,** on the southwest corner of High and Pleasant streets.

Built in 1790, this two-story Georgian structure was the home of Colonel William McCleery, an Irish immigrant who was active in settling this area and who enjoyed a distinguished political career in the state.

McCleery had first settled in western Pennsylvania after emigrating from County Tyrone, where he had been born in 1741. In the early 1780s he was a lieutenant of a company of rangers protecting the frontier and served as a county justice and a representative in the Pennsylvania Assembly. About 1784 he moved with his wife to Morgantown, possibly because he could not legally retain possession of his six slaves under Pennsylvania's new constitution of 1780.

(McCleery's wife – Isabella Stockton – was famous for the epic proportions of her early life: captivity by Indians, education in a Canadian convent, a love affair with a young French Canadian who accompanied her on a dangerous journey to visit her parents in Virginia, an elopement, the beginning of the return trip to Canada, and the assassination of her young husband en route.)

By 1788, meanwhile, William McCleery had become the first lawyer in Randolph County and the state attorney for Harrison County, both in western Virginia. He later was appointed district judge for Monongalia and represented that county in the state legislature. In addition, he was a federal tax collector under President Washington and was a deputy attorney general and the clerk of the district court. (While a federal tax collector during the Whiskey Rebellion in 1794, McCleery disguised himself as a slave in order to escape an angry crowd come to tar and feather him.)

In the meantime, McCleery had acquired 18,000 acres and had invited Mathew Gay, his Irish-born nephew, to come to America. The young man studied law in McCleery's office and succeeded to his uncle's practice when the latter retired in 1807. By that date, however, the older man had lost most of his land holdings because of his failure to pay taxes on the property. Additional financial reverses caused him to borrow $1,400, for which he mortgaged his two residence lots in Morgantown, various furnishings, some livestock, and three of his slaves.

At the time of his death in 1821, McCleery was an elder of the local Presbyterian congregation, to which he had donated property for a church and a cemetery. According to the old African-American slaves who survived their master, McCleery's ghost was often seen roaming through the rooms of his former residence.

PARKERSBURG

¶ **Blennerhassett Hotel,** 4th and Market streets.
Named for Hermann Blennerhassett, an eccentric Irishman who became involved with Aaron Burr's infamous conspiracy, this brick building was constructed in 1889 while Parkersburg was an oil-refining center. The hotel was restored in 1986 and features antiques from various parts of the country.
§ Phone: 304-422-3131.

¶ **Blennerhassett Island Historical State Park,** Blennerhassett Island, 2 miles south in the Ohio River.
This 500-acre park on an island in the Ohio River contains a reconstruction of a two-story mansion built about 1800 by Hermann Blennerhassett, a wealthy if somewhat naive Irishman. The original house burned to the ground in 1811. The present structure was built on the original foundations, which were uncovered in the mid 1970s.
Although born in England, Blennerhassett was the son of an Irish gentleman who claimed to be a direct descendant of King Edward III. After attending Trinity College in Dublin, the younger Blennerhassett was admitted to the Irish bar in 1790. He was described as a cultured man, having made the "Grand Tour" of the Continent and possessing a more than average talent for music and a particular fondness for science. According to his contemporaries, he was blessed with "all sorts of sense except common sense."
In 1796 Blennerhassett arrived in the United States with his new wife, who, it was discovered in 1901, was his niece. During that first year he wrote a letter to his nephew in Ireland, describing his impressions of America and the journey from Long Island to Philadelphia. Betraying a sense of self-importance, the uncle reported that the "only great person I regret not having become acquainted with is the President [George Washington]. He unfortunately set off for home two days after my arrival, which prevented my attending to his levee; but the day before his departure we were so fortunate as to be seated at church in the pew opposite to him."
Within two years the Irishman had settled on this island in the Ohio River, where it seems he intended to live the life of a country squire. After purchasing the upper portion of the island for $4,500, he continued to expend a considerable portion of his wealth in building an estate here. The wooden two-story central building which he erected measured fifty-two feet by thirty-six feet and was flanked by two wings – one with his

The Blennerhassett Mansion.

library and his laboratory, the other with offices, the servants' hall, and the kitchen. The lawn was several acres in extent and sloped away from the house, which was surrounded by a carriage road, graveled walks, a two-acre garden, and 100 acres of crops and orchards.

Once the interior of the mansion was furnished, Blennerhassett had further reason to brag. He boasted that "The house and offices I occupy stand me in upward of thirty thousand dollars, not mentioning gardens and shrubbery, in the English style, hedges, post fences, and complete farm-yards, containing barns, stables, overseers' and negro houses." Another writer described the elegant interior of the house in some detail: "Foreign frescoes colored the ceilings – the walls were hung with costly pictures, and the furniture, imported from Paris and London, was rich, costly, and tasteful. Splendid mirrors, gay colored carpets, and elegant curtains em-bellished their apartments. Massive silver plate stood on the sideboard. The drawing-room resembled the richest Parisian *salon* in the heyday of Louis XIV."

Although the incongruity of an Irish lord in the American wilderness had aroused the resentment of his neighbors, Blennerhassett caused addi-tional trouble for himself by his initial dealings with Aaron Burr. While the latter maintained until his death that he never entertained "any de-sign to separate the Western from the Eastern States," the popular concep-tion was otherwise. In addition, Blennerhassett was believed to have writ-ten a series of articles in the *Ohio Gazette* predicting the possibility of such a separation. Although the articles presented reasons why the West might separate from the Atlantic states in a peaceful and constitutional way, they were interpreted as secessionist and supportive of Burr's alleged plan. Whatever his intention, Blennerhassett continued to act unambiguously, supervising the construction of a supply boat and fifteen barges, contributing funds for the purchase of a tract of land which Burr intended to colonize, and allowing his island to be used by armed recruits. In response the local militia took possession of the Irishman's island and looted his mansion in December 1806. The fugitive Blennerhasset hastened to join Burr at the mouth of the Cumberland River but was arrested and temporarily detained by authorities in Mississippi Territory.

After his release Blennerhassett was rearrested and escorted to Richmond, Virginia, for trial. In a prison journal which he began in August 1807, he confided that he had endorsed bills drawn by Burr to the amount of $10,000 but that he had become disillusioned with the former vice president as early as the previous January. In a letter dated October 19, 1807, he addressed his wife from jail, obviously contrasting the kindness of strangers with the fickleness of disingenuous friends: "It will not surprise you to learn that I have had the unsolicited offers of horses and money, which I have declined. No less than three Irishmen have come forward in this way; namely, Jas. O'Hennessey, a Kerry-man who never spoke to me until he rode hither, 105 miles to see me; Mr. Pat. Hendren, a lawyer, in easy circumstances, settled thirty miles from hence; and Mr. Pierce Butler, whom I have never seen, who resides in Philadelphia, is very wealthy, and has made an unlimited offer through [another]. . . . Thus we find a few choice spirits to compensate for the inconstancy of false friends. May they reconcile us to the world."

The trial itself, of course, centered on the nature of Burr's scheme. One witness testified that Blennerhassett had told him that the object of the scheme was an invasion of Mexico, which Burr would subsequently rule as king. William Wirt, the prosecuting attorney, argued that the evidence supported the belief that the plan involved secession of the western states, a Mexican invasion, and creation of a western empire centered around New Orleans.

Wirt reached exceptionally oratorical heights in attempting to depict the gullible and newly ambitious accomplice. "Who is Blennerhassett?" he asked. "His history shows that war is not the natural element of his mind . . . . Possessing himself of a beautiful island in the Ohio, he rears upon it a palace and decorates it with every romantic embellishment of fancy[:] music that might have charmed Calypso . . . an extensive library . . . a philosophical apparatus [that] offers to him all the secrets and mysteries of nature . . . [and] a wife, who is said to be lovely even beyond her sex and graced with every accomplishment . . . . The prisoner [Burr] in a more engaging form, winding himself into the open and unpractised heart

of the unfortunate Blennerhassett, found but little difficulty in changing
the native character of that heart and the objects of its affection. . . . In a
short time the whole man changed. . . . Greater objects have taken possession of his soul – his imagination has been dazzled by visions of diadems,
and stars and garters and titles of nobility: he has been taught to burn
with restless emulation at the names of Cromwell, Caesar, and Bonaparte.
His enchanted island is destined soon to relapse into a desart [sic]; and in
a few months, we find the tender and beautiful partner of his bosom . . .
shivering, at midnight, on the winter banks of the Ohio, and mingling her
tears with the torrents that froze as they fell."

At the end of the trial, Chief Justice Marshall ruled that charges of
treason against the United States be dropped against Burr and
Blennerhassett but that the pair be tried for conspiracy against Spain.
Marshall concluded that the preponderance of evidence supported the
opinion "that the enterprise was really designed against Mexico. But there
is strong reason to suppose that the embarkation was to be made at New
Orleans, and this, it is said, could not take place without subverting for a
time the Government of the Territory, which it is alleged would be treason." But such treason, he continued, "would arise incidentally, and would
not be the direct object for which the men originally assembled." He then
ordered that the pair be held for trial on the charge of misdemeanor. (Although Burr and Blennerhassett were indicted in January 1808 for conspiracy against Spain, the charges were never tried in court.)

After the trial Blennerhassett moved with his wife to Mississippi to
take up the life of a cotton planter. As if to signify his desire to forget the
past, he named his plantation *La Cache* or "hiding place." His subsequent
economic success is evident in the advertisement of sale describing his
estate eight years later: 1,000 acres of land, a dwelling, an orchard, a cotton gin, and twenty-two African-American slaves. With the $25,000 he
received for his property and slaves, he paid off his creditors, moved with
his wife to New York City, and later practiced law in Montreal. While in
that Canadian city, his wife penned "The Deserted Isle," a lament over the
fate of her former home on the Ohio. Two stanzas of the lengthy poem
appear below.

> There rose the seat, where once, in pride of life,
> My eyes could mark the queenly river's flow,
> In summer's calmness, or in winter's strife,
> Swollen with rains, or battling with the snow.
> Never, again, my heart such joy shall know.
> Havoc, and ruin, rampant war, have pass'd
> Over that isle, with their destroying blast.
> . . . .
> And, oh! that I could wholly wipe away

The memory of the ills that worked thy fall;
The memory of that all-eventful day,
When I return'd, and found my own fair hall
Held by the infuriate populace in thrall,
My own fireside blockaded by a band
That once found food and shelter in my hand.

§ Accessible only by sternwheeler from Point Park at 2nd and Ann streets. Open early May-Labor Day, Tuesday-Sunday 10-5:30; day after Labor Day-October 31, Thursday-Sunday 10-5:30. Fee for boat ride and mansion tour. Phone: 304-428-3000 or 800-225-5982.

¶ **Blennerhassett Museum,** 2nd and Juliana streets.

Among the museum's exhibits are Ice Age tools found on Blennerhassett Island as well as furnishings belonging to the Blennerhassett family.

§ Open May-Labor Day, Tuesday-Sunday 9:30-6; day after Labor Day-October 31, Tuesday-Sunday 9:30-5; November-December, Tuesday-Saturday 11-5, Sunday 1-5. Fee. Phone: 304-428-3000 or 800-225-5982.

POINT PLEASANT

¶ **Point Pleasant Battle Monument State Park,** Tu-Endie-Wei Park, on the southwest corner of Main and 1st streets at the juncture of the Ohio and Kanawha rivers.

A granite shaft, erected in 1909 and standing eighty-four feet high, marks the site of what some authorities call the "First Battle of the Revolution." The sides of the monument are engraved with the names of the casualties in that engagement.

Here on October 10, 1774, 1,000 colonial troops under Colonel Andrew Lewis scored a decisive victory against Ottawa and Shawnee Indians led by Chief Cornstalk. While the Virginians suffered eighty dead and 140 wounded, the Indian tribes lost 200 of their braves. The victory broke the power of the Indians in the Ohio Valley and prepared the way for General George Rogers Clark's campaign of 1778-79.

Andrew Lewis, who was born in Donegal, Ireland, had come to Virginia with his parents in 1732. He later became a justice of the peace and a representative in the colonial assembly. During the French and Indian War, he served in the militia and was wounded twice while serving with Colonel George Washington at Fort Necessity in western Pennsylvania. After Washington's surrender of the fort to the French, Lewis defused a situation which could have caused more bloodshed. As the French took over control of the fort, an Irish soldier cursed an Indian ally of the French, called him a "copper-skinned scoundrel," and aimed his musket at him.

Although Lewis, who was nearby, could walk only with great difficulty because of his wounds, he was able to knock the Irishman's gun from its sight, thereby saving the Indian and preventing a retaliatory massacre of the Americans.

Lewis is best known, however, for his victory at Point Pleasant. Perhaps because of that victory, Washington regarded Lewis as the best military tactician in America and suggested that he be named commander-in-chief of the Continental Army in 1775. Although Congress selected Washington instead, it commissioned Lewis as a brigadier general. In 1776 the Irishman commanded an army which drove Virginia's royal governor from the colony.

§ Every year on the weekend closest to October 10, Point Pleasant commemorates Lewis's 1774 victory over Chief Cornstalk with the Battle Days Celebration.

SWEET SPRINGS

¶ Lynnside Site, on State 3.

Although now in a dilapidated state, this low brick house was built about 1835 by William Lewis II and was the home of Lewis family members for five generations. The house was constructed in a Jeffersonian Greek Revival style and apparently was named for its builder's grandmother, Margaret Lynn.

The Lewis family was descended from John Lewis, an Irishman who had fled Donegal, Ireland, in 1720 after killing his landlord with a shillelagh. It seems that when Lewis was unable to pay the newly raised rents, the landlord and his posse came to the Lewis house intent upon doing violence. Seeing that his brother had been killed when the posse fired indiscriminately into the house, John ran outside with his shillelagh, struck the landlord a mortal blow, and chased after the posse. Although a £500 bounty was placed on Lewis's head, various influential Protestant families protected him until he could escape from Ireland. He first sailed to Portugal but from there headed for Philadelphia. After his wife (Margaret Lynn) and their sons, William and Andrew, joined him in America, they moved west to Lancaster, Pennsylvania, and then to what became Augusta County, Virginia. In 1774 Andrew led a victorious American force at the battle of Point Pleasant. (See entry above.)

¶ Sweet Springs Spa, on State 3/311.

The original Sweetsprings Hotel on this site was established in 1792 by *William Lewis, whose father, John, was the first family member in this part of the state. The fashionable spa boasted seventy-two rooms – each with a fireplace but without bath.

The resort reached the zenith of its popularity after 1833, when Lewis constructed the present structure in the Jeffersonian style. Although it was visited during its heyday by the likes of *John C. Calhoun, Henry Clay, Martin Van Buren, Franklin Pierce, and Millard Fillmore, its popularity declined after World War I. Although at one time it was the Andrew S. Rowan Home for the Aged, today it stands empty.

WELLSBURG

¶ **Patrick Gass Burial Site,** Brook County Cemetery, 22nd Street, Lot 43, Section H.

This is the grave of Patrick Gass, Wellsburg's most illustrious – if little known – inhabitant and the last Caucasian survivor of the Lewis and Clark expedition. He was also the first member of the expedition to publish an account of the famous trek to the Pacific coast.

Born on the Pennsylvania frontier, Gass was of Irish parentage. According to an 1859 biography, this Celtic ancestry "probably accounts for his patriotic proclivities, as he seems to [have] inherit[ed] the hatred of British domination so common to the sons of the Green Isle, and which appears to be transmitted by hereditary descent." Although the youngster attended school for only nineteen days, he somehow learned to read and write. After traveling to New Orleans, Cuba, and Philadelphia, he returned to his home in Wellsburg.

In 1803 Gass joined Lewis and Clark's expedition as a private but was soon advanced to the rank of sergeant by a vote of his companions, perhaps because, at thirty-two, he was the oldest member of the party except for Clark. At the conclusion of this historic trek, he received from Lewis a written testimonial of his fortitude and dependability. With the help of David McKeehan, an Irish schoolmaster, he prepared for publication the journal which he kept of his travels across half the continent. The original 262-page work was published in 1807 and was soon translated into French and German.

Gass's later life only confirmed the stories of his remarkable stamina. Besides serving in the War of 1812, he fought with *Andrew Jackson against the Creek Indians and lost an eye during the campaign. In 1831, at the age of fifty-eight, he married for the first time, taking as his wife a young woman named Maria Hamilton. The decision to marry caused his biographer, G. J. Jacob, to marvel: "He who had fought the wild bears of the mountains, slept with the buffalo on the plains, straddled the Missouri, and lived for months on unseasoned dog-meat, then faced the British at Lundy's Lane and Erie, and fought his way through blood and flame, it was little thought would ever surrender his manhood to weak woman's wiles and winning ways." When his military friends joked with him about the seven children born to him and his young wife, he replied in a witty manner. Jacob paraphrased the response thus: "as all his life long he had striven to do his duty, he would not neglect it now, but by industry make amends for his delay."

While in his eighties, Gass traveled to Washington, D.C., to request a more generous pension. When that was denied him, he lived the remaining years of his life on his annual allowance of $96 and help from his children and friends. Even at the age of eighty-eight, though, Gass was still surprisingly fit. "Although now, somewhat bowed and slightly crippled with the rheumatism," his biographer wrote, "he is a remarkably alert and active walker and can make the four miles from his residence to Wellsburg in about as good time as most of those one fourth his years."

In the meantime Gass was baptized into the Campbellite sect, having undergone a conversion which was probably responsible for overcoming his longstanding fondness for liquor. When he died in 1870, just shy of his ninety-ninth birthday, he was the last known survivor of the Lewis and Clark expedition except for Sacajawea's son.

WESTON

¶ **Jackson's Mill Museum,** at the first gate near the West Fork River on the grounds of the State 4-H Conference Center, 4 miles north on U.S. 19 from Interstate 79.

The old sawmill that is the centerpiece of this museum was constructed in 1837 on this site, originally the five-acre farm of Colonel Edward Jackson, the grandfather of *Thomas "Stonewall" Jackson. Two eighteenth-century log cabins and a working gristmill are also on the grounds.

Between the ages of six and sixteen, the young Jackson lived here with his grandfather. As soon as he was capable, the boy joined the other workers in felling trees, grinding grain, breaking flax, and tending sheep. From here he walked three miles to attend school in Weston. Eager to learn more than the short school sessions offered, he promised to teach a slave how to read and write if the latter supplied him with fire wood so he could read each night. The slave later escaped to Canada via the Underground Railroad.

The teenage Jackson was also employed in the construction of the Parkersburg and Staunton Turnpike and each Sunday walked three miles to attend church. The local justice of the peace was so impressed by Jackson's sense of responsibility that he obtained for the seventeen-year-old boy an appointment as a constable. The following year Jackson enrolled in the U.S. Military Academy.

§ Open Memorial Day weekend-Labor Day, Tuesday-Sunday noon-5. Fee. Phone: 304-269-5100.

WYOMING

BUFFALO

¶ **Fort Kearny State Historic Site,** between Buffalo and Sheridan, 2 miles off Interstate 90 exit 44W.

Named for the Irish-American Civil War officer Philip Kearny, this outpost was one of three built in the late 1860s to protect travelers along the Bozeman Trail. Exhibits about the history of the fort are on display in the visitor center on the site.

The fort, which consisted of a wooden stockade and two blockhouses, held off frequent attacks by the Sioux under Chief Red Cloud. Under the command of Captain William Fetterman, the garrison suffered eighty-one fatalities. In 1868 the post was abandoned under the terms of a treaty with local tribes.

§ Open mid May-September 30, daily 8-6; April to mid May and October-November, Wednesday-Sunday noon-4. Fee. Phone: 307-684-7629.

CODY

This town of 8,000 inhabitants in the western part of the state was established as the result of a development scheme capitalizing on the popularity of "Buffalo Bill" Cody.

Although in 1895 the famous scout was traveling with his Wild West Show, a group of developers thought it expedient to utilize his name recognition. One of the investors expressed the group's motivation: "[W]e concluded that as Cody was probably the best advertised man in the world, we might organize a company and make him president." Three years later, when it was decided to move the town to its present location, Buffalo Bill offered his own name for the site. After the company adopted the suggestion, a spokesman said, "This did no harm to us, and it highly pleased the colonel."

Near the end of his life, Cody said, "I don't want to die and have people say, 'Oh there goes another old showman[.]' I want the people of Wyoming who are living on the land that had been made fertile by my work and expenditure to remember me and say, 'This is the man who opened up Wyoming to the best of civilization.'" Following his death in 1917, 25,000 people viewed his body as it lay in state in the capitol in Cheyenne.

• The city of Cody annually sponsors the Buffalo Bill Birthday Ball on the Saturday closest to February 27, the famous Westerner's birthday.

¶ **Buffalo Bill Boyhood Home,** on the grounds of the Buffalo Bill Historical Center. (See entry below.)

This frame clapboard house was moved to Cody in 1933 from Le Claire, Iowa, where William Cody was born in 1846. Although the claim by Cody's grandmother Lydia Martin that her ancestors were of Irish nobility was most likely an exaggerated one, Cody was probably of Irish ancestry. In a biography that was produced during his life and which was sold at his famous Wild West Shows, it was asserted that Cody's Irish ancestors had immigrated to America in 1747. In addition, genealogists doing research on another Cody family derived the surname from the Irish Odo, a name that the passing of time transformed into MacOdo, then Codo, and finally Cody.

When William Cody's father died, the eleven-year-old youngster went to work to support his family. After a year as a mounted messenger for two freight lines, the boy attended school – apparently for the first time – learning to write his name and read at an elementary level. The following spring, however, he tried his luck in the Colorado gold fields until his lack of success in that venture forced him to accept a job as a Pony Express rider. Although still only in his teens, he served as a scout during the Civil War, primarily with the 9th Kansas Cavalry against the Comanches and Kiowas.

After the war Cody was still in demand as a scout, and it was at this time that he earned his nickname "Buffalo Bill." After briefly serving as a civilian scout and guide for the U.S. cavalry at Fort Leavenworth and Fort Hays, the twenty-one-year-old was hired to supply twelve head of buffalo per day to feed 100 workers constructing the Kansas Pacific Railroad. His technique was ingenious: while hunting from his mount, he close in on the lead buffalo, killed it with his .50-calibre Springfield rifle ("Lucretia Borgia"), turned the rest of the herd in a milling circle, and picked off the rest of his quota. In his autobiography Cody claimed to have killed 4,280 buffalo during a period of less than eighteen months.

Beginning in 1868, Cody was employed as chief scout for the 5th Cavalry. In one year he guided seven expeditions and took part in nine military engagements. Although in 1872 he was awarded the Congressional Medal of Honor for his services in the Indian wars, he was considered a friend by many Native American tribes. In 1878 he wrote: "Every Indian outbreak that I have ever seen has resulted from broken promises and broken treaties by the government." That same year a former commander of the 5th Cavalry commented that Cody's eyesight was better than a field-glass, his knowledge of terrain was perfect, and his stamina was legendary. Cody was regarded as such an expert rider that the *New York World* wrote that he could ride with a cup of water on his head and not spill a drop. He assumed such epic proportions that his story was told in 700 dime novels, the *Buffalo Bill Weekly* (which ran for seventeen years), and a best-selling autobiography.

In 1872 Cody began the acting career that marked the later years of his life. After Buffalo Bill's premiere in *The Scouts of the Prairies*, one critic complained of its "execrable acting, . . . intolerable stench, scalping, blood and thunder." Eleven years later Cody opened his famous Wild West "Exhibition" in Omaha, Nebraska. For the next thirty years the Wild West train transported 600 Indians, broncobusters, cowboys, and sharpshooters as well as 500 cattle, bison, and elk to thousands of towns and cities in the U.S. and Europe. When the show arrived in England, the *Birmingham Gazette* noted that "Additional interest is attached to the buffaloes by the fact that they are almost the only survivors of what is nearly an extinct species. According to Colonel Cody there are not so many buffaloes on the whole American continent as there are in the exhibition."

¶ **Buffalo Bill Dam,** west of town.
     Erected in 1910 and originally called Shoshone Dam, this local landmark was renamed in 1946 for the famous Wild West stuntman, who helped raise money for its construction. The dam's original height of 325 feet made it the tallest such structure in the world. It recently underwent construction to raise the height and rebuild the power plant.

¶ **Buffalo Bill Historical Center,** at the junction of U.S. 14/16/20 and 720 Sheridan Avenue.
     This sprawling complex houses four museums devoted to the history, art, and culture of the American West.
     • The Buffalo Bill Museum contains 5,000 items and memorabilia, including a stagecoach used in Buffalo Bill's Wild West Show, his Congressional Medal of Honor (awarded in 1872 for his part in the Indian Wars), and gifts from Queen Victoria and Grand Duke Alexis of Russia. The museum also displays firearms and gloves belonging to Annie Oakley and a handgun owned by *James Butler "Wild Bill" Hickok.
     • Among the paintings and sculptures in the Whitney Gallery of Western Art are works by Albert Bierstadt, George Catlin, *Thomas Moran, Frederic Remington, and Charles Russell. One of the art works is Robert Lindneux's painting of a shootout between Buffalo Bill Cody and the Sioux chief Yellow Hand. (See Van Tassel, Wyoming.)

¶ **Buffalo Bill Statue,** at the west end of Sheridan Avenue.
     This bronze equestrian statue of the famous scout was cast from a mold made in 1924 by Mrs. Harry Payne Whitney. Cody is depicted sitting astride his favorite mount, Smoky, holding his Winchester rifle above his head to announce the discovery of enemy tracks. In making the twelve-foot-high horse, the sculptor shipped Smoky to New York and photographed the horse in both fast and slow motion.

¶ **Irma Hotel,** 1192 Sheridan Avenue.

This two-story stone and brick hotel was constructed in 1902 by *William "Buffalo Bill" Cody to accommodate the sightseers, big-game hunters, and wealthy ranchers who visited the town.

The famous hotel – named for one of Cody's four children – boasts a huge carved cherrywood bar, a French import which Cody brought by rail to Red Lodge, Montana, and by wagon to Cody. The $100,000 bar was given to Cody as a gift from Queen Victoria in appreciation for his Wild West Show.

§ Phone: 307-587-4221.

DANIEL

¶ **Rendezvous Park,** at the juncture of the Green River and Horse Creek.

During the 1820s and 1830s this site was the location of the annual gathering of as many as 1,500 trappers. The first rendezvous in this area occurred in 1824 under the leadership of Thomas ("Broken Hand") Fitzpatrick, the famous Irish-born trapper, scout, and Indian agent. During the rendezvous season trappers and traders exchanged goods and amused themselves with horse racing, wrestling, gambling, and shooting contests.

Fitzpatrick was born in County Cavan about 1799 and came to America as a teenager. During the 1820s and 1830s he became forever identified with the Rockies, first as an explorer and then as a trapper. While living with the Crow Indians in the fall of 1823, he learned of a relatively accessible route through the Rockies, apparently first used in 1812 but subsequently forgotten. In March 1824 he led a band of Mountain Men through the pass and down to the Green River a tributary of the Colorado, thus earning the nickname "Discoverer of the South Pass." Six years later he formed the Rocky Mountain Fur Company with James Bridger and three other Mountain Men. After the company was dissolved in 1834, he worked for the American Fur Company, continuing to inhabit that twilight world between eastern civilization and western savagery.

The terror which invested that world is evident in the episode which caused the whites to call Fitzpatrick "White Hair." In 1832 Fitzgerald eluded hostile Indians by hiding in a cave. Although his pursuers came within inches of finding him, he managed to slip from their sight. His brushes with death continued as he almost drowned while crossing the Snake River in a makeshift raft and escaped a pack of wolves only by climbing a tree, remaining there until dawn. Although the next day he found and cooked a buffalo carcass, his subsequent efforts to find food were generally fruitless. As a result, he lost so much weight that he could not walk. The two scouts who finally found him were shocked by the thirty-three-year-old trapper's emaciated face and a mane that had turned white almost literally overnight.

Four years later, while exploring the desert regions of the Rocky Mountains, the Irishman was pursued by a party of Blackfeet until he and his stead were forced to jump from a forty-foot precipice into the Yellowstone River. Hardly had he emerged on a sand bar on the opposite bank when the savages were again at his heels. In his haste to pull off the cover on his rifle, he accidentally discharged the weapon, whose contents shattered his left wrist. Undaunted, he reloaded and fired, killing two of his pursuers before running into the woods and eventually shaking them off his trail. From then on, he was known as "Broken Hand" among the Indians.

Beginning in the 1840s, Fitzpatrick's name became associated with the nation's westward migration. In 1841 he served as guide for the first emigrant train to head for Oregon and California through northern Montana. Although he stayed with this group only as far as Fort Hall, he continued to the Flathead country of northeastern Montana with the missionary Father Pierre De Smet. Seven years later the Jesuit priest had occasion to recall his western trek with Fitzpatrick: "The captain is identified with the whole of that region, having spent the greater part of his life in it. He knows the localities well, and is acquainted with all the tribes who reside in it. . . . I had the pleasure and happiness of traveling in his company during the whole summer of 1842, being my second expedition to the mountains, and every day I learned to appreciate him more and more."

In 1843-44 the Irish Mountain Man served as guide for Charles Fremont's second and longest expedition. The thirteen-month trek took the young Fremont from Kansas Landing to Idaho, across the Sierra Nevada to Sutter's Fort, south through the San Joaquin Valley, and back across the Sierras into Utah and then home to Missouri. During that time he had more than sufficient opportunity to observe the experienced Fitzpatrick.

After hardly a breathing space, "White Hair" Fitzpatrick was again heading west, this time on two successive expeditions with *Colonel Philip Kearny. In 1845 the Mountain Man accompanied Kearny and his 1st Dragoons as guide along the Oregon Trail to South Pass and then to Bent's Fort. The following year he guided Kearny's Army of the West to Santa Fe. Kearny later described Fitzpatrick as "an excellent woodsman, one who has been much west of the mountains, and who has a good, if not a better, knowledge of that country than any other man in existence."

In 1848, following the American victory in the Mexican War, Fitzgerald was appointed Indian agent to the Arapahoes, Cheyennes, and Sioux in the Upper Platte. During the next five years he helped negotiate treaties with various Plains tribes north of the Platte. So successful was he that Fremont wrote to his father-in-law, Senator Thomas Benton: "[Fitzpatrick] is a most admirable agent, entirely educated for such a post, and possessing the ability and courage necessary to make his education available. He thus succeeded in drawing out from among the Comanches the whole Kiowa nation, with the exception of six lodges, and brought over among them a considerable number of lodges of the Apaches and Comanches. When we arrived [at Big Timber, about thirty miles south of Bent's Fort,] he was holding a talk with them, making a feast and giving them a few presents. . . . In a few years he might have them all farming here on the Arkansas." In 1865 Chief Little Raven of the Arapahoes described Fitzpatrick as "the one fair agent" they had ever had.

Despite his deserved reputation for fairness toward the Native Americans, Fitzpatrick held no romantic illusions about them. His letters to the Indian Office reflect keen insight into the psychology of his charges, particularly one report which cautions that "whenever I found them . . . professing great friendship, [I was inclined] to double the guard and become more vigilant in guarding against surprises." He was not persuaded that the atrocities committed by the Indians were invariably due to provocation by whites. In fact, he believed that Indian attacks upon whites could be stopped only by reciprocal force: "I am aware that great violations of justice have been committed on both sides; but the Indians of whom I now speak (the wild tribes of the prairie) have always kept far ahead of the white man in the perpetration of rascality; and I believe it is only in order to keep peace and hold his own against the Indian, that the white man is often obliged to resort to many mean practices."

Fitzpatrick was equally opinionated about the role of missionaries. Although he disapproved of much which these innovators did, he believed that missionaries could have a beneficial effect on the aborigines by teaching them hygiene, moral principles, and industry. But instead, he lamented, "nearly the first thing the missionary performs is to baptise the subject. The Indian, thinking the ceremony some great 'medicine' which will render him invulnerable or produce some good luck, will submit to the ceremony with a good grace until he finds that those who have passed through all the ceremonies of religion have no better luck in hunting and war than they had before, and comes to the conclusion that the white man's 'medicine' is not so strong as his own and therefore loses all faith in it."

Fitzpatrick's career had left such an impression on the Western mind that within five years of his death he had become legendary. According to an account in the New Orleans Delta of January 2, 1859, he "had one day got separated from his companions and was pursuing his game alone in the wilderness; and, as ill luck would have it, he was seen by a war party of Indians. . . . He happened to know that these savages, who as yet were little acquainted with the use of firearms, had several times, when they had taken white hunters prisoners, put the muzzle of their rifles close to their breasts, and fired them by way of experiment to see what would come of it. He therefore thought it prudent to extract the bullet from his [rifle, but the Indians] very soon overtook him; and then they disarmed him and tied him to a tree. One of the warriors, who it appeared understood how to pull a trigger, then seized the rifle, placed himself a few paces in front of the owner of it, took aim at his breast, and fired; but when the Indians looked eagerly through the smoke toward where Fitzpatrick stood they saw he was safe and sound in his place, and he quietly took out of his pocket the bullet he had previously placed there. . . . They declared he had arrested the bullet in its flight, was an invulnerable and wonderful conjurer and . . . that some great misfortune would most likely befall the tribe if they did not set him free immediately, and they therefore cut his bonds and made off as fast as possible. . . ."

Allusions to Fitzpatrick's legendary life have persisted well into the twentieth century. A reference to one of the most famous episodes in his life appeared in "Broken Hand, Chief of the Mountain Men," written in 1929 by Ann Woodbury Hafen. A portion of the lengthy poem describes an unexpected encounter:

> On frosted nights,
> When the Great Bear turns in his starry bed,
> The trapper creeps from his furry roll
> To feed the midnight fire.
> At an hour when the moon back-tracks the dawn,
> Where then and now hold breathless rendezvous,
> The Mountain Men come back.
> I built a camp beside a mountain stream.
> And when the night was silent as spent fire
> A hand reached from the past to feed the coals.
> Pines cones that leaped to flaming ghosts revealed
> A horny hand spread out to catch the warmth –
> A grease-smeared hand, three fingers stubbed.
> "Why, you – you're Broken Hand, the trapper-chief!"
> Scarred fingers fed the cones
> But not a word the Mountain Man replied. . . .

FORT LARAMIE

¶ Fort Laramie National Historic Site, 3 miles southwest.

The origin of this famous frontier fort on the Laramie River dates from 1834, when William Sublette and Robert Campbell, a native of Ireland, established a trading post on this site and called it Fort William. When the fort later came into the possession of the American Fur Company, the post was enlarged, fortified with adobe blockhouses and bastions, and renamed Fort John. Use of the fort's present name began when a clerk in Campbell's supply house in St. Louis marked a box "Fort Laramie" instead of "Fort John on the Laramie."

In 1851 the fort was the site of a mammoth peace conference attended by 10,000 Plains Indians, the famous explorer Jim Bridger, and the Irish-born Indian agent Thomas Fitzpatrick. (See Daniel, Wyoming.)

Although the fort was abandoned in 1890, eleven structures have been restored and furnished in period, among them the officers' club, the enlisted men's barracks, the stone guardhouse, and the sutler's store. This last building was described by a visitor in 1866 as "a scene of seeming confusion not surpassed in any popular, overcrowded store of Omaha itself . . . soldiers . . . teamsters, emigrants, speculators, half-breeds, and interpreters. Here, cups of rice, sugar, coffee, or flour were being emptied into the looped-up skirts or blankets of a squaw; and there, some tall warrior was grimacing delightfully as he . . . sucked his long sticks of peppermint candy."

§ Open June 1-Labor Day, daily 8-7; rest of the year, daily 8-4:30. Closed January 1, Thanksgiving, and December 25. Fee. Phone: 307-837-2221.

MEDICINE BOW

¶ **Owen Wister Cabin,** on the grounds of the Medicine Bow Museum, 405 Lincoln Highway.

During the summer of 1885, this cabin was home to Owen Wister, the famous author. His mother was the daughter of the English actress Fanny Kemble and her husband, Pierce Butler, a descendant of one of the Irish-born signers of the Declaration of Independence. (See St. Simons Island, Georgia.)

Like his friend and college classmate *Theodore Roosevelt, Wister had come west to improve his impaired health. He became so enamored of the country that he returned during four consecutive summers. In 1891, after returning to Philadelphia from his last western sojourn, he was asked why no fiction writer had portrayed the West as Roosevelt had done in his prose articles. "I'm going to try it myself," Wister reportedly replied. "I'm going to start this very minute." That evening he composed "Hank's Woman," his first western story.

¶ **Owen Wister Monument,** across the street from the Virginian Hotel, 404 Lincoln Highway.

This monument of petrified wood commemorates Wister and his most famous western work, *The Virginian*, written in 1902 to depict the cowboy as an epic folk hero. The book inspired two stage plays, two silent motion pictures, a "talking" film, and a television series in the 1960s.

Despite his glorification of the cowboy, Wister's description of Medicine Bow in the novel was less flattering: A "wretched husk of squalor . . . Houses, empty bottles and garbage. . . . They seemed to have been strewn there by the wind and to be waiting till the wind should come again and blow them away. Yet serene above their foulness swam a pure and quiet light . . . they might be bathing in the air of creation's first morning."

When Wister had first arrived in Medicine Bow in 1885, he was unable to find lodgings. As a result, he spent that first night at the counter of the town's general store. A quarter century later Medicine Bow boasted the Virginian Hotel, named for the author's famous novel and still accommodating guests today.

RANCHESTER

❡ **Ranchester City Park,** off Route 14 West.

The site of this park was the scene of a major confrontation in 1865 between hostile Arapaho and Brigadier General Patrick Connor, an Irish native.

The battle was one encounter in the Powder River Indian Expedition, undertaken to secure the Bozeman Trail from Indian incursions and to retaliate for earlier Indian attacks against army troops. Connor described the goal more bluntly: "to kill all male Indians over the age of twelve."

Connor had come to this part of Wyoming from Fort Laramie, in command of about 900 men and with his guide, Jim Bridger. After establishing Fort Connor (later Fort Reno), the Irishman led about 200 men in a surprise attack against an Arapaho village. In the subsequent battle of Tongue River, Connor counted only eight American casualties but thirty-five slain Indians, 500 captured horses, and 200 destroyed lodges. Although his was a notable victory, Connor was quickly made the scapegoat for the reverses suffered by the other two columns and was relieved of his command. Eight months later he was honorably discharged. (See Colonel Connor Statue, Salt Lake City, Utah.)

RAWLINS

This town and a nearby spring were named for John Rawlins, an officer of Scotch-Irish descent who served as aide-de-camp to *General Ulysses S. Grant during the Civil War. In 1867, while accompanying the chief engineer of the Union Pacific Railroad to Salt Lake City, Rawlins discovered a spring in this area, calling it "the most gracious and acceptable of anything" in the vicinity. He told General Grenville Dodge that if anything were ever to be named for him, he would prefer that it be a spring.

Rawlins and Grant had met while living in Galena, Illinois, where the former had helped organize the 45th Illinois Infantry soon after the fall of Fort Sumter. During the war Rawlins not only was an advisor to Grant but also helped moderate the general's fondness for drink. When the war was over, Rawlins sought the dry climate of the western plains in the hope that it would alleviate his tubercular condition. It was on that trek west that he discovered the spring named after him.

SHERIDAN

⌡ Sheridan Inn, Fifth and Broadway streets.

For two decades after its construction in 1892, this elongated structure was the center of the valley's social life, hosting such famous personalities as *William Jennings Bryan, Calamity Jane, John J. Pershing, *Theodore Roosevelt, Charles Russell, and Leonard Wood.

Its most famous guest, however, was *William "Buffalo Bill" Cody, who made the inn his home when he was not on tour with his Wild West Show. He briefly owned the Sheridan in the mid 1890s. During his visits here Cody could be seen sitting on the wide porch interviewing Indians and cowboys who were interested in joining his world famous troupe.

The hotel, which was modeled after a typical Scottish country inn, is 130 feet long and has so many dormer windows that it was nicknamed the "House of 69 Gables." During the inn's heyday the livery stable and barns of the Cody Transportation Company were located to the rear. These facilities were operated by "Buffalo Bill" and the hotel management.

§ Open Memorial Day-Labor Day, Monday-Saturday 9-8, Sunday 10-4; rest of the year, daily 9-3. Fee. Phone: 307-674-5440.

⌡ Trail End Historic Center State Historic Site, 400 East Clarendon Avenue.

This Flemish-style mansion was constructed between 1908 and 1913 as the home of Governor John Kendrick, the "Cowboy Senator." The eighteen-room house is noted for its ballroom, stained-glass, English Gothic library, central vacuuming system, and oak and mahogany paneling (shipped by rail in thirty-six boxcars).

John Kendrick was born in Texas in 1857, the son of a rancher and Anna (Maye) Kendrick, a native of Ireland who had arrived in New Orleans about 1846. At the age of twenty-two, Kendrick began a career in the cattle business, at first trailing herds from Texas to Wyoming and then acquiring and expanding his own stock. In the early 1900s he moved to Sheridan, where he became a well known rancher and was elected president of the Wyoming Stock Growers. From this position he launched a political career that saw his election to the state legislature in 1910 and to the governorship four years later. Among his achievements as chief executive was the creation of a public service commission and of state surveys to seek out reclamation sites. In 1915 he joined the legislature's protest when *President Woodrow Wilson withdrew public lands containing mineral rights. During seventeen subsequent years in the U.S. Senate, the "Cowboy Senator" urged the investigation of the Teapot Dome scandal and lent his support to meat-packing legislation. He was buried in Mt. Hope Cemetery in Sheridan.

§ Open June-August, daily 9-6; rest of the year, daily 1-4. Closed December 15-March 31. Donations. Phone: 307-674-4589 or 307-777-7014.

SOUTH PASS CITY

❡ **South Pass Overlook,** Route 28, fourteen miles southwest.

From this vantage point one can see the twenty-five-mile-wide pass through which as many as 400,000 settlers crossed the Rockies in the middle of the nineteenth century. The pass, which is 7,550 feet high, was first discovered in 1812 but remained forgotten until "rediscovered" twelve years later by Jedediah Smith and the Irishman Thomas Fitzpatrick. (See Daniel, Wyoming.)

VAN TASSELL

❡ **Cody-Yellow Hand Fight Site,** 20 miles east to a point where Nebraska, South Dakota, and Wyoming meet.

Here in 1877 *Colonel William "Buffalo Bill" Cody and a detachment of soldiers from the 5th U.S. Cavalry encountered a half dozen Indians. In a face-to-face shootout between Cody and the Sioux chief Yellow Hand, the Indian's horse fell dead while Cody's mount stumbled and fell after stepping into a badger hole. The two combatants continued firing at each other until Yellow Hand fell dead from a bullet to his brain. According to some versions of the tale, Cody then removed the Indian's warbonnet and scalped him, offering it in tribute to the dead at the Little Bighorn by saying, "The first scalp for Custer."

YELLOWSTONE NATIONAL PARK

❡ **Pahaska Tepee,** 2 miles from the park boundary on Route 14/16/20.

Despite its name, this "tepee" is a log lodge built in 1904 and christened with the Sioux word for "Longhair," the Indians' name for *William "Buffalo Bill" Cody. (The famous scout's friend Iron Tail – the Indian whose image is on the Buffalo nickel – suggested the name.)

Although now a visitor center, the two-story building was formerly a hunting lodge where Cody entertained military officers, politicians, and foreign figures such as the prince of Monaco.

§ Phone: 307-527-7701.

Works Consulted

Abernathy, Thomas Perkins. *The Burr Conspiracy*. New York: Oxford University Press, 1954.

Aitken, Jonathan. *Nixon: A Life*. Washington, D.C.: Regnery Publishing, Inc., 1993.

Anthony, Katharine. *Dolly Madison: Her Life and Times*. Garden City, N.Y.: Doubleday & Company, Inc., 1949.

Arthur, Stanley Clisby. *Old Families of Louisiana*. New Orleans: Harmanson, 1931.

Ashe, Samuel A'Court. *History of North Carolina*. 2 vols. Greensboro, N.C.: Charles L. Van Noppen, 1925.

――――, ed. *Biographical History of North Carolina*. 7 vols. Greensboro, N.C.: Charles L. Van Noppen, 1905-1908.

Ayres, Alex, ed. *The Wit and Wisdom of Will Rogers*. New York: Penguin Books, 1993.

Ayers, Edward L. *The Promise of the New South: Life After Reconstruction*. New York: Oxford University Press, 1992.

Bacon, James. *How Sweet It Is: The Jackie Gleason Story*. New York: St. Martin's Press, 1985.

Bagley, Clarence B. *History of Seattle From the Earliest Settlement to the Present Time*. 3 vols. Chicago: The S. J. Clarke Publishing Company, 1916.

Bailey, Paul. *Sam Brannan and the California Mormons*. Los Angeles: Westernlore Press, 1959.

Bancroft, Hubert Howe. *Chronicles of the Builders of the Commonwealth*. 7 vols. San Francisco: The History Company, 1891-92.

Barbour, Philip L., ed. *The Jamestown Voyages Under the First Charter 1606-1609*. Works Issued by the Hakluyt Society. Series 2, vol. 136. Cambridge: Cambridge University Press, 1969.

Barnes, John. *Irish-American Landmarks*. Detroit: Visible Ink, 1995.

Barnes, William C. *Arizona Place Names*. Rev. & ed. by Byrd H. Granger. Tucson: University of Arizona Press, 1960.

Barovick, Robin. "The Choctaw Tribe and the Irish Famine." *Irish America* (September/October 1995): 23-25.

Basten, Fred E. *Beverly Hills: Portrait of a Fabled City*. Los Angeles: Douglas-West Publishers, 1975.

Bateman, Newton, et al., eds. *Historical Encyclopedia of Illinois*. 2 vols. Chicago: Munsell Publishing Company, 1925.

Baudier, Roger. *The Catholic Church in Louisiana*. New Orleans: n.p., 1939.

Beckner, Lucien. "John Finley: The First Pathfinder of Kentucky." *The His-*

tory Quarterly of the Filson Club 1 (April 1927): 111-122.

Bell, Malcolm Jr. *Major Butler's Legacy: Five Generations of a Slaveholding Family*. Athens, Ga.: University of Georgia Press, 1987.

Benton, Thomas H. *Thirty Years' View; or A History of the Working of the American Government for Thirty Years, from 1820 to 1850*. 2 vols. New York: D. Appleton and Company, 1858.

Biographical Directory of the United States Congress 1774-1989. Washington, D.C.: U.S. Government Printing Office, 1989.

Birmingham, Stephen. *Real Lace: America's Irish Rich*. New York: Harper & Row, 1973.

Blade, Robert E. *Pioneer Presbyterian Congregations*. Philadelphia: Presbyterian Historical Association, 1989.

Blair, Edward. *Leadville: Colorado's Magic City*. Boulder: Pruett Publishing Company, 1980.

Blanco, Richard, ed. *The American Revolution 1775-1783: An Encyclopedia*. 2 vols. New York: Garland Publishing, Inc., 1993.

Blessing, Patrick J. *The Irish in America: A Guide to the Literature and the Manuscript Collections*. Washington, D.C.: Catholic University of America Press, 1992.

Boatner, Mark Mayo, III. *The Civil War Dictionary*. New York: David McKay Company, Inc., 1959.

———. *Encyclopedia of the American Revolution*. New York: David McKay Company, Inc., 1974.

———. *Landmarks of the American Revolution*. Harrisburg, Pa.: Stackpole Books, 1973. p. 503

Bob Villa's Guide to Historic Homes of the South. New York: Lintel Press, 1993.

Bothwell, Margaret Pearson. "The Astonishing Croghans." *The Western Pennsylvania Historical Magazine* 48 (April 1965): 119-144.

Bottom, Raymond B. "John Mitchel." *Virginia Historical Magazine* 60 (April 1952): 326-328.

Boylan, Henry. *A Dictionary of Irish Biography*. New York: Barnes & Nobles Books, 1978.

Brewster, S. W. "Reverend Father Paul M. Ponziglione." *Transactions of the Kansas State Historical Society* 9 (1905-06): 19-32.

Brown, John Howard, ed. *Lamb's Biographical Dictionary of the United States*. 7 vols. Boston: James H. Lamb Company, 1900-1903.

Browning, Peter. *Yosemite Place Names*. Lafayette, Calif.: Great West Books, 1988.

Bruccoli, Matthew J. *Some Sort of Epic Grandeur: The Life of F. Scott Fitzgerald*. New York: Harcourt Brace Jovanovich, 1981.

Bruce, Philip Alexander. *History of the University of Virginia 1819-1919*. 5 vols. New York: The Macmillan Company, 1920-22.

Buckbee, Edna Bryan. *The Saga of Old Tuolumne*. New York: The Press of the Pioneers, 1935.

Buffalo Bill Historical Center, Cody, Wyoming. San Diego: Oak Tree Publications, 1984.

Burchell, R. A. *The San Francisco Irish 1848-1880.* Berkeley: University of California Press, 1980.

Burlingame, Merrill G. *The Reader's Encyclopedia of the American West.* New York: Thomas Y. Crowell Company, 1977.

Bushe, Andrew. "Without a Trace." *Irish Echo* 15-21 November 1995: 27.

Bushong, Millard Kessler. *Historic Jefferson County.* Boyce, Va.: Carr Publishing Company, Inc., 1972.

Butler, Phyllis Filiberti. *The Valley of Santa Clara: Historic Buildings, 1792-1920.* San Jose, Calif.: The Junior League of San Jose, Inc., 1975.

Byington, Lewis Francis, ed. *The History of San Francisco.* 3 vols. Chicago: The S. J. Clarke Publishing Company, 1931.

Cabell, Margaret C. *Sketches and Recollections of Lynchburg.* Richmond, Va.: C. H. Wynne, 1859.

Cadwallader, Anne. "Dispute Over Clinton Roots." *Irish Echo* 23-29 August 1995: 1

Caldwell, Chris, and Tad Ames, eds. *Puerto Rico.* Hong Kong: APA Publications, 1989.

Callahan, Bob, ed. *The Big Book of American Irish Culture.* New York: Penguin Books, 1989.

Callahan, James Morton. *History of the Making of Morgantown, West Virginia.* Morgantown: West Virginia University Studies in History, 1926.

Campbell, Charles, ed. *Some Materials to Serve For a Brief Memoir of John Daly Burk.* Albany: Joel Munsell, 1868.

Candaele, Kelly. "Ulysses S. Grant: The Irish Visit, 1879." *Irish America* 12 (March/April 1996): 70-72.

Capers, Gerald M. *The Biography of a River Town. Memphis: Its Heroic Age.* Chapel Hill: The University of North Carolina Press, 1939.

Carpenter, Aurelius O., and Percy H. Millberry. *History of Mendocino and Lake Counties, California.* Los Angeles: Historic Record Company, 1914.

Carson, Herbert N. *Cyrus Hall McCormick: His Life and Work.* Chicago: A. C. McClurg & Company, 1909.

Cashin, Edward J. *The Story of Augusta.* Augusta, Ga.: Richmond County Board of Education, 1980.

Cassal, Hilary. "Missionary Tour in the Chickasaw Nation and Western Indian Territory." *The Chronicles of Oklahoma* 34 (Winter 1956-57): 397-416.

Castle, Henry A. "General James Shields, Soldier, Orator, Statesman." *Collections of the Minnesota Historical Society* 15 (1915): 711-730.

Caughey, Bruce, and Dean Winstanley. *The Colorado Guide.* Rev. ed. Golden, Colo.: Fulcrum Publishing, 1991.

Chalker, Fussell M. "Fitzgerald: Place of Reconciliation." *The Georgia Historical Quarterly 55 (Fall 1971): 398-402.

Champlin, John Denison. *Cyclopedia of Painters and Painting*. New York: C. Scribner's Sons, 1886-87.

Chittenden, Hiram Martin. *The American Fur Trade of the Far West*. 2 vols. New York: The Press of the Pioneers, Inc., 1935.

Christensen, Dr. Lawrence O., and Jack B. Ridley. *UM-Rolla: A History of MSM-UMR*. Rolla, Mo.: University of Missouri Press, 1983.

Clark, Allen C. *Life and Letters of Dolly Madison*. Washington, D.C.: W. F. Roberts Company, 1914.

Clark, Dennis. *Hibernian America: The Irish and Regional Cultures*. Westport, Conn.: Greenwood Press, 1986.

Clarke, Charles G. *The Men of the Lewis and Clark Expedition*. Glendale, Calif.: The Arthur H. Clark Company, 1970.

Clarke, Joseph I. C. "The Fighting Race." *The Journal of the American Irish Historical Society* 10 (1910-11): 87-88.

——. *My Life and Memories*. New York: Dodd, Mead and Company, 1926.

Clarke, Thomas D. "Finley, John." *The Reader's Encyclopedia of the American West*. New York: Thomas Y. Crowell Company, 1977.

Clary, Raymond H. *The Making of Golden Gate Park, The Early Years: 1865-1906*. San Francisco: California Living Books, 1980.

Clement, J., ed. *Noble Deeds of American Women*. Buffalo: George H. Derby and Company, 1852.

Clifford, Howard. *The Skagway Story*. Anchorage: Alaska Northwest Publishing Company, 1975.

Clum, John P. "Nellie Cashman." *Arizona Historical Review* 3 (January 1931): 9-34.

Coffin, Joshua. *A Sketch of the History of Newbury, Newburyport, and West Newbury, from 1635 to 1845*. Boston: Samuel G. Drake, 1845.

Cohalan, Daniel F. "Andrew Jackson." *The Journal of the American Irish Historical Society* 28 (1929-30): 173-187.

Coit, Margaret L. *John C. Calhoun*. Boston: Houghton Mifflin Company, 1950.

Coleman, J. Winston, Jr. *Sketches of Kentucky's Past*. Lexington, Ky.: Winburn Press, 1979.

Collins, Lewis. *Historical Sketches of Kentucky*. Maysville, Ky.: Published by the author, 1848.

Colonel Robert Campbell: Mountain Man to Millionaire. Produced by Barlow Video Productions, 1985. Videocassette.

Condon, William H. *Life of Major-General James Shields*. Chicago: Press of the Blakely Printing Company, 1900.

Conmy, Peter Thomas. *Stephen Mallory White, California Statesman*. [San Francisco]: Dolores Press, 1956.

Connally, John, and Mickey Herskowitz. *In History's Shadow: An American Odyssey*. New York: Hyperion, 1993.

Connelley, William Elsey, and E. M. Coulter. *History of Kentucky*. 5 vols. Chicago: The American Historical Society, 1922.

Conrad, Barnaby. *San Francisco: A Profile with Pictures*. New York: The Viking Press, 1959.

Conyngham, D. P. *The Irish Brigade and Its Campaigns*. Boston: William McSorley & Company, 1867.

Core, Earl L. *The Monongalia Story: A Bicentennial History*. Parsons, W.Va.: McClain Printing Company, 1976.

Cottman, George S. *Centennial History and Handbook of Indiana*. Indianapolis: Max R. Hyman, 1915.

Coues, Elliot. "Memoir of Patrick Gass" in *History of the Expedition Under the Command of Lewis and Clark*. 3 vols. Edited by Elliott Coues. New York: Francis P. Harper, 1893.

Coulter, Tom. "Gaffey Legacy More Than a Street." *San Pedro News-Pilot* 19 August 1981: A3-A8.

Couper, William. *One Hundred Years at V.M.I.* 4 vols. Richmond, Va.: Garrett and Massie, Inc., 1939-40.

Crampton, C. Gregory. *Land of Living Rock: The Grand Canyon and the High Plateaus*. New York: Alfred A. Knopf, 1972.

Craven, Bvt. Lieut.-Col. John J., M.D. *Prison Life of Jefferson Davis*. New York: Carleton, 1866.

Crimmins, John D. *Irish-American Miscellany*. New York: Published by the author, 1905.

Cromie, Alice. *Restored America: A Tour Guide*. New York: American Legacy Press, 1979.

———. *A Tour Guide to the Civil War*. Chicago: Quadrangle Books, 1965.

Cronin, Bernard Cornelius. *Father Yorke and the Labor Movement in San Francisco, 1900-1910*. Washington, D.C.: The Catholic University of America Press, 1943.

Curley, Rev. Michael J. *Church and State in the Spanish Floridas (1783-1822)*. Washington, D.C.: The Catholic University of America Press, 1940.

Current, Richard N., ed. *Encyclopedia of the Confederacy*. 4 vols. New York: Simon & Schuster, 1993.

Cushman, Clare, ed. *The Supreme Court Justices: Illustrated Biographies, 1789-1993*. Washington, D.C.: Congressional Quarterly, 1993.

Custer, Elizabeth B. *Following the Guidon*. New York: Harper & Brothers, 1890.

Da Costa, Beverley, ed. *Historic Houses of America*. New York: American Heritage Publishing Company, Inc., 1971.

Dale, Harrison Clifford, ed. *The Ashley-Smith Explorations and the Discovery of a Central Route to the Pacific 1822-1829*. Cleveland: The Arthur H. Clarke Company, 1918.

Daniels, Josephus. *The Life of Woodrow Wilson 1856-1924*. [n.p.: W. H. Johnston, 1924].

David, Lester. *The Lonely Lady of San Clemente*. New York: Thomas Y. Crowell Publishers, 1978.

Davie, Michael. *Titanic: The Death and Life of a Legend*. New York: Alfred A. Knopf, 1986.

Davis, Burke. *Sherman's March*. New York: Random House, 1980.

Davis, John H. *The Kennedys: Dynasty and Disaster, 1848-1983*. New York: McGraw-Hill, 1984.

Davis, Robert G., ed. *The Diary of William Barret Travis*. Waco, Tex.: Texican Press, 1966.

Davis, Varina. *Jefferson Davis, Ex-President of the Confederate States of America: A Memoir by His Wife*. New York: Belford Company, 1890.

Davis, William C. *Breckinridge: Statesman, Soldier, Symbol*. Baton Rouge: Louisiana State University Press, 1974.

———. *Jefferson Davis: The Man and His Hour*. New York: Harper Collins, 1991.

"The Death of Daniel Healy." *The Leadville Daily Chronicle* 27 May 1912.

deFord, Miriam Allen. *They Were San Franciscans*. Caldwell, Id.: The Caxton Printers, Ltd., 1941.

DeGregorio, William. *The Complete Book of U.S. Presidents*. 4th ed. New York: Barricade Books, Inc., 1993.

Delaney, John J. *Dictionary of American Catholic Biography*. Garden City, N.Y.: Doubleday & Company, Inc., 1984.

de Mare, Marie. *G. P. A. Healy: An American Artist*. New York: David McKay Company, Inc., 1954.

Demeter, Richard. *Primer, Presses, and Composing Sticks: Women Printers of the Colonial Period*. Hicksville, N.Y.: Exposition Press, 1979.

Derr, Mark. *The Frontiersman: The Real Life and the Many Legends of Davy Crockett*. New York: William Morrow and Company, Inc., 1993.

Descriptive Catalogue of Painting and Sculpture in the National Museum of American Art. Boston: G. K. Hall & Company, 1983.

Des Moines and Polk County, Iowa. 2 vols. Chicago: The S. J. Clarke Publishing Company, 1911.

DeVoto, Bernard. *The Year of Decision 1846*. Boston: Little, Brown and Company, 1943.

Dickson, Samuel. *The Streets of San Francisco*. Stanford: Stanford University Press, 1955.

Dillon, Richard. *Great Expectations: The Story of Benicia, California*. Benicia: Benicia Heritage Book, Inc., 1980.

———. *Iron Men: California's Industrial Pioneers: Peter, James, and Michael Donahue*. Point Richmond, Calif.: Candela Press, 1984.

Dillon, William. *Life of John Mitchel*. 2 vols. London: Kegan Paul, Trench & Company, 1888.

Dooley, Agnes W. *Promises To Keep: The Life of Doctor Thomas A. Dooley*. New York: Farrar, Straus and Company, 1962.

Dorris, J. T. "Michael Kelly Lawler: Mexican and Civil War Officer." *Journal of the Illinois State Historical Society* (Autumn 1955): 366-401.

Dorset, Phyllis Flanders. *The New Eldorado: The Story of Colorado's Gold and Silver Rushes*. New York: The Macmillan Company, 1970.

Dorsett, Lyle W. *The Pendergast Machine*. New York: Oxford University Press, 1968.

Dowling, Patrick J. *California: The Irish Dream*. 2nd ed. San Francisco: Golden Gate Publishers, 1989.

Downs, Robert, et al. *Memorable Americans 1750-1950*. Littleton, Colo.: Libraries Unlimited Inc., 1983.

Draper, Lyman C. *King's Mountain and Its Heroes*. Cincinnati: Peter G. Thomson, 1881.

Dufour, Charles L. *Nine Men in Gray*. Garden City, N.Y.: Doubleday & Company, 1963.

Dunn, Jerry Camarillo, Jr. *The Smithsonian Guide to Historic America: The Rocky Mountain States*. New York: Stewart, Tabori & Chang, 1989.

Durham, Michael S. *The Smithsonian Guide to Historic America: The Desert States*. New York: Stewart, Tabori & Chang, 1990.

———. *The Smithsonian Guide to Historic America: The Mid-Atlantic States*. New York: Stewart, Tabori & Chang, 1989.

Durham, Nelson Wayne. *History of the City of Spokane and Spokane County, Washington*. 3 vols. Spokane: The S. J. Clarke Publishing Company, 1912.

Durkin, Joseph T., ed. *John Dooley, Confederate Soldier: The War Journal*. [Washington, D.C.]: Georgetown University Press, 1945.

Eastman, John. *Who Lived Where: A Biographical Guide to Homes and Museums*. New York: Facts on File Publications, 1983.

Editors of American Heritage. *The American Heritage Book of Great Historic Places*. New York: American Heritage Publishing Company, Inc., 1957.

Ehrlich, Eugene, and Gorton Carruth. *The Oxford Illustrated Literary Guide to the United States*. New York: Oxford University Press, 1982.

Eleuterio-Connor, Susan K. *Irish American Material Culture*. New York: Greenwood Press, 1988.

Eliot, Alexander. *Three Hundred Years of American Painting*. New York: Time Incorporated, 1957.

Elliott, Lawrence. "Legend of the Four Chaplains." *Reader's Digest* (June 1989): 65-70.

———. *The Long Hunter: A New Life of Daniel Boone*. New York: Reader's Digest Press, 1976.

Emerson, Mrs. B. A. C. *Historic Southern Monuments*. New York: The Neale Publishing Company, 1911.

Emmons, David M. *The Butte Irish: Class and Ethnicity in an American Mining Town, 1875-1925*. Urbana: University of Illinois Press, 1989.

Engstrand, Iris H. W. *San Diego: Gateway to the Pacific*. Houston, Tex.: Pioneer Publications, Inc., 1992.

Everhart, William C. *Vicksburg National Military Park*. Washington, D.C.: National Park Service, 1954.

Faherty, William Barnaby, S. J. *The Great Saint Louis Cathedral*. St. Louis: St. Louis Cathedral, 1988.

———. *The Saint Louis Portrait*. Tulsa, Okla.: Continental Heritage Inc., 1978.

Father Albert, O.F.M. Cap. "How Sean Heuston Died." *The Capuchin Annual 1966*: 305-306.

Father Canice, O.F.M. Cap. "Some Who Have Gone." *The Capuchin Annual 1936*: 49-67.

"Father Ryan, Poet-Priest of the Confederacy." *Missouri Historical Review* 36 (October 1941): 61-66.

Federal Writers' Project of the Works Progress Administration. *Florida: A Guide to the Southernmost State*. American Guide Series. New York: Oxford University Press, 1939.

———. *Iowa: A Guide to the Hawkeye State*. New York: The Viking Press, 1938.

———. *Kansas: A Guide to the Sunflower State*. American Guide Series. New York: The Viking Press, 1939.

———. *Kentucky: A Guide to the Bluegrass State*. American Guide Series. New York: Harcourt, Brace and Company, 1939.

———. *Mississippi: A Guide to the Magnolia State*. American Guide Series. New York: The Viking Press, 1938.

———. *Montana: A State Guide Book*. American Guide Series. New York: The Viking Press, 1939.

———. *Nebraska: A Guide to the Cornhusker State*. New York: The Viking Press, 1939.

———. *New Orleans City Guide*. Rev. ed. Boston: Houghton Mifflin Company, 1952.

———. *New Orleans City Guide*. American Guide Series. Boston: Houghton Mifflin Company, 1938.

———. *North Carolina: A Guide to the Old North State*. American Guide Series. Chapel Hill: The University of North Carolina Press, 1939.

———. *North Dakota: A Guide to the Northern Prairie State*. American Guide Series. Fargo, N.D.: Knight Publishing Company, 1938.

———. *Rhode Island: A Guide to the Smallest State*. Boston: Houghton Mifflin Company, 1937.

———. *Tennessee: A Guide to the State*. American Guide Series. New York: The Viking Press, 1939.

Ferrier, William Warren. *The Story of the Naming of Berkeley*. Berkeley, Calif.: n.p., 1929.

Fike, Claude E. "The Gubernatorial Administrations of Governor Gerard Chittocque Brandon, 1825-1832." *The Journal of Mississippi History* 35 (August 1973): 247-265.

Filson, John. *The Life and Adventures of Colonel Daniel Boon*. Brooklyn: C.

Wilder, 1823.

Fink, Gary M., ed. *Biographical Dictionary of American Labor Leaders.* Westport, Conn.: Greenwood Press, 1974.

Finn, John. *New Orleans Irish Arrivals-Departures.* Jefferson, La.: Published privately, 1983.

Fitch, Raymond E., ed. *Breaking with Burr: Herman Blennerhassett's Journal, 1807.* Athens, Ohio: Ohio University Press, 1988.

Fitzgerald, Margaret E., and Joseph A. King. *The Uncounted Irish in Canada and the United States.* Toronto: P. D. Meany Publishers, 1990.

Fitzgerald, Sally. "Root and Branch: O'Connor of Georgia." *The Georgia Historical Quarterly* 64 (Winter 1980): 377-387.

Fitzgerald, Sister Mary Paul. *Beacon on the Plains.* Leavenworth, Kans.: The Saint Mary College, 1939.

"Five Iowa Brothers Lost in Pacific Battles." *New York Times* 13 January 1943: 10.

"5 Sullivans Died, Survivor Writes." *New York Times* 15 January 1943: 7.

Flannery, John Brendan. *The Irish Texans.* San Antonio: The University of Texas Institute of Texan Cultures, 1980.

Fleming, Thomas, ed. *Chronicles: A Magazine of American Culture* (August 1995): 6.

Fogdale, Alberta Brooks. *Royal Family of the Columbia: Dr. John McLoughlin and His Family.* Fairfield, Wash.: Ye Galleon Press, 1978.

Foster, Morrison. *Biography, Songs and Musical Compositions of Stephen C. Foster.* Pittsburgh: Published by the author, 1896.

Franklin, John Hope, ed. *Reminiscences of an Active Life: The Autobiography of John Roy Lynch.* Chicago: The University of Chicago Press, 1970.

French, Hiram T. *History of Idaho.* 3 vols. Chicago: The Lewis Publishing Company, 1914.

Fryxell, Fritiof, ed. *Thomas Moran: Explorer in Search of Beauty.* East Hampton, N.Y.: East Hampton Free Library, 1958.

Gallagher, Tag. *John Ford: The Man and His Films.* Berkeley: University of California Press, 1986.

Gallier, James. *The American Builder's General Price Book and Estimator.* New York: Stanley & Company, 1833.

Galloway, John Debo. *The First Transcontinental Railroad.* New York: Simmons-Boardman, 1950.

Garland, Hamlin. *Ulysses S. Grant: His Life and Character.* New York: The Macmillan Company, 1920.

Garwood, Darrell. *Crossroads of America: The Story of Kansas City.* New York: W. W. Norton & Company, Inc., 1948.

Gebhard, David, and Deborah Nevins. *200 Years of American Architectural Drawings.* New York: Whitney Library of Design, 1977.

Gentry, Curt. *The Dolphin Guide to San Francisco and the Bay Area.* Rev. ed. Garden City, N.Y.: Dolphin Books, 1969.

Gerstle, Mark. *1906: Surviving San Francisco's Great Earthquake and Fire*. San Francisco: Chronicle Books, 1981.

Gibbons, James. *A Retrospective of Fifty Years*. 2 vols. Baltimore: John Murphy Company, 1916.

Glasscock, C. B. *The War of the Copper Kings: Builders of Butte and Wolves of Wall Street*. New York: The Bobbs-Merrill Company, 1935.

Gleeson, John. *The Book of Irish Lists and Trivia*. Dublin: Gill and Macmillan Ltd., 1989.

Goode, James M. *The Outdoor Sculpture of Washington, D.C.* Washington, D.C.: Smithsonian Institution Press, 1974.

Goodwin, Doris Kearns. *The Fitzgeralds and the Kennedys*. New York: Simon and Schuster, 1987.

Gordon, Alice, et al. *The Smithsonian Guide to Historic America: Texas & the Arkansas River Valley*. New York: Stewart, Tabori & Chang, 1990.

Gower, Herschel, and Jack Allen. *Pen and Sword: The Life and Journals of Randal W. McGavock*. Nashville: The Tennessee Historical Commission, 1959.

Grant, Frederic James, ed. *History of Seattle, Washington*. New York: American Publishing and Engraving Company, 1891.

Greenberg, Ronald M, ed. *The National Register of Historic Places 1976*. 2 vols. Washington D.C.: U.S. Department of the Interior, 1976.

Greenhow, Rose O'Neal. *My Imprisonment and the First Year of Abolition Rule at Washington*. London: Richard Bentley, 1863.

Grehan, Ida. *Irish Family Histories*. Boulder, Colo.: Roberts Rinehart Publishers, 1993.

Griffin, William D. *The Book of Irish Americans*. New York: Times Books, 1990.

Griswold, Don L., and Jean Harvey. *The Carbonate Camp Called Leadville*. Denver: The University of Denver Press, 1951.

Guinn, J. M. *Historical and Biographical Record of Los Angeles and Vicinity*. Chicago: Chapman Publishing Company, 1901.

Gwathmey, Edward M. *John Pendleton Kennedy*. New York: Thomas Nelson and Sons, 1931.

Hafen, LeRoy R. *Broken Hand: The Life of Thomas Fitzpatrick, Mountain Man, Guide and Indian Agent*. Denver: The Old West Publishing Company, 1973.

———, ed. *The Mountain Men and the Fur Trade of the Far West*. 10 vols. Glendale, Calif.: The Arthur H. Clarke Company, 1969.

Hagood, Hurley, and Roberta Hagood. *Hannibal Yesterdays*. Marceline, Mo.: Jostens, [n.d.].

Hall, James Norman, and Charles Bernard Nordoff, eds. *The Lafayette Flying Corps*. 2 vols. Boston: Houghton Mifflin Company, 1920.

Haltigan, Patrick J. *The Irish in the American Revolution and their Early Influence in the Colonies*. Washington, D.C.: Published by the author, 1908.

Hammer, Kenneth, ed. *Custer in '76: Walter Camp's Notes on the Custer Fight.* Norman, Okla.: University of Oklahoma Press, 1990.

———. *Men With Custer.* Fort Collins, Colo.: The Old Army Press, 1972.

Hanchett, William. *Lincoln Murder Conspiracies.* Chicago: University of Illinois Press, 1983.

Hanna, Charles A. *The Scotch-Irish or The Scot in North Britain, North Ireland, and North America.* 2 vols. New York: G. P. Putnam's Sons, 1902.

———, ed. *The Wilderness Trail.* 2 vols. New York: G. P. Putnam's Sons, 1911.

Hansen, Gladys. *San Francisco: The Bay and Its Cities.* New rev. ed. American Guide Series. New York: Hastings House, 1973.

Hansen, Harry. *California: A Guide to the Golden State.* American Guide Series. New rev. ed. New York: Hastings House, 1967.

———. *Texas: A Guide to the Lone Star State.* American Guide Series. New rev. ed. New York: Hastings House, 1969.

Harbert, Nancy. *New Mexico.* Oakland, Calif.: Compass American Guides, Inc., 1992.

Hardy, Gordon, et al., eds. *Above and Beyond.* Boston: Boston Publishing Company, 1985.

Harmon, Nolan B., Jr. *The Famous Case of Myra Clark Gaines.* Baton Rouge: Louisiana State University Press, 1946.

Hart, Herbert M. *Old Forts of the Northwest.* Seattle: Superior Publishing Company, 1963.

Harting, Emilie C. *A Literary Tour of the United States: Northeast.* New York: William Morrow and Company, Inc., 1978.

Hawley, James H., ed. *History of Idaho: The Gem of the Mountains.* 3 vols. Chicago: The S. J. Clarke Publishing Company, 1920.

Healy, George P. A. *Reminiscences of a Portrait Painter.* Chicago: A. C. McClurg and Company, 1894.

Hearst, William Randolph, Jr. *The Hearsts, Father and Son.* Niwot, Colo.: Roberts Rinehart Publishers, 1991.

Hebért, Rachel Bluntzen. *The Forgotten Colony: San Patricio de Hibernia.* Burnet, Tex.: Eakin Press, 1981.

Henry-Ruffin, M. E. "Home of Father Ryan: Poet-Priest." *Historic Houses of Alabama and Their Traditions.* Birmingham: Birmingham Publishing Company, 1935.

Henry, William A., III. *The Great One: The Life and Legend of Jackie Gleason.* New York: Doubleday, 1992.

Herbermann, Charles George, et al. *Catholic Encyclopedia.* 15 vols. New York: Appleton, 1907-12.

Herron, Don. *The Literary World of San Francisco and its Environs.* San Francisco: City Lights Books, 1985.

Heymann, C. David. *A Woman Named Jackie.* New York: Carol Communications, 1989.

Historic Charleston Guidebook. Charleston, S.C.: The Junior League of Charleston, 1965.

Cutler, Harry Gardner. *History of Florida Past and Present*. 3 vols. Chicago: The Lewis Publishing Company, 1923.

History of Marin County, California. San Francisco: Alley, Bowen & Company, 1880.

The History of St. Patrick's Parish and Church. Hackensack, N.J.: Custombook, Inc., 1976.

History of the State of Nebraska. Chicago: The Western Historical Company, 1882.

Hofstadter, Richard. *The American Political Tradition and the Men Who Made It*. New York: Vintage Books, 1974.

Hogrefe, Jeffrey. *O'Keeffe: The Life of an American Legend*. New York: Bantam Books, 1992.

Holdredge, Helen. *The Woman in Black: The Life of Lola Montez*. New York: G. P. Putnam's Sons, 1955.

Holli, Melvin G., and Peter d'A. Jones, eds. *Biographical Dictionary of American Mayors, 1820-1980*. Westport, Conn.: Greenwood Press, 1981.

Holman, Frederick V. *Dr. John McLoughlin, the Father of Oregon*. Cleveland: The Arthur H. Clark Company, 1907.

Hoover, Mildred Brook et al. *Historic Spots in California*. Rev. ed. Stanford: Stanford University Press, 1990.

Horan, James D. *Mathew Brady: Historian with a Camera*. New York: Bonanza Books, 1955.

House, Boyce. *San Antonio: The City of Flaming Adventure*. Rev. ed. San Antonio: The Naylor Company, 1968.

Howard, John Tasker. *Stephen Foster: America's Troubadour*. New York: Thomas Y. Crowell Company, 1953.

Hoyt, William Henry, ed. *The Papers of Archibald D. Murphey*. 2 vols. Raleigh, N.C.: E. M. Uzzell & Company, 1914.

Hubbell, Jay B. *The South in American Literature 1607-1900*. Durham, N.C.: Duke University Press, 1954.

Hudson, Patricia L., and Sandra L. Ballare. *The Smithsonian Guide to Historic America: The Carolinas and the Appalachian States*. New York: Stewart, Tabori & Chang, 1989.

Hume, Major Edgar Erskine. "Colonel Theodore O'Hara: Author of The Bivouac of the Dead." *Southern Sketches* 6 (1st Series): 3-57.

Hunt, Rockwell D. *California's Stately Hall of Fame*. Stockton, Calif.: College of the Pacific, 1950.

Illustrated Guide to the Treasures of America. Pleasantville, N.Y.: The Readers' Digest Association, Inc., 1974.

Interview between Neely Grant II and Mrs. Barton Lee Mallory, March 21, 1962.

"Irish Officer Made History at Battle of Little Bighorn." *The Irish Tribune*

13 June 1993: 25.

Irvine, Leigh H. *History of Humboldt County, California*. Los Angeles: Historic Record Company, 1915.

Isenberg, Michael T. *John L. Sullivan and His America*. Urbana: University of Illinois Press, 1988.

Jackson, Mary Anna. *Memoirs of Stonewall Jackson*. Louisville, Ky.: The Prentice Press, 1895.

Jackson, Ronald Vern, and Altha Polson. *American Patriots*. N.p.: n.p., 1981.

Jacob, G. J. *The Life and Times of Patrick Gass*. Wellsburg, W.Va.: Jacob & Smith, 1859.

James, Dorris Clayton. *Antebellum Natchez*. Baton Rouge: Louisiana State University Press, 1968.

James, Edward T., ed. *Notable American Women 1607-1950*. Cambridge: The Belknap Press of Harvard University Press, 1971.

James, William F., and George H. McMurry. *History of San Jose, California*. San Jose: A. H. Cawston, 1933.

"Jesse James May Prove Dead Men Do Tell Tales." *Los Angeles Times* 18 July 1995: A5.

Johnson, Allen, et al., eds. *Dictionary of American Biography*. 28 vols. New York: C. Scribner's Sons, 1928-88.

Johnson, John. *The Defense of Charleston Harbor*. Charleston, S.C.: Walker, Evans & Cogswell Company, 1890.

Johnson, Patricia Givens. *General Andrew Lewis of Roanoke and Greenbrier*. Christiansburg, Va.: Published by the author, 1980.

Johnson, Robert C. *John McLoughlin: Patriarch of the Northwest*. Portland, Ore.: Metropolitan Press, 1935.

Jones, Ernest. "The Battle of Sabine Pass." *Blue & Gray Magazine* 4 (August-September 1986): 19-24, 47-53.

Jones, Maldwyn Allen. *American Immigration*. 2nd ed. Chicago: The University of Chicago Press, 1992.

Josephson, Matthew. *Edison: A Biography*. N.p.: John Wiley & Sons, Inc., 1992.

Keithley, Ralph. *Buckey O'Neill: He Stayed With 'em While He Lasted*. Caldwell, Id.: The Caxton Printers, Ltd., 1949.

Kelly, Giles M. *A Genealogical Account of the Descendants of John Kelly of Newbury, Massachusetts, U.S.A.* Albany, N. Y.: Joel Munsell's Sons, 1886.

Kelly, Mary Pat. "All Aboard: The U.S. Navy's Irish American Connection." *Irish America* (November/December 1995): 28-29.

Kelly, Sister Mary Gilbert. *Catholic Immigrant Colonization Projects in the United States, 1815-1860*. New York: The United States Catholic Historical Society, 1939.

Kemble, Frances Anne. *Journal of a Residence on a Georgian Plantation in 1838-1839*. Edited by John A. Scott. New York: Alfred A. Knopf, 1961.

Kemp, Louis Wiltz. *The Signers of the Texas Declaration of Independence*. Houston: The Anson Jones Press, 1944.

Kenneally, James J. *The History of American Catholic Women*. New York: The Crossroad Publishing Company, 1990.

Kennedy, John F. *Profiles in Courage*. New York: Harper & Row, 1961.

Kersey, Dr. Harry A., Jr. *The Stranahan House: A Site History*. N.p.: Fort Lauderdale Historical Society, n.d.

Ketchum, Richard M. *Will Rogers: The Man and His Time*. New York: Simon and Schuster, 1973.

Kidd, Barbara Ruth. "The History of Sweet Springs, Monroe County, West Virginia." *West Virginia History* 21 (July 1960): 234-268.

Kilmer, Joyce, ed. *Anthology of Catholic Poets*. Garden City, N.Y.: Halcyon House, 1947.

King, Joseph A. *Winter of Entrapment: A New Look at the Donner Party*. Toronto: P. D. Meany Publishers, 1992.

King, Joseph A. *Winter of Entrapment: A New Look at the Donner Party*. Rev. ed. Lafayette, Calif.: K & K Publications, 1994.

Klotter, James C. *The Breckinridges of Kentucky 1760-1981*. Lexington: The University Press of Kentucky, 1986.

Kobles, John J. *F. Scott Fitzgerald's Minnesota: His Homes and Haunts*. St. Paul: Minnesota Historical Society Press, 1978.

Koch, Margaret. *Santa Cruz County: Parade of the Past*. Fresno, Calif.: Valley Publishers, 1973.

Komar, Charlene, and Greg Storey. "Clarke's Window Finds a Place in the Sun." *Irish America* 12 (March/April 1996): 74-77.

Kruh, David, and Louis Kruh. *Presidential Landmarks*. New York: Hippocrene Books Inc., 1992.

Kuhlman, Thomas A. "The Captain Cornelius O'Connor House in Homer: A Symbol of the Dakota County Irish." *Nebraska History* 63 (Spring 1982): 16-32.

Kupperman, Karen Ordahl. *Roanoke: The Abandoned Colony*. Totowa, N.J.: Rowman & Allanheld, 1984.

Kurzman, Dan. *Left To Die: The Tragedy of the USS Juneau*. New York: Pocket Books, 1994.

Laird, Archibald. *Monuments Marking the Graves of the Presidents*. No. Quincy, Mass.: The Christopher Publishing House, 1971.

Lake, Benjamin J. *The Story of the Presbyterian Church in the United States of America*. Philadelphia: Westminster Press, 1956.

Lamar, Howard R., ed. *The Reader's Encyclopedia of the American West*. New York: Thomas Y. Crowell Company, 1977.

Lavender, David. *The Fist in the Wilderness*. Garden City, N.Y.: Doubleday & Company, Inc., 1964.

Lea, Tom. *The King Ranch*. 2 vols. Boston: Little, Brown and Company, 1957.

Lee, Fred J. *Casey Jones: Epic of the American Railroad*. Kingsport, Tenn.:

Southern Publishers, Inc., 1939.

Lee, Thomas Z. "American Irish Historical Notes." *The Journal of the American Irish Historical Society* 25 (1926): 218-222.

Leiding, Harriette Kershaw. *Historic Houses of South Carolina*. Philadelphia: J. B. Lippincott Company, 1921.

Lesesne, Thomas Petigru. *Landmarks of Charleston*. Richmond, Va.: Garrett & Masie, 1932.

Levin, H., ed. *The Lawyers and Lawmakers of Kentucky*. Chicago: The Lewis Publishing Company, 1897.

Levingston, Steven E. *Historic Ships of San Francisco*. San Francisco: Chronicle Books, 1984.

LeVot, Andre. *F. Scott Fitzgerald: A Biography*. Garden City, N.Y.: Doubleday & Company, Inc., 1983.

Lindsley, John Berrier, ed. *The Military Annals of Tennessee, Confederate*. Nashville: J. M. Lindsley & Company, 1886.

Linehan, John C. "The Irish Pioneers of Texas." *The Journal of the American Irish Historical Society* 2 (1899): 120-138.

———. "The New Hampshire Kellys." *The Journal of the American Irish Historical Society* 5 (1905): 32-52.

Logan, William Bryant, and Vance Muse. *The Smithsonian Guide to Historic America: The Deep South*. New York: Stewart, Tabori & Chang, 1989.

Logan, William Bryant, and Susan Ochshorn. *The Smithsonian Guide to Historic America: The Pacific States*. New York: Stewart, Tabori & Chang, 1989.

Lonn, Ella. *Foreigners in the Union Army and Navy*. Baton Rouge: Louisiana State University Press, 1952.

Legends of Loudoun: An Account of the History and Homes of a Border County of Virginia's Northern Neck. Richmond, Va.: Garrett and Massie Inc., 1938.

Luce, Edward S. *Keogh, Comanche and Custer*. St. Louis: John S. Swift Company, Inc., 1939.

Lynch, Alice Clare. *The Kennedy Clan and Tierra Redonda*. San Francisco: Marnell & Company, 1935.

Mace, O. Henry. *Between the Rivers: A History of Early Calaveras County, California*. Sutter Creek, Calif.: Gold Country Enterprises, 1991.

MacManus, Seumas. *The Story of the Irish Race*. Rev. ed. New York: The Devin-Adair Company, 1968.

"The Mallorys, Neelys and the Fine Victorian Mansion." *The Memphis Commercial Appeal* 19 June 1977: G6-7.

Malone, Russ. *Hippocrene U.S.A. Guide to Irish America*. New York: Hippocrene Books, 1994.

Marshall, Charlotte Thomas. "Robert Taylor and His Relatives and Descendants." *Speech to the Athens Historical Society* (May 17, 1970).

Mason, Yvonne. "Believe It – John T's Tavern is Open." *Random Lengths* 6 July 1990.

Matthews, Janet Snyder. *Edge of Wilderness: A Settlement History of Manatee River and Sarasota Bay 1528-1885*. Sarasota, Fla.: Coastal Press, 1983.

Mathews, Mazine. "Old Inns of East Tennessee." *The East Tennessee Historical Society's Publications* 2 (1930): 22-33.

Matson, Robert William. *William Mulholland: A Forgotten Forefather*. Stockton, Calif.: University of the Pacific, 1976.

Maynard, Theodore. *The Story of American Catholicism*. New York: The Macmillan Company, 1954.

McCann, James H. "Towers of Silence Speak." *The Journal of the American Irish Historical Society* 30 (1932): 134-163.

McCarran, Sister Margaret Patricia. "Patrick Anthony McCarran." *Nevada Historical Society Quarterly* 11 (Fall-Winter 1968): 5-66; 12 (Spring 1969): 5-75.

McClatchy, Eleanor, and Roy V. Bailey. *Private Thinks by C. K. and Other Writings of Charles K. McClatchy*. New York: The Scribner Press, 1936.

McConnell, W. J. *Early History of Idaho*. Caldwell, Id.: Idaho State Legislature, 1913.

McCoy, Michael. *Montana: Off the Beaten Path*. Old Saybrook, Conn.: The Globe Pequot Press, 1993.

McDowell, Jack. *San Francisco*. Menlo Park, Calif.: Lane Magazine & Book Company, 1969.

McEnery, Thomas, ed. *California Cavalier: The Journal of Captain Thomas Fallon*. San Jose, Calif.: Inishfallen Enterprises Inc., 1978.

McEniry, Sister Blanche Marie. *American Catholics in the War with Mexico*. Washington, D.C.: The Catholic University of America, 1937.

McGrew, Clarence Alan. *City of San Diego and San Diego County*. 2 vols. New York: The American Historical Society, 1922.

McGuire, Edward J. "Memorial of Joseph I. C. Clarke." *The Journal of the American Irish Historical Society* 24 (1925): 227-240.

Meigs, William M. *The Life of John Caldwell Calhoun*. 2 vols. New York: The Neale Publishing Company, 1917.

Meleney, John C. *The Public Life of Aedanus Burke: Revolutionary Republican in Post-Revolutionary South Carolina*. Columbia: University of South Carolina, 1989.

Michelin Green Guide to Ireland. 1992 ed.

Miller, David Humphreys. *Custer's Fall: The Native American Side of the Story*. New York: First Meridian Printing, 1992.

Miller, Robert Ryal. *Shamrock and Sword: The Saint Patrick's Battalion in the U.S.-Mexican War*. Norman, Okla.: University of Oklahoma Press, 1989.

Mizener, Arthur. *Scott Fitzgerald and His World*. New York: G. P. Putnam's Sons, 1972.

Mobile Travel Guide: Middle Atlantic. New York: Prentice Hall General Reference and Travel, 1994.

Mobile Travel Guide: Northwest and Great Plains. New York: Fodor's Travel

Publications, 1995.

Mobile Travel Guide: Southeast. New York: Prentice Hall General Reference and Travel, 1994.

Monaghan, James, ed. *The Book of the American West*. New York: Julian Messner, Inc., 1963.

Montgomery, Richard G. *The White-Headed Eagle*. New York: The Macmillan Company, 1934.

Moore, Charles. *The Family Life of George Washington*. Boston: Houghton Mifflin Company, 1926.

Moore, John Trotwood, and Austin P. Foster. *Tennessee: The Volunteer State 1769-1923*. 4 vols. Chicago: The S. J. Clarke Publishing Company, 1923.

Morrel, Martha McBride. *"Young Hickory": The Life and Times of President James Polk*. New York: E. P. Dutton & Company, Inc., 1949.

Morton, J. Sterling, et al. *Illustrated History of Nebraska*. 3rd ed. 2 vols. Lincoln, Nebr.: Western Publishing and Engraving Company, 1911.

Mosher, Leroy E., ed. *Stephen M. White: His Life and His Work*. 2 vols. Los Angeles: The Times-Mirror Company, 1903.

"Mother's Tears for Her Five Heroic Sons Christen New Destroyer 'The Sullivans.'" *New York Times* 5 April 1943: 11.

"Mrs. W. J. McNamara Died This Morning; Funeral Tomorrow." *The Victoria Daily Advocate* 22 February 1917: 3.

Muir, Andrew Forest. "Railroads Come to Houston 1857-1861." *The Southeastern Historical Quarterly* 64 (July 1960): 42-63.

Mulkerns, Helen. "The Man Who Made Westerns." *Irish Echo* 8-14 November 1995: 25.

Mulligan, Tim. *Virginia: A History and Guide*. New York: Random House, 1986.

Murphree, Dennis. "Hurricane and Briarfield, the Davis Plantations." *The Journal of Mississippi History* 9 (January-April 1947): 98-107.

Murphy, Virginia Reed. "Across the Plains in the Donner Party (1846)." *The Century Illustrated Monthly Magazine* 42 (May-October 1891): 409-426.

"Name 'The Sullivans' Set for Destroyer." *New York Times* 10 February 1943: 16.

Nash, Charles Edward. *Biographical Sketches of Gen. Pat Cleburne and Gen. T. C. Hindman*. Little Rock, Ark.: Tunnah & Pittard, Printers, 1896.

National Cyclopaedia of American Biography. 81 vols. New York: J. T. White Company, 1893-1978.

National League of American Pen Women. *Historic Houses of Alabama and Their Traditions*. Birmingham: Birmingham Publishing Company, 1935.

National Portrait Gallery, Smithsonian Institution, Permanent Collection Illustrated Checklist. Washington, D.C.: National Portrait Gallery, 1987.

Neider, Charles, ed. *The Autobiography of Mark Twain*. New York: Harper & Brothers, 1959.

Nelson, Mike. "Catholic Cemeteries Home to Many Celebrities." *The Tidings* 15 May 1994: 10-11.

Nesbit, Robert C. *"He Built Seattle": A Biography of Judge Thomas Burke*. Seattle: University of Washington Press, 1961.

Nevins, Allan, and Frank Ernest Hill. *Ford: Expansion and Challenge 1915-1933*. New York: Charles Scribner's Sons, 1957.

Newmark, Harris. *Sixty Years in Southern California 1853-1913*. 3rd rev. ed. Edited by Maurice H. and Marco R. Newmark. Boston: Houghton Mifflin Company, 1930.

Niethammer, Carolyn. "The Lure of Gold." *The Women Who Made the West*. New York: Doubleday & Company, 1980.

Niehaus, Earl F. *The Irish in New Orleans 1800-1860*. Baton Rouge: Louisiana State University Press, 1965.

"Notes and Documents: Confederate Necrology." *Georgia Historical Quarterly* 20 (September 1936): 263-269.

Nuckols, Mrs. S. V. "History of William Poage and His Wife, Ann Kennedy Wilson Poage Lindsay McGinty." *The Register of the Kentucky State Historical Society* 11 (January 1913): 101-103.

Oberste, William H. *Texas Irish Empresarios and Their Colonies*. Austin: Von Boeckmann-Jones Company, 1973.

O'Brien, Michael J. "Burke's Garden, Virginia." *The Journal of the American Irish Historical Society* 26 (1927): 58-69.

———. *George Washington's Associations with the Irish*. New York: P. J. Kenedy & Sons, 1937.

———. "The Irish Ancestors of Theodore Roosevelt." *The Journal of the American Irish Historical Society* 17 (1918): 144-145.

———. *Irish Settlers in America*. 2 vols. Baltimore: Genealogical Publishing Company, Inc., 1979.

O'Connell, Philip. "A Kilmore Missionary in Mexico: The Rev. Dr. Michael Muldoon." *The Irish Ecclesiastical Record* 49 (January-June 1937): 252-254+

Oldt, Franklin T., ed. *History of Dubuque County, Iowa*. Chicago: Goodspeed Historical Association, 1911.

O'Laughlin, Michael C. *Irish Settlers on the American Frontier*. Kansas City: Irish Genealogical Foundation, 1984.

O'Neal, Bill. *Encyclopedia of Western Gun-Fighters*. Norman, Okla.: University of Oklahoma Press, 1980.

O'Neall, John Belton. *Biographical Sketches of the Bench and Bar of South Carolina*. Charleston: S. C. Courtenay & Company, 1859.

O'Reilly, John Boyle. *Selected Poems*. New York: P. J. Kenedy & Sons, 1913.

Owen, Thomas McAdory. *History of Alabama and Dictionary of Alabama Biography*. 4 vols. Chicago: The S. J. Clarke Publishing Company, 1921.

Parkinson, R. R. *Pen Portraits*. San Francisco: Published by the author, 1878.

Parks, Joseph H. "Memphis Under Military Rule, 1862 to 1865." *The East Tennessee Historical Society's Publications* 14 (1942): 331-58.

Parmet, Herbert S., and Marie B. Hecht. *Aaron Burr: Portrait of an Ambitious Man*. New York: The Macmillan Company, 1967.

Parrish, William E. *David Rice Atchison of Missouri: Border Politician*. Columbia: University of Missouri Press, 1961.

Parsons, Mark, and R. E. Burnett. *Landmark Inn State Historic Site: Archaeological Investigations, Medina County, Texas, 1975-1980*. Austin: Texas Parks & Wildlife Department, 1984.

Pendleton, William C. *History of Tazewell County and Southwest Virginia 1748-1920*. Richmond, Va.: W. C. Hill Printing Company, 1920.

Perkins, William Rufus. *History of the Trappist Abbey of New Melleray*. Iowa City: State University of Iowa, 1892.

Peters, James Edward. *Arlington National Cemetery: Shrine to America's Heroes*. Kensington, Md.: Woodbine House, 1986.

Pictorial and Biographical Memoirs of Indianapolis and Marion County, Indiana. Chicago: Goodspeed Brothers, 1893.

Piggott, Michael. "Irish Pioneers of the Upper Mississippi Valley." *The Journal of the American Irish Historical Society* 9 (1910): 301-330.

"Pioneer Manufacturer Victim of Infirmities." *Louisville Times* 27 February 1914: 1.

Placzek, Adolf K., ed. *Macmillan Encyclopedia of Architects*. 3 vols. New York: The Free Press, 1982.

Plummer, Mary H., and Gerald W. Gillette, eds. *On Holy Ground: American Presbyterian/Reformed Historical Sites*. Philadelphia: Presbyterian Historical Society, 1982.

Plunkett, Josephine Mary. "Joseph Mary Plunkett's Last Message." *The Capuchin Annual 1966*: 303-304.

Pollack, Queena. "An Irish Innkeeper and His Internationally Known 'Innkeeper's Daughter.'" *The Journal of the American Irish Historical Society* 28 (1929-30): 94.

Portrait and Biographical Record of Arizona. Chicago: Chapman Publishing Company, 1901.

Potter, George. *To the Golden Door: The Story of the Irish in Ireland and America*. Boston: Little, Brown and Company, 1960.

Powell, William S., ed. *Dictionary of North Carolina Biography*. 6 vols. Chapel Hill: The University of North Carolina Press, 1979-1994.

Preece, Harold. *The Dalton Gang: End of an Outlaw Era*. New York: Hastings House Publishers, 1963.

Prendergast, Thomas F. *Forgotten Pioneers: Irish Leaders in Early California*. San Francisco: The Trade Pressroom, 1942.

The Princeton Language Institute. *The 21st Century Dictionary of Quotations*. New York: Dell Publishing, 1993.

"The 'Prison Journal' of Stephen F. Austin." *The Quarterly of the Texas State*

Historical Association 2 (January 1899): 183-210.

Proctor, Be H. *Not Without Honor: The Life of John H. Reagan.* Austin: University of Texas Press, 1962.

Purcell, L. Edward. *Who Was Who in the American Revolution.* New York: Facts on File, Inc., 1993.

Purdue, Howell, and Elizabeth Purdue. *Pat Cleburne: Confederate General.* Hillsboro, Tex.: Hill Junior College Press, 1973.

Pyle, Joseph Gilpen. *The Life of James J. Hill.* 2 vols. Garden City, N.Y.: Doubleday, Page & Company, 1917.

Pyron, Darden Asbury. *Southern Daughter: The Life of Margaret Mitchell.* New York: Oxford University Press, 1991.

Quinn, Charles Russell. *The History of Downey, California.* Downey: Elena Quinn, 1973.

Quinon, Stephen. "Careers of the Croghans." *The Western Pennsylvania Historical Magazine* 5 (July 1922): 215-219.

Raider, Perry Scott. "The Romance of American Courts: Gaines vs. New Orleans." *The Louisiana Historical Quarterly* 27 (January 1944).

Randall, E. O. "Blennerhassett." *Ohio Archaeological and Historical Society Quarterly* 1 (September 1887): 127-163.

Randall, J. G., and David Donald. *The Divided Union.* Boston: Little, Brown and Company, 1961.

Read, Thomas Buchanan. *The Poetical Works of T. Buchanan Read.* New rev. ed. Philadelphia: J. B. Lippincott & Company, 1883.

Reagan, Ronald. *An American Life: The Autobiography.* New York: Simon and Schuster, 1990.

Reading, June Allen, ed. *Consignments to El Dorado: A Record of the Voyage of the* Sutton *by Thomas Whaley.* New York: Exposition Press, 1972.

Reed, Merrill A. *Historic Statues and Monuments in California.* Burlingame: Merrill Reed, 1956.

Reese, M. Lisle, ed. *South Dakota: A Guide to the State.* 2nd rev. ed. American Guide Series. New York: Hastings House, 1952.

Refugio County Advantage Press, 22 February 1995: 14.

Register of Debates in Congress. 14 vols. Washington, D.C.: Gales & Seaton, 1825-1837.

Reiter, Joan Swallow. *The Old West: The Women.* Alexandria, Va.: Time-Life Books, 1978.

"Reminiscences of Mrs. Annie Fagan Teal." *Southwestern Historical Quarterly* 34 (April 1931): 317-328.

"Review of *The Woods-McAfee Memorial Containing an Account of John Woods and James McAfee of Ireland and Their Descendants.*" *The Virginia Magazine of History and Biography* 13 (January 1906): 333-334.

Richards, Rand. *Historic San Francisco: A Concise History and Guide.* San Francisco: Heritage House Publishers, 1991.

Richards, Sandy, ed. *Stranahan House: Frank and Ivy Stranahan, New River*

Pioneers. N.p.: Stranahan House, 1995.

Robinson, Blackwell P., ed. *The North Carolina Guide*. Chapel Hill: The University of North Carolina Press, 1955.

Robinson, Roxana. *Georgia O'Keeffe: A Life*. New York: Harper & Row, 1989.

Roche, Richard. *The Texas Connection: The Story of the Wexford Colony in Refugio*. Wexford, Ire.: The Print Ship, 1989.

Rolle, Andrew F. *California: A History*. 2nd ed. New York: Thomas Y. Crowell Company, 1969.

Roosevelt, Theodore. *The Rough Riders*. New York: Charles Scribner's Sons, 1899.

Ross, Ishbel. *First Lady of the South: The Life of Mrs. Jefferson Davis*. New York: Harper & Brothers Publishers, 1958.

Rothensteiner, John. *History of the Archdiocese of St. Louis*. 2 vols. St. Louis: [n. p.], 1928.

Rothrock, Mary U., ed. *The French Broad-Holston Country*. Knoxville: The East Tennessee Historical Society, 1946.

Rowland, Dunbar, ed. *Jefferson Davis, Constitutionalist: His Letters, Papers and Speeches*. 10 vols. Jackson, Miss.: Mississippi Department of Archives and History, 1923.

Rowland, Eron. *Varina Howell: Wife of Jefferson Davis*. New York: The Macmillan Company, 1927.

Russell, Don. *The Lives and Legends of Buffalo Bill*. Norman: University of Oklahoma Press, 1960.

Ryan, William Morris. *Shamrock and Cactus: The Story of the Catholic Heroes of Texas Independence*. San Antonio: Southern Literary Institute, 1936.

Sacks, Benjamin. *Carson Mansion & Ingomar Theatre*. Fresno, Calif.: Valley Publishers, 1979.

Sadie, Stanley, ed. *The New Grove Dictionary of Music and Musicians*. 20 vols. London: Macmillan Publishers Limited, 1990.

Safford, William H., ed. *The Blennerhassett Papers*. Cincinnati: Moore, Wilstach & Baldwin, 1864.

Santa Fe, Taos & Albuquerque. New York: Access Press, 1993.

Satterfield, Archie, and Dianne J. Boulerice Lyons. *Washington Handbook*. 4th ed. Chico, Calif.: Moon Publications, Inc., 1994.

Schlesinger, Arthur M., Jr., ed. *The Almanac of American History*. New York: Bramhall House, 1986.

Scott, Mary Wingfield. *Houses of Old Richmond*. Richmond, Va.: The Valentine Museum, 1941.

Shackford, James Atkins. *David Crockett: The Man and the Legend*. Chapel Hill: The University of North Carolina Press, 1956.

Shannon, William V. *The American Irish*. Rev. ed. New York: The Macmillan Company, 1966.

Sheaffer, Louis. *O'Neill: Son and Artist*. Boston: Little, Brown and Company, 1973.

———. *O'Neill: Son and Playwright*. Boston: Little, Brown and Company, 1968.

Shenkman, Richard, and Kurt Reiger. *One-Night Stands With American History*. New York: William Morrow & Company, Inc., 1980.

Shepherd, Donald, and Robert F. Slatzer. *Bing Crosby: The Hollow Man*. New York: St. Martin's Press, 1981.

Shepherd, Donald, et al. *Duke: The Life and Times of John Wayne*. Garden City, N.Y.: Doubleday and Company, 1985.

Sherr, Lynn, and Jurate Kazickas. *Susan B. Anthony Slept Here: A Guide to American Women's Landmarks*. New York: Times Books, 1994.

Sifakis, Stewart. *Who Was Who in the Civil War*. New York: Facts on File Publications, 1988.

Silka, Henry P. *San Pedro: A Pictorial History*. San Pedro: San Pedro Bay Historical Society, 1993.

Simon, Ted. "They Don't Make 'Em Like That Anymore." *Los Angeles Times* 14 January 1996: Book Review 1+.

Simpson, Harold B. *Audie Murphy: American Soldier*. Dallas: Alcor Publishing Company, 1982.

Smith, Justin. *The Annexation of Texas*. New York: The Baker and Taylor Company, 1911.

Smith, Page. *The Nation Comes of Age: A People's History of the Ante-Bellum Years*. New York: McGraw-Hill Book Company, 1981.

———. *A New Age Now Begins. A People's History of the American Revolution*. New York: McGraw-Hill Book Company, 1976.

———. *The Shaping of America: A People's History of the Young Republic*. New York: McGraw-Hill Book Company, 1980.

———. *Trial by Fire: A People's History of the Civil War and Reconstruction*. New York: McGraw-Hilll Book Company, 1982.

Smith, Valerie Electra. "Who Was John T. Gaffey." *San Pedro Weekly* 27 October-9 November 1989: 14.

Smylie, James H. *American Presbyterianism: A Pictorial History*. Philadelphia: Presbyterian Historical Society, 1985.

Smythe, William E. *History of San Diego 1542-1908*. 2 vols. San Diego: The History Company, 1908.

Snyder, Gerald S. *In the Footsteps of Lewis and Clark*. Washington, D.C.: The National Geographic Society, 1970.

Sobel, Robert, and John Raimo, eds. *Biographical Dictionary of the Governors of the United States 1789-1978*. 4 vols. Westport, Conn.: Meckler Books, 1978.

Soltis, Stephen. *The Insider's Guide to Metropolitan Washington, D.C.* Richmond, Va.: Richmond Newspapers, Inc., 1993.

Sorensen, Theodore C. *Kennedy*. New York: Harper & Row, 1965.

Spalding, William A. *History of Los Angeles City and County, California*. 3 vols. Los Angeles: J. R. Finnell & Sons Publishing Company, 1931.

Sparkman, Robert S. "The Woman in the Case: Jane Todd Crawford, 1763-1842." *Annals of Surgery* 189 (May 1979): 529-545.

Speech of Mr. T. J. Rusk, of Texas, on The Mexican War, delivered in the U.S. Senate, Feb. 17, 1848. Washington: n.p., 1848.

Stanton, William A. "The Irish of Memphis." *The West Tennessee Historical Society Papers* 6 (1952): 87-118.

Starr, Kevin. *Inventing the Dream: California Through the Progressive Era.* New York: Oxford University Press, 1985.

Starr, S. Frederick. *Southern Comfort: The Garden District of New Orleans.* Cambridge, Mass.: The M.I.T. Press, 1989.

Stellman, Louis J. *Sam Brannan: Builder of San Francisco.* New York: Exposition Press, 1953.

Stephen, Leslie, and Sidney Lee, eds. *Dictionary of National Biography.* 66 vols. London: Smith, Elden, & Company, 1885-1901.

Stephens, Francis X., Jr. "The Mullanphys of St. Louis." *The Journal of the American Irish Historical Society* 29 (1930-31): 173-182.

Stevens, Walter B. *St. Louis: History of the Fourth City 1764-1909.* 3 vols. Chicago: The S. J. Clarke Publishing Company, 1909.

Stewart, George R. *Ordeal by Hunger: The Story of The Donner Party.* Boston: Houghton Mifflin Company, 1960.

Stewart, John J. *The Iron Trail to The Golden Spike.* Salt Lake City: Deseret Book Company, 1969.

Stick, David. *Roanoke Island: The Beginnings of English America.* Chapel Hill: The University of North Carolina Press, 1983.

Stookey, Dr. Walter M. *Fatal Decision: The Tragic Story of the Donner Party.* Salt Lake City: Deseret Book Company, 1950.

"Streets of San Francisco." *Irish Echo* 14-20 July 1993: 26.

Sweeny, William M. "Brigadier-General Thomas W. Sweeny, U.S.A. – A Biographical Sketch – 1820-1892." *The Journal of the American Irish Historical Society* 2 (1899): 193-201.

———. "Theodore O'Hara." *The Journal of the American Irish Historical Society* 25 (1926): 202-206.

Talbert, Charles G. "The Life of William Whitley." *The Filson Club History Quarterly* 25 (April 1951): 101-121.

Tebeau, Charlton W. *A History of Florida.* Coral Gables, Fla.: University of Miami Press, 1971.

Teggart, Frederick J., ed. "Diary of Patrick Breen, One of the Donner Party." *Academy of Pacific Coast History* 1 (July 1910): 3-16.

Thomas, Bob. *The Once and Only Bing.* New York: Grosst & Dunlap, 1977.

"Thomas M. Brennan, Manufacturer, Dead at 74." *Louisville Courier Journal* 28 February 1914: 1.

"Thomas M. Brennan Suddenly Stricken." *Louisville Herald* 28 February 1914: 7.

Thomas, Samuel. "The Restoration of Locust Grove." *The Western Penn-*

sylvania Historical Magazine 48 (April 1965): 145-150.

———. "William Croghan, Jr. (1794-1850): A Prominent Pittsburgh Lawyer from Kentucky." *The Western Pennsylvania Historical Magazine* 51 (July 1968): 213-227.

Thornton, Francis Beauchesne. *Sea of Glory: The Magnificent Story of Four Chaplains.* New York: Prentice-Hall, 1953.

Thrapp, Dan L. *Encyclopedia of Frontier Biography.* 4 vols. Spokane: The Arthur H. Clarke Company, 1988-94.

Thum, Marcella. *Exploring Literary America.* New York: Athenaeum, 1979.

Thwaites, Ruben Gold, ed. *Early Western Travels 1748-1846.* Vol. 14, *Part I of James's Account of S. H. Long's Expedition, 1819-1820.* Cleveland: The Arthur H. Clark Company, 1905.

Tolbert, Frank X. *Dick Dowling at Sabine Pass.* New York: McGraw-Hill Book Company, Inc., 1962.

Tucker, Phillip Thomas. *The Confederacy's Fighting Chaplain: Father John B. Bannon.* Tuscaloosa, Ala.: The University of Alabama Press, 1992.

Tucker, Wilma, and Don Tucker. "Mendocino – From the Beginning." *Mendocino Historical Review* 16 (Winter 1992): 34-35.

Turnbull, Andrew. *Scott Fitzgerald.* London: The Bodley Head, 1962.

Turner, Martha Anne. *William Barrett Travis: His Sword and His Pen.* Waco, Tex.: Texican Press, 1972.

Turner, Wallace. "Rep. Phillip Burton, Democratic Liberal, Dies on Visit to California." *New York Times* 11 April 1983: B6.

Twain, Mark. *Roughing It.* Edited by Bill Hamlin. New York: Penguin Books, 1981.

Tyler, Lyon G., ed. *Encyclopedia of Virginia Biography.* 5 vols. New York: Lewis Historical Publishing Company, 1915.

———, ed. *Men of Mark in Virginia.* 5 vols. Washington, D.C.: Men of Mark Publishing Company, 1906-09.

Warrum, Noble. *Utah Since Statehood.* 4 vols. Chicago: The S. J. Clarke Publishing Company, 1919-20.

Vandiver, Frank E. *Mighty Stonewall.* New York: McGraw-Hill Book Company, 1957.

Varble, Rachel M. *Jane Clemens: The Story of Mark Twain's Mother.* Garden City, N.Y.: Doubleday & Company, Inc., 1964.

Vincent, A. W. B. "A Little Bit of Ireland in the Heart of California." *Ireland of the Welcomes* 44 (July/August 1995): 9-11.

Volwiler, Albert T. *George Croghan and the Westward Movement.* Cleveland: The Arthur H. Clarke Company, 1926.

Von Hinueber, Caroline. "Life of German Pioneers in Early Times." Edited by Rudolph Kleberg Jr. *The Quarterly of the Texas State Historical Association* 2 (January 1899): 227-232.

Waddell, Joseph A. *Annals of Augusta County, Virginia, from 1726 to 1871.* Staunton, Va.: C. Russell Caldwell, 1902.

Wakin, Edward. *Enter the Irish-American*. New York: Thomas Y. Crowell Company, 1976.

Walker, Dale L. "O'Neill, William Buckey." *The Reader's Encyclopedia of the American West*. New York: Thomas Y. Crowell Company, 1977.

Walker, Henry Pickering. *The Wagonmasters: High Plains Freighting from the Earliest Days of the Santa Fe Trail to 1880*. Norman, Okla.: University of Oklahoma Press, 1966.

Wallace, Robert. *The Old West: The Miners*. New York: Time-Life Books, 1976.

Waln, Robert, Jr. *The Biographies of the Signers of the Declaration of Independence*. 9 vols. Philadelphia: R. W. Pomeroy, 1824.

Walser, Richard, ed. *The Poems of Governor Thomas Burke of North Carolina*. Raleigh, N.C.: State Department of Archives, 1961.

Walsh, Henry L. *Hallowed Were the Gold Dust Trails: The Story of the Pioneer Priests of Northern California*. [Santa Clara, Calif.]: University of Santa Clara Press, 1946.

Walsh, Richard J., and Milton S. Salsbury. *The Making of Buffalo Bill: A Study in Heroism*. Indianapolis: The Bobbs-Merrill Company, 1928.

Walworth, Arthur. *Woodrow Wilson: World Prophet*. 2 vols. New York: Longmans, Green and Company, 1958.

Ward, Geoffrey C. *The Civil War: An Illustrated History*. New York: Alfred A. Knopf, 1990.

Waring, Alice Noble. *The Fighting Elder Andrew Pickens 1739-1817*. Columbia: University of South Carolina Press, 1962.

Warner, Ezra J. *Generals in Blue: Lives of the Union Commanders*. [Baton Rouge]: Louisiana State University Press, 1964.

Waterbury, Jean Parker, ed. *The Oldest City: St. Augustine, Saga of Survival*. St. Augustine, Fla.: The St. Augustine Historical Society, 1983.

Wayne, Aissa. *John Wayne: My Father*. New York: Randon House, 1991.

Webb, Walter Prescott, et al., eds. *The Handbook of Texas*. 3 vols. Austin: The Texas State Historical Association, 1952-76.

Weber, Francis J. *California: The Catholic Experience*. [Hong Kong: Printed by Libra Press, 1981?].

——. *Catholic California: Some Historical Reflections*. [N.p.: n.p.], 1992.

——. "Interfaith in Action." San Buenaventura, Calif.: Junipero Serra Press, 1976.

——, ed. *Mission Dolores: A Documentary History of San Francisco Mission*. [San Francisco]: Francis J. Weber, [1979?].

——, ed. *The Precursor's Mission: A Documentary History of San Juan Bautista*. [Mission Hills, Calif.]: Francis J. Weber, [1978].

——. *Vignettes of California Catholicism*. Mission Hills, Calif.: [Francis J. Weber], 1988.

Webster's American Military Biographies. Springfield, Mass.: G. & C. Merriam Company, 1978.

Wecter, Dixon. *Sam Clemens of Hannibal*. Boston: Houghton Mifflin Company, 1952.

Weichmann, Louis J. *A True History of the Assassination of Abraham Lincoln and of the Conspiracy of 1865*. Edited by Floyd E. Risvold. New York: Alfred A. Knopf, 1975.

Weil, Tom. *Hippocrene USA Guide to America's South: A Travel Guide to the Eleven Southern States*. New York: Hippocrene Books, 1990.

Weyand, Leonie Rummel, and Houston Wade. *An Early History of Fayette County*. Burnet, Tex.: Eakin Press, 1936.

Wheeler, John H. *Reminiscences and Memoirs of North Carolina and Eminent North Carolinians*. Baltimore: Genealogical Publishing Company, 1966.

White, Kate. "Father Ryan – The Poet-Priest of the South." *South Atlantic Quarterly* 18 (January 1919): 69-74.

Whiting, Charles. *Hero: The Life and Death of Audie Murphy*. Chelsea, Mich.: Scarborough House, 1990.

Who Was Who in America. Vol. 1 (1897-1942). Chicago: The A. N. Marquis Company, 1942.

Who Was Who in American History: Arts and Letters. Chicago: Marquis Who's Who, Inc., 1975.

Wibberly, Leonard Patrick O'Connor. *The Coming of the Green*. New York: Henry Holt and Company, 1958.

Wiencek, Henry. *The Smithsonian Guide to Historic America: Virginia and the Capital Region*. New York: Stewart, Tabori & Chang, 1989.

Wiley, Samuel T. *History of Monongalia County, West Virginia*. Kingwood, W.Va.: Preston Publishing Company, 1883.

"William J. McNamara." *The Victoria Daily Advocate* 8 May 1903.

Williams, Amelia. "A Critical Study of the Siege of the Alamo and of the Personnel of its Defenders." *The Southwestern Historical Quarterly* 37 (July 1933): 1-44; (October 1933): 79-115; (January 1934): 157-184; (April 1934): 237-312.

Williams, Marjorie L., ed. *Fayette County: Past & Present*. 2nd printing. La Grange, Tex.: n.p., 1976.

Williams, Michael W. *The African American Encyclopedia*. 6 vols. New York: Marshall Cavendish, 1993.

Williams, William H. "The History of Carrollton." *The Louisiana Historical Quarterly* 22 (January 1939): 181-215.

Wilson, Charles Reagan, and William Ferris, eds. *Encyclopedia of Southern Culture*. Chapel Hill: The University of North Carolina Press, 1989.

Wilson, D. Ray. *Kansas Historical Tour Guide*. 2nd ed. Carpentersville, Ill.: Crossroads Communications, 1990.

Wilson, James Grant, and John Fiske, eds. *Appleton's Cyclopaedia of American Biography*. 8 vols. New York: D. Appleton and Company, 1887-1918.

Wilson, Samuel, Jr., and Leonard Huber. *The St. Louis Cemeteries of New Orleans*. New Orleans: St. Louis Cathedral, 1990.

Winckler, Suzanne. *The Smithsonian Guide to Historic America: The Great Lakes States*. New York: Stewart, Tabori & Chang, 1989.

———. *The Smithsonian Guide to Historic America: The Plains States*. New York: Stewart, Tabori & Chang, 1990.

Winther, Oscar Osburn. *The Story of San Jose 1777-1869*. San Francisco: California Historical Society, 1935.

Wirt, William. *The Two Principal Arguments of William Wirt, Esquire, on the Trial of Aaron Burr, for High Treason, and on the Motion to Commit Aaron Burr and Others, for Trial in Kentucky*. Richmond, Va.: Samuel Pleasants, Jr., 1808.

Wittke, Carl. *The Irish in America*. Baton Rouge: Louisiana State University Press, 1956.

———. *We Who Built America: The Saga of the Immigrant*. Rev. ed. Cleveland: The Press of Western Reserve University, 1964.

Wolle, Muriel Sibell. *Montana Pay Dirt: A Guide to the Mining Camps of the Treasure State*. Denver: Sage Books, 1963.

Wood, Robert L. *Across the Olympic Mountains: The Press Expedition, 1889-1890*. Seattle: The Mountaineers and The University of Washington Press, 1967.

———. *Men, Mules and Mountains: Lieutenant O'Neil's Olympic Expeditions*. Seattle: The Mountaineers, 1976.

Wooster, Ralph. "Foreigners in the Principal Towns of Ante-Bellum Texas." *The Southeastern Historical Quarterly* 66 (October 1962): 208-220.

Workman, Boyle. *The City That Grew*. Los Angeles: The Southland Publishing Company, 1936.

Writers' Program of the Work Projects Administration. *Alabama: A Guide to the Deep South*. American Guide Series. New York: R. R. Smith, 1941.

———. *Arkansas: A Guide to the State*. American Guide Series. New York: Hastings House, 1941.

———. *Atlanta: A City of the Modern South*. American Guide Series. New York: Smith & Durrell, 1942.

———. *Colorado: A Guide to the Highest State*. American Guide Series. New York: Hastings House, 1941.

———. *Copper Camp*. New York: Hastings House, 1943.

———. *Georgia: A Guide to its Towns and Countryside*. 2nd printing. American Guide Series. Athens, Ga.: University of Georgia Press, 1946.

———. *Houston: A History and Guide*. American Guide Series. Houston: The Anson Jones Press, 1942.

———. *Louisiana: A Guide to the State*. American Guide Series. New York: Hastings House, 1941.

———. *Louisville: A Guide to the Falls City*. American Guide Series. New York: M. Barrows and Company, Inc., 1940.

———. *Maryland: A Guide to the Old Line State*. American Guide Series. New York: Oxford University Press, 1940.

———. *Missouri: A Guide to the "Show Me" State*. American Guide Series. New York: Duell, Sloan and Pearce, 1941.

———. *Nevada: A Guide to the Silver State*. American Guide Series. Portland, Ore.: Binfords & Mort, 1940.

———. *New Mexico: A Guide to the Colorful State*. American Guide Series. New York: Hastings House, 1940.

———. *The Ohio Guide*. New York: Oxford University Press, 1940.

———. *Oregon: End of the Trail*. American Guide Series. Portland, Ore.: Binfords & Mort, 1940.

———. *Puerto Rico: A Guide to the Island of Boriquén*. American Guide Series. New York: The University Society, Inc., 1940.

———. *South Carolina: A Guide to the Palmetto State*. American Guide Series. New York: Oxford University Press, 1941.

———. *Texas: A Guide to the Lone Star State*. American Guide Series. New York: Hastings House, 1940.

———. *Utah: A Guide to the State*. American Guide Series. New York: Hastings House, 1941.

———. *Virginia: A Guide to the Old Dominion*. American Guide Series. New York: Oxford University Press, 1941.

———. *Washington: A Guide to the Evergreen State*. American Guide Series. Portland, Ore.: Binfords & Mort, 1941.

———. *West Virginia: A Guide to the Mountain State*. American Guide Series. New York: Oxford University Press, 1941.

———. *Wisconsin: A Guide to the Badger State*. American Guide Series. New York: Duell, Sloan and Pearce, 1941.

———. *Wyoming: A Guide to its History, Highways, and People*. American Guide Series. New York: Oxford University Press, 1941.

Wyllys, Rufus K. *Arizona: The History of a Frontier State*. Phoenix: Hobson & Herr, 1950.

Younger, Calton. *Ireland's Civil War*. London: Frederick Muller Ltd., 1968.

Site Index

*Although some of the statues and monuments in this list do not honor Irish or Irish Americans, they are included because they were created by sculptors of Irish descent.

Y

Subject Index